March 13: The Soviet Congress of People's Deputies repeals the Communist party's monopoly on political power.

March 18: In East German elections, voters back the pro-unification party allied with Kohl.

April 13: Gorbachev threatens an embargo of Lithuania.

May 4: The Latvian parliament declares independence and is branded illegal by Gorbachev.

May 29: Yeltsin is elected parliamentary leader of the Russian Republic.

May 30–June 2: Bush-Gorbachev summit is held in Washington and at Camp David. Gorbachev privately concedes that it should be up to the German people to decide "whether or not they're to be in NATO."

July 12: Yeltsin resigns from the Communist party.

July 16: Gorbachev and Kohl agree that the unified Germany will belong to NATO.

Aug. 1: Baker, in Irkutsk, tells Shevardnadze of a CIA bulletin warning that Iraq might be preparing to invade Kuwait: "We hope you'll try to restrain these guys."

Aug. 2: Iraq invades Kuwait.

Aug. 3: Baker and Shevardnadze issue a joint condemnation of the invasion.

Sept. 9: Bush meets with Gorbachev in Helsinki to discuss the Persian Gulf and secretly promises to support an international conference on the Middle East when the crisis is over.

Oct. 3: East and West Germany unite.

Nov. 16: Yeltsin attacks Gorbachev for trying to accumulate too much power.

Nov. 19: NATO and Warsaw Pact leaders in Paris sign a treaty on Conventional Forces in Europe (CFE). Gorbachev dines with Bush and assures him, "We've been with you since Day One on the Gulf, and we'll continue to be with you."

Nov. 23: Gorbachev proposes a new Union treaty that will loosen ties between the central Soviet government and the fifteen republics.

Nov. 27: The UN passes Security Resolution 678, authorizing the use of force in the Persian Gulf.

Dec. 20: Shevardnadze resigns, warning of a hard-line "dictatorship."

Dec. 26: Gorbachev chooses Gennadi Yanayev as Soviet vice president.

1991

Jan. 2: Soviet troops seize buildings in Vilnius.

Jan. 13: "Bloody Sunday" in Vilnius: fifteen Lithuanians are killed.

Jan. 16: The Persian Gulf War begins with an air attack on Baghdad.

Jan. 18: Gorbachev calls Bush and demands a halt to the bombing of Baghdad, saying the UN coalition has "made its point."

Jan. 20: "Bloody Sunday" in Riga: Soviet "Black Beret" troops kill four Latvians.

Feb. 6: Six Soviet republics announce they will boycott the referendum on Gorbachev's new Union treaty.

Feb. 18: Gorbachev meets with Iraqi Foreign Minister Tariq Aziz in Moscow in a last attempt to broker a settlement and avert a ground war.

Feb. 23: The allies launch a ground assault.

Feb. 27: Bush announces that "Kuwait is liberated."

March 17: Soviet citizens vote in favor of Gorbachev's Union treaty.

March 28: Defying Gorbachev's ban, 100,000 Yeltsin supporters demonstrate in Moscow.

April 9: Gorbachev's hard-line prime minister, Valentin Pavlov, unveils an "anticrisis program," reasserting the power of the central government.

April 23: Gorbachev shifts back toward the reformers and holds conciliatory talks with the leaders of nine republics.

June 12: Yeltsin is elected to the newly created presidency of Russia.

June 20: Baker warns Soviet Foreign Minister Alexander Bessmertnykh in Berlin of a hard-line coup against Gorbachev. In a telephone conversation with Bush, Gorbachev brushes the warning aside.

July 17: Bush and Gorbachev complete the START treaty in London; Bush fends off Gorbachev's demands for Western economic aid.

July 19: Bush receives a secret Soviet message imploring him not to visit Kiev during his upcoming Moscow summit with Gorbachev.

July 29–Aug. 1: In Moscow, Bush and Gorbachev sign the START treaty and announce their co-sponsorship of a Middle East peace conference. Afterward Bush visits Kiev and denounces "suicidal nationalism."

Aug. 18–21: Hard-liners stage a coup against Gorbachev.

Aug. 24: After the collapse of the putsch, Gorbachev resigns as head of the Communist party.

Aug. 29: The Soviet parliament bans Communist party activities.

Sept. 2: Bush recognizes the independence of the Baltic states.

Oct. 30: Gorbachev sees Bush at the Middle East conference in Madrid but is clearly preoccupied by troubles at home.

Nov. 19: Gorbachev reappoints Shevardnadze as foreign minister.

Dec. 1: Ukrainians vote for independence.

Dec. 8: Yeltsin meets with the leaders of Ukraine and Belarus in Minsk to declare the formation of the new "Commonwealth of Independent States."

Dec. 15: Baker sees Yeltsin and Gorbachev in Moscow and realizes that the Soviet military has thrown its support to Yeltsin.

Dec. 25: Gorbachev resigns and calls Bush to assure him, "You may feel at ease as you celebrate Christmas." The USSR ceases to exist.

AT THE HIGHEST LEVELS

PREVIOUS BOOKS BY MICHAEL R. BESCHLOSS

Kennedy and Roosevelt: The Uneasy Alliance (1980)

Mayday: Eisenhower, Khrushchev and the U-2 Affair (1986)

The Crisis Years: Kennedy and Khrushchev, 1960–1963 (1991)

PREVIOUS BOOKS BY STROBE TALBOTT

Endgame: The Inside Story of SALT II (1979)

The Russians and Reagan (1984)

Deadly Gambits: The Reagan Administration and the Stalemate in Nuclear Arms Control (1984)

Reagan and Gorbachev (1987)
(with Michael Mandelbaum)

The Master of the Game: Paul Nitze and the Nuclear Peace (1988)

Translator-editor:

Khrushchev Remembers (1970)

Khrushchev Remembers: The Last Testament (1974)

AT THE

The Inside Story

HIGHEST LEVELS

of the End of the Cold War

MICHAEL R. BESCHLOSS
and
STROBE TALBOTT

LITTLE, BROWN AND COMPANY
Boston   Toronto   London

First Edition

Library of Congress Cataloging-in-Publication Data

Beschloss, Michael R.
    At the highest levels: the inside story of the end of the cold
war / Michael R. Beschloss and Strobe Talbott. — 1st ed.
        p.   cm.
    Includes index.
    ISBN 0-316-09281-9
    1. United States — Foreign relations — Soviet Union. 2. Soviet
Union — Foreign relations — United States. 3. Cold War. 4. United
States — Foreign relations — 1989–   . 5. Soviet Union — Foreign
relations — 1985–1991. 6. Bush, George, 1924–   . 7. Gorbachev,
Mikhail Sergeyevich, 1931–   . I. Talbott, Strobe. II Title.
E183.8.S65B4685   1993
327.73047′09′048 — dc20   92-36336

10   9   8   7   6   5   4   3   2   1

MV-NY

Published simultaneously in Canada by Little, Brown & Company
(Canada) Limited

Printed in the United States of America

To our wives, Afsaneh and Brooke

CONTENTS

Preface   xi

1   "His Heart Is in the Right Place"   3
2   "I Don't Want to Do Anything Dumb"   19
3   "More! You Must Do More!"   43
4   "Look, This Guy *Is* Perestroika!"   69
5   "The Makings of a Whole New World"   101
6   "I'm Not Going to Dance on the Wall"   126
7   "Eye to Eye"   153
8   "I'm Going to Hold a Seminar on Germany"   172
9   "I Don't Want to Make the Wrong Mistakes"   196
10   "Two Anchors Are Better"   215
11   "A Fantastic Result"   231

12   "This Is No Time to Go Wobbly"   244
13   "You Can't Back Off"   268
14   "I Want to Preserve the Relationship"   298
15   "You've Got to Understand"   321
16   "He's All They've Got"   345
17   "I Really Hit Him over the Head"   362
18   "Business Is Business"   374
19   "We're Counting on You"   393
20   "We're Not Going to Let Him Use Us"   411
21   "I'm Afraid He May Have Had It"   421
22   "What We Have Accomplished Will Last Forever"   442
     Epilogue   465

     Selected Bibliography   475
     Index   477

PREFACE

At the beginning of 1989, we decided to write a book about relations between the United States and the Soviet Union over the next three years. No one could have foretold that our story would encompass the liberation of Eastern Europe, the disbanding of the Warsaw Pact, the suspension of the Soviet Communist party, the death of the Soviet Union, and the end of the Cold War.

The title of this book reflects its central theme: in managing the U.S.-Soviet relationship during its climactic phase, George Bush and Mikhail Gorbachev relied on understandings reached "at the highest levels," often in secret and in consultation with only their very closest advisers. They developed what they came to call a "partnership." The term suggests how they transformed the East-West rivalry. They were able to preserve and strengthen their cooperation despite international crises and flare-ups of domestic opposition on both sides.

Still, conducting state-to-state relations in this highly personal fashion had its costs. Bush and Gorbachev were so closely attuned to each other that it eventually caused both men to lose touch with their domestic constituencies.

Gorbachev came to believe that it was more important for him to cultivate his relationship with Bush and his fellow Western leaders than to reach an accommodation with Boris Yeltsin and other champions of democratization, decentralization, and free-market economics.

Bush was so intent on shoring up Gorbachev that he was slow to perceive that by the summer of 1991, the Soviet leader was largely a spent force. Bush created the impression that he cared more about his friend in the Kremlin than about the principles of freedom and independence. His ties to Gorbachev — and his reluctance to support Yeltsin — ultimately became a political liability in Bush's campaign for reelection.

Early in our work, we quietly asked a large number of American and Soviet officials if they would speak with us on a regular basis about what was happening within and between their two governments; many consented, on the condition that we not identify them as sources. We made similar arrangements with officials of other NATO and Warsaw Pact states.

For more than three years, we kept in frequent touch with contacts in Washington, Moscow, and several European capitals. We often saw our sources within days — sometimes even within hours — of the closed-door meetings, negotiating sessions, telephone calls, and other diplomatic exchanges described in these pages. The information they provided was not just reproduced from fresh memory but often drawn from written talking points, memoranda of conversations, reporting cables, and other documents. We have used direct quotations only when our sources had firsthand, immediate knowledge of what was said. As far as possible, we have checked information about each meeting, conversation, or episode with a variety of sources.

Just as the official written record of these events will eventually be declassified, so we are placing our research and interview notes in the Williams College Library in Williamstown, Massachusetts, under time seal for use by future scholars.

Since so many of our sources must remain anonymous, we cannot acknowledge our debt to them here, but our gratitude to them is immense.

Among those we can thank are several officials responsible for informing the public about the workings of government. In Washington: Marlin Fitzwater, the presidential press secretary, his deputy, Roman Popadiuk, and their colleagues in the White House and National Security Council staff press offices; Margaret Tutwiler of the State Department; Pete Williams of the Defense Department; Captain Jay Coupe and Colonel William Smullen of the office of the chairman of the Joint Chiefs of Staff; and E. Peter Earnest of the Central Intelligence Agency.

In the Soviet government: Vitali Ignatenko, Igor Malashenko, and Andrei Grachyov of the Kremlin; Gennadi Gerasimov of the Ministry of Foreign Affairs; and Boris Malakhov, Leonid Dobrokhotov, and Georgi Oganov of the Soviet embassy in Washington.

We also appreciate the assistance we received from the Institute for the Study of the U.S.A. and Canada, its director, Academician Georgi Arbatov, and its Washington representative, Vladimir Pechatnov.

For help in making our way through the thickets of arms control, we would like to thank Spurgeon Keeny, Jack Mendelsohn, Matthew Bunn, Dunbar Lockwood, and Lee Feinstein of the Arms Control Association in Washington.

Several editors at *Time* supported our efforts and guided into the pages of the magazine excerpts from our work while it was still in progress: Henry Muller, John Stacks, Ron Kriss, James Kelly, Johanna McGeary, and Brigid Forster. Michael Duffy, Dan Goodgame, Michael Kramer, and J. F. O. McAllister were generous with their counsel and the fruits of their own reporting.

We are especially grateful to Walter Isaacson, who encouraged this project from its inception and gave us an expert and detailed critique of the final manuscript.

The Moscow bureau of *Time* — John Kohan, Jay Carney, and Felix Rosenthal — were most hospitable during our frequent intrusions. Yuri Zarakhovich helped us with a variety of queries while we were finishing the book.

Several friends — notably James MacGregor Burns, Elizabeth Drew, William Hamilton, Richard Holbrooke, Priscilla Johnson McMillan, Don Oberdorfer, and Louise Walker — provided us with substantive advice and moral support at key moments. Two others, both masters of the subject of East-West relations, William G. Hyland and Michael Mandelbaum, read early versions of the manuscript and gave us useful comments.

We express a special debt to Maryam Mashayekhi, Martha Clark, and Galit Zolkower, who helped in gathering research material for this book and aided us in innumerable other ways. Vladislav Zubok and Kathy Lavinder provided us with additional research.

Thanks, also, to Ed Turner, Gail Evans, Bernard Shaw, Frank Sesno, Charles Bierbauer, Steve Hurst, Claire Shipman, Patrick Reap, and Jill

Neff of CNN, to Newton Minow and Yvonne Zecca of the Annenberg
Washington Program, and to Patricia Lee Dorff of *Foreign Affairs*.

We relied particularly on the professionalism of our literary agents,
Timothy Seldes and Esther Newberg. Their confidence in us kept us
going. We also feel very lucky to have ended up in the honorable and
capable hands of Charles Hayward and William Phillips at Little, Brown
and Company. Our editor there, Roger Donald, along with his colleagues Dorothy Straight and Geoffrey Kloske, saw our manuscript
through to publication with great skill, high standards, and good cheer.

Finally, we are grateful to all members of our households who had
to live with this project for four years. Devin and Adrian Talbott took
an active interest in the subject and indulged their father in his preoc-
cupations. Our wives, Afsaneh and Brooke, encouraged our collaboration with each other even when it strained our collaborations with
them. They also read large portions of the manuscript at various stages
and gave us the benefit of their excellent advice. For those and many
other reasons, this book is dedicated to them.

Michael R. Beschloss
Strobe Talbott
Washington, D.C.
November 4, 1992

AT THE HIGHEST LEVELS

CHAPTER 1

"His Heart Is in the Right Place"

On Thursday, December 10, 1987, at the end of his first visit to the United States, Mikhail Gorbachev stepped out of the White House, bade farewell to Ronald Reagan, and then slipped into the backseat of his black ZIL limousine, where he was joined by Vice President George Bush.

As the car rolled down the White House driveway, under a soft rain, for the trip to Andrews Air Force Base, Bush told Gorbachev that he had something on his mind and would prefer that Gorbachev never publicize what he was about to say. Gorbachev nodded.

Even though the presidential election year of 1988 would not begin for another three weeks, the vice president was already campaigning hard for the Republican nomination. His party's Senate leader, Robert Dole of Kansas, was running ahead of him in several polls.

Bush said, "There's a good chance that I'm going to win the presidential election next year. Dole looks pretty dangerous right now, but I think I'll get the Republican nomination. If I'm elected — and I think I will be — you should understand that I want to improve our relations."

Bush said that during his seven years as Ronald Reagan's vice president, he had had to keep his moderate views to himself. He explained that Reagan was surrounded by "marginal intellectual thugs" who would be delighted to seize on any evidence that the vice president was a closet liberal. Therefore, during the 1988 campaign, he would have to do and say many things to get elected. Mr. Gorbachev should ignore them.

Gorbachev said that he understood. Long afterward, he recalled this conversation as the "most important talk Bush and I ever had." Over the next four years, each time the Soviet leader's close aides complained that Bush was pandering to Republican conservatives, Gorbachev would remind them of their talk in the limousine, saying, "Don't worry. His heart is in the right place."

The first forty-six years of George Bush's life gave him only occasional opportunities to deal with the Soviet Union. As Richard Nixon's ambassador to the United Nations in 1971 and 1972, he took his Soviet counterpart, Yakov Malik, to see the New York Mets (owned by his friend Joan Whitney Payson), without notable diplomatic result.

When Bush was director of the Central Intelligence Agency in the administration of Gerald Ford, conservative critics of détente and proponents of an American arms buildup accused the agency of having consistently underestimated the Soviet military threat. Rather than standing up for the professional intelligence officers over whom he presided and shielding the agency from political pressure, Bush tried to mollify the right wing. He invited a group of outsiders to serve as a kind of visiting committee to monitor the CIA's methods. He gave them security clearances and authorized them to prepare a report second-guessing the agency's evaluation of top-secret intelligence data on various Soviet activities.

Predictably, the group, called Team B, pronounced the CIA guilty of being soft on the USSR and added its voice to the rising chorus calling for new American weapons programs. One of Bush's CIA lieutenants recalled that his boss "never showed deep convictions when reviewing strategic estimates. His main concern was to try to reconcile differences of opinion. . . . He's a problem solver. 'Get the goddamned problem solved. If it takes a Team B, do it.' "

After Ford was defeated, in 1976, Bush offered to stay on as CIA director, but Jimmy Carter refused. In the fall of 1978, Bush flew up from Houston for a private dinner in New York. Other guests included eminent figures in the Northeastern foreign policy community, most of them Democrats. After dessert, Bush denounced Carter's failure to stand up to the Soviet threat. He cited Communist advances in Somalia and Ethiopia and the president's waffling over deployment of the neutron bomb.

One Democratic alumnus of the Kennedy-Johnson State Department derided Bush's monologue as "simplistic" and "ignorant." Bush angrily retorted that the Democrat was "arrogant" and "soft," just like the liberal foreign policy establishment he represented — no wonder it was in trouble!

The Team B experience and Ronald Reagan's nearly successful challenge to Ford in 1976 had demonstrated that the Republican party's soul had moved toward the Southwest and the Right. The internationalist, Atlanticist wing of the party was losing ground to its more conservative elements. In 1978, Bush publicly resigned from the Trilateral Commission and the Council on Foreign Relations, which he pronounced "too liberal."

When Bush was sworn in as vice president in 1981, he knew that both his ideological purity and his mettle were objects of suspicion among the Reaganites. Reagan was determined to put Moscow on notice that there was a new, hard-line regime in Washington. He did not wish to dilute that message by giving prominence in foreign affairs to Bush, with his reputation for moderation.

The vice president admitted, though only in private, that he was uncomfortable with some of Reagan's harsh rhetoric and gestures toward the Soviets at the start of their first term. In November 1982, when Leonid Brezhnev died, Bush and his wife, Barbara, were traveling in Africa. Bush hoped that Reagan would choose him to represent the United States at the Moscow funeral, but he did not wish to seem to be grabbing at it. He barked at his national security aide Admiral Daniel Murphy, "No planning!"

When Reagan gave him the assignment, Bush flew to Frankfurt, where he was briefed by a young CIA Soviet analyst, Robert Blackwell. Blackwell scoffed at widespread rumors that the new Soviet leader, Yuri Andropov, the former chairman of the KGB, was a closet Americanophile who gorged himself on Jacqueline Susann novels and guzzled scotch: Andropov could be expected to use strong leadership and his "formidable intellect" to reassert "socialist order and discipline" after years of drift under Brezhnev, Blackwell believed.

When Bush met Andropov in Moscow, he joked that as former intelligence chiefs, the two of them had been "in the same business."

Afterward, the vice president retired with Ambassador Arthur Hartman, Secretary of State George Shultz, and their aides for caviar and champagne at Spaso House, the official U.S. residence. Hartman reminded the others that the old mansion was bugged. The vice president said he had found the new leader hard-nosed and abrasive: "I feel he's intelligent. Maybe we can deal with him. But let's be careful."

In February 1984, when Andropov died of kidney failure, Reagan asked his vice president to fly back to Moscow. In Bush's private quarters aboard *Air Force Two,* Robert Blackwell gave him a cursory CIA report on the new Soviet leader, Konstantin Chernenko. He confessed that the agency was startled that Chernenko had won the top job in the Kremlin, especially after losing out to Andropov in 1982.

Many in Washington recalled Chernenko as the man who had lighted Brezhnev's cigarettes for him when Brezhnev was trying to cut down on his smoking. The CIA considered him a "weak sister." But even Chernenko had made a speech in 1982 in Tbilisi, the capital of Soviet Georgia, warning that the Soviet Union was on the precipice of an internal crisis.

Bush's national security aide Donald Gregg, a former CIA man, told him that Finnish intelligence was predicting that the seventy-two-year-old Chernenko would be a transitional figure. After his passing there would be a mammoth struggle for the future of the Soviet Union, between the regressive, hard-drinking Leningrad party chief, Grigori Romanov, whom the Finns by proximity knew all too well, and someone who might be a change for the better, "this new guy Mikhail Gorbachev."

In Moscow, after seeing the ailing Chernenko atop the Lenin Tomb and at close range, the vice president expected to be back soon for another funeral. He gave Ambassador Hartman's wife, Donna, a photograph of himself, inscribed, "Next time the funeral's on me (Don't show this around)." To embassy staff members he cracked, "See you again, same time, next year!"

The change in Soviet leadership and the approaching 1984 presidential election moved Reagan to seek a summit with Chernenko, preferably in July, just before the two political conventions. The Democrats were already complaining that American-Soviet relations were in crisis, and that Reagan was the first president since Herbert Hoover who had not met with his Soviet counterpart.

Bush encouraged the president to pursue a summit. To sound out the Soviets, he suggested that Reagan send General Brent Scowcroft, who had been Gerald Ford's national security adviser, to Moscow with a private letter from the president to Chernenko. Reagan agreed. When Scowcroft arrived in Moscow, however, not a single high Soviet official would see him. One asked Ambassador Hartman, "If they've got something to tell us, why don't they tell us officially?" Chernenko wrote the president to refuse his summit offer.

In March 1985, Chernenko died. In Geneva, on his way to Moscow, Bush learned that the new chief would be Gorbachev. When Robert Blackwell met the vice president in Moscow, he reported that the CIA had been predicting Gorbachev's succession for months: Gorbachev was already the number two man in the Soviet Communist party; Andropov had been his principal patron.

Members of Bush's party joked about how well they knew the funeral routine by now: the viewing of the corpse, the military parade in Red Square, the reception in Saint George's Hall, the spaghetti dinner prepared by the excellent Italian chef at Spaso House.

The vice president and Blackwell were startled by how glad Muscovites seemed to be rid of their "doddering old men." Not more than thirty minutes after the funeral procession, they saw workmen tearing down Chernenko posters and throwing them into the trash. Bush said that their hosts seemed hardly able to wait to get the old man buried and to turn the fate of their country over to their new, fifty-four-year-old leader.

Gorbachev received Bush and Secretary of State Shultz in Saint Catherine's Hall. In a forty-five-minute monologue, he said that the Soviet Union was not interested in confrontation with the United States. He hoped that Washington would negotiate seriously in Geneva with the Soviets over nuclear arms. When Bush and Shultz brought up human rights, however, Gorbachev, like his predecessors, reacted with indignation at the American attempt to "interfere in the internal affairs of the USSR."

After the meeting, Blackwell predicted to Bush that Gorbachev would move fast. One clue was Gorbachev's obvious self-confidence; also, the military was already less visible on Soviet television than it had been before. The vice president agreed that there was "something different" here. Unlike Brezhnev, Andropov, and Chernenko, Gorbachev was "very smooth. He's young, tough, wants to change the Soviet Union, testy on human rights. A formidable man."

Asked by reporters whether such a vigorous Soviet leader was good for the West, Bush said, "That depends on us. We clearly want the

Soviet Union to change. Here's a man who wants to change it. But how he does so depends in part on how we interact with him. The challenge is not to 'help' him but to put forward U.S. interests in a way that affects his policy the way we want."

In October 1986, Reagan met Gorbachev at Reykjavik, where the Soviet leader sprang a surprise proposal to reduce drastically both countries' nuclear arsenals. The two men could not agree on final terms, but both endorsed the idea of eliminating all offensive strategic arms within ten years, a plan that would revolutionize the system of mutual deterrence that had kept the peace since the 1950s.

When Bush, who had stayed behind in Washington, learned about what had happened in Reykjavik, he was appalled that Reagan would deal on such fundamental issues without preparation or consultation with his Western allies. But he did not hint publicly at his disapproval.

In December 1987, Gorbachev made his visit to Washington, where he and Reagan signed a treaty banning intermediate-range nuclear missiles. During the three-day summit, Bush went to the Soviet embassy on Sixteenth Street for a breakfast of blinis and caviar with the Soviet leader. Gorbachev kept him waiting for almost two hours, which made the vice president furious.

Bush was accompanied at the breakfast by supporters from his upcoming presidential campaign, including John Sununu, the combative, deeply anti-Soviet governor of New Hampshire, who regularly observed Hungarian Freedom-fighters Day and Lithuanian Freedom Day — causes that in 1987 still had a quaint, quixotic ring. Avoiding controversy, Sununu rhapsodized to Gorbachev about American and Soviet accomplishments in science.

After the meeting, Gorbachev offered Bush a lift back to the White House in his limousine. "Welcome to my tank!" he said as they got in. The vice president said, "It's too bad you can't stop and go into some of these stores, because I think you'd find warm greetings from the American people."

When they passed crowds at the corner of Connecticut Avenue and L Street, Gorbachev told his driver, "Stop the car!" He emerged from the limousine and cried in Russian, "I want to say hello to you!" Some of the onlookers gasped. As Gorbachev shook hands, Bush climbed out of the car and posed with him for photographers, but the cameras — and the crowds — were clearly focused on Gorbachev.

As they drove on to the White House, Bush, obviously impressed by the visitor's mastery of public relations, asked, "Do you do this a lot?" Gorbachev said, "I do it in Moscow and I do it every time I go to the provinces. . . . Leaders should be equal to the people."

Bush's chief campaign pollster, Robert Teeter, advised the vice president that the more anxious Americans were about whether their next president was up to dealing with Gorbachev, the better it was for Bush; he should, therefore, play up the Soviet threat. In January 1988, Bush began using the kind of public rhetoric that he had just privately asked the Soviet leader to ignore. He told the National Press Club that Gorbachev was not a "freedom-loving friend of democracy" but an "orthodox, committed Marxist."

As Reagan approached the end of his presidency, he unwittingly served as a smiling, glad-handing foil for Bush's efforts to appear less captivated by Gorbachev's charm and more inclined to drive hard bargains with the Kremlin. In a famous incident during Reagan's visit to Moscow in June 1988, Gorbachev had picked up a small boy in Red Square and asked him to "shake hands with Grandfather Reagan." A reporter asked Reagan if he still believed that the Soviet Union was an "evil empire." The president said, "No, I was talking about another time, another era."

Vacationing at his family home in Kennebunkport, Maine, Bush sounded a very different note. He warned reporters, "The Cold War isn't over." The following month he cautioned against a "euphoric, naively optimistic view about what comes next." Privately he was disturbed by Reagan's "sentimentality" about Gorbachev. He felt that the president and Secretary of State Shultz were "crashing too hard" to make a final deal with the Soviets before Reagan left office.

In September 1988, Bush invited Gorbachev's foreign minister, Eduard Shevardnadze, to a breakfast at his official residence on Massachusetts Avenue. Except for a State Department interpreter, the only other American present was Shultz. In the spirit of his limousine conversation with Gorbachev the previous December, Bush told Shevardnadze that after he was elected, he hoped to continue the relationship forged under President Reagan.

Bush knew that Reagan, as the nation's most popular conservative, had more latitude to make deals with the Kremlin than he himself would have once he came into office. Therefore he quietly urged Shevardnadze to finish as much business as possible with the outgoing administration. Terrified that a leak of his relatively conciliatory remarks might be used against him in the campaign, he asked Shultz to give him the interpreter's notes of the session and to make no copies.

During the fall campaign, Bush said that he wished to keep the "pressure on Moscow to change." He opposed cuts in the defense budget or the Strategic Defense Initiative, Reagan's pet project for a space-based antimissile shield. In his first debate with the Democratic nominee, Michael Dukakis, Bush insisted that "the jury is still out on the Soviet experiment."

Viewing the campaign from the Kremlin, Gorbachev wondered whether Bush was backing away from the assurances he had offered in the limousine. His advisers reminded him that Bush had to placate his right wing; the vice president had to show some "muscles." Once he was elected, they said, Bush would probably resume Reagan's policies.

In December 1988, after the election, Reagan met Gorbachev for the final time as president over luncheon at the U.S. Coast Guard station at Governors Island in New York Harbor. Bush had agreed to attend, but only in a supporting role.

That morning, Gorbachev had given a fateful speech at the UN. He declared that the "use or threat of force" could no longer be an "instrument of foreign policy." He pledged to shift the USSR's military doctrine to a purely defensive stance and to cut half a million Soviet troops as well as many tanks, artillery pieces, and war planes in Eastern Europe.

Before the luncheon, when reporters asked for comment on Gorbachev's initiative, Reagan said, "I heartily approve." Bush took the same line he had taken for eight years, this time with a hint of smug irony: "I support what the president said." Eager to ingratiate himself with the president-elect, a beaming Gorbachev said, "That's one of the best answers of the year!"

Bush's advisers had warned him to assume a remote air of toughness and skepticism with the Soviet leader; he must not prejudice the negotiations that would begin once he was president. Once the doors were closed, Reagan's spokesman Marlin Fitzwater was shocked to notice that Gorbachev treated Reagan almost like a piece of furniture. The only American that Gorbachev seemed to be interested in was Bush, who kept trying to dodge his questions and turn the attention back to his chief.

When Reagan noted that a recent poll showed that 85 percent of Americans supported the new relationship with Moscow, Gorbachev aimed his reply at Bush: "I'm pleased to hear that. The name of the game is continuity." After more chatter, the vice president finally burst out: "What assurance can you give me that I can pass on to American businessmen who want to invest in the Soviet Union that *perestroika* and *glasnost* will succeed?" Gorbachev glared at him and snapped, "Not even Jesus Christ knows the answer to that question!"

He went on to lecture Bush: "I know what people are telling you now — that you've won the election, you've got to go slow, you've got to be careful, you've got to review, that you can't trust us, that we're doing all this for show. You'll see soon enough that I'm *not* doing this for show, and I'm not doing this to undermine you or surprise you or take advantage of you.

"I'm engaged in real politics. I'm doing this because I need to. I'm doing this because there's a revolution taking place in my country. I started it. And they all applauded me when I started it in 1986, and now they don't like it so much. But it's going to be a revolution nonetheless. . . . Don't misread me, Mr. Vice President."

That day an earthquake had devastated Soviet Armenia, killing twenty-five thousand Armenians and leaving almost a half million homeless. The next morning, Gorbachev canceled visits to the Metropolitan Museum of Art and other New York landmarks to fly back to the Soviet Union. Soon after, at Christmas, Bush sent his son Jeb and his twelve-year-old grandson George to Armenia to inspect the damage and assess how the United States might help.

Bush had not achieved his life's ambition by taking large chances or questioning conventional wisdom, particularly on the Soviet Union. Thus, at the end of 1988, his natural instinct was to apply the brakes to the Soviet-American relationship, pull over to the side of the road, and study the map for a while.

Bush's old Houston friend and two-time campaign manager, James Baker, whom he had promptly named as his secretary of state, shared and reinforced his instinctive caution. In several private conversations, Baker and Bush reviewed the experience of previous administrations with an eye to the near future.

They concluded that those presidents who had encountered trouble in Soviet-American relations had often moved too quickly. The principal examples of this were John Kennedy, who had let himself be rushed into an early, bruising summit with Nikita Khrushchev, and Jimmy Carter, who had proposed an ill-considered "comprehensive" arms-control plan to the Kremlin after only two months in office.

Baker now told the president-elect, "Part of the challenge is to avoid rashness." He added that the biggest mistakes, particularly at the beginning of an administration, were "frequently those of commission, not omission."

Bush's new national security adviser, Brent Scowcroft, was, if anything, even more cautious. The quiet, modest, steady son of a Utah wholesale grocer had gone to West Point and flown for the air force during World War II. In 1948, during a training exercise, Scowcroft's P-51B Mustang crashed in a New Hampshire forest. His back broken, he was hospitalized for two years.

Scowcroft had served as air attaché in the U.S. embassy in Belgrade in the late 1950s and then, after teaching stints and further air force service, had risen on Richard Nixon's National Security Council staff to become Henry Kissinger's deputy. When Gerald Ford stripped Kissinger of his NSC portfolio in November 1975, Scowcroft succeeded him as national security adviser.* Bush liked to joke that during those years, as director of the Central Intelligence Agency, he had "worked for" Scowcroft.

In the 1980s, Scowcroft was a senior officer of Kissinger's consulting firm, Kissinger Associates, and was a member of the presidential panel appointed by Ronald Reagan to investigate the Iran-*contra* scandal. After the 1988 election, Bush asked him to return to the White House.

Since the death of the Nixon-Ford-Kissinger détente in the mid-1970s, Scowcroft had worried about vacillations in both U.S. policy and public opinion toward the Soviet Union. Détente, as even some of its own proponents acknowledged, had been oversold. Despite the improved atmosphere of relations between Washington and Moscow and a series of agreements on arms control and other issues, the Soviets continued to persecute dissidents, build new weapons, and throw their considerable weight around internationally.

As a result, many Americans became disillusioned; they felt their own government had been taken in. Now that Scowcroft was back in office, he worried that the United States and its allies faced, in Gorbachev, a new, more effective version of what Scowcroft called the "clever bear syndrome" — the old Brezhnev practice of pursuing expansionist goals while lulling the West into lowering its defenses. The West could keep up its guard, Scowcroft believed, "only when we've

---

* Kissinger remained as secretary of state for the rest of Ford's term.

been scared to death"; Gorbachev was all the more formidable an opponent precisely because he was so unfrightening and reassuring.

A wise leader, said Scowcroft, must pay attention to his adversary's
capabilities, not his intentions. Unless and until the Soviet war-making
capability changed, Americans must still be suspicious of Gorbachev.

On Sunday, December 18, 1988, Henry Kissinger slipped into Bush's small
West Wing vice presidential office for a quiet meeting with the president-
elect, Baker, and Scowcroft. He told Bush that he was about to become
"the first president with a real opportunity to end the Cold War."

Why not discreetly negotiate a deal? Kissinger suggested. Gorbachev
would promise not to use violent force to suppress reform and liberalization in Eastern Europe; in exchange, the West would promise not to
exploit any economic or political changes that occurred there at the
expense of "legitimate" Soviet security interests.

For example, said Kissinger, the West might pledge not to use Eastern
Europe as a base from which to run covert intelligence operations
against the Soviet Union. It might forswear any effort to lure Eastern
European countries out of the Warsaw Pact. Shorn of his military option, meanwhile, Gorbachev would be more likely to let Eastern Europe
have the political breathing room it needed to reintegrate itself with the
West.

The proposal was classically Kissingerian: the use of secret high-level
diplomacy to reach a bargain based on the balance of power. He made
it clear that he would not object to acting as emissary to Gorbachev,
which would thrust him back into the center of the American-Soviet
relationship — especially with Scowcroft, his old friend and protégé
from the Nixon and Ford administrations, at the National Security
Council, and with the foreign-policy neophyte Baker at State.*

Bush was intrigued by Kissinger's idea, so much so that he authorized him to take a letter over his signature to Gorbachev in Moscow.
The former secretary of state was delighted. In January, a week before
the inauguration, Kissinger flew to the Soviet capital.

---

* During the 1988 campaign, Kissinger had wondered aloud with intimates whether
Bush might appoint Baker chief of staff for his first year as president (in order to get the
White House in shape) and put Kissinger at State — just for a year. However, he glumly
noted that in Bush's slender campaign autobiography, *Looking Forward* (1987), he was
the only person "criticized by name." In fact, Bush's comments about him in the book
were very mild.

*   *   *

Events in Eastern Europe were already beginning to confirm Kissinger's concern about a coming confrontation between newly stirring democratic forces and the diehard regimes. On Monday, January 16, 1989, demonstrators in Prague were arrested for observing the twentieth anniversary of the suicide of Jan Palach, the young student who had set himself on fire to protest the 1968 Soviet invasion.

Eight hundred people were arrested. Among them, and sentenced to nine months in prison, was a dissident playwright charged with "inciting disorder." This was Vaclav Havel.

That same day, in Moscow, Kissinger saw Gorbachev's close aide Alexander Yakovlev at the Kremlin. Yakovlev was one of the key members of Gorbachev's brain trust, a principal advocate and theoretician of *glasnost,* the policy of openness and official honesty. Having been an exchange student at Columbia University in the late 1950s and ambassador to Canada in the early 1980s, he spoke excellent English.

Yakovlev told Kissinger that Gorbachev was anxious about the Bush administration's seeming reluctance to pick up quickly where the Reagan administration had left off. He and Gorbachev could understand that the new leaders in Washington might wish to take some time to assess their options, he said, but a failure to reaffirm their improved relations might arouse concern around the world.

Yakovlev warned Kissinger that certain Communist party hard-liners were unhappy with Gorbachev's policies. In closed-door meetings, they lacerated him for abandoning socialism and selling out to the West. Yakovlev implied that Gorbachev and his fellow reformers needed Western recognition and encouragement as well as reciprocal concessions to maintain support for their program at home. If the Bush administration retreated from the progress made under Reagan, Gorbachev's conservative opponents would benefit.

Kissinger replied that improvements in U.S.-Soviet relations under Reagan had been largely cosmetic. It was time to introduce more substance. He said he was well acquainted with Bush and had recently met with the president-elect and his key advisers. He further said that he had a proposition to make, which should be considered semiofficial in that it had Bush's personal blessing.

The situation in Europe, Kissinger said, was dangerously fluid. The political evolution there could well turn into a revolution that could eventually provoke an international confrontation. He conjured up a twofold specter that he knew would frighten any Soviet: Eastern Europeans straining against the ties binding them to the Soviet Union, coupled with a resurgence of German nationalism that was likely to make the Federal Republic all the more eager to exploit tensions between East Germany and the Kremlin.

Kissinger suggested that if faced with the prospect of "losing" Eastern Europe — especially East Germany — the Soviet Union might feel compelled to use force to reassert itself in the region. This would provoke some kind of powerful reaction from the United States. Kissinger recalled that at the beginning of the twentieth century, the Great Powers had had no intention of starting World War I yet still had set off a chain reaction of crises because no one knew what the limits were.

To avert such a danger now, Kissinger proposed a high-level U.S.-Soviet negotiation to reach a cluster of understandings — some formal, some informal. They would set limits on what the Soviet Union could do to defend its interests in Eastern Europe, in exchange for a Western pledge to do nothing that would accelerate the changes in the East, particularly if such action might threaten the Kremlin's sense of its own security.

Kissinger said that the superpowers could not stop history, but they could prevent events from blowing up. He repeated that he had discussed his idea with people in the incoming administration. They were ready for a dialogue in good faith. What answer should he take back to Washington?

Yakovlev replied that the Kremlin was ready to undertake detailed discussions with the Bush administration aimed at managing the process of change in Europe and minimizing the disruptive effect of that change on East-West relations. He noted that one of the standard themes in Kissinger's writings was the need to preserve a balance of power. Sometimes this meant maintaining the status quo in international relations.

Yakovlev said that he endorsed that idea; the United States and Soviet Union had common interests in preserving the status quo in Europe during the period immediately ahead. Kissinger agreed, though he added that it was difficult to put the matter that way in the United States: American public opinion would never allow the U.S. government to explicitly accept the need for Eastern Europe to remain under Soviet domination.

Two days later, on Wednesday, January 18, Gorbachev called Kissinger to his grand office in the Kremlin. The only other Soviets present were an interpreter and Anatoli Dobrynin, the twenty-three-year ambassador to the United States, who had worked closely with Kissinger during their years in power together in Washington. He was now an adviser to Gorbachev.

Kissinger handed Gorbachev the letter from Bush, which pledged to continue the progress begun under Reagan — though not immediately. The president-elect had written that he hoped Gorbachev would understand if the new administration took some time to assess the relationship and consider its options.

Kissinger explained his proposal for an understanding on Eastern Europe. Might there be any Soviet interest in such an agreement? Gorbachev leaned forward, arched an eyebrow, and gave a half-smile. "I detect that there's another question behind that question," he said. He suspected that Bush, using Kissinger as a go-between, was trying to trick him into revealing how willing he was to abandon Soviet control over Eastern Europe.

Kissinger responded that he had "no hidden agenda"; the idea was very much his own, though the president-elect had expressed interest and authorized him to seek Gorbachev's reaction. Reassured, Gorbachev told him that the notion might be worth pursuing; if there should be a back-channel negotiation on the matter, Kissinger should deal with his old friend Dobrynin. Kissinger was encouraged enough to think that his plan might have some chance.

After Kissinger's departure, Gorbachev reread Bush's letter. He was joined by his chief foreign policy aide, Anatoli Chernyayev, a veteran of the party apparatus, primarily the international department, whom he had known since the 1950s. Chernyayev was the kind of bureaucrat who preferred keeping his head down. He had never distinguished himself as an advocate of reform, though people who had known him during the Khrushchev period remembered him as having privately expressed relatively liberal views and having maintained some friendships with political dissidents.

Chernyayev said that Bush's letter contained "a certain contradiction": Bush promised continuity yet suggested that he might change American policy. Gorbachev chose to be encouraged that Bush had wasted no time in communicating with him: what other newly elected U.S. president had written to a Soviet leader even before he could use White House stationery? He wrote out a reply urging Bush to work together with him for "world peace."

Gorbachev's personal aide for Eastern Europe, Georgi Shakhnazarov, advised him to support the Kissinger plan. He felt that if the Bush administration was interested in consultations and understandings that could keep problems in Eastern Europe from spilling over into other areas of Soviet foreign policy, so much the better.

On Thursday, January 19, Bush called Meredith Price, editor of his prep school's alumni magazine, the *Andover Bulletin,* in response to Price's request for an interview. Asked what he hoped historians would say about his presidency, Bush said, "Left things a little better than when I found them. Kept America strong and kept the inexorable move toward democracy going forward.

"And I say 'inexorable' because when you look around the country, I don't think any serious student of world politics thinks that socialism or communism is on the rise. I think most people see that incentives and ownership and the freedoms that we think of when we think of democracy are on the move, and I'd like to keep those trends going with the United States at the forefront. And so I guess in the end, I'd hope they would say, 'He made a difference. He did his best.' "

In his inaugural address, delivered the next day, Bush used a word picture to convey his values and his sense of the world mood: "The day of the dictator is over. The totalitarian era is passing, its old ideas blown away like leaves from an ancient, lifeless tree. . . . We know what works: *freedom* works. We know what's right: *freedom* is right. We know how to secure a more just and prosperous life for man on earth — through free markets, free speech, free elections, and the exercise of free will unhampered by the state."

On Sunday, January 22, Brent Scowcroft quickly made it clear that he and his boss were under no illusions about Gorbachev. Appearing on ABC's "This Week with David Brinkley," he said that Gorbachev seemed "interested in making trouble within the Western alliance. And I think he believes that the best way to do it is a peace offensive, rather than to bluster, the way some of his predecessors have."

Scowcroft warned that Gorbachev's foreign policy might be secretly intended to throw the West off its guard and give the Soviet Union time to restore its economy and build new military power before a new world Communist offensive.* "Until we have better evidence to the contrary," he said, "we ought to operate on that expectation. . . . I think the Cold

---

* Adherents of this theory sometimes used the Russian word *peredyshka* (breathing space).

War is not over. There may be, in the saying, light at the end of the tunnel. But I think it depends partly on whether the light is the sun or an oncoming locomotive."

Having allowed Scowcroft to play bad cop, Bush once again played good cop. On Monday morning, January 23, he asked Scowcroft to arrange a telephone call to Gorbachev in the Kremlin. Bush said that he wanted to "establish contact, just check in with the guy."

For a president to telephone a Soviet leader was unusual, but the call was characteristic of Bush. When he looked at the globe, he thought of the ultimate Rolodex. For him, the splotches of color meant not just countries but presidents, kings, and prime ministers, many of whom he knew well and referred to by their first names. When a crisis erupted, his first instinct was to reach for the telephone.

When his call was put through to Moscow, Bush reassured Gorbachev that while he intended to make a broad reassessment of American relations with the Soviet Union, he would not allow any "foot-dragging." He thanked the Soviet leader for the warm reception given his son and grandson in Armenia.

Hearing what he wanted to hear, Gorbachev later told aides that he was encouraged by the call. For years he had been eager to have an American interlocutor with whom he could argue and bargain freely.

Although he had been affected by Reagan's warmth and goodwill, Gorbachev was tired of the lack of spontaneity, the anti-Soviet jokes, the Hollywood stories, the incessant recitation — always as if for the first time — of the Russian proverb *Doveryai, no proveryai* (Trust, but verify), which Gorbachev took as an insult.* Gorbachev told several aides after Bush's call that the new American president seemed ready to deal with historical forces and world issues not in the abstract, but directly, "as one human being to another."

---

* In his address at the signing of the treaty eliminating intermediate-range nuclear missiles at the White House in December 1987, Reagan delivered the hackneyed line again. As if he could stand it no longer, Gorbachev came close to the edge of public rudeness, piping up, "You repeat that at every meeting." The Soviet laughter in the East Room was not entirely without malice. Reagan defused the moment by retorting good-naturedly, "I *like* it!"

CHAPTER 2

"I Don't Want to Do Anything Dumb"

ON FRIDAY, January 27, 1989, Bush held his first news conference as president. Watching in his office at the State Department, Baker playfully addressed the image on the television screen: "Pull your tie up, George."

A reporter asked the president about Scowcroft's pessimism about the Soviet Union. Bush replied that the administration's position was "Let's take our time now." He said that he did not like using the term "Cold War": "That doesn't properly give credit to the advances that have taken place in this relationship. . . . Do we still have problems, are there still uncertainties, are we still unsure in our predictions on Soviet intentions? I'd have to say, 'Yeah, we should be cautious.' "

The next day, Kissinger arrived at the White House and reported to Bush, Baker, and Scowcroft on his talk with Gorbachev in Moscow. Afterward Baker asked the assistant secretary of state for Europe, Rozanne Ridgway, and her deputy for the Soviet bloc, Thomas Simons, for a confidential assessment of Kissinger's idea for a superpower negotiation on Eastern Europe.

Both career foreign-service officers who had spent eight years as part of the Reagan administration, they hated the Kissinger plan. Simons said that negotiating with the Soviets on Eastern Europe would legit-imize their role there. Moreover, "Why buy what history is giving you for free?" He noted that Soviet power was waning in Eastern Europe. There was no need for the United States to make concessions to the Kremlin in order for that process to continue. Ridgway warned that leaders in both Eastern and Western Europe would be furious at the idea of the Americans and Soviets negotiating their fate over their heads.

Baker's close adviser Dennis Ross told him that Ridgway and Simons were overreacting. Forty years old, Ross was an intense, quiet-spoken Berkeley political scientist with no strong commitment to conservatism or the Republican party. In 1972, just out of college, he had worked for the presidential campaign of George McGovern. With his semi-Beatles haircut and his preference for blue jeans when he worked on weekends, he looked slightly out of place among the other men and women around Bush and Baker. The walls of his office were decorated with the kindergarten-modern artwork of his children.

In 1988, after working in the Carter Pentagon and on the Reagan NSC staff, Ross had served as foreign-policy adviser to the Bush cam-paign, traveling with the candidate and helping him shape answers to questions from the press and responses to his Democratic opponent, Michael Dukakis. Immediately after the election, Ross was Scowcroft's first choice to be deputy national security adviser, but Baker insisted that he come with him to State instead.

The new secretary of state was concerned about what he saw as the traditional isolation of his department from the White House, and its long-standing rivalry with the NSC. Having at his side a key aide who already had an established relationship with the president would help. Scowcroft was determined to avoid a replay of the conflict that had so often broken out between the NSC and State in the past, notably during the Reagan administration, so he deferred to Baker. Ross became direc-tor of the State Department's policy planning staff.

In that post, Ross displayed the passion for anonymity that had often been prescribed for effectiveness as a senior staff aide. When his sec-retary once slipped him a *U.S. News & World Report* story that he was being considered for the Moscow embassy, he wrote in tiny letters on the clipping, "No thanks!" Three years into the Bush administration, David Hoffman wrote in the *Washington Post* that "despite his central role," Ross remained "one of the least public of Washington figures." Baker appreciated this quality, along with Ross's intelligence, his loy-alty, and his mordant sense of humor.

In response to Kissinger's proposal, Ross told his boss that to discuss the future of Eastern Europe with the Soviets in a serious, sustained, high-level dialogue would be only "common sense." Baker agreed, but he and Ross set the gambit aside for now.

In the Oval Office in late January, Bush told Scowcroft that he wanted to have an answer to the question of "what the world should be like in the next century, and what we should do to get there. I want to do something important, but I want to proceed prudently. I don't want to do anything dumb." He wished to "sit down with some of our best experts on the Soviet Union and see what they think — get their sense of Gorbachev."

Scowcroft gave the job of organizing the seminar to his thirty-four-year-old staff Soviet expert, Condoleezza Rice, a Stanford professor of political science.* Born in segregated Birmingham, Alabama, she had been a classmate of one of the four girls killed in the bombing of a black church in 1963. As a child, she had driven to Washington with her family and been barred from many motels and restaurants en route. When they arrived, her father photographed her in front of the White House. She told him, "One day I'm going to be in it."

After once aspiring to be a concert pianist, Rice had switched to political science at the University of Denver and earned a doctorate by writing a dissertation on the armed forces of Czechoslovakia, later specializing in the Soviet General Staff. When she lectured in the Soviet Union, her audiences were unprepared to hear an American black woman tell them things they did not know about their own country's military command — and in excellent Russian.

Rice now drew up a list of academic experts on Soviet affairs and penciled in a session for March. On Friday, February 10, after flying back to Kennebunkport, Maine, from Ottawa and his first foreign visit as president, Bush decided not to wait that long, and asked Scowcroft to hold the seminar that weekend. Rice worked the telephone.

Bush had spent every summer of his life but one in the house built on Walker's Point in 1903 by his maternal grandfather, George Herbert Walker. He called the house "our family strength," a "sacred place."

---

* Rice's parents adapted the name Condoleezza from an Italian musical phrase meaning "with sweetness."

On Sunday, February 12, clad in a baseball cap, a sweater, worn dungarees, and running shoes, Bush ushered a half-dozen Soviet specialists into his master bedroom, one of the few parts of the house that the Bushes kept heated during the winter. In addition to Rice, the group included Adam Ulam of Harvard, Marshall Goldman of Wellesley and the Harvard Russian Research Center, Stephen Meyer of MIT, Robert Pfaltzgraff of Tufts, and Ed Hewett, then of the Brookings Institution. Since most of the academics taught at universities in and around Cambridge, Massachusetts, they had been easily summoned to Maine on short notice.

With the icy Atlantic waters and gray-white skies visible through the steamy windowpanes over his shoulder, the president said, "We've got to take a hard look at our Soviet policy. I want to hear your views on what's happening over there. I'm not so much interested in policy recommendations per se. Those can wait. First we need to know what's going on, what we're dealing with."

The experts agreed that Gorbachev was committed to drastic reforms that would make the Soviet Union a more humane and agreeable member of the world community. The president said, "Suppose, God forbid, that his heart stops tomorrow. Is there *perestroika* after Gorbachev?"

Most in the bedroom nodded: Gorbachev had launched a process larger than himself, one that would be difficult for the hard-liners to reverse should he die or be ousted. While criticizing Stalin's personality cult, he had created his own "cult of power," with himself as the embodiment of *perestroika*, and was using the power of that cult to reduce the authority of the party and the Moscow apparatus. Rice said, "It would be hard for anyone who replaced Gorbachev to put all that back into the bottle."

With a faint smile, Scowcroft cautioned, "Never say never!" The academics conceded that *perestroika* might produce a backlash — a coup d'état against Gorbachev by hard-liners in the party, the army, and the KGB. The Soviet system might well turn out to be unreformable.

"The Achilles' heel of Gorbachev's program might turn out to be Eastern Europe," said Rice. She noted that just the day before, Hungary's Communist leaders had, astoundingly, consented to the formation of rival parties. She said that Gorbachev was taking the risk that the economic experimentation and other forms of independence he was encouraging in Eastern Europe might fuel anti-Communist and anti-

Soviet emotions that could sweep the satellite countries out of his control.

Bush asked whether the Soviets might at some point use troops to reassert their control over Eastern Europe. Several of the experts replied that the political cost for Gorbachev would be "astronomical." Goldman said that even short of such a crackdown, if change came too fast to Eastern Europe, it could "blow back" into the Soviet Union. The Soviet republics might demand liberalization and autonomy.

The president remarked that the experts seemed to agree that the sagging Soviet economy had compelled Gorbachev to turn his back on the war in Afghanistan. Could the United States use its leverage to extract concessions on human rights? Goldman and Hewett warned against any ostentatious attempt to exploit Soviet weakness; that could turn out to be a gift to Soviet hard-liners.

They cited the Jackson-Vanik Amendment. Imposed by Congress in the mid-1970s and still in force, this measure linked American economic favors such as the granting of "most favored nation" status to the Kremlin's easing of restrictions on the emigration of Soviet Jews. Irate over U.S. "blackmail," Leonid Brezhnev had responded by drastically reducing the Jewish exodus.

Hewett argued that since Soviet Jews were now emigrating again in large numbers, the United States should reward the Soviet reform movement by suspending Jackson-Vanik. He added, "We must not adopt a policy that ties us to Gorbachev as a man. This would inflate public expectations in the West and put the U.S. in an awkward position if Gorbachev's heart should stop." Scowcroft nodded vigorously.

During a relaxed moment in the kitchen, the president put issues of high policy aside and gave his impressions of some Soviet personalities he had met. He told his guests of his encounters with Gorbachev's hard-driving, strong-willed wife, Raisa, whom he had found to be "not exactly a charmer." A few days later, when Bush returned to the Oval Office, he told aides that the Sunday seminar was one of the best such sessions he had ever had: "If I can get that much good stuff on my day off, think how productive we can be around here when we're supposed to be working!"

In Moscow, Gorbachev was shown Bush's Kennebunkport guest list, which was published in the U.S. press. He was taken aback to see the name of Marshall Goldman, who had become well known among Western Kremlinologists for his repeated predictions that Gorbachev's days in power were numbered. Gorbachev feared that if Bush expected him to be deposed, he would be unlikely to take the risk of serious bargaining with Moscow.

On Monday, February 13, sitting at a desk carved from the timbers of the HMS *Resolute,* which had been used by John Kennedy and been restored to the Oval Office by Ronald Reagan, Bush put on his rimless aviator glasses and looked at a four-page secret directive drafted for his signature.

It said that America's forty-year policy of containment had been "vindicated." The United States and the Soviet Union "might stand at the door of a new era" of reduced military forces and peaceful resolution of nagging issues. Yet the USSR remained "an adversary with awesome military power." It would be "thoughtless to abandon policies that have brought us this far." Was it in the U.S. interest "to 'help' Gorbachev as he pursues *perestroika?*" Would such help "induce the USSR to pay a political price"?

Drafted by Scowcroft and his staff, the directive asked the State Department to conduct a "national security review" of U.S. policy toward the Soviet Union, suggesting changes that Bush might implement over the next four to eight years. Designated NSR-3, the recommendations should be on the president's desk by mid-March.

After a careful reading of Scowcroft's draft, Bush added a sentence of his own: "My own sense is that the Soviet challenge may be even greater than before because it is more varied." He told Scowcroft that he wanted to think about a period longer than eight years: "Let's see if we can't come up with something more forward-looking. Let's push it out at least into the next century."

Two days later, Scowcroft returned to the Oval Office with a revision that included the question, "What kind of relationship do we wish to see in the year 2000?" Bush approved and signed the directive. He told aides that he recognized that Gorbachev was a "historically formidable person"; yet they must remember that he was "still a Russian and a Communist, which counts for more in the final analysis."

No president had ever had to deal with a Soviet Union whose leadership and future were less certain. Bush hoped that NSR-3 would buy him time in which to ponder Soviet relations at the start of his term, protected from the buffeting of public opinion and events. He wanted to ensure that his policy would survive any eventuality.*

---

* Earlier presidents had used a similar technique. In 1952, Dwight Eisenhower was nominated by a largely isolationist Republican party and elected after a campaign in

Scowcroft told colleagues, "The Marxist-Leninist threat is over as an ideological and economic challenge. We won that one. It's still a considerable military threat, but even that is changing. So it's not good enough just to have four more years, modifying the basic approach we inherited. There's a new world out there. We've got to ask where we'd like to be at the end of the century and what policies will get us there."

Scowcroft's deputy Robert Gates told a private group that it was time to turn away from the Reagan manner of dealing with the Soviets: "A lot has happened in the relationship in an ad hoc way. We've been making policy — or trying to — in response to what the Soviets are doing, rather than with a sense of strategy about what we should be doing." He said that the Bush administration needed a "conscious pause" on Soviet policy for several months while it "looks over the landscape and reconsiders its position."

Gates warned those working on the policy review, "Don't be so dazzled by Mikhail Gorbachev, Superstar, that you forget we're in the business of making policy toward a country, not an individual. Bear in mind that the guy who's running the Soviet Union now may not be running the Soviet Union ten years from now." Gates believed that Gorbachev would probably turn out to be a historical aberration, "an exception that would prove the rule."

Robert Blackwill, the NSC official who was responsible for Europe and the Soviet Union, passed out Bush's directive to officials from State and other agencies.* Except for stints as a political officer in Nairobi and Tel Aviv, Blackwill had spent most of his foreign-service career working on European security and arms control.

He was a stubborn Atlanticist who tended to see East-West relations almost exclusively in terms of keeping NATO together. Blackwill attributed his deep aversion to taking chances to the experience of growing up on a farm in western Kansas. He liked to note that a gambling man bet the farm on a new combine, only to be wiped out by a hailstorm

---

which he and the man he would make his secretary of state, John Foster Dulles, extravagantly promised to "roll back" the tide of world communism. In fact, Eisenhower intended to practice neither isolationism nor rollback. With few modifications, he wished to continue Harry Truman's containment of the Soviet Union. He bought time by appointing three panels to study and report on the merits of hard, soft, and moderate approaches to Moscow.
* Early in the administration, Blackwill was sometimes confused in the press with Robert Blackwell of the CIA.

just before harvest; a gambling girl went behind a haystack and ended up in a shotgun wedding.

Blackwill saw Mikhail Gorbachev as a gambler who threatened to disrupt NATO. He needed no convincing about the wisdom of going slow in U.S.-Soviet relations. Of the policy review, he told an interagency group, "I can promise that this president will read every word of the final paper. All of us are going to have to learn to write for a president who has real expertise in this area." Playing on the title of Dean Acheson's memoir about the origins of the Cold War, he told them that they had the chance to be "present at the creation" of a new epoch in American diplomacy.

Some at State suspected that Scowcroft had sold NSR-3 to the president in order to mire down their department while the NSC consolidated its hold over the Bush administration's foreign policy. Rozanne Ridgway was convinced that the review would be used as a crowbar with which to dismantle and discredit the policies of her old chieftains Reagan and Shultz. For this she blamed James Baker.

As recently as the fall of 1988, many political leaders and journalists had predicted that the Bush presidency would be tantamount to Ronald Reagan's third term. Some presumed that the new president would retain so many Reagan personnel and policies that it would be difficult to discern that the fortieth president had actually left Washington.

But Bush and his circle had quickly made it clear that a new man was in charge. Hundreds of Reagan appointees were told that their services were no longer required.* Nowhere was this more true than at the State Department, where the incoming secretary wasted no time in cleaning house. Baker told aides, "Remember, this is *not* a friendly takeover."

He had installed five people to help him quickly dominate the department's bureaucracy. To attack the most urgent issues, along with Dennis Ross, Baker chose Robert Zoellick, a thirty-six-year-old Harvard-trained lawyer who had served under him at Treasury. To deal with the press, he appointed Margaret Tutwiler, a onetime Birmingham debutante who had been a Baker aide since his White House days. The

* The only cabinet members to be kept on were Nicholas Brady of Treasury, Richard Thornburgh of Justice, and Lauro Cavazos of Education, all appointed by Reagan in 1988 at Bush's urging.

veteran diplomat Lawrence Eagleburger and Robert Kimmitt, who had served on the Carter and Reagan NSC staffs, were to run the bureaucracy and deal with other topics.

Of these, only Eagleburger, the deputy secretary of state, was a professional diplomat, and he had retired from the foreign service in 1984.

Eagleburger's selection was intended largely to cement good relations with the White House, since he and Brent Scowcroft had been close friends and colleagues for nearly thirty years. They had both served in the American embassy in Belgrade early in their careers, and their paths had crossed again under Henry Kissinger at the NSC staff in the Nixon-Ford years. When Kissinger became secretary of state, in 1973, he took Eagleburger with him to help manage the bureaucracy. During that period Scowcroft and Eagleburger met frequently and talked on the phone many times a day. For old times' sake — and to the consternation of their colleagues — they often used snatches of Serbo-Croatian, which they had learned in Yugoslavia.

Both had followed Kissinger into private life, serving, respectively, as vice chairman and president of Kissinger Associates.

When Baker was Ronald Reagan's chief of staff in 1983, his allies argued that if he were to be made national security adviser, he could help the president score one international success after another, which would make Reagan seem indispensable in the 1984 campaign, just as Nixon had seemed indispensable in 1972. Baker in 1989 had a similar strategy for himself and for Bush. As with Nixon, the cardinal issue would have to be the new administration's relationship with the Soviet Union.

But Nixon had had the advantage of dealing with a Soviet leadership that was relatively stable and predictable. Baker had no idea what policies Gorbachev would be following two months hence, not to mention how long he would stay in power or what kind of Soviet leaders would follow him. Baker knew that if American-Soviet relations suddenly collapsed and Bush seemed too soft, the president would not be able to count on the kind of Teflon protection against right-wing criticism that Reagan had enjoyed.

Baker thought that Shultz had been a flabby negotiator during his final year in office, paying for Soviet concessions that Gorbachev might have made for free. It became fashionable for Bush administration officials to denounce Shultz to reporters — anonymously — as the "worst secretary of state since Stettinius."*

In his seventh-floor office at the pinnacled, Stalin-Gothic Foreign Ministry tower on Smolensk Square in Moscow, Eduard Shevardnadze was briefed on the whispering campaign being carried out in Washington against Shultz. It worried him. He had cherished his years dealing with Shultz; he remembered being happily surprised at their second meeting, in New York in 1985, when Reagan's secretary of state had stood up and said, "Here is my hand. Give me yours!"

Shevardnadze felt that he and Shultz had forged a new American-Soviet relationship. He recalled that when the two of them negotiated, "nothing prevented us from remaining ourselves in outlining our positions and trying to bring them closer. If one of us said, 'I can't go any farther than that,' the other understood: 'That's how it really is. He isn't bluffing.' "

Unlike their predecessors, Shevardnadze and Shultz had visited each other's homes and met each other's grandchildren. Once Shultz had taken Shevardnadze and his party down the Potomac on a yacht, as a banjo player, honoring the foreign minister's Georgian background, played "Georgia on My Mind."

Shevardnadze was informed that the man behind the whispering campaign against Shultz was the new secretary of state. Valentin Falin, chief of the international department of the Communist party's Central Committee, advised Shevardnadze that Bush and Baker were "dismissive of past achievements in Soviet-American relations."

Gorbachev and Shevardnadze privately referred to Bush's policy review as the *pauza* — the pause.† Combined with the *pauza,* the anti-Shultz campaign in Washington made them wonder whether the best years in Soviet-American relations might not now be behind them.

Shevardnadze ordered his staff to prepare a background dossier on Baker. Why were Baker and Bush turning their backs on the administration of which they had both been such a vital part? Were these two men so obsessed with protecting themselves from domestic right-wing critics that they were going to throw away the new opportunities in

---

* Edward Stettinius, a steel executive with no foreign-policy experience, was appointed by Franklin Roosevelt in 1945, three months before he died. Harry Truman fired him soon after taking office.
† Robert Gates used the same term ("the pause") to describe this period — but with approval.

American-Soviet relations, the very opportunities that made *perestroika* possible?

The dossier tried to put the best face on Baker: he was disciplined, efficient, well organized. He was a "pragmatist," not a "zoological anti-Communist." But Shevardnadze was not impressed. He told Gorbachev that Baker seemed like a "cold fellow," in whom it would be difficult to find the humanity he had so valued in Shultz. Why else would he "deliberately suspend" diplomacy with the Soviet Union?

Falin warned Gorbachev that the Americans might be using the *pauza* as a "pretext for preparing to dismantle" what Shevardnadze and Shultz had built; the pause might "betray a desire in Washington to use the complexity of the situation inside the Soviet Union to gain advantages for the U.S. on every point in the relationship."

Shevardnadze's principal deputy, Alexander Bessmertnykh, who had been the number two Soviet in Washington during Reagan's first term, predicted to his boss that after the *pauza*, Bush would embrace a policy of "constructive continuity." He saw the *pauza* as a "natural development in a new administration as it finds its bearings." The Soviet Union should not be tempted to exploit the hiatus. It was a "reflection of the new, more mature, more civilized nature of the relationship."

Bessmertnykh and other *amerikanisti* in the ministry argued that sooner or later Bush would resume the kind of diplomacy practiced under Reagan and Shultz. After all, the new president was moderate, pragmatic, and obviously sensitive to public opinion in both Europe and the United States, where Gorbachev was so popular. There was every reason to expect "favorable mental chemistry" once Bush met Gorbachev at a summit. *"Dai im vremya,"* said Bessmertnykh: Give them time.

Gorbachev and Shevardnadze were not the only ones impatient with Washington. When Baker made his first tour of Europe as secretary of state, in February, one head of government after another told him that Bush must not hold back with the Soviets. The British prime minister, Margaret Thatcher, told Baker that she was concerned about the policy review and the "apparent air of relaxation" in Washington. "And I'm sure Mr. Gorbachev is, too," she added.

Thatcher had been the first Western leader to say in public that Gorbachev was a different kind of Soviet leader. In the fall of 1984, when it was clear that Chernenko was not long for this world, she had invited to London the two men who were thought to be the leading contenders in the succession: Gorbachev and Grigori Romanov. When Gorbachev accepted, the British took it as a sign that he was more likely to get the job.

During their first conversation at Chequers, her official country retreat, in December 1984, Thatcher had given the presumptive next Soviet leader a Tory lecture on how to run a modern society: "Mr. Gorbachev, you *must* decentralize power. Don't let the economic ministries run everything!"

Gorbachev had listened intently, waving away aides who interrupted to remind him that he was late for his next appointment. He asked the prime minister what the Americans were really up to. Wasn't the Reagan administration bent on humiliating and finally destroying the Soviet Union? Thatcher replied that Reagan was more reasonable than his public rhetoric would indicate. Besides, the Soviet Union had itself to blame for such a long record of menacing behavior, she insisted.

After their talk, in a television interview, the prime minister uttered nine words carefully chosen by her foreign-policy aide Charles Powell: "I *like* Mr. Gorbachev. We can do business together." This commendation from the "Iron Lady of Capitalism," as she was called by the Soviet press, reassured Western leaders who had been nervous about the Soviet succession.

After Gorbachev took power, his chemistry with Thatcher was nourished not only by her willingness to vouch for him before the world but also by the candor with which they argued about politics, ideology, economics, and international relations. Both leaders were self-confident and forceful to the point of imperiousness. Like many heads of government, they appreciated these characteristics in each other far more than they did in their own citizens and colleagues.

Thatcher would tear into Gorbachev about what a "frightful thing" communism was. The Soviet Union, she maintained, was to blame for much of what had gone wrong in the twentieth century. Gorbachev would respond by denouncing Britain and the West for their mass unemployment and poverty. When she complained about Angola, Afghanistan, or Nicaragua, he would retort, "And what about Northern Ireland?"

In the early 1960s, Prime Minister Harold Macmillan had tried and failed to carve out a role for Britain as mediator between the Soviet Union and the United States. Ironically, it was the firebreathing Thatcher who finally succeeded in that task. She was just as frank in advising Reagan, Shultz, and other Americans about dealing with the Soviets as she was with Gorbachev himself.

In February 1989, she told Baker, "Don't let things linger. Don't let them lie fallow." The new U.S. administration must not allow the rapprochement with the Soviets to slow down. Nor must Gorbachev be permitted to win the battle for world opinion. The British foreign secretary, Geoffrey Howe, told Baker that the United States must "get back in the game."

Baker shook his head and said, "The stakes are too high, the issues too complicated for us to go off half-cocked. Besides, we've got time. If what's going on in the Soviet Union is as important as you think, it's not going to end by next Tuesday." He argued that every single day, Gorbachev's reforms were moving closer to the point at which reversal would be impossible. Responding to Gorbachev did not necessarily mean meeting him halfway: "He's *coming* our *way*. Let's *keep* him coming."

Nevertheless, after flying home to Washington, Baker told the president that their Western allies were getting restless. Bush replied that he would not be shoved by Gorbachev.

That month, Shevardnadze was touring Arab capitals. His ostensible purpose was to campaign for a Middle East peace conference, but he also hoped that the trip would jar Bush and Baker out of their lethargy. At the White House, a reporter asked Bush about Shevardnadze's Middle East trip and the "widespread impression" that the U.S. president had "no foreign policy."

The president's temper flared: "Well, I've never heard such outrageous hypotheses!" A ripple of nervous laughter swept the room. Bush went on, "I don't worry about that. And we *have* a foreign policy. . . . I don't want to be rushing out because Mr. Shevardnadze went to the Middle East. I'd like for the first step we take of that nature to be a prudent step."

Coming home late from a Saturday at the office, Robert Blackwill watched panelists on the television program "The McLaughlin Group" complain that after a month, the administration still lacked a policy toward the Soviet Union. He asked colleagues, "What would Herodotus make of this? We're trying to produce a policy for the next century, and they're saying our time's up after a few weeks!"

Bald, bespectacled, built like a fireplug, the old Soviet hand Jack Matlock, the U.S. ambassador to the Soviet Union, had ascended through the Foreign Service during thaws and freezes in the Cold War. Some officials in the Bush administration tended to associate him with what they saw as the softheadedness of Reagan's last year in office. They planned to replace him before long.

On the Bush-Baker shortlist for Matlock's job was Donald Kendall of Pepsi-Cola, whose history with Moscow dated back to Pepsi's introduction into the Soviet Union in the late 1950s. Another possibility was James Billington, the Librarian of Congress and a historian of Russian politics and culture.

But as time went on, Bush and Baker came to regard Matlock as a known commodity, a symbol of continuity and a signal that Washington was taking its time in deciding how to put its own mark on the relationship. He remained at his post for two and a half years of the Bush administration.

Matlock appreciated the magnitude of what Gorbachev was doing. He had watched Nikita Khrushchev preside over an early version of *glasnost* in the late 1950s, only to crack down on artists and writers in the early 1960s. Similarly, Khrushchev's measures to decentralize agriculture and industry and to reduce the size of the military, which Soviets now called the "first *perestroika,*" had been denounced as "harebrained schemes" by the orthodox Communists who ousted him in 1964.

Fluent in Russian, Matlock heard the testimony of Soviet citizens whose lives were changing dramatically. His consular officers reported to him at the end of a long day how many Soviet citizens were suddenly receiving permission to come to the West. He would go home to Spaso House, turn on the television, and see an investigative reporter jab a microphone into the face of an unhappy local party boss and demand to know why social services were so abysmal — or a talk show on which a white-bearded Russian Orthodox priest explained Christian doctrine on the immortality of the human soul.

On flights between Moscow and Washington, Matlock carried stacks of newspapers and journals. He read articles in *Sovietskaya Kultura* about the absurdity of state monopoly of production and distribution, in *Pravda* about the once-heretical notion that humankind's common interests superseded the conflicting interests of the working class and the bourgeoisie, in *Izvestia* about how the West had been justified in feeling threatened by Stalin's foreign policy after World War II.

Still, Matlock soon fell into line with the position that was emerging back in Washington. Like others, he believed that the improvements in the Kremlin's behavior were a direct result of forty years of consistent pressure from the West, and particularly, for the previous eight years, from the Reagan administration. Wasn't Gorbachev simply acknowledging what Western critics had always said was wrong with the Soviet system?

The ambassador felt that there was no need to overhaul American objectives just because Gorbachev preached — and seemed to practice — "new thinking." On the contrary, because Gorbachev was leader both of the ruling elite and of the opposition, steady criticism and demands for further change from the outside would help him force through his radical remedies on the inside.

Matlock was pessimistic about Gorbachev's chances for success and survival in power. He thought that Gorbachev's effort to reform the country was sure to exacerbate the already considerable stringencies of Soviet life. In the first week of January 1989, the Politburo had approved an economic austerity package that reduced state investment and pegged many workers' salaries to productivity.

Perestroika would have to mean price reform, which would lead to inflation. Increased competitiveness in industry would bring unemployment. *Glasnost* meant that the press would report and complain about these social miseries. With democratization, meanwhile, citizens who were paying higher prices or were out of work would be able to elect deputies to the Soviet parliament, who would shake their fists at Gorbachev and his ministers.

Still, Matlock believed that whatever happened to Gorbachev or to the specifics of the program he sponsored, the Soviet system had already changed in basic, encouraging ways, and that it would continue changing no matter who next held the top post in the Kremlin. He believed that whatever happened in Soviet domestic affairs would preoccupy the Kremlin too much to permit a return to a militant, expansionist foreign policy.

In late February, Matlock retreated for several days to the American embassy dacha, located on a five-acre compound on the banks of the Klyazma River at Tarasovka, forty-five minutes outside Moscow. There, in a sitting room looking out on a birch and pine forest, he drafted three long messages that he later sent by cable to Washington.

The first concerned the internal situation; the second outlined Soviet foreign policy; the third contained Matlock's own recommendations for a U.S. response. For security reasons, he wrote in longhand and kept the sheaf of paper with him at all times: U.S. officials presumed that the KGB bugged all embassy property and could reconstruct, from electronic impulses, anything typed out on an electric typewriter.

Matlock's cables emphasized economics. He argued that the United States was underestimating its "leverage" with Gorbachev — that is, its capacity not to "help" the Soviet leader but to nudge him further in the direction he was already going. By adopting a more positive tone about improvements in bilateral trade and Soviet participation in the world economy, the Bush administration could coax the Soviet Union toward a free-market economy.

Returning to Washington in early March, Matlock commended the 1988 Reagan-Gorbachev summit to Robert Blackwill of the NSC as a model for one to be held between Gorbachev and Bush. Blackwill replied, "I don't know, Jack. Maybe it wasn't such a great idea for the president to have said the evil empire was a thing of the past. Did you ever think that kind of statement lets the Soviets off the hook?"

Matlock replied that letting the Soviets off the hook was exactly what the United States should *not* do. But keeping them on the hook required increased political and economic engagement.

Matlock made his case to the president in the Oval Office on Friday, March 3. The ambassador presented Bush with a new Soviet edition of his campaign autobiography, *Looking Forward*. Scowcroft joked, "You sure it wasn't pirated, Jack?"*

The president gave Matlock twenty minutes of his time, which the ambassador used to urge a summit with Gorbachev before the end of 1989. If too many months passed between summits, he felt, the American-Soviet agenda would grow clogged. The public would expect too much. Better to enshrine the notion of annual summits — what the ambassador called "normal diplomacy at the highest level."

The president politely brushed Matlock off, saying, "Interesting. Let's think about it." Scowcroft frowned. Back at the State Department, Matlock bitterly told colleagues, "Our marching orders are clear: 'Don't just do something, *stand there!*' "

That week, Baker flew to Vienna for his first meeting as secretary of state with Eduard Shevardnadze. In the baroque splendor of the Hofburg Palace, thirty-five delegations were assembled to discuss conven-

---

* Soviet publishers were turning away from their old tendency to republish Western books in Russian without permission. The Soviet copyright agency VAAP had bought the Soviet rights to *Looking Forward* from Doubleday.

tional forces in Europe (CFE) — the size of armies as well as the number and kinds of armaments that faced each other along the Iron Curtain.

In 1979, NATO had resolved to deter the Warsaw Pact from attacking Western Europe by deploying a new generation of intermediate-range nuclear forces (INF). These new American missiles, poised against the Soviet Union, were intended to counterbalance a new class of Soviet missiles already aimed at Western Europe. The Kremlin made a huge effort to thwart the American plan.

During his first year in office, Ronald Reagan offered a "zero option": NATO would cancel its deployment if the Soviets would eliminate all of their similar missiles. The Soviets refused: why should they destroy a system already in place in exchange for the mere cancellation of a Western plan for the future? Vice President Bush shored up support for the zero option in Western Europe, where there was widespread opposition to the new U.S. missiles. In January 1983, in West Berlin, Bush won a standing ovation when he read out an "open letter" from Reagan to the people of Europe, in which the president offered to meet with Yuri Andropov to persuade him of the merits of the arrangement. In late 1983, when the United States, on schedule, startled installing the missiles, the Soviets walked out of INF talks in Geneva.

When Gorbachev took power, he was far more amenable to the zero option, which conformed to his wish to scale back Soviet defense spending and the Soviet Union's debilitating rivalry with the West. In the spring of 1987, he proposed broadening the definition of "intermediate-range" to include missiles designed to strike targets as close as three hundred miles away. Reagan agreed.

Many Western European leaders worried that Reagan was getting carried away: perhaps the president might even accede to the complete "denuclearization" of Europe. Under the forty-year-old NATO doctrine, U.S. nuclear weapons were considered vital to offset two perceived Soviet advantages: the Soviet Union was geographically closer to Western Europe than was the United States, and the Warsaw Pact had more men under arms and more tanks and artillery than NATO.

To allay these anxieties, the Reagan administration pledged not only to leave its short-range nuclear forces in Europe but also to upgrade the eighty-eight U.S. Lance missiles based in West Germany. While this position reassured many strategists in Washington, London, Paris, and Brussels, it upset those in Bonn.

The West German chancellor, Helmut Kohl, knew that if the Lances were ever fired, it would probably be because NATO was losing the early phase of a war and Western commanders were trying to stop Soviet armored columns that were already thrusting deep into West Germany. The resulting devastation would kill more West Germans than invaders. Kohl feared that even if the Lances were not fired, they would be irresistible targets for preemptive strikes by advancing Warsaw Pact forces, perhaps including Soviet nuclear weapons.

Unlike Brezhnev, Gorbachev was not the sort of Soviet leader who by his bloviation and bullying inadvertently helped American leaders make the case for new nuclear weapons in Europe. Gorbachev wanted a treaty on shorter-range nuclear forces (SNF) that would not only prevent the upgrading of the Lances but require the removal of the old missiles from West Germany.

By January 1989, the United States and its Western allies seemed to be on a collision course. The United States was pressing to deploy new SNF missiles, over the growing objections of the West Germans.

The president and Baker used the dispute to put Soviet propagandists, the "softheads" of Western Europe, and the U.S. Republican Right on notice that the new administration would stand firm not only against the Soviet adversary but also against Western allies, if necessary. At the start of the Bush administration, Robert Blackwill privately predicted that the Lance missiles would be the "defining security issue of the next couple of years."

When Baker met with his staff in February, he said that "any concession" on Lance "would be a classic slippery slope" that would lead to a nuclear-free Europe, risking the "entire strategy that has served NATO well for forty years."*

With American INF missiles gone from Europe because of the zero option and the remaining SNF missiles for West Germany in jeopardy, NATO defense planners became even more concerned about the Warsaw Pact's numerical advantage in nonnuclear, or conventional, forces. By 1989, no NATO member had the will or the desire to make a major increase in its contribution to the defense of Western Europe. On the contrary, Western Europeans were eager to see U.S. troops leave their continent, as were budget-minded U.S. congressmen.

---

* This was an overstatement. Under an SNF agreement, U.S. nuclear weapons would still defend Western Europe. Four hundred U.S. submarine-launched warheads were "dedicated" to NATO, as were numerous other weapons in the area. It was long-standing American policy to threaten the use of all of its strategic forces if the Warsaw Pact attacked any NATO member state.

This left the option of stepping up the effort to reach a bargain with the Eastern bloc to reduce the number of troops on both sides of the Iron Curtain. Talks on conventional forces had been bogged down for years. The West knew that any soldiers and weapons the Kremlin withdrew from Eastern Europe could be quickly sent back in a crisis. The United States, by contrast, would have to move its men and materiel across the Atlantic. The West therefore argued that the Warsaw Pact must make disproportionate cuts in order for the deal to be truly equitable.

In April 1987, Gorbachev had surprised the West by conceding this point. At the UN in December 1988, he announced dramatic cuts in Soviet forces. In response to these unilateral concessions, the United States had to adjust its own position. Even before Bush was sworn in, he and Scowcroft held what they called "look-ahead" sessions — relaxed, private conversations about possible future troubles and opportunities — and one of the topics they discussed was what should be done about American forces in Europe.

Pressures were building on both sides of the Atlantic to reduce these forces, and tensions were growing over the issue of "burden sharing" — that is, whether the Western Europeans were contributing sufficiently to their own defense. Public-opinion polls indicated that NATO was seen increasingly as an anachronism, and an expensive one. Gorbachev was doing everything he could to encourage such sentiment, using what Scowcroft derisively called his "proposal-a-day" strategy.

Scowcroft said, "There's a concatenation of events, all going in one direction, all harmful. We've got to do something to get out ahead." The administration should come up with an arms-control initiative that did what Gorbachev himself did so skillfully: make a virtue out of the necessity of reducing forces in Europe.

NATO heads of state and government were scheduled to meet in Brussels in the middle of 1989. The meeting would be Bush's debut as leader of the alliance. Both the president and Scowcroft knew that it could turn into a disastrous, unruly debate over the terms and pace of American retreat from Europe — and the dismantlement, if not the collapse, of the postwar order. Scowcroft said that the United States needed to "do something fairly dramatic to get out of this whole mess."

Following his own advice to his staff to come up with new ideas, and Bush's exhortation to "think big," Scowcroft suggested that the United States propose the removal of both superpowers' armies from Europe: American troops stationed in Western Europe would be brought back across the Atlantic, while Soviet troops would be withdrawn from Eastern Europe.

The United States had forces in Western Europe solely to protect its allies there from an attack coming from the East. Soviet forces, by contrast, were in Eastern Europe to enforce the Kremlin's subjugation of the Warsaw Pact. Soviet influence over Eastern Europe was almost exclusively the result of the Soviet military presence there, while American influence over Western Europe was the result of commerce, culture, and shared political values and institutions.

Therefore, if both superpowers pulled their armies out of Eastern and Western Europe, the United States and the West would reap the lion's share of the benefit. If the Soviet army could be induced to end its occupation of Eastern Europe, the nations of that region might finally be able to move toward genuine self-determination and perhaps even reintegration with the West. This constituted a zero option for CFE.*

Soon Scowcroft began to have second thoughts. Blackwill pounded away at what he called, only half jokingly, Scowcroft's "harebrained scheme." He teased Scowcroft by suggesting that he had spent so much of his professional life on nuclear strategic issues that he had forgotten the basics of conventional defense: "It's warm bodies that fight wars, and therefore warm bodies that deter them. As long as the Soviet Union is on the Eurasian landmass and the U.S. is not, we'll need our troops over there. Maybe if the USSR moves to the Bahamas, we can consider bringing our forces back onto this side of the ocean, but not before."

Noting that Scowcroft's plan would remove American ground forces but leave some air force units in Europe, Blackwill joked that the general was betraying the parochialism of his own air force background: "What we've got here is the fly-boy's answer to arms control: Bring the army home so you guys can provide air cover for those folks who stay behind!"

Beyond his objection to the substance of Scowcroft's plan, Blackwill

---

* Scowcroft saw additional, more technical attractions in the idea of removing U.S. ground forces from Europe. He believed that equity, economics, and logistics all argued for the Western European countries' providing a much larger share of the ground forces in NATO. It would be both fairer and cheaper for the Western Europeans to supply the manpower necessary for their own defense, and it would be much easier to mobilize units during a crisis if the reinforcements came from the local population rather than from across the Atlantic.

did not want the United States to be drawn into a bidding contest with Gorbachev: "We shouldn't try to go head to head against Gorbachev in the boldness sweepstakes." Such arguments gave Scowcroft an accurate though probably mild taste of the opposition he could expect from the national security establishment if he went public with his idea. He quickly backed away from it.

Gorbachev had followed up his spectacular UN speech of December 1988, in which he promised to cut Soviet forces by half a million troops and ten thousand tanks over the next two years, by announcing a 10 percent cut in defense spending.* The Kremlin had also published detailed figures on the size of its armed forces and begun the pullout of troops from Warsaw Pact countries.

Now, in Vienna, Shevardnadze proposed that NATO and the Warsaw Pact set equal ceilings on their military hardware and reduce their troops by 25 percent. He added that the introduction of Lance missiles would "destroy the fragile trust that has just begun to emerge in Europe."

Baker was in the awkward position of having to explain why the United States was still refusing to reciprocate Gorbachev's initiatives. Dennis Ross and Robert Zoellick had pressed the State Department bureaucracy hard for new ideas on SNF. They warned Baker, "Your speech won't be received well compared to what Shevy will say." But Baker chose not to take risks. In his address, he placed the burden on Gorbachev: the *Soviets* were the ones who would have to "let the 'new thinking' " sweep away the "era of stagnation" once and for all.

Baker's speech drew only tepid applause. Afterward he told Ross, "I guess we bombed out there today, didn't we?" Ross said, "Not really. If you look at the substance of what's happening, the Soviets are accepting our position. According to their own proposal, they've got to cut like crazy to come down to where we are right now."

Baker was not consoled by Ross's answer. "I'm not talking about the numbers," he said. "I'm talking about the politics of it all. Look who's getting the big cheers. Then look at who's getting the big yawns."

*   *   *

* Erich Honecker, the party boss of the most orthodox Soviet satellite, East Germany, knew that Gorbachev was not kidding. In January 1989, to keep on the Soviet leader's good side and, he hoped, preserve the old order, Honecker proclaimed that his armed forces would be cut by ten thousand troops, six hundred tanks, and fifty combat planes. Like Gorbachev, he cut his defense budget by 10 percent.

The next day, Tuesday, March 7, Shevardnadze called on Baker at the U.S. ambassadorial residence where Khrushchev had confronted Kennedy in 1961. Under a Gilbert Stuart portrait of George Washington, the two foreign ministers sat down at a green-baize-draped table in the embassy dining room, joined by Matlock and the U.S. ambassador to Austria, Henry Grunwald, the former editor-in-chief of Time Inc., who was born in Vienna and fled the Nazis in the 1930s.

Baker and Shevardnadze soon withdrew with their interpreters to the wood-paneled library, which was dominated by a large Milton Avery seascape. Smarting from what he saw as his failure the previous day, Baker was determined to impress Shevardnadze with his initial presentation on arms control. The Soviet foreign minister asked him for assurance that the Bush administration, like its predecessor, was "serious about moving forward in the improvement of the relationship."

Baker replied that *perestroika* was "good for the USSR and good for the rest of the world. We really hope that you succeed. But your success depends on you, not on us."

Shevardnadze concurred. He said he would ask only that the United States continue to nurture world developments that made it possible for the Soviet Union to devote the attention and resources necessary to internal reform. Baker said that the Bush administration would do just that.

When he returned to Moscow, Shevardnadze expressed amusement to his aides that during their meeting, Baker had relied on a thick sheaf of background papers and marked-up talking points, with passages underlined and notes scrawled in the margins.

The new secretary of state may have been articulate and forceful, said Shevardnadze, but when interrupted with a question or remark that did not fit the script, he had seemed uncertain of himself. Baker would riffle through his papers and then, if he could not find what he was looking for, improvise without much coherence.

Shevardnadze concluded that Baker was intelligent and diligent, but his lack of experience showed. Still, he added, at no point had the new secretary of state tried to score cheap debating points.

The foreign minister reported to Gorbachev that there had not been much personal warmth between him and Baker, but there was plenty of time for that to develop: "I think I'm going to do fine with this fellow. . . . This is a man I can accomplish things with."

Shevardnadze's favorable assessment of Baker did not please the hard-liners in the Soviet leadership. Vladimir Kryuchkov of the KGB and Dimitri Yazov, the defense minister, predicted that Bush's policy review would have a sinister outcome. Shevardnadze, they complained, had become the chief apologist for the Americans: he was exploiting his intimate relationship with the Soviet president to undermine competing foreign-policy advice from the party, the secret police, and the military.

Gorbachev defended his foreign minister, but only to a point. On occasion Shevardnadze would return to his office from the Kremlin, collapse in his upholstered chair, and tell his aides that there had been yet another "real struggle" with the military and the KGB. Gorbachev was still accepting his benign view of the *pauza*, but Shevardnadze did not know how much longer he could hold out.

When Baker returned to Washington, he gave Bush his own version of the meeting in Vienna. No longer would Shevardnadze have the luxury of playing to a pushover like Shultz; gone were the days when a secretary of state would nod while Shevardnadze parroted Gorbachev's self-congratulatory rhetoric about his contributions to the future of mankind. This time, he said, the foreign minister had seemed almost a supplicant.

Still, Baker conceded that he had been unsettled by Shevardnadze's public-relations triumph. He had come out of the 1988 campaign worried about the Republican Right's opposition to Bush, but now his political radar had swung toward Europe. He felt that the position he had had to present in Vienna was "much too static, very proforma."

Baker exhorted the president to "get off the dime." The longer the United States seemed to be hunkering down, the harder it became to keep the Western allies "on board." The Soviets needed only slight encouragement to keep dealing on essentially Western terms.

He reported that Shevardnadze seemed "obsessed with continuity." All the United States had to do was resume the process that the rest of the world had understood to be under way before Bush's election. The American hand was very strong. Baker believed that he could make headway not only in arms control but also on regional conflicts and human rights.

He told Bush that Gorbachev and Shevardnadze needed foreign

successes: "They're desperate to keep bringing home the bacon in foreign policy, since they're having so much trouble putting bacon on the table in their economy. Much of what they're doing is ad hoc. I'm not sure how much time they've got. Nor am I sure *they* know how much time they've got." Gorbachev should welcome "proposals and initiatives that we might generate." He was clearly "in a real hurry."

CHAPTER 3

"More! You Must Do More!"

ON TUESDAY, March 14, 1989, one day before the deadline, the result of the much-heralded policy review landed with a thud on the president's gold-embossed green-leather desktop.

Bush was not a devoted reader. When asked whether the president read memos, his former aide Pete Teeley said, "Yes, but make it short." Like Franklin Roosevelt and Ronald Reagan, Bush preferred to gather information through conversation.

One exception to this rule was the daily secret report from the CIA. As director of Central Intelligence in the mid-1970s, Bush had sometimes brought these documents to President Ford by hand, along with models of missiles and bombers to illustrate Soviet military developments. (At least once, as a prank, he called on Ford in a disguise provided by the agency's clandestine service.)

The final version of NSR-3 was thirty-one single-spaced pages, six pages over the limit Blackwill had set with State.* The highly classified document began portentously: "We are in a transition period

---

* To keep the document even this short, the State Department had had to use a smaller typeface than usual.

potentially as important as the immediate postwar period." There was only a "small chance" that the Soviet Union would "return to draconian autocracy."

The United States must try to "make reforms irreversible" in the Soviet Union while introducing "no irreversible shifts" in American policy. The president must remember that Moscow still aspired to become a "more competitive superpower." Gorbachev's "desire for less confrontational relations" was a "double-edged sword" that could rend the Western alliance.

Nevertheless, "*perestroika* is in our interest": Gorbachev's new approach "gives us sources of leverage we did not have eight years ago." American policy must be designed not to "help" Gorbachev but rather to "challenge" the Soviets in such a way as to "move them in the direction we want."

Further, U.S. policy should try to help "institutionalize" Soviet reform so that it could not be suspended or reversed if Gorbachev or a successor should attempt a return to the Ice Age. The United States should seize the initiative and establish the criteria by which to decide whether or not the Soviet Union should be admitted to the community of civilized nations.

The Soviets' anxieties "that they will not be competitive in the twenty-first century" were responsible for a "dynamic toward democratization." This was "consistent with our goal of seeing a Soviet Union that increasingly recasts its values and priorities in terms of the quality of life of its people rather than expansion abroad — and where there are internal political constraints on the power of the Soviet leadership and the Party."

Buried deep in the NSR was a list of desiderata for change in the Soviet Union: increased institutional safeguards for civil, political, and economic freedoms; more liberal laws and election practices, including a secret ballot; an independent judiciary; a "more critical press"; "flourishing unofficial organizations"; more freedom of movement; progress "toward the establishment of economic liberty" through decentralized decision making; the right to own land and capital; an end to the command economy; and, most ambitious, "the ending of the monopoly of the Communist Party and the dissolving of the police state."

The authors of this report cannot have imagined that all of this and more would actually come to pass within three years. The recommendations for U.S. policy, however, were hardly bold or even very specific. Alexander Vershbow, the director of the State Department's Soviet desk, called the recommendations "status quo plus." He knew that there would be a long tug-of-war between those who wanted to emphasize the status quo and those who wanted to stress the "plus."

At the White House, Scowcroft found the conclusions hedged and much too cautious — a "big disappointment." During brainstorming sessions in his office at the end of the day, he kept telling members of his staff that he wished them to "stretch," to break out of old habits and patterns. He chided them for their "lack of imagination about where to take America. . . . You're being too conservative. You've become a bunch of old curmudgeons."

But in his own public statements on the Soviet Union, Scowcroft continued to sound like a curmudgeon himself. He considered it to be one of his duties to deflate excessive public expectations so that they did not harm the president.

The policy review also disappointed Bush and Baker. For three weeks, the president did not even bother to schedule an NSC meeting for its formal consideration. Distancing himself from NSR-3 and the Reagan holdovers who had drafted it, Baker complained to Bush that after all its huffing and puffing, the bureaucracy had produced not a cannon but a popgun. Rozanne Ridgway and the others had simply "dredged up" ancient positions. Couldn't anyone come up with anything "creative or new"?

In late March, Baker was irritated by the lassitude of his bureaucracy and the familiar experience of reading articles suggesting that he was in over his head. The conservative *National Review* reported that the secretary of state's "decidedly listless debut" had left his admirers "gnashing their teeth in frustration."

Baker decided to "goose the people around here to expand their minds a bit" and remind them that he was not a "prisoner of this building." He took Kissinger's proposal for an American-Soviet negotiation over Eastern Europe out of mothballs.

On Tuesday, March 28, the *New York Times* reported on its front page that the secretary was "considering" the Kissinger plan — with a caveat. In an interview with the newspaper's diplomatic correspondent, Thomas Friedman, Baker said, "I think it is important that any such idea, to the extent that it is going to be pursued, be pursued carefully, so that you do not send a signal that somehow we are getting together with the Soviet Union and carving up Eastern Europe."

Yet this was just the implication that many felt the plan inevitably conveyed. In the corridors of State, old enemies of Kissinger's and new ones of his plan sardonically dubbed it "Yalta II." This label was the equivalent of a poison warning. At Yalta in 1945, Franklin Roosevelt, Winston Churchill, and Joseph Stalin had divided Europe into two armed camps. For many in the West, the code word *Yalta* had come to be synonymous with acquiescence in Stalin's enslavement of Eastern Europe.

After reading the *Times* piece, indignant foreign ministers in Europe demanded "clarification." Reflecting both his own views and those of angry Hungarian officials, the U.S. ambassador in Budapest, Mark Palmer, denounced the proposal in his cables to Washington. At the White House, Blackwill told Scowcroft that the West Germans were saying that such a bargain would be viewed as an effort to rein in the independence movements in Eastern Europe — especially in East Germany.

The British ambassador in Washington, Sir Antony Acland, climbed into his Bentley and was driven to the State Department. He marched in and informed Lawrence Eagleburger that Her Majesty's government was strongly opposed to "any possible deal between the United States and the Soviet Union on Eastern Europe."

Eagleburger assured Acland that the idea was "not under serious consideration" and that the administration was "aware of all the down sides." He said that Baker had only been expressing his personal view that the plan was "interesting as an intellectual exercise." He added that the "merit in the Kissinger proposal, if any, is that it gives us a chance to think through the implications of dramatic change in Eastern Europe."

Furious, Kissinger was convinced that Baker had deliberately ambushed him, first by killing the idea with kindness in the *Times,* then by ordering his staff — his longtime aide Larry Eagleburger, no less — to administer the coup de grace with Allied diplomats.

During a private White House luncheon in late March, Baker nudged the president further toward a more active approach to Gorbachev. He noted the recent election of a Soviet Congress of People's Deputies: here was new evidence that Gorbachev was "really serious about opening up the system. With every step of this kind that he makes, it's harder and harder to imagine him going backward."

In their first taste of electoral democracy, from one end of the Soviet Union to the other populist, liberal, nationalist challengers had defeated the careerists of the Communist party establishment. Some party candidates had lost even when running unopposed, for voters were allowed in effect to cast vetoes.

One victor was Boris Yeltsin, the onetime Moscow party chief whom Gorbachev had fired in 1987 for demanding reforms that were too radical. Now Yeltsin had captured 89 percent of the vote for Moscow's at-large seat in the new congress. Many members of the Soviet embassy in Washington, including several KGB officers, had cast their absentee ballots for him. Some analysts at the CIA saw Yeltsin as an important potential source of support for Gorbachev's program, and, if Gorbachev should falter, a possible successor.

On Saturday, April 1, Scowcroft's deputy Robert Gates warned in a speech in Brussels that neither Gorbachev nor his power structure was irrevocably committed to reform. Gates said that he expected "prolonged turbulence" in the Soviet Union.

With his small stature, smooth face, neatly combed white hair, and singsong Kansas voice, the forty-five-year-old Gates gave the impression of a well-behaved and precocious youngster. He radiated a skepticism about Gorbachev that was so intense that his bureaucratic foes sometimes thought it contained a barely disguised nostalgia for the bygone era when Soviet leaders had glowered, stonewalled, bullied, and otherwise behaved according to stereotype. Gates was the administration's chief doubting Thomas in the debate over whether Gorbachev was "for real" or "good for us."

Gates had earned his doctorate from Georgetown and joined the CIA as an analyst specializing in the Communist world. After a stint on the NSC staff under Ford and Carter, he returned to the agency and eventually became deputy director for intelligence and then deputy director. During the Reagan-Gorbachev years, he oversaw a series of agency reports questioning whether anything fundamental had changed in the Soviet Union. Summaries of these assessments, and sometimes the documents themselves, found their way into the hands of conservative senators and congressmen, who used them to tar the State Department as "soft" on Gorbachev.

Exasperated, George Shultz had several times complained to the

White House that the CIA was overstepping the boundaries between analysis and advocacy. He held Gates largely responsible. When William Casey was incapacitated in 1986 by a deadly brain tumor, Reagan chose Gates to succeed him as director of Central Intelligence. The president withdrew the nomination when senators complained that Gates had failed to notify Congress about the diversion to the Nicaraguan *contras* of profits from the administration's covert sale of arms to Iran.

Soldiering on as deputy director to Reagan's fallback choice, William Webster, Gates had gone public in January 1988 with his bleak assessment of Gorbachev. In a Dallas speech he predicted, "A long, competitive struggle with the Soviet Union still lies before us." That October, at a meeting of the American Association for the Advancement of Science, he issued the most ringing declaration yet put forth by any U.S. official of the case against Gorbachev. The Soviet leader's real purpose, he said, was to use détente to grab Western technology and improve the Soviet military machine: "The dictatorship of the Communist party remains untouched and untouchable." Should the United States want to help revitalize the Soviet system? "I think not."

After hearing about the speech, Shultz had called Gates and reprimanded him: the CIA's deputy director had no right to comment in public on policy. Such "name-calling" would be "personally offensive to Gorbachev."

In April 1989, Baker had much the same reaction to Gates's latest pronunciamento. It was out of harmony with the secretary's growing belief that the change in the Soviet Union was profound. Privately Baker complained, "The deputy director of the NSC shouldn't be out giving policy speeches on the Soviet Union, especially so early in the administration. You shouldn't have everybody and his dog out there giving political speeches."

The previous month, Bush had nominated the conservative Wyoming congressman Dick Cheney as secretary of defense, in place of former Texas senator John Tower, whose nomination had been defeated by the Senate. On Tuesday, April 4, Cheney told reporters that he was a "believer" in the notion that Gorbachev wanted changes in the Soviet economy that would demand "certain political reforms" such as elections. Gorbachev was "serious" about cutting back on military spending.

Baker welcomed Cheney's remarks. Delighted Soviet officials attributed Cheney's apparent friendliness to his experience as Gerald Ford's chief of staff during the heyday of détente. Actually, Cheney had been more influenced by the Soviet ambassador, Yuri Dubinin, who had come to his huge Pentagon office shortly after his swearing-in and given him chapter and verse about the Congress of People's Deputies and the "birth" of "normal politics" and "real democracy in our country."

Within hours, a Russian translation of Cheney's comments was handed to Gorbachev, who exclaimed with delight, "This from the chief of the Pentagon!"

In early April, Gorbachev left Moscow for his first trip to London as supreme Soviet leader. Given his warm relationship with Margaret Thatcher, he would nowhere be better equipped to exploit growing Western European impatience with the Americans.

Before Gorbachev's departure, the Pentagon leaked a report that the Soviets were sending new long-range bombers to Libya. On the day of Gorbachev's principal London address, at the Guildhall, where General Dwight Eisenhower had given a famous speech after the Allies' victory in Europe, the State Department announced that two months earlier the KGB had been caught trying to bug the U.S. consulate in Leningrad.

Shevardnadze sputtered to the press that the Americans were waging an "old and disagreeable kind of campaign against us." He presumed — correctly — that some officials in Washington were trying to generate doubts that Gorbachev was really a new kind of Soviet leader.

At Number Ten Downing Street, when the doors closed behind Gorbachev and Thatcher, the Soviet president opened fire on the Americans. He said that Bush's policy review was about to become an "obstacle" to the relationship, perhaps even a deliberate "braking mechanism." Why should it take so long for a new president who had been part of the previous administration to work out his own approach?

The improvement in East-West relations, Gorbachev said, "isn't just based on my ideas or policies. These are matters of mutual interest and joint agreement." He reminded the prime minister that she had several times privately vouched for Bush. Hadn't she promised him that the new president would pick up where Reagan had left off? Well, nothing was happening — nothing except a lot of petty harassments! The whole situation was "intolerable."

Thatcher urged Gorbachev to be patient. But immediately after their talk, she fired off a message to Bush saying that Gorbachev was worried and upset, and with reason: the policy review was indeed taking an awfully long time.

*   *   *

On Wednesday, April 5, the strategist, diplomat, and scholar George Kennan testified before the Senate Foreign Relations Committee. He charged that Bush had been "unresponsive" to recent "encouraging initiatives and suggestions from the Soviet side": "Whatever reasons there may once have been for regarding the Soviet Union primarily as a possible, if not probable, military opponent, the time for that sort of thing has clearly passed."

Senators, the audience, and even the committee stenographer responded with a standing ovation. Kennan was the dean of American Sovietologists and the intellectual father of the concept of containment.* His testimony poked another hole in the seawall that the president had tried to build around himself with his policy review.

Gorbachev announced two days later that he would stop production of weapons-grade uranium and shut down two plutonium plants. Asked by the press for a reaction, Bush was petulant: "We'll be ready to react when we feel like reacting and when we have prudently made our reviews upon which to act."

Privately the president was worried about the mounting pressure for action on the Soviet Union. Marlin Fitzwater and Roman Popadiuk, a career foreign-service officer who handled press relations for the NSC, wrote him a series of memos on the "perceptual problem" and the need to "put the ball back in Gorbachev's court."

In Los Angeles, Ronald Reagan was telling friends of his "uneasy" feeling about Bush's "foreign-policy indecisiveness." The former president felt that Bush's "hesitancy" about the Soviet Union had allowed Gorbachev to regain the initiative in world opinion and create a "needless crisis" in NATO.†

---

* Kennan had predicted in the late 1940s that eventually a "contained" Soviet Union would "mellow": it would give up on its quest for world domination and turn inward to deal with the strangulating consequences of its ideology and its political system.

† On May 6, a column to this effect appeared in the *Washington Post*. The author was Lou Cannon, a veteran political correspondent who was working on a book about the Reagan presidency. Reagan was concerned, wrote Cannon, that Bush's "excessively cautious approach" to arms control and his "hesitancy" had enabled Gorbachev "to regain the political initiative in the battle for European public opinion and created a needless crisis in NATO." These insights into the ex-president's thinking were attributed to "Reagan's friends." Those who considered themselves witting in the ways of journalism presumed that Cannon had the story from Reagan himself.

It was widely believed that Reagan had decided to let his feelings be known because he detected and resented the implicit criticism of him in many of the caveats coming out of the new administration. In fact, Cannon wrote the column just *before* he conducted

Bush told Scowcroft that they had better "get moving, at least in the way we talk about this thing. We've got to make clear that we know important stuff is happening and we're not just sitting here on our duffs."

On Sunday, April 9, Scowcroft dutifully had himself booked to appear on "Meet the Press." Ten weeks earlier, he had insisted on a similar program that the Cold War was not over. This time he said, "What we're seeing now is evidence . . . that the West has won." Nonetheless, the American people must be neither euphoric nor complacent. There was no need for any "sharp, dramatic change" in U.S. policy toward the USSR.

That same day, in the streets of Tbilisi, capital of the Soviet republic of Georgia, Soviet troops broke up a throng of ten thousand Georgian nationalists. More than two hundred people were injured, and nineteen killed, sixteen of them women. Some were beaten to death with shovels.

The information rattling out of teletypes in the White House basement was fragmentary. Scowcroft told his aides, "We're like a physician that can't do a lot of help but we've got to take an oath not to do harm. Almost whatever we say will be used to stir up trouble over there on one side or another." Condoleezza Rice agreed: "We don't want to give Gorbachev's conservative critics a stick to beat him with."

Robert Blackwill made the same point to Scowcroft. "It's obviously in our interest for internal reform to go forward. So what do we say when there are bumps on the road, including really bad ones like this? Uttering cosmic banalities doesn't do much except make us feel good."

Scowcroft needed little persuading: "We've got no dog in this fight. For everyone's sake, the less said, the better." The Voice of America was ordered to avoid any broadcasts that would inflame the situation in Georgia.

In the briefing room, the president's spokesman, Marlin Fitzwater, read out a statement drafted by Condoleezza Rice and checked with State: "We are following the situation closely. We regret any loss of life, but we'll have no further comment." Afterward Fitzwater kidded Rice, "Gee, Condi, that thing was so bland I could have written it myself."

---

an interview with Reagan. It was, just as he said in print, based on conversations with friends of the former president, who had recently talked to Reagan themselves and to whom he had indeed expressed himself along the lines that Cannon reflected in his piece. Cannon's book, *President Reagan: The Role of a Lifetime,* was published in 1991 by Simon & Schuster.

She replied, "Believe me, Marlin, I don't know what happened, and neither do you. When a situation is this unclear and there's blood in the streets, we wouldn't be helping with a lot of preaching or finger-waving."

In Tbilisi, Zviad Gamsakhurdia, a popular pro-independence fire-brand and the son of Georgia's best-known writer, charged that Bush had made a secret Faustian pact with Gorbachev: in return for Soviet concessions, the United States would look the other way as the Kremlin used indiscriminate cruelty to suppress the republics.*

Gorbachev sent Shevardnadze to his native Georgia to calm the situation. Angered, jolted, and deeply moved by what he had heard about the crackdown, the foreign minister proclaimed to his countrymen, "You are already not the same people you were yesterday. But I too have changed."

Shevardnadze's closest personal aide, Sergei Tarasenko, stayed behind in Moscow to monitor the Voice of America and other Western news media. He called his boss in Tbilisi and told him that the Americans had chosen a "nonprovocative" response. Shevardnadze was delighted to hear that Bush and Baker had been so "sensitive and attentive" to his and Gorbachev's dilemma: "This is a powder keg down here," he said. "A few sparks from the Americans could set off an explosion."

Shevardnadze was chagrined when Gorbachev refused to call Soviet military commanders to account for their role in the bloodshed. He threatened to resign, but Gorbachev talked him out of it.

The only senior American official who publicly lambasted the Kremlin for the crackdown in Georgia was the vice president of the United States. Traveling in the Far East three weeks after the event, Dan Quayle repeated an unverified charge aired by the Georgian press that Soviet troops had used poison gas against the demonstrators in Tbilisi.

Back in Washington, some administration officials at the State Department and the NSC dismissed Quayle's comments as evidence of how "out of the loop" he was. Others, including the White House chief of staff, John Sununu, smiled knowingly at how effectively the vice president was covering the administration's right flank. Sununu said, "Quayle's playing tough cop to Bush's good cop. And with these guys in Moscow, we need plenty of tough cops."

---

* Gamsakhurdia later became the president of an independent Georgia and was subsequently deposed, largely because of his authoritarian methods and repressive policies.

*   *   *

While violence was erupting in Georgia, Poland was being transformed peacefully. In January, the country's Communist president, General Wojciech Jaruzelski, had lifted the official ban on Solidarity, the first independent trade union behind the Iron Curtain, led by Lech Walesa. At a round table in a Warsaw palace, Walesa and other dissidents joined with Polish officials to remake the country's political and economic system.

Jaruzelski told the U.S. ambassador in Warsaw, John Davis, that he was consulting frequently with Gorbachev, who fully supported his policies of conciliation. When Baker went to Vienna in March for the CFE talks, he was startled to hear Polish delegates debating among themselves whether to opt for a French or an American-style presidency. On the flight home, he told his aides that there was a "sense of a new beginning" among the diplomats from Eastern Europe: "There are going to be some good opportunities there if we play our cards right."

Secretary of the Treasury Nicholas Brady, the former New York investment banker who was almost as close to the president as Baker, urged caution. In the early 1970s, he recalled, the West had vainly tried to help by throwing good money down the rathole of a Polish economy based on central planning, subsidized prices, and inefficiency.

At a series of interagency meetings, Dennis Ross and Thomas Simons of State joined with Blackwill and Rice of the NSC to urge U.S. investment in Polish "reform communism."* A Treasury man rolled his eyes and grumbled, "We did that already, in 'seventy-four!" Rice shot back, "I was in *college* in 'seventy-four. Things change!" She and Blackwill wrote the president to argue that the Warsaw roundtable agreements were the death knell of a divided Europe: the United States must now offer economic rewards to keep reform going.

Before an NSC meeting on Friday, March 24, Scowcroft discarded his usual caution. He told Bush that for the first time, he had a chance of accomplishing what earlier presidents had only dreamed of: returning Eastern Europe to the Western fold. "Nick Brady will tell you that we

---

* As Bush's State Department escort during the then vice president's 1987 trip to Poland, Simons had advocated a policy of U.S. financial incentives for Polish political reform. Bush's Treasury escort, David Mulford, wanted to limit the United States to rhetorical encouragement. The vice president brokered a compromise: promise Jaruzelski that serious progress toward democratization would bring a positive (though unspecified) U.S. response in trade and finance. While arguing with Treasury through 1989, Simons repeatedly cited Bush's verdict: "George Bush cannot forswear himself!"

can't do this," Scowcroft said. "He'll tell you we can't afford it. But what we really can't afford is to let this opportunity go by."

Scowcroft won the argument. On Monday, April 17, Bush flew to Hamtramck, Michigan, a largely Polish-American suburb of Detroit, and spoke from the steps of city hall: "My friends, liberty is an idea whose time has come in Eastern Europe." The "true source of tension" between East and West was "the imposed and unnatural division of Europe." The roundtable agreements were a "watershed": "If Poland's experiment succeeds, other countries may follow."

The president pledged that further economic and political reforms would bring new American trade and credits. John Sununu had wanted to call this the Bush Doctrine, but Scowcroft had scotched the idea, saying that while it was up to presidents to make policy, it should be left to others to name doctrines after them. Thus the president's men referred to his new principle as the Hamtramck Concept. A few weeks later, Scowcroft privately predicted that Bush might in time apply the same concept, linking aid with reform, to the Soviet Union.

On Saturday, April 29, Dick Cheney appeared on a CNN interview program hosted by the syndicated columnists Rowland Evans and Robert Novak. They asked him about Gorbachev's prospects for political survival.

Cheney had been criticized by the Right earlier in the month for his friendly public comments about the Soviet leader. Now, badgered by the two fiercely conservative columnists, he made what he later privately called a "horseback" decision to avoid being "nailed" again. He declared that if he had to "guess today," he would say that Gorbachev would "ultimately fail" to reform his economy and make the Soviet Union an "efficient, modern society." Gorbachev himself would then be replaced by someone "far more hostile" to the West.

Cheney's gloomy prediction made Sunday headlines. Shevardnadze called the statement "incompetent and not serious." General Mikhail Moiseyev, chief of the Soviet General Staff, denounced the Americans to several of his comrades: "Are we sure we know what we're doing with these people? Are we sure we haven't made a mistake in believing that we could do business on a mutual basis with them?"

In Washington, Baker was even angrier about Cheney's latest remarks than he had been about Gates's Brussels speech. He shared Cheney's skepticism about Gorbachev's survival, but he discussed it only with the president and his own close aides. He worried that if the administration allowed Cheney's remarks to stand in public, it might seem to reflect fresh U.S. intelligence or, alternatively, alarm the Soviets into thinking that U.S. policy was about to harden.

Cheney had always been more ideological than Baker. Now came the inevitable conflicts between a secretary of state who was eager to exploit the new climate with Moscow by using the vigorous horse-trading of which he was capable, and a secretary of defense who wanted the Pentagon to remain handsomely funded by Congress during a period when the Soviet threat appeared to be shrinking.

Baker later came to feel that April 1989 was the month that gave birth to a "disconnect" between him and Cheney. He was convinced that it would take Cheney years to explain away his indiscreet remarks on "Evans and Novak." After hearing about the program, Baker called Scowcroft at the White House and said, "Dump on Dick with all possible alacrity."

At Scowcroft's behest, on Monday, May 1, Marlin Fitzwater told reporters that Cheney's "personal observations" on Gorbachev did not reflect the administration's views. In an economics speech that day to the U.S. Chamber of Commerce, Bush inserted a gratuitous line of praise for the Soviet leader: "I made clear to Mr. Gorbachev up there in New York — Governors Island, when we met [in December 1988] — that we wanted to see *perestroika* succeed."

Designed as an antidote to Cheney's remarks, this sentence was the most forthright public statement of support for Gorbachev's reforms that Bush had yet made as president.

That week, Baker was preparing for his first visit to Moscow and his first private conversation with Gorbachev. He decided that it was time to assert his primacy as the president's spokesman on Soviet relations.

On Thursday, May 4, in a speech at the Center for Strategic and International Studies in Washington, he went public with the warning he had been stressing for two months in the Oval Office: the United States was in peril of seeming "passive in the face of the great strategic changes" in the world. To assert itself, it must "test the application of Soviet 'new thinking' " again and again.

There was irony here. As an interim slogan for its handling of the Soviet Union, the administration was adopting a term originally devised for none other than Michael Dukakis. The idea of "testing" the Soviet

Union had been advanced in a fall 1988 *Foreign Affairs* article by Graham Allison, the dean of Harvard's Kennedy School of Government, a well-practiced intellectual entrepreneur.

As a Democratic foreign-policy adviser, Allison had persuaded Dukakis to work the phrase into several of his speeches late in the 1988 presidential campaign. The defeat of his candidate that November did not stop Allison from promoting the notion of testing Gorbachev: early the next year he took it to Robert Zoellick, a former student at Harvard, who gave it to Baker. The secretary of state felt that to American ears, the word *testing* sounded appropriately skeptical and hardheaded.

There was no question which set of issues best lent itself to the concept of testing in early 1989. It was not arms control, where the new administration did not yet know exactly what it wanted, but that other troublesome subject, regional conflicts.

The Soviets had already ended their military occupation of Afghanistan. Elsewhere they were, in Baker's words, "showing signs of willingness to be part of the solution rather than part of the problem." The Kremlin was using its influence to win a withdrawal of Vietnamese troops from Cambodia and an end to the long-simmering and interrelated struggles in Namibia and Angola.

However, to official eyes in Washington, the new look of Soviet foreign policy was least evident in the region that mattered most to the United States: Central America. The Soviet Union and its thirty-year client, Cuba, were still backing the Sandinistas in Nicaragua, who in turn were supporting a leftist insurgency in El Salvador.

For the United States, Communist activity of any kind in Latin America had long been a neuralgic issue. The most serious crisis of the Cold War had occurred in 1962, when Nikita Khrushchev placed nuclear missiles in Cuba. During the Reagan administration, U.S. support for anti-Communist *contra* guerrillas in Nicaragua had not only failed to topple the Sandinista regime but also led to a rancorous domestic political battle and the most damaging scandal of Reagan's presidency — the Iran-*contra* affair.

Soon after taking office, Bush and Baker had moved quickly to shift their reliance from the *contras* to the peace process that had been under way in the region since 1987, when five Central American presidents signed a treaty in which the Sandinistas promised to stop subverting El Salvador and move toward free elections in Nicaragua in 1991. Later, the Sandinistas had agreed to accelerate the timetable of their elections by a year and hold them in February 1990, in exchange for a plan to demobilize the U.S.-backed *contras*.

Baker's assistant secretary for Latin America, Bernard Aronson, had impressed him with a secret memo urging that the administration make Central America the number one test of Soviet behavior: Gorbachev and the Soviets must see "tangible signs that they will pay a real price in bilateral relations if they obstruct our Central American diplomacy."

At the White House, Baker told the president that they should "subject the Soviets to Chinese water torture on this subject. We'll just keep telling them over and over — drop, drop, drop — that they've got to be part of the solution in Central America, or else they'll find lots of other problems harder to deal with."

Gorbachev was scheduled to fly to Havana in early April for a three-day visit with Fidel Castro.* On Monday, March 27, Bush sent the Soviet leader a secret letter: "It is hard to reconcile your slogans . . . with continuing high levels of Soviet and Cuban assistance to Nicaragua. There is no conceivable military threat that justifies that assistance. And now, at a point when we are clearly charting a new course, your assistance is almost certain to be used to undercut [our] diplomatic effort. . . .

"A continuation of [this] practice in this region of vital interest to the U.S. will . . . inevitably affect the nature of the [U.S.-Soviet] relationship. . . . An initiative by the Soviet Union and Cuba to shut off the assistance pipeline feeding armed conflict in the region would pay large dividends in American goodwill. It would suggest that the Soviet Union was prepared to promote a political settlement in the region through deeds and not simply slogans."

Gorbachev left for Cuba without replying to Bush. During their private sessions, Castro made the normally loquacious Soviet leader seem tongue-tied by comparison as he poured out data on the achievements of socialism in Cuba. Trying to get a word in edgewise, Gorbachev politely urged him to view socialism "in the world context" and to see Marxism-Leninism as a "living, evolving organism that must adapt to a changing environment."

Castro was not interested. He let fly another burst of statistics on the dramatic improvements in Cuban literacy and infant mortality rates since his 1959 revolution, then asked barbed questions about the bad

* The visit had originally been planned to follow Gorbachev's trip to the UN in December but had had to be postponed because of the Armenian earthquake.

news he had been hearing about Gorbachev's *perestroika*. Was it true that workers were terrified of being unemployed? That corruption and street crime were rampant? That sugar was nowhere to be found in Soviet stores? (Sugar was Cuba's principal export to the Soviet Union.)

Gorbachev changed the subject. He stressed the improvements in East-West relations and the need to reduce Cuban tensions with the United States. Castro made it clear that he required no advice from this Johnny-come-lately. Over and over he cried, "I know the Yanquis!" Bush and his circle were not much different from the ultramilitaristic "clique" that had surrounded Ronald Reagan.

Prompted by Bush's letter, Gorbachev several times tried to bring up the Cuban arms pipeline to the leftist Sandinista regime in Nicaragua and the Salvador rebels. Now it was Castro who changed the subject. He was outraged that the U.S. government was funding a Cuban exile television station, TV Marti, which was about to start broadcasting its capitalist, imperialist propaganda from Florida. This was a "new provocation against us," an "act worse than psychological warfare. It's aggression against the sovereignty of our airwaves!"

He suggested a quid pro quo: if Gorbachev used his influence to get the Yanquis to abolish TV Marti, Cuba might be willing to curtail its "fraternal assistance" to the Sandinistas. Gorbachev promised to urge Washington to observe the principle of noninterference of all kinds. Castro leaned into Gorbachev's face: "That's not what I'm talking about!" he insisted. He wanted no vague talk about "principles"; he wanted the plug pulled on TV Marti!

On Gorbachev's arrival, the two men had embraced. At his departure, they merely shook hands. Gorbachev publicly denounced the "export of revolution and counterrevolution," implicitly chastising Cuba for aiding the Salvador rebels and the United States for funding the Nicaraguan *contras*. But Castro's deputy foreign minister vowed that there would be "no change" in Cuba's support for "revolutionary movements and countries," and the Soviet ambassador to Havana ruled out any reduction in Soviet aid to Cuba.

By early May, on the eve of his trip to Moscow, Baker and his aides had concluded that while eager to get credit for saying things that were pleasing to American ears, Gorbachev was either unwilling or unable to stop Castro from making trouble in the hemisphere. The CIA informed the president that Gorbachev evidently felt that "Castro's policy is useful geopolitically to the Soviet Union because it allows keeping leverage on the U.S."

*   *   *

Gorbachev now replied to Bush's March letter: "Some circumstances prevented me from replying earlier. Nevertheless, on the eve of Secretary Baker's arrival, I would like to inform you of our position on the questions you have raised."

He reported some "positive trends in Central America," and especially in Nicaragua, where agreements had been reached to end the civil war and hold elections, in accordance with "the intention of your administration and the U.S. Congress to 'give diplomacy a chance.'" (Here Gorbachev was needling Bush by reminding him that U.S. congressional and public support for the *contras* was dwindling.)

"To promote a peaceful settlement of the conflict, since 1988 the USSR has not been supplying arms," Gorbachev continued. He said that he could not offer this assurance without noting that the "attacks by the *contras* against the territory of Nicaragua have stopped." (This allowed him to say to the Cubans, the Sandinistas, and his own colleagues that he was merely reciprocating an American concession.)

"I must tell you that I found the Cuban leader an intellectually strong person, wise with many years of experience in statesmanship, a mature, well-informed and responsible political figure who gives in-depth and realistic analyses of the situation in his own country, in Latin America and throughout the world. As he told me, Cuba was and is in favor of normalizing its relations with the U.S."

Gorbachev was essentially asking Bush to solve the Castro problem himself: if the United States ended the economic blockade and resumed diplomatic relations, Castro would not need to rely so much on Moscow. Perhaps then his behavior in the hemisphere would improve.

Bush, Baker, and Scowcroft rejected Gorbachev's premise that the road to peace in Central America ran through Havana, not through Moscow. They discounted his claim that all Soviet military aid to Central American leftists had stopped. U.S. intelligence showed otherwise. Still, they were happy to hear his implicit pledge that such shipments would now end.

Flying aboard an air force plane to Moscow, along with his wife, Susan, and his aides, Baker told the traveling press corps that if the Soviets turned out to be "serious about new global behavior," the United States would "seek diplomatic engagement" with the Kremlin: "We want to test the new thinking across the whole range of our relationship. *If* we find that the Soviet Union is serious about new global behavior, *then*

we will seek diplomatic engagement in an effort to reach mutual ben-
eficial results."

Dennis Ross privately explained that the purpose of "testing" the
Soviet Union was to avoid passivity, to show that the United States was
not naive, to give Gorbachev and "Shevy" a push to "do the right thing
and overcome their bureaucracy," which would in turn compel the
United States to respond.

The reporters on the plane did not know that in Baker's briefcase
was a new letter from Bush to Gorbachev. In it the president noted that
at the UN in December 1988, Gorbachev had said that the aim of
perestroika was "to make the Soviet Union a stronger power." Bush
conceded, "That is entirely understandable. Equally understandable is
our concern that a stronger Soviet Union could translate into a more
assertive military power."

Bush asked Gorbachev to assure the United States that the Soviet
Union would eschew military interference in the Western hemisphere:
"Given the lingering deep-seated differences between us, a constructive
contribution by your government in support of a diplomatic solution
in Central America will be a key near-term test."

The appeal of the verb "to test" was that in the context of American
policy at the time, it sounded active, though in fact it was passive. It
implied that the onus for bringing about further improvements in the
relationship still lay squarely on the USSR, and that the standards used
to judge those improvements would be established by the West. "Testing" was part of the vocabulary of the *pauza*.

So Shevardnadze had noticed. Shortly before Baker's arrival in Moscow, Ambassador Jack Matlock reiterated Washington's complaint
about Cuban aid to the Sandinistas. Angrily, the foreign minister replied
that the most serious problem in Central America was the refusal of
the United States to alter its own policy there in any fundamental respect. He said that he was annoyed by Baker's use of the word *test* in
his recent public statements. It suggested that the Soviet Union had to
jump through hoops to please the United States.

After his meeting with Matlock, Shevardnadze fumed to his aides,
"Are the Americans willing to do *nothing* to help us? Are *we* the ones
who have to make all the moves? We take these huge steps and all we
hear from Washington is, '*More! More! You must do more!*'" He suspected that negotiating with the Bush administration was going to be a
"one-way transaction: We give, they take!"

*   *   *

In the Lenin Hills outside Moscow on Wednesday, May 10, Baker met Shevardnadze at a Foreign Ministry guesthouse. The two foreign ministers shared little in the way of background or temperament. During the 1960s and 1970s, while Baker was practicing corporate law in Houston, Shevardnadze had served as interior minister in Tbilisi. Baker's father had been a part of the Houston establishment; Shevardnadze's had narrowly escaped being murdered by Stalin.

Baker was tight and programmed — charming, but usually for a purpose. Shevardnadze, by contrast, often seemed burdened and distracted by an inner sadness. The deep black wells around his eyes betrayed his melancholy. He often struck those around him as being preoccupied by the sad and turbulent history of his Georgian homeland.

What the two men had in common was a civilized manner, a certain oversensitivity to what was written about them in the press, a canny intellect, and bargaining skills. They were both old and intimate friends of their bosses. And in May 1989, both Baker and Shevardnadze were privately urging those bosses to pay less heed to domestic hard-liners.

Baker began his formal opening statement by insisting to Shevardnadze that the United States was not "imposing tests" on Soviet behavior after all. (This language had been suggested by Ross, who had anticipated Shevardnadze's objections to the word *test*.) Baker said that he wanted to create a "basis for true cooperation" with the Soviets on regions of conflict around the world. He understood the "value of having the Soviet Union actively involved in settlements."

But "with that kind of inclusion comes responsibility," he maintained. The Kremlin must press the Sandinistas to accept a U.S.-sponsored peace agreement. It must "lend its support, through deeds as well as words, to convince Managua and Havana — in whatever manner you choose — to halt aid for subversion in Central America."

Baker said that if the Kremlin refused to cooperate in achieving a political solution, it would pay a price. "We have all seen in the past how events in other regions changed the political atmosphere in which treaties agreed to by both sides were considered." Surely Shevardnadze remembered that the Soviet invasion of Afghanistan in 1979 had turned the U.S. Senate against the ratification of the SALT II treaty.

If, on the other hand, the Soviets played ball on Central America, Baker could promise not to "plan" military attacks on Nicaragua. The United States might offer Managua economic aid. If the Sandinistas won the February 1990 elections fair and square, the United States would not only stop making war on them, it would even help them rebuild their country. In that case, the Soviets could "take credit for, in effect, ensuring the long-term survival of the Sandinistas." All this would constitute a "new approach," allowing politics to replace bombs and guns.

Shevardnadze replied by asking why the United States could not simply deal directly with Castro. Why couldn't Washington approach relations with Havana in the same generous, forward-looking spirit that the secretary had just conveyed about Nicaragua? Baker answered, "I'm afraid that doesn't work." He said he understood that after President Gorbachev's April visit to Cuba, Castro had made it plain that he was still committed to the export of revolution.

When Shevardnadze brought up Afghanistan, Baker braced himself. He expected the Soviet foreign minister to demand that the United States stop sending arms to the *mujahadeen* anti-Communist guerrillas before the Kremlin cut off military aid to the Sandinistas. If he did, Baker planned to say that neither the Kabul nor the Managua regime was legitimate, that both had come to power by force, in defiance of the will of the people: thus the Afghan *mujahadeen* and the Nicaraguan *contras* were both fighting for just causes.

But Shevardnadze amazed and delighted Baker by resisting the temptation to link Afghanistan to Nicaragua. He even suggested that the Soviets might not insist on keeping Mohammad Najibullah, their puppet leader in Kabul, as part of a coalition government after a settlement.

Baker assured Shevardnadze that the United States merely wanted Afghanistan to be a neutral country once again, not a thorn in the Soviet Union's side: "We have no interest in seeing a regime in Kabul hostile to the USSR. That isn't in our interest either."

Next on the agenda was the Middle East. The Israelis had recently put a new proposal on the table: the election by Gaza and West Bank Palestinians of delegates to negotiate with Israel over self-rule. The Palestinians were refusing to cooperate. They felt the plan would prejudice their claim to an independent state. In this they were supported by most of the Arab world, including the Soviet client Syria.

Baker asked Shevardnadze to support the Israeli plan and use his influence on Damascus to do the same. The foreign minister surprised him by saying yes — but for a price: the United States must endorse a "parallel" process that would lead to an international conference on the Middle East, chaired by the United States and the Soviet Union.

The Soviets had peddled this idea since the days of the preeminent old thinker Andrei Gromyko. Such a conference would ensure that the Kremlin, representing radical Arab clients including Syria, Iraq, and Libya, would help to shape any settlement of the Arab-Israeli dispute. Israel and the United States were not interested in helping Moscow achieve this aim.

If Shevardnadze was hoping for some reciprocity for his own concession, he was disappointed. The Americans made it clear that an international conference would be a distraction from, and an impediment to, the elections proposed by the Israelis, which the U.S. side considered to be the only realistic avenue available for launching a peace process.

At the end of the day, Baker privately told his aides, "No reason to encourage this conference business. Sooner or later it'll go away. I doubt Shevardnadze has his heart in it."

That evening the Shevardnadzes invited James and Susan Baker to dinner at their apartment, which was elegant by Moscow standards. The foreign minister had not issued the invitation idly. He felt that in their formal meetings he had failed to get through to the taut, businesslike Texan, who was known to be much more intimate with Bush than Shultz had been with Reagan.

Shevardnadze knew how acutely Baker was attuned to American domestic politics. Perhaps the secretary of state would be more candid and more sensitive to Gorbachev's diplomatic requirements if he had a better understanding of the Soviets' internal predicament.

Nanuli Shevardnadze showed the Bakers around the apartment. Her guests were startled to learn that she was an outspoken partisan of independence for her native republic. She said, "Georgia must be free!" Having been briefed on Baker's passion for hunting turkey on his ranch in Pearsall, Texas, Shevardnadze presented the secretary of state with a twelve-gauge shotgun.*

They sat down to a Georgian dinner of spicy lamb and vegetable stew, accompanied by wine and vodka. Almost as soon as he raised his fork, the foreign minister discarded the old Soviet prohibition against discussing internal problems with outsiders. During the Cold War, Soviet officials had felt that such confessions might weaken their standing

---

* The gun's value exceeded the gift limit set by American law for U.S. officials. Shevardnadze never found out that his present ultimately went into the State Department gift collection.

against the West. Now Shevardnadze hoped that a frank description of what he and Gorbachev were compelled to deal with might not only break the ice but also help him to pry some concessions out of the secretary of state.

In excruciating detail, he described the madhouse Soviet economy of 1989: repairmen taking payment in vodka, taxi drivers demanding their fares in foreign cigarettes, subsidized bread so cheap that it was fed to pigs, corn rotting in the fields. He acknowledged that Gorbachev and his colleagues had underestimated some of the problems and mishandled others.

Fascinated, Baker replied that one thing was clear: the Soviet Union would have to reform its currency and pricing system radically, and do it quickly. Shevardnadze reminded him that reform meant raising prices: "Our people already have had to suffer a great deal. Now we're asking them to put up with inflation, too."

Baker said, "At the risk of sounding gratuitous, I served as finance minister of the number one country in the world for three and a half years, and I learned a few things about economics and also about politics." One lesson, he said, was that if a government was going to administer strong, sour-tasting economic medicine, it should do so early in its term, so that it could blame the ensuing discomfort on its predecessors. Therefore, the Soviets should move as soon as possible on price reform.

Baker urged Shevardnadze to press his colleagues for "military *glasnost*": "Publish your defense budget, so that when you announce fourteen- or nineteen-percent reductions, we know what baseline you're reducing from."

"Well, you know, we'd like to know that information too," said the foreign minister. "And I think we're going to have to find it out and reveal it, because we're going to be required to say something on this subject to the Congress of People's Deputies."

This comment impressed Baker as evidence that the Politburo was serious about the movement toward democracy that had begun with the March elections. Perhaps the new parliamentary process would help to erode the Soviet government's old secretiveness and domination by the military.

Baker proposed an official channel between their departments for "exchanging" information and analysis on internal developments within their two countries. Behind the fig leaf of a reciprocal exercise to benefit both sides, he was suggesting a dignified means for the Soviets to obtain advice from the United States on how to reform their economy.

Before the evening ended, Baker showed off pictures of his new fifteen-hundred-acre ranch near Pinedale, Wyoming, with its trout stream and vast fields. His face fell when he saw Shevardnadze slipping the pictures into his pocket. Later he sent Dennis Ross to Sergei Tarasenko with a message: "Please send my pictures back. They're the only ones I've got!"

The next morning, Gorbachev received Baker alone in Saint Catherine's Hall at the Kremlin, the same great chamber where he had first met Bush, in 1985. The only other people present were interpreters. Gorbachev had been briefed by Shevardnadze on his dinner conversation with Baker. Referring to handwritten notes, Gorbachev spoke of the dangers he saw in the radical price reform that his country so obviously needed: "If we decontrol prices, that means things will cost more, and that will take money out of people's pockets."

Baker replied that on the contrary, letting prices float to their natural level would stimulate production and put money *into* people's pockets. Gorbachev frowned and shook his head in doubt. Turning quickly to foreign policy, he said that the USSR needed a new international climate in order to conduct the "huge and vitally important task of transforming itself. . . . Certain principles that we are establishing in our internal life — principles of mutual respect and self-accountability and self-determination — must also apply in our approach to international life."

Gorbachev admitted that there was "disagreement" within the Soviet leadership and "resistance" to *perestroika*. Referring to Dick Cheney's pessimistic comments a fortnight earlier, he said, "I understand there are those on your side who question our prospects. I understand that because there are those here, too, who question where we are headed."

He went on, "Things have moved more slowly than we thought they would. In a big and complex country like ours, no one can expect the process to be easy, especially in a period of revolutionary change. Perhaps we are now passing through the most difficult moment."

Baker tried to be reassuring: "The president has said, and I have said, that we have no wish to see *perestroika* fail. To the contrary, we would very much like it to succeed." This would create new possibilities in U.S.-Soviet relations. One example was Central America: was Mr. Gorbachev willing to let him announce that the Soviet Union had pledged to cut off arms to Nicaragua?

This suggestion put Gorbachev on his guard. He and Shevardnadze had frequently discussed the Americans' determination to get something for nothing. Now he told Baker that the main point of his letter to Bush had been the recommendation that Washington deal directly with Havana. If Baker would announce publicly that the United States was willing to enter such negotiations, then the Soviets could proclaim a cutoff of Soviet arms.

Baker had no intention of publicizing the Soviets' Cuban ploy, so he let the matter of an announcement drop.

After the two men had talked alone for an hour, their colleagues were ushered into the room. When he was introduced to Robert Gates, Gorbachev said, "I understand that the White House has a special cell assigned to the task of discrediting Gorbachev. And I've heard that you are in charge, Mr. Gates." He turned to Baker and added, "Perhaps if we are able to work out our problems, Mr. Gates will be out of a job."

Gates chuckled. He was flattered to know that the leader of the country he had studied all of his professional life knew that he existed; and besides, it might be useful for Gorbachev to know that someone in the White House who had constant access to Bush would be watching him closely and skeptically.

Baker's aides were on guard when they saw that the Soviet delegation included the uniformed Marshal Sergei Akhromeyev, the former chief of the General Staff who was now Gorbachev's main adviser on military matters. They took Akhromeyev's presence to mean that Gorbachev was going to spring one of his flashy arms-control proposals.

They were right. After everyone sat down, Gorbachev stressed that reducing the size of Soviet armed forces was a crucial part of *perestroika*. He and the leadership had decided on one-sided cuts, but it would be easier for him to get his own military to accept such sacrifices if they were part of an American-Soviet agreement to scale down both military establishments.

Gorbachev revealed that he was about to announce that the Soviet Union would reduce its short-range nuclear forces in Eastern Europe by five hundred missiles. Baker and his people groaned to themselves: here was one more initiative designed to display Gorbachev to the world as the master peacemaker. How many Americans or Western Europeans would understand that this cut was almost meaningless, leaving roughly 95 percent of such forces in place?

Gorbachev went on to say that he hoped his gesture would improve prospects for the elimination of all remaining short-range nuclear forces and, of course, prevent the deployment of the new American Lance missiles. He would also be proposing some new Soviet concessions at the CFE talks in Vienna. These gestures were made in a "constructive spirit of goodwill." They were not "in any way politically motivated."

"It sure looks like politics to *me*," said Baker. "What you're trying to do is play on an issue that has some sensitivity on our side." He was referring to West German public opposition to the Lance missiles. Leaving the meeting, Baker consoled himself with the thought that he would have several days to brief Western allies and prepare his response before Gorbachev's diplomats presented the proposal in Vienna.

Gorbachev had indicated to Baker that he was giving him a confidential preview. He asked Baker not to disclose the proposal because he had not yet consulted his East European allies. But right after the Kremlin meeting, Shevardnadze held a press conference and revealed the broad outlines of the new Soviet position.

In his private stateroom on the air force plane flying out of Moscow, Baker sputtered to his aides that Gorbachev and Shevardnadze had set him up. They had "ambushed" him, "blindsided" him, "sandbagged" him. In an effort at spin control, he composed himself and strolled back to the press section. Affecting unconcern, he briefed reporters in detail on Gorbachev's proposal, acknowledging, "He's extraordinary. . . . We expected something from him, but I can't say we expected this."

Baker soon discovered that he had made a rare error in dealing with the press. He had hoped that his first mission to Moscow would be reported as a successful attempt to shift the focus from arms control to regional conflicts. Instead, by giving out more details than the Soviets had offered in Moscow, he guaranteed that the first wave of stories on the visit would focus on arms control, comparing American "stubbornness" to Soviet "flexibility" — and contrasting the amateurish secretary of state with the experienced Soviet president.*

At the White House, Scowcroft brought a brief Associated Press report on Gorbachev's new initiative to the Oval Office. Bush demanded, "What is it exactly he's done? Find out right now!"

After gathering further information, Scowcroft told the president that Gorbachev's gesture was a gimmick to stir up new opposition to

---

* For example, the headline over a column by Robert Novak, who was traveling with the secretary's press entourage, was "Gorbachev Rolls Baker."

the Lance and make the United States look bad for refusing to bargain over short-range nuclear forces. As for the new CFE offer, Gorbachev was up to his old tricks, trying to divide the West.*

On his return to Washington, Baker complained to Bush that the irritating Soviet public-relations exercise had been "vintage Gorbachev."

---

* The persistent Soviet effort to include aircraft in a CFE deal was certain to arouse new objections in London and Paris, where the governments were determined to protect their bombers from being limited under the terms of the treaty.

CHAPTER 4

"*Look, This Guy* Is *Perestroika!*"

O N FRIDAY, May 12, 1989, the president traveled to Texas A&M University to give a commencement speech that was billed as the unveiling of the administration's policy toward the Soviet Union. At the heart of the speech were several phrases that figured prominently in the presidential order that had emerged from National Security Review number 3.

In March, after the policy review was completed, Scowcroft had asked Robert Blackwill and Condoleezza Rice to "improve on" and "push beyond" the bland document. They drafted a so-called National Security Directive designated NSD-23, each of whose seven pages was stamped SECRET.

NSD-23 asserted that "containment was never an end in itself. It was a strategy born of the conditions of the postwar world." Recent Soviet change suggested that a "new era may now be upon us. We may be able to move beyond containment to a new U.S. policy that actively promotes the integration of the Soviet Union into the international system." Like the policy review that preceded it, the directive languished for months before Bush signed it.* Numbered copies were locked up in safes.

But as Scowcroft and his aides began working on the Texas A&M address, they kept returning to the phrase "beyond containment." During a speechwriting session in Scowcroft's office, Blackwill, along with James Cicconi and David Demarest of the White House staff, wondered whether the phrase might be advertised as a Bush Doctrine. Scowcroft shook his head. Once again he said that presidents should not name doctrines after themselves: let the press confer such labels.

Nonetheless, Blackwill urged that administration officials do everything they could to ensure that the phrase was pounded into the public mind. He promised dinner in an excellent Washington restaurant to anyone who used the slogan "beyond containment" on television after the president made his speech.

Flying to Texas with the president aboard *Air Force One*, Scowcroft carried out his customary assignment of lowering public expectations. He said to reporters, "We can't celebrate, because the Soviet Union, you know, is still a massive military power. We still have big problems with them, and change at this point can be reversed."

"Containment worked," Bush declared to the graduates. "Our review indicates that forty years of perseverance have brought us a precious opportunity. And now it is time to move beyond containment to a new policy for the 1990s — one that recognizes the full scope of change taking place around the world and in the Soviet Union itself."

No one should doubt "our sincere desire to see *perestroika,* this reform, continue and succeed." But American security "must be based on deeds, and we look for enduring, ingrained economic and political change."

Mindful of the ridicule he had endured during the 1988 campaign and afterward for his shortcomings as a conceptualizer, the president declared that the years ahead required a "sweeping vision. Let me share with you that vision." He saw a Western Hemisphere "no longer threatened by a Cuba or a Nicaragua armed by Moscow," and a Soviet Union reducing "ties to terrorist nations."

Bush called on the Soviets to cut Warsaw Pact forces, "tear down the Iron Curtain," work with the United States to solve regional conflicts, achieve "lasting political pluralism and respect for human rights," and "join with us in addressing pressing global problems, including the

---

* He finally got around to signing it on September 22, 1989.

international drug menace and dangers to the environment." Should the Soviets ease their emigration laws, he would try to see to it that they were granted most-favored-nation trade status.

Told to expect a major Bush initiative, the White House press corps had speculated on what it could be. At the close of the president's speech they found out: "Open Skies." The president had exhumed and slightly augmented a plan that Dwight Eisenhower had first proposed at a 1955 meeting with Khrushchev in Geneva.

The original plan would have allowed both sides to overfly each other's territories to assure themselves that they were not in danger of a surprise attack. Khrushchev had denounced the idea as a "bald espionage plot."

It had been Blackwill's idea to try it again. During the preparations for the Texas A&M speech, he had asked a group of experts from various departments of the government whether a "reprise of Open Skies" might not be a good way to establish the direct relevance of *glasnost* to international relations. Virtually all the experts dismissed the idea, pointing out that aircraft overflights were all but pointless in an age of sophisticated spy satellites.

"But what if Gorbachev proposes it?" asked Blackwill. The group acknowledged that the United States would have to agree to it. Blackwill said, "So why don't we propose it first?" There were shrugs all around, and George Bush's first initiative was born — or, more to the point, resurrected, after thirty-four years.

For those in the audience at Texas A&M and the millions more around the world who were waiting to see what he was willing to do in response to Gorbachev's initiatives, the president had pulled out of his hat not a live rabbit but a dead mouse — a stale proposal conceived by the CIA in the bitterest days of the Cold War. David Hoffman of the *Washington Post* wrote that the speech "offered no new responses" to Gorbachev. A *New York Times* editorial agreed that it was "short on content." So much for Bush's attempt to rebut those who said he lacked the "vision thing."

In Moscow, Gorbachev thought that the address must have lost something in translation. He privately told an aide, "It's hard to know exactly what to make of all this. Let's see what else they have to say." Anatoli Dobrynin strained hard to find "hints of change, hints that Bush is thinking in a more realistic way."

Shevardnadze's aide Sergei Tarasenko, however, told his boss that the speech did indeed suggest a "major change" in U.S. policy, "because it means that the Americans will no longer by reflex be seeking to oppose everything we do and counter every move we make."

Andrei Grachyov, chief of a newly established "Division of New Political Thinking" within the secretariat of the Central Committee, concluded that "beyond containment" was either good news or bad: it was either a sign of American willingness to stop treating Soviet relations as a zero-sum game, or a U.S. proclamation of victory in the Cold War, following which it would begin to dictate the terms of surrender.

Back in the Oval Office, the president could not help but be miffed by the contrast between the worldwide praise for Gorbachev's latest arms-control proposals and the raspberries that had greeted Open Skies.

Baker's aides tried to yank public attention back to the new American-Soviet cooperation on regional conflicts. Citing sources high in the State Department, Don Oberdorfer of the *Washington Post* revealed the happy news that Gorbachev had assured Bush that the Soviets had stopped supplying weapons to Nicaragua. Oberdorfer published the story on Tuesday, May 16.

The problem was that Baker's circle had not shared the same news with the professionals of the State Department's Bureau of Inter-American Affairs. Asked for comment, they prepared for public release a sanitized intelligence summary showing that the Sandinistas and Salvador rebels were still receiving military aid from the Eastern bloc and Cuba, and perhaps directly from the Soviet Union as well.

Baker's aides realized that this information contradicted the story they had already put out. They ordered that the summary not be released. This put State in a double bind: it had leaked a story that was favorable to the Kremlin, then suppressed one that was unfavorable.

Angry hard-liners on the White House staff did not distinguish between Baker's staff and the worker bees of the Latin American bureau: here was the State Department, true to form, putting out the soft line, doing the Kremlin's dirty work. John Sununu asked, "Whose side are those guys on, anyway?" Gates said, "The Sovs are deliberately sending mixed signals, and State is amplifying them!"

Marlin Fitzwater tried to undo the damage by shifting the blame to the Kremlin. Asked how the United States would respond to Gorbachev's latest "initiative" on Central America, Fitzwater told reporters that Gorbachev was playing "a P.R. game," not matching "words with deeds." American policy was "very careful and methodical." People should contrast that with the Soviet approach "of throwing out in a kind of drugstore-cowboy fashion one arms control proposal after another."

Using the intelligence material prepared and then suppressed by the State Department, the White House spokesman went on, "At this point we don't see any evidence of any cutoff. The military aid is still coming in." Having dismissed Gorbachev as a flashy charlatan, he was now calling him a liar.

Fitzwater returned to his office and closed the door, telling aides, "You won't believe what I just did!" They worked out a public qualification saying that the "drugstore-cowboy" comment had not been "intended to go to the heart of reform"; Fitzwater had been referring only to its "P.R. externals."

The Senate majority leader, George Mitchell, denounced the administration's "name-calling." Ambassador Dubinin complained to the State Department: "What are we to make of this? Our foreign ministers have a positive meeting, and now there's this abuse!" In the senior ranks of State, there was little sympathy for Fitzwater. Lawrence Eagleburger exclaimed, "Some cowboy! For that matter, some drugstore!"

But when Dan Quayle heard about Fitzwater's barb, he said, "Great! Good for him!" He remarked to reporters over breakfast that he found "nothing troubling" in the characterization: "A drugstore cowboy, in a sense, connotes a bit of phoniness, and there is a bit of phoniness about the propaganda." Gorbachev was "perceived as making radical proposals out there," but they were "really marginal."

Told that the ever-controversial vice president had risen to his defense, Fitzwater smacked his forehead and said, "Oh boy! I guess now I'm in *real* trouble!"

On Sunday morning, May 21, the president and his wife awoke in their Kennebunkport bedroom. Behind their heads was a white-painted wooden headboard-bookcase crammed with duck decoys, family snapshots, and books. Bush read newspapers that contained new reminders that he was losing ground to the leader of the Soviet Union in the contest for approval in the eyes of the world.

A *New York Times* editorial said, "Imagine that an alien spaceship approached earth and sent the message: 'Take me to your leader.' Who would that be? Without doubt, Mikhail Sergeyevich Gorbachev." David Broder wrote in the *Washington Post* that what made Gorbachev's feat

"all the more extraordinary" was that he had achieved his world position "while acknowledging, and perhaps because he admits, that the
nation he leads is far weaker than anyone had reckoned."

Bush confided to Scowcroft that he was "sick and tired of getting
beat up day after day for having no vision and letting Gorbachev run
the show. This is not just public relations we're involved in. There's real
danger in jumping ahead. Can't people *see* that?" The president privately told other advisers that if the opportunities Gorbachev offered
were real, they would not vanish. If they vanished, then they were not
real, in which case, "We'll end up realizing we were lucky — and
smart — that we didn't move faster."

By now, Baker was not so sure. He was beginning to conclude that
the uncertainty in the Soviet Union argued for a swift effort to "lock
in as much as possible of what we like about what's happening over
there." The West, led by the United States, should take full advantage
of the current regime in Moscow by making deals that would limit the
options of any later government that might seek to undo reform.

In previous weeks, the president had become more receptive to
Baker's calls for a bold stroke to reestablish American leadership. Bush
had shifted somewhat from his initial concern with "prudence" and
had begun to talk instead about the "need to do something to get the
ball rolling."

As was often the case, it took a deadline to concentrate the president's mind: at the end of May, Bush was to make his debut as leader
of the free world when he attended a NATO summit in Brussels. Baker
had already experienced the perils of going to a major international
gathering with nothing but old policies and old rhetoric; Bush would
face the same sort of embarrassment if he went to Brussels empty-
handed. He knew that unless he did something to capture the diplomatic high ground in Brussels, the spotlight on intra-alliance quarrels
over SNF and Lance would be more glaring than ever. He decided to
take a gamble on CFE.

In March, Scowcroft had watched Dick Cheney torpedo his idea
about removing American and Soviet ground troops from Europe.
The defense secretary had said that the proposal would widen the divisions that Gorbachev's "peace offensive" had already caused within
NATO.

Now, in the Oval Office, Bush asked Cheney and the chairman of
the Joint Chiefs of Staff, Admiral William Crowe, to draft their own

proposal to "energize" the CFE process. Cheney was reluctant to alter the existing NATO position. He wanted NATO to keep on rejecting Gorbachev's efforts to include limits on aircraft and troop numbers in a CFE treaty.*

Scowcroft, meanwhile, was pushing for an adjustment that would cover troops as well as armor. The Iron Curtain, after all, was enforced not by the motorized hunks of metal in the East but by the Soviet troops there: "Whatever we come up with has got to focus attention on the fact that the Cold War started with the Soviet occupation of Eastern Europe," Scowcroft argued. He insisted that the West's new proposal must call for the removal of U.S. and Soviet troops, not just NATO and Warsaw Pact forces.

Crowe worried that such a proposal would aggravate the long-standing anxiety of NATO allies that the two superpowers were negotiating their fate over their heads.

Baker sided with Scowcroft in this dispute. After returning from Moscow in mid-May, he had told Bush that in accepting most NATO ceilings on armor and artillery in exchange for the inclusion of aircraft and manpower in a deal, Gorbachev's surprise proposal "gives us something we can grab on to."

This impressed Bush, as did a private letter that soon arrived from Gorbachev, spelling out the Soviets' willingness to go much further than halfway to meet Western concerns. The president told his aides, "This guy's really serious, isn't he?"

He increased the pressure on his advisers: "Time's a-wasting, Brent! . . . We've gotta push." He ordered Cheney and Crowe to come up with a plan that was "front-loaded" with lower troop levels on the Western side as well as the Warsaw Pact side. Cheney and Crowe continued to worry about the military consequences and about clearing the plan with their NATO counterparts.

Eager to obtain the maximum impact on world opinion, Baker wanted the largest cuts possible. At the White House, he suggested a CFE agreement that would achieve a 25 percent reduction of almost everything on the Western side, both men and machines. Bush would not yet commit himself to a target number but said, "We've got to get ahead of the problem by the time of the NATO meeting. We've got to

---

* Because it was difficult to count heads and verify manpower limits, the Pentagon preferred to let lower troop levels be a consequence of the removal of equipment rather than a stipulation of a CFE treaty.

be in the position of making a proposal that is really serious and that is taken really seriously."

Crowe reminded his fellow chiefs that for years Congress had been demanding that Western European governments share a larger portion of their continent's defense burden. Here was a way to meet those demands. Any U.S. withdrawal would be partial and gradual. He asked the chiefs to provide the "kind of give the president is looking for" by relaxing their old refusal to allow aircraft to be included in a CFE agreement. At the same time, Crowe said that cuts as large as those that Baker wanted would "make a mockery of forward defense and jeopardize the alliance."*

At Kennebunkport, on the weekend before Bush's trip to Brussels, Crowe told the president that 5 to 10 percent reductions were "doable," but Baker's preferred 25 percent cuts would require a "whole new strategy" for Western Europe. Moreover, even if Baker got his way, "we would only have made a minor dent in the Soviet Union's overall strength. Most importantly, we would provoke one hell of an argument in NATO councils."

Bush replied, "I'm planning to go to NATO and say, 'Here's a *possible* proposal. What do you think? I'm not imposing it on you.' "

For nearly thirty years, France had been the most independent member of the alliance, the most likely to complain about American high-handedness. Yet its president, François Mitterrand, was less concerned about having an American proposal foisted on him than he was about the danger of continuing inertia in Washington.

While Bush was consulting with the leaders of the Pentagon, Mitterrand flew to Kennebunkport. He was upset about the quarrel within the alliance over short-range nuclear forces. He feared that by forcing new Lances on West Germany and resisting the elimination of all SNF missiles, the United States and Britain were risking a debacle in Brussels. Margaret Thatcher was even more adamantly opposed than was Bush to any hint of willingness to sacrifice the Lance deployment to arms control.

Helmut Kohl wished to wring from his NATO colleagues an endorsement of new negotiations that would not only obviate the need for

---

* This was true only if the Eastern European states remained what they had been for forty-four years — heavily armed Soviet satellites ready to act at the Kremlin's behest. Even in May 1989, this was a questionable assumption.

the upgraded Lances but do away with all short-range nuclear weapons stationed on German soil. Thatcher had for some time been publicly scolding Kohl on this issue, which Mitterrand regarded as trivial compared to the changes under way in the East and between East and West.

In Kennebunkport, Mitterrand told Bush that he thought Thatcher was being "foolish" for pushing Kohl, and that the United States had to do something in a hurry to rescue NATO from "this poisonous debate." Under Mitterrand's influence, Bush's focus shifted from the reasons for doing less in CFE, which were military, to the reasons for doing more, which were diplomatic and political.

In a meeting with the president and his top national-security advisers in the Cabinet Room on Monday, May 22, Baker asked for a CFE initiative that would have "impact" and "punch." Crowe replied that the United States could propose a major reduction in the number of U.S. troops actually stationed in Europe. But it had better preserve the access to bases, the supplies, and the infrastructure that could support a quick return of massive American force, if necessary. "We should be able to say to NATO, 'If we're needed, we can come back,' " said Crowe.

Annoyed, Bush glared at Crowe and Cheney and complained, "You guys aren't helping me much. You've got all these reasons why I *can't* do things. I want to show that the United States is leading the alliance."

Baker renewed his recommendation for a 25 percent cut: "That sounds more like a round number, less like a trim at the edges." Crowe put his cards on the table and said he would accept 20 percent: "We can go that far and not upset our strategy."

The president said, "Okay, I think I hear that we can do twenty percent." He turned to Cheney and Crowe and asked them, "Now, is twenty percent all right? You can live with that?" They nodded. Siding with Scowcroft, Bush overruled Cheney's request that the troops be cut from NATO as a whole, not just from U.S. forces in Europe: "I want something that the U.S. can do alone, by itself, on its own," he said.

Bush sent Baker's and Scowcroft's deputies, Lawrence Eagleburger and Robert Gates, on a secret mission to the key capitals of Europe with a presidential letter laying out the proposal.

The centerpiece of the U.S. position on CFE was a proposed limit of about 275,000 on the number of soldiers that either superpower could station in other countries' territory anywhere in Europe. If the terms were accepted, it would mean that the Soviets would probably have to return to civilian life some 350,000 men — more than ten times as many as the United States would be bringing home. Still, the U.S. initiative was basically a compromise between the Western CFE proposal that was already on the table in Vienna and the Soviet scheme that Gorbachev and Shevardnadze had previewed for Baker in Moscow.

As Eagleburger and Gates had expected, they encountered some resistance on the inclusion of aircraft, particularly in Paris.* Fortunately, Mitterrand overrode his own military high command and the Quai d'Orsay. Having complained to Bush only a few days earlier about Thatcher's letting adherence to the fine points of strategic theology obscure an opportunity for a diplomatic breakthrough, he was not about to let his own government make the same mistake.

Margaret Thatcher's position was similar to Mitterrand's. To her, the plan for troop reductions seemed a bit overambitious. But having been the most vocal of the allies in urging Bush to respond more vigorously to Gorbachev, she was reluctant to quibble with the substance of the proposal.

Bush was scheduled to give a national security speech on Wednesday, May 24, at the Coast Guard Academy in New London, Connecticut. When he read the draft submitted to him, he found it flat and too cautious. "Can't we tilt this forward a bit?" he asked. "You know, juice it up? It's too much of a downer, too military." Amplifying his boss's objections, Sununu denounced the draft as "junk . . . oatmeal . . . unpresidential crap."

When the West Wing speechwriters came up with a new draft, Bush polished it himself, pounding on the IBM electric typewriter he kept in the study adjoining the Oval Office. The final version included a line inserted by the president: "Our policy is to seize every — and I mean *every* — opportunity to build a better, more stable relationship with the Soviet Union, just as it is our policy to defend American interests in light of the enduring reality of Soviet military power."

---

* Eagleburger and Gates explained that the president's proposal would be designed in such a way as to exempt British and French bombers. The Soviets wanted to include carrier-based planes and "dual-capable" land-based fighters that could drop bombs as well as act as interceptors and carry out strafing missions. Washington was now willing to include certain kinds of aircraft but wanted to exclude carrier-based planes and dual-capable fighter-bombers, such as the American F-111s based in Britain as well as the French Mirage IVs and 2000s. Several French officials objected that even a partial and carefully circumscribed concession on the issue of aircraft constituted an American "betrayal" on an important point of principle.

*   *   *

Before flying to Brussels on Sunday, May 28, the president sent a message to Gorbachev in which he revealed the main features of his plan.

By the time Bush arrived in Brussels, Kohl's diplomatic aides were trying to work their will against Lance by suggesting that if there was enough movement on CFE, there might be SNF negotiations. When the Canadian external-affairs minister, Joe Clark, supported the Anglo-American opposition to such a move, the West German foreign minister, Hans-Dietrich Genscher, snapped, "How many nuclear missiles do you have on *your* soil?" Baker produced a compromise: CFE progress might set the stage for a "partial reduction" of SNF later on.

But just as Bush and Baker had hoped, the bickering over SNF faded when the NATO Council turned its attention to the CFE proposal that Bush put before the group. Thatcher, now exuding beneficence, said that Bush's initiative had "transformed" the meeting from a squabble into a show of unity, as it had the potential to transform the very structure of European security.

Mitterrand then asked for the floor. The others were startled. Ever since President Charles de Gaulle had withdrawn France from the military structure of the alliance, French presidents had tended toward stony silence at meetings of the NATO Council.

Somberly, Mitterrand said that he knew there was a good deal of interest in his government's position, particularly because of France's well-known concern with preserving its independent deterrent. After a theatrical pause, he said that it was extremely important that everyone in the room understand what he was about to say. He cast his eye around the entire company as though to make sure no one was nodding off.

Bush's proposal, he said, was "good for the alliance because we can't give the impression of merely standing in place. . . . We need innovation. The president of the United States has displayed imagination — indeed, intellectual audacity of the rarest kind. . . . Those advising me said 'no' to aircraft. . . . But I told them they were wrong. I told them we must be bold, as the American president wants us to be. President Bush, I again congratulate you."

The European press suddenly turned friendly to Bush. The *Guardian* of London said that the U.S. president had ridden "to the rescue like the proverbial U.S. cavalry, at the last possible minute."

At a news conference after the NATO Council meeting, Bush

congratulated his colleagues, and himself, for having achieved what he called the "double hit" of regaining the initiative in CFE and suppressing the squabble over SNF. "Whatever political arrows might have been fired my way, it's all been worth it, because I think we have something sound and solid to build on now," he said.

With his trademark awkward friskiness, he went on, "Here we go now, on the offensive, with a proposal that is bold and that tests whether the Soviet Union will move toward balance." On Wednesday, May 31, after boarding a helicopter to Bonn, Bush told his aides that he was "on a real high." At the NATO summit he had scored the first major foreign-policy success of his presidency.

The president's letter to Gorbachev proposed a deadline that was as difficult for the diplomats to swallow as the suggested reductions would be for the military: the talks should produce a treaty within six to twelve months, and the treaty should be implemented by 1992 or 1993. The Soviets, who were certain to have much more trouble absorbing demobilized soldiers into their rigid, stagnant economy, had been talking about completing conventional-force reductions by 1997; Bush's ambitious timetable was pure one-upsmanship.

In Moscow, General Mikhail Moiseyev, the chief of the General Staff, and his colleagues were already unsettled by Gorbachev's moves toward demilitarization and disarmament. Now they were even more upset at the notion that officers who had signed up for lifetime careers would have to face a forced return to civilian life.

Alexander Bessmertnykh told Ambassador Matlock, "If you're serious about breaking the habit we've both been in of scoring cheap points off each other, you shouldn't be proposing deadlines for propagandistic effect, especially ones that aggravate the already serious problems that exist within our own society between our military and political leaders."

Marshal Akhromeyev groused to Gorbachev that Bush's rhetoric in Brussels had been "gloating and provocative." But Shevardnadze insisted that Akhromeyev was overreacting. Bush's CFE proposal was, he said, a vindication of his optimistic assessment of the *pauza*. He told his boss, "We were right to be patient. Now we can begin in earnest."

In Europe, John Sununu told reporters that Bush's "game plan" for this trip was to "whip Western Europe into line, then turn everyone's attention to Eastern Europe." The vehicle was to be a presidential speech in Mainz, West Germany.

At the city's Rheingoldhalle, Bush declared, "Let Europe be whole and free." Forty years before, he said, this had been a "distant dream": "Now it's the new mission of NATO. . . . The world has waited long enough." The president called for free elections and political pluralism in Eastern Europe, cooperation in cleaning up the environment in the East, and a "less militarized Europe." He noted that the reform government of Hungary had begun dismantling the barbed-wire fence along its border with neutral Austria: "Let Berlin be next! Let Berlin be next!" he exclaimed.

Bush said that in a Europe that was "whole and free," the openness of markets and the untrammeled flow of people, ideas, and goods would create a web of mutual respect and interdependence. This would not threaten the Soviets: "Our goal is not to undermine their legitimate security interests." Noting Gorbachev's insistence on a "common European home," Bush said, "There cannot be a common European home until all within it are free to move from room to room."*

Stopping in London, the president called on Margaret Thatcher at Number Ten Downing Street. As was often the case, she was slightly disconcerted by Bush, with his occasional references to the "blond bimbos" of television journalism and his odd habit of asking her, "If I were a TV reporter, what would you say about such-and-such?"

Thatcher found Bush much more open and sympathetic about Gorbachev in private than he was in public. She had read the Mainz address closely and urged him to take the next possible opportunity to reassure the Soviet leader that he had nothing to fear from the West if he pursued reform. She later sent Gorbachev a message describing her conversations with Bush, adding that she hoped the president's inner views would soon be revealed in U.S. policy.

In an interview granted to Don Oberdorfer and Ann Devroy of the *Washington Post* before he left London, Bush declared that for the Soviets to move beyond containment, there would have to be a "significant shift in the Soviet Union," as well as a "lightening-up on the control in

---

* Bush was especially sensitive to the danger of provoking the Kremlin's insecurities. In September 1983, during a visit to Budapest, Vice President Bush praised the Hungarian Communist party boss Janos Kadar for his economic reforms and advances toward human rights. Kadar's aides later said that this kind of praise made their lives more difficult with Moscow.

Eastern Europe," which would free them "to move down the democratic path much more." As Thatcher had suggested, Bush asserted that
it was "part of my responsibility" to persuade the Soviets that they
faced no threat from the West.

The next morning, in his Kremlin office, Georgi Shakhnazarov, Gorbachev's chief adviser on Eastern Europe, studied a Russian translation
of Bush's words. Shakhnazarov was an Armenian who, like Gorbachev,
had once been a protégé of Yuri Andropov. He was a longtime champion of reform, advocating in particular the need to diminish the influence of Marxist ideology on Soviet foreign policy.

Jotting notes and making check marks in the margins of the document, he told an American visitor that Bush's comments were "extremely important and positive" — especially his emphasis that change
in Eastern Europe would not threaten the Soviet Union: "It almost
doesn't matter that there are no details about what this assurance means
in practice. What matters is that Bush says it, he says it repeatedly, and
he seems sincere in saying it."

Shakhnazarov pondered the U.S. president's list of hopes for the future. As far as he was concerned, "all of Bush's conditions can be fulfilled." The Poles and Hungarians could "do what they want"; there
was no reason Solidarity could not come to power. "The only exception
is Germany," he said. Here was a "special case," but not one that Gorbachev would have to worry about anytime soon. Unlike Poland and
Hungary, East Germany was showing few signs of revolutionary fer-
ment in the summer of 1989.

Besides, the division of Germany was "a common question," one on
which Soviet views were not that different from those of several Western
governments, notably France and Britain. Shakhnazarov insisted that
with Germany's history of belligerence, few in the West would be eager
to see it united. He felt that Bush's interview justified the Kremlin's
increasing tendency to see the U.S. president as "serious, decent, sensible." "Even if he's not a terribly bold leader or a great orator, we can
trust him as a partner," he concluded.

In recent weeks Gorbachev and his advisers had been thinking hard
about how to describe the relationship they hoped to establish with
Bush. They settled on the word *partnership*. This suggested that the two
nations were moving from "negative peace" — that is, the effort to
avoid a nuclear conflagration — to joint efforts that could make the
entire world more secure.

At the Kremlin on Wednesday, June 21, Gorbachev himself used the term during a private meeting with Admiral Crowe, who was reciprocating a trip Akhromeyev had made to the United States the previous year. The startled chairman of the Joint Chiefs of Staff had never before heard any responsible figure on either side describe the Soviet-American relationship as a partnership.

In China, a confrontation had been building between the people and their leaders since mid-April, when the government announced the death of Hu Yaobang, the former chairman of the Communist party. In the context of Chinese politics, Hu had been a political reformer — too much so for the tastes of the country's senior leader, Deng Xiaoping, and his latest protégé, Li Peng. Students at Beijing University mounted a series of protests mourning Hu as a martyr to the cause of democracy.

Gorbachev's arrival in Beijing in mid-May for the first Sino-Soviet summit meeting in decades helped to trigger an escalation of the protests, culminating in the occupation of Tiananmen Square, in the heart of the capital. Chinese authorities had to move Gorbachev's welcoming ceremony from the square to Beijing Airport.

At the White House, John Sununu had for months watched Gorbachev lead what seemed to be a charmed life. Now, after hearing about the disruption of the Soviet leader's reception in China, he gleefully said to his aides, "Well, I guess he's really been upstaged and embarrassed this time, hasn't he?"

In fact, the Chinese upheaval only served to dramatize the impact that Gorbachev's policies were having. As he walked off his plane to a twenty-one-gun salute, workers, intellectuals, policemen, soldiers, and other citizens poured into Tiananmen Square to join the students. A quarter of a million people were gathered there by the end of the day.

Next to the newly erected *Goddess of Democracy,* a huge figure modeled on the Statue of Liberty, posters demanding Deng's ouster were waved alongside ones displaying Gorbachev's face, over legends asking him to come to the square and be hailed. Banners in Chinese, Russian, and English read "Democracy Is Our Common Dream. . . . In the Soviet Union They Have Gorbachev. In China, We Have Whom?"

Gorbachev told his aides that of the senior officials he met, he felt sympathy only for Hu's successor as party leader, Zhao Ziyang, who favored conciliation with the students and political reforms to match the economic ones that were under way. After the Soviet leader left for Shanghai, Zhao was stripped of his post.

After midnight on Sunday, June 4, Chinese government troops launched a massive assault on Tiananmen Square. Through the night of blood and flame, hundreds were massacred on the spot, and hundreds more were hauled off to be executed out of camera range.

In Moscow, some scholars, foreign policy experts, and others who had regular contact with Westerners worried that henceforth they should be more careful about talking to foreign visitors. Tiananmen was a reminder of what a crackdown might look like.

On the same day as the massacre in Beijing, Poles voted for a new parliament under an accord reached in April. This was arguably the best news to come out of Eastern Europe in half a century. As a result, Communists were routed and Solidarity candidates elected.*

Despite the Poles' joy over the election, the grim news from China touched a deep chord in their collective memory. In 1968, 1970, 1976, and 1981, Poles too had poured into the streets to defy their Communist government and demand freedom. They too had been thwarted by troops of their own country. Through the spring, the Polish reformers had frequently warned of the danger of *katastrofa* if Solidarity pushed too far and the regime panicked. Now they began to call it by a different name: *Tiananmen.*

Gorbachev was in a position to decide whether the regime of General Jaruzelski could count on Soviet military might to enforce Polish Communist rule. By now Jaruzelski knew that the answer was no. For just that reason, the Polish president had been negotiating with Solidarity and the Catholic church over the new political order.

Two days after the election, Jaruzelski asked Solidarity to join the Communists in a coalition. Lech Walesa refused. Instead, another negotiation led to a follow-up election to fill those parliamentary seats that were still vacant. Few doubted that the outcome would be another Solidarity landslide, leading to a Solidarity government. The custodians

---

* All one hundred seats in the upper house, the Senate, were contested; Solidarity won ninety-two outright. In the lower house, Solidarity was permitted to field candidates for only 35 percent of the seats, 161 in all, of which it won 160. The remaining 299 seats were reserved for the Communist party and its allies. Although the Communists ran unopposed and were able to use the party's nationwide apparatus as a campaign machine, only five of them received enough votes to qualify. Across Poland, citizens exuberantly crossed Communist names off ballots. The Western press described the elections as "partially open" or "semi-free." More bluntly and accurately, they were rigged in favor of the Communists, who managed to lose anyway.

of the totalitarian system were no longer merely compromising with their democratic opponents; they were capitulating to them.

Bush was scheduled to visit Poland and Hungary in early July. With Tiananmen on their minds, representatives of both Solidarity and the Polish government told American diplomats and members of the White House advance team that the president should avoid saying anything that might strike the Soviets as too gloating or critical. They cited Marlin Fitzwater's "drugstore-cowboy" remark as a case in point.

Obligingly, the president called three Polish journalists — two from the official press and one from the Solidarity newspaper *Gazeta Wyborcza* (Electoral Gazette) — to the Oval Office and told them, "We're going in a constructive vein, not in some critical vein or not in some mode of trying to complicate things for somebody else. . . . I will not be trying to inflame change. . . . I'm not going to deliberately do anything that is going to cause a crisis."

The president noted that Gorbachev had recently been mobbed in Bonn by adoring crowds chanting "*Gorbi! Gorbi!*" and that he had spoken to the Council of Europe in Strasbourg on his vision of a "common European home." Bush told the Polish reporters, "I have no hangups when Gorbachev goes to Germany or France. Fine, let him go." His syntax in characteristic disarray, he said, "The better hand he gets, the better he is received there — they're saying, ' 'Attaboy! Keep it up!' Keep what up? Keep *reforming* up!"

Then, almost in passing, the president added, referring to Poland, "I would like to see a continuation that would result in the Soviets' feeling comfortable taking their troops out of there." It was this last sentence that made headlines in the West and dominated the special summary of foreign news that was placed before Gorbachev in Moscow the next day.

On Sunday evening, July 2, the Soviet leader attended a recital by the pianist Van Cliburn, whose concerts in Moscow in 1959 and in the White House during the Reagan-Gorbachev summit of 1987 had provided background music for earlier thaws in the Soviet-American relationship.

Gorbachev invited Jack Matlock to join him in his box at the concert hall. He took the ambassador aside and told him that he was not happy about Bush's implication that the USSR should withdraw its troops from Poland. Matlock cabled a warning to Washington that the president had already managed to rile the Kremlin about his trip.

With Matlock's message in mind, Bush told his speechwriters, "Whatever this trip is, it's *not* a victory tour, with me running around over there pounding my chest." Whatever they gave him to say, "I don't want it to sound inflammatory or provocative. I don't want what I do to complicate the lives of Gorbachev and the others. . . . I don't want to put a stick in Gorbachev's eye."

On Friday, July 7, in Bucharest, Gorbachev gave a speech to Warsaw Pact leaders in which he seemed to accept the reforms in Poland and Hungary. He asked his "fraternal" allies for "tolerance" and "independent solutions of national problems."

The meeting's host, Nicolae Ceausescu, a despot in the Stalinist mold, openly complained of "disunity" in the alliance. The only other unreconstructed hard-liner who was still in power, East Germany's seventy-seven-year-old Erich Honecker, collapsed and had to return home. The medical cause was believed at the time to be a kidney or gall-bladder ailment, but Poles and Hungarians joked that it was Gorbachev's words that had made Honecker sick.

In Poland, as a result of the runoff parliamentary elections, Solidarity now held ninety-nine out of the one hundred seats in the upper house and all 161 seats allotted to the non-Communist opposition in the lower house. To the surprise of almost everyone, Jaruzelski had announced that he would not run for president in the national elections scheduled for later in the year.

On Sunday, July 11, Bush left for Europe. After takeoff from Andrews Air Force Base, he summoned Robert Blackwill and Dennis Ross to his narrow forward cabin to talk about Poland.

In September 1987, just before announcing his presidential candidacy, Bush had traveled to Poland along with a film crew hired by his campaign aides. The Polish people adored the Reagan administration for its strong opposition to the Communist regime's imposition of martial law in 1981, and the White House was sure that the trip would yield politically useful footage.

When Bush met with Jaruzelski on that earlier trip, he urged him to accelerate liberalization, to make Solidarity legal and bring it into the process of reform. Jaruzelski replied that such a course would be "suicidal" for his government.*

---

* During the same 1987 trip, in a bleak, driving rain, Bush had also visited the Birkenau

Now, nearly two years later, Bush asked Blackwill and Ross about the "personalities behind the politics" of Poland. What, really, was Lech Walesa all about? And why was Jaruzelski refusing to run for the new Polish presidency?

Like most others in the West, Bush admired Walesa as a hero of freedom and had condemned Jaruzelski for having imposed martial law on Poland in 1981. Still, back in 1987, Jaruzelski had treated him with genuine courtesy and discretion; Bush said it had been a "real class act." Now that Jaruzelski was negotiating with Solidarity, he felt sympathetic toward him.

The velocity and unpredictability of the Polish transformation was making Bush uneasy. He was in no hurry to see Jaruzelski swept aside in favor of Walesa. He told his aides that a sudden collapse of the Communist regime might be "more than the market can bear."

Bush's apprehension had been fanned by Walesa himself. During Bush's 1987 Warsaw trip, in a meeting with Walesa, the then vice president had asked whether Solidarity would ever be legalized. Walesa replied that if this "improbable" event occurred, it could "cause a lot of trouble for us" because Solidarity might be blamed for the sagging Polish economy.

Here was a hint of the essential George Bush. There was little in his intellectual life or political experience to give him an understanding of revolutionaries such as Walesa. Unlike most of the other Cold War presidents — including Truman, Eisenhower, Kennedy, and Nixon — Bush had read little of world history. He tended to be uncomfortable with political figures whose manners and aspirations seemed exotic. In his lexicon, *solid, proven,* and *reliable* were adjectives of high praise. Names like Walesa and Yeltsin did not find their way into Bush's Rolodex as easily as Jaruzelski or Gorbachev.

Bush's sympathy for Jaruzelski and his misgivings about Walesa suggested an almost emotional preference for familiar processes and gradual, orderly change, even at the sacrifice of democratic ideals. It was wholly consonant with his increasing desire to form a tacit alliance with Mikhail Gorbachev against Boris Yeltsin and others who seemed to be extremists in the context of Soviet politics.

Bush asked Ross and Blackwill whether Jaruzelski might not be a

---

concentration camp, where he solemnly viewed the gas chambers and crematoria. Using words that did him little good, he said, "Strong — wow — powerful! That's something, isn't it?"

"stabilizing force for the future" of Poland — at least the near future. Wouldn't it be preferable for the Communists, not Walesa and Solidarity, to bear the brunt of Polish impatience with the hardships of reform? Bush did not seem to consider the possibility that extending Jaruzelski's political life might ultimately delay or even prevent the transformation of the Polish system into a democracy.

On Sunday evening, *Air Force One* landed in Warsaw. Sweating from the heat as he waited on the tarmac, Jaruzelski mopped his forehead. Bush told the cameras that Americans had a "fervent wish: that Europe be whole and free." But in the way he conducted himself throughout his visit, Bush made it clear that he was in no hurry to see that day come. Quite to the contrary, he was nervous about how rapidly the Iron Curtain was coming unraveled, and he tried to use his influence to shore up the holdovers of the old regime, whom he saw as forces for gradual change, against the longtime dissidents, who struck him as being recklessly impatient.

The crowd was sparser than it had been for his 1987 visit. During the era of Soviet domination, Poles had cheered Western leaders as a way of thumbing their noses at the Communist regime. (In an effort at spin control, Scowcroft urged the traveling White House press corps to keep in mind that greeting a U.S. president was no longer an "expression of opposition to the government.") Also, now that Bush was here again, the Poles wanted to know how much aid he was going to offer their country before they gave him a wholehearted welcome.

On Monday morning, Bush surprised Jaruzelski by turning what was supposed to be a brief, pro forma encounter into a private conversation that lasted over two hours. Several times he said that he appreciated Jaruzelski's "steadying" influence on Polish politics. Jaruzelski relaxed and leaned forward, as if to absorb the U.S. president's soothing words.

Here Bush was playing to his strength. His civility — the historical and geopolitical equivalent of good sportsmanship — enabled him to make Jaruzelski feel like a statesman guiding his country through a difficult passage, rather than a defeated soldier desperately trying to preserve his side's dignity as he negotiated the terms of surrender.

Bush went on to say that he was not interested in winning a contest with the Soviets over Poland. Instead, he wished to "assist in a process, an evolution." Jaruzelski, he said, had already played an important part in that evolution; perhaps he might continue to do so in the future.

Bush's public efforts to prop up Jaruzelski further cooled his reception by the Poles. Uninterested in the pragmatic case for preserving Soviet dignity, they remembered only that this general was still the head of a party that had served as a Soviet truncheon for forty-four years, and that he had ordered Polish troops to fire on Polish citizens.

Later that day, Bush told the Polish parliament, "Poland is where the Cold War began, and now the people of Poland can help to bring the division of Europe to an end." He said that he would ask Congress for $100 million for a special fund to underwrite Polish private enterprise, and another $15 million to cleanse the polluted air and water of Krakow; in addition, he would request new World Bank loans and U.S. support for rescheduling Poland's foreign debt.

Infuriating the Poles, John Sununu told an American television reporter that given more aid, Poland would be like a "young person in a candy store" who lacked the "self-discipline" to spend his money wisely. He repeated the analogy several times during the trip.

After speaking in Warsaw, Bush traveled to Gdansk, where he met privately with Walesa in his two-story stucco house. Walesa complained about what he considered to be the paltry U.S. offer of aid. He said that Poland deserved "better treatment" than this. Asking for $10 billion over three years, he warned that if Polish reforms led to surging unemployment and poverty, "we will have a civil war. We are at the end of our rope."*

Buoyed by Bush's encouragement, Jaruzelski decided to run for president after all. White House aides worried that their boss had given Jaruzelski the impression that he was not only Moscow's man but Washington's as well. They denied to reporters that Bush had actually talked Jaruzelski into running, though they conceded that the general might have changed his mind after enjoying the limelight and new respectability bestowed on him by the president's Warsaw visit.

After hearing that Jaruzelski would run, Bush told his staff in private that he was relieved: it would be much better for the general to "hang in there and see this thing through."†

Air Force One landed in Budapest on Monday evening, July 10. Ten thousand Hungarians waited at the airport amid thunder, lightning, and

---

* That fall, Bush nearly doubled the size of the U.S. benefits earmarked for Poland.
† Jaruzelski ultimately won the election by a single vote in parliament, thanks to the absence of several Solidarity delegates.

rain. Ignoring the weather, the figurehead president, Bruno Straub, read out a fifteen-minute welcoming speech.

While Straub droned on, the first U.S. president ever to visit Hungary played to the crowd. He waved away his wife's offer of an umbrella, as if to join his hosts in braving the elements. When he finally pulled on a raincoat, the onlookers applauded, waved, and made V-for-victory signs. Called on to speak, Bush ostentatiously tore up his prepared text, doffed his coat, and plunged into the midst of the cheering Hungarians.

Power in Hungary was still concentrated in the nation's Communist party and its boss, Karoly Grosz. During Reagan's second term, the CIA had tagged Grosz as a reformer who might lead Hungary for years to come. In early 1989, just as Jaruzelski was capitulating to Solidarity one step at a time, Grosz had approved the formation of independent Hungarian political parties.

But by the time Bush arrived in Budapest, in July, Grosz's fellow Communists had concluded that he was moving too slowly. Determined to survive in free elections but fearful that Grosz's ouster would provoke the Kremlin, they named him to a new four-man presidium on which he was outnumbered by three more vigorous reformers: Rezso Nyers and Miklos Nemeth, both free-market economists, and Imre Pozsgay, the party's most popular figure, who had been chosen to run for president in the upcoming election.

On Wednesday morning, July 12, in a room overlooking the Danube, Bush privately met with Grosz, Nyers, and Nemeth. They told him that their party was transforming itself into a Western-style union of social democrats that would take its chances at the polls. But their ability to continue the experiment, they said, would depend on Gorbachev's benevolence.

The president set aside his talking points, typed on index cards. He said, "We're with you. What you're doing is exciting. It's what we've always wanted. We're not going to complicate things for you. We know that the better we get along with the Soviets, the better it is for you."

Amplifying what he had told Jaruzelski, Bush said that he had no intention of forcing Eastern European leaders to "choose between East and West." He did not want to exploit what was happening in Eastern Europe. All nations, including the Soviet Union, had much to gain from the changes that were sweeping the area.

Bush said he recognized that the "general quality" of U.S.-Soviet relations would affect the outcome of that process: the better the relationship between Washington and Moscow, the greater the latitude for reform in Hungary. To describe what he wanted American policy to be, he kept using the word *constructive*.

Like Jaruzelski, Bush's Hungarian hosts leaned forward in their chairs, the relief evident on their faces. Condoleezza Rice was so fascinated to hear the president improvising that she almost forgot she was supposed to be taking notes.*

The leaders of Czechoslovakia had once bid for Woodrow Wilson's support by modeling their first constitution on Wilson's famous Fourteen Points. Now, in similar fashion, the Hungarians told Bush exactly what they knew he wanted to hear.

"We have to get rid of the dead hand of statism," said Nyers. "The great test for our party is whether we're willing to put our case before the people in an election."

Hungary, he added, had finally achieved the stage of political development that the United States had reached in 1776. But no one should forget that it was Gorbachev's tolerance of Hungarian reform that had made this possible. The liberation of Eastern Europe could continue only as long as *perestroika* continued in the USSR. Thus Gorbachev's survival was crucial to their success.

Bush said, "We don't want to make things more difficult for you — *or* for Mr. Gorbachev."

That afternoon, at the residence of the U.S. ambassador to Hungary, Mark Palmer, Pozsgay told the president and Baker that his three colleagues had painted too rosy a picture of the situation. "What our party is doing may be too little, too late," he said. He doubted that the Communists would remain in power once truly democratic elections were held. He himself would leave the party if it did not "catch up with the people and their insistence on real reform."

Pozsgay's brashness disconcerted Bush. The president asked him how anyone could be sure that the transition to a post-Communist era would be orderly. He wondered if the new leaders would have the experience and the tactical skill to manage the delicate relationship with Moscow.

During a private meeting later that afternoon, representatives of Hungary's non-Communist opposition informed the president and Baker that if anything, Pozsgay had soft-pedaled the public's impatience

---

* She scrawled, "Improved relations with the U.S.S.R. reduce pressure on the nations of Eastern Europe, especially those on the cutting edge of reform." Rice later gave these notes to the White House speechwriters to work into a speech that Bush was planning to give in the Dutch city of Leiden at the end of the trip.

with and disdain for the current leadership. Bush replied, "Your leaders are moving in the right direction. Your country is taking things one step at a time. Surely that's the prudent thing to do."

Once again the president was promoting his own most cherished attitudes: caution in the face of the unknown, prudence in the face of change. After the meeting he said, "These really aren't the right guys to be running this place. At least not yet. They're just not ready." He told Baker that of the leaders he had met, Nyers and Nemeth seemed the best equipped to lead Hungary into an era combining reform communism with democracy.

During their flight to Paris, on Thursday morning, the president, Scowcroft, and Fitzwater walked down the aisle to the back of the plane, where reporters were jammed into narrow seats. Bush said that the pace of reform in Eastern Europe had "absolutely amazed" him. Echoing Nyers, he stressed that it was the "leadership of the Soviet Union and the leaders in these countries themselves" who had made it all possible.

Returning to his private forward stateroom, he told his aides, "If there were no Gorbachev, there would be nothing of what we've just seen in Poland and Hungary." With his tendency to describe profound events in self-consciously trendy language, he said, "There's big stuff, heavy stuff going on here."

The City of Light was celebrating the two hundredth anniversary of the French Revolution. François Mitterrand had suggested that the leaders of the seven major industrial democracies — the so-called Group of Seven, or G-7 — plan their annual economic summit to coincide with the national pageant.

From Moscow, Gorbachev almost stole the show. When the seven leaders and their ministers sat down in private, Mitterrand read out a letter he had received from the Soviet president, saying that the Soviet Union wanted to join in promoting worldwide growth and easing the indebtedness of the Third World.

"*Perestroika,*" wrote Gorbachev, "is inseparable from a policy aimed at our full participation in the world economy." In effect, Gorbachev was applying for associate membership in the club whose executive committee was then in session in Paris.

At first, Gorbachev's appeal infuriated the Americans. They had come to Paris to talk about Eastern Europe, and suddenly everyone else wanted to talk about the Soviet Union. Robert Blackwill, hearing of Gorbachev's letter, murmured that it reminded him of Shirley Temple's playing a waif in a dirty, tattered dress, pressing her nose against the window of a pastry shop.

Baker exclaimed, "Gorbachev is trying to hijack the summit! He's butting in, screwing up what we want to accomplish here." More calmly, he added, "Gorbachev will keep pressing because he seeks acceptance and help, and if he doesn't get it from us, he'll get it from the Europeans." Scowcroft agreed that the letter was "pure grandstanding."

Their president was more philosophical. He noted that Gorbachev's letter implicitly accepted the invitation that Bush himself had issued at Texas A&M in May, when he called on the Soviets to join the world economic system.

During a lull in the summit, wearing a T-shirt and running shorts, Bush returned to the U.S. ambassador's residence on the Place Vendome and jogged around the sumptuously landscaped grounds. Then he sat down with Baker and Scowcroft on the rear veranda.

With little preamble, the secretary of state told his friend of thirty-two years that it was time for him to propose a private meeting between himself and Gorbachev. By now Baker had concluded that Gorbachev and Shevardnadze were "pretty much for real," and he knew Bush well enough to sense that in the afterglow of his visit to Eastern Europe, the president was ready to entertain the idea of a face-to-face talk with Gorbachev.

Bush agreed that it was time to "get engaged" with Gorbachev: "What good would it do to hold back now?" He noted how quickly Eastern Europe was being enveloped by change, and conceded, "I don't think we should wait until the next summit to talk to the Russians about all this. What's going on is so remarkable that maybe an informal meeting with Gorbachev would be a good idea."

In fact, Scowcroft was the one who needed convincing. Worried as ever about excessive public expectations, he said, "We've got to slow this thing down. We can't let ourselves be driven by Moscow at breakneck speed here."

But Bush was plainly attracted by Baker's suggestion. He rejected Scowcroft's objections, saying that a meeting with Gorbachev would allow him to regain control of the relationship: "Better for us to talk one-on-one than to be lobbing proposals and speeches and letters back and forth at each other. I want to see him up close, get a chance to feel him out, make sure he's got the right read on me."

Scowcroft reminded the president that it might be dangerous to be drawn into supporting Gorbachev the man, as opposed to *perestroika* the policy. Exasperated, Bush replied, "Look, this guy *is perestroika!*"

He insisted that any meeting with Gorbachev must not be turned into a full-fledged summit, with lavish ceremony and prepackaged accomplishments. Negotiations with the Soviets over time and place must be kept as secret as possible. Only at the last moment should the event be revealed to the world.

Aboard *Air Force One* en route to Washington on Tuesday morning, July 18, Bush called for a sheet of White House stationery and scrawled out in longhand an invitation to Gorbachev to meet with him in advance of their first full-dress summit, which was tentatively scheduled for 1990.

Bush wrote, "Let me get quickly to the point of this letter. I would like very much to sit down and talk to you, if you are agreeable to the idea. I want to do it without thousands of assistants hovering over our shoulders, without the ever-present briefing papers and certainly without the press yelling at us every 5 minutes about 'who's winning,' 'what agreements have been reached' or 'has our meeting succeeded or failed.' "

Bush did not send the letter on to Moscow through Jack Matlock, his ambassador there, for fear that its contents would be leaked. Instead, he waited ten days and gave the sealed envelope to Gorbachev's military adviser, Marshal Sergei Akhromeyev, during an Oval Office visit. On his return to Moscow, Akhromeyev presented the envelope to Gorbachev. When Gorbachev opened it, he was delighted at the evidence that Bush was finally ready to deal with him face to face.

In late July, Baker returned to Paris for a nineteen-nation conference called to mediate an end to the civil war in Cambodia. The meeting accomplished almost nothing, but it gave Baker an excuse to see Shevardnadze in private.*

---

* In 1989, under Kremlin prodding, Vietnam removed most of its troops from Cambodia. The Cambodian regime agreed to a series of negotiations on a peace settlement under UN auspices. The Paris conference collapsed after a month, largely over the participants' inability to agree on a formula that would prevent the return to power of the

On Saturday, July 29, Shevardnadze recieved the secretary of state for a meal at the residence of the Soviet ambassador in Paris. Baker could smell the food being cooked in the kitchen and hear the chef noisily clanking his pots with the radio turned up loud. At times the Americans could scarcely hear the words of Shevardnadze's bald, fine-boned, mustachioed interpreter, Pavel Palazhchenko, who performed the same function for Gorbachev.

As he had during his dinner with the Bakers in May, Shevardnadze discoursed for two hours on his country's internal politics. He reported that Gorbachev was dealing with crises not only among contending ethnic groups but also over economics.

In Siberia in early July, for example, coal miners had gone on strike against poor wages, wretched living conditions, and shortages of consumer goods. Soon the strike spread to the Ukraine. Gorbachev began bargaining with the miners, but the Soviet people were growing more impatient and unhappy by the day — and not just the minorities along the Soviet periphery, but ethnic Russians in the heartland.

Shevardnadze said that the trouble in the coal fields showed that civil unrest and official violence like that in Tbilisi in April could recur anywhere in the Soviet Union — and perhaps on a much larger scale. In time, there could be a danger of civil war and dictatorship.

Shevardnadze intended his gloomy monologue to do more than merely inform Baker about conditions in the Soviet Union. By raising the possibility of future internal strife — and future efforts by the Soviet military to put it down, as in Tbilisi — he was inviting Baker to give him some idea of what Bush's response would be.

Consulting his index cards, Baker replied with careful language. He said that he felt compelled to express a growing concern among Americans. It would be "tragic" if their two governments' progress toward a new international order were thwarted by a vicious cycle of Soviet civil unrest and official repression. However, he added, the U.S. government drew a distinction between "preserving law and order" and "preventing free expression."

Baker said he would understand if the Kremlin had to use force to deal with "irrational bloodletting and national hatreds." But "it would not be understood by us" if Soviet authorities used violence to "put down strikes and other forms of political activity." If that happened,

---

Khmer Rouge guerrillas, whose reign of terror had devastated the country and decimated its population in the 1970s.

"you will re-create in our country the reaction to Tiananmen Square — and this will create a logic of its own."

Using his written talking points, Baker went on to tell Shevardnadze that the United States and the Soviet Union were "poised on the threshold of a new era." He and the president wanted Gorbachev to succeed in his program. Quoting Bush, Baker said, "We don't want to put a stick in President Gorbachev's eye." He went on, "We have made very clear that in supporting the process of reform, we're not trying to create problems for the Soviet Union."

Speaking of Soviet internal unrest, Shevardnadze pledged, "We're going to handle this in a way that advances the cause of what we're trying to do. We have a lot of difficulties, but we're determined to prevail — and prevail without resorting to violent force."

He admitted that the Soviet "political mechanism is way ahead of the economic mechanism." Still, the situation was not as bad as it might seem from the West. Look at Kazakhstan, he said. In that vast Central Asian republic, a forty-nine-year-old Gorbachev-style reformer, Nursultan Nazarbayev, was enjoying much success in bringing free-market economics to agriculture.

"Our task is to extend the experience of Kazakhstan to other regions," Shevardnadze said, and he noted that the coal strikers had carried placards endorsing Gorbachev and his reforms. What was happening in the Soviet Union was a "true revolution," with Gorbachev at its head. Come what might, Gorbachev was determined to keep the revolution peaceful.

Shevardnadze conceded to Baker that ever since Soviet troops had massacred Georgian demonstrators in Tbilisi in April, he had had a "complex" about the danger of the nationality problem in the Soviet Union exploding into violence. He now uttered a statement that he would repeat to Baker in almost every one of their subsequent meetings: "If we were to use force, then it would be the end of *perestroika*. We would have failed. It would be the end of any hope for the future, the end of everything we're trying to do, which is to create a new system based on humane values. If force is used, it will mean that the enemies of *perestroika* have triumphed. We would be no better than the people who came before us. We cannot go back."

Baker was moved by what he heard. He felt that Shevardnadze had "opened up completely on his internal problems." Later he looked back on this meeting as the start of what he called his "bonding" with Shevardnadze. Baker noted that their next ministerial meeting was scheduled to take place in the United States, and he reminded Shevardnadze of the pictures of his ranch that he had showed him in May. "Perhaps we might have a ministerial in Wyoming," he suggested. "Would you have any interest in that?"

Shevardnadze was delighted with the idea of going to the American Old West. Baker said that what he had in mind was the same kind of easygoing, wide-ranging, feet-on-the-table exchange that Bush had proposed to have with Gorbachev in the message he had just sent through Marshal Akhromeyev.

Shevardnadze sat up with a start. He had no idea what Baker was talking about. When Baker elaborated on the message, Shevardnadze was irate that Bush had used Akhromeyev as the channel instead of him. But he did his best to suppress his fury and not let Baker know that Gorbachev had failed to inform him about such a major matter.

Ross, who had not known about Akhromeyev's role as courier, later told Baker that he had been "absolutely the wrong guy to use." The marshal could be expected to "use this with Gorbachev to gain an even more special position, seeking to be a special channel to the U.S." They could not assume that Akhromeyev "would even tell Shevy what he was doing."

After the Americans departed, Shevardnadze exploded. He shouted at Tarasenko that the Americans were deliberately "bypassing" him. Why else would they use Akhromeyev to carry such a message? The marshal was one of the chief enemies of Shevardnadze's approach to foreign policy, especially on arms control. He could imagine how pleased Akhromeyev and the generals must be to have the U.S. president communicating with Gorbachev through them.

Tarasenko tried to calm his boss down. He suggested that Bush had been understandably concerned with the secrecy of a sensitive communication. Perhaps Baker had suspected that the residence was bugged by any number of intelligence services. Perhaps that was why he had referred so cryptically to a message that he assumed Gorbachev had already shared with Shevardnadze.

Shevardnadze was not mollified. He grumbled that if the Americans were going to "play a double game" and go behind his back, they would be sorry: there were things he could do back in Moscow to block U.S. initiatives! He later complained to Baker, who quickly apologized, saying that the slight had been unintentional. "It won't happen again," Baker promised.

*   *   *

During the Paris meetings, Tarasenko called on Dennis Ross at his suite at the Inter-Continental Hotel, near the Louvre. He reported that within a few days, he and Shevardnadze would be flying to Tehran. Did Baker wish them to take any message to the Iranians on behalf of the Americans?

Ross, who handled the Middle East as well as the Soviet Union for Baker, replied that the U.S. hostages held by pro-Iran extremists in Lebanon remained the biggest obstacle to better relations between Washington and Tehran. It would be helpful if Shevardnadze could tell the Iranians that the Soviet Union wanted the hostages set free. Tarasenko agreed, adding, "If we learn anything interesting, we'll get back to you."

Shevardnadze and Tarasenko were as good as their word. Their feeler in Tehran did not lead to immediate release of the hostages, but it put the radical government of Iran on notice that it could no longer expect to play the United States and the Soviet Union off against each other.

The secretary of state and his aide welcomed the opening of this back-channel to the highest level of the Soviet foreign ministry. The Iran gambit proved to be the first of many occasions on which Ross and Tarasenko would do important secret business together.

After his appointment in 1985, Shevardnadze had searched the foreign ministry for intellectual talent and seized upon Tarasenko. As a young diplomat, Tarasenko had been posted in Cairo in the 1960s and in Washington in the mid-1970s; he had been with the ministry in Moscow since 1977.

In the months that followed, Ross would come to see Tarasenko as the "Soviet equivalent of me, [Robert] Zoellick and Margaret [Tutwiler] rolled into one." When the foreign minister traveled, Tarasenko was almost always at his side. Like his boss, he was a determined fighter for reform in Soviet foreign policy. He told Ross, "Change will be very hard, but for us there is no alternative."

Baker could not banish Shevardnadze's somber picture of Soviet society from his mind. Returning to Washington with his aides, he said, "We've got to ask ourselves: What happens if Gorbachev loses, if things go to hell in a handbasket over there?"

He ventured an answer to his own question: "One thing that might happen is that they would begin to move externally again — start looking for a bogeyman to blame all their troubles on and to consolidate their position at home. Therefore, the question for us is: How can we help? For starters, and at a minimum, we've got to proceed in Eastern Europe in a way that makes clear we're not trying to take advantage of the Russians' troubles. But that's a matter of what we *shouldn't* do. What can we do *actively?*"

Baker did not want to go empty-handed to the Wyoming meeting with Shevardnadze in September: "We've got to thread a needle here. On the one hand, we've got to get the message through loud and clear to the Soviets that they're not going to be eligible for the memberships they want unless and until they make structural changes in their system. At the same time, we've got to make clear to them that we genuinely want them to succeed."

Scowcroft's deputy Robert Gates was giving Bush almost the opposite advice. He told the president that the United States should make no more moves of its own until the Soviet internal situation was far clearer and more stable: it was much too soon for Washington to cast its lot with Gorbachev.

Gates warned, "Gorbachev might be succeeded not by another Gorbachev but by another Stalin." Another possibility was that "this Gorbachev might become a very different Gorbachev, one much less to our liking." If the Soviet Union had its own version of the Tiananmen massacre, how differently might Gorbachev act from Deng Xiaoping?

Gates urged a "steady" policy toward Moscow, one that could weather the lurch from reform to repression that he considered to be virtually predestined by a thousand years of Russian history. After first coming to power, in 1985, Gorbachev had managed to convert some of his Western popularity into credit at home. But Gates reminded the president that that was no longer the case.

Now, he said, Gorbachev's international superstardom was hurting him among the Soviet people. They were complaining that it brought them no clothing, no housing, no food. There were already rumors in Moscow that during the coming winter, the Kremlin would have to ration more than twenty basic foodstuffs. Mass hunger and chaos could trigger a hard-line backlash against Gorbachev. Gates said that the United States must be prepared.

On his return from Paris, Baker told the president, "Gorbachev unquestionably has more problems than you or I would wish on our worst enemy. The odds are he won't succeed, although of course we can't say that. However, his failure wouldn't necessarily mean the failure of reform. You can't get the genie back into the bottle." In any event, the

U.S. government should not "sit around and look as though we're *expecting* the guy to fail."

Bush took his August family holiday at Kennebunkport, where he received Thomas Watson, Jr., a family friend who was a former chairman of IBM and had been Jimmy Carter's ambassador to Moscow. Watson lobbied the president for a more activist policy toward Gorbachev: the United States should reward him for what he had done already, he urged, and help to "save *perestroika* from its many enemies."

The president told Watson that he felt torn. He was groping for some way of "engaging with reform" and "helping Gorbachev pull it off." Still, he was worried that U.S. aid intended to boost Gorbachev might wind up benefiting the Soviet military or giving Soviet hard-liners an excuse not to reform their economy.

CHAPTER 5

"The Makings of a Whole New World"

O N FRIDAY, August 18, 1989, twenty days after Baker's private talk with Shevardnadze, Gorbachev's close adviser Alexander Yakovlev held a press conference on the subject of the three Baltic republics. Yakovlev "unequivocally" condemned the 1939 Hitler-Stalin pact that had led to the Soviet annexation of Latvia, Lithuania, and Estonia.

However, he insisted that the Kremlin still considered the Baltics as much a part of the Soviet Union as any of the other twelve republics and left no doubt that the Soviet government would resist any effort to dislodge them from the USSR.

Four days after Yakovlev's pronouncement, the Lithuanian parliament declared the Soviet annexation "illegal." Sensing that the Kremlin's will was weakening, Baltic nationalists wanted to push quickly for as much independence as they could get. Secessionist organizations asserted their "right" to be free of Moscow. A million people formed a human chain four hundred miles long, linking the three Baltic capitals of Tallinn, Riga, and Vilnius. The Baltics and the Kremlin were on a collision course.

*   *   *

Bush and Baker now had to deal with a dilemma for U.S. policy. For fifty years, the United States had refused formally to recognize that the Baltic states were part of the Soviet Union. Anti-Communist emigrés from the three republics maintained legations in Washington and New York. American officials avoided visiting the Baltics because such visits required permission from Moscow.

If this was the public American position, however, the private position was very different. U.S. officials from the president on down worried that a sudden outbreak of separatism would bring on violence and possibly even a civil war, in which portions of the Soviet Union might break away, leaving nuclear weapons under uncertain control.

Bush, Baker, and Scowcroft all hoped that the Baltic leaders would not press Gorbachev too hard for independence, at least for now. "It is not necessarily in the interest of the United States to encourage the breakup of the Soviet Union," said Scowcroft — in private. Had he said such words in public, the American Right would have been after his scalp, accusing him of acquiescence in the Soviet occupation of the Baltics.

Meanwhile, in Poland, Jaruzelski's handpicked Communist prime minister failed to form a government. He called on a prominent Solidarity activist, Tadeusz Mazowiecki, to assemble a coalition. Communist hardliners balked until Tuesday, August 22, when Gorbachev telephoned the Polish party leader, Meiczyslaw Rakowski, and persuaded him to cooperate in the transfer of power to the first non-Communist-led government in Eastern Europe since the 1940s.

Returning to Washington from his Wyoming vacation, Baker whistled at what had happened while he was away. "Gorbachev's obviously riding a tiger, but it's almost as though he's spurring the tiger on," he noted.

On Tuesday, September 12, thirty minutes behind schedule, Boris Yeltsin arrived by limousine at the basement entrance of the White House West Wing. The firebrand of the Congress of People's Deputies was visiting the United States for the first time, on an eight-day speaking tour of New York, Baltimore, Washington, Chicago, Philadelphia, Minneapolis, Indianapolis, San Francisco, and Los Angeles.

The trip was sponsored by the Esalen Institute of California and a Soviet foundation supporting AIDS-related research and treatment programs. Yeltsin's lecture fee ranged up to twenty-five thousand dollars.

Bush was not eager to receive him. He feared that a formal meeting might prompt Gorbachev to suspect that the United States was dabbling in Soviet domestic politics at his expense. Bush considered Yeltsin to be a loose cannon on the slippery, rolling deck of Soviet politics, with his reputation for heavy drinking, intemperate behavior, and impolitic outbursts. What if he should turn the meeting into some kind of spectacle that would embarrass both Bush and Gorbachev?

Feeling uneasy as ever about what he called the "Gorbocentric" strain in U.S. policy, Robert Gates had asked the president to meet with Yeltsin. Fritz Ermarth, the chairman of the National Intelligence Council, had seconded the suggestion. Skeptical about Gorbachev's political longevity and his commitment to radical reform, Ermarth was impressed by Yeltsin's comeback. He told Condoleezza Rice that though Yeltsin might be eccentric and bumptious, he was showing great courage — much more than Gorbachev — on behalf of positions that the United States should support.

Scowcroft agreed that there should be some kind of low-key meeting between Bush and Yeltsin. In 1975, when Scowcroft was his national security adviser, President Gerald Ford had to decide whether to see Alexander Solzhenitsyn, the iconoclastic novelist and Nobel laureate who had been expelled from the Soviet Union the previous year. Secretary of State Henry Kissinger had argued that for Ford to receive such a prominent critic of the Kremlin would be "disadvantageous," and Ford concurred. Solzhenitsyn was kept out of the White House, to the outrage of many conservatives.

Now Scowcroft reminded his aides how he and Ford had been "burned" by the Solzhenitsyn affair. Refusing to let himself and Bush be put in a similar position over Yeltsin, he asked Blackwill and Rice to devise a formula that would keep everyone happy. They came up with a plan that called for Scowcroft to receive the visitor in his West Wing corner office. Since Yeltsin, as a mere parliamentarian, had no automatic claim on the president's time, Bush and Quayle could each simply "drop by" — with no need for publicity or substantive discussion.

When Rice greeted him at the side entrance, Yeltsin snapped, "This isn't where visitors arrive who are going to see the president." She said, "Your appointment is with General Scowcroft." Yeltsin crossed his arms in defiance and replied, "I'm not going anywhere unless you assure me

I'm going to see the president!" Speaking in Russian, Rice tried to coax him into the building, but Yeltsin would not budge.

Finally she said, "I'm afraid General Scowcroft is very busy, and if we're not going to go see him, we should let him know." Yeltsin relented. "Well, all right, let's go," he said.

She took him to Scowcroft's office, with its tall French windows looking out on the old gray Executive Office Building and the North Grounds of the White House. Bush stopped in for about fifteen minutes and made a point of stressing his "very positive relationship" with Gorbachev: the American people shared the Soviet leader's hope for the "success of the reform movement in the Soviet Union," he said. Yeltsin was on his best behavior. Afterward Bush told his aides that the guest had seemed a "jolly fellow."

After Bush left the room, Scowcroft asked Yeltsin a single question: "What are your objectives on this trip?" Yeltsin's reply went on nonstop for nearly an hour, as he unreeled his thoughts on price reform, the convertibility of the ruble, and the possibility of a joint U.S.-Soviet mission to Mars. He would solve Moscow's housing shortage by "inviting" Western developers to build a million apartment units. He would encourage Western investment by reserving 15 percent of the Soviet economy for private ownership.

Halfway through the monologue, Scowcroft fell sound asleep. Yeltsin seemed barely to notice. Before the meeting ended, Quayle came in for about ten minutes. Alluding to embarrassing stories in the U.S. press about both Yeltsin and himself, he said, "I've been reading your press reviews. Have you read mine?" Yeltsin laughed.

Scowcroft had choreographed the meeting to avoid news stories saying that Bush had engaged in any serious dialogue with Gorbachev's most prominent critic. But Yeltsin emerged from the West Wing to tell the press corps that he had presented Bush and Quayle with a "ten-point plan" to "rescue *perestroika*." Inside, Scowcroft complained that Yeltsin was "devious" and a "two-bit headline-grabber."

Yeltsin's next stop was the State Department. Scowcroft had informed Baker about the Soviet visitor's steamroller tactics at the White House. In a performance that was even more studied than usual, the secretary of state repeatedly interrupted Yeltsin, challenging his naïveté on economics and offering his own homilies on the need for price reform and a convertible ruble.

After the meeting, Baker exclaimed to his aides, "What a flake! He sure makes Gorbachev look good by comparison, doesn't he? And you've also got to sympathize with Gorbachev if that's what he's got to deal with." Ross said that Yeltsin had not proved to be as bad as Scowcroft had warned. Baker replied, "That's true, but he certainly doesn't know anything about market economics. He makes Gorbo look like an expert!"

Following the president's lead, high-ranking U.S. officials privately contrasted Yeltsin's earthy manner and his drinking with the "Western" behavior of Gorbachev. One even joked that the most important American Yeltsin seemed to have met on his trip was Jack Daniel.

In January 1989, Kissinger had scoffed at the Gorbachev reforms as "atmospherics." As late as September, one could still fairly argue that Gorbachev had not seriously changed Soviet behavior around the world.

In Afghanistan, the armies of the Soviet-backed Kabul regime were on the offensive. They used heavy armaments supplied by Moscow in January, after the Kremlin withdrew its soldiers, to break the control of the U.S.-backed *mujahadeen* over Jalalabad, the nation's second-largest city. In Cambodia, though the Vietnamese were pulling out, civil war was raging. In the Middle East, Syria remained entrenched in Lebanon, where its troops and Muslim forces fought Christian militias.

Central America, too, was as turbulent as ever. On this trouble spot Bush and Baker had invested more effort than on any other. Over the course of the summer, Assistant Secretary of State Bernard Aronson and his Soviet counterpart, Yuri Pavlov, had been bargaining about the free and fair elections that were to be held in Nicaragua in Febuary 1990. But in the meantime, Soviet and Warsaw Pact weapons continued to flow into the Sandinista arsenal.

When Pavlov blamed this stockpiling on Castro, Aronson replied that the Soviets could rein in the Cuban leader if they wished to. Pavlov said, "Castro doesn't take orders from anyone. Has it ever occurred to the United States that some of our friends have no interest in seeing an improvement between our own governments?"

As Condoleezza Rice put it in a meeting with other U.S. officials, "We keep telling them to knock it off, but the Soviets are still putting military equipment into every nook and cranny of the Third World. I think we've got to re-ask ourselves the tough question: What are the tangible differences from the old days?" She said that Gorbachev's "new thinking" might prove to be simply "another cover for power politics":

"It's as much an instrument for hardball foreign policy as old thinking was. . . . So why, given all this, should we help them?"

Scowcroft, Gates, and Blackwill agreed. They wondered whether the best thing might not be to give the Soviets no serious aid — to let Moscow stew in its own juices for a while. They felt that if the Soviet internal crisis came to a head, it might force a decisive confrontation between the reformers and the reactionaries. Conversely, if the West helped the Kremlin, it might inadvertently reduce the pressure for reform.

On Wednesday, September 13, Deputy Secretary of State Lawrence Eagleburger spoke at Georgetown University about Europe. The continent had been his life's work. Having served as an American diplomat in Yugoslavia in the early 1960s and again in the late 1970s, he was especially sensitive to the danger that whatever change came to Eastern Europe, especially the Balkans, might turn ugly.

Eagleburger's tone was very different from that of the president's lyrical speeches in Europe in July. He asserted, "For all its risks and uncertainties, the Cold War was characterized by a remarkably stable and predictable set of relationships among the great powers." A sudden end to the East-West standoff could bring disorder, leading to government crackdowns, the reestablishment of dictatorships, and war.

"Already we are hearing it said that we need to take measures to ensure the success of Gorbachev's reforms," said Eagleburger. But this was not the task of Western foreign policy. It would be better to maintain the "security consensus which has served the West so well over the past forty years until the process of democratic reform in the East has truly become irreversible."

Two days later, Bush told a group of media executives that on the subject of the Soviet Union, "I'm like the guy from Missouri: show me. . . . Europe has had peace for some forty years now, and if you look at your textbooks, why, you'll see that that's a long time in an area of the world . . . that has involved us in this century in two massive wars."

In Moscow, Gorbachev worried that Yeltsin's visit to the White House and the statements by Eagleburger and Bush might betoken a new hardening in American policy toward the Soviet Union. The Soviet Foreign Ministry spokesman, Gennadi Gerasimov, publicly asked, "Are these statements consistent with the concept of breaking out of the policy of containment, or do they reflect the inertia of the Cold War period?"

The Democratic leader of the Senate, George Mitchell of Maine, accused the president of having a "basic ambivalence" about Gorbachev's changes: the administration seemed "almost nostalgic about the Cold War," he charged.

Stung, the president told his aides, "It sounds like that 'timidity' stuff that was going around last spring."

Astounded that his speech had attracted so much notice, Eagleburger apologized to the secretary of state. Baker shrugged it off. At his first formal press conference since taking office, he insisted that the Bush administration was "fully engaged across an increasingly broadened agenda" and wished to make a "constructive contribution to *perestroika*."

Baker then took a swing at Mitchell: "When the president of the United States is rocking along with a 70 percent approval rating on his handling of foreign policy, if I were the leader of the opposition, I might have something similar to say."*

Soon Baker was sorry he had spoken out. His words ignited a lingering doubt as to whether he was really cut out to be a statesman or whether he was still a political operative at heart. Some had speculated that he was running foreign policy merely as an epilogue to the 1988 campaign and a prologue to one in 1992 (or 1996, the year in which Baker was suspected of having an interest in running for president himself); now the secretary seemed to be saying that Bush's Soviet policy was sound because the polls showed that the American voters liked it.

Scalded by the press, Baker told his aides, "Well, between Larry and myself, I guess we really managed to screw up this week!" Ross replied, "You'll get no argument on that from me, Bob [Zoellick], or Margaret [Tutwiler]."

Margaret Thatcher stopped in Moscow on her way back from a visit to Tokyo. She had received a letter from Bush asking her to make three points on his behalf when she saw Gorbachev. First, he supported *perestroika* — personally and without reservation. Second, he was not alarmed by predictions that Soviet reform was about to collapse. Third, his policy toward Eastern Europe would not threaten the Soviet Union or exploit its difficulties there.

* Around the same time, Baker told visitors in the privacy of his office, "I know polls don't mean that much, but this president has the highest approval rating in history." Referring to Jesse Helms, the hard-line Republican senator from North Carolina, he said, "No one but Helms is giving us a hard time."

When Thatcher delivered the message, Gorbachev was skeptical of Bush's third point. He told Thatcher that he wanted to see democracy and self-determination flourish in Eastern Europe, but not if it jeopardized Soviet security, which he continued to define as keeping the Warsaw Pact intact.

Earlier that month, Ukrainian nationalists had marched through the streets of Kiev, demanding independence for Ukraine, which was the Soviet Union's second-largest republic and its chief source of food. Gorbachev responded by purging the hard-line Ukrainian party boss Vladimir Shcherbitsky from the Politburo. At the same time, he delivered a blistering attack on the outbreak of separatism in the republics. This was classic Gorbachev, straddling a position between the foot-draggers of the Right and the radicals of the Left.

Over luncheon with Thatcher, Gorbachev dismissed the problem of nationalism with a sweep of his hand. Recalling Charles de Gaulle's remark on how difficult it was to preside over a country that manufactured more than 120 different kinds of cheese, he said, "Imagine how much harder it is to run a country with over a hundred and twenty different nationalities."

"Yes!" interjected Leonid Abalkin, a deputy prime minister who served as economic adviser to Gorbachev. "Especially if there's no cheese!"

On Thursday, September 21, Shevardnadze came to the White House for the first time since Bush had taken office. The two men had last seen each other exactly a year before, in their breakfast meeting at the vice presidential residence. In the Oval Office, the president showed Shevardnadze to one of the white-upholstered chairs next to the fireplace and took the other for himself. Baker and American and Soviet aides sat on two white sofas.

After the television cameramen and photographers left the room, Bush repeated the three-point message he had sent to Gorbachev through Margaret Thatcher. Shevardnadze urged the president not to be disconcerted by reports of Gorbachev's domestic troubles: the Soviet president was firmly in charge and committed to further reform. Alluding to Yeltsin, Bush replied that another recent Soviet visitor had offered him a contrary assessment. Shevardnadze gave a thin smile and said, "Well, don't believe everything you hear."

The foreign minister did not deny that the challenges to Gorbachev from all sides were growing more dire every week. Taking a very different approach than Gorbachev had with Thatcher in Moscow, he referred to the "painful" nationalities problem: "We on our side are fully aware of the extent to which improved relations between states depend on domestic stability."

When Bush reviewed the Shevardnadze meeting with Scowcroft afterward, he made clear the depth of his commitment to the status quo in the East bloc. He told Scowcroft that it would be "very stupid" for the United States to make statements or pursue policies aimed at hastening the breakup of the Warsaw Pact or encouraging centrifugal forces that might tear the Soviet Union apart.

Scowcroft basically agreed: "It's in our interest that the nationalist debate be tempered. Perhaps some kind of federation would be better than having all these republics arc off and go their own ways."

Bush said, "It's tempting to say, 'Wouldn't it be great if the Soviet empire broke up?' But that's not really practical or smart, is it?"

Scowcroft warned that for the United States to encourage the secessionists might provoke a "severe crackdown" and "change the character of the central government," making it far more militaristic and authoritarian. If some of the Soviet republics seceded, the United States would still have to deal with a Russia that was deeply hostile to the West, armed with twenty-five thousand nuclear weapons, and able to make plenty of trouble around the globe.

Bush repeated that he wanted to see the "situation over there slow down and settle down a bit." He wished to give Gorbachev and Shevardnadze "some time to keep all these things under control and moving in the right direction."

After Shevardnadze's meeting with Bush, Baker brought the Soviet foreign minister back with him to the State Department. Prominently displayed on the bookshelves of his small private office were volumes written by friendly journalists and public figures, as well as a framed and autographed photograph of Baker strolling with Ronald Reagan.

With a homey flourish, Baker showed his guest a framed color aerial photograph of his Wyoming ranch, where they would be holding their in-depth talks. The picture rested on a wooden end table next to a much-used telephone with direct lines to Eagleburger, Tutwiler, Ross, and Zoellick.

That evening, Shevardnadze and Baker went to Andrews and boarded an Air Force plane bound for Jackson Hole. At the behest of their boss, the secretary of state's aides had arranged the most relaxed visit ever between American and Soviet foreign ministers. On Baker's ranch, the two men would go fly-fishing, stroll along trails, and assess the world from the tranquil setting of Jackson Lake and the Snake River Valley, with the pale-violet, snow-capped Grand Tetons beyond.

Aboard Baker's jet, Shevardnadze reminisced over the engine noise about how, as party boss of his native Georgia in 1978, he had stood up to the Kremlin. Always worried about nationalist rebellions, Leonid Brezhnev and his colleagues had demanded that Russian be designated the official language of all Soviet republics. Shevardnadze explained to Baker that Georgians had always felt passionately about their native tongue.

Afraid that rioters might burn down Tbilisi, Shevardnadze had gone into the city square, despite assassination threats, and shouted through a bullhorn that he would consider the nationalists' demands. Then he called Brezhnev and hammered out a compromise. He boasted to Baker, "We Georgians led the way in establishing the principle that Russian is the federal language but not the republican language."

During the four-hour flight to Wyoming, Baker asked Shevardnadze how Gorbachev was planning to deal with the problem of secessionism throughout the Soviet Union. He knew that in recent months the Soviet president had drawn on his foreign minister's experience in dealing with nationalism in Georgia, the Baltics, and elsewhere.

Shevardnadze responded with a variation of the mantra he had frequently uttered in private since their Paris meeting in late July: "If we have to put down internal dissidence by force, it would be the end of *perestroika*. Therefore, it's not an option."

He went on, "We must deal with the problem without forcing it to become violent. We must learn one of the lessons of the past, which is to avoid as much as possible inadvertently causing an escalation. In the measures we take, we must not turn protests into riots and riots into bloodshed."

Shevardnadze argued that in none of the Baltic republics did a majority endorse complete separation from the Kremlin: "The Baltic peoples are too closely bound to the Soviet Union to stand completely alone."

Baker replied, "If you're so sure of that, why not let them hold a referendum on secession? Even if you were wrong about the majority view there, and the referendum passed, you'd end up with a lot of

Finlands around you. Cut the Baltics loose! You'd be better off with three little Finlands."

Following Yakovlev's August line, Shevardnadze said that complete independence for the Baltics was out of the question. He and Gorbachev believed that the nationalists would settle for "maximum political and economic autonomy" within the USSR, especially if *perestroika* produced a higher standard of living. Gorbachev hoped that the Baltics would prove to be a "laboratory for *perestroika*," demonstrating to the rest of the Soviet Union that the great experiment of economic reform could indeed bring a better life for the citizenry.

Shevardnadze believed that if the peoples of the non-Russian republics were liberated from the most inefficient and repressive aspects of Soviet rule, they might be willing to remain part of a union or federation. Thus, the ability to keep the nationalities problem under control hinged on the success of *perestroika*, which in turn hinged on the willingness of the capitalist world to help tide over the Soviet Union during the inevitable traumas of adjustment.

Baker and Shevardnadze were joined in the forward compartment of the plane by Nikolai Shmelyov, an economist on the staff of the Institute for the Study of the U.S.A. and Canada in Moscow, a member of the Supreme Soviet, and an outspoken proponent of rapid, sweeping economic reform.*

Shmelyov was in favor of the Soviets' introducing a free market not only in goods and services but in currency as well. He advocated letting the ruble find a natural rate of exchange against the currencies of the West, a measure that would result in a massive devaluation. Baker found Shmelyov obsessed with the notion that a convertible ruble would be a panacea for all that ailed the Soviet economy.

Still, the inclusion of an outsider and gadfly such as Shmelyov in Shevardnadze's party was a clever tactic. Baker had been stressing for months that the Soviet Union had to make fundamental changes in the Soviet economy. Here was an economist who agreed with him, traveling in the entourage of the foreign minister.

Shevardnadze hoped that Baker would take Shmelyov's presence as a sign that even the most radical proposals had become respectable in Moscow. This was exactly Baker's interpretation.

The plane landed at Jackson Hole after sundown. The two diplomats

---

* Shmelyov had briefly been married to Nikita Khrushchev's granddaughter.

emerged into the evening chill and walked down a dark-red carpet imported by the town fathers from five hundred miles away. Wyoming's governor, Michael Sullivan, presented Baker and Shevardnadze with Stetson cowboy hats. Sullivan's aides had asked the Soviet embassy for the foreign minister's hat size, in vain. They finally got it from the CIA: 7½.

Over the next two days, the two men took walks along trails through stands of lodgepole pine, yellow aspen, and cottonwood. Shevardnadze was thrilled. He told his host that the beauty of the setting was a "miracle."

At Cattleman's Bridge on the Snake River, they fished for trout. When Shevardnadze picked up his spinning rod, Baker could tell that his guest had no idea how to use it but was too proud to ask for help. The NBC television news anchor Tom Brokaw, who owned a nearby property, waved at Baker and chuckled when he saw Shevardnadze struggling with his line. The foreign minister caught nothing, but that did not seem to impair his enjoyment of the outing.

On Friday evening, the men were joined by their wives for a local dinner of fresh trout and salmon. On Saturday, they dined on ribs and buffalo steaks during a hoedown at the Jackson Lake Lodge, where employees passed out straw hats, bandannas, and bucking bronco pins, and a band played country and western music.

In the privacy of a mountain lodge, the two diplomats finally got down to business — the old business of nuclear arms control. They argued over the chief issue on the agenda: START, the nearly finished treaty on strategic arms reduction that Bush had inherited from Reagan. Before the rise of Gorbachev, arms control had been virtually the only major problem that the United States and the Soviet Union could bargain over with any result.

In August 1968, Lyndon Johnson had arranged to make a dramatic flight to Leningrad, where he and the Soviet leaders would open the first serious negotiation between the two powers over nuclear arms and delivery systems.* But on the eve of the announcement, Soviet tanks rolled into Czechoslovakia, and Johnson never made the trip. It was

---

* Not inconsequentially, Johnson had also anticipated that this journey would boost the fortunes of the 1968 Democratic presidential nominee. Who that would be was still undecided. It has been speculated that despite his announcement that he would not seek the prize, Johnson hoped that by starting the first serious round of arms control talks ever, he would help to make himself seem so indispensable that the Democrats at Chicago would draft him to run again.

not the last time that progress in arms control would fall victim to "linkage" between diplomacy and Soviet behavior.

After Richard Nixon took office, and for the next dozen years, the two sides conducted strategic arms limitation talks (SALT). The results — the SALT I accords (1972) and the SALT II treaty (1979) — were not intended to stop the arms race; rather they were meant to function as rules for the road, by imposing limits on the number and size of intercontinental ballistic missiles (ICBMs) and other strategic weapons that each country could deploy.

Ronald Reagan loathed the SALT process. Part of this was the ultra-conservative's complaint that Nixon, Ford, Kissinger, and Carter had given away the store; but after Reagan took office, in 1981, it became clear that he also had genuine moral objections to the idea of mutual deterrence, which he called a "suicide pact," and would prefer to abolish the two arsenals.

Reagan did not content himself with fine-tuning the balance of terror; he wished to end it. Americans who voted for Reagan in 1980 had little idea that on this issue they were electing a radical, a heretic, an idealist, a romantic, a nuclear abolitionist.

The first dramatic sign of Reagan's seriousness about nuclear disarmament came in March 1983, when he unveiled his vision of an impregnable space-based shield that would render offensive missiles "impotent and obsolete." What Reagan called his strategic defense initiative (SDI), the press dubbed Star Wars, reflecting the view of many technical experts that the idea was science fiction.

Had the Kremlin gerontocracy in 1985 selected as the new leader a more traditional Soviet politician than Gorbachev, Reagan's dreams of abolishing nuclear weapons would probably have remained empty rhetoric. Reagan's critics would have continued to charge that he was using this posture as an excuse to resist any further steps toward arms control.

As it happened, though, Reagan's new Kremlin counterpart had similar ambitions. Gorbachev knew that going beyond arms control to actual disarmament would serve his campaign to reduce the drain of military spending on the Soviet economy. Nonetheless, he was also under heavy pressure from his generals to do everything he could to block SDI, which they feared because of the superiority of U.S. technology.

In October 1986, at Reykjavik, Reagan and Gorbachev agreed in principle to major reductions in strategic offensive forces. However, a final deal fell through because Gorbachev insisted on linking these reductions to the cancellation of SDI, which Reagan refused to consider. Still, by the end of Reagan's presidency, negotiators in Geneva were within striking distance of a treaty based on the Reykjavik talks.

When it came to the all-important issue of how to keep the nuclear peace, George Bush was as much a traditionalist as Reagan was a revolutionary. Much as Churchill had once said of democracy, Bush believed that mutual nuclear deterrence was the worst possible arrangement, except for any other.

Nor did Bush share Reagan's fervor for SDI. In March 1983, the vice president's chief of staff, Admiral Daniel Murphy, had rushed into his office with an advance copy of Reagan's speech announcing the program. Murphy said, "We've got to take that out! If we go off half cocked on this idea, we're going to bring on the biggest arms race that the world has ever seen."* Murphy shared the view of many experts that the expansion of U.S. defenses would only provoke the Soviets to increase their offenses — thus accelerating the vicious cycle of the arms race.

Bush refused Murphy's plea to try to talk Reagan out of SDI. He knew how strongly Reagan felt about the program and did not wish to cross him. Murphy said, "Then, Jesus Christ, at least you *personally* should stay neutral. You don't want to be way out on a limb and then cancel it if you become president of the United States."

Through the remaining years of the Reagan presidency, SDI became a litmus test for Republican conservatives, whose support Bush would need for the 1988 nomination. The vice president never discussed the subject with Murphy again. In public, when necessary, he recited the Reagan administration's catechism on SDI: defense was "moral," offense "immoral." Better an effective, purely defensive shield than the threat of mass murder. But Bush's heart was never in it. In private, he told one aide, "The less I have to say on this thing, the better."

As vice president, Bush was also uneasy about START. For analysis of the negotiations, he often relied on Samuel Watson, a retired army colonel on his staff. A hard-liner, Watson warned Bush that the more strategic weapons the U.S. had to give up, the greater the danger that

* Murphy was especially sensitive to this problem because he was an expert on antisubmarine warfare and thus familiar with the tendency of breakthroughs in defensive technology to spur additional offensive deployments.

the Soviets would hide missiles they were supposed to destroy, in order to use them in a crisis and tip the balance of power in their favor.

Once Bush became president, his qualms about START were renewed by his national security adviser. Brent Scowcroft said that nuclear weapons were "like fire insurance — you buy them even if you don't want to use them." Scowcroft felt that Reagan's rush toward disarmament had been a "mighty dubious objective for grown-ups in this business."

Scowcroft believed that START was a matter of "seeing how much you can shave from deterrence and still keep it in effect. I think this is playing with fire." He worried that the unfinished treaty that Reagan had bequeathed to Bush had some dangerous loopholes.* In part because of his air force background, Scowcroft defined U.S. national security largely in orthodox military terms: preventing the Kremlin from having even the theoretical ability to defeat the United States in a single crushing, preemptive strike.

By the late 1970s, hawkish analysts were convinced that the United States was rapidly growing vulnerable to a nuclear Pearl Harbor. They cited the adverse ratio of highly accurate Soviet ICBM warheads to underground silos containing America's thousand Minuteman missiles. Because these silos were stationary and in the sights of Soviet war planners, it was feared that in the desperate atmosphere of an American-Soviet crisis, they might actually *invite* a "bolt-from-the-blue" attack, rather than deter one.

In 1983, Reagan had chosen Scowcroft to chair a presidential commission on the future of U.S. strategic forces. The commission's report recommended two steps to reduce U.S. vulnerability to a first strike: a START agreement that would lower the ratio of Soviet warheads to U.S. ICBM silos, and the deployment of new U.S. weapons that would be less vulnerable to Soviet attack. These included a new ICBM, the Midgetman, which would be armed with a single warhead and mounted on a mobile vehicle that would be harder for the Soviets to target.

The Pentagon, however, pressed for a larger, ten-warhead mobile ICBM called the MX. Early in 1989, Scowcroft advised Bush to stall the START negotiations in Geneva until the administration had a clearer

---

* Besides cutting the overall number of Soviet warheads and reducing by 50 percent the largest, mightiest Soviet missiles, the treaty would also reduce the number of U.S. ICBM silos. Some U.S. analysts charged that the ratio of Soviet missiles and warheads to U.S. silos would actually increase — a result they considered dangerous.

idea of what weapons would make up the next generation of U.S. deterrent forces. Bush's newly appointed START negotiator, Richard Burt, tried and failed to devise a proposal that would both satisfy Scowcroft and get the talks moving.*

In June 1989, when the START negotiations finally resumed in Geneva, Bush sent Gorbachev a private list of proposals. Almost every one demanded the lion's share of compromise from the Soviets. Gorbachev was so offended that he did not even send the president a direct reply.

Fearing an impasse before the negotiations even began, Burt devised another approach — one that offered a bit more inducement for the Soviets to sign a treaty before Bush had to run for reelection.†

Dick Cheney, who was as skeptical about START as Scowcroft, complained to Baker about Burt's "overeagerness." For his part, Burt warned Baker that Cheney was obstructing an "important opportunity": "We're stopped dead in our tracks." He asked the secretary of state to allow him some flexibility. "That way we'll be able to steal a march on Shevardnadze," he said, "because you can be sure he'll be bringing something of his own to Wyoming."

But Baker lacked the stomach for a showdown with Scowcroft and Cheney. He was hopeful that a START treaty could eventually be signed without any major U.S. compromises. He noted that the Soviets had

* Burt's plan, which he entrepreneurially referred to as the "strategic stability reductions initiative," called for writing an "escalator clause" into the draft treaty, which eventually would make room for the Midgetman and a similar Soviet missile, the SS-25. It would ban the MX and its Soviet counterpart, the SS-24, which had multiple warheads, and prohibit testing of the giant SS-18. This was so that in time the SS-18's reliability would erode: the missiles would, in effect, rust away in their silos. Campaigning for his idea at the State Department, Burt said it was a "way to win over Scowcroft by helping lock in Midgetman as a successor to Minuteman, while locking in MX as a bargaining chip."
† Burt's proposed compromise was an attempt to reconcile the U.S. and Soviet positions on cruise missiles. Because these weapons were so small, they were easier to conceal from the other side's spy satellites than bombers and ballistic missiles. On the traditional arms control principle that all permitted weapons should be "verifiable," cruise missiles should thus have been subject to strict constraints — or so the Soviets insisted. But cruise missiles were a category of weaponry in which the United States had a marked technological advantage, and therefore also a category that the Pentagon sought to "protect" from arms control. The U.S. Air Force was equipping its bombers with air-launched cruise missiles (ALCMs) to ensure their ability to penetrate Soviet antiaircraft defenses; the U.S. Navy wished to put sea-launched cruise missiles (SLCMs) on submarines and surface ships for use against enemy vessels, and as a means of projecting power into various regions of the globe. (The suitability of SLCMs for "land-attack" missions was spectacularly demonstrated in January 1991, at the outset of Operation Desert Storm, when the United States began fighting to oust Iraq from Kuwait.)

come to every recent meeting with arms control concessions of their own: why not let them do so again now?

Baker proved to be correct. When Shevardnadze landed in Washington for his White House visit with Bush, he was carrying a nine-page letter from Gorbachev suggesting that the Soviets were willing to make new concessions.

These concerned primarily SDI. Since 1985, the Soviets had refused to sign a START treaty unless the United States reaffirmed the 1972 SALT I antiballistic missile (ABM) treaty, which, in their view, precluded SDI. Gorbachev's advisers understood that Bush did not share Reagan's passion for Star Wars; they doubted that the Bush administration would pursue the program with anything like the vigor Reagan had displayed.*

During the summer of 1989, the Soviets privately debated about how to strengthen the hand of those in the administration who, left to their own instincts, would let SDI fade away. Should the Kremlin persist in linking START to the reaffirmation of the ABM treaty and thus to the repudiation of SDI? This would provide the "more reasonable Americans" with a strong argument against Star Wars. Or should the Soviets earn some points with the United States by backing off from their adamance on the still-hot issue, trusting Bush not to make them sorry by forging ahead with SDI?

Shevardnadze pushed hard for the latter course. He had his staff organize secret seminars at which leading Soviet scientists advocated "unlinking" START from SDI. The group included the nuclear physicist Yevgeni Velikhov and the longtime Soviet space chief Roald Sagdeyev, both of whom Gorbachev respected. On so esoteric an issue as anti-missile

* For example, during his turbulent and unsuccessful confirmation hearings in January 1989, Bush's first nominee for defense secretary, John Tower, had dismissed as "unrealistic" Reagan's dream of comprehensive, impregnable space-based defenses. Dick Cheney several times said that SDI had been "oversold," and two days after the inauguration, Brent Scowcroft, who had repeatedly criticized SDI as a private citizen, said on ABC's "This Week with David Brinkley" that he opposed "moving forward with this massive program until we understand clearly how it fits into what we are trying to do." At his first press conference, Bush asserted that SDI would not provide a "shield so impenetrable" that it would eliminate the "need for any kind of other defense." With that cautious statement, Bush repudiated the essence of what had attracted Reagan to SDI. Among the administration's upper ranks, only Vice President Quayle remained genuinely enthusiastic about the program.

defenses, the scientists, who tended to be liberals, found it easy to out-argue the hard-liners in the military and the party, for the simple reason that they knew so much more about the topic.

In the September 1989 letter that Shevardnadze brought to Bush, Gorbachev wrote, "Let us set aside, for the time being, our conceptual argument about whether the placing of weapons in space ... will strengthen strategic stability or have the opposite effect. Let us not allow this issue to make the already complex talks more difficult."

In the Oval Office, Shevardnadze also suggested to Bush that the Kremlin might dismantle a huge radar station near Krasnoyarsk, in Siberia, which American experts had long charged was a violation of the ABM treaty. U.S. hawks had denounced the radar as a symbol of persistent, flagrant Soviet cheating on arms control treaties.* Shevardnadze's talk of destroying the facility amounted to an admission of Soviet guilt that reflected, as the foreign minister told Bush, a "political decision."

Shevardnadze's statement implied that Gorbachev had overruled the military's objections, but in fact it was Shevardnadze himself who had rammed these concessions through in Moscow. During the intense arms control negotiations with the Reagan administration, the foreign minister had grown frustrated with the reflexive tendency of the Defense Ministry and the General Staff to block almost any modification of the Soviet negotiating position. He found that he could deliberately exceed his authority by short-circuiting the decision-making process in Moscow and bypassing the generals altogether.

Shevardnadze had refined the practice of asking his own arms control experts to come up with new initiatives, which he would propose to the Americans himself. After they accepted his terms, he would take the breakthrough back to Gorbachev for his approval, and only then would he present it to the military — as a fait accompli. Precisely because this gambit worked so often and so well, Shevardnadze was despised in the highest ranks of the Soviet military.

It was in this bold fashion, capitalizing on his intimacy with Gorbachev, that Shevardnadze had decided, as he privately told his aides, to "lance the boil" of the radar at Krasnoyarsk. Convinced that the military would never admit Soviet guilt on this issue, he did so on his own.

* In fact, it was one of the USSR's very few unambiguous and serious violations.

*   *   *

During the talks in Baker's log cabin, Shevardnadze expanded on the hint in Gorbachev's letter that START and SDI could finally be unlinked: the Soviet Union would be willing to sign and implement a START treaty without a separate accord limiting space-based defenses.

Having made that large concession, Shevardnadze suggested that the Americans reciprocate by agreeing to hold separate talks on what aspects of SDI might be compatible with the ABM treaty. This was a variation on a proposal that the Soviets had floated during the Reagan administration.

Baker knew that diehard proponents of SDI, led within the government by Vice President Quayle, would oppose subjecting any part of the program to negotiated limits. Therefore, he told Shevardnadze, "We've seen this before, and we've turned it down before."

Shevardnadze was disappointed. Instead of prompting U.S. flexibility, his concessions had resulted in American stonewalling. It was clear to him that Baker and his people had concluded that all they needed to do now was sit back, pocket what the Kremlin had to offer, and wait for more.*

If Bush and Baker were less than enthusiastic about START, which they looked on as unfinished business from the Reagan administration, they were eager to make progress as quickly as possible on treaties that they could call their own. One example was a ban on chemical weapons, which the president had once decried as an "awful, silent death."

As vice president, Bush had twice flown to Geneva to present the U.S. position on a worldwide chemical weapons ban. In the 1980s, the dictatorship of Saddam Hussein in Iraq used chemical weapons against its own rebellious Kurdish minority as well as against Iran. Bush was especially moved by a much-reprinted color photograph of the corpse

---

* Shevardnadze also agreed to drop the Kremlin's long-standing insistence that sea-launched cruise missiles (SLCMs) be limited under START. Instead he proposed that SLCMs be consigned to a separate negotiation. Aware of the U.S. Navy's protectiveness toward the SLCM program, Baker held firm against any limits, even outside the START framework. On the issue of mobile ICBMs, Baker was more flexible, though his concessions were conditional. Rather than lifting the ban on such systems altogether, as Burt had urged, Baker told Shevardnadze that the treaty might permit them, but only after the U.S. Congress decided which kind it wanted.

of a woman lying in the street with a dead child in her arms. Both were victims of a gas attack by the Baghdad regime on the Kurdish town of Halabja.

By the summer of 1989, the chief obstacle to an international agreement on chemical weapons was concern over verification. Deadly chemicals were easy to hide; stockpiles could not be monitored with anything like the precision with which spy satellites could keep track of missile sites.*

Bush told Scowcroft to press ahead with negotiations anyway. The general replied, "You realize that this means we're kicking the can of verification down the road." The president said, "Yeah, I know. But my gut just tells me that the danger of proliferation" — that is, the chance that poison-gas weapons might find their way into other countries' arsenals — "is more important than the risk of Soviet cheating."

Cheney and Admiral Crowe of the Joint Chiefs of Staff were concerned that the Soviets might try to extend this more relaxed standard for verification to the treaties on conventional and nuclear arsenals. Bush waved their caution aside. With great secrecy, he assigned the problem to Baker, who proposed a prompt agreement to reduce existing chemical weapons stockpiles by 80 percent while negotiating a "follow-on" treaty that would reduce them even further.†

In Jackson Hole, Baker discussed the plan with Shevardnadze, who was glad to find an area in which the United States was willing to budge from long-held positions. After the session, an amazed Tarasenko told his boss, "This is really something new and important. The Americans are no longer quite so obsessed with our cheating."

Two days after Shevardnadze left Wyoming, Bush unveiled his plan at the United Nations, saying, "The U.S. is ready to destroy nearly all —

---

* Bush himself told the UN Committee on Disarmament in 1984, "For a chemical weapons ban to work, each party must have confidence that the other parties are abiding by it. . . . No sensible government enters into those international contracts known as treaties unless it can ascertain — or verify — that it is getting what it contracted for." Thus the U.S. draft treaty that he unveiled there on behalf of the Reagan administration contained complex provisions for comprehensive and intrusive on-site inspections. The Soviet Union immediately objected, as it had to similar proposals over the years, on the grounds that the United States was "asking nations voluntarily to sanction intelligence activities by the other side on their territory."

† Good soldiers both, Cheney and Crowe did not obstruct the exercise with the kind of damaging leaks that had been common during arms control talks under Reagan. When the proposal was announced, the president and Baker took a good deal of heat from right-wing critics for what was considered to be their shocking nonchalance about verification.

98 percent — of our chemical weapons stockpile, provided the Soviet Union joins the band. And I think they will."

The next day, Shevardnadze went before the UN General Assembly to urge the immediate elimination of the superpowers' poison-gas stockpiles and to call for a ban on further production of chemical weapons. In the past, U.S. officials would have accused Shevardnadze of practicing one-upsmanship. But in the new atmosphere, Bush and Shevardnadze were seen to be coming together rather than vying with each other for propaganda points.

After their September meetings, Shevardnadze felt that both he and Baker had solidified their rapport and their trust in each other and that they "would like to go further toward constructive cooperation."

More than ever before, Baker was fascinated by Shevardnadze: "Unlike so many diplomats, he can be influenced if you make a good argument. He'll listen to it, he'll make a hard decision, and later he'll defend it at home with Gorbachev and the military."

Once again, Baker could not get over the Soviet diplomat's candor about Soviet mistakes and problems. Baker told his aides, "In the past, their insecurities kept them from admitting their weaknesses, partly because they were afraid that we'd exploit those weaknesses. Now they've got enough confidence in themselves and enough trust in us to be honest. The situation has got the makings of a whole new world."

Over the next three weeks, Baker twice made new public efforts to extend a hand to Gorbachev. He told the Senate Finance Committee on Wednesday, October 4, that the outlook for Soviet reform was "promising." That week, his aide Robert Zoellick accompanied U.S. Federal Reserve Chairman Alan Greenspan on a five-day trip to Moscow, where they advised Gorbachev's economic experts on how to build a market-oriented financial system.

In New York on Monday evening, October 16, Baker told the Foreign Policy Association, "It would be a mistake to conclude that the challenges are too daunting or that the impediments to success are too great. So far, Gorbachev has secured greater power over the years, and he reveals every intention to 'stay the course.' "

No longer did Baker speak of "testing" Soviet intentions; now he said that he and the president would search for "points of mutual advantage."

Taken together, Baker's Senate testimony and his New York speech constituted the most enthusiastic official endorsement thus far of Gorbachev and his policies. Baker stressed that the common denominator of virtually all of Gorbachev's policies was freedom. He noted that the Kremlin now granted the individual citizen unprecedented freedom of speech as well as free choice in electing the Congress of People's Deputies. *Perestroika* was inching toward free markets. By applying the "new thinking" to Eastern Europe, the Soviet leaders even seemed willing to free the satellites.

Baker was implicitly refuting the prophets of Gorbachev's doom within the Bush administration. When Robert Gates learned of Baker's oblique reference to those who felt that the "challenges" were "too daunting," he knew whom the secretary of state had in mind.

At the same time, Baker was careful not to raise expectations about the scope of what the United States or the West could do to help Gorbachev economically. He tried to cast the U.S. position as consistent with the Kremlin's own disclaimers on the subject: the success of *perestroika* depended on the Soviets themselves, not on foreign assistance.*

Subordinates at the State Department picked up Baker's cautiously upbeat theme. Curtis Kamman, the deputy assistant secretary of state for Europe, said in a speech at a U.S.-Soviet conference in Pittsburgh that the two nations were no longer adversaries but rather "cooperative partners in certain respects." An official of the Bush administration was now defining the relationship in the same terms that Gorbachev himself had used with Admiral Crowe in Moscow three months before: *partnership*.

The vice president of the United States was not happy with what he was hearing. Three days after Baker's Senate testimony, Dan Quayle told a television interviewer that Gorbachev was a "master of public relations," and *perestroika* merely a "form of Leninism."

The day after the New York address by Baker — conceivably a rival for the Republican nomination in 1996 — Quayle cautioned a Los Angeles audience against those "who say the Cold War is over." Improvements in Soviet relations were "neither inevitable nor irreversible." Weren't the Soviets still making mischief in Afghanistan, North Korea, Cambodia, and Central America? "Let them reform themselves!" the vice president demanded.

* Baker also quoted Ed Hewett of the Brookings Institution, who had briefed the president in Maine in February: "However strong Western feelings may be about the possible outcome of this reform effort, Western policymakers should see that their 'influence' on this process can be no more than modest."

As usual, Scowcroft stayed out of the public debate. But after reading an advance text of Baker's New York speech, he feared that it was a mistake to emphasize only the positive developments in the Soviet Union and the U.S.-Soviet relationship. Like Eagleburger, he remained apprehensive about the prospect of a post–Cold War world, which he expected to be "confused, even chaotic."

On the paramount issue, the military competition between the United States and the Kremlin, Scowcroft was not willing to conclude that the Soviets were ready to accept American terms. He noted that the Soviets were sending "mixed signals" on START: it was "too early to say" whether Shevardnadze's Wyoming concessions represented real progress or whether Gorbachev and his foreign minister were merely "reshuffling the deck chairs on the *Titanic*."

On Monday, October 23, Scowcroft privately said, "It would be dumb if we decided the Cold War is over, or that the Soviets aren't a threat anymore, or that we don't need NATO and we can use our defense budget to straighten out our domestic economic order."

Striking a position somewhere between Baker's and Quayle's, Scowcroft said that he wanted to be "skeptically hopeful" but not "prejudge the outcome of what's going on over there." Above all, he said, "whatever we do, we can't tie our policy to Gorbachev."

That same day, in Moscow, Shevardnadze admitted publicly for the first time that the Soviet invasion of Afghanistan in 1979 had violated "general human values."* In Budapest, the acting Hungarian president, Matyas Szuros, declared that the Soviet invasion of Hungary in 1956 had been illegal. Szuros depicted his government as the successor to the "national independence movement" that the Soviet Union had once crushed with tanks.

At the State Department, Baker told his aides that the Moscow and Budapest statements were the "stuff of which watersheds are made. We just can't sit over here and appear to be churlish. If we keep saying he can't pull it off, it'll begin to sound as though that's what we want. And if it happens that the pessimists are right and Gorbachev does get

---

* Shevardnadze was careful to establish where blame did *not* belong. He noted that in December 1979, when the Brezhnev regime launched the invasion, "M. S. Gorbachev and I were candidate members of the Politburo. I found out about what had happened from radio and newspaper reports. A decision that had very serious consequences for our country was made behind the back of the party and the people. We were confronted with a fait accompli."

thrown out on his ear, there'll be a lot of people who will say we got into the business of self-fulfilling prophecy."

Baker had observed to his staff as recently as July that in all his years in government, he had never seen a U.S. administration so free of intramural combat as Bush's. Now he detected the emergence of the old problem of internecine bickering over policy. After hearing about Quayle's speech, Baker told Scowcroft, "We don't need this kind of free-for-all in what we're saying publicly. I don't care whether it's seen as good cop–bad cop or Baker versus Quayle. *We don't need it!*"

The secretary ordered his aides to tell the press that the vice president was "off the reservation" on this issue, and that the president had approved Baker's New York speech in advance. On background, Dennis Ross told reporters that Baker's address had been designed "to show that the accomplishments of the Wyoming ministerial didn't come out of a vacuum, and to make it clear that the president has one spokesman on this issue — and it's Baker."

Robert Gates asked the State Department to clear an address he was planning to give at a conference in Bethesda, Maryland. He had been polishing the text for months. Profound, lasting Soviet reform, it said, would defy not only seventy-two years of communism but a millennium of Russian history as well. Gorbachev was basically a disciplinarian of the Andropov mold: "Every element of political reform seems to have been designed to increase Gorbachev's personal power."

Gorbachev was trying to make the old system work, Gates argued, not establish a new one. He intended not to liberate Eastern Europe from communism but rather to turn it over to new-breed Communists like himself. He had "rigged" the Soviet elections earlier that year and would never tolerate a genuine opposition party.

State sent back Gates's draft with a polite suggestion that perhaps it was "too pessimistic." Slyly, Gates revised it by including material from Baker's own gloomy pronouncements on Gorbachev the previous spring. This made Baker all the angrier. He called Scowcroft at the White House and asked him to muzzle Gates. Scowcroft passed the bad news along to his deputy, who slipped the text of his undelivered speech into the top drawer of his desk.

Baker also struck back at the skeptics in public. In San Francisco, he told an audience, "Any uncertainty about the fate of reform in the Soviet Union is all the more reason, not less, for us to seize the present opportunity. . . . The president and I have both said that we want *perestroika* to succeed."

Scowcroft's spokesman Roman Popadiuk joked with White House reporters, "Baker is back!"

Gates privately told colleagues, "As long as Gorbachev is behaving himself — relatively speaking — Jim Baker's sunny approach will carry the day. But if Gorbachev shows his dark side, the points some of the rest of us have been trying to make won't seem quite so farfetched."

In Helsinki, Gorbachev affected a lordly detachment from the wrangling in Washington. He told the Finnish president, Mauno Koivisto, that Baker's recent public statements showed that Bush's government had finally "come around to a realistic assessment both of what is happening in the USSR and of what is possible in international relations. The Americans have made up their minds, and now they seem ready to proceed."

CHAPTER 6

"I'm Not Going to Dance on the Wall"

B Y LATE OCTOBER 1989, only a dozen people in the U.S. government knew that Bush had three months earlier secretly approached Gorbachev to propose a get-acquainted meeting.

Most U.S. presidents like to spring surprises on the public for diplomatic and political advantage. Bush carried this instinct to an extreme. One reason was that planning in secrecy reminded him of his halcyon days as director of the Central Intelligence Agency. Another was that he enjoyed catching the media off guard. Still another reason was that he hoped a major surprise might help overcome his reputation for orthodoxy and cautiousness, especially in relations with the Soviet Union.

Thus the president had ordered that the plan for the meeting be divulged only to those who needed to know: Quayle, Baker, Scowcroft, Gates, Sununu, and Fitzwater. William Webster of the CIA, a Reagan holdover, was kept in the dark. So was Dick Cheney.

Scowcroft shared the secret with Robert Blackwill early on, largely to stop Blackwill from bombarding him with memos urging exactly the kind of meeting that the president had already proposed. But Scowcroft warned, "If there's a leak, Bob, the president will go ballistic, and I'll make sure we start with a presumption of your guilt!"

Blackwill brought Condoleezza Rice into the charmed circle to help with preparations. He presumed that Baker had similarly confided in Robert Zoellick. In October, when the two men discussed the timing for a visit to Moscow by the secretary of agriculture, Clayton Yeutter, Zoellick suggested the first few days of December. Blackwill said, "But that'll conflict with the other meeting." Zoellick was puzzled: "*What* other meeting?" Blackwill gulped and changed the subject.

Back in July, when Bush first wrote to Gorbachev, Scowcroft and Gates had worried that the Soviet leader might pull "another Reykjavik," arriving with dramatic proposals for instant negotiation. Scowcroft and Gates were not entirely confident that Bush, with his tendency to overemphasize the importance of personal compatibility, would be able to resist Gorbachev's formidable powers of persuasion.

They worried that the president's new enthusiasm for "helping Gorbachev" might make him vulnerable to some kind of Soviet gambit on START. The last thing Scowcroft wanted to see was "premature and illusory" progress on arms control — which would give congressional Democrats the excuse to pull the plug on the MX, the B-2 "Stealth" bomber, and other components of the U.S. "strategic modernization" program.

In the Oval Office in late September, Scowcroft tried gently to make this point to his boss. Bush smiled and assured the general that he could be trusted to sit in the same room with Gorbachev "without giving away the store. Besides, you'll be there to keep an eye on me, Brent."

The secret negotiations between Moscow and Washington over what was variously called the "presummit," "mini-summit," "nonsummit," or "interim informal meeting" had not been easy. Bush and Gorbachev had to exchange cables four times. Shevardnadze bargained with Matlock in Moscow, and Dubinin with Scowcroft in Washington. In August, Shevardnadze's deputy, Alexander Bessmertnykh, came to Washington on the pretext of preparing for the Wyoming ministerial between Baker and Shevardnadze, but he actually spent more of his time on the Bush-Gorbachev get-together.

The first problem was timing. The Americans did not want to commit themselves to a date until Gorbachev promised to attend a full-scale summit in Washington in 1990. A number of the president's advisers, particularly Scowcroft, were concerned that without such an arrangement, the first meeting would become a deadline for progress on START, putting the American side under pressure to compromise. But Baker was so impressed by the arms control concessions Shevardnadze brought with him to Wyoming that he felt it was safe to agree to a Washington summit in mid-1990, and hence an informal meeting in early December 1989.

The second problem was venue. In the spirit of his recent meetings with other heads of government such as Mitterrand, Thatcher, and Kohl, Bush was eager to lure Gorbachev to a rustic hideaway where he and his visitor could combine statesmanship with outdoorsmanship, pitching horseshoes and "shooting the breeze."

He had in mind a setting like Kennebunkport or Camp David, or perhaps a wilderness outpost in Alaska, which would have the advantage of being roughly halfway between Moscow and Washington. The president told his staff in September that he hoped to "work on the chemistry with the guy," in an environment that would "give us both a chance to put our feet up on the table."

But holding the meeting anywhere on American soil was a problem for Gorbachev, since it would require him to make three trips in a row to the United States.* This would flout protocol and make him look like a supplicant. Thus the Soviet leader insisted that his first encounter with Bush be on neutral ground. Since Gorbachev was already scheduled to make a state visit to Italy in early December, the Soviets suggested a site somewhere in or near the Mediterranean.

The Americans suggested holding the meeting in Sicily. The Soviets refused, since Italy was a member of NATO. Both sides were also concerned about possible terrorism by the Red Brigade or some other ultra-leftist organization that might regard the Soviet reformer and the U.S. president as a two-for-the-price-of-one target. Cyprus was in turn rejected because of the long-simmering conflict between its Greek and Turkish communities and its dangerous proximity to the permanent crisis zone of the Middle East.

The president's younger brother William, nicknamed Bucky, had another idea. In September, Bucky Bush traveled to Malta, where, acting as the president's personal representative, he attended ceremonies marking the twenty-fifth anniversary of Maltese independence and called on the prime minister, Eddie Fenech Adami. On his return he reported to

* He had come in December 1988 and would be coming again in 1990.

the president that the Maltese were eager to attract international attention and investment. When Bush revealed that he was pondering a site for a meeting with Gorbachev, Bucky pushed hard for Malta.

Rumors later circulated in Europe that the younger Bush, a business consultant, was in a position to reap financial gain from helping to locate the meeting in Malta. The White House denied the charge, which had the potential to embarrass a president who always made a point of his concern for avoiding "even the appearance of an ethical violation." No proof ever emerged that the president's brother made money off the summit. However, well-placed officials in Malta and Italy insisted that he had steered investors toward projects sponsored by the Italian hotel firm CIGA, which was contemplating the construction of a resort on the Maltese island of Gozo.*

At the president's behest, the U.S. negotiators suggested Malta to the Soviets, who promptly accepted: the island was a longtime member of the Non-Aligned Movement, and it was close to Italy and thus convenient for Gorbachev, who would be visiting Rome and Milan in early December. The president proposed that the meeting be held on Soviet and U.S. ships in Marsaxlokk Bay. He told his aides that this would help keep his conversations with Gorbachev "away from the press . . . and I want a Camp David atmosphere on board."†

---

* This was not the first time Bush had risked the appearance of mixing public and private interests. In September 1977, he traveled to China for two weeks as a private citizen with J. Hugh Liedtke, who in 1953 had joined him in founding Zapata Petroleum and who was now chairman of Pennzoil. In Beijing, Bush met for 90 minutes with the senior Chinese leader, Deng Xiaoping, and took Liedtke, who wanted to sell the Chinese oil equipment and management and technical advice, to see the minister of foreign trade, Li Chiang. Shortly afterward, in January 1978, Bush had Liedtke to dinner at his Houston home, along with an official delegation of visiting Chinese oil experts. Later that year, when Liedtke returned to China with a proposal for drilling in the South China Sea, the Chinese allowed his associates to see geological studies that had previously been kept secret.

While there is no evidence that Bush received any direct financial reward for opening doors in China for Liedtke, there is no question that he used the influence he enjoyed as a result of his government service to help a personal friend and former business partner.

† With his tendency to frame world affairs in the language and atmospherics of World War II, Bush may also have been thinking of Franklin Roosevelt and Winston Churchill, who proclaimed the Atlantic Charter on two ships off Newfoundland in August 1941, when Bush was a senior at Andover. In February 1945, Roosevelt and Churchill met at Malta on their way to see Stalin at Yalta, where the three leaders would divide up Europe.

Gorbachev approved a shipboard encounter, recalling that he had stayed on a Soviet vessel during his Reykjavik meeting with Reagan in 1986. The U.S. Secret Service was delighted with the arrangement, reasoning that it would be easier to protect Bush on board a ship than on an island perilously close to Muammar Qaddafi's Libya.

A final sticking point was Malta's insistence that its territorial waters be respected as a nuclear-free zone. The U.S. Navy customarily refused to inform local governments during port calls whether or not its ships bore nuclear weapons. In the end, the Maltese were so eager to host the meeting that they did not press the issue.

No one on the American side of the negotiations raised serious questions about the site. Of the few involved in the actual bargaining, none had been to Malta. When the secret reached the ears of Lena Steinhoff, a secretary on the staff of the National Security Council who had served in the U.S. embassy in Malta for two years, she was puzzled and told colleagues, "Gee, that's kind of odd, especially doing it on ships. The weather can be really awful at that time of year."

Hoping for maximum publicity when he finally unveiled the secret, Bush planned simultaneous announcements in Washington and Moscow on Tuesday, October 31. Over the weekend before, White House officials prepared briefings for Congress and the press, while Baker had State draft cables to allied leaders.

On Monday evening, October 30, Scowcroft and Gates left the West Wing to dine with the Bushes in the presidential residence and talk about the great secret that was to be sprung upon the world the next day. The general said, "I think this story may actually hold."

He was wrong. That evening, when Condoleezza Rice returned to her apartment off Connecticut Avenue, the telephone was ringing off the hook. It was the NSC press spokesman, Roman Popadiuk, who had been left out of the planning. He had just received a call from David Hoffman of the *Washington Post*. Popadiuk said to Rice, "I need some help on something. I'll make it simple. If I said, 'The president is going to meet Gorbachev in the Mediterranean,' what would you say? Just give me one word — true or false?"

"Damn!" said Rice. Popadiuk said, "That's not one of the choices, but I guess it means 'true.' " She told him to stonewall, then informed the president. When Bush learned that the press would have the first word after all, he went on what was by his standards a rampage, calling up aides and lambasting them for their failure to keep his cherished secret.

On Halloween morning, when Ambassador Dubinin arrived at the White House to put the finishing touches on the joint announcement, Scowcroft and his colleagues were unable to disguise their mortification over the leak. Dubinin said, "Oh, don't worry. Frankly, we were surprised that you kept it quiet as long as you did." That hardly made the Americans feel better.

In Moscow, Shevardnadze gave the Americans a tweak of his own. He reminded the world that even in the era of *glasnost,* the Soviets remained better at keeping secrets. He began his announcement by saying, "This will come as no surprise to those of you who get the *Washington Post.*"

Bush met with the press in the White House briefing room at ten o'clock in the morning. When a reporter said, "It sounds like you were stampeded into this, because it wasn't in the works, and you had projected — ," the president interrupted, "You mean, *since July* it's been in the works."

"Has it?" the reported asked.

"Yes," the president gloated. "You just haven't been told." Bush said that he wanted to talk to Gorbachev "about their economy, our economy, a wide array of subjects. And I've said over and over again, we want to see *perestroika* succeed." Asked if one of his purposes was to give Gorbachev a "political boost" at home, the president said, "If it does, fine."

Then he added a metaphor suitable to both the setting of the upcoming event and his concern about the larger strategic stakes involved: "I don't want to have two gigantic ships pass in the night because of failed communication."

The enthusiasm of the world press and the public for the Malta meeting did not keep Bush from nursing his grudge against the media and the mysterious leakers. A fortnight later, the *Washington Post,* which had first broken the story, reported that the president would be taking "fewer than twenty" U.S. officials to Malta. Bush called Marlin Fitzwater and exploded, "Twenty, my ass! It's going to be more like *four!*"

As it turned out, however, the president did not have much time to worry about who had spoiled his secret. By the time he shook hands with Gorbachev thirty-two days later, the Berlin Wall had been punctured, and the satellites of Eastern Europe were flying out of the Kremlin's orbit.

On Thursday, November 9, the East German government announced that its citizens could leave the country without special permission. After nightfall, tens of thousands surged through the suddenly ruptured Berlin Wall, many for the first time. Jazz bands played under searchlights originally installed to help catch fugitives. East and West Berliners leapt atop the ugly twenty-eight-year-old partition; raising glasses of champagne and beer, they sang, danced, hacked off pieces of the wall, and wept with joy.

Watching the scene on a television set in his small study adjoining the Oval Office, Bush knew what this meant. He told his aides, "If the Soviets are going to let the Communists fall in East Germany, they've got to be really serious — more serious than I realized."

Begun in Poland and Hungary, the revolution of 1989 had spread to East Germany in August, when 130 East Germans won asylum at the West German mission in East Berlin. The next month, fifty-five hundred took refuge at the mission in Prague. When Hungary opened its borders, a thousand East German tourists fled into Austria.

The East German Communist boss Erich Honecker had only just returned to work after surgery for what was now identified as a cancerous gallbladder. He demanded that the exodus be stopped, but to no avail. The Hungarian government had obtained the Kremlin's tacit assent in advance. As the Soviet Foreign Ministry spokesman, Gennadi Gerasimov, coyly put it, Hungary's action was "very unexpected, but it does not directly affect us."

Demonstrations spread through East Germany. In Dresden, ten thousand people tried to stop a train bound for the West so that they could climb aboard. From East Berlin, at Honecker's behest, the hard-line Soviet ambassador, Vyacheslav Kochemasov, fired off cables imploring the Kremlin to "save" Honecker from the deluge, but Gorbachev told his aides that he was "disgusted" with Honecker's "inept" handling of the problem.

In the first week of October, Gorbachev flew to East Berlin to attend the fortieth-anniversary celebration of the Communist regime. In a preparatory visit the previous summer, Alexander Bessmertnykh had called on Honecker at his country house outside the East German capital. Honecker rhapsodized about East Germany's "spectacular" economic progress and showed Bessmertnykh the latest figures to prove that all was well.

Driving away from the meeting, an East German official had told Bessmertnykh that Honecker's figures were "inflated," a "fantasy." Bessmertnykh reported to Gorbachev and Shevardnadze that Honecker was living in a dream world. Moreover, it was a sign of how fast discipline was breaking down under his leadership that a midlevel subordinate would feel free to contradict him behind his back to a visitor from Moscow.

Now, in East Berlin, during a private confrontation with Honecker, Gorbachev told the old man that the way to stop the demonstrations throughout his country was to introduce a German version of *perestroika;* if he did that, the people might yet be won over to the side of the leadership.

Honecker scoffed. During his last visit to the Soviet Union, he said, he had looked in on some stores and been shocked to find the shelves so bare. The Soviet economy was in shambles, while East Germans were the most prosperous citizens in the socialist world. How dare Gorbachev tell him how to run his country!

At the anniversary ceremonies, Gorbachev gave a speech urging East Germans to adopt Soviet-style reforms. As though to emphasize where responsibility for the future lay, he added that East German policy should be made "not in Moscow but in Berlin." Honecker stood at his side, looking acutely unsettled.

When Gorbachev returned to Moscow, he privately told his aides that Honecker would have to go, as soon as possible: "The [East German] leadership can't stay in control." He ordered his General Staff to make sure that Soviet troops stationed in East Germany did not get involved in the strife that was sure to envelop the country.

On the weekend of October 7, on Honecker's orders, the East German security police used rifles and tear gas to put down demonstrations in several cities. With no assurance of the Kremlin's backing on the crackdown, Honecker's opportunistic state security chief, Egon Krenz, opposed Honecker's decision. The following Monday, Krenz let fifty thousand protesters march through Leipzig.

Other members of Honecker's regime could also see which way the wind was blowing. Adopting a new slogan — "Change and Renewal" — they abruptly replaced their old boss with Krenz and released hundreds of demonstrators from jail. At the fifty-ninth minute of the eleventh hour, Krenz was making his bid to become the East German Gorbachev.

*   *   *

On Wednesday, October 25, during a visit to Helsinki, Gorbachev had publicly said that the Soviet Union had "no right, moral or political," to interfere in the events in Eastern Europe, adding, "We assume others will not interfere, either." He pointedly hailed Finland, a neutral country that had broken free of Russian and Soviet expansionism, as a model of stability and independence.

In the spring of 1989, as one "test" of Gorbachev's sincerity, the Bush administration had demanded the repeal of the Brezhnev Doctrine — the Soviet Union's claim, at the time of its 1968 invasion of Czechoslovakia, that it had the right to provide "assistance, including assistance with armed forces," to any Communist nation in which "the people's socialist gains" were in jeopardy.

Now Gerasimov told reporters in Helsinki, "I think the Brezhnev Doctrine is dead." In its place, he quipped, would be the "Frank Sinatra Doctrine." This referred to the final line in the singer's signature ballad: "I did it my way."

On Tuesday, October 31, Krenz had called on Gorbachev at the Kremlin. By now, his death's-head visage looked more frightened than frightening. He knew better than to ask for Soviet military support to restore order in his country; Gorbachev had already ruled that out. Instead, he asked the Soviet leader for political help in fending off a challenge from the reformist Dresden party chief Hans Modrow.

Gorbachev consented. After their meeting, Krenz told reporters that the demonstrations throughout his homeland were a "good sign" of the imminent "renovation of socialism." However, he hastened to add, the Berlin Wall was still needed as a "protective shield" between "two social systems" and "two military blocs."

This reiteration of their new leader's commitment to the continued division of Europe — and Germany — merely called forth even more demonstrators than before. In desperation, Krenz announced more conciliatory measures. He fired his entire cabinet and two thirds of his Politburo, but that was not enough. He called Gorbachev at the Kremlin and asked him what to do. On Shevardnadze's strong recommendation, Gorbachev advised Krenz to open his borders. This would "let off steam" and "avoid an explosion."

After the Berlin Wall began to crumble, Marlin Fitzwater called reporters and television cameramen into the Oval Office. Bush sat at his desk, twisting a pen in his hand.

A reporter asked whether this meant the end of the Iron Curtain. The president rambled, "Well, I don't think any single event is the end of what you might call the Iron Curtain, but clearly this is a long way from the harshest Iron Curtain days — a long way from that." Had he ever imagined such a development? "Now, I didn't foresee it, but imagining it? Yes."

Told that he did not sound elated, Bush replied defensively, "I am not an emotional kind of guy. . . . I'm very pleased. And I've been very pleased with a lot of other developments. . . . And so, the fact that I'm not bubbling over — maybe it's getting along towards evening, because I feel very good about it."

In their analysis of the day's extraordinary developments, a number of commentators complained about Bush's failure to express the American people's joy over an event demanded by every president since Kennedy. They imagined how Reagan, with his mastery of the showmanship that bolstered statesmanship, might have risen to the occasion.

The majority leader of the House of Representatives, Richard Gephardt of Missouri, said, "Even as the walls of the modern Jericho come tumbling down, we have a president who is inadequate to the moment." Senator George Mitchell of Maine demanded to know why Bush did not immediately rush over to see the breach in the wall for himself.

On the satirical NBC television program "Saturday Night Live," the comedian and Bush impersonator Dana Carvey stood in front of videotaped scenes of Berliners celebrating at the wall. Mimicking Bush's penchant for speaking in sentence fragments, he explained why he was avoiding jubilation: "Wouldn't be prudent." Affecting the familiar lopsided grin and weakness for slogans, he pointed at himself and said, "Place in history? Se–cure!"

The president himself quickly realized that he had flubbed a chance to capitalize on the happy news. He told his staff, "Maybe I should have given 'em one of these." Leaping into the air like the delighted car owner in a Toyota commercial, he cried, "Oh, what a feeling!"

The aides laughed sympathetically. They knew that Bush's restraint had a larger purpose: he was determined not to rub Gorbachev's nose in the defeat of world communism. He was also worried that a Western celebration of the wall's collapse might encourage a backlash by hardliners in East Berlin and Moscow.

On several occasions, both in public and in private, Bush said, "I'm not going to dance on the wall." Remembering Hungary in 1956, when American propaganda had encouraged the revolutionaries to expect

Western intervention, he did not want the East Germans to count on the U.S. military to rescue them if their regime should try to turn back history with a massacre like the one in Tiananmen Square.*

In Moscow, asked to assess Bush's response to the opening of the wall, Gerasimov said, "I think he's handling it as a real statesman." He tried to depict this latest development in East Germany as a sign of socialist self-confidence — "a positive and important fact," compatible with "what President Gorbachev is trying to accomplish here and what he wants to see elsewhere."

At the White House, Scowcroft told colleagues that by letting his people go, Krenz was "buying time for himself, and for the system." He saw no reason yet to presume that either Moscow or East Berlin would allow the East German people to "go their own way and take the state with them." Scowcroft could not imagine that Gorbachev would permit East Germany to leave the Warsaw Pact: "The basic reality — East Germany as a Communist state within the Soviet sphere — hasn't changed and probably won't change."

Robert Blackwill suggested, "With the new task of redrawing the map of Europe, we could use another person around here." Scowcroft smiled and joked, "Oh, so now you want a staff cartographer? I don't think we're quite to that point yet. Let's see how all this plays out."

As soon as the wall was breached, both Germanys bloomed with banners demanding that they be united. Bush was at least outwardly relaxed about the prospect. At a state dinner for Philippine President Corazon Aquino on the day the wall collapsed, Bush told a guest at his table, "The Germans aren't any kind of a threat at all. They are a totally different country from what they used to be."

Western officials had long routinely needled the Kremlin by demanding German unification, even though many of them, especially in Europe, privately hoped that it would never happen. They feared that a united Germany would be too big and powerful, and that it would inevitably throw its weight around. Twice in the twentieth century, German militarism and expansionism had plunged the world into war. Russians, Poles, and other neighbors of Germany were not eager to test the

---

* Within a day of the rupture of the Berlin Wall, the seventy-eight-year-old Bulgarian party boss Todor Zhivkov was replaced by Petur Mladenov, who promised to establish a "modern, democratic, and law-governed state." Gorbachev sent the new leader effusive congratulations. Bulgaria had been the most loyal and thoroughly Sovietized of the satellites; now it was testing the Sinatra Doctrine.

proposition that 1914 and 1939 were aberrations; nor were the British, French, and other peoples who had suffered directly at German hands.

As for Gorbachev himself, he was far from enthusiastic about the possibility that the opening of the wall might lead to early unification. In his December 1988 speech at the UN, the Soviet leader had maintained that self-determination should extend to Germans as well. But the following September, when he saw Margaret Thatcher in Moscow, he admitted that "no reasonable person" could fail to be anxious about the prospect of an immense, unified German power in the heart of Europe.

The British prime minister had replied that her people, like Gorbachev's, had suffered in the war. She agreed that the process of change in Germany might be moving a bit too quickly; better if the whole process were to slow down a bit, "so that we can all take careful stock of the implications."

During his October visit to Moscow, Egon Krenz had dismissed German unification as an "illusion" that must be shattered lest it undermine an "integral aspect of a stable Europe." Gorbachev agreed.

Back in the spring, when Bush had spoken of a Europe "whole and free," a number of Soviet officials had presumed that the U.S. president wished to see Western Europe serve as a magnet that would pull East Germany out of the Soviet orbit and unite it with the Federal Republic. Now they could imagine precisely that happening.

After the wall came down, Gerasimov issued a public warning against "recarving the boundaries of postwar Europe": East Germany must remain a member of the Warsaw Pact and a Soviet "strategic ally," he argued. During a meeting in Moscow, Shevardnadze told the French foreign minister, Roland Dumas, that demands for a single Germany were causing him and Gorbachev "great anxiety."

In a private letter to Bush, Gorbachev sounded uncharacteristically alarmed. The Soviet Union, he wrote, had vital interests in the future of Germany, and the United States must pay attention to those interests. The victorious powers of World War II — the United States, the Soviet Union, Britain, and France — were still responsible for Germany. They would have to collaborate if at any time the situation turned into a crisis.

Bush said to his aides, "The guy's really upset, isn't he?" In his reply to Gorbachev, he wrote that he endorsed the recent steps toward a "Europe that is whole and free" but stressed that the United States also had an interest in keeping the situation "calm and peaceful."

                              *   *   *

On Monday evening, November 13, Bush dined at the White House
with Henry Kissinger, who had concluded, without great joy, that German unification was now "inevitable." Kissinger warned the president,
"If the Germans see us as obstructing their aspirations, we'll pay a price
later on."

A Jewish refugee from Nazi Germany, Kissinger felt more than a
little ambivalent about unification, but he insisted that for the president
to adopt a two-Germanys policy would be "disastrous." This would
give Gorbachev a golden opportunity to side with Helmut Kohl against
the United States in the pursuit of quick unification. Since there was no
stopping unification, and any attempt to slow it down would only stir
up resentment among Germans both East and West, it would be best
for the U.S. president to move in virtual lockstep with the West German
chancellor.

Bush replied that he had "no great hangup" about German unification. Still, he did not wish to create the impression that the United States
was in any way pushing it; instead, he preferred a "prudent evolution."
He knew how the issue unsettled many Europeans. He told Kissinger
that he believed one of the "red lines" Gorbachev could not cross was
"losing" East Germany — especially if the resulting united state remained in NATO. His own position was not much different: if neutrality was the price of German unification, Bush, like his predecessors,
was reluctant to pay it.

The president had been hoping, too, that Bonn would take the lead
in financing the reconstruction of all the Eastern European states that
were now emerging from the long night of communism. He did not
want to see West Germany's resources devoted almost exclusively to its
poor relation to the east.*

A week after Bush's dinner with Kissinger, Kohl's foreign minister,
Hans-Dietrich Genscher, flew to Washington to present the president
with a piece of the Berlin Wall. In public, Genscher and Bush were all
smiles, sharing a moment of triumph for the transatlantic alliance.

In private, however, Genscher made it clear that there might be com-

---

* During this dinner, Kissinger, who was just back from a visit to China, also strongly
recommended that Bush move quickly to repair a relationship that was under considerable strain because of the Tiananmen massacre in June. Bush subsequently dispatched
Scowcroft and Eagleburger — the two people in his administration with the closest ties
to Kissinger — on a fence-mending mission to Beijing.

plications and even strains within the West because of what had happened in the East. He put Bush on notice that the Lance missile program would be a casualty of recent events: "Surely you understand, Mr. President, that no government in Bonn can consider any system that might result in nuclear weapons' being targeted on Dresden or Leipzig."

In Bonn, Kohl was telling his aides that while unification could not be ruled out, it would not happen for at least three or four more years. Publicly he was more circumspect, asking the Bundestag merely to consider some kind of "confederative structures" with East Germany. Even this statement, vague and mild though it was, greatly irked the Soviet Foreign Ministry, which criticized the Bonn government for pushing East German reform "in a nationalist direction."

In Scowcroft's West Wing office, Blackwill acknowledged that the ability of the United States to influence the situation inside East Germany was marginal. "But what we convey to the Soviets about our policy is *not* marginal," he said. "We've got to reassure them that we're not eager to exploit the situation to their disadvantage."

Scowcroft concurred: "This is one of those times when the best thing we can do is mess out." Noting that several columnists had suggested that Bush see Krenz in East Berlin on his way to Malta, Blackwill rolled his eyes and laughed: "Krenz? Who's he? Eight weeks from now he'll be history."*

Bush was already deep into his homework for the Malta meeting with Gorbachev. Scowcroft gave him a menu of twenty topics to choose from. The president asked for briefings on all, saying, "It's back-to-school time, Brent."

Tutorials were held in the Oval Office and at Camp David by government specialists, outside experts, and former officials. CIA analysts gave Bush up-to-the-minute information about the Soviet economy, the nationalities issue, and the entrenched centers of Soviet power.

The president was briefed on the Soviet military and its attitude toward *perestroika* by Henry Rowen, a veteran Pentagon strategist; Arnold Horelick, the RAND Corporation's chief Kremlinologist; and

---

* This bold-sounding prediction was not audacious enough for 1989: Krenz lasted less than a month. On December 1, the East German parliament abolished the leading role of the Communist party. Shortly afterward, the entire Politburo, including Krenz and his rival Hans Modrow, resigned, although the two remained, briefly, president and prime minister, respectively.

Stephen Meyer of MIT, who had participated in Bush's first such session, at Kennebunkport in February. Alan Greenspan and Robert Zoellick reported on their trip to Moscow.

Former high officials such as Richard Nixon, James Schlesinger, and Jeane Kirkpatrick offered advice based on their own experience with the Soviets. Partly to score a few points with the Right, the White House also sought help from the Heritage Foundation, a think tank established by the right-wing Colorado beer magnate Joseph Coors.

Zbigniew Brzezinski, who had just returned from the Soviet Union, told Bush during a private luncheon that political freedom without serious economic reform was producing "social despair" among the Soviet people, who were now able to vent their anger and frustration at the government. Brzezinski had served as Jimmy Carter's national security adviser, but he was welcome in this White House because, dismayed by what he saw as the leftward drift of his fellow Democrats, he had endorsed Bush for president in 1988.

During his visit to the Soviet Union, Brzezinski, with his reputation as an outspoken anti-Communist, had been given almost a hero's welcome. He addressed a standing-room-only crowd at the Foreign Ministry's Diplomatic Academy on the banks of the Moscow River, and was enthusiastically applauded for denouncing the regime that most of those in the audience had served loyally for decades.

Brzezinski was allowed to visit Katyn Forest, near Smolensk, the site of an infamous massacre of Polish officers by Stalin's troops early in World War II. Officially, Moscow maintained its claim that Hitler had been responsible for the atrocity, but by permitting the Polish-born Brzezinski to expose this lie at the scene of the crime, Gorbachev, Yakovlev, and Shevardnadze were preparing the public for the truth.

Bush asked Brzezinski, "Are the masses still behind Gorbachev and *perestroika*?" The visitor said, "Probably, but they are impatient to see political reform yield material benefits."

The president asked about the chances for "another Tiananmen" in Red Square. Brzezinski replied that there was indeed a distinct danger of backlash. But whereas in China the democracy movement had grown up from the grass roots, with the dissident leadership concentrated in one public square in the capital, in the Soviet Union democratic reforms had been imposed from the top down and were spreading throughout the country. Hence the Kremlin had its own stake in the process.

Bush wondered how much change Gorbachev and his comrades seemed willing to brook in Eastern Europe. Brzezinski said that they would probably insist that the Eastern states — especially East Germany — remain in the Warsaw Pact.

The president said, "Okay, now you're the president of the United States. What do you want out of Malta? If you could design what I should say to Gorbachev, what would it be?" Half answering his own question, he said he did not feel there was much he could do for Gorbachev besides encouraging him to persist in his reforms.

Bush added that he was, however, willing to consider aid to improve Soviet public health and clean up the Soviet environment, since these measures "couldn't be used against us if Gorbachev is overthrown." He paused and then asked, "Will the Europeans consider me miserly if that's all I do?" Brzezinski bluntly answered, "Yes, I think they will." The president looked chagrined.

By now John Sununu had joined them. He snapped at Brzezinski, "Are you proposing a *bailout* for the Soviet Union?" Brzezinski gave Sununu a withering look, then replied that the president might want to "dangle something in front of Gorbachev" as an incentive for further reform.

Sununu recited one of his pet theories about a future Soviet-Japanese conspiracy against the United States. Brzezinski strained hard to be polite, silently hoping that Bush was not relying too heavily on his chief of staff for counsel in foreign affairs.

Under Reagan, the CIA had begun the practice of preparing a film on Gorbachev before the president attended a Soviet summit. Out of deference to what was thought to be Reagan's short attention span and his impatience with detail, the film was usually kept to about ten minutes. Bush asked for one that was more comprehensive. The resulting documentary ran for roughly half an hour; it was the saga of a determined reformer struggling with monumental problems.

Bush also studied a highly classified National Intelligence Estimate (NIE) prepared under the supervision of Robert Blackwell, who had served as his CIA briefer during his three trips to Moscow as vice president. By now Blackwell's title was National Intelligence Officer for the Soviet Union.

Stamped SECRET and headed "Key Judgments," Blackwell's paper predicted that the economic dilemma would make 1990–91 one of the most tumultuous periods in Soviet history. Gorbachev would probably be able to stay in control of the process; his policy of limited, evolutionary reforms would continue and very likely succeed. While the

Kremlin might occasionally have to use tough measures to handle ethnic unrest or secessionism, the recourse to repression was unlikely to be so harsh or so extensive that it would derail reform. Blackwell felt that Gorbachev was "in for the long haul" and deserved American support.

During the drafting of the paper, a number of Blackwell's colleagues in the CIA's Office of Soviet Analysis (SOVA) had parted company with him. Among this group was SOVA's senior political analyst, Grey Hodnett, who in September had completed another paper, entitled "Gorbachev's Domestic Gambles and Instability," which took a discordant line.

Hodnett and his allies believed that either Gorbachev's reforms would destroy him or he would desperately try to save himself by returning to some form of "old thinking." They argued that while the reforms that had been instituted to date, particularly those under the general heading of *glasnost,* were radical enough to allow the Soviets to vent seventy-two years' worth of discontent, *perestroika* itself was too limited to fulfill people's expectations. Those who subscribed to this view also felt that unless Gorbachev brokered some kind of special status for the Baltics, a direct confrontation between these republics and Moscow was almost inevitable.

Hodnett and like-minded CIA analysts predicted that if Gorbachev failed to stabilize Soviet finances and ram through a true free-market system, the deterioration of the economy would bring social unrest and perhaps even outright revolution. This would give hard-liners a pretext to retake the Kremlin and resurrect a more orthodox totalitarian regime. Another possibility was the "Ottomization" of the Soviet Union, with one republic after another breaking away; this, too, might increase the hard-liners' incentive to overthrow Gorbachev.

Gorbachev's quasi-reforms were the "worst of all possible worlds — all pain and no gain," Hodnett believed. He was much more impressed by Boris Yeltsin's ideas. Hodnett conceded that more radical reforms of the kind Yeltsin was urging might cause short-term chaos in the Soviet Union, but he argued that in time they would stand a better chance of creating a "social equilibrium" than Gorbachev's half-measures.

This harsh critique of Gorbachev was endorsed by Hodnett's immediate boss, George Kolt, the director of SOVA, and also by Blackwell's superior, Fritz Ermarth of the National Intelligence Council. The director of the CIA, William Webster, acceded to Ermarth's recommendation that a pessimistic, cautionary "alternative view" of Gorbachev by Kolt and Hodnett be sent to the President along with Blackwell's relatively sanguine NIE.

In a private White House meeting, Webster tried to gloss over the dispute among his subordinates: "What we've got here is a little healthy disagreement between a glass-is-half-full guy and some others who think it's half empty."

In fact, the disagreement was more serious than that. In making the case that Gorbachev might succeed on his own terms, Blackwell's NIE was also implicitly arguing for maximum U.S. support of the Soviet leader. Hodnett, Kolt, and Ermarth were, by contrast, advocating that the United States begin shifting toward Yeltsin instead.

The division within the intelligence community was mirrored at the NSC. Blackwill and Rice took a position close to the one presented in Blackwell's NIE, while Gates leaned toward the SOVA dissent, though he was careful to make his preference known only to Scowcroft and the president.

On one important point almost everyone was agreed: the U.S. must not try to make Gorbachev's life any more difficult than it already was. If Bush did anything that Soviet hard-liners could portray as an attempt to exploit Soviet internal or external troubles, Gorbachev would be all the more vulnerable to a backlash and perhaps even a coup. This was something that no U.S. official wanted — especially the principal consumer of Blackwell's and Hodnett's "product" in the Oval Office.

Bush complained to Scowcroft that the experts and briefing papers that the general was sending into the Oval Office were "great on the big-picture stuff but a little short on specifics."

In October, the president had insisted that Malta would be nothing more than a get-acquainted meeting. But the opening of the Berlin Wall and the rush toward change in Eastern Europe convinced him that he must be seen as having reciprocated Gorbachev's initiatives in some serious way. The NSC's Blackwill told colleagues, "The question now is how to satisfy the wild beast of public opinion."

Blackwill, Rice, Zoellick, and Ross thought it unlikely that Gorbachev would "pull a Reykjavik" and spring a major surprise proposal. But they wanted Bush to be ready for one, just in case. They asked the CIA to anticipate what Gorbachev might offer or seek in eighteen different areas, from negotiations on the control of chemical weapons to possible Soviet membership in world financial institutions.

The four advisers suggested to the president that he dominate the agenda from the outset with a glittering "basket of initiatives" that made up in quantity what they lacked in substance. Some of these were simply recycled versions of old proposals.

When Bush asked Robert Gates what Gorbachev wanted from Malta, Gates said, "He wants added momentum for the relationship as a whole and for arms control in particular. He hopes for a START agreement and a summit in the U.S. in late spring or early summer of 1990, and a conventional-forces agreement later in the year." Gates explained that a CFE agreement, along with unilateral Soviet cuts, would allow Gorbachev to transfer from the Soviet military complex to the civilian sector more money than he could ever hope to get in economic aid from the West.

At the State Department in late November, Baker's subordinates gave him a list of arms control initiatives for Malta. Most of these were familiar proposals, such as ways to resolve lingering disputes over START, but one was new: a proposed ban on mobile ICBMs with multiple warheads, or MIRVs (multiple independently targetable reentry vehicles).

Over the years, as U.S. and Soviet defense planners had modernized their missile forces, the trend had at first been toward developing rockets with multiple warheads. The next development was the introduction of mobile launchers, followed by a combination of MIRVing and mobile systems, such as the U.S. Air Force's railroad-based MX and its approximate Soviet counterpart, the SS-24.

Officials at State had for some time favored giving up the MX in exchange for eliminating the SS-24, but Pentagon officials had always refused. The MX's mobility made it less vulnerable to Soviet preemptive attack, they argued, and its MIRVing made it a highly cost-effective way of deploying — and delivering — ten warheads.

Now that Malta was approaching, with a new premium on dramatic-sounding proposals, Richard Burt, the chief START negotiator, and Reginald Bartholomew, the under secretary of state with overall responsibility for arms control, suggested a ban on MIRVed mobile missiles. Dennis Ross endorsed the idea. He suspected that Gorbachev might make just such a proposal — and "it would be nice to be one jump ahead of him for a change."

Baker had not forgotten his embarrassment at being "outproposaled" by Gorbachev in May. He knew that Scowcroft was an advocate of "de-MIRVing" and of the single-warhead Midgetman, as were some key congressmen, such as Representative Les Aspin and Senator Sam Nunn, the Democratic chairmen of the House and Senate Armed Services committees. Proposing a ban on MIRVed mobile missiles would put a "Bush stamp" on the arms control process and at the same time draw bipartisan congressional applause. Baker said in a staff meeting that it was a "real twofer."

But would the president go along with it? The secretary of state worried about his old friend's cautiousness and fear of criticism from the Right, especially on national defense. But this time Bush surprised him. He not only accepted the plan but went even further: he would propose a ban on *all* MIRVed ICBMs — stationary as well as mobile.

While such a proposal would have been certifiably bold and unquestionably controversial among defense experts, it would also have aroused opposition from the Soviets. MIRVed ICBMs were the strongest element in the Soviet arsenal, larger and more numerous than their American counterparts. Therefore banning MIRVed ICBMs would tilt the balance of the military competition in favor of the United States, as it would allow the U.S. Navy to keep its submarine-launched MIRVs, a category of weaponry in which the U.S. was superior to the USSR.*

The president was pushed in this direction by Scowcroft, who had been growing impatient with what he called the "tame, stand-pat stuff" coming out of the bureaucracy. Scowcroft had begun to see a way out of the logjam in July, when he met with Marshal Akhromeyev in Washington. The two generals were pleased to find that they could talk bluntly about basic issues.

One of the topics they had discussed was the superpowers' heavy investment in MIRVed ICBMs, which suffered from the strategic double jeopardy of being both vulnerable and threatening. Akhromeyev seemed surprisingly open to the idea of coming to grips with what Scowcroft regarded as the curse of land-based MIRVs; Scowcroft told Bush after the meeting that it had been the "best conversation I've ever had with a Russian on arms control."

Now Scowcroft reminded the president of his encounter with Akhromeyev: "If the United States is going to commit itself to the goal of de-MIRVing, let's have the courage of our convictions. Let's follow the

---

* If written into the START treaty, this proposal would require the United States to give up the MX, both on rails and in silos, as well as the three-warhead Minuteman ICBM, while the Soviets would have to give up not just the mobile SS-24 but their silo-based SS-18s, with ten warheads each, and also the six-warhead SS-19s and four-warhead SS-17s.

logic of our own position. Why limit de-MIRVing to mobiles? Let's go all the way!" Bush replied, "Okay, let's go for it."

Scowcroft knew that the Pentagon would put up a fight. Traveling abroad, Dick Cheney learned of the proposal only at the last minute. On his return, over breakfast with Baker and Scowcroft, he worked hard to contain his anger but made it clear that he felt they had blind-sided him on an issue central to the interests of the Defense Department.

He noted that the administration was already fighting an uphill battle in Congress to save the MX program. An offer to trade the missile away in START, even if conditioned on Soviet willingness to give up the SS-24, would give the program's opponents a fresh excuse to withhold funding.

Besides, Cheney continued, there was no certainty that Scowcroft's cherished Midgetman — the single-warhead alternative to MX — would ever come into being. Precisely because each Midgetman warhead required a separate rocket, it was an expensive proposition, probably too costly for Congress to support over the long run. Did the United States really want to propose a ban on the missiles it had — the MX and the three-warhead Minuteman — without any certainty that it would ever have new systems to replace them?*

Baker and Scowcroft quickly marched backward. They were not about to proceed with the de-MIRVing proposal over the objections of the secretary of defense. They crossed it out in the president's Malta briefing book. Returning to State from the White House, Baker told his aides, "It turned out to be more than the traffic could bear."

The failure of the MIRV initiative diminished Bush's chances of making the START treaty a document over which he could feel much pride of authorship. Once again, his negotiators were consigned essentially to completing the unfinished business of their predecessors in the Reagan administration.

No such hectic intramural dickering occurred in Moscow. Gorbachev's advisers took the Americans at their word about Malta. In contrast to

* Richard Burt was also worried by the proposal, but for a different reason. Since the Soviets had many more MIRVed ICBMs than did the United States, Gorbachev's military advisers were sure to tell him that the initiative would not be to his advantage. The Soviets would likely carry the logic of Scowcroft's position a step further, saying, If we're going to be truly serious about de-MIRVing, why stop at the water's edge? Why not ban MIRVs on submarine-launched ballistic missiles (SLBMs) as well? Burt felt that in that case, the START talks would quickly degenerate: "The result is that we'll never get a treaty, certainly not by next year [1990], when we want one."

their behavior at Reykjavik, they assiduously avoided anything that might strike Bush as a diplomatic sneak attack.

Gorbachev read a briefing paper prepared by Georgi Arbatov, the director of the Institute for the Study of the U.S.A. and Canada, and his deputy Andrei Kokoshin. Arbatov was the best-known Soviet specialist on the United States, a leading impresario of seminars and less formal exchanges on U.S.-Soviet relations. His institute had served as a sanctuary for advocates of relative liberalization as well as a point of contact between the superpowers during good times and bad.

The paper drew on Arbatov and Kokoshin's analysis and on confidential discussions they had held with various American government officials, including Blackwill, Ross, Nunn, and Aspin. The memorandum claimed that it was the prevailing view in Washington that with Gorbachev's UN address of December 1988, Soviet foreign policy had reached, and probably passed, the peak of its dynamism. Now there must be not startling initiatives from the Soviet side but rather a "consolidation" of progress in START and other negotiations.

Arbatov and Kokoshin reported that while Bush's people had overcome their initial doubts about Gorbachev's sincerity, they increasingly questioned his ability to accomplish what he intended. They even doubted his ability to remain in power. The issue of Gorbachev's political future would be central to American strategy for the next several years.

The Arbatov-Kokoshin paper went on to say that the Bush administration seemed to be split between two camps: men like Gates and Cheney, who wanted to exploit Soviet internal weaknesses in order to extract as many concessions as possible before a more truculent regime replaced Gorbachev's; and Baker and others, who were concerned that excessive U.S. demands could contribute to Gorbachev's fall.

Arbatov and Kokoshin implied that Bush himself was somewhere in the middle. They urged Gorbachev to use the Malta meeting to give the U.S. president a greater sense of his country's stake in the success of *perestroika* and in Gorbachev's own survival.

The memorandum advised Gorbachev not to make any dramatic arms control proposals. This was not only because Blackwill and Ross had warned Arbatov and Kokoshin against "another Reykjavik," but also because the two Soviets feared a backlash from hard-liners in the Defense Ministry, the party apparatus, and elsewhere. These "old thinkers" were already complaining that under the influence of the much-resented Shevardnadze, the Soviet Union had already made too many unilateral concessions.

Gorbachev should neither seek nor appear highly receptive to American economic aid, counseled Arbatov and Kokoshin. The Soviet leader's critics in Moscow were already depicting him as too willing to play the supplicant caretaker of a "superpower in decline" and too eager to throw himself on the mercy of the Americans.

They wrote that Gorbachev must do everything he could to give the impression that he was meeting Bush as an equal. He should expand on the concept of a U.S.-Soviet partnership. The meeting's leitmotif must be "mutual understanding and, if possible, mutual actions" to thwart potential instability in the international system — not just in the Soviet bloc but around the world.

Arbatov and Kokoshin assured Gorbachev that this approach would not only appear appropriately dignified at home; it would also appeal to Bush, whom they described as the sort who preferred predictability to spectacular breakthroughs, evolution to revolution.

Gorbachev accepted the advice to forgo any blockbusters. But no one told him that he had to eschew grand public gestures while stopping in Rome before his meeting with Bush. He strolled past the Colosseum and broke through his security cordon to kiss babies and shake hands with fans who shouted *"Gorbi! Gorbi!"* Members of the crowd told reporters that Gorbachev was *"molto simpatico,"* a leader of "cosmic dimensions," even "evangelical."

Once again the Soviet leader tried to create an illusion of benevolent mastery over events, playing the weakest of hands as though he were holding four aces. At the City Hall, under a statue of Julius Caesar, he urged that the Conference on European Cooperation and Security (CSCE) be reconvened in 1990.

CSCE had begun with an international conference in Helsinki in 1975, largely at Soviet initiative. It was part of Leonid Brezhnev's attempt to get the West to accept the division of Europe. But over time, Western leaders had managed to turn the so-called Helsinki process into a mechanism for pressuring the Kremlin and its satellite regimes in Eastern Europe to respect human rights.

Gorbachev now hoped to make a different use of CSCE, and, by recasting it as a substitute for the Warsaw Pact and NATO, to advance his goal of a neutral Europe. He added ominously that the West would be making a serious mistake if it sought to exploit the change in Eastern

Europe to achieve the "collapse of socialism." That evening he proclaimed that the Cold War was ending "not because there are victors and vanquished, but precisely because there are none of either."

In fact, it was already clear that as the general secretary of the Communist party, as commander in chief of the Warsaw Pact, as the lineal successor of Lenin, Stalin, Khrushchev, and Brezhnev, Gorbachev was himself a grand historical loser. Yet rather than accepting the role of representative of a defeated power, he cast himself instead as a spokesman for the bravest hopes of mankind. At the City Hall, he declaimed, "We need spiritual values. We need a revolution of the mind."

Gorbachev called on Pope John Paul II in the library of the sixteenth-century Apostolic Palace. As a Pole, the Pope had long been regarded by the Soviets as a sinister and provocative figure. Addressing his host as "Your Holiness," Gorbachev invited him to visit the Soviet Union, agreed to reopen diplomatic relations with the Vatican, and promised that the Soviet Union would "shortly" pass a new law guaranteeing religious freedom for all believers.

From Rome, Gorbachev flew briefly to Milan, where he declared that the "Prague Spring" of 1968 had been an "acceptable movement for democracy, renewal, and humanization of society. It was right then, and it is right now."

As the Soviet leader spoke, his aides began to grow nervous. Fog was descending on Milan. Weather reports said that a major storm was sweeping across southern Europe and the Mediterranean toward Malta.

When White House aides in Washington heard that Gorbachev had proposed reviving CSCE, they were not surprised. CSCE was on the list of possible Gorbachev initiatives that they had drawn up for the president. Blackwill boasted to colleagues, "Whatever more he's got in his bag of tricks, we're ready for him."

Some of Bush's aides, especially the ever-combative Sununu, talked of the president's mission to Malta as though it were a bombing run. They were going to "drop a big one on Gorbachev," "send him reeling": he would "never know what hit him." Of the initiatives Bush was taking to Malta, Blackwill said, "The Soviets are totally unprepared for all this. Their eyes are going to pop out." Sununu exulted to the president, "We're going to beat the timidity rap once and for all." Bush replied, "That's right! We're coming on like gangbusters!"

Bush's principal personal goal in going to Malta was to elevate his own standing, but he also wanted to bolster Gorbachev and his commitment to reform. On Thursday, November 30, before departing for Malta, he privately told his cabinet and the NSC, "I don't want to be begrudging. I don't want to seem halfhearted. The purpose of what I'm going to be doing over there is to show Gorbachev that I support him all the way."

Before kissing his wife good-bye and boarding a helicopter on the South Grounds, the president stopped in the Rose Garden to address several hundred officials who had gathered to see him off. He said that Gorbachev's "rousing reception" in Italy showed "how deeply the people of Europe want to see change and reform continue to move forward."

Bush expressed his hope that Malta would represent a large step toward "a Europe that is, indeed, whole and free." He and Gorbachev wanted to "build a sustained relationship for real achievements over the long term. He is looking for ways to keep those reforms moving forward, and I'm looking for ways to promote democracy and freedom. And the one way is to support his efforts toward reform."

During the flight to Malta, Bush was repeatedly awakened for intelligence reports from Manila, where President Corazon Aquino was fighting a coup attempt by military dissidents. This was the fifth such mutiny against her presidency, and the most serious. Bush ordered U.S. Air Force jets to seize control of the skies over Manila, in a show of force that ultimately helped to defeat the coup.

On Friday morning, when the president stepped off the plane at Valetta, his face was ashen and his eyes were red. Torn between concern for what was happening in Manila and anxiety over the next day's meeting with Gorbachev, he summoned up his reserves of politeness for the obligatory discussion of U.S.-Maltese relations with Prime Minister Adami. Looking out the window of the Presidential Palace, Bush saw torrential rain and winds lashing the waters of the Grand Harbor.

That afternoon, the storm grew more furious. The president retired to his quarters on the USS *Belknap,* a guided missile cruiser that was the flagship of the U.S. Sixth Fleet. Four-foot waves tossed the Maltese patrol boats and the dinghy full of U.S. frogmen assigned to guard against terrorists or assassins.

In the wardroom of the *Belknap,* Bush joined his advisers to cram for the next day's encounter. Scrutinizing a talking paper drafted by Blackwill and Rice, he told Scowcroft that he wanted something "more direct and less bureaucratic." For example, the script called for him to offer Gorbachev observer status in the structure designed to preserve liberal trade policies — the General Agreement on Tariffs and Trade (GATT) — but only if Gorbachev instituted price reform.

The president said, "Let's just give it to the Soviets straight, without strings. We want 'em to learn about the international trading system. Besides, remember: I was at the UN. I know something about observer status. There's not that much trouble they can cause even if they wanted to, which I suspect they don't."

Bush also decided to drop part of the qualification built into his offer to waive the Jackson-Vanik amendment. The paper had him withholding the waiver until Soviet legislation guaranteeing the right to emigrate was "faithfully implemented." The president said, "Why is this stuff in here about implementation? They're already implementing the right to emigrate. Let's just drop it."

On several points he paused and asked, "What will Gorbachev say in response? Is there anything to his point of view on that?" One example was the civil war in Cambodia. The paper called for Bush to urge Gorbachev to stop sending arms to the Communist regime in Phnom Penh. The president knew that Gorbachev would counter by reminding him that the Kremlin had proposed a moratorium on outside arms shipments to all parties in the Cambodia conflict.

Since the United States and its allies were providing military assistance to several factions in the Cambodian imbroglio, Bush said, "I'm not completely comfortable getting into a wrangle on that. Let's concentrate our fire on Central America, where we *know* we've got a good case."

The Sandinistas had just provided him with a new piece of evidence of their ongoing export of revolution. A week earlier, a twin-engine Cessna aircraft had crashed in a bean field in eastern El Salvador, loaded with automatic rifles, mortars, antitank weapons, and antiaircraft missiles. Destined for the guerrillas of El Salvador, the cargo had almost certainly come from the Sandinista government in Managua.

Baker suggested to Bush, "You can point out to Gorbachev that the whole question of what we do on trade policy — whether we lift the Jackson-Vanik amendment, for instance — is important within the U.S. You can make clear to him that if there's continuing turmoil and violence in Central America, our public is going to ask, 'Why are we helping the Soviets economically when they're pumping a billion dollars into Central America?'"

After the president left the meeting, Blackwill, Rice, Zoellick, and

Arnold Kanter, the NSC's arms control expert, worked into the night to refine the paper so that it would be ready when Bush took his motor launch to the Soviet missile cruiser *Slava* to see Gorbachev at ten o'clock the next morning.

Outside, in the blackness, the winds had reached gale force. They tore Soviet and American flags from their staffs and sent scaffolding set up for television network commentators crashing to the ground. Maltese officials said it was the worst storm they had seen in five years.

CHAPTER 7

"Eye to Eye"

B Y DAWN, the storm was even more menacing. The Soviets moved the first meeting from the bobbing *Slava,* anchored at the mouth of the harbor, to the *Maxim Gorky,* a heavier cruise ship anchored at dockside, on which Gorbachev had spent the night.

At 10:00 A.M., a small launch pulled up next to the *Gorky.* Gripping the rails to steady themselves, Bush, Baker, Scowcroft, Sununu, Fitzwater, and Zoellick boarded the Soviet ship. The secretary of state wore an antiseasickness patch behind one ear. Fitzwater denied to reporters that Baker had been vomiting.

On the *Gorky*'s promenade deck, Gorbachev nervously paced the hastily converted card room. Standing nearby were Shevardnadze, Alexander Yakovlev, Anatoli Dobrynin, and other aides. On one wall were bookshelves; on another was a stern portrait of the ship's namesake, the early-twentieth-century author, smoking a pipe.

As Sergei Tarasenko later recalled, Gorbachev and Shevardnadze "had a very keen feeling that we had to accomplish a huge maneuver without losing time. We felt that the Soviet Union was in free fall, that our superpower status would go up in smoke unless it was reaffirmed by the Americans. With the avalanche of 1989 almost behind us, we wanted to reach some kind of plateau that would give us some time to catch our breath and look around."

Smiling broadly, Bush strode into the card room and shook Gorbachev's hand. As reporters scribbled in notebooks and photographers snapped pictures, the president portrayed himself as an old sailor, claiming that the jostling of the *Belknap* all night had not disturbed his sleep: "Piece of cake!"

Gorbachev joked that the storm was part of a secret Soviet plan to disarm the U.S. Sixth Fleet. Bush seemed taken aback: was this a signal that Gorbachev intended to dominate their meetings by throwing him off balance? His smile vanished, and he turned businesslike. He noted that the weather outside seemed to be calming down, which was a "good sign." Putting on his aviator glasses, Bush said, "Let's go to work." The press was ushered out.

Sitting with his delegation across from the Americans at a long, narrow table, Gorbachev said, "I don't know who should start. You are a guest on my ship. On the other hand, you invited me to this meeting."

Some of the Americans grimaced at what they saw as another sign of Gorbachevian one-upsmanship — his way of putting the burden on Bush to reveal why he had asked Gorbachev to come all the way to Malta.

Bush took the opening and began. Feeling somewhat nervous, he spoke in a reedy, high-pitched voice, telling Gorbachev that he had "some boilerplate" involving their need to seize the opportunities offered by the momentous changes in the world. Gorbachev nodded and wrote in a small orange notebook as Pavel Palazhchenko murmured a simultaneous translation into his ear.

Bush went on, "You're dealing with an administration that wants to see the success of what you are doing. The world will be a better place if *perestroika* succeeds."

Looking down at his two-page list of initiatives, he said, "Here are some ideas." He repeated his offer to waive Jackson-Vanik. He would also "explore with Congress" the suspension of the Stevenson amendment, which impeded U.S. Export-Import Bank loans to the Soviet Union. He would encourage a "dialogue" between Moscow and the Organization of Economic Cooperation and Development.

Bush further promised to urge the organization that ran the General Agreement on Tariffs and Trade to grant the Soviets observer status. "Exposure to GATT and its workings should be very helpful to *pere-*

stroika," he noted. He hoped that Gorbachev would hasten to overhaul his economy — especially the Soviet pricing system.

He handed Gorbachev a list of areas in which the United States might provide "technical cooperation" — a euphemism for assistance — that would help the Soviet Union establish a banking system, a stock market, and other free-market institutions. "Look these over," he said. "We'll be happy to pursue any of them with you." Gorbachev leaned forward and nodded.

Bush had been advised by Gates that what Gorbachev wanted most from Malta was conclusion of the START and CFE treaties in 1990. He said, "Let's really get going on this." He suggested a number of specific START goals that Baker and Shevardnadze could begin working on in January.* He conceded that there were still "blanks" in the U.S. proposal because his own government had not yet reached complete agreement within its own ranks, but he promised that by the time Baker met with Shevardnadze, "we'll have our own position resolved."†

Bush also proposed a multination CFE summit, attended by himself and Gorbachev, before the end of 1990. "If we impose a sense of deadline, it'll help move the negotiations forward," he said.

He augmented the chemical weapons offer he had presented in September at the UN. Earlier, while vowing to destroy 80 percent of existing American stocks, he had reserved the option of continuing to produce chemical weapons as a hedge against terrorists and "outlaw states." Now he said that the United States would stop all production as soon as the forty nations that were considered capable of manufacturing such weapons agreed on a ban.

Repeating a point that Baker had made to the Soviet leader in May, Bush urged Gorbachev to extend *glasnost* to the Soviet military by exchanging data with Washington on military spending and production. He pushed a pile of Pentagon documents across the table and said, "Here's a first step toward an exchange, although as a former CIA man, I'd be very disappointed if the KGB didn't give you all this stuff anyway." Gorbachev chuckled.

Bush did not limit his presentation to the seventeen initiatives he had brought with him to Malta. Having softened Gorbachev up, he turned

---

* These included breaking the impasse on air-launched cruise missiles and coming up with ways to count and limit ballistic missiles in storage and to make sure that one side's use of codes in missile tests did not impede the other's ability to verify treaty compliance.
† This referred mainly to the thorny issue of sea-launched cruise missiles.

tough on Central America, declaring that Soviet and Cuban adventurism in the Western Hemisphere was the "single most disruptive element" in Soviet-American relations, and a "gigantic thorn in your shoe as you try to walk smoothly along."

Bush said that he simply could not understand how the Soviet leadership could allow the Sandinistas' assistance to the guerrillas of El Salvador to drive a wedge between the United States and the Soviet Union. The Costa Rican president, Oscar Arias, who was spearheading a promising effort for peace, had specifically asked him to prevail upon Gorbachev to stop Soviet support for Castro.

"Castro is embarrassing you," Bush said sternly. "He's detracting from your credibility, violating everything you stand for. The one thing, sir, you must understand is that Americans cannot accept your support for Havana and Managua."

The president cautioned Gorbachev not to underestimate how strongly he, the Congress, and the American people felt on this issue. Following Baker's advice, he warned that the United States would not lift the Jackson-Vanik amendment or take any other step to help the Soviet economy until the Kremlin stopped making mischief in Central America. Given the Soviet Union's tolerance toward the amazing changes in Eastern Europe, how could Gorbachev allow himself to be associated with the "old thinkers" in Central America?

Gorbachev replied that he had tried to persuade Castro to adopt some form of *perestroika,* "but we cannot dictate to him." The Soviet Union respected other countries' right to self-determination. "I've told Castro that he's out of step with us and that he should be doing what the Eastern Europeans are doing. But he's his own man," he said. As for Nicaragua, the Soviet government had contacted Managua about the plane loaded with guns and missiles, and the Sandinistas had denied any involvement.

"Well," Bush said, "they're lying to you." Gorbachev bit his lip. He was unwilling to be drawn into an argument in front of the two delegations. He decided to return to the subject later, when he and Bush were alone.

Among the proposals that Bush handed to Gorbachev was the idea of holding the Olympic Games in Berlin in the year 2004. Gorbachev immediately saw a trap: he presumed that Bush was trying to put him on record as supporting the notion that Berlin would by then be the capital of a united Germany. He made no direct response to the suggestion, wishing neither to accelerate German unification, which he feared, nor to antagonize the West Germans, who wanted a unified Germany as soon as possible.

Later in the day, members of Gorbachev's party confronted the Americans and denounced what one called "this cheap trick that seems almost calculated to rub our noses in the most sensitive single foreign policy and international security issue that we face."

In their separate talks, Shevardnadze confided to Baker that there was "deep unease" within his government about German unification. He complained that the West Germans still hoped to regain territory lost in World War II, mainly in Poland: "We are hearing revanchist statements coming from the West German side."

Gorbachev told Bush, "We have inherited two Germanys from history. History created this problem, and history will have to solve it." Adopting what he had been told was Bush's favorite word, he said, "Where the question of Germany is concerned, I have a *prudent* and cautious policy."

Bush responded that it was important for change in all parts of Eastern Europe to proceed in a way that was orderly and did nothing to threaten "anyone's legitimate security interests" — including, obviously, those of the Soviet Union.

Gorbachev began his own formal presentation with his usual hortatory abstractions. The world was changing, and the United States and the Soviet Union had to change with it. They must deal with each other in new ways. New times required new thinking. He was pleased by Bush's decision to start with economic issues — especially with proposals that demonstrated the United States' desire to assist in Soviet reform.

Flipping through his orange notebook and reviewing his record of Bush's remarks, Gorbachev said, "You tell me you support *perestroika*. I have no doubt about this. But until now, I've been looking for a tangible demonstration. During your presentation, I heard it. I was going to ask you today to go beyond words. But you have done so."

During his hourlong discourse, Gorbachev suggested that he was willing to go more than halfway on some issues. On-site arms control inspection? "You can have as many inspectors as you want." Drastic reductions in the number of Soviet troops in Eastern Europe? "We're aware that our troops are unwelcome there anyway."

Following the practice of his predecessors, Bush gave Gorbachev a list of about twenty Soviets who wanted to leave the Soviet Union.

Gorbachev said, "Let us know how many immigrants you want, and we'll send them to you!" Bush replied, "Let's set a goal that by next year's summit we won't have another list to give you."

The president was underscoring a larger message: the more accommodating the USSR was on ideological and humanitarian issues, the more help it could expect from the United States on the economic front.

At noon, Bush and Gorbachev excused their aides for a one-on-one conversation at which their interpreters and note-takers were the only others present. Now the Soviet leader felt free to mix it up with Bush on some of the more contentious issues that had arisen that morning.

He went on the offensive, making full use of the more argumentative talking points that he had refrained from using during the larger meeting. Why was the United States so self-righteous about Central America, he asked, when U.S. armed forces were at that very moment "intervening" in the Philippines?

Bush replied that U.S. air actions to support President Aquino were "just exercises. We're not shooting at anybody."

Gorbachev was not appeased. He said that in word and deed, he had shown once and for all that the Brezhnev Doctrine was dead. Now the United States was pursuing "what my colleagues tell me is the Bush Doctrine!"

Bush said that there was a "big difference" between Brezhnev's actions in Czechoslovakia and what the United States was doing for Aquino: "We were invited by the government to help." To Gorbachev this may have sounded ironically similar to the Kremlin's old insistence that its adventures in Czechoslovakia and Afghanistan were in response to appeals from those countries for "fraternal assistance."

Besides, Bush went on, there was a "problem" with a "crazy colonel" in the Philippines—a reference to Colonel Gregorio "Gringo" Honasan, the leader of the attempted coup. Gorbachev retorted that the Kremlin had plenty of "crazy colonels" among its allies around the world, "but we don't intervene!" As proof, he asked Bush to consider what was happening in Eastern Europe, where governments were responding to pressure from their own populations, not from Moscow. "Events in Eastern Europe reflect what we are trying to do in the Soviet Union," he asserted.

At the same time, he said, "all parties" must recognize that the Eastern Europeans were going to make their own decisions. The United States and the West had better not "exploit" the situation.

After their aides rejoined them for lunch, Gorbachev shifted the focus to his internal economic troubles. As liveried waiters passed around silver bowls of caviar, Gorbachev railed about his budget problems: "Our deficit was bad enough before, but then we had this awful run of bad luck." He spoke of the devastating expense of recovery after the Chernobyl nuclear disaster and the Armenian earthquake. To make matters worse, low world oil prices were depleting the Soviet Union's hard-currency earnings.

The "ultimate test" of his policies, he said, would be whether he could end his country's shortage of consumer goods. To accomplish this, he would have to do more than merely fix the broken structures of the Soviet economy: he would have to change his people's attitude toward work.

Resuming his customary air of self-certainty, Gorbachev then went on to say that the Soviet Union was moving from state ownership of enterprises toward "collective ownership." He had in mind the "Swedish model," he explained, because Swedish socialism was fairer and more public-spirited than American capitalism.

Bush said, "But it's still the *private sector* in Sweden that makes the money, not the public."

Gorbachev replied that anything owned collectively, by more than one person, could be excluded from the category of private property: "I know and you know that there is almost no private property in the United States. . . . Why, some of your firms have as many as twenty thousand shareholders!"

Bush politely refrained from pouncing on this new evidence of Gorbachev's ignorance of Western economics. Instead he told the Soviet leader of his experiences as an oil wildcatter in the Gulf of Mexico: when he and his partners lost an oil rig, they lost their entire investment. "But it didn't cost the American taxpayer a single penny, except for the tax writeoff."

Palazhchenko had a hard time translating the term "tax writeoff." When he finally succeeded, Gorbachev looked more perplexed than ever. He complained about the bad advice his economists had been giving him. Bush laughed and said, "I've had that experience, too!"*

* Bush later told Senator Richard Lugar, the Indiana Republican, about Gorbachev's

To help ensure that Gorbachev did not ask him for direct financial aid — a request that he would have had to refuse — Bush noted with approval Shevardnadze's recent public comment that the Soviet leadership was not "looking for handouts" because it was "proud." Bush said, "I understand you're proud, and so are we."

After luncheon, Bush was scheduled to go back to the *Belknap* for three hours of "private time" before returning to the *Gorky* for another session with Gorbachev at 4:30 P.M. The two leaders would end their day together with a working dinner on the *Belknap.*

The seas looked so violent that Gorbachev proposed that Bush stay on the *Gorky* to ensure that their talks could continue. Bush declined. The shuddering presidential launch had to make a dozen passes before it succeeded in tying up alongside the *Belknap;* once Bush and his party were on board, his advisers and Secret Service detail insisted that the president remain on the ship until the weather improved.

The result was that Bush never saw Gorbachev again that day. When Bush failed to return to the *Gorky* for the afternoon session, Gorbachev urged that the dinner be held on the Soviet ship. The Americans claimed that a "broken ladder" would prevent Bush from leaving the *Belknap.* Gorbachev snapped, "Better teach your navy how to repair it!"

Georgi Arbatov, a member of the Soviet official party, said, "Bush made a mistake. He shouldn't have gone back to that bloody ship!" Onshore, the international press learned that the storm had severed a communications cable to the *Belknap.* Fitzwater had to issue a denial that Bush had been cut off from the world. The "Malta White House" announced that Soviet and American weather forecasters were "sharing information."

The whole event was in danger of turning into a debacle. With the entire world watching, the leaders of the United States and the Soviet Union had traveled to a barren island in the middle of nowhere, only to risk being tossed into the ocean by sixteen-foot seas.

In the absence of any real news, the weather quickly became the principal story out of Malta, embellished by the inevitable metaphors about superpowers' being rocked by forces beyond their control. Tom Brokaw told his NBC audience that the Malta meeting should be called the "seasick summit."

"ignorance" of basic economics, adding that he was eager to "help educate the guy." Bush's tone seemed to Lugar to be one more of sympathy than of condescension.

In the public relations contest, the Soviets had the advantage. Because Gorbachev and his aides were at dockside aboard the *Gorky*, they were able to feed material on the morning session to Soviet briefers, who disseminated it with their own self-serving interpretation. For the American version, the reporters turned to Roman Popadiuk, who had been given no serious information. Exasperated, he called Fitzwater on the *Belknap* and complained, "I'm dead meat here! I've got nothing to tell these people, and they're howling mad."

Baker's spokeswoman, Margaret Tutwiler, called her boss from a U.S. communications shack on the pier. Over the roar of the winds, drenched by the rain, she shouted in her Alabama drawl, "Mr. Baker, this is a drownin' rat callin' for help. I know you and the president are out there all by yourselves, sippin' champagne or whatever, and you can't know what's goin' on here on the mainland. But I'm gonna tell you: we're gettin' crucified. We're gettin' absolutely stomped!"

For full dramatic effect, Baker and Fitzwater had planned to wait until the summit's climax on Sunday to announce the United States' list of seventeen initiatives to the world. Now Baker yelled into the telephone, "Dump!" and Popadiuk and Tutwiler started telephoning influential American correspondents in their hotel rooms.

Throughout the afternoon, the president of the United States sat in the admiral's quarters, surrounded by photographs of the Sixth Fleet, and glumly stared out through a porthole at the fog and wet. At one point, he took Scowcroft out onto the *Belknap*'s deck to peer in the direction of the *Gorky*, just a thousand yards away, where Gorbachev and the other Soviets were throwing a sixty-sixth birthday party for Yakovlev.

That evening, Bush and those of his aides who felt up to it drank white wine and consumed a dinner that the president pronounced "wonderful." He told the stewards that he was sorry Gorbachev would not be able to "get an idea of what U.S. Navy food is like."

By Sunday dawn, the storm had begun to abate. The morning session was scheduled for the *Belknap*, but both sides now agreed to use the more stable *Gorky* instead. When his launch arrived at the Soviet ship, the president was wearing his own antiseasickness patch.

Asked by a reporter whether the storm had ruined the meeting, Bush cried, "Hell, no! Hell, no! The summit's going just fine, thanks." With the same forced gaiety, he bounded up the stairs of the Soviet ship, thrust out a hand to his host, and said, "Good morning!" Beaming,

Gorbachev replied, in carefully rehearsed English, "Long time no see!"

The day before, eager to build a relationship with Bush, Gorbachev had constrained his competitive instincts and refrained from discussing his qualms about what was happening to Soviet power and Soviet-style communism around the world. Now Gorbachev told Bush that he wanted to get something "off my chest."

He complained that certain aspects of U.S. rhetoric and policy were "one-sided" and "unhelpful to what I'm trying to accomplish." Talk in the West about the "collapse of socialism" was "provocative and even insulting." The effect on Moscow and other "socialist capitals" was comparable to the effect that old Communist rhetoric about the "export of revolution" and the "crisis of capitalism" had once had on the West. And, he added petulantly, why must Bush repeatedly assert that what was happening in Eastern Europe was a "triumph of Western values"?

Bush asked, "Why does that bother you so much? I see *glasnost* as a Western value, openness as a Western value, representative government as a Western value, pluralism as a Western value."

"We have these values, too," said Gorbachev. "Why don't you call them *Eastern* values?"

Ever the lawyer searching for mutually acceptable language, Baker piped up, "What about calling them *democratic* values?"

"That's good!" said Gorbachev. "*Democratic* values! That's it!"

During their talk on Saturday, Gorbachev had demanded "meaningful naval arms control." By this he chiefly meant limits on sea-launched cruise missiles, or SLCMs. He asked, "How can we really have a big START agreement that does not restrict an entire category of nuclear weapons?"

Bush knew that such weapons were easy to hide and that the only viable means of verification — shipboard inspections by experts from the other side — was unacceptable to the U.S. Navy. He replied, "It just doesn't work."

Now Gorbachev handed Bush a blue and white map prepared by Marshal Akhromeyev, showing the Soviet Union's "encirclement" by American bases as well as U.S. aircraft carriers and battleships. The map's purpose was to underscore the Soviet General Staff's contention that U.S. vessels armed with SLCMs posed an especially lethal threat to the Soviet Union.

For a moment, Bush was at a loss for words. Tartly Gorbachev said, "I notice that you seem to have no response."

"That's because what you're saying gives me a lot of trouble," said Bush. "Naval arms control is going to be hard to get." He pointed out that the Soviet landmass was shown on the map as a giant white empty space, with no evidence of the imposing military complex that the U.S. forces were intended to deter: "Maybe you'd like me to fill in the blanks on this. I'll get the CIA to do a map of how things look to us. Then we'll compare and see whose is more accurate."

"We are encircled by your navy," said Gorbachev. "As we go to lower levels in these other weapons systems [land-based missiles and bombers], you need to reduce naval weapons as well. Geography is a special factor in all of this."

Historically, Gorbachev continued, the Soviet Union had always been mainly a land power, while the United States had used its navy to protect its interests on the far side of two oceans. In time both NATO and the Warsaw Pact would take on a cast that was less military and more political. He even acknowledged that America could serve as an agent of peaceful change in Europe.

"We don't consider you an enemy anymore," Gorbachev told Bush. "Things have changed. We want you in Europe. You ought to be in Europe. It's important for the future of the continent that you're there. So don't think we want you to leave."

Baker considered this the most vital and hopeful statement that Gorbachev had made all weekend. He later told his aides that Gorbachev had finally "stopped playing one-upsmanship games," such as trying to trick or pressure the United States into getting out of Europe.

Baker was right. Gorbachev realized that his policy of loosening the Soviet grip on Eastern Europe would unleash competing and potentially disruptive forces there. The Western Europeans would not be able to restrain and control those forces alone; they would need the help of the United States. Therefore, it was in the interests of the Soviet Union for the U.S. to remain a powerful presence on the Continent.

After dismissing their aides, Bush and Gorbachev spoke about the most sensitive and potentially the most explosive matter on their agenda: the fate of the Baltic states. Bush noted that during the press conference at the end of the summit, the subject was sure to be raised.

Gorbachev replied that he would be ready for any questions that might be asked about the Baltics. Echoing what Shevardnadze had been saying to Baker for months, he told Bush that the Kremlin was "determined" to avoid repression if at all possible. The use of force "would be the end of *perestroika*."

He said that he and his colleagues were "prepared to be innovative in our solutions" to the problem: "We'll look at any form of association [between the Baltic states and the central Soviet government] that meets mutual interests." The Kremlin would not, however, tolerate unilateral Baltic secession from the Soviet Union. The Soviet Union had a constitution to deal with precisely this issue; the prescribed process would be neither easy nor swift.

Speaking with great care and trusting in the confidentiality of the conversation, Bush reminded Gorbachev that in forty-nine years, the United States had never recognized the Soviet annexation of the Baltics. Nor had it relinquished its desire for Baltic independence. Still, he was ready to "respond to the generosity of your position" — that is, Gorbachev's repeated promise not to use force against the Baltics.

Bush said that if the central Soviet authorities caused an outbreak of violence in the Baltics, it "would create a firestorm" of anti-Soviet feeling in the United States. But if Gorbachev kept his word and avoided violence, the U.S. government would reciprocate with restraint in what it said on the subject, because, as Bush put it, "we don't want to create big problems for you."

Gorbachev took this to mean that Bush would not press the issue of Baltic independence, and that as long as Soviet tanks did not roll, the U.S. president would not engage in demagogy on the issue or try to embarrass his Soviet counterpart.

Had it been revealed to the world at the time that Bush had implied such an accommodation, the American Right would doubtless have cried that his captivation by Gorbachev had caused the president to make some kind of secret bargain to sell out the Baltics. But the conversation did not become public.

At the end of their talks, Bush and Gorbachev appeared before reporters in the *Gorky*'s discotheque for the first joint press conference in the history of superpower summitry. Their only point of sharp disagreement was Central America, which had the look of a messy legacy from an unfortunate past. It seemed evident that the months ahead would produce CFE and START treaties to be signed in 1990.

The two men even found a way to make a rhetorical virtue out of the weather. Gorbachev said, "This whole incident shows we can adjust well to changing circumstances." Arriving in Brussels to brief NATO allies on his way home, Bush declared, "The seas were as turbulent as our times."

As usual, the Foreign Ministry spokesman, Gennadi Gerasimov, had a tag line for the occasion: "We buried the Cold War at the bottom of the Mediterranean Sea."

On his return to Moscow, Gorbachev told *Pravda* that Malta had shown the "importance of contacts at the highest levels." In private conversation with his inner circle, he recalled his talk with Bush in the limousine in Washington in 1987. That was the first time he had felt that he could "trust" Bush, he said. He had wondered about him during the aggravating *pauza* of 1989, but "in Malta I became firmly convinced that my original instinct had not deceived me."

Malta had made Gorbachev optimistic that Bush would not hold the entire U.S.-Soviet relationship hostage to whatever the Soviets did about the Baltics. He was also glad that the president seemed disinclined to push hard for early German unification. According to Alexander Bessmertnykh, Gorbachev was "extremely relieved" that at Malta Bush had promised not to "trap" or "undermine" him in his dealings either with the Baltics or with the rest of Eastern Europe. Two years later Bessmertnykh recalled, "If it were not for Malta, the Soviet Union would never have so smoothly surrendered its control of Eastern Europe and the Baltics."

Finally, the summit suggested to Gorbachev that Bush was at last emerging from his fear of the American Right. Still riding high in U.S. public opinion polls, and newly confident of his political standing, Bush would not need to play tough with the Soviet leader for domestic political reasons. Gorbachev even hoped that in time Bush might be willing to offer the Soviet Union some serious financial help — not just technical assistance — for *perestroika*.

The long year of 1989 had carried Bush beyond his original intentions. In January, he had resolved that despite the demands of American public opinion, Western leaders, and the Soviets themselves, his relationship with the Soviet leader would be far cooler than his predecessor's.

At the start of the year, Bush had been determined to position himself in such a way that if Gorbachev were deposed at any time in a right-wing coup, no one could ever claim that the U.S. president had gotten carried away and offered concessions to Moscow that had proved to be reckless and premature.

Bush had also felt that his keeping Gorbachev at arm's length would prevent the American people from vesting excessive hopes in the new relationship with Moscow. He knew that the Republican defeat in the 1976 election could be attributed in part to public disillusionment with détente and therefore with the two presidents, Nixon and Ford, who had nurtured the policy.

Bush's original intentions had been altered by three unexpected developments. The first was the steady buildup of pressure on him from the American people and the Western allies for serious engagement with Gorbachev. This might not have had such a powerful impact on Bush had it not been impressed upon him by a secretary of state who was at once one of his best friends, a political operative deeply sensitive to public opinion, and an ambitious fledgling diplomat who did not enjoy having to apologize to his new NATO colleagues for the president's caution.

The second was the revolution of 1989 in Eastern Europe. Before the fall of that year, Bush had been able to argue, as Kissinger had done before the inauguration, that the changes wrought by Gorbachev were "cosmetic" and easily reversible. But with the Berlin Wall down and Eastern Europe as a whole leaving the Soviet sphere, it was almost impossible to maintain that the world was in imminent danger of returning to the Cold War as everyone had known it. The public's disappointment over Bush's tepid reaction to the opening of the wall was a warning: if the president continued his public reserve toward Gorbachev, he would be at risk of seeming out of touch with both the American people and the march of history.

The third development was Malta. Meeting for the first time as president with Gorbachev, Bush found that he actually liked and — as Margaret Thatcher had predicted — could do business with the Soviet leader. Bush was affected more than most world leaders by personal relations. He always placed great importance on the orchestration of foreign leaders' visits, telling aides, "These visits can alter how people respond to you." In the mid-1970s he had been impressed by the careful planning of such trips by the Chinese, who assigned their best foreign service officers not to negotiations but to protocol.

In this, Bush was nearly the opposite of Richard Nixon, who observed, "Bush believes, far more than I, in the effectiveness of personal diplomacy. He believes that if you have a good personal relationship, it helps on substance. I believe that unless leaders' interests are compatible, a personal relationship doesn't mean anything."

When he returned from Malta to the White House, the president told his aides that he had been startled by how much more willing Gorbachev was to discuss human rights at Malta than he had been during their first encounter, in Moscow, in 1985. Even on such thorny issues as Central America, there had been a "twinkle in his eye, and sometimes even an actual wink."

Bush noted that the "way we [the American delegation] clicked off our list of things that we wanted to accomplish didn't exactly disarm him, but it did show him that we were ready to move forward on a lot of things he wanted. He may have been pleased it wasn't going to take hours to drag them out of us."

Recalling Gorbachev's complaints about the Philippines, the president observed, "He's really got a problem with anything that makes it look as though we're on the march while he's on the retreat, doesn't he? I sort of knew that, but hearing it from *him* was somehow still different."

Gorbachev's warnings not to exploit the changes in Eastern Europe had helped Bush understand "in my gut what his concern is." Bush had been "absolutely blown away," he said, by how little Gorbachev knew about economics, and by how much of what he thought he knew was incorrect. He was relieved that he had not been forced to refuse a request from Gorbachev for a "bailout" of the Soviet economy.

On December 6, in a telephone interview with Hugh Sidey of *Time*, Bush said that his new relationship with Gorbachev was "very personal": "I'll find ways to contact him in a very quiet fashion. I can write him. I can call him. I'm not going to be a pen pal, but we can communicate."

More than anything else, what Malta suggested to Bush was that Gorbachev would prove to be a reliable partner in the new climate between Washington and Moscow. In manners, appearance, and rhetorical style, he was nearly indistinguishable from the leaders of Western Europe. He also had a domestic political problem with which Bush could in some ways identify: dangerous critics and rivals on the left and right.

For Bush, who recoiled from the notion of rapid, uncontrolled political change and from emotional, mercurial leaders such as Walesa and Yeltsin, Gorbachev represented the best hope for reshaping the Soviet status quo in an orderly fashion.

For the next twenty months, Bush structured American policy toward the Soviet Union on four principles: helping Gorbachev to remain in power; keeping him on the track of "reform," however vaguely defined; "locking in" agreements favorable to the United States, which would be much more difficult to reach with a tougher Kremlin regime; and conceding nothing that would injure the United States should Gorbachev be suddenly deposed by Soviet hard-liners.

Covering his domestic flank, the president briefed conservative leaders and experts from Washington think tanks on his meetings with Gorbachev in Malta, stressing the tough message he had delivered on Central America. At a dinner for the House Republican leader, Robert Michel, on December 6, he said, "I was very up-front with him about the things we don't like that they're doing."

After listening to Bush recount Gorbachev's absorption in his domestic problems, Vice President Quayle remarked, with what struck some present as glee, "Poor Gorbachev! He doesn't stand a chance!" Playing to fellow conservatives during an interview on CNN, Quayle warned against "getting caught up" in Gorbachev's "magnetic personality." He reminded the conservative *Washington Times* that the Soviet Union still had a "totalitarian system."

Quayle's spokesman David Beckwith denied that the vice president was parting company with Bush: "You can call it a difference in tonal quality. We're all singing from the same songbook, but there are different parts. Some people are singing bass, some alto."

During the very weekend that Bush and Gorbachev were together in Malta, Communist rule in East Germany had begun its final collapse. The Communist party's "leading role" was revoked. A special parliamentary committee accused Honecker and other deposed leaders of corruption and expelled them from the party. Egon Krenz resigned and was replaced by a more reformist party leader, Gregor Gysi.

At a Moscow summit of Warsaw Pact leaders in early December, Gorbachev manfully declared that the alliance would still have an important role in the new Europe: the Warsaw Pact and NATO both provided "elements of security." He did not need to spell out what he meant: maintaining both alliances would, he hoped, impede the early unification of Germany. On this subject, he said, "Bush is formulating his positions slowly, thoughtfully." Gorbachev said that on Germany, his views and Bush's were very close.

At almost the same time, in the Oval Office, Bush was telling his aides, "I think Gorbachev and I basically see eye to eye on German unity. It's coming, but it doesn't have to come tomorrow." The president said that given a choice between the success of *perestroika* and German unity in the near future, he himself would choose *perestroika:* "That's what's driving the things we like in Soviet foreign policy."

Bush and Baker assumed that German unification would come slowly, and that the administration would not have to begin to commit itself to an approach before the East German elections, scheduled for May 1990. Advised that his ambassador to Bonn, Vernon Walters, had forecast, with seeming boldness, that Germany would be reunited "within five years," the president looked acutely uncomfortable. He told reporters, "I am not into the predicting of time on the question of Germany."

On Monday, December 11, Bush sent Walters to West Berlin to meet with representatives of the other World War II victors — France, Britain, and the Soviet Union. With Bush's support, the Four Powers issued a statement stressing the importance of maintaining "stability" in and around Berlin. For those Germans impatient for unification, this statement was intended as a flashing yellow light.

At the Warsaw Pact summit of early December, every visiting delegation save one was led by a self-styled reformer who had come to power in 1989.*

The exception was Romania, whose Stalinist tyrant, Nicolae Ceausescu, complained to his new colleagues that the Americans and Western Europeans were stepping up their old campaign for world domination: "They're out to liquidate socialism!" he cried. He proposed a new Warsaw Pact meeting in Bucharest to plan a counteroffensive on behalf of the "proletarian parties."

The other leaders did their best to ignore him. They endorsed a Czechoslovak proposal to condemn the 1968 Soviet invasion that had

---

* Bulgaria was represented by Petur Mladenov, who had replaced Todor Zhivkov, the party strong man of thirty-five years. For Czechoslovakia, Karel Urbanek had taken the place of Milo Jakes, who had resigned in the face of mass demonstrations; while the Warsaw Pact summit was under way in Moscow, 200,000 people were protesting in Prague against Urbanek's government. The East German delegation was nominally led by a subdued and distracted Egon Krenz, who had just quit as general secretary of the party, and by Hans Modrow, the prime minister. The head of the Hungarian group was Rezso Nyers, whose party had changed its name from Communist to Socialist and disavowed Leninism. The Poles who came to Moscow were under the leadership of their new non-Communist prime minister, Tadeusz Mazowiecki, though President Jaruzelski and the party leader Mieczyslaw Rakowski were also part of the delegation.

crushed the Prague Spring as an "illegal act that had long-term negative consequences." This resolution drove still another stake through the heart of the Brezhnev Doctrine. Ceausescu refused to sign it.

Three weeks later, Ceausescu and his wife were executed, their bodies riddled with bullets in the bloodiest of the Eastern European upheavals. After the dictator's death, his security forces continued their rampage. Some Romanians turned their guns on ethnic Hungarians who lived in the western part of the country. Lawrence Eagleburger warned Baker that the civil war and ethnic violence might spread far beyond Romania's borders. The gloomy view of post–Cold War Europe that Eagleburger had expressed to catcalls and criticism in September suddenly seemed all too prescient.

Some of those who had overthrown Ceausescu went so far as to call on Gorbachev to send in Soviet troops to stop Ceausescu's secret police from maintaining a dictatorship. In Washington, Baker mused that the Soviets "have got the incentive and the capability to do something to stop the bloodshed." On Sunday, December 24, he said on NBC's "Meet the Press" that the United States would not object "if the Warsaw Pact felt it necessary to intervene" in Romania.

The moment was laden with irony. On the tenth anniversary of Brezhnev's invasion of Afghanistan, and only weeks after Gorbachev's renunciation of the Brezhnev Doctrine, here was a secretary of state suggesting that the United States might look favorably on a Soviet decision to order troops back into an Eastern European nation.

Baker may have had an additional motive beyond his desire to stop the bloodshed. The United States had just launched a massive invasion of Panama, called Operation Just Cause, whose chief aim was to remove the country's dictator, General Manuel Noriega, from power and bring him back to Miami to stand trial on drug-trafficking charges.

Gorbachev's sending troops to buttress freedom in Romania might provide a useful counterpoint to the United States' actions in the Philippines and Panama. This would tacitly establish a new American-Soviet doctrine under which both powers would have the right to provide military support for "just causes" in their areas of influence.

By cable, Baker asked Ambassador Matlock in Moscow to sound out the Soviets on their attitudes on and intentions in Romania.

When Matlock went to the Central Committee and the Foreign Ministry, some Soviet officials wondered whether the Americans were laying a "trap" or engaging in a "provocation." They suspected that Bush and Baker might be coaxing the Soviet Union to revert to the kind of behavior that had caused so much trouble in the past. Then, if Soviet forces entered Romania, the United States would publicly condemn the intervention and reap huge gains in world opinion.

Shevardnadze took a less conspiratorial view. He told Matlock that he found Baker's suggestion not sinister but merely "stupid." He was "categorically opposed" to any outside intervention. The Romanians' revolution was "their business," and no one else's. Any kind of Soviet meddling would only "make a martyr out of Ceausescu."

Citing Panama, Ivan Aboimov, one of Shevardnadze's deputies, remarked to Matlock, with unconcealed bitterness, "It seems that we've turned the Brezhnev Doctrine over to you!"

CHAPTER 8

"I'm Going to Hold a Seminar on Germany"

A TELEVISION CAMERA was rolled into Gorbachev's offices in the Kremlin for the taping of his New Year's message to the Soviet people. Sitting at a desk, he looked into the lens and said that 1989 had been the "year of the ending of the Cold War." While the 1990s promised to be the "most fruitful period in the history of civilization," the Soviet Union had "lived through a difficult year, the most difficult year of *perestroika*." He asked for "reason and kindness, patience and tolerance."

Next Gorbachev taped a New Year's greeting to Americans: "During the Malta meeting, President Bush and I agreed that it was essential to get away from the Cold War and also to abandon the weapons of Cold War, so that the 1990s can open a period of genuine cooperation." He warned against another disruption of U.S.-Soviet relations like the *pauza* of the previous year. In 1990, Americans must not be distracted by "hesitations, wait-and-see attitudes, doubts, and suspicions."

That week, Gorbachev canceled several meetings scheduled for January 1990 with foreign leaders, including one with the British Labour party leader, Neil Kinnock. "Political events in the Soviet Union," he said, required his "personal attention."

The most serious problem he faced was the growing clamor for independence in Lithuania. Earlier in December, the Lithuanian Communist party had broken off its relations with Moscow and demanded freedom for the republic. Furious, Gorbachev had telephoned the Lithuanian Communist leader, Algirdas Brazauskas, and ordered him to revoke the request: "I have the means to stop you and can remove you, if necessary." Brazauskas replied, "You cannot remove me. I am the leader of an independent party."

Gorbachev met behind closed doors with the Central Committee in Moscow. Hard-liners demanded that he use force against Vilnius, lest the breakaway of Lithuania lead to the dissolution of the entire Soviet Union. Gorbachev refused, saying, "I won't have blood on my hands."

At Gorbachev's behest, Yakovlev called Brazauskas and warned, "Thunderclouds are gathering over Gorbachev's head." He asked Brazauskas whether the Lithuanians really wished to provoke the Soviet leader's replacement by someone who would really crack down on them.

Gorbachev persuaded the Central Committee to suspend the issue for the time being, while a delegation from Moscow was sent to Vilnius to ask local party leaders to listen to reason. Boris Yeltsin, wanting to keep the onus squarely on his rival, proposed that Gorbachev head the delegation himself. The Central Committee agreed.

After the meeting, Gorbachev emerged and told reporters in a quavering voice that the Soviet leadership would oppose unilateral moves toward independence by Lithuania or any of the fourteen other Soviet republics. "Otherwise," he said, "we would be deliberately seeking the breakup of the Soviet Union."

Accompanied by an entourage of forty, Gorbachev flew to Vilnius on Tuesday, January 11. More than 200,000 angry Lithuanians were gathered outside the main Catholic cathedral, chanting "Independence!" One of their banners read "LENIN RECOGNIZED LITHUANIA, STALIN TOOK AWAY ITS INDEPENDENCE — AND GORBACHEV?"

Gorbachev's three-day visit marked the first time a supreme Soviet leader had ever set foot in Lithuania. Wading into the crowds, he cried, "Independence? Let's have it! At the workplace, in cities, in the republics, *but together!*" Still, what had worked for Gorbachev in Washington in 1987 did not work here: the crowds argued with him, sometimes abusively.

Gorbachev cautioned party members, factory workers, collective farmers, and intellectuals that if Lithuania became an independent state, it would go "nowhere": "If there's anyone here who thinks that it's all so easy that today or tomorrow you just have an election, get together and raise your hands, and leave the Soviet Union, well, this is not politics. It doesn't even remotely smell of politics. It's simply not serious."

He warned that if Lithuania seceded, its ethnic minorities (he did not need to specify that this meant primarily the large group of Russians living in the Baltics) would lose their rights. In order to secede, Lithuania would have to pay back the Soviet central government for the money it had poured into Lithuanian housing, factories, and other construction over the previous half century. Without subsidized oil, gas, and other resources, Lithuania would fall into a "mud puddle." Besides, Gorbachev continued, from the Soviet Union's point of view, Lithuania was the site of crucial ports and communications lines: "Our security lies here."

Gravely Gorbachev declared, "Today I am your friend, but if you choose to go another way, then I will do everything I can to show that you are leading people to a dead end." Lithuanians must not "look for conflict, or you'll get real trouble." Any "provocations" would invite a crackdown by the Soviet military and bring an end to *perestroika:* "If even the slightest suppression occurs, or a misunderstanding in, say, Estonia or Moldavia, it will spill over to the rest of the country."

Still, he hinted that compromise was possible: "We need a mechanism on how a republic might withdraw from the Soviet Union. We need to discuss such questions as the time frame for leaving, defense, and communications." This was the first time a Soviet leader had ever spoken publicly with even faint tolerance about the secession of a Soviet republic.

Gorbachev even went so far as to suggest that he might tolerate opposition parties within the Soviet Union. A year before, he had called the idea "rubbish"; now he said that such a development would be "no tragedy," adding, "We should not fear a multiparty system the way the devil fears incense."

Vytautas Landsbergis, the professor of musicology who had become the leader of the Lithuanian independence movement, remained as committed as ever to a free Lithuania. Speaking before crowds in Vilnius, he insisted, "What has been stolen should be given back!"

In Washington, Bush kept the promise he had privately made to Gorbachev at Malta. He reminded Scowcroft and Baker several times that he wanted official American rhetoric about the Baltics to "stay cool."

Marlin Fitzwater informed the press that although the United States had never recognized the Soviet Union's annexation of the Baltics, "We don't want to take any positions that are not helpful to either side." Meanwhile, several State Department officials told reporters that, as one put it, "the Soviet leadership at the highest levels is of the opinion that it can't let Lithuania go."

No sooner did Gorbachev return from Vilnius to Moscow than he had to contend with even worse trouble in the Caucasus. There the republics of Armenia and Azerbaijan were simultaneously in conflict both with the central Soviet government and with each other.

For decades, Armenian and Azeri nationalism had been held in check by the iron-fisted rule of Moscow. Emboldened, like the Lithuanians, by Gorbachev's reforms, citizens of both republics were now asserting their long-suppressed claims to independence. In Baku, throngs led by the Popular Front of Azerbaijan, demanding secession from the USSR and union with their ethnic kinsmen in northern Iran, blockaded the local headquarters of the Communist party and Soviet television.

Complicating matters further was the region of Nagorno-Karabakh, an Armenian enclave inside the boundaries of Azerbaijan. Fearing what would happen to them if Azerbaijan achieved independence, its people now wanted to secede from that republic and join with Armenia itself. The result was a new outbreak of an old feud — Christian Armenians and Muslim Azeris had been at each other's throats since at least the eighth century — and the worst eruption of violence in the Soviet Union since World War II.

To deal with the crisis, Gorbachev sent Yevgeni Primakov to Baku. A onetime *Pravda* correspondent in the Middle East with close ties to the KGB, Primakov had risen through the ranks of the Soviet academic establishment to succeed Yakovlev in 1985 as director of the influential Institute of World Economy and International Relations.

In the late 1980s, Primakov had become increasingly active in politics as an ally of Gorbachev's in the Congress of People's Deputies and the Supreme Soviet. By 1990 he was a member of Gorbachev's inner circle. In advising the Soviet leader on economic, defense, and foreign policy issues, Primakov emphasized his background as a specialist on the Arab and Islamic worlds. When violence broke out in the Caucasus, he was thus the natural choice to be Gorbachev's man on the scene.

In Baku, Primakov told crowds that the Soviet forces were there merely to protect the minorities. He was booed. Soviet Defense Minister Dimitri Yazov and Interior Minister Vadim Bakatin flew to Azerbaijan and took up positions in a military command post outside Baku, where Soviet troops were girding themselves for a fight. Supporters of the Popular Front arranged buses and trucks in crude barricades against the "invaders" from Moscow.

Before dawn on Saturday, January 20, columns of army and Interior Ministry troops broke through the barricades and stormed the city, exchanging fire with demonstrators armed with rifles and submachine guns. While the official death toll was 120, members of the Popular Front claimed that as many as 1,000 had in fact died.

The previous July, Baker had privately told Shevardnadze that the United States would understand if Gorbachev had to use the Soviet military against "irrational bloodletting and national hatreds." From Gorbachev's point of view, the situation in Baku certainly qualified.

On television, the Soviet leader defended the crackdown. The militants, he said, were "irresponsible pirates and black-market dealers. *Perestroika* is like a thorn in their flesh. They are unable to launch a frontal attack on it, so they turn to ethnic struggles."

That same week, George and Barbara Bush held a small private dinner at the White House for Susan Eisenhower, granddaughter of the thirty-fourth president, and Dr. Roald Sagdeyev, an eminent Soviet space scientist, who were soon to be married in Moscow.

Ambassador Yuri Dubinin was one of the guests. During the evening, Bush expansively told Dubinin that he supported Gorbachev "completely" in what he had had to do in Baku: sometimes a leader had to use force to protect the rights of minorities and keep the peace. On their way out, Dubinin remarked to Eisenhower and Sagdeyev, "Isn't it wonderful that the president supports us?" They were concerned that Dubinin might think Bush's views on Baku extended to Lithuania.

That week the president gave an interview to *Newsweek*. He said he would "love" to have seen the use of force avoided in Baku, "but here you have a situation where the Soviet Union is trying to put down ethnic conflict, internal conflict." Gorbachev's "extraordinarily difficult" problems would "not be made easier by a lot of pontificating from leaders in other countries."

Asked if Gorbachev would survive the rise of Soviet secessionism, he declared, "I hope that he not only survives but stays strong." More than at any time before Malta, Bush now publicly allied himself with Gorbachev against the nationalists of the USSR. He felt that Gorbachev was "really the best hope" for U.S. interests: "I think we have a lot at stake in continuing to deal with this man."

Privately, Bush and Baker were more worried than ever that the Soviet leader might not be long in power. Shevardnadze had been forced to postpone his next ministerial meeting with Baker, originally scheduled for Moscow in February, so that Gorbachev could hold a two-day Central Committee meeting in hopes of strengthening his hand. Boris Yeltsin was publicly forecasting that Gorbachev's government "might collapse within several months."

Fearing that the West might pull back from Gorbachev, Shevardnadze assured the foreign press corps in Moscow that his boss was not in danger of being overthrown: "Gorbachev and the political leadership of this country on the whole enjoy the support of the bulk of the Soviet people, even though we are experiencing great difficulties — empty shelves in stores and a host of other social, economic, and interethnic problems."

On Wednesday morning, January 31, Bush spoke to Gorbachev on the telephone. It had been almost exactly a year since their first such conversation, just after Bush's inauguration. The president had hoped to build a relationship with Gorbachev by letter but had received only cold, institutional replies. He complained to his staff, "The Soviets are so bureaucratic!"*

Once Bush had decided to telephone his Soviet counterpart, Scowcroft asked Dubinin to find out when Gorbachev would be free to talk. The Kremlin insisted on initiating the call, which went first to the Signal Corps installation in the White House and then to the Oval Office. An interpreter and a note-taker listened in on extensions in the basement situation room. As they spoke, Bush took his own notes, which were later transcribed by his secretary, Patty Presock.

Rather than interrogating the Soviet leader about the many domestic troubles facing him, Bush chose to use this conversation to fortify

---

* Explaining why he felt "driven" to telephone Gorbachev, Bush once told a journalist, "If there are going to be disagreements between the Soviet Union and the U.S. — and there will be — I want to be sure they're real and they're based on fact, not on misunderstanding. If he knows the heartbeat a little bit from talking, there's less apt to be misunderstanding. . . . Part of the reason for phone calls is that you can build a relationship that is confidential, where you can speak freely, frankly discuss differences."

Gorbachev's morale. The president said he was considering making a proposal for further cuts in U.S. and Soviet combat forces in Europe; unless Gorbachev said the reduction was out of the question, he would present the idea that evening in his State of the Union address. The Soviet leader welcomed the initiative in principle, since he was eager to reduce his own military spending.

Gorbachev was spending the week at his dacha at Novo-Ogarevo, half an hour's drive outside Moscow. Built in 1956, with a four-columned portico and steepled Victorian bays, the two-story stucco mansion was modeled on the early-nineteenth-century houses of the Russian gentry. Equipped with a billiard room, a solarium, and a movie theater, it was a secret to most Muscovites.

Aides motored out to the dacha to help Gorbachev prepare a major address to the Central Committee on party reform. Moscow was buzzing with rumors that Gorbachev was going to announce that he would quit the party. When a version of this story was broadcast by CNN, Gorbachev issued a public denial.

Many of his countrymen hoped that the rumors were true. On Sunday, February 3, hundreds of thousands marched through Moscow, demanding an end to the Communist monopoly on Soviet power. Crowds gathered in front of the Moskva Hotel, where many Central Committee members were staying, and cried, "Resign! Resign!" Placards said, "SO-VIET COMMUNIST PARTY, WE'RE TIRED OF YOU!" and "72 YEARS ON THE ROAD TO NOWHERE." Addressing the demonstrators, Boris Yeltsin said, "This is the last chance for the party."

On Monday morning, February 5, Gorbachev addressed the closed-door Central Committee meeting. He asserted, "The Party will be able to fulfill its mission as a political vanguard only if it drastically restructures itself . . . and cooperates with all forces committed to *perestroika*."

Gorbachev recommended changing the Soviet constitution to end the Communist party's lock on political power and open the way to a multiparty system. He called for economic reforms, a 20 percent reduction in the size of the Central Committee itself, and a new executive office — the presidency — which would give him more authority. As one pro-Gorbachev member of the Central Committee explained, "With the presidency independent of the party, there cannot be a coup."

While Shevardnadze and Yakovlev defended Gorbachev and his program at length, others attacked him from the right and the left. In the end, however, the only vote against the platform was cast by Boris Yeltsin, who complained that Gorbachev was still "trying to write his proposals with both his right hand and his left hand — always compromising."

On Wednesday, February 7, as the Central Committee plenum dragged on, Baker's air force 707 landed in Moscow in a dense fog. The secretary of state was unable to stay in his usual Spaso House quarters because Ambassador Matlock had turned the mansion over to Susan Eisenhower for her wedding to Sagdeyev and the reception that followed.

The Baker party encamped at the modern Mezhdunarodnaya Hotel, built by Armand Hammer in anticipation of the 1980 Olympics, which the United States and other Western countries had ended up boycotting to protest the Soviet invasion of Afghanistan. Baker's first meeting with Shevardnadze was scheduled for 7:00 P.M., but the Central Committee was still closeted, so Shevardnadze's aides asked the secretary to come to the Foreign Ministry an hour later instead.

Baker wondered whether Shevardnadze would be too preoccupied with Soviet internal politics to be able to concentrate on international issues. As he jotted down notes for his opening presentation, he structured his points in a way that he hoped would help Shevardnadze to shift his focus.

He assumed that Shevardnadze's ability to make concessions would be constrained. Throughout the Central Committee plenum, Gorbachev and Shevardnadze had been on the defensive, as one speaker after another criticized them for giving in too often to Washington. On the flight to Moscow, Baker had told his aides that he wanted to help Gorbachev and Shevardnadze by providing an "explanation of what we're asking for and of how it's in their country's interests, too."

When he met Shevardnadze at eight, Baker was startled to find him energetic and even relaxed, despite the day's ordeal. Baker began the session by lauding the changes in the American-Soviet relationship. This time he deliberately went one step beyond his earlier statements to Shevardnadze about how he and Bush wanted *perestroika* to succeed. Now he said, "We believe that the process of Soviet renewal is in our interest. It is important and positive."

Renewal was exactly the word that Gorbachev and Shevardnadze had been using to define their policies. The secretary of state and Dennis Ross had worked out the new phraseology to strike a responsive chord;

Shevardnadze, in turn, knew what he was hearing and was grateful.

Baker went on, "We want to see you succeed. We really mean that. We know there are limits to what we can do to help. As the general secretary has said, a stable international environment is necessary for the renewal process to succeed."

Shevardnadze's face lit up. "You know," he said, "I used those precise words yesterday, in my speech to the plenum! I see we are approaching this in the same way."

"We know that there must be a stable world on the outside for *perestroika* to go forward," Baker said. He then turned to several trouble spots in the outside world, complaining particularly about recent Soviet shipments of MiG-29 war planes to Cuba. Shevardnadze looked pained and made it clear that his heart was not in the task of defending his country's continued support of Castro.

On Afghanistan, Baker said that the United States would drop its long-standing insistence that Mohammed Najibullah, the pro-Soviet president of the country, be removed before negotiations could begin on ending the civil war.

The very mention of Najibullah — a personification of the bad old days of Soviet foreign policy — caused Shevardnadze to blurt out, "Sometimes I wish all these people would just kill each other and end the whole thing." Then, regaining his composure, he acknowledged that it would be helpful to let Najibullah remain at his post for a while longer. He had enough troubles at home without being perceived as helping to topple old Kremlin clients: "It would be very difficult for us to force him to go, but it might be acceptable if he decided to leave on his own."

Baker also made note of the changes in Eastern Europe since the Malta meeting. He mentioned that after Moscow he was planning to visit Romania and Bulgaria. Shevardnadze said, "That's a good idea. It will boost the reformers in those countries. I was there for thirty-six hours, and I think it would be good if you did it. We would like to hear your impressions."

It was an extraordinary exchange. The American secretary of state and the Soviet foreign minister were coordinating their efforts to promote the liberation of Eastern Europe from Soviet control.

Shevardnadze went on, "We think the process of change in Eastern Europe is uneven. In Poland, we are confident that the changes will go forward in a stable way because that government reflects the will of the people. But in Romania that is less clear. The new leaders are like night and day from Ceausescu — philosophically, ideologically, emotionally, socially. But no political culture has been permitted there for all these years. A dictator dominated everything."

The two men agreed on a Bush-Gorbachev summit to be held in Washington that summer, and on a chemical weapons ban that would embrace all the elements of the plan Bush had proposed at the UN in September. Shevardnadze had earlier told reporters that he would give Baker an answer on Bush's proposal for a 195,000-troop limit in central Europe; now he said that the answer would come from Gorbachev himself when he received Baker on Friday. Sensitive to Baker's past indignation at Gorbachev's attempts to trump the Americans with headline-grabbing new initiatives at the arms control table, he grinned at the secretary and added, "It's a *counterproposal,* not a *counteroffensive.*"

As for the U.S. position, Baker said that he and the president were ready to expand on their Wyoming offer on START. He offered some slight concessions on the restriction of air-launched cruise missiles and on several other highly technical issues, and indicated that the administration might also be willing to negotiate limits on sea-launched cruise missiles, provided the matter was dealt with outside the bounds of the START treaty.

Shevardnadze replied, "You have presented very positive elements. Our experts will have to look at them. Then we will make a judgment. They will work through the night. It is important to get all this behind us."

Arms control, once the centerpiece of U.S.-Soviet diplomacy, was increasingly being treated as underbrush that had to be cleared away before Baker and Shevardnadze could make progress on more immediate, more important, and more interesting issues.

On Thursday evening, February 8, the Shevardnadzes entertained the Bakers at their Moscow apartment. During dinner (another Georgian meal), Shevardnadze conceded to Baker that the deterioration of the Soviet economy posed a serious threat to Gorbachev's survival. However, he said, the greatest domestic danger was not the economy but the rise in nationalism and ethnic tensions.

Baker noted that he had been hearing about increasing anti-Semitism in the Soviet Union. In January, thugs shouting "Kill the Yids!" had beaten several delegates at a meeting of liberal writers, and Russian ultranationalists were complaining that under *glasnost,* a "Jewish conspiracy" was transforming Russia into a "robot deprived of all elements of human life." Baker asked about rumors that pogroms were about to begin.

The foreign minister dismissed Baker's query: there *were* ethnic problems, but the Jews were not being singled out. The anti-Semitic, ultranationalistic organization Pamyat, he said, was a "fringe group" that did not really threaten the Jews.

Shevardnadze said that although the new openness demonstrated at that week's Central Committee plenum might seem refreshing, in fact it created new problems. Before, no one would have dared to question Soviet foreign policy; now, at party meetings, people were standing up and calling out, "Why did you and Gorbachev lose Eastern Europe? Why did you surrender Germany?"

After his talk with Shevardnadze, Baker told his aides, "With the Central Committee session, Gorbachev has strengthened himself, but that may not be a blessing. The more power he gathers to himself, the harder it will be to lay off blame on anyone else when things go badly."

Still, Baker had been shaken by Shevardnadze's bleak account of Gorbachev's problems: "The odds have got to be against his survival, although we aren't about to say that in public. The more we talk about the odds' being against his survival, the more it becomes a self-fulfilling prophecy. The danger to Gorbachev is not that he'll be thrown out in some palace coup, but that it'll come from the streets. The freedom genie is out of the bottle. They're not on track to cure their economic problems or their ethnic problems, so it'll come from below."

He concluded, "We should help Gorbachev *when it is to our mutual advantage*. We can gain a great deal if we lock in agreements that are in the U.S. interest. We don't risk anything by hitching our star to Gorbachev. As long as he's there, he's the one we should be focused on."

On Friday morning, February 9, Baker sat down with Gorbachev and Shevardnadze at the long, ornate table in St. Catherine's Hall at the Kremlin. This time there was none of Gorbachev's usual chaff and badinage. Unlike Shevardnadze, the Soviet leader looked frazzled after the struggles of the week.

Usually Gorbachev began such sessions by meeting alone with Shevardnadze and Baker, later expanding the group to include aides. This time, he reversed the order. Soon the Americans realized why. In the larger session, with Marshal Akhromeyev present, Gorbachev plodded through a perfunctory discussion of START, haggling over arcane matters such as counting rules for air-launched cruise missiles.

Baker presumed that this monologue was intended for internal consumption. He felt that by now arms control had become for Gorbachev little more than a symbol of the management of the East-West relationship. The big domestic savings the Soviets so desperately needed would come not from START but from CFE, which would lead to cost-saving reductions in military manpower and conventional armaments. Nevertheless, Baker and Shevardnadze subsequently agreed on several disputed issues in START.*

On CFE, Gorbachev told the Americans that he could not tolerate the 30,000-troop U.S. advantage in Europe that would be the result of the latest U.S. proposal. He would accept an equal ceiling but not an asymmetrical outcome favoring the West. Echoing Shevardnadze's careful wording of the day before, he said, "I want you to consider this a counterproposal, not a counteroffensive."

Baker replied that he would have to consult U.S. allies over the next few days, but he found Gorbachev's ideas "very interesting."

Gorbachev then dismissed Akhromeyev and the other aides and got down to what really concerned him: the momentous changes in the world, especially in Germany. He warned that German unification might destabilize Europe.

Germany might not be forever satisfied with its current borders, he said. How could he be certain that West German leaders would not renege on their current reassuring statements once they had won back their eastern territory? He insisted that German unification must be "managed"; the "lessons of history" showed that the Soviet Union must play an active part in that process.

Gorbachev's qualms about a unified Germany in NATO were not only political but also emotional. The Nazis had occupied his own home region late in 1942. Compelled to hand their meager food supplies over to their conquerers, some villagers nearly starved. Gorbachev's father fought on the Ukrainian front for five years, and three of his uncles died in the war.

When Baker spoke with Gorbachev about Germany, he was mindful of the old Soviet tendency to play Washington and Bonn off against

---

* One of these was the question of how to limit ALCMs. The Soviets also accepted the U.S. approach on SLCMs: instead of seeking verifiable limits, each side would simply declare to the other once a year the number of weapons it planned to deploy.

each other. Thus he took care to say nothing that the Soviets could leak to Kohl as evidence that the United States was secretly opposed to quick unification and was dealing behind his back.

Baker told Gorbachev that the United States was "sensitive" to Soviet concerns, but unification was "inevitable." Events were moving fast. Unification had been an American goal for forty years and remained so. However, while no one except the Germans could decide the fate of Germany, the "external aspects" of unification were a "different matter," since they involved the security of other nations. Therefore the Soviet Union could indeed reasonably expect to be part of the process of establishing a new, post–Cold War order in Europe.

Since the collapse of the Berlin Wall, in November, Gorbachev and Shevardnadze had publicly acknowledged that Germany might someday be unified, but they had maintained that this should not happen soon, nor should a unified Germany be a member of NATO.

In Washington, Bush and Baker had assumed that they could defer this prickly problem for a while. But throngs of East Germans were racing to the West — 75,000 in January alone. The East Germans moved up their elections to mid-March. Realizing that the victors were sure to be those candidates who were in favor of unification, Bush told his aides that they had better come up with a plan, and quickly.

On the seventh floor of the State Department, Robert Zoellick took the lead in advising Baker on Germany. He and Dennis Ross felt that the Big Four Yalta-style process was outmoded, and the thirty-five-member CSCE too unwieldy. Instead they settled on what they called a "Two-plus-Four" mechanism.

Under this scenario, Germany's legal, political, and economic future would be decided by the leaders of the two Germanys and the four victorious powers of World War II. First, the East and West German leaders would meet to resolve internal aspects of the new state, in a session to be held, most probably, just after the East German elections. The two German powers would then join the Big Four to discuss the external problems of unification.

Ross and Zoellick liked this plan because, as Zoellick observed, it could be a "mechanism for involving us with the Germans" throughout the process; Ross felt that it would allow Gorbachev to say that the Soviets were an integral part of the machinery managing unification. They proceeded to try to win over the State Department bureaucracy and the NSC staff.

When Baker shared the idea with the British foreign minister, Douglas Hurd, Hurd said that he would prefer "Four-plus-Zero" — that is, leaving the Germans out — but would consent to the American plan. In a Washington meeting, the West German foreign minister, Hans-Dietrich Genscher, told Baker that he liked the idea but wished to ensure that it would indeed be "Two-plus-Four," not "Four-plus-Two": Genscher meant that the German people must now have pride of place in any formula that would decide their destiny.

Baker reassured him. He and Genscher agreed to press hard for early German unification and full NATO membership, while promising the Soviets that they had "no interest in extending NATO to the east." In other words, East Germany was a special case. There was no Western plan to encourage the rest of the Warsaw Pact to defect to NATO.

In his talk with Gorbachev on February 9, Baker proposed the Two-plus-Four mechanism to deal with the "external aspects" of German unification. They had to rule out a body composed solely of the four World War II allies, since the "Germans would never accept it." Baker acknowledged the Soviet suggestion to refer the problem to CSCE, but he argued that that apparatus was "far too unwieldy and cumbersome." Two-plus-Four was the "most realistic way to proceed."

Gorbachev allowed that such a mechanism might be "suitable for the occasion," but he refused to commit himself.*

Baker did not exclude the possibility that Germany might ultimately have some more amorphous link to the alliance than full membership, perhaps like that of France, which had political but no military ties to NATO. But in his discussion with Gorbachev, he stressed that the United States favored a "united Germany remaining in NATO and not being neutral," an approach that was "strongly" backed by Bonn. The Soviet Union must not reject the idea out of hand; it was "unrealistic" to expect an economic power the size of a united Germany to be neutral. Moreover, the Soviets should be wary of Germany's seeking neutrality because in that case it would also have to provide for its own security.

The secretary of state knew that Gorbachev and his colleagues were worried mainly about a recurrence of Germany's historical ambition to seize territory to its east. He asked Gorbachev, "Would you prefer to see a united Germany outside of NATO and with no U.S. forces, perhaps

---

* The idea had earlier been mentioned to one of Shevardnadze's deputies, who seemed already to know about it — "maybe because we were tapped," said one Baker aide.

with its own nuclear weapons? Or would you prefer a unified Germany to be tied to NATO, with assurances that NATO's jurisdiction would not shift one inch eastward from its present position?" Baker prodded Gorbachev to agree that only NATO could make sure that Germany would not move eastward.

Gorbachev replied, "Certainly any extension of the territory of NATO would be unacceptable." He spoke of the deep Soviet fear of the Germans, the impact of the Nazis, the deaths of tens of millions of Soviets. From this Baker concluded that Gorbachev might be willing to accept a united Germany as a NATO member if the territory of the former East Germany could be excluded from NATO deployments and maneuvers.

Gorbachev then said, "Well, I'm thinking about the German issue. In fact, I'm going to hold a seminar on Germany." A number of options would be assessed in this forum. Gorbachev repeated to Baker that Germany always evoked strong emotions within Soviet society; if German unification led to a new burst of German nationalism of the kind that had led to two world wars earlier in the century, "our people could move toward Russian nationalism."

Baker did not know how ferocious a struggle Gorbachev and Shevardnadze were already fighting with their Kremlin colleagues over Germany. Yegor Ligachev and other conservative members of the Politburo were still furious that Gorbachev had let East Germany go; the prospect of a united Germany in NATO was salt in the wound.

Even one of Gorbachev's closest aides, Andrei Grachyov, lamented the "reappearance of anti-Communist, anti-Soviet feelings in Eastern Europe, the destruction of Lenin statues, the desecration and acts of barbarism against our cemeteries of Soviet soldiers. It's all very painful." He noted that "our European neighbors are eager not to aggravate the Germans, not to repeat the mistake of the Versailles Pact. But they must be careful not to put the Soviet Union in the position of Weimar Germany — especially since we were not defeated in a war."

Andrei Gromyko's retired deputy Georgi Kornienko, the Soviet Germanicist Valentin Falin, and his deputy in the Central Committee secretariat, Nikolai Portugalov, all demanded that Yakovlev and others "stop" Gorbachev and Shevardnadze from handing Germany over to the Americans.

But Yakovlev had other priorities: he wanted the Soviet government to be able to concentrate on its immense domestic problems undistracted by an endless dispute over the future of Germany. He not only refused to second his colleagues in their anxieties about a united Germany, but told them, "What is so wrong or terrible about that?"

On Saturday, February 10, Chancellor Kohl and his foreign minister, Hans-Dietrich Genscher, flew to Moscow. Baker pointedly refrained from meeting with Kohl and Genscher in order to avoid the public impression that the United States, the Soviet Union, and West Germany were deciding Germany's future in the absence of the British and French.

However, to help prepare Kohl for his meeting with Gorbachev, Baker had entrusted to the West German ambassador in Moscow a three-page, for-your-eyes-only letter for the chancellor. It described Gorbachev's possible openness to a Two-plus-Four mechanism and outlined his concerns about a united Germany, stressing the need to reassure the Soviets that Germany's borders were permanent.*

Baker had informed Bush that Kohl was "anxious and full of suspicion" about the private talks on Germany between the U.S. secretary of state and the Soviet leader. Baker felt that Kohl must be reassured that they were not dealing behind his back. To calm the chancellor and convey the United States' support for quick unification, Bush wrote him an effusive letter, saying that his heart was with Kohl as he took part in the "most important" meeting between a German and a Soviet leader "in decades." If the result of Kohl's session with Gorbachev in Moscow was speedier German unification, that could only mean that "our dream will be here sooner." Bush implored Kohl to insist to Gorbachev that Germany should remain in NATO.

However sincerely U.S. presidents after World War II may have favored a reunited Europe, and whatever their Cold War public rhetoric, most of them had mixed emotions about a united Germany that once again might dominate the continent. Truman, Eisenhower, Kennedy, and Nixon, all well read in history, knew that one did not need to be anti-German to be concerned about the German militarism and expansionism that had led the world into two costly wars.

Bush was largely indifferent to that history. He accepted at face value the argument that the German people of 1990 had no serious relationship to the German people of 1914 or 1939. Now that German

---

* Later Kohl sent a warm and grateful message to Baker, saying that he had used the memo for talking points in his meeting with Gorbachev.

unification seemed inevitable, he wanted to be on the record as one of
the first Western leaders to jump onto the bandwagon: once Germany
became a world power, Helmut Kohl or his successor would remember
who his friends had been.

Not surprisingly, Kohl was overjoyed by Bush's letter. He told his
aides that it was "one of the most important documents in the history
of U.S.-German relations." In his talks with Gorbachev, bolstered by
the letters he had received from Bush and Baker, Kohl pushed the Soviet
leader to agree that it was the "sole right of the German people to
decide for themselves whether they wish to live together in a single
state."

Kohl conceded that unification could only take place if it coincided
with the "legitimate interests of our neighbors, friends, and partners in
Europe and the world." When he asked Gorbachev and Shevardnadze
about their attitude toward a united Germany in NATO, the Soviets
were equivocal.

This Kohl took as an encouraging sign. He and Genscher offered
several inducements, suggesting that Bonn might be willing to provide
financial support for those Soviet troops who remained in eastern Germany; honor all East German commercial contracts with Moscow;
and cut the size of the German army as part of a treaty on European
security.

Bush and Baker were concerned that given a choice between staying in
NATO and proceeding full throttle toward unification, Kohl might bid
NATO good-bye. Hence they sought to create what Robert Blackwill
privately called a "Western cocoon" around Kohl. "If ever he is confronted with the choice of leaving NATO or else breaking with the
Russians," said Blackwill, "Kohl will be surrounded. There will be a
Western chorus standing beside him saying, 'We're with you.' We'll
remind him that whatever happens on Germany this year, Germans will
look back on Bismarck, Adenauer, and Kohl as leaders of equal rank."

As for Gorbachev, the Americans looked for ways to reward him for
his willingness to tolerate a united Germany in NATO. Blackwill answered his own question: "How can we help Gorbachev deal with his
domestic situation? When he comes to Washington in June, let's stage
the most stupendous American-Soviet summit of the postwar era."

The summit would be "Christmas in June" for Gorbachev: "He
could address a joint meeting of Congress. We'll have agreements on

START, CFE, CSCE, chemical weapons, a commercial trade agreement, so that he can go back to Moscow and show his own people what he's gotten from his relationship with the West." Along with those prizes for good behavior would come warnings: Gorbachev would "have to be reminded that he can't split NATO without doing damage to the relations that are bringing him so much. We'll have to remind him that the Senate has to be persuaded to ratify all these treaties. They won't like it if he's just busted up NATO."

Gorbachev would also be reminded that the Soviet Union had its own interest in allowing U.S. troops to remain in Europe, where they could keep an eye on the newly united Germans.

On Sunday evening, February 11, Baker's air force plane landed in Ottawa. Twenty-three NATO and Warsaw Pact foreign ministers were gathering in the Canadian capital to discuss Bush's Open Skies proposal and other arms control matters. On his arrival, Baker told Shevardnadze that he had spoken to Bush about Gorbachev's "counterproposal" on troops in Europe, but he and the president preferred "to stick with our own proposal." The United States, as usual, was hanging tough, insisting on an "asymmetrical" CFE treaty, heavily weighted in favor of the West.

While arms control was on the agenda, Germany was on everyone's mind. In private meetings in corridors, side rooms, and heavily guarded hotel suites, Baker, Hurd, Dumas, and Genscher debated the Two-plus-Four notion. Over breakfast at the West German embassy on Tuesday morning, the four diplomats decided that if they could persuade Shevardnadze to agree now, they should do it. Events in Germany were moving too fast for them to wait.

At a formal session of the Open Skies conference, Baker strolled over to Shevardnadze with a scrap of paper on which he had scrawled language for a Two-plus-Four announcement. Shevardnadze's translator copied it down in Russian. The foreign minister said that he would have to "check" with Gorbachev.

"Oh, by the way," Shevardnadze added, Gorbachev was ready to drop his latest insistence on symmetrical force levels in Europe — provided both sides agreed that the American advantage not exceed 30,000 troops. Astonished, Baker grinned and said, "No problem at all." While Shevardnadze telephoned his boss in Moscow, Baker called Bush, who was equally startled and delighted.

Raymond Seitz, the assistant secretary of state for Europe, felt that the Soviets were "desperate for a CFE agreement. The faster, the better. It's a matter of economic life or death."

Baker agreed: "The Soviets are so determined to get a CFE agreement this year that political decisions are overruling everything else."

Bush knew that Kohl and Genscher, though coalition partners, were far from being close friends or political allies.* Scowcroft told the president he was not sure that Kohl was "on board" Two-plus-Four: "We might be moving too fast on this. You ought to talk to Kohl yourself." Bush called the chancellor and asked, "Do you have any problem with the Two-plus-Four and going ahead with an announcement now?" Kohl said, "No, it's a good idea." After the call, Bush told Baker to move full speed ahead.

Shevardnadze informed Baker that Gorbachev had accepted the Two-plus-Four idea, with some slight changes in the language of the announcement.†

When Two-plus-Four was announced, the Dutch, Italians, and Belgians in Ottawa were furious at being presented with a fait accompli. In a heated meeting, Baker's party politely reminded them that this was a matter for those Allied powers who had legal rights in Germany, "and nobody else." Genscher upbraided the Italian foreign minister, Gianni De Michelis, telling him, "You're not a player in this game."

Kohl declared that Germany was "jumping with a single leap" toward unification: "We have never been so close to our goal, the unity of all Germans in freedom, as we are today."

In Moscow, Valentin Falin was as horrified and belligerent as Kohl was jubilant. He told reporters, "If the Western alliance sticks with its demand of NATO membership for all of Germany, there won't be any unification."

On Saturday, February 24, Kohl and his wife, Hannelore, arrived at Camp David for a weekend with the Bushes and their grandchildren. During the weekend, Bush wore running shoes and a blue flight jacket adorned with the presidential seal and his name in embroidery. A Kohl

---

* They led different parties that had joined in a governing coalition.
† He said that it must not mention the mid-March East German elections or suggest that these would trigger the Two-plus-Four meeting. Gorbachev did not want his East German allies to presume that he had abandoned them. And to mollify the Poles, the text should specify that the Two-plus-Four talks would deal with "issues of security of the neighboring states."

aide marveled at Bush's success in getting his boss to doff his tie: "Can you imagine this happening in Europe?"

The president liked to screen films on Saturdays after dinner. Guests were told that after the lights went down, they could slip away whenever they wished without embarrassment. This evening's selection was a cops-and-corruption thriller called *Internal Affairs,* starring Richard Gere. The president had not been warned that the opening dialogue included the word *motherfucker.* Mrs. Bush disappeared after three minutes, and the Kohls soon afterward.

In their talks over the weekend, Bush and Kohl looked at German unification from various angles, laboring to anticipate every possible Soviet anxiety and objection. Would a united Germany have nuclear weapons? How large an army would it need? Would it guarantee the Polish border?

Genscher reminded Bush that the Bonn government wished to offer the Soviet Union a package of incentives for it to accept unification: financial aid, food supplies, a commitment that existing commercial contracts would be honored, troop cuts, and maximum use of the CSCE process to involve the Soviet Union in the new Europe.

The last item on this list slightly unnerved Bush and Baker, who wondered whether after unification the Germans might try to build up CSCE as a replacement for NATO. They were willing to let Kohl use CSCE to convince Gorbachev that the West did not intend to exploit the Soviet Union's loss of Eastern Europe, but they did not want to accept it as a substitute alliance.

On almost every other issue, there was little disagreement between the two leaders, except about the Oder-Neisse Line, which separated Germany from Poland. With elections ahead, Kohl was reluctant to commit himself to a position that would lose votes. He knew that seven to ten million Germans had family ties to such places as East Prussia and the Sudetenland, now part of the Soviet Union and Czechoslovakia, respectively, and were therefore reluctant to give up the idea of those lands' someday being returned to Germany.

Kohl's stance frustrated Bush, but he decided not to press the matter, not wanting to risk a conflict. He presumed that the chancellor would be more pliable once the German elections were behind him.

The two leaders agreed that U.S. troops should remain stationed in Germany "as a continuing guarantor of stability." To mollify Gorbachev, they resolved that the territory of what would soon be the former East Germany "should have a special military status" that would take account of the "legitimate security interests of all interested countries, including the Soviet Union."

On Saturday, Blackwill gave Kohl's aide Horst Telschik a one-and-a-half-page statement that Bush intended to read at Sunday's joint press conference at Camp David. The text included a sentence asserting that the united Germany should remain a "full member" of NATO, and that this status would include "participation in its military structure." Bush suspected that Kohl would not wish to go that far in public, but on Sunday morning, Telschik told Blackwill, "The statement looks fine."

At their news conference, Kohl refused to pledge that a united Germany's eastern border would not be changed. He said that the question would be "settled definitely by a freely elected, all-German government." Bush said, "I think we're in alignment."*

The veteran UPI correspondent Helen Thomas asked Bush who NATO's enemy was now that the Soviets were "less and less" of a problem: was NATO's new mission "to keep the Germans down"? Adopting a formulation suggested to him by Scowcroft, Bush replied, "No, the enemy is *unpredictability*. The enemy is *instability*."

This statement was both important and problematic. For more than four decades, there had been no question as to who was the principal enemy of the United States and its allies: the Soviet Union and Soviet communism. Yet out of that enmity had come a degree of both predictability and stability. The Cold War, though it had threatened to turn hot over Berlin and Cuba, was also a period of sustained peace between the two mightiest powers on earth.

Now the U.S. president was acknowledging that the old enemy was gone, and with it the order that had come with the Cold War. Moreover, he was identifying as the new enemy not a single, identifiable country or camp of countries but a pair of abstractions: unpredictability and instability. How was the United States or NATO to cope with this new, unsettled state of affairs? No one asked Bush that question, which was just as well because he had no answer.

* Baker said privately, "I don't want to complicate Kohl's domestic political situation on the Polish border." Later a Polish deputy foreign minister complained about Kohl's silence on the eastern German border. He asked Robert Blackwill, "Did you tell Kohl it wasn't good enough?" Blackwill said no, adding, "We don't lecture our friends in public." On March 6, Kohl endorsed a proposal for the East and West German parliaments to renounce any territorial claims to Poland and to instruct a future unified Germany to place a "final seal" on the issue. Gorbachev welcomed the "correction."

*   *   *

On Tuesday, February 27, the Supreme Soviet considered a bill granting Gorbachev the sweeping presidential powers he had requested. He had charged opponents of the bill with "cheap demagoguery." The bill passed by a vote of 306 to 65.

On Wednesday morning, Bush telephoned Gorbachev to congratulate him and also to report on his weekend with Kohl. Both he and the chancellor, he said, felt that a unified Germany should be a "full member of NATO."

"Well," Gorbachev replied, "this is a problem for us, and I'll have to think about it."

Bush was encouraged not to have received a flat no. He thanked Gorbachev for seeing Baker earlier in the month and assured him that he intended to keep his Malta promise to complete START negotiations before their June summit in Washington. He added that he was grateful for Gorbachev's public pledge to support the newly elected Nicaraguan government of Violeta Chamorro.*

On Sunday, March 4, Soviet citizens cast ballots in the first competitive elections for seats in local councils and parliaments in the Russian Republic, Ukraine, and Byelorussia. The best-known candidate was Boris Yeltsin, who defeated eleven rivals from his hometown of Sverdlovsk, winning more than 70 percent of the vote in his race for the Russian parliament.

Yeltsin had campaigned on a platform calling for a free-market system and the liberalized laws on private property that Gorbachev had backed away from the previous December. Now he hoped to persuade his new colleagues to elect him president of the Russian Republic, in place of the incumbent Brezhnev-style Communist Vitali Vorotnikov. In that post, he could challenge Gorbachev and the Soviet leadership from the left.

On Monday, March 12, the Lithuanian parliament unanimously voted formally to "reestablish" the independence their country had lost fifty

---

* In their joint Moscow communiqué, Baker and Shevardnadze had pledged to "respect the results of free and fair elections" in Nicaragua. Assistant Secretary of State Bernard Aronson asked the Soviet diplomat Yuri Pavlov if the Soviets would continue denying weapons to the Sandinistas if Chamorro won; Pavlov said yes.

years before. They chose as their new president Landsbergis, who declared, "We are not asking anyone's permission to take this step."

At the White House, Bush knew that the situation in Lithuania had the potential to derail his relationship with the Soviet Union and Gorbachev. He asked his aides and the State Department to devise language that would allow him to walk the delicate line between Washington's old refusal to concede Lithuania's annexation and his own desire not to create trouble for Gorbachev.

In an Oval Office interview with reporters, Bush refused to allow himself to be pinned down. Asked about the actions of the Lithuanian parliament, he said, "We rejoice in this concept of self-determination. And beyond that, we think it's very important that whatever happens be peaceful."

Of Moscow's hints that the price for Lithuanian secession should be a payment of $34 billion in hard currency to the Soviet government, Bush insisted, "I'll not get into all that, and there are claims on both sides, and that's a matter for them to sort out peacefully. The main thing I keep coming back to — peaceful, peaceful change."

Fitzwater told the press that the United States would not offer Vilnius diplomatic recognition: to be recognized by the U.S., a government must be in control of its own territory and destiny. There were still Soviet divisions on Lithuanian soil, and they could strike at any moment against the local government. On behalf of the president, Fitzwater was warning Landsbergis not to appeal to the United States to fight his battles; instead, he was implying, Landsbergis should work out the best deal he could with the Kremlin.

Gorbachev learned about the situation in Vilnius on the fifth anniversary of his installation as leader of the Soviet Union. At that moment, the Congress of People's Deputies was poised to ratify the Supreme Soviet draft law for a strong, five-year executive presidency and a multiparty political system.*

Appearing before the Congress, Gorbachev rejected the notion of "negotiation" with Vilnius: "You carry out negotiations with a foreign country." The "alarming" Lithuanian declaration was "illegal and invalid," he maintained. The Congress of People's Deputies voted to instruct him to ensure that Soviet laws were enforced in Lithuania.

After being sworn in as the Soviet Union's first executive president,

---

* The bill passed by a vote of 1,817 to 133, with 61 abstentions.

Gorbachev endorsed a "mutually respectful dialogue" with Vilnius: "My idea is to preserve the Union on the basis of a different approach to each republic, on the basis of a new Union treaty."

Then, on Friday, March 16, in his first presidential decision, Gorbachev sent Landsbergis (whom he privately disparaged as "that piano player") a harsh ultimatum: renounce the independence declaration by Monday, or else.

Soviet military planes and helicopters buzzed the rooftops of Vilnius during impromptu "maneuvers" and dropped handbills calling Landsbergis a "tool" of "those who once owned bourgeois Lithuania and disposed of the fates of its people, sold its land and factories to foreign capital, and cost hundreds of thousands of Lithuanians their jobs."

Landsbergis told his parliament that he would not retreat. Like the Hungarians of 1956 who challenged Kremlin rule in vain, he cabled Western governments pleading for "political and moral support."

Even Gorbachev's conservative rival Yegor Ligachev said, "We must resolve this by political means. Tanks will not help in this matter."

But during a private meeting in Moscow with Admiral William Crowe, the former chairman of the U.S. Joint Chiefs of Staff, Defense Minister Yazov made it clear that some military commanders, at least, were eager to move in with the tanks. The Soviet Army was ready to "crush" Lithuania, said Yazov, adding, "If one republic secedes, Gorbachev is through. And if he has to use force to prevent one from leaving, he's out, too."

Gorbachev was receiving conflicting advice: his political comrades were telling him to limit himself to political means against the Lithuanians, while his military comrades were pushing military means. His instinct, as usual, was to tack in one direction one minute and in the other the next — to play both good cop and bad cop almost simultaneously. But he also had to keep in mind his promise to Bush at Malta that he would do everything he could to avoid cracking heads and spilling blood on the streets of Vilnius.

CHAPTER 9

"I Don't Want to Make the Wrong Mistakes"

GORBACHEV'S DEADLINE for Lithuania's surrender was Monday, March 19, 1990. In anticipation, Kremlin ministries were ordered to increase their "protection" of Soviet installations in the renegade republic and forbidden to conduct "any negotiations whatsoever" with Vilnius. Lithuania and the other Baltic states of Estonia and Latvia were warned against issuing their own currency, establishing independent foreign trade relations, or trying to seize Soviet property in their territory.

In Moscow, Gorbachev repeated that he would not bargain with Landsbergis but said he would accept a "dialogue" with the Lithuanian people. The Kremlin would base its next step, he said, on the "character and content" of Landsbergis's reply to his demands.

At the White House, Marlin Fitzwater told reporters that the United States was concerned about the Soviets' "intentions and purposes." Still, he added, "we should be a force for encouraging a peaceful process of development of democracy there and not one of trying to stir up any trouble." In Vilnius, Landsbergis complained that the Bush administration had "sold us out" in favor of its relations with Gorbachev. To a significant degree, Landsbergis was right: Bush believed that the survival of a unified USSR was more important to international peace and stability than an independent Lithuania.

On Tuesday, March 20, Baker saw Shevardnadze in Windhoek, Namibia, where both were attending ceremonies celebrating Namibian independence. During a private meeting, Baker asked the foreign minister what the Soviets were planning to do in Lithuania.

Shevardnadze replied, "To cover the issue fully, I'd need from now until tomorrow morning. We aren't going to use force against Lithuania. We will engage in a dialogue with the Lithuanian leaders. But they need to become more serious about the realities of the situation.

"Who would actually be worse off after independence? Economically, they'd collapse tomorrow if we stopped subsidizing their oil and gas. We have important military facilities there. They can't simply impose independence. We're prepared to take account of their interests, but they have to take account of ours. I'm confident we'll work this out. We will not use force unless they attack our garrisons." Referring to his fellow Georgians, Shevardnadze said, "Our people are really different from the Baltic peoples. The Lithuanians are calm. Ours would probably attack the garrisons."

Baker repeated his familiar warning that the American-Soviet relationship would be affected by whatever happened in Lithuania: "If you use force or coercion, there would be all sorts of consequences. We wouldn't be able to control them." To this Shevardnadze responded, "We've taken note of the nuances in your public statements, and we appreciate them."

Baker said, "We can't continue these nuances forever. If you ratchet up the pressure on this issue, we can't sustain them."

Shevardnadze remarked ominously that the Soviet military was taking a tougher line than ever on Lithuania. Furthermore, having been excluded from the decision-making process on Germany and Eastern Europe, the KGB, the generals, and many party leaders were now demanding "with much emotionalism" that there be no concessions on the Baltics.

On START, the foreign minister indicated that for the moment his hands were tied. Baker concluded that the bureaucracy and the military were pressuring Gorbachev to stand up to the Americans (and to Shevardnadze) on this issue, especially with Germany moving toward unification.

Shevardnadze said he was looking forward to seeing the South African reformist president, F. W. de Klerk. He asked whether de Klerk was sincere. Was Pretoria's movement away from apartheid irreversible? Baker was struck that Shevardnadze was asking the same questions about the South African leader that people in the West often asked about Gorbachev.

Shevardnadze mentioned the African National Congress: "We've known the ANC people for years, but they're different now. They're emphasizing a peaceful, political approach." Once again, the foreign minister seemed to be grasping for a hopeful analogy to the situation in his own country: perhaps the newly unleashed forces of democratization and nationalism in the Soviet Union would, like those in South Africa, be willing to compromise with a reformist regime.

On Germany, Shevardnadze noted that the previous Sunday, voters in the first free East German parliamentary elections had voted in a conservative alliance tied to Kohl's Christian Democrats, making clear their preference for speedy unification with West Germany.

Shevardnadze told Baker that the pace of German unification was "too fast": "We understand that a neutral Germany is a problem. We don't want to see a neutral Germany. We want to see your troops remain. But we have a problem with NATO. It's an imagery problem. It would look as if you had won and we had lost.

"The short-term problem is, how can we explain this domestically? The long-term problem is, how do you know that what we'll see ten years from now is going to be what we want? I have no problem with any current German leaders, but my nagging doubt is about who will replace them. The lessons of history suggest that we cannot be relaxed about the Germans."

As the Baltic crisis swelled, the U.S. press and Congress increased the pressure on Bush to stand up to Gorbachev. "We are playing out one of the great moral moments in modern history," wrote William Safire in the *New York Times*. Rowland Evans and Robert Novak worried that the president's "sweet talk and body English" might be "teaching the Soviet leader that military force can work."

Senators and congressmen demanded immediate diplomatic recognition for Lithuania. Brent Scowcroft noted with regret that even Senator Nancy Kassebaum, the moderate Kansas Republican, was "beating the drums for Lithuanian independence."

Responding to the mounting pressure, Scowcroft warned Ambassador Dubinin that if the Kremlin used force against Lithuania, the president might cancel the June summit with Gorbachev: "Any actions which increase tension or tend to intimidate are not only counter-productive but can affect the entire relationship between the United States and the Soviet Union."

Publicly, however, the administration kept its comments temperate and conciliatory. In Moscow, Gorbachev told his aides that he was grateful for Bush's refusal to raise the temperature of American rhetoric: Western criticism would only make it harder for him to adhere to a "middle course" between nationalists in the republics and hard-liners in Moscow.

On Wednesday, March 21, he issued his first edict as executive president of the Soviet Union: all Lithuanian citizens must give up their weapons for "temporary storage." He also directed the KGB to tighten security on the Soviet-Lithuanian border. Landsbergis rejected the order as intimidation by a "foreign power," enforceable "only through brutal, armed force." He said that the "ghost of Stalinism" was "walking in the Kremlin."

In the Senate, Jesse Helms demanded immediate U.S. recognition for Vilnius. To the relief of both the White House and the Kremlin, the resolution failed by a vote of 59 to 36.

On Thursday, March 22, at a news conference, Bush repeated that the United States had never recognized the Soviet annexation of Lithuania. "However," he allowed, "there are certain realities in life — the Lithuanians are well aware of them — and they should talk, as they are, with the Soviet officials about these differences."

He went on, "We're not here to sit here and say who in Lithuania ought to talk to whom in Moscow. How presumptuous and arrogant that would be for any president! . . . Lithuanians have got elected leaders, and clearly the Soviets have a strong leader. They can figure that out without fine-tuning from the United States."

The next day, Soviet paratroopers occupied Communist party buildings in Vilnius. The commander of Soviet Army ground forces, General Valentin Varennikov, assured Landsbergis by telephone that his men would not seize the Lithuanian parliament building that night. That was his only promise. On Saturday, March 24, a convoy of Soviet tanks and armored personnel carriers rolled past the parliament to a garrison at the edge of the capital.

At the Kremlin on Monday, March 26, Gorbachev received Senator Edward Kennedy of Massachusetts. Primed by Bush in a private meeting before his departure for Moscow, Kennedy asked Gorbachev under what circumstances the Soviet Union would use force against Lithuania. In his reply, Gorbachev tried to appease his American visitor while keeping the pressure on the Lithuanians: force "would be used only if there is violence that threatens the lives of others."

Gorbachev intended this ambiguous formulation to suggest that it was the Lithuanians themselves who were to blame for the prospect of violence. In fact, the leaders and the people of Lithuania had been entirely peaceful in campaigning for independence. Gorbachev called the Lithuanian declaration of independence a "palace coup d'état" — a ludicrous characterization in light of the overwhelming support shown for the declaration both in the parliament and throughout Lithuania.

Kennedy warned Gorbachev of the "high risk" to Soviet-American relations "if there is a Tiananmen Square in Vilnius." Gorbachev responded that he was "committed" to a peaceful resolution of the conflict, but he insisted that Lithuania was an "internal matter." Then he added, "You don't know what pressure I'm under. Many in our leadership want us to use force right now."

In several conversations with his advisers, Bush recalled Dwight Eisenhower and Hungary in 1956 and said, "I am not going to be a president who gives subject peoples the false impression that if they rebel, they are going to get help." He did not want U.S. rhetoric to encourage Landsbergis to adopt an uncompromising position that could lead only to bloodshed.

However, in larger groups with outsiders present, the president took a somewhat tougher line. On Tuesday, March 27, he told Republican leaders that he intended to hold Gorbachev to his pledge not to use force against Lithuania. He noted that the Soviet leader was working on a new secession law that would establish a five-year waiting period after a republic-wide plebiscite for independence. "Let's give the situation a chance to work itself out peacefully," Bush said. Even Newt Gingrich, the combative House Republican Whip and a frequent Bush critic from the right, agreed to back the president, provided there was no bloodshed.

In the privacy of his office that day, Scowcroft read the cables on Kennedy's meeting with Gorbachev and on Admiral Crowe's talks with Soviet generals, who had said that unlike Eastern Europe, Lithuania "would not be let go." Scowcroft was surprised that Gorbachev had implied to Kennedy that he was keeping open the option of using force. It was almost as though the Soviet leader had decided to go along with those who wanted to stage a violent incident that would serve as a pretext for Soviet troops to move into Vilnius.

There was no question in Scowcroft's mind that what he called the "emotional" appeal of Baltic independence must be subordinated to the "hardheaded realities" of American-Soviet relations. For the United States to seem to be actively engaged in encouraging the breakup of the Soviet Union would be "highly provocative," and suggesting to the Russians that it was a "U.S. enterprise" might well increase their determination to crush minorities throughout the Soviet Union.

In private, Scowcroft said what he could not say in public: Americans could do no more than wish the Balts well, since there was a "lot more at stake" in terms of U.S. national interests.

Bush fully agreed. During a meeting with Scowcroft and other aides, he said, "I don't want people to look back twenty or forty years from now and say, 'That's where everything went off track. That's where progress stopped.' "

The obvious question was how to use American influence to restrain Gorbachev. Bush and Scowcroft's answer was to turn down even further the volume of what they were saying from the White House podium, while Bush addressed Gorbachev personally and confidentially with a renewed statement of concern.

On Wednesday, March 28, during a telephone conversation, Bush and Margaret Thatcher agreed that further public pressure on Gorbachev would not be "productive."

The president ordered Fitzwater to halt his slowly escalating criticism of the Soviet Union's actions in Lithuania. As Fitzwater later recalled, "We kept saying we're 'deeply concerned,' we're 'seriously concerned,' we're 'gravely concerned.' It was clear we couldn't keep doing this. So we said that we couldn't comment on Lithuania every day although we might actually have strong feelings about what was going on."

On Thursday evening, March 29, after Kennedy reported personally to Bush on his meeting with Gorbachev, the president sent the Soviet leader a private letter, their first direct communication since the beginning of the Baltic crisis. He emphasized that he was not trying to make Gorbachev's dilemma more difficult. Thus, he was keeping his end of their Malta bargain by refraining from engaging in propaganda or public finger-wagging at Soviet expense. Now it was up to Gorbachev to make good on his own promise at Malta by defusing a situation that was looking more explosive with every passing day.

Jack Matlock was then on his way to Washington. Baker ordered him to return immediately to Moscow and "personally follow up" on the president's letter to Gorbachev. In particular, he was to pursue the notion that the Soviets might solve the Baltic problem by endorsing the results of a plebiscite on independence.

On Saturday, March 31, Gorbachev offered to enter into a dialogue with Landsbergis if the Lithuanian declaration of independence was repealed. Landsbergis asserted it was "both legally and morally" impossible to revoke the declaration. The Presidium of the Lithuanian parliament, however, replied to Gorbachev that it was ready for negotiations "at any level."

Shevardnadze arrived in Washington on Tuesday, April 3, for a three-day meeting with Baker to plan the summit scheduled to begin in late May. Baker asked whether, if Vilnius were to suspend — not repeal but suspend — its independence decree, the Soviets would be ready to start a "meaningful, serious dialogue" and "lift the sanctions."

Deflecting Baker's question, Shevardnadze said, "The Lithuanians will come around. There is a split in the Lithuanian leadership. Things will work themselves out." Yet again, he assured Baker that Moscow would not use military force.

Baker replied, "That's not enough. We have to have a real dialogue. What would it take to get you to agree to one?" Shevardnadze gave another vague answer. After the meeting, Dennis Ross told Tarasenko, "You say you want a dialogue, but we see no indication that you're serious about it."

Tarasenko responded, "We're willing to go along with your idea of a suspension of the independence decree. But the Lithuanians have to be willing to come to Moscow. Gorbachev felt humiliated when he asked Landsbergis to come to Moscow and Landsbergis refused." When Ross asked, "Does the minister [Shevardnadze] feel that way, too?" Tarasenko said, "Not as strongly."

Baker conveyed this message to Landsbergis. The Lithuanian president was relieved that the Soviets were finally showing signs of flexibility, but he was as firm as ever about his own position. Suspending the declaration of independence, he said, would mean that Lithuania would have to operate under Soviet law. However, if the Soviets were willing to go along with a "temporary" suspension, "that might be a way to resolve the problem."

The Bush administration was now thoroughly established as a mediator between Moscow and Vilnius. It was an odd role in several respects. For one thing, the Kremlin, which still considered Lithuania to be an integral part of the USSR, was allowing another country to help in its dealings with what it regarded as an obstreperous province. After many decades of angrily rejecting any American action that smacked of "interference in the internal affairs" of the Soviet state, the Kremlin was now tacitly welcoming American diplomatic intervention. And for good reason: Gorbachev knew that the more Landsbergis listened to the cautionary advice he was getting from Washington, the more time there would be to work out a compromise that might keep the union together. Since that goal still by and large conformed to Bush's desires as well, the United States was actually a less-than-neutral go-between: Bush was more on Gorbachev's side than on Landsbergis's.

Shevardnadze had been accompanied to Washington by Marshal Akhromeyev and Major General Alexander Peresyokin of the Soviet General Staff. During this period, Akhromeyev was complaining to almost anyone who would listen that the Americans were "taking advantage" of the Soviets. They were "winning too much of the time." He was "getting sick and tired of the Americans' always having their way."

He had told Admiral Crowe in March that he and his fellow military officers were "very disillusioned" with Gorbachev's policies and their effect: "I had no idea that *glasnost* would bring out this much disaffection among the Soviet people. There is no basis for it. It demonstrates that our people aren't mature or disciplined enough."

When Shevardnadze and Baker turned to arms control, it became clear that the Soviet military was in a state of near rebellion against its civilian leadership. The foreign minister was forced to renege on several important concessions he had made on cruise missiles during his and Baker's February meetings in Moscow. Baker's face turned white. He said, "I'm not sure what the point of our getting together is if we work out an agreement and then your military backtracks and you say the agreement no longer exists."

After the meeting, Tarasenko confirmed to Ross that his minister was under fierce military pressure. The generals, he said, were angrier than ever about the extent to which Gorbachev's reforms were upending their preeminent place in Soviet society. They were irate about the loss of Eastern Europe and especially East Germany, and furious about secessionism in the Baltics and other republics. Tarasenko told Ross that the military had to be "given the chance to get what they want" in arms control.

When Ross reported Tarasenko's explanation to Baker, the secretary of state wondered whether Gorbachev still had the political authority to make arms control deals. He now doubted that a START agreement could be finished before the Washington summit.

On the Baltics, Gorbachev, in his usual fashion, soon resumed the appearance of moving toward both confrontation and compromise. On Tuesday, April 10, his spokesman, Arkadi Maslennikov, announced that the Soviet government would not insist that Vilnius repeal its declaration of independence. But the Lithuanians must "at least" stop passing laws that contradicted the Soviet constitution.

Then, three days later, Gorbachev sent Landsbergis a letter threatening an economic blockade unless this order was obeyed within forty-eight hours. Baker warned Shevardnadze by telephone that an economic embargo against Lithuania would endanger American-Soviet negotiations on a range of issues, from trade to civil aviation.

On Tuesday, April 17, the Kremlin informed Vilnius that unless its demand was met, Soviet natural gas would be cut off within twenty-four hours, and shipment of oil supplies to Lithuania's main oil refinery halted.

That evening, Bush called Baker, Cheney, and Scowcroft to the White House. Together they decided that if the blockade went forward, the United States should reduce its commercial contacts with Moscow, including a pending commercial trade treaty, since, as Baker said, these were "more directly in their interest than in ours." They resolved that talks on arms control and regional issues should proceed, however, since they were at least as much in the interest of the West as in that of the USSR. The next day, Baker called Shevardnadze and told him that there were "limits" to the administration's patience.

But Gorbachev concluded that as long as he kept up at least the semblance of the "dialogue" that the Americans wanted between Moscow and Vilnius — and as long as he stopped short of outright bloodshed — he could keep turning the screws of economic pressure.

The Kremlin quietly proposed to Landsbergis that Vilnius suspend its declaration of independence for two years while negotiations went forward. Landsbergis replied, "If somebody authorized by Moscow to negotiate presented us with a package of proposals including this, we could have a discussion."

Meanwhile, Moscow extended its economic embargo to metals, wood, tires, sugar, and other materials. On Saturday, April 21, foreign ministers of the European Community, meeting in Dublin, asked the Soviet Union to lift the blockade but, out of respect for the "very difficult position of President Gorbachev," refused to support Vilnius by pledging to send substitute supplies.

In the Cabinet Room on Monday evening, April 23, Bush convened an NSC meeting on the Baltics. Baker reported that none of the twenty U.S. allies consulted favored punitive sanctions against Moscow. Baker, Nicholas Brady of Treasury, Clayton Yeutter of Agriculture, and the president's special trade representative, Carla Hills, all argued that sanctions would be an excessive response — unless Gorbachev resorted to violence on a large scale.

Bush agreed. As Condoleezza Rice observed later that day, "He's afraid to light a match in a gas-filled room." Nevertheless, the president decided to let Gorbachev know that if the Baltic crisis had not been resolved by the time of the Washington summit, the United States would withhold final approval on the American-Soviet commercial trade agreement. This document was nearly completed and was of great domestic political and economic importance to Gorbachev.

The next morning, Bush told a group of contractors who were visiting the White House, "I don't want to do something that would inadvertently set back the progress that has been made in Eastern Europe. . . . And so it is delicate. . . . I'm old enough to remember Hungary in 1956 and where we exhorted people to go to the barricades, and a lot of people were left out there alone." Bush said he wanted to see "progress in the Soviet Union go forward without having some elements that are opposing Gorbachev on all of this crack down and set the clock back to a day that we all remember of a Cold War mentality and confrontation. . . . I love the old expression of Yogi Berra's. You say, 'What happened to the Mets, Yogi?' He said, 'Well, we made the wrong mistakes.' I expect in this job I'll make plenty of mistakes, but I don't want to make the wrong mistakes." Bush believed that adding to the pressures already on Gorbachev would so qualify.

In Vilnius, Landsbergis said, "The Soviets are strangling our nation like a boa constrictor." He declared his land the victim of "another

Munich." This reference to Neville Chamberlain's appeasement of Hitler further reduced Bush's sympathy for Landsbergis. Like many of his generation, Bush regarded Munich as one of the greatest political follies of the century. As a combat pilot in World War II, he had risked his life to help undo its consequences.

Bush sent Gorbachev another private letter warning that the crisis in Lithuania could kill their trade agreement. He wrote that his inability to move forward with the pact did not mean that he had abandoned his support for *perestroika;* it simply reflected political reality. An outraged Congress would be unlikely to ratify the document in any case.

On Thursday, April 26, François Mitterrand and Helmut Kohl wrote Landsbergis to urge that he suspend the independence declaration and bargain with Moscow. Bush had encouraged them to draft the letter. He welcomed this opportunity to give the French and Germans a sense of involvement in one of the first tests of post–Cold War diplomacy.

Primed by the Americans, Lithuanian Prime Minister Kazimera Prunskiene endorsed the Kohl-Mitterrand proposal, an act that solidified her reputation in the West as a more reasonable alternative to Landsbergis. Gorbachev's spokesman, Maslennikov, likewise forewarned by Washington, said that the letter was "not far from the line that the Soviet leadership has been pursuing." As evidence of its sincerity, the Kremlin said that it might consider reducing its natural gas embargo against Lithuania by 50 percent.

On Tuesday, May 1, the Senate resolved by a vote of 73 to 24 to withhold U.S. trade benefits from Moscow until the embargo on Lithuania was lifted and negotiations were begun with Vilnius. Making it clear which Lithuanian leader he preferred, Bush scheduled a White House meeting with Prunskiene. He had not even replied to a letter he had received from Landsbergis.

On Thursday afternoon, May 3, a Lincoln Continental bearing Prunskiene pulled up at the White House gate. A truck was parked there, blocking the way. Prunskiene was compelled to emerge from her car, show her red Soviet passport to a guard, allow her purse to be searched, and walk through a metal detector and up the White House driveway. Her brother, who was accompanying her, was turned away and forced to wait across the street, in Lafayette Park.

While Bush considered Prunskiene preferable to Landsbergis, he was not eager to receive any opposition leaders from the Soviet Union.

White House staff members later claimed that the driveway gate had been broken, but there was an obvious similarity to the way Yeltsin had been treated during his own White House visit the previous September.

Unlike Yeltsin, Prunskiene was at least admitted to the Oval Office. She wisely expressed "regret" to the president for Landsbergis's comment about "another Munich." She also offered to postpone the full implementation of independence until 1992 if negotiations with Moscow were proceeding constructively. Bush praised her patience and foresight.

On Friday evening, May 4, Baker met Shevardnadze in Bonn, where they and the other Two-plus-Four foreign ministers opened discussions on Germany. Waving aside a barrage of questions on Lithuania, Shevardnadze told reporters, "The Cold War is over. Our planet, this world, all of Europe are embarking now on a new road. This is going to be a peaceful period."

At the Kremlin the previous week, the new East German prime minister, Lothar de Maiziere, had irked Gorbachev by saying that he would be willing to see a unified Germany enter NATO if the Western alliance were "changed." Neutrality, he said, was "no solution" because a united Germany should not serve as a "buffer zone." As if in response, NATO took a small but symbolic step to make itself more benign: the alliance formally approved Bush's cancellation of plans for a new generation of Lance missiles and nuclear artillery for Germany.

Shevardnadze told the other five delegations in Bonn that the Soviet Union was ready to agree to quick German unification as long as Britain, France, and the United States postponed for several years a decision on what military ties Germany would have. Kohl rejected this as "negotiation poker."

In a private session with Baker, Shevardnadze praised Bush's decision on Lance but said that it was not enough to make Gorbachev change his mind about accepting a united Germany in NATO. Baker pressed him: "What is it *specifically* that you need?" Shevardnadze could not answer. Baker sensed that his friend and partner had been all but paralyzed by the shift to the right in Moscow.

Baker asked Shevardnadze about a new round of rumors that there would be a pogrom against the Jews the next day in Moscow. "This is a matter of concern to us," he said.

Having dismissed the matter when Baker first raised it, in February, Shevardnadze now seemed to take the danger seriously: "We're doing everything we can. The security forces and the MVD are on a high level of alert. We're watching people who might do such a thing. We've called many of them in. Although we're doing all we can, we can't guarantee that there won't be individual incidents." He added that elements of Pamyat had been prominent when Gorbachev and his colleagues were heckled off Lenin's Tomb during the May Day parade earlier that week.

Shevardnadze obviously now feared that with the Soviet Right ascendant, anything could happen. In raising the possibility of the Soviet authorities' using force to protect Jews against pogroms, Shevardnadze may have been trying to remind Baker that there might also soon be cases in which the Kremlin would be justified in using force to protect ethnic Russians in the non-Russian republics.

Turning to Lithuania, Shevardnadze said, "It is only because of the relationship that you and I have developed that we're prepared to discuss this issue. In other times and with other countries, we would have said that this was an internal issue. We draw a distinction with you."

The foreign minister said that just as the Bush administration had to deal with its own domestic concerns, so he and Gorbachev were under severe pressures: "We need a little more time on Lithuania. We'll be patient. We won't use force. We'll find a political solution."

Baker noted that Shevardnadze seemed less anxious about Lithuania than before. He wondered whether perhaps his Soviet counterpart might be too complacent about the problem. "We've heard you talk about a dialogue, but we've still seen no signs of it," he said. Shevardnadze replied, "The Lithuanians have to take the first step."

Baker said, "Your problem is that they don't believe you'll follow them. It's in your interest to convince them." Why was it so difficult to sign an agreement with Vilnius? Shevardnadze insisted, "Things are moving in the right direction. But we want to wait to see more signs of seriousness from the Lithuanians."

The next day, Ross took Tarasenko aside and said, "What I heard last night was someone who seemed quite relaxed about Lithuania. Shevardnadze almost seemed to feel that everything will work itself out now." Tarasenko said, "Yes, we're past the point of crisis."

Ross concluded that the Soviets were seeing a fissure in the Lithuanian leadership between Landsbergis and the more accommodating Prunskiene. Perhaps Gorbachev also felt that he was finally striking a stable balance between the forces on either side of him in the Soviet government.

When he and Shevardnadze met again that day, Baker warned that because of the continuing confrontation between Moscow and Vilnius, it would be "very difficult" to sign a trade agreement at the Washington summit. He and Bush were not imposing any "formal linkage," but getting a trade pact through Congress during an economic blockade against Lithuania would be "tough, maybe impossible."

Calling what he hoped was Baker's bluff, Shevardnadze replied, "We won't be pleased if there's no trade agreement, but it won't be any tragedy. We didn't have it before. We won't dramatize it. If you can't do it, you can't do it. This will be a symbol of the state of our relations, but we won't play it up."

On arms control, Baker chose not to take Shevardnadze to task for his April backtracking on START. Instead he told him that Bush had approved some new American compromises on cruise missiles to answer some of the Soviet military's objections. He hoped that Shevardnadze could now sell a final deal to his own side.

On Monday, May 14, Helmut Kohl took another big step toward German unification. Discarding his earlier insistence on delaying an all-Germany election until 1991, he announced that he was "open" to a date later in 1990.

This decision had been hastened by a local election defeat for Kohl's Christian Democratic Union the previous day. Germans were beginning to comprehend how much unification would cost; the longer the process took, Kohl knew, the less popular it would become. Kohl was also growing anxious that the disgruntlement of the Soviet military might affect the Kremlin's willingness to tolerate German unification. Genscher agreed, saying, "History does not repeat its offers."

That same day, in Moscow, Kohl's aide Horst Telschik slipped into the Kremlin and pledged to Gorbachev that after unification, Bonn would undertake to finance and provision the 360,000 Soviet troops in East Germany for several years, and would then build housing for them when they returned to the Soviet Union.

Gorbachev gave Telschik the impression that he would look more kindly on early unification if Kohl were willing to take the lead in persuading Western countries to aid the Soviet Union. Telschik reminded Gorbachev that the year before, he had invited the chancellor to visit his longtime home in Stavropol. Perhaps now was the time for Kohl to take up that invitation — and to hold face-to-face talks with Gorbachev.

*   *   *

In Moscow on Tuesday, May 15, Baker met with Shevardnadze in the gloomy, castellated Spiridonovka Palace, once the official Moscow residence of Stalin's foreign minister, Vyacheslav Molotov. Baker and his aides wondered whether Shevardnadze would be his old cooperative self or the melancholy, querulous figure of April and early May.

Once again, the Baltic crisis shadowed their talks. On April 11, the Estonian parliament had abolished the conscription of Estonian citizens into the Soviet Army. On May 4, the Latvian parliament had declared independence from the Soviet Union.

Gorbachev had been trying desperately to prevent these other two Baltic states from slipping away, even promising loosened ties to Moscow if they would only remain part of a Soviet confederation. But once it became clear that Latvia and Estonia were as intent on complete independence as Lithuania, Gorbachev hurled more thunderbolts, proclaiming the new actions null and void and threatening more economic sanctions.

Baker now told Shevardnadze, "I want to remind you of what I said in Bonn — that it will be difficult to get a trade agreement unless there is a positive change in the Baltics."

Shevardnadze replied, "Remember what *I* said. If you can't sign it, we won't make you sign it." He acknowledged that with the Estonian and Latvian developments, "the situation has changed since we last spoke." Then he added, "Ask Gorbachev about it."

As Shevardnadze briefed Baker on the trouble Gorbachev was having with *perestroika*, his feistiness returned. "There will be no turning back!" he vowed: Gorbachev was "committed." Still, the transition to a "regulated market economy" would be very difficult indeed.

Baker and his aides noted the new phrase "regulated market economy." They judged it to be more Gorbachevian hokum, some sort of hybrid between a genuine free market and a socialist economy that would allow Gorbachev to insist that he had not abandoned communism. As Baker later said, the fundamental problem was Gorbachev's inability "to fish or cut bait on economic reform."

Shevardnadze went on to say that *perestroika*, if it continued, would be accompanied by disruptions and hardships. The Soviet Union would need $20 billion in credits and other Western aid to cushion Soviet society against these shocks. The West, he suggested, should show its support of *perestroika* "at a moment when it counts."

Baker did his best to lower Shevardnadze's expectations about how much help the USSR could expect from the West: for now, any U.S. aid could only be in the form of expertise and technical cooperation. "Loans will be hard to do at a time when the Soviet Union is sending billions of dollars to Cuba and other troublemakers," he said.

On Thursday, Baker and Shevardnadze dined at the Moscow home of a Georgian artist. Also invited was Yevgeni Primakov. Saying that he was growing "tired," Shevardnadze hinted that he might soon leave the Foreign Ministry. Baker presumed from Primakov's presence at this meal that he might be in line to succeed Shevardnadze; rumors to that effect had been circulating for some time, and Primakov, who met frequently with Western visitors, had done nothing to discourage such speculation.

On Friday morning, May 18, Baker saw Gorbachev at the Kremlin. Like Shevardnadze, the Soviet leader seemed more positive about the showdown in the Baltics than he had in the past.

Gorbachev had met the day before with Prunskiene. In doing so, he backed away from his insistence that he would see no Lithuanian official until the Vilnius regime accepted Soviet authority over Lithuania. He saw Prunskiene partly in response to American calls for "dialogue" and partly to exploit the tension between her and Landsbergis. During a strained meeting, Gorbachev promised to open direct talks between Moscow and Vilnius, but with the usual condition: only if the Lithuanian parliament suspended its declaration of independence.

Now Gorbachev told Baker, "I had a good discussion with Mrs. Prunskiene. She will go back to her parliament and argue for suspension of the declaration of independence. I hope she'll manage to get it through."

Baker reminded Gorbachev that he and Bush did not have a "lot of room to maneuver": so long as the Kremlin was using pressure tactics against the Baltics, the U.S.-Soviet trade agreement was in jeopardy.

Gorbachev said he wanted to "change the climate." But there would be "difficult problems" to solve: "We'll set up committees on the economy and security. It'll take some time, but we'll do it. . . . I still think independence is a mistake for them, but we're not going to prevent it. . . . We'll go along with the Lithuanians and work out whatever status they want."

He listed other complications. Several Soviet republics had claims on Lithuania, and his own citizens were pressuring him not to permit secession and to protect ethnic Russians in the Baltics. The letters were pouring in. The president of the United States would never tolerate such a move by one of the fifty states, Gorbachev declared; in such a case, President Bush would go to great lengths to guard Americans in danger. He himself had the same obligation toward Russians in Lithuania.

Baker mentioned that on Wednesday evening, he had met with fifteen Soviet Jews who had been refused exit visas. Gorbachev said that he was under pressure from even the moderate Arab states to slow the emigration of Soviet Jews to Israel, since they were being used to populate the occupied territories of the West Bank and the Gaza Strip. His Kremlin colleagues were complaining that he was throwing away years of Soviet diplomacy in the Middle East. "I'm being attacked," he said.

Gorbachev, Shevardnadze, and Akhromeyev were now joined by Primakov and General Branislav Omelichev, the second-most-powerful general in the Soviet Union. Baker suspected that Omelichev was there to act as a military watchdog, to make sure that Gorbachev gave nothing away in CFE or START. He noted that Gorbachev paid ostentatious attention to the general and virtually ignored Akhromeyev.

Still, when the secretary of state raised a technical issue of arms control, Gorbachev called on Omelichev like a schoolboy to answer the question. The general seemed so nervous even to be at such a meeting that he did not know whether to remain seated or stand at attention.

Baker told Gorbachev that he was "disappointed" that they had recently taken "no meaningful steps" toward CFE. Turning to START, he addressed some issues that had arisen since February. The most immediate was a new American air-launched cruise missile (ALCM) called Tacit Rainbow, which the U.S. Air Force hoped to deploy by the thousands. Since it was designed to carry a conventional warhead, the air force was arguing that it should not fall under the terms of a nuclear arms treaty.

Baker proposed that Tacit Rainbow be excluded from the provisions of a START treaty on new weapons since the missile already existed. Noting their concurrence on other points, he said, "You've got a deal — and we close ALCMs — provided that Tacit Rainbow is grandfathered." Gorbachev replied, "Yes, we've got a deal." He and Baker shook hands.

However, when U.S. negotiators arrived at a state guesthouse a few hours later to draw up language for the treaty, the Soviets were back to demanding restrictions on Tacit Rainbow.* Baker blew up at Shev-

---

* They wanted limits on the missile's future modernization and guarantees that it would not later be transformed into a nuclear weapon.

ardnadze, charging him with negotiating in bad faith. "How can we do business this way?" he fumed.

Shevardnadze said, "There's no need to get angry." After the meeting, Tarasenko came up to Ross and told him that Shevardnadze knew the problem was largely the fault of the Soviets. He would try to find a way out, he said: "Could you send us a letter describing Tacit Rainbow's capabilities?"

The next day, Baker complied and settled the matter.* On the flight back to Washington, he told reporters in the back of his plane that Gorbachev was still "very much in charge." But privately he was more worried than ever about the pressures on Gorbachev from the right. He even wondered whether the Soviet president might renege on the agreements they had just reached when he came to Washington for the summit with Bush a fortnight hence.

As the summit approached, Ambassador Dubinin dutifully went about the task of preparing for Gorbachev's arrival. The Americans had come to respect him. Speaking virtually no English when he took up his post in Washington in 1985, he had learned the language with extraordinary speed and since then had proved a fairly reliable conduit of messages between Moscow and Washington.

Dubinin was not without a sense of humor, though it was always in keeping with the official line. That spring, the White House wanted to know whether Gorbachev would consent to come to Kennebunkport so that Bush could offer him the same informal hospitality he had shown other foreign leaders, among them Helmut Kohl. They asked if Gorbachev had any hobbies: did he fish, for example, or play tennis? Dubinin replied, "Gorbachev has only one hobby — *perestroika!*"

Back in Moscow, however, Dubinin had long been the object of sniping, particularly from Alexander Bessmertnykh, who had served in Washington before and wanted to return as ambassador. Bessmertnykh even committed the diplomatic indiscretion of asking American visitors to Moscow whether Dubinin was "up to the job."

A week before the summit, Gorbachev abruptly sent Bessmertnykh to replace Dubinin, who was transferred to Paris. When Dubinin went to the White House for a farewell talk with Bush, the president took

---

* He told Shevardnadze that he would provide a written description of the missile's capabilities and limits on its planned deployment without specific promises about the future.

him for a walk around the White House grounds. There were tears in Dubinin's eyes. Afterward, he told an aide, "I started out skeptical about Bush, but I don't feel that way anymore. He may be inarticulate, but he hasn't made a mistake yet in our relations."

When Bush greeted Bessmertnykh for the first time as ambassador, he recalled his earlier service in Washington and said, "Welcome back home!"

When the Supreme Soviet of the Russian Republic met in Moscow in late May, Boris Yeltsin shifted his campaign for the post of supreme leader of the new Russian government into high gear. He promised to champion Russian sovereignty: under him, Russia would run its own economic affairs, have its own foreign policies, and sign treaties with the other Soviet republics.

On May 24, Gorbachev's prime minister, Nikolai Ryzhkov, presented the Kremlin's latest package of economic reforms, approved by Gorbachev's Presidential Council. It quickly became clear that the "Ryzhkov plan" would in time triple the price of bread, which almost instantly disappeared from stores all over the Soviet Union as citizens rushed to hoard supplies. The growing resentment of Gorbachev's policies made Yeltsin all the more popular.

Gorbachev went before the Russian parliament and accused Yeltsin of trying to "excommunicate Russia from socialism" and to break up the Soviet Union by "rejecting the principles established by Lenin." When balloting began for chairman of the Russian parliament, Gorbachev endorsed the old Russian Republic prime minister, Alexander Vlasov, who promptly quit the race to avoid certain defeat.

Yeltsin's chief remaining rival was Ivan Polozkov, one of Gorbachev's most conservative critics. Alarmed that Yeltsin was fast becoming the most popular political figure in the Soviet Union, Gorbachev quietly endorsed Polozkov, instructing his people to do everything they could to stop Yeltsin.

When Yeltsin failed to win a majority on the first and second ballots, Polozkov dropped out and Vlasov resumed his candidacy. On Tuesday, May 29, the day of the climactic vote, Gorbachev led his large party onto a fleet of Aeroflot jets bound for North America.

CHAPTER 10

"Two Anchors Are Better"

GORBACHEV was eating his lunch somewhere over the North Atlantic when he was informed that the new president of Russia would be Boris Yeltsin. "Well," he told his aides, "we're going to have to negotiate with him. I won't bear grudges."

But on his arrival in Ottawa, he declared to reporters, "If Yeltsin is playing a political game, then we are in for difficult times." During the Soviets' stopover, Canadian Prime Minister Brian Mulroney called Bush three times to warn that Gorbachev was in a "sarcastic and grumpy" mood. He advised the president not to start formal talks as soon as Gorbachev got to the White House: better to "walk him around the grounds" first and try to get him to relax a little.

At 6:50 on Wednesday evening, May 30, 1990, Gorbachev's blue and white jet landed at Andrews Air Force Base. Looking harried, Gorbachev emerged from the forward door of the plane, with his wife, Raisa, clutching his right elbow. They walked down the ramp and shook hands with Baker. A motorcade took them into the capital city past demonstrators holding a variety of placards: "SUPPORT GORBACHEV" . . . "QUIT LITHUANIA" . . . "STOP ATTACKING ARMENIANS."

The contradictory exhortations were a reminder of the several competing strains in U.S. domestic attitudes toward the USSR: widespread approval for Gorbachev and his policies contrasted with the more critical views of various ethnic groups, such as Baltic- and Armenian-Americans, who saw the Soviet leader as an oppressor of their kinsmen who were still inmates in the "prison of nations."

On Thursday morning, Gorbachev's armor-plated limousine rolled up to the South Portico of the White House. In the ninety-degree heat, the Soviet president was welcomed by a salute of howitzers, martial music, and a fife and drum corps in colonial dress.

Bush had prepared for this summit with briefings on internal Soviet politics, the Soviet economy, and the nationalities problem. On Memorial Day weekend, Robert Gates had flown up to Kennebunkport with two fat briefing books for the president. The Baltic crisis had long before put an end to the idea that Gorbachev might address a joint session of Congress.

Fitzwater had predicted that Bush's approach to Gorbachev at the summit would be one of "tough love." He borrowed the term from an American movement that advocated dealing with problem children through a combination of emotional reinforcement and strict discipline.

In his welcoming address, Bush asked Gorbachev to help further the "process of building a new Europe, one in which every nation's security is strengthened and no nation is threatened. . . . And as I've said many times before, we want to see *perestroika* succeed."

Gorbachev's formal reply included a barbed reference to past Soviet suffering at German hands: "I come to the United States with the impression still fresh in my mind of how our people are celebrating the forty-fifth anniversary of the victory over nazism, and of my meetings with war veterans."

Heeding Mulroney's advice, Bush casually strolled off with Gorbachev toward the Oval Office, where they had a tête-à-tête. Their first talk was philosophical — where they were, where they were going — but intense. Bush did not check his wristwatch until twenty minutes past the time the meeting was supposed to end.

Gorbachev told him that they were in a "new era," with "much uncertainty but much promise." They were "moving beyond our enemy status." He gloomily described the crisis in the Soviet economy: Western aid was "really needed." He hoped that Bush was "serious" about wanting *perestroika* to succeed.

The Soviet leader said that he realized that a trade agreement would bring the Soviet people little immediate practical relief, but he felt it would be an important symbol that his policy of cooperating with the West was bringing rewards. He confessed, "I *need* this."

The official U.S. position had long tied normalized economic relations with Moscow — including most-favored-nation (MFN) benefits — to a new Soviet law allowing citizens to emigrate freely. Along with Congress, Bush and Baker had specifically linked the signing of the trade agreement to the lifting of Soviet sanctions against Lithuania.

The Kremlin had promised Washington that an emigration bill would be passed at the end of May, but the hard-liners had dug in, asking why the United States should be rewarded for improving trade relations when such improvements were presumably in the interests of both countries. Others in Moscow had begun to comprehend the effects of the bill beyond the exodus of Soviet Jews: they could easily imagine a "brain drain" that would deprive the Soviet Union of its most educated citizens.

A few days before Gorbachev's arrival, Baker had learned that enactment of the Soviet emigration bill was being postponed until the fall. Moreover, the blockade against Vilnius was still on. At Baker's behest, his assistant secretary for Europe, Raymond Seitz, called Bessmertnykh and informed him, "The trade agreement will not be signed at this summit." The Soviets clumsily replied that if there was no trade agreement, they might retaliate by scuttling a pending grain agreement much desired by American farmers. The Americans shrugged off the threat; the USSR, with its permanent crisis in agriculture, needed to import grain more than the United States needed access to the Soviet market.

Now, in the Oval Office, Bush told Gorbachev that on the trade agreement, his hands would be tied until the Soviet Union passed an emigration law. Even then, it would be "extremely difficult" for him to persuade the Senate to approve the pact unless the Kremlin eased its sanctions against Lithuania.

Gorbachev said that he could not do so "just yet": it would encourage the secessionists and enrage his own hard-liners. But in keeping with his pledge at Malta, he repeated that he did not intend to use force against the Baltic states; he still hoped to solve the crisis through dialogue.

Bush responded that he wanted to be "helpful" to *perestroika,* but "we have concerns": the U.S. administration did not feel "entirely comfortable" with the Soviet positions on aid to Cuba, German unification, and internal economic reform.

Baker met separately with Shevardnadze. When the secretary of state ran down the list of agreements that he thought they could sign before the summit was over, Shevardnadze said, "I see that the trade agreement isn't there." Baker replied, "As I said in both Bonn and Moscow, it would be difficult for us to send it to Congress unless you change the Lithuanian situation."

Shevardnadze had the same air of resignation he had displayed in Bonn and Moscow. Almost pleading, he said, "I must tell you how important it is to us that we conclude this agreement at this summit. Otherwise, how can we explain it to our people in Moscow when we return?"

Baker had never seen the foreign minister more emotional. Playing his own strong hand, he said dryly, "I don't know why you can't simply use the argument that in light of Lithuania, the U.S. can't conclude this."

Shevardnadze confided that Gorbachev needed something to show at home for his standing in the West: "I've rarely spoken like this with you, but it's just *extremely important* that this be done."

Never before had Gorbachev's domestic difficulties made him so desperate for the benefits of good relations with the United States. Never before had Shevardnadze made it so clear to Baker how much Gorbachev depended on Bush's indulgence and support.

The official schedule had Bush showing Gorbachev his horseshoe pit outside the Oval Office, and perhaps even tossing a few with him. But the morning session ran forty minutes long, and Gorbachev had to make his apologies and rush back to his embassy, where he was to host a luncheon in the rococo ballroom for sixty American "intellectuals and opinion leaders."

The embassy staff had been told that Raisa Gorbachev wished to meet movie stars and other celebrities. The guests at the luncheon included Jane Fonda, Ted Turner, Isaac Asimov, Van Cliburn, Douglas Fairbanks, Jr., Pamela Harriman, Dizzy Gillespie, Armand Hammer, Jesse Jackson, and Andrew Wyeth. Frank Sinatra and Robert Redford sent their regrets. John Kenneth Galbraith told Gorbachev that as an economist he represented a "profession that has surely caused the world more suffering than any other." The host laughed. He jokingly referred to Henry Kissinger as "my contentious old friend."

As Kissinger mingled with the Soviets who were present, he was astounded that Gorbachev's own aides seemed willing to bad-mouth their boss barely out of his earshot. When he asked Primakov whether the Soviets had realized what the consequences of tearing down the Berlin Wall would be, Primakov replied that they had had "no idea," adding that it wasn't "our" decision at all. He pointed at Gorbachev: "It was *his!*"

Gorbachev gave a disjointed, testy speech warning that no one should try to pressure him or the Soviet Union on the misconceived notion that it was "enfeebled." Talk of weakness was "just not serious." He said that for Americans, "it is all so easy. You have all the mechanisms and institutions in place." But in Moscow, "Oh, how we have to twist our brains!"

That afternoon, Gorbachev met with Bush and their advisers in the Cabinet Room. Bush and Baker gave Gorbachev and Shevardnadze a list of "assurances" intended to make a unified Germany in NATO more tolerable for the Soviets.*

Gorbachev replied by suggesting that Germany be a member of both NATO *and* the Warsaw Pact. He cited the president's U.S. Navy background: "You are a sailor. You will understand that if one anchor is good, two anchors are better." Bush said that he did not understand "how two anchors could work"; German membership in NATO alone was a better idea.

Gorbachev then delivered a confused and meandering statement on Germany. The Soviet people, he said, could not accept that Germany, their enemy in World War II, and NATO, their enemy in the Cold War, should now be joined: "We know why NATO exists. . . . It is a Cold War organization."

Still, he wondered whether it "shouldn't be the German people who decide whether or not they're to be in NATO." Just as a united Germany was "consistent with the principle that people should have the right to

---

* They were as follows: U.S. willingness to consider limitations on a united Germany's armed forces; acceleration of talks on short-range nuclear forces in Europe; transitional arrangements for Soviet troops to remain in East Germany for several years; a ban on nuclear, chemical, and biological weapons for Germany; German border guarantees; strengthening of CSCE; renovation of NATO to make the alliance seem less menacing to Moscow; and arrangements for Bonn to finance the remaining Soviet troops in East Germany and their housing in the Soviet Union on their return home.

choose their alliances," so the "external relationships" of the German people "should be up to the Germans."

Bush pressed the Soviet president for specifics on such a referendum but failed to elicit any. He welcomed Gorbachev's admission that a united Germany should be able to decide for itself with which alliance it wished to be associated. Seizing the opening, he asked Gorbachev if he would be willing to repeat what he had just said in a public statement.

Gorbachev nodded. Listening to this exchange, several members of the Soviet delegation were conspicuously appalled — especially Valentin Falin, long the Kremlin's senior expert on Germany. Shevardnadze took his boss aside for an intense, quiet discussion while Falin filibustered.

When Gorbachev resumed speaking for the Soviet side, he began to back away from what he had said. Robert Gates concluded that Gorbachev had "gone beyond his brief." In an obvious attempt to delegate a matter on which he was now in trouble with his own comrades, Gorbachev three times asked Shevardnadze to work with Baker on the German problem.

At first Shevardnadze bluntly refused, saying, "This is an issue to be solved by the heads of government. . . . We need some political direction here." Finally, however, he relented.

The Americans were astonished. Never before had a Soviet foreign minister so baldly resisted his chief in their presence. They reasoned that Gorbachev was trying to get Shevardnadze to take the heat for whatever happened on Germany, and that the foreign minister was unwilling to go along.

Going even further than he had at Malta, Gorbachev specifically declared his hope that the U.S. military would remain in Europe for a long time. He told Bush, "I want you to know that I regard this as in your interest and our interest. And that, I *am* willing to say publicly."

As they listened to Gorbachev's soliloquy, several of the Americans felt that for the moment, at least, he had lost his usual ability to pretend that he had all the answers. Robert Blackwill noted how much less controlled, exacting, and commanding Gorbachev seemed than he had at Malta.

Bush brought up his Open Skies proposal, which had been languishing along with other arms control issues: "I feel bewildered that you haven't signed up. We don't understand. If the problem is technology, we'll sell you the technology you need." Gorbachev said, "That sounds pretty close to our position. Isn't that right, Marshal Akhromeyev?"

The marshal shook his head vigorously and insisted, "No, we cannot open all areas of the Soviet Union unless we have the right to fly over U.S. bases in the Philippines and other areas of the world!" The Americans were struck by this additional instance of insubordination and this new hint that Gorbachev was losing control over his military.

When Gorbachev emerged from the West Wing late that afternoon, he characteristically gave an impromptu press conference to describe the day's meetings in a light most favorable to himself. U.S.-Soviet differences on Germany had "somewhat narrowed," he said, but now it was for Baker and Shevardnadze to take up the matter, as "I think it is not here that the German question will be resolved." Annoyed at Gorbachev's showboating, Bush watched the performance on television.

On his way back to the embassy, Gorbachev stopped his limousine and got out at Fifteenth Street and Pennsylvania Avenue. He was eager to re-create the magic of December 1987, a simpler and better time for him. When the crowd cheered and applauded, Gorbachev drank in the adulation. Through his interpreter, he shouted, "I feel really at home!" It was an odd but telling remark, for back home he would have received nothing like this reception from his own people.

Bush's aides coaxed their boss into the Rose Garden to put his own spin on the day. "The tone was positive," Bush told the press, but he added pointedly, "Differences remain. . . . When he says this whole German question will not be solved in a meeting of this nature, I would agree with that."

That evening, the Bushes honored the Gorbachevs at a state dinner, with entertainment by the mezzo-soprano Frederica von Stade. Unlike the Americans, who were dressed in black tie and formal gowns, Gorbachev wore a business suit — and tried to do business during the meal, lobbying his hosts to go ahead and sign the Soviet-American trade pact.

The next morning, Bush called Chancellor Kohl in Bonn to assure him that he had cut no secret deal with Gorbachev on Germany. At the Soviet embassy, over breakfast with twelve U.S. congressional leaders, Gorbachev complained about the Bush administration's "rigid position" that a "united Germany must belong to NATO."

When Senator George Mitchell asked him about the prospects for *perestroika* and Western investment, Gorbachev droned on for twenty-eight minutes about various kinds of property, leaseholds, private ini-

tiatives, and entrepreneurship. Even as he appealed for normalized economic relations, he allowed his frustration over the Baltics — and
Western criticism of his policies there — to come pouring out: "What
do we need to do for you to give us MFN? Maybe we should introduce
presidential rule in the Baltics and at least fire some bullets!"

He went on, "Why did you let your administration intervene in Panama if you love freedom so much? . . . It would be humiliating if we
were to beg for something from you."

At eleven o'clock, Gorbachev was driven to the White House. To
keep him from making another unplanned television appearance, Bush's
aides diverted him from reporters.

Watching Gorbachev's breakfast with the legislative leaders on television, Bush had been affected by the Soviet president's appeal for signature of the trade treaty. Now, during their morning meeting, he told
Gorbachev that he was "exploring" the possibility of signing the trade
agreement that afternoon, but once again he emphasized that it would
be very difficult to get Congress to approve it without a peaceful settlement of the Lithuanian situation.

The two men agreed to quicken the pace of the CFE talks, but they
could not overcome the final obstacles to a START treaty. They sent
Baker and Shevardnadze out to work on the arms control logjam with
their experts at the State Department, but with General Omelichev en-
forcing Soviet intransigence, they made little progress.

So great was Gorbachev's thirst for public affection and proof of his
stature in the West that he devoted four hours of the afternoon to
accepting five awards from various organizations, one at a time.* As
Gorbachev beamed, representatives of each group solemnly entered the
Soviet embassy's ornate reception hall, hung its banner on the wall,
and lavished him with praise before Soviet and American television
cameras. Condoleezza Rice later said that when she saw these four
hours on the schedule, "That's when I knew that things must be hard in
Moscow!"

The White House East Room was being prepared for a televised ceremony at five o'clock, at which Gorbachev and Bush would sign those
agreements they had been able to complete.† When the arms control

---

* They were the Albert Einstein Peace Prize, the Franklin Delano Roosevelt Freedom
Medal, the Martin Luther King, Jr., Non-Violent Peace Prize, the Man of History Award,
and the Martin Luther King, Jr., International Peace Award.
† These included agreements on chemical weapons, nuclear testing, student exchanges,

sessions at the State Department ran overtime, the ceremony was post-poned for an hour.

Throughout the afternoon, Bush's economic advisers pressed him to normalize trade relations with Moscow as soon as possible, as a stimulus both to internal Soviet reform and to East-West commerce. His political aides, however, cautioned against any move that might be interpreted as a favor or reward to Gorbachev at a time when he was still bullying the Balts.

Moved by Shevardnadze's emotional appeal the day before, Baker advised the president in a midafternoon telephone call to sign the commercial trade treaty. Bush consented, on the condition that Gorbachev renew his promise to settle the Baltics crisis through peaceful dialogue, not through the use of force. His decision was made so late that no one had thought to bring the documents themselves to the White House; a courier had to be sent to the Commerce Department to fetch them.

At six o'clock, the American and Soviet delegations, congressmen, senators, and others took their places in the East Room. Before following Bush into the chamber, Gorbachev asked him, "Are we going to sign the trade agreement?" Bush said, "Yes." Smiling broadly, Gorbachev said, "This really matters to me."

Bush warned him that he would not send the pact to Congress or grant MFN status before the Soviet emigration law was passed and the blockade on Lithuania lifted. He said that he was inclined to explicitly mention both linkages in his public statement.

Gorbachev pleaded with him not to link the agreement to Lithuania; that would make him appear weak and subject to outside pressure in the eyes of hard-liners at home. With great reluctance, Bush agreed to this request.

The two leaders then walked into the East Room and sat down at the exquisite carved wooden table that had been used to sign other treaties dating back to the Kellogg-Briand Pact of 1928, an attempt to commit the great powers not to resolve their controversies by war. Much of the audience was still in suspense over whether Bush would sign the trade agreement.

Bush tipped his hand in a single sentence near the end of his opening statement: "President Gorbachev and I are also signing a commercial

---

the peaceful use of atomic energy, and a future international park on Alaskan and Siberian land along the Bering Strait, as well as a compromise joint statement on the still-unfinished strategic arms treaty.

agreement and are looking forward to the passage of a Soviet emigration law."

It was a classic example of Bush's preferred way of dealing with Gorbachev — and a good illustration of why that way was often so effective. Bush had granted the Soviets something they desperately wanted, and he had made the favor conditional on a major concession on their part. Yet by treating the whole issue in such a low-key, almost offhand manner — and by not rubbing Gorbachev's nose in the Soviet concession — he had managed to impose exactly the sort of linkage between U.S.-Soviet trade and the Kremlin's policies toward its own citizens that previous Soviet leaders had always found not only objectionable but unacceptable.

That evening, Bush's motorcade roared up to the Soviet embassy in a blur of sirens and flags for a return dinner hosted by the Gorbachevs. This time all the men were in business suits. The Bushes were escorted up the grand staircase, past the huge portrait of Lenin, to the second floor, where they were greeted by their hosts.

In his toast, Gorbachev said, "What happened today . . . has been made possible only in the environment produced by our meeting with President Bush at Malta." Bush said, in turn, "Yesterday we welcomed the Gorbachevs back to Washington still filled with memories of the things we shared in Malta — friendship, cooperation, seasick pills!"

After the laughter died down, he turned serious: "Mr. President, I learned that the name of your hometown in the northern Caucasus, Privolnoye, can mean 'spacious' or 'free.'" Gorbachev said, "Thank you for mentioning it."

"Well," continued Bush, "it reminded me of the new breeze, the new spirit of freedom that we've seen sweep across Europe and around the globe."

Mindful of their leader's aversion to small talk, the Soviets had declined Bush's invitation for an overnight trip outside Washington. The most they would allow was eight hours at Camp David on Saturday.

On Saturday morning, Bush found that Gorbachev was nervous about flying by helicopter; it took him several minutes to persuade his guest not to make the fifty-five-mile trip by motorcade. During the flight, an air force major sat next to the two leaders in the wood-paneled Sikorsky. Strapped to his wrist was the "football," the doomsday briefcase that enabled a president of the United States to launch nuclear missiles. Elsewhere in the cabin, one of Gorbachev's aides carried the Soviet equivalent — the *chemodanchik,* or "little suitcase."

Looking down at the suburbs, Gorbachev saw houses with swimming pools and tennis courts. Bush explained how an American bought a house. Gorbachev asked how much these homes cost and who lived there. He was taken aback by the extraordinary wealth of "average" Americans.

After they landed, Bush drove Gorbachev by golf cart from the helicopter pad to Aspen Lodge. As the two first ladies strolled hand in hand through the oak and chestnut forest, Bush, Gorbachev, Baker, Shevardnadze, Scowcroft, and Akhromeyev sat down at a glass-topped table outside the lodge, overlooking the pool, golf course, and putting green. Bush suggested that everyone remove his tie and coat to enjoy the day. Gorbachev's aides thought it an immense accomplishment to get their boss out of his tie and into a V-necked gray sweater.

Over a luncheon of hot sorrel soup, the two leaders discussed what Gorbachev called "the planet and its flash points." Region by region, Bush asked, "What problems do you see?" and "How might we deal with that?" At several points, Bush asked, "What can we do to help you meet your problems?"

They discussed Afghanistan, Cambodia, southern Africa, Nicaragua, Cyprus, Korea, and Cuba. Bush remonstrated with Gorbachev for continuing to send $5 billion annually to Castro. Gorbachev lamely replied, "We don't really give them aid. We give them large subsidies — oil at prices way below the market. We buy their sugar at inflated prices. But during the coming year, we're going to normalize the relationship."

On one subject, their views were nearly identical. Bush and Gorbachev shared a deep frustration with the policies of Israeli Prime Minister Yitzhak Shamir, whose Likud government continued to build settlements on Israeli-occupied territories and to resist compromise with the Arabs. They lamented that the Labor opposition leader, Shimon Peres, was having such trouble returning to power. They agreed on the need for persistence, patience, and cooperation on the Israeli-Palestinian problem.

Bush praised Gorbachev for permitting far more Soviet Jews to emigrate than had any of his predecessors: "What you've done is remarkable, letting these people go. Let's keep it going." He then presented a list of dozens of Soviet Jews who were still being refused exit visas.

Gorbachev said that he was under great pressure from even the moderate Arabs to end the exodus.* His own hard-liners gave him trouble when he did things that seemed to favor the Jews: "I have to weigh denouncing anti-Semitism against the danger of provoking Russian nationalism."

Bush raised the subject of Boris Yeltsin: what role would he have in Soviet politics now that he was the head of the Russian parliament? Gorbachev emotionally replied that Yeltsin was "not a serious person" but rather an "opportunist," adding, "Yeltsin could have been with us, but now he's become a destroyer."

During the retreat at Camp David, with Bush as his passenger, Gorbachev took the controls of a golf cart. Passing John Sununu's cabin, the Soviet leader took his hands off the wheel and waved. The cart took a hard left and swerved off the asphalt, but both Gorbachev and Bush grabbed the wheel before the cart could turn over and perhaps injure them. Gorbachev's interpreter, Pavel Palazhchenko, quipped, "You see how the leaders of the two great powers are cooperating to avoid disaster and keep everything on proper course!"

Bush noted that there were "lovely trails here we can walk on if we decide to do it." Gorbachev said that he and Raisa "often go for long walks in the woods." When Bush took Gorbachev for a stroll, they ended up at the horseshoe pit; Gorbachev tossed three, making a ringer on his first try.

That night, the American and Soviet delegations dined on salmon at a large E-shaped table in Laurel Lodge. Bush offered a toast: "These meetings haven't been all sweetness and light. It's very important for me to do well in sports. I like to win. So you can imagine how I felt when I learned that my visitor, throwing a horseshoe for the first time in his life, got a ringer!" He reached under the table and pulled out a plaque on which Gorbachev's winning horseshoe had been hastily mounted.

Touched by the gesture, Gorbachev replied that in his country, too, a horseshoe mounted over a door meant good luck. Brandishing his plaque, he said, "May this one be over the door of your house and my house and over the door of the American people and give us good

---

* On May 29, Shamir had written Gorbachev a private letter insisting that Israel had no policy of "directing" Soviet Jews to occupied Arab lands, and claiming that only a few had settled there. He praised the Soviet Union, "under your leadership, for the opening of gates for the Jews who yearn for their historic homeland."

fortune." During their telephone conversations over the next year and a half, Bush would frequently refer to Gorbachev's prowess at horseshoes as a means of reestablishing the friendliness of their encounter at Camp David.

The previous evening, after the treaty signing, Scowcroft had asked Akhromeyev what he thought of the summit. The marshal had coolly answered, "It's all right. Nothing special." But the atmosphere at Camp David had improved the mood even of the caustic old soldier. At dinner, he told the Americans, "This is the most special day in the history of our relations. Nothing will be the same again." As Robert Blackwill later observed, "The atmosphere would have been a lot chillier if the trade agreement hadn't been signed."

Bush and Gorbachev were to hold a joint press conference at ten o'clock on Sunday morning in the East Room of the White House. The day before, in honor of the closer American-Soviet relationship, Blackwill had given an advance copy of Bush's planned opening statement to Bessmertnykh, so that Gorbachev could prepare his own remarks knowing what Bush would say.

Blackwill told Bessmertnykh, "We're not asking for you to approve this statement, but we ordinarily show such things to our friends." Buried within the boilerplate was a sentence saying that Bush and Gorbachev were "in full agreement" that alliance membership was a "matter for the Germans to decide."

The Americans were taking advantage of the opening that Gorbachev had given Bush on the first day of the summit. They knew that the people of a united Germany would choose to be affiliated with NATO; they presumed that the Soviets would see the sentence as a trap and object accordingly.

Late into Saturday night, Condoleezza Rice waited by her telephone for the Soviets to call and demand its deletion. At one in the morning on Sunday, she called Blackwill and said, "I haven't heard from them yet."

Bessmertnykh finally called to say that he had no objection to Bush's remarks. Whatever the dissension within its own ranks on the subject, the Soviet leadership had tacitly accepted that Germany would stay in NATO after unification.

At the Sunday-morning press conference, Gorbachev was asked about the Arab-Israeli dispute and its implications for Kremlin policy. He replied that unless Soviet Jews were barred from settling in the occupied territories, the Soviet Union might have to "postpone issuing exit visas." This threat startled the Americans; it went beyond anything Gorbachev had told Bush privately at Camp David. They suspected that he was playing to the conservatives back home.

Afterward, when the Bushes saw the Gorbachevs off, the presidents' wives kissed on both cheeks and embraced. As the visitors got into their limousine, Bush called out, "Good-bye! Good luck!" The Gorbachevs and the other Soviets were driven to the brilliantly sunlit grounds of the Washington Monument, where several helicopters were waiting to whisk them off to Andrews Air Force Base. A band played, and howitzers fired a salute.

Over the din, Baker leaned over to Shevardnadze and said, "I think they were good meetings." Shevardnadze feigned surprise: "Do you have any doubt?" Back at the White House, Bush told his aides, "I think I improved my personal relationship with Gorbachev, but I wouldn't want to overdo it."

The qualifier was telling. Bush knew that during the months ahead, his ability to influence Gorbachev might prove critical — especially his ability to keep him from letting the hard-liners loose on the Baltics. At the same time, however, the summit had provided several stark indications that Gorbachev might be losing his grip on power, even among his own closest associates. Insofar as Gorbachev's control over events was diminishing, Bush's influence on him was losing its political value. Therefore, better not to "overdo" the relationship or rely too much on it as an instrument of American policy.

Flying west, Gorbachev stopped in Minneapolis and toured Control Data, which in 1968 had sold the Soviet Union its first large U.S. computers. He met with a number of corporate leaders — including Lee Iacocca of Chrysler, James Robinson of American Express, and Donald Kendall of Pepsico — and toured a "typical Minnesota family farm." He also joined the rapscallion British tycoon Robert Maxwell in announcing a "Gorbachev-Maxwell Foundation," to which Maxwell had pledged millions of dollars.*

In San Francisco, the Gorbachevs received Ronald and Nancy Reagan for coffee. To scotch the old stories of a feud between them, the two wives made a point of embracing.

---

* As the British press baron grew more enmeshed in financial troubles, he quickly forgot his pledge. The foundation died almost as soon as it was born.

Then the Gorbachevs were driven to Stanford University, where they were greeted by George Shultz, who now taught there. Gazing at the magnificent campus, Gorbachev told Shultz, "Well, George, I see you now live in paradise. . . . You should all have to pay a tax on this weather." Students cried, "Gorby! Gorby!" Gorbachev gave a speech that struck a familiar note: "The Cold War has been left behind," he said, "and it is not worth squabbling over who won."

Returning to San Francisco from Palo Alto, he lunched with 150 business and civic leaders and held an unprecedented meeting with South Korean President Roh Tae Woo. Largely out of deference to their North Korean comrades, Soviet officials had long refused to deal with South Korea; in agreeing to meet with Roh, Gorbachev was breaking that taboo. He wished to send a strong signal to the world that Soviet foreign policy would no longer be driven or limited by the ideological imperatives of the Cold War. Gorbachev also hoped that the normalization of relations with Seoul would bring him South Korean investment and financial aid.

The Gorbachev-Roh meeting was arranged on the Soviet side primarily by Anatoli Dobrynin, who was then still serving as an adviser to Gorbachev. In reporting back to the Kremlin, Dobrynin bypassed the Soviet Foreign Ministry entirely. He and several other Gorbachev aides were concerned that much as Arabists in the ministry were making it difficult for the USSR to cooperate with the United States in the Middle East, so the ministry's career Asia hands would resist and perhaps even sabotage the dramatic shift in Soviet policy from North to South Korea.

When Shevardnadze learned about the San Francisco meeting, he was outraged — not because he disagreed with the policy, but because he felt personally humiliated that Gorbachev and Dobrynin had not seen fit to include him in such a major diplomatic development.*

As the Gorbachevs boarded their jet to fly home, a Cossack-attired choral group on the tarmac sang a Russian rendition of "I Left My Heart in San Francisco." Raisa Gorbachev savored this last reminder of the adoration her husband was receiving in the West; she knew that back home he could expect only more trouble and criticism. Within

---

* The Gorbachev-Roh meeting gave a strong boost to a diplomatic process that would eventually lead to the exchange of ambassadors, the admission of South Korea to the UN, an increase in South Korean capital flowing to the Soviet Union, and the buildup of world pressure on North Korea to accept international controls on its nuclear program.

earshot of Jack Matlock, she muttered, "The thing about innovations is that sooner or later they turn around and destroy the innovators."

In Copenhagen on Tuesday, June 5, Baker met with Shevardnadze during a session of the Conference on Security and Cooperation in Europe (CSCE). The secretary of state complained about Gorbachev's unexpected threat in Washington to halt Jewish emigration to Israel: "We can't give you MFN if you insist on doing this. If you're thinking of it, you had better know that this will cause big problems." Baker noted that among Israelis — who disagreed among themselves on almost everything — the "one clear consensus" was that "no one must do anything to jeopardize Soviet Jewry."

Shevardnadze replied, "We're very concerned about what Shamir and the Israelis are doing. But what Gorbachev said was just a warning. There has been no change in our policy, and we have no plans for any change."

To allay Soviet fears about a united German state within NATO, Baker raised some new ideas for enhancing the role of CSCE, limiting the size of the German army, and planning for the future of Soviet troops in eastern Germany. These were all amplifications of the nine "assurances" he and Bush had offered the previous Thursday afternoon in the Cabinet Room.

Replying with none of the hesitancy that Gorbachev had shown in Washington, Shevardnadze took another giant step toward Soviet acceptance of the unification of Germany within NATO. He said that if the American assurances could be codified, the Soviet Union could agree to Germany's unification by the end of 1990. Such a state would, of course, be free to choose its own alliances. With these assurances, the Soviet Union could have "good relations" with the new Germany.

Baker had to struggle to contain his jubilation. It was clear to him that Gorbachev had resolved the frictions that had been so apparent among his entourage when the subject was raised in Washington. That evening Baker called Bush and said, "The Soviets are coming around on Germany." He then called Hans-Dietrich Genscher, who was also in Copenhagen. Told that the German foreign minister had retired for the night, Baker insisted that he be woken up to hear the news: the USSR was finally "on board."

CHAPTER 11

"A Fantastic Result"

ON TUESDAY, June 12, in Moscow, Gorbachev declared to the Supreme Soviet that he would accept a united Germany as a NATO member if there was a transition period during which military forces in the current East Germany retained "associate membership" in the Warsaw Pact.

Once again, the Soviet leader was trying to make a cave-in to the West looked principled and tough. He said, "If we have the feeling that our interests are not being taken into account on the German issue, then the positive processes in Europe will be in real jeopardy. This is no bluff." He added that if NATO leaders should decide to make their alliance less military and more political, then the problem of German unification would be a great deal easier to solve.

In Washington, Bush told reporters that his position was "well known" to Gorbachev: he wanted a unified Germany in NATO "with no conditions." As long as Gorbachev was playing the good loser, the American president was delighted to be magnanimous in victory. He said that he expected his Soviet counterpart to float other new ideas: "We'll listen and we'll discuss them without rancor."

On Sunday, June 17, the East German parliament voted to consider using a provision in Bonn's constitution to accelerate a merger of the two nations: instead of the two governments' having to negotiate, East Germany could simply vote to join with West Germany. Helmut Kohl now said that a December date for the first all-German elections in more than a half century was "coming near to being very, very likely."

On Friday, June 22, Baker was in East Berlin for another Two-plus-Four session.* The East German foreign minister, Markus Meckel, relayed the Soviets' latest effort to make unification more palatable to the Kremlin: they proposed that NATO and the Warsaw Pact declare themselves no longer enemies and renounce the use of force. This proposal made no sense. Not only was the Warsaw Pact collapsing before their eyes, but for a military alliance, to renounce the use of force was to render itself impotent. Baker dismissed Meckel's suggestion.

When the Two-plus-Four foreign ministers convened, Shevardnadze produced a surprise proposal: the Four Powers should continue to oversee Germany for a three-to-five-year transition period, during which they would help "limit the strength of Germany's armed forces" and "make sure that they are rendered incapable of offensive operations."

Under this plan, a "review commission" would then judge whether or not Germany deserved full sovereignty. In the meantime, the Four Powers should enforce a "ban on the resurgence of Nazi political ideology" and the "preservation of memorials commemorating those who were killed in the fight against fascism." Apologetically, Shevardnadze said that his proposal was a "draft" that was "not regarded by us as the final truth. We are ready to seek compromise approaches."

Baker, Dumas, Hurd, and Genscher all objected. Noting that the Soviet plan "would restrict German sovereignty for some years," Baker protested that a united Germany should not be "singularized or discriminated against."

Four times during his presentation, Shevardnadze said that a "great deal" would depend on the NATO summit to be held in London in July. "Gorbachev is very concerned about how the London summit will define what NATO will mean in the context of a new Europe," he explained. Baker urged him, "Tell us what you want so that you will be

---

* The previous day, the two German legislatures had endorsed the idea of swift economic union and vowed to sign a treaty confirming once and for all the post–World War II border with Poland, ending any hint of future German claims on Polish territory.

reassured that your security won't be damaged, and we'll tell you whether we can give you those assurances."

That evening, Baker complained to Shevardnadze, "I told my boss that you guys were coming around, and now you're backing away!" Almost sheepishly, Shevardnadze confessed that what he had presented was "not Gorbachev's and my statement" but rather a "Politburo document."

He said that "any progress on Germany" would now have to wait until after a crucial Soviet party congress in July. At that meeting, Gorbachev expected the hard-liners to blame him and Shevardnadze for losing Eastern Europe and dangerously weakening the Soviet Union. Shevardnadze told Baker that Germany had become a serious domestic political problem. Afterward, Ross declared to Baker that he had rarely seen Shevardnadze look so "beleaguered."

Tarasenko later confided to Ross that Shevardnadze had been forced to "go through the motions" with the "military, hard-line document" to render Gorbachev less vulnerable to the charge of selling out to the West. He went on to say that a united Germany in NATO would be easier for the Soviets to accept if, in addition to NATO's becoming more benign, "conflict-resolution centers" were established within the CSCE, and the two sides reached a common understanding of European security.*

Ross advised Baker to help Gorbachev manage the run-up to the party congress. "If he comes out of the party congress all right," he concluded, "we should finally have a united Germany in NATO."

On Saturday, June 30, in response to Bush's signing of the U.S.-Soviet trade pact four weeks earlier, the Soviet government lifted its embargo against Lithuania.

Two days later, the Twenty-eighth Congress of the Soviet Communist Party began. Gorbachev had hoped to reduce the party's administrative control over Soviet society, but the party establishment, understanding what was at stake, stacked the session with its own people, who could be counted on to obstruct reform. Delegates complained that Gorbachev

---

* This idea was based on the "nuclear risk reduction centers" created in 1988 by the U.S. and Soviet governments for the purpose of exchanging information that would reduce the possibility of nuclear war by accident or miscalculation, and producing data required by arms control treaties. In 1991, a new multilateral communications center was opened in the Hague, to link the thirty-eight members of the CSCE.

and his allies had undermined the Warsaw Pact, lost the Baltics, fractured the ideological foundations of the party, and encouraged the collapse of the Soviet Union.

Shevardnadze defended his foreign policy by stressing the waste of billions of rubles on the arms race. As for Germany, he said, the Soviet Union had to make a choice: either use the Soviet troops in East Germany to block unification, or work with the West to build a secure Europe. Many delegates booed. Shevardnadze felt dejected and angry that Gorbachev did little to defend him at the meeting.

Boris Yeltsin, too, charged that Gorbachev had failed to "neutralize" the conservative forces that were now "on the offensive." If the party failed to reform itself, it would lose any "serious" role in society, he said. He proposed a change of name, to the "Party of Democratic Socialism," and a new identity as a democratized party whose cells in the army and the KGB, in factories and in enterprises, would be abolished.

Gorbachev was busy defending himself against demands that he "stop traveling abroad and concern himself with the country." After threatening to resign, he was reelected general secretary by a vote of 3,411 to 1,116. He proposed his candidate for deputy party leader Vladimir Ivashko, first secretary of Ukraine. Challenged by the conservative firebrand Yegor Ligachev, Gorbachev's man won by a vote of 3,109 to 776, after which Ligachev announced his retirement from politics.

On the next-to-last day of the congress, Yeltsin rose and announced that he was quitting the party: he could not be president of the Russian republic and fairly serve all Russians under the constraints that the party imposed. He strode down the center aisle and out of the hall to scattered boos and catcalls.

Nevertheless, by the end of the congress, Gorbachev could claim a mandate for himself and his programs. Having gotten this ordeal out of the way, he was now free to settle once and for all, in his own fashion, the question of German unification.

While the party congress was still in session, on Wednesday evening, July 4, Bush flew to London for the NATO summit. Having squeezed in a golf game on Wednesday morning, he emerged from *Air Force One* looking tired, with puffy eyes and a slower stride than usual. He sneezed and blew his nose.

At the White House in June, in preparation for the London meeting, Robert Blackwill had given Scowcroft a memo on "what a new NATO should look like." It began with the sentence "The Cold War is over" and floated a variety of ideas for a declaration to come out of the London summit.

The proposals called for Eastern European states to send permanent representatives to NATO; for Gorbachev to attend a session of NATO's Atlantic Council; and for the West to press for faster progress in CFE. There should be an integrated European army with a permanent U.S. component, which was the "best possible way to insure against the U.S. military being kicked out of Germany."

Blackwill hoped that such proposals would "give the new democracies in Eastern Europe the prospect for a home port in the coming storm," even as they offered Gorbachev "every possible excuse to acquiesce in a united Germany in NATO."

Blackwill was confident, too, that the proposals would boost the Bush administration's stock with Helmut Kohl. If the Soviets accepted the package, the result would be accelerated unification; if they rejected it, then Kohl could blame the Kremlin for impeding the process, and could say, "We did everything possible to be reasonable."

Bush approved. Blackwill urged him to get as much of the proposal as possible accepted by allied leaders before it was leaked to the press: "Keep in mind that the day after the NATO summit opens, Gorbachev will get his morning news summary just as you do. That will tell him what part of your proposal has made it through. He'll personalize it. He'll use this to judge how successful you've been in managing the alliance."

Bush agreed that it was only a matter of time before the plan leaked. When that happened, he said acidly, he hoped that the "blond bubbleheads" on television would perceive the importance of what he was doing. He sent a three-page letter to Kohl, Thatcher, Mitterrand, Italian Prime Minister Giulio Andreotti, and NATO Secretary-General Manfred Woerner.

Kohl loved Bush's proposals for transforming NATO, and after reading the president's letter, Woerner sent a personal note: "I usually take coffee at 8:30 A.M., but when I read your message, George, I reached for the champagne."

Margaret Thatcher, however, registered her unmistakable skepticism about Bush's plans for NATO. Worried as ever about German unification, she pointedly mentioned when she greeted Bush and other NATO colleagues in London that in preparation for this meeting of the alliance,

she had read Alan Clark's *Barbarossa* — a none-too-subtle hint that
Germany's 1941 invasion of the Soviet Union was much on her mind,
as were other instances of the German propensity for aggression, such
as the Battle of Britain.

Baker tried to soften up the prime minister by praising her role in
breaking the deadlock in negotiations over Namibia: "You know, that
whole Namibia thing almost broke down. You were in the region. I
want you to know how much we all appreciate your work in helping
to put things together." With no trace of levity, Thatcher replied, "Yes,
it's lucky I was there." Baker tried to keep from rolling his eyes.

It had been only a year since Gorbachev informed Western leaders
in Paris that he neither wanted nor needed direct Western aid. Now he
sent Bush, Thatcher, and many of their colleagues a plea for long-term
credits and other help: "Without this radical step, a further renewal of
our society will be impossible," he wrote. In effect, Gorbachev was
attempting to extract a bribe for consenting to a united Germany in
NATO and proceeding with his own reforms.

Scowcroft told Bush, "I think it's partly a ploy. It's a clever thing to
do, to try to co-opt the West into helping him with his program."
Frantic to keep Gorbachev from turning against German unification,
Kohl advised his colleagues that he was so impressed by Gorbachev's
letter that he wished to send the Soviets up to $15 billion in aid. Bush,
eager not to alienate Kohl, did not object.

The NATO leaders signed a declaration based on Bush's proposals,
which committed their alliance to sign a nonaggression pact with individual Warsaw Pact nations. Gorbachev and the other Eastern European leaders were invited to send regular envoys to NATO, and the
Western alliance promised to eliminate nuclear-tipped artillery shells in
Europe if the Soviet Union would reciprocate.

Using language proposed at the last minute by Kohl, the leaders also
resolved to set a firm limit on the size of Germany's armed forces under
a CFE agreement. This was a departure from the chancellor's previous
insistence that any Western declaration on conventional forces must not
single out Germany. From his talks with Shevardnadze, Baker had concluded that this might be the key that would unlock Soviet approval of
a united Germany in NATO.

On his way out of the hall, Bush told reporters that Gorbachev could
claim credit for the great change in NATO. When asked about his own
role, the president saw an opening to gibe his critics. He replied jovially,
"Leadership. Maybe even vision."

Baker had sent an advance copy of the London NATO declaration to Shevardnadze, saying, "This is a draft. I think we can get it, and I'm going to work hard to get it, but it's a draft and it could change." This allowed him and Bush an escape hatch in case the allies changed the language, but at the same time it gave the Soviets an incentive to promise that Gorbachev's response would be glowing.

Shevardnadze was grateful for the gesture. Tarasenko later confided to Ross, "If we had been caught by surprise, Akhromeyev would have torn it apart."

After the declaration was issued in London, the Soviet Foreign Ministry spokesman, Gennadi Gerasimov, announced that it should help Gorbachev win over the opponents to German unification: "Now we can show them they are wrong."

In Houston on Monday, July 9, Bush welcomed the leaders of the seven major industrialized democracies with a barbecue and indoor rodeo at the Astrodome. Once the group got down to business, the issue of aid to the Soviet Union was near the top of the agenda.

During Bush's Camp David meeting with Gorbachev, Dennis Ross had asked Primakov, "How much do you really need?" Primakov had replied, "About twenty billion dollars a year for three years." In Houston, given a similar figure, Kohl and Mitterrand lobbied their colleagues for $15 to $20 billion in aid to Moscow, which they justified as a sign of Western confidence in Gorbachev and his reforms.

Bush, Thatcher, and Japanese Prime Minister Toshiki Kaifu all balked at the sum. Bush argued that until the Soviet economy was restructured and Soviet military spending and foreign aid were reduced, Gorbachev could not use the money wisely. Brian Mulroney replied that if Gorbachev were to be "chucked out" of office, "we would be in an infinitely worse position than we are today."

To avoid a shouting match, Bush suggested sending experts to help the Soviet Union rebuild its rail and communications networks, grain storage sites, food distribution systems, and other essential services. Finally the seven leaders agreed to send Gorbachev a letter expressing encouragement for *perestroika* and promising to expedite international studies of the Soviet economy as a prelude to possible Western aid. It was a polite but thinly disguised rejection of the kind of large-scale, concrete assistance Gorbachev was looking for — and a vivid indication that there were limits to how far Bush would go in propping up his friend in the Kremlin.

*   *   *

On Saturday, July 14, Kohl flew to Moscow. He was prepared to offer
a ceiling on German forces of 400,000, about 100,000 fewer than West
German troop strength in 1989. He had already pledged $3 billion in
German credits to the Soviet Union and $730 million to pay for Soviet
troops in East Germany.

On Sunday morning, at an official guesthouse on the outskirts of
Moscow, Gorbachev told the chancellor, "We've got a few small nuts
to crack, but we have very good teeth." He said that he was ready to
move toward swift German unification. In a characteristic effort to
claim that he had been on Kohl's side all along, he added that with the
party congress over, he was now free to follow his own instincts.

That afternoon, Gorbachev took Kohl by air to Stavropol, which
had been occupied by the Germans during World War II. During the
flight, the two men haggled over the size of the future German army.
When they arrived in his hometown, Gorbachev showed Kohl the office
he had used as local party leader and led him on a stroll through the
city square.

At the Caucasus resort village of Arkhyz, the two leaders bargained
late into the night. Gorbachev said that NATO's recent changes made
it easier for him to tolerate a united Germany that would choose its
own external alliances.

In response, Kohl pledged to hold formal talks on the withdrawal of
Soviet troops from East Germany and reductions in a future all-German
army. He promised that the Soviets would have a grace period of three
to four years in which to remove their troops from Germany. When the
troops left, Germany would contribute financially to their reentry into
Soviet society. Gorbachev said that he hoped no nuclear weapons or
foreign troops would be based in eastern Germany.

The next day, at a joint news conference, Gorbachev declared,
"Whether we like it or not, the time will come when a united Germany
will be in NATO, if that is its choice. Then, if that is its choice, to some
degree and in some form, Germany can work together with the Soviet
Union." Kohl said, "This is a breakthrough, a fantastic result."

If there was a single point at which the Cold War ended, it was
probably this, the moment when Gorbachev acceded to German unification within NATO. The division of Germany had been at the heart
of the nearly half-century-long division of Europe: Stalin's conquest of
Eastern Europe in effect began when the Red Army surged into eastern

Germany, captured Berlin, and made out of the Soviet zone of occupation a new state, the German Democratic Republic, the jewel in the crown of the Soviet empire.

Then, too, some of the most frightening moments of the Cold War had been caused by East-West disputes over the status of Germany and Berlin; confrontations between the superpowers over West Berlin had in the late 1950s and early 1960s brought the world close to a third world war. Despite Gorbachev's repeated protestations that there were no winners or losers, he had capitulated on the single most troublesome and dangerous issue of the Cold War.

An aide told Baker of Gorbachev's statement on Germany while the secretary of state's plane was being refueled at Shannon Airport, Ireland, on its way to Europe. Baker was stunned. He had expected that Gorbachev's troubles with his hard-liners would keep him from backing down on Germany until August at the earliest. Reading a memo about the Gorbachev-Kohl meeting before its outcome was known, he had scribbled in the margin, "This is a nonevent."

Reporters on his plane needled Baker for having been caught off guard. He tried to defend himself: "This is a delightful surprise — to the extent that it is a surprise." Baker presumed that having decided to allow Germany to belong to NATO, Gorbachev wanted to move as quickly as possible to reap full credit from the Germans, who would now dominate Europe.

Some of Shevardnadze's aides had advised him to share the decision making on Germany with others in the Soviet government — especially Germanicists such as Falin and Nikolai Portugalov in the Central Committee secretariat and Yuli Kvitsinsky in the Foreign Ministry. That way, they would have to bear some of the responsibility for the final decision.

But Shevardnadze had worried that involving officials who opposed German unification might prove an impediment, and in the end he was virtually alone in persuading Gorbachev to swallow the notion of Germany as a full member of NATO.

Portugalov later traced the decision back to what he judged to be Gorbachev's inept performance in discussing Germany with Bush at the White House: "What happened was so unprofessional, so unexpected, that all of us were startled. Of course, now it looks like 'tout est pour le mieux.' But then it looked awful, scandalous. We could and should have asked Kohl to accept a French-style military status for Germany. That was not done because Shevardnadze was pressing Gorbachev with his 'concessions to the Americans' line.'"*

The old Germanicist Valentin Falin told colleagues that Shevardnadze had sold Gorbachev a "bill of goods" on German unification within NATO. Angry at having been shut out of the deliberations, Falin privately charged that Shevardnadze had received "some kind of secret financial payoff" from West German industrialists, and castigated him as "the Americans' most powerful agent of influence."

A year later, Bessmertnykh recalled this moment as a milestone in Gorbachev's relationship with the hard-liners: "The acceptance of a united Germany in NATO was one of the most hated developments in the history of Soviet foreign policy, and it will remain so for decades."

At the White House, Bush declared that Gorbachev's decision was "in the best interests of all the countries of Europe, including the Soviet Union." But privately he was piqued that in the end Kohl and Gorbachev had worked out the matter on their own. Was this a glimmering of the new world to come?

On Tuesday morning, July 17, Bush spoke with Gorbachev by telephone for forty-five minutes. His pretext was to brief Gorbachev on the London summit, but his main purpose was to keep the Soviets and Germans from making a habit of bypassing Washington in their diplomatic collaborations.

He reminded Gorbachev that he had been the "architect" of the NATO declaration and said he wished to "reassure" him about the alliance's peaceful intentions. This was a hint that the more intimately the United States was involved in European security affairs, the less likely it was that Germany would supplant it as senior partner of the alliance.

Gorbachev acknowledged that the London declaration had been a "very important impulse" that had influenced his decision on Germany. "I take such pride in the way Europe is moving into this new era of freedom," he added.

Bush commiserated with him about the attacks at the party congress from the left and the right. He said that he sometimes felt similarly whiplashed by his own Congress in Washington. But when Gorbachev

---

* "French-style military status" referred, again, to France's unique position as part of NATO's political structure but not its military command.

took the opportunity to ask once again for Western financial aid, Bush politely put him off.

The U.S. president believed that in the absence of more radical economic reform in the USSR, cash infusions of the sort Gorbachev was begging for would simply be a matter of pouring good money after bad. They would do the Soviet Union no lasting good — and therefore would not really help Gorbachev at all.

By the summer of 1990, Bush and Baker had quietly resolved to begin reaching out seriously to other current and potential Soviet leaders beyond Gorbachev.

The previous September, when Boris Yeltsin had come to Washington as a mere member of parliament, they had been able to argue that he deserved no entree to the Oval Office. But now that Yeltsin was the leading figure in the Russian Republic and was vowing to wrench Russia free of the Soviet Union, the president and secretary of state could no longer afford to do Gorbachev the favor of keeping his rival at arm's length.

Yeltsin's emergence as parliamentary leader of Russia had ratified his position as the most popular figure in the Soviet Union and a likely succcessor to Gorbachev, at the head either of the Soviet government or of an independent Russia. Unless the Americans made peace with him soon, his memory for political slights would predispose him against Washington.

In the past, when foreign governments had suddenly changed, U.S. presidents had often been criticized for refusing to make contact with the opposition until it was too late. Thus Eisenhower was caught flat-footed when the Cuban people overthrew Fulgencio Batista in favor of Fidel Castro, and Carter was slow to adjust when the Iranians replaced their shah with Ayatollah Ruhollah Khomeini. Bush did not wish to suffer similar criticism if and when Gorbachev was supplanted by Yeltsin.

The president and Baker felt that their making contact with leaders on Gorbachev's left, including mayors Gavril Popov of Moscow and Anatoli Sobchak of Leningrad, would increase the pressure on him to push for reform. Moreover, their reaching out to secessionist leaders such as Prime Minister Prunskiene of Lithuania would help to counterbalance the influence of the hard-liners in Moscow who were demanding that Gorbachev use force to hold the Soviet Union together.

When Baker met with Shevardnadze in Paris on Wednesday, July 18, he informed the foreign minister that the United States intended to increase its contacts with Yeltsin and other representatives of the reform and independence movements throughout the Soviet Union.

The news did not upset Shevardnadze. He knew that the new U.S. policy would help induce Gorbachev to press for reform and to tolerate more freedom for the republics — two causes to which Shevardnadze himself was more sympathetic than his president.

Shevardnadze did not need to say that Gorbachev would be irritated by this development. His boss would regard it as an attempt on Bush's part to hedge his bets on Gorbachev's survival. It would weaken his claim to be the Soviet Union's indispensable channel to the West — and to Western aid — and at the same time increase the pressure on him from the right: once Bush and Baker began dealing seriously with secessionists such as Landsbergis and Prunskiene, the KGB's Kryuchkov and other hard-liners would cite it as proof of their belief that the CIA was engineering the breakup of the Soviet Union.*

The foreign minister told Baker that he understood why he and Bush had to reach out beyond Gorbachev to other leaders. He praised the younger generation of oppositionists, such as Popov and Sobchak, who were pushing for faster political and economic change. He noted that U.S. politicians had informed him that they sometimes set aside their partisan differences and stood behind their president. "In the Soviet Union," said Shevardnadze, "we unfortunately have people who always want to say, 'Dump the president.' . . . We haven't developed your kind of political maturity."

Shevardnadze reported that Gorbachev had emerged stronger from his recent party congress, but he admitted that they were "in a position where we need to move" on the economic crisis. Baker gave him a detailed paper outlining areas in which the United States could provide expertise, including the distribution of food and consumer goods and a few other areas not previously offered, such as housing, banking, and tax administration.

Before the secretary of state flew back to Washington, he and Shevardnadze agreed to meet a fortnight later in Irkutsk. There, on the shore of Lake Baikal, which the Soviets considered one of the natural wonders

---

* In Moscow, Gorbachev's spokesman Arkadi Maslennikov publicly warned the U.S. against offering Gorbachev's foes "encouragement or assistance"; this was "interference" in Soviet "internal affairs" that "would hardly be tolerated."

of the world, Shevardnadze would reciprocate Baker's Wyoming hospitality.

At the end of July, Baker flew from a meeting in Singapore to Irkutsk, where Shevardnadze was waiting for him. The foreign minister pressed for a second Bush-Gorbachev summit, this time in Moscow, before the end of 1990. He hoped that this would help bolster Gorbachev against the many challenges he was facing from the right and the left, as well as the economic and ethnic turmoil that threatened to overtake his country.

At Lake Baikal, Shevardnadze was determined to overcome the embarrassment of catching no fish on Jackson Lake nearly a year before. When he and Baker climbed onto a speedboat to go fishing, he was accompanied by a professional Soviet fisherman armed with the latest high-tech angling gear.

In their formal talks in Irkutsk, Baker and Shevardnadze bargained over START, European security, and Cambodia, and neared a final settlement of the dispute over Afghanistan. During one exchange, Shevardnadze shared what he called a "premonition": the end of the Cold War might create dangerous power vacuums in various regions of the world, which local dictators would then be tempted to fill.

On Wednesday morning, August 1, Baker awoke to find a CIA bulletin from Washington reporting that Iraqi forces were massing ominously on the border of Kuwait. He did not confide the news to Shevardnadze until noon, waiting until they were alone in the foreign minister's ZIL limousine on their way to a luncheon.

As they rode through the streets of Irkutsk, the secretary of state told Shevardnadze what he had learned. "Things are looking bad," he said, adding that the CIA was predicting an invasion of Kuwait. Baker noted that Shevardnadze and his colleagues had known and dealt with Iraqi President Saddam Hussein for years. "We hope you'll try to restrain these guys," he said.

Shevardnadze reasoned that if Saddam Hussein were indeed about to invade Kuwait, Iraq's allies in Moscow would have been told about it. He scoffed at the notion that Saddam would do something as irrational as invading Kuwait. However, that afternoon, in a message to the Foreign Ministry in Moscow, Shevardnadze asked his deputies to use quiet channels to ensure that Saddam's troops remained on their own side of the border.

CHAPTER 12

"This Is No Time to Go Wobbly"

IT WAS 7:45 in the morning in Irkutsk on Thursday, August 2, 1990, when Baker received a call from Robert Kimmitt, his under secretary for political affairs, who was back in Washington. They were speaking over an open telephone line, so Kimmitt used opaque language, but his message was clear: the CIA was now absolutely convinced that Iraq was about to invade Kuwait.

When they met an hour later, Baker passed the word to Shevardnadze, who still refused to believe it. He said, "The crisis is being defused." Baker took this to mean that somehow Saddam Hussein had assured the Soviet Union that he would not cross the Kuwaiti border.

At the end of their talks that afternoon, following their custom, the two men wrapped up several items of business in private, with only their interpreters and closest aides present. Shevardnadze was startled when Margaret Tutwiler broke in; he knew she would disturb them only in case of an emergency. She handed Baker a message. He read it and said, "Gentlemen, the State Department has received information that Iraq has crossed the border into Kuwait."

"I can't believe that's true!" said Shevardnadze. "We haven't heard anything about that. There's simply no logic to it." He told Tarasenko to look into the matter. Tarasenko called Moscow and confirmed the report. Shevardnadze was furious that the KGB had failed to predict the invasion.

Baker wondered whether the Iraqis were "going all the way" to Kuwait City or "just taking the disputed stuff" — islands and oil-rich land that Iraq and Kuwait had been haggling over for years. Shevardnadze said that a massive invasion would be "completely irrational." He noted that in the past, Saddam had flaunted his might by sending his army on brief excursions over the Kuwaiti border. But anything on a larger scale would contradict "any notion of common sense."

Shevardnadze decided to fly to Moscow at once. Baker was scheduled to travel to Ulan Bator for a ground-breaking visit to Mongolia, which he was reluctant to cancel. Since Dennis Ross and Robert Zoellick were already scheduled to return to Moscow, they could keep in close touch with the Soviets.

Baker pressed Shevardnadze for an embargo on Soviet arms shipments to Iraq. Shevardnadze agreed that something must be done, but he said he could make no promises until he spoke to Gorbachev.

Still reeling from the news, the foreign minister observed that although Saddam was "willful, tough, and domineering," he was also "shrewd." Yes, he had gone to war against Iran, dropped chemical weapons on the Kurds, and used mass terror to crush internal rebellion. But that was all before the end of the Cold War, when he could expect to play the Soviets off against the Americans. Attacking Kuwait now would be tantamount to "committing suicide," Shevardnadze suggested.

Just before Baker and Shevardnadze boarded their planes, Dennis Ross informed them that Saddam's armies had marched all the way to Kuwait City.

From his plane en route to Ulan Bator, Baker called Bush, who agreed that he should not cancel his trip to Mongolia: there was no need to further alarm the world. Bush asked whether the Soviets might be persuaded to join the United States in condemning the invasion. Baker replied that Ross and Zoellick were raising the matter with Soviet officials in Moscow.

On his arrival in Ulan Bator, Baker walked through the scheduled ceremonies, but his mind was on Kuwait. Spending much of the night on the telephone to the president and Scowcroft, he emphasized that the UN could prove to be supremely important in this instance. The

United States should take the lead in getting the Security Council to denounce the invasion and impose immediate sanctions.

Scowcroft was concerned about their relying too heavily on the UN. He relayed the worry of the chairman of the Joint Chiefs, General Colin Powell, that UN sanctions might hamper the Pentagon's war planning. But Bush sided with Baker. By telephone, the secretary of state asked his under secretary for political affairs, Robert Kimmitt, to have the U.S. ambassador to the UN, Thomas Pickering, start drafting a resolution for the Security Council.*

Aboard the Soviet plane flying toward Moscow, Ross and Zoellick had found Shevardnadze and Tarasenko receptive to the idea of a Soviet-American stand against Saddam's action. When they landed, Ross's aide Peter Hauslohner suggested that the United States and the Soviet Union issue a joint statement denouncing Saddam's invasion. Ross thought it a "terrific idea."

He called Baker in Ulan Bator and suggested that such a joint statement "would demonstrate U.S.-Soviet partnership." It would show that the world had changed and would make it impossible for Saddam to "hide behind a possible U.S.-Soviet split," which he would "use to keep the Arab world divided."

Ross said, "I think that not only should we have a joint statement, but also you should come back here to give it with Shevardnadze, because that will give it real drama. And that will demonstrate for the world to see that the United States and the Soviet Union are right together."

Baker replied, "If it looks for sure as if we can get a joint statement, then I'll cut short the balance of my trip and return to Washington through Moscow. . . . Go ahead, but be sure it's a good statement."

Tarasenko took Ross to the Soviet Foreign Ministry and up in the elevator to his seventh-floor office, where he said, "Let's find out the latest information." Ross expected him to summon an intelligence briefer; instead, Tarasenko turned on CNN.

An English-language typewriter was found, and one of Ross's deputies, Andrew Carpendale, used it to tap out a draft statement. Ross rewrote it and read it to Tarasenko, who liked it and read it to Shev-

---

* Enacted as Resolution 660 by a vote of 14 to 0, with Yemen abstaining, it condemned the invasion, demanded Iraq's immediate and unconditional withdrawal, called for negotiations between Iraq and Kuwait, and reserved the option of taking "further steps to ensure compliance with the present resolution."

ardnadze over the telephone. The foreign minister said, "Sounds good. Let me call Gorbachev."

Vacationing at Foros, his Black Sea retreat, Gorbachev instructed Shevardnadze to check the statement with other members of his new Presidential Council, which included Prime Minister Valentin Pavlov, Defense Minister Dimitri Yazov, and KGB chief Vladimir Kryuchkov.

Through the night, Shevardnadze argued with these men. He held out for a solution "that would restore sovereignty, territorial integrity, and legitimate rule to Kuwait," feeling that "if the world community could not stop the aggression against Kuwait, then it would have gained nothing from the end of the Cold War."

Pavlov, Yazov, and Kryuchkov maintained that it was more important to preserve the warm Soviet relationship with Iraq. They cited the Soviet Union's Treaty of Friendship and Cooperation with Baghdad. Iraq was the most important Soviet client in the Gulf. The Kremlin had invested billions of rubles in resisting U.S. influence in the Middle East; what was more, they said, in this time of economic hardship, it must not be forgotten that the Soviet Union had sold Iraq and other Middle Eastern states about $17.5 billion worth of weapons since 1986.

Shevardnadze also had to cope with resistance from Arabists within the Foreign Ministry who were protective of the Soviet Union's long-standing ties to Iraq, deeply suspicious of American motives in the Middle East, and dead-set against a U.S.-led military buildup in the region. The foreign minister's critics complained that once again he was being seduced by his American friends: had they invested in the Middle East for all these years merely to become the tail on the American dog? They warned them that when the Americans bombed Iraq, as surely they would, "you will have blood on your hands."

Shevardnadze called Gorbachev, who approved in principle a joint American-Soviet statement of some kind but refused to side with Shevardnadze against the other ministers. The foreign minister was irate. Just as he had done with arms control and German unification, Gorbachev was forcing him to carry the full burden of an unpopular policy.

On Friday morning, August 3, Tarasenko brought a watered-down version of the joint statement to Ross at Spaso House. When Ross read it, his heart sank. He asked Tarasenko to tell Shevardnadze that tougher language was needed: "The statement's got to be strong if Baker is going to fly back here."

Ross tried to telephone Baker to tell him to postpone his trip from Ulan Bator to Moscow until the language was strengthened. He was chagrined to hear that the secretary was already airborne and that there were communications problems: Baker could not be reached on his plane.

After a quick trip back to the Foreign Ministry, Tarasenko brought another version of the statement to Spaso House. Ross told him that it was still too ambiguous: "If we put out this statement, we'll send exactly the wrong message to Saddam Hussein. It'll be obvious that we *aren't* together on this."

Together they sharpened the language, which Tarasenko promised to "sell to our side." He succeeded, with one exception: the Soviets still balked at declaring a joint arms embargo.

Exhausted, Baker arrived at Vnukovo Airport outside Moscow on Friday afternoon. Shevardnadze and his wife, Nanuli, greeted the secretary of state and Susan Baker as they stepped off the airplane ramp. The communications problems had kept Ross from speaking with his boss for seven hours; now Ross took Baker aside and explained to him what he would have to accomplish with Shevardnadze.

When the two men withdrew into the airport's VIP lounge, Baker argued with Shevardnadze for the arms embargo: "This statement has to have teeth in it. It has to be clear to Saddam Hussein and the world that we're together."

The foreign minister required little persuading but stressed that the Soviets would not acquiesce in American "gunboat diplomacy." Baker assured him that Bush would not take unilateral military action against Iraq unless American citizens were harmed.

Finally, the doors to the room were flung open, and the two men walked across the gleaming marble floor to a lectern, where a crowd of reporters was waiting. With Shevardnadze at his side, Baker announced the "unusual step" of "jointly calling upon the rest of the international community to join with us in an international cutoff of all arms supplies to Iraq."

Baker flew on to Washington, arriving on Saturday morning, August 4. He immediately took a helicopter to Camp David, where he joined the president, Quayle, Scowcroft, Cheney, Powell, and other officials at a long table in the wood-paneled conference room.

Outside the room was a souvenir of the administration's last major military exploit: a framed, life-size photograph of Bush, riddled with bullet holes, which had been seized the previous December at General Manuel Noriega's private rifle range in Panama.

Richard Haass, a Harvard political scientist who was Scowcroft's principal aide for the Middle East, observed that there was a "palpable sense of history" in the room: everyone knew that this was the "first test of the post–Cold War era."

Lawrence Eagleburger warned that if they allowed Saddam's aggression to stand, it would set "all the wrong standards for the new world order." It would tell the Muammar Qaddafis and the Kim Il Sungs that with the removal of one of the two superpowers, "pipsqueaks like Saddam Hussein can do more rather than less because they aren't constrained by their Big Brother." By the end of the session, Bush had resolved to send 200,000 U.S. troops to Saudi Arabia, if the Saudis agreed.

That day in Washington, the Soviet embassy delivered a letter from Shevardnadze to Baker. As soon as Baker read it, he realized how great a domestic price Shevardnadze was having to pay for acceding to their joint statement in Moscow: it was obvious that he was now being forced to cut his losses with his comrades.

The letter said that the Soviet Union would not support any further UN resolutions against Iraq until it was clear that Iraq had refused to comply with Resolution 660. Saddam should be given some time to withdraw from Kuwait. Shevardnadze wrote that he was "alarmed" by reports that the United States was pushing to halt commercial air service to Iraq, as that would "jeopardize" the possible evacuation of Soviet and other foreign nationals.

At the White House on Monday morning, August 6, having gained Saudi approval for the airlift, dubbed Operation Desert Shield, Bush, Baker, and Scowcroft discussed how to break the news to Moscow that hundreds of thousands of U.S. troops were about to go to the Gulf.

The three men agreed that it would be "disastrous" if the Soviets publicly criticized the airlift. Such an exchange could even spark a classic Cold War–style crisis, in which Saddam would try to play off one power against the other. Scowcroft was eager to establish an American-Soviet partnership, but only so long as the Soviet Union was distinctly the junior partner.

At the president's behest, Baker telephoned Shevardnadze, who was resting at his dacha outside Moscow. He ran through the latest U.S.

intelligence estimates of the Iraqi buildup: more than 100,000 troops, armed with tanks, artillery, and surface-to-surface missiles. He reported that in response to a Saudi request, Bush was going to send U.S. forces to the Gulf. He insisted that Washington was not trying to exploit the crisis to enhance its influence in the Middle East.

Baker said that the president would issue a secret order that afternoon, with troops to begin moving the following day. On Wednesday, the administration would announce the action to the world. Baker said he was calling now so that Gorbachev and Shevardnadze would not be taken by surprise.

Irritated, Shevardnadze said, "Are you *consulting* us or are you *informing* us?"

"We're informing you, I guess, but isn't there *something* we can do together here? I have no authority to offer this, but what would you think of contributing naval forces or ground forces yourself? How can we work together on this?"

Shevardnadze said he had nothing to offer. Baker persisted: "Look, is there *anything* else we can do to cooperate on this?"

Shevardnadze improvised: "How about the Military Staff Committee of the Security Council?"

Over the previous three days, the Moscow hard-liners had discussed how they might prevent the United States from taking unilateral action against Iraq. One possibility they had considered was this moribund UN committee, which Moscow had long been attempting to revive as a means of enhancing Soviet influence. The hard-liners felt that involving the committee in the Gulf crisis might give the Soviet Union an effective veto over a U.S. military attack on Baghdad.

Baker promised to raise the idea with Bush. He reported to the president that Shevardnadze was "plenty pissed" that he had not been consulted in advance about the decision to send U.S. troops to the Gulf. Both Bush and Powell were worried about the idea of using the Military Staff Committee, for precisely the same reasons that the Soviet hard-liners supported it: it would give the Soviet Defense Ministry a say in the Gulf operation. But on second thought, the two men realized that it might actually help enmesh the Soviets in an eventual military attack on Iraqi forces.

Baker telephoned Shevardnadze and said that the United States had "absolutely no problem" with a Soviet naval or land presence in the Gulf. Shevardnadze replied, "If President Bush is interested, then I'll raise the matter with President Gorbachev."

When Baker suggested such American-Soviet cooperation to the State Department, however, he provoked much the same kind of complaints that Shevardnadze had stirred in the Foreign Ministry. U.S. diplomats fired off memos warning that to invite the Soviet Union to send forces to the Gulf region was to discard four decades of diplomacy aimed at keeping the Soviets out.

Shevardnadze called Baker back to say that he and Gorbachev could not go along with the suggestion that Moscow deploy military forces in the crisis zone. One reason was that memories of Afghanistan — the last instance in which the Soviet Union had intervened militarily in the Islamic world — were still too fresh in Moscow. Baker was nevertheless able to persuade the foreign minister to endorse a new UN resolution imposing severe trade and military sanctions on Iraq.*

By endorsing the possibility of a revived Military Staff Committee, Baker felt that he had gone a long way toward quelling Soviet doubts about American good faith in the Gulf. He told Shevardnadze about the flak he was getting from his own bureaucracy and encouraged him to inform his Arabists that their decision to break with Iraq had already paid off: for the first time, the United States had invited the Soviet Union to be militarily and politically involved in the Gulf.

But the two countries were still a long way from being in lockstep. On Wednesday morning, August 8, after Bush announced that elements of the 82nd Airborne Division and key U.S. Air Force units were assuming "defensive positions" in Saudi Arabia, an official Soviet spokesman in Moscow cautioned against U.S. "muscle-flexing."

During the week that followed, Baker and Shevardnadze spoke by telephone almost daily, collaborating on another UN resolution opposing Saddam's "annexation" of Kuwait.

On Thursday, August 16, Baker wrote Shevardnadze of his anxiety over U.S. citizens' being rounded up in Kuwait and held as hostages. He was concerned that the nearly eight thousand Soviet citizens working in Iraq could likewise be taken hostage if the situation were to deteriorate further — and if the Kremlin were seen to be siding with the White House against Saddam. Shevardnadze agreed to still another

* Resolution 661, which was enacted on August 6, embargoed Iraqi and Kuwaiti imports and exports, established a Security Council committee to monitor its implementation, and promised further "efforts to put an early end to the invasion by Iraq."

UN resolution, this one demanding that Iraq allow the "immediate departure" of foreign citizens.*

The next day, Gorbachev interrupted his Black Sea vacation to view a Soviet army exercise in Odessa. In a televised speech, he called the invasion of Kuwait a "blatant violation" of international law; only "collective efforts" and "political methods," he said, would keep it from "escalating into a full-scale military confrontation."

Defending his government's cooperation with Washington, he declared, "For us to have reacted in a different way would have been unacceptable, since the act of aggression was committed with the help of our weapons, which we had agreed to sell to Iraq to maintain its defense capability, rather than to seize foreign territories and whole countries."

Bush and Baker were delighted by Gorbachev's speech, especially because they knew that American-Soviet solidarity was about to be tested in a way that might fracture the partnership almost as soon as it had begun.

An Iraqi tanker was steaming toward Yemen, where it was expected to unload Iraqi oil. A U.S. frigate fired warning shots, but the tanker refused to reverse course. In Baghdad, an official spokesman warned of "grave consequences" if the United States did not leave the ship alone.

From his Wyoming ranch, Baker called Shevardnadze. He said that he had asked the president to hold off on ordering U.S. naval action against the ship, but only if the Soviet Union endorsed a new UN resolution that would authorize military action to enforce the embargo.

Baker felt that the United States already had the right to use force under Article 51 of the UN charter, but he knew that unless specific authorization was given by the Security Council, the Soviets and other partners might pull out of the anti-Saddam coalition. Still, if the United States and its partners waited too long for a resolution, it might be too late to enforce the sanctions.

On Monday, August 20, the Iraqi deputy premier, Saadoun Hammadi, met with Shevardnadze in Moscow. Shevardnadze demanded Saddam's unconditional withdrawal from Kuwait and the release of all foreign nationals held in Iraq.

---

* Resolutions 662, proposed on August 9, and 664, proposed on August 18, were enacted unanimously.

Hammadi scrutinized Shevardnadze's language for signs that Saddam might split the Americans and Soviets apart. He found none, but members of his staff, after talking privately to Arabists in the Foreign Ministry, told him that there was widespread concern that Shevardnadze might be too far out on a limb. Hammadi returned home to Baghdad with a definite sense that there were tensions within the Soviet government that could be exploited in Iraq's favor.

Shevardnadze sent Baker two detailed reports of the talks, saying, "Let us see what happens when Hammadi reports to Saddam Hussein." He asked Baker for another five days to give Hammadi time to persuade his boss: "We think we have a chance to get the Iraqis to pull out and live up to the terms of Resolution 660 — to withdraw unconditionally — but we need a little time to do it."

Nervous about the delay, Baker replied that Scowcroft and the Pentagon were calling for the use of force with or without a new UN resolution. "There's not a lot of time," he said. "We have this early test. It's important for us to stay together. It's important for us to do this on the basis of Security Council resolutions if we can, but not at the price of either allowing them to break the coalition or allowing them to think they can separate us."

Baker suggested that they come to a decision within three days: "Otherwise, the ships will have moved to a point where we can't do anything to stop them." Shevardnadze promised, "I'll get back to you." In the meantime, at the UN, Pickering circulated several drafts of a possible use-of-force resolution to the other four permanent members of the Security Council.

In Kennebunkport, sitting at a round table near the rocky edge of Walker's Point, Bush held a meeting on the problem. Scowcroft and Powell argued for moving against the Iraqi tanker right away, without waiting for a UN resolution. They cited heavy pressure from Margaret Thatcher, the media, and Congress. Scowcroft said, "If we don't act now, after all our strong statements, we'll look like a paper tiger. You can't back down at the outset."

On Baker's behalf, Eagleburger said, "At least give us a chance to see if we can't bring the Soviets along." Bush resolved the matter in Baker's favor but said that it was a "tough call" and that he felt "very frustrated."

When the Iraqi tanker finally made its way to Yemen, the United States held its fire. Bush tried to mollify Thatcher in a call to London.

When it came to standing up to aggressive dictators, the prime minister considered herself the reincarnation of Winston Churchill. She was proud of having locked horns with Argentina over its invasion of the Falklands, and of having won that contest. Now, agitated by what Bush was telling her, she said, "All right, George, all right, but this is no time to go wobbly."

On Wednesday, Baker called Shevardnadze and turned up the heat. Iraq was ignoring existing UN resolutions, he said, so it was time for a new, tougher provision. Shevardnadze replied that Saddam had yet to give the Soviets his final answer, but since Baker felt so strongly, they would agree to a new UN resolution by Saturday if Saddam did not yield before then.

Baker said, "The president doesn't want this to drag on indefinitely. . . . Can you guarantee your support for the resolution if we delay the vote until Saturday?"

"We'll have to do a complete review of the situation," said Shevardnadze. "We want to put more political pressure on Iraq. We also don't want to do anything precipitous that might harm Soviet nationals in Iraq. Our review will be over by early Friday, Moscow time. We will tell you then how we'll act in the Security Council. I'll be in touch with you if there are differences between the Soviet position and the draft resolution."

Baker bore down: "We'll give you your three days. But will you promise me now that if we *do* move on Saturday, we'll have your support?"

Shevardnadze refused to commit himself. Instead, he took the offensive, complaining about charges made by American newspapers that the Soviet Union had known about and approved of Saddam's invasion in advance. He noted that one American conservative think-tank expert, writing on the *New York Times*'s op-ed page, seemed to have gotten this idea from highly placed sources in U.S. military intelligence.*

Shevardnadze said, "I know that newspapers are newspapers and journalists are journalists. But this kind of thing cannot help but cause serious anxiety and concern here in Moscow. . . . We are always puzzled and alarmed by such stories where unnamed officials and sources are concerned."

Flipping through a folder of press clippings on his lap, Baker struck back. He read aloud from an article in the conservative *Washington*

* That morning's *New York Times* op-ed page included a piece by Peter Schweizer of the conservative American Foreign Policy Council, entitled "Is Moscow Playing Cute on Kuwait?"

Times charging that the Soviet military was still aiding the Iraqi army. Both men were playing good cop, pointing ominously over their shoulders at the bad cops in their own military establishments.

Shevardnadze told Baker, "Probably people in both of our countries would like to move back to old thinking if given the opportunity to poison the well."

Early on Thursday morning, August 23, Bush took Scowcroft aboard his blue-hulled speedboat *Fidelity* off Kennebunkport. As Scowcroft later recalled, "It hadn't been a great summer for bluefish. The fish weren't biting. We got the chance to talk the way we so rarely do in Washington. You're out there on a boat in the ocean. There's absolutely nothing to do."

During the four-hour outing, away from the pressures of decision, Bush mused about Shevardnadze's "courage" in standing up to the Soviet military on the Gulf. Gorbachev's support for the UN resolutions had shown a "fundamental shift" in Soviet policy, he said. Until now, the United States could not have been sure how the Soviets would react in a Third World crisis like the one in Kuwait.

Bush told Scowcroft that the Gulf crisis had helped to crystallize some of his own ideas about foreign policy and the UN. A new world system really seemed to be in the making; perhaps the UN could finally assume the role it was designed for in 1945, with the United States and the Soviet Union acting as partners in a global scheme of collective security. The "good news" about the situation in the Gulf, he said, was that it was showing the world the "real possibility" of cooperation with the Soviet Union.

Bush said that Saddam was just the kind of villain who could force "civilized nations" to see the importance of stopping "another Hitler." If handled properly, this crisis could deter other acts of "naked aggression" and set the stage for other instances of international cooperation. To Scowcroft's surprise, amid these geopolitical ruminations, the president caught three bluefish.

On Friday, August 24, Shevardnadze called Baker in Wyoming to say that the Soviet government's "review" of the Gulf crisis was finished. Gorbachev had just sent Saddam a private message that "categorically" asked how Iraq planned to respond to the existing UN resolutions. He had demanded a same-day response.

"Frankly, we don't expect a major change in the Iraqi position,"

Shevardnadze told Baker. "But we have a moral obligation to give him one last chance to pull back. We'll inform the United States as soon as we hear from him."*

The foreign minister added that he and Gorbachev "basically" approved of the draft resolution that Pickering was circulating in New York, though "we'll have a few changes to propose. Some might make it even stronger and more flexible, expanding the scope of the means to enforce the resolutions. . . . We'll send instructions to our UN representative, assuming that the Iraqi reply is hopeless. We'll be working late tonight here in Moscow."

On Friday evening at 9:45 Moscow time, Shevardnadze's deputy Alexander Belogonov summoned Matlock to the Foreign Ministry and presented him with a letter from Shevardnadze to Baker. It said that Shevardnadze had hoped to telephone the secretary of state but was tied up at the Kremlin. Gorbachev had received Saddam's reply, which was "completely unsatisfactory": "I do not believe it would be worth commenting on," wrote the foreign minister. "We have given instructions to our UN representative to see Ambassador Pickering."

Before dawn on Saturday, the Security Council approved Resolution 665 by a vote of 13 to 0, with Yemen and Cuba abstaining. To accommodate Soviet sensitivities, the resolution did not call outright for the use of force but instead provided for "measures commensurate to the specific circumstance" to enforce the four previous resolutions on Kuwait.

Shevardnadze reached Baker later and said, "President Gorbachev wants to convey to President Bush how satisfied he is with our joint work in the Security Council."

"We agree," said Baker. "This is unprecedented. . . . We can only overcome this thing if we and the international community show sufficient resolve."

Shevardnadze noted that he was soon to see the French foreign minister, Roland Dumas, and said, "I will pass along your regards, if you don't object." Shevardnadze was doing more than engaging in courtesies: he was underscoring for Baker how closely he, as foreign minister of the Soviet Union, was collaborating with two different NATO governments.

That day, the United States initiated a full naval blockade of Iraq.

---

* Sergei Chetverikov of the Soviet embassy briefed Kimmitt at the State Department on the text of Gorbachev's demarche.

*   *   *

Although Gorbachev had gone along with it in the end, Shevardnadze's role in the passage of Resolution 665 lent still more weight to the arguments of Kryuchkov, Yazov, and other competitors for Gorbachev's ear that Shevardnadze was much too sympathetic toward the Americans. Over the past year, the Soviet generals had suffered one reversal after another, and now 200,000 U.S. troops were massed only seven hundred miles from the Soviet border. Whatever the Americans said, who knew when they would leave?

In Moscow, Gorbachev told reporters in late August that the sooner a political settlement of the Gulf crisis allowed the U.S. to withdraw its troops, "the calmer we all will feel. . . . We know that an escalation of the military situation is fraught with unknown consequences."

Yevgeni Primakov had by now appointed himself spokesman for those in Moscow who were worried about the U.S. military presence in the Gulf. He wished to resolve the crisis "by political means" — by reaching a compromise that would leave Saddam with at least some of his territorial gains.

The highly ambitious Primakov now saw an opportunity to position himself for the moment when Gorbachev grew so tired of Shevardnadze's unpopularity that he would decide to sack him and choose a new foreign minister. Already there were rumors in Moscow that Gorbachev was ready to give Shevardnadze a new, largely ceremonial portfolio as "adviser" on the nationalities problem, or perhaps as the first Soviet vice president.

Bush and Baker knew that dislodging Saddam from Kuwait might take military action, and that getting Soviet consent for such action would not be easy. The Soviets kept refusing U.S. requests for even token participation in the coalition force — for example, just one warship in the multinational flotilla.

In an Oval Office briefing, Condoleezza Rice advised Bush that below the second echelon of the Soviet Foreign Ministry, there was a "pretty clear lack of support" for Soviet cooperation with the United States on the Gulf.

The president worried that Gorbachev was less willing than Shevardnadze to accept the huge U.S. military deployment in the Gulf. By the end of August, the one major coalition leader with whom Bush had yet to talk by telephone was the president of the Soviet Union.

To invigorate his relations with Gorbachev, Bush decided to ask him for a meeting in a neutral European capital. At Malta and in Washington, his private powers of persuasion had helped to relieve Gorbachev's anxieties about American intentions toward the Baltics and Germany. Another personal meeting would, he hoped, allow him to assure the Soviet leader that the United States had no wish to be a permanent military presence in the Gulf, and show him how the crisis could help to fulfill his vision of an interdependent world based on the rule of law.

With his belief in personal gestures, Bush presumed that Gorbachev would be flattered that he would take the trouble to come so far to see him on such short notice. By now he was also prepared to offer some modest form of financial aid that would demonstrate to the Soviet people the value of a close relationship with the United States.

Bush realized that Gorbachev's support for the U.S. position on the Gulf might ultimately hinge on American acceptance of a postcrisis role for the Soviet Union in the Middle East. The United States might have to give in to some version of the old Soviet demand for an international conference to settle the Israeli-Palestinian dispute and other outstanding Middle East issues.

Under the new world order he had sketched out for Scowcroft on the *Fidelity,* the president had no objection to accommodating the Soviets in this matter, though he could not say so in public. If Bush were to proclaim that he was ready to accept increased Soviet influence in the region, his own domestic critics, like Gorbachev's, would doubtless say that he had paid too high a price for cooperation.

Furthermore, if Bush were to publicly announce his acquiescence in the formation of a postcrisis international conference of the kind that the United States and Israel had long opposed, he would provoke domestic accusations that he had given in to Saddam's demands and sold out the Israelis in order to pursue his relationship with Gorbachev. This would be especially damaging coming at a time when much effort was required to build support among the American people for a possible war with Iraq.

Gorbachev seized upon Bush's proposal for a meeting. Since the Finns were best equipped to host such an event with little advance warning, Helsinki was nominated as the venue. Bush would be paying Gorbachev the compliment of traveling all the way to the doorstep of the Soviet Union.

On Saturday, September 1, on the lawn of his house at Kennebunkport, Bush announced the meeting to reporters, who had already learned of the possibility from a leak the previous day to the *Washing-*

ton Post — the second time in a year that the *Post* had broken the story of a Bush-Gorbachev meeting before the president could make it official.* A White House spokesman told reporters that the "concept of ad hoc, confidential contacts at the highest level" matched the "new spirit of the Soviet-U.S. dialogue."

Three days later, in a speech given in the Pacific port city of Vladivostok, Shevardnadze tried to recoup some of his own domestic standing by taking a public position on the Gulf that was close to Primakov's. He hinted broadly that the crisis should be explicitly linked to an international conference on the Israeli-Palestinian dispute, saying that Iraq's seizure of Kuwait was "one of several highly complex, interlocking problems" in the Middle East that demanded a "coordinated solution."†

The words *interlocking* and *coordinated* caused heartburn in Washington. They smacked of exactly what the United States was determined to avoid: linkage between the resolution of two very different issues — namely, Saddam's aggression against Kuwait and Israel's occupation of the West Bank, the Gaza Strip, and the Golan Heights.

The Bush administration had decided that it could stomach an international peace conference cosponsored by the United States and the Soviet Union, but it was more unwilling than ever to play along with Saddam's attempt to condition his withdrawal from Kuwait on Israel's withdrawal from the occupied territories. It was one thing to reward the Soviet Union for the many genuine and spectacular improvements in its international behavior; it was quite another to appear to be rewarding Saddam for undoing his act of aggression.

Baker tried to paper over the issue. He said on NBC that with the "extraordinary degree of international consensus" on Iraq, an international conference was "almost" in effect already. He went on to say, however, that "we would like to see a little bit more of what the Soviets have in mind."

The next day, Israeli Foreign Minister David Levy met with Baker in Washington for the first high-level American-Israeli meeting since the crisis began. In a subtle public signal to the Soviets, Baker said afterward, "We agreed it is very important in the context of the overall

---

* Buried inside the paper was a story headlined "U.S.-Soviet Meeting Rumored for Sept. 8."
† So much for Baker's May 1989 prediction that Shevardnadze's interest in an international conference on the Middle East would, in time, "go away."

situation in the Middle East that there be a credible peace process under way."

Trying to erase the unwanted implication of what Shevardnadze had said at Vladivostok, Baker added that he and Levy had also agreed that "we should not link the situation between Israel and the Palestinians with the situation in the Persian Gulf, as some have suggested."

On Friday evening, September 7, at Andrews Air Force Base, Bush boarded for the first time the new specially built Boeing 747 that had just been designated *Air Force One*. Shortly before takeoff, the president told reporters that he planned to "go to sleep right away. I got no news."

Helen Thomas of UPI was unhappy to discover that on the new plane, the president was even more insulated from the press than he had been on the old one. Barbara Bush quipped with good-natured sarcasm, "Yes, we have been complaining about that!"

On Saturday, the huge plane landed at Helsinki Airport. There were puddles on the tarmac, but the rain had stopped. At the nineteenth-century Presidential Palace on the waterfront, Bush lunched with Finnish President Mauno Koivisto. The two men had known each other since 1983. Koivisto was a Russian-speaking student of the Soviet Union, and he and Bush had compared their impressions of that country over the years.

This time, Bush told Koivisto that he was very worried about the future of Gorbachev and *perestroika:* "Even in a capitalist system, you can't tell people in advance that they're going to have to put up with unemployment and inflation.

"Gorbachev's been so honest with the Soviet people about the sacrifices they're going to have to make that he's increased the chances of failure. He's put people in a dark mood. They're taking out their fears and frustrations on him." Koivisto was struck by how much more pessimistic Bush was about Gorbachev in private than he was in public.

After the luncheon, the president went to the U.S. ambassador's residence, where seventy-five employees and their families waited with punch and cookies under a large blue and white tent. Mixing with the crowd, he referred to the U.S. military buildup in the Gulf in classic Bush-speak: "Lotta air force down there. Lotta planes down there. Lotta knowledge. Hopefully it'll keep Saddam Hussein from doing anything reckless."

* * *

At the Soviet embassy in Helsinki, late on Saturday evening, Gorbachev told Shevardnadze, Primakov, Akhromeyev, and other aides that he had not given up on the idea of exactly the sort of linkage that the Americans — and the Israelis — so wanted to avoid. Perhaps it was time, he said, to step up efforts to solve the Palestinian problem "in the context" of dislodging Iraq from Kuwait "by political means."

Primakov favored doing everything possible to find Saddam a dignified way to back out of Kuwait. At the same time, he worried that Saddam might be so stubborn that he would pass up the chance to play the Palestinian card, in which case his hand would be weaker than ever. If the Soviet Union succeeded in overcoming American objections and establishing linkage, and Saddam still refused to withdraw, he would have to bear "grave responsibility" for blocking a resolution to the Palestinian problem.

Akhromeyev was already thinking about what would happen when "political means" failed and the Gulf was plunged into war. He reminded Gorbachev that military action would bring "colossal destruction and human casualties." The allies would not be able to dislodge Saddam "by an air strike alone"; they would have to conduct a bruising, prolonged ground war.

Akhromeyev pointed out that the Iraqi army had more than three thousand tanks in Kuwait and Basra, in southern Iraq. If war began, these could push into Saudi Arabia. Furthermore, the Iraqi army was battle-hardened: with eight years of fighting experience against Iran, it had proved that it was "not afraid of losses."

While Gorbachev met with his aides, Baker briefed Bush and Scowcroft on a quick trip he had just made to the Middle East. He asked Ross to draft a joint U.S.-Soviet statement on the Gulf that would be "pithy, unbureaucratic, quotable, and unmistakable." It should signal that once the Gulf crisis was resolved, the United States would be willing to proceed toward a Middle East peace conference — as a reward not to Saddam but to Gorbachev, for his role in the resolution.

The next morning, Bush and Gorbachev met in the second-floor Yellow Salon of Koivisto's Presidential Palace. Gorbachev denounced Saddam's "barbaric attack" on Kuwait but also gibed Bush for his hasty dispatch of 200,000 troops to the Gulf without consultation with Moscow.

Then Gorbachev said, "Why don't we push for an international conference on the whole Middle East? This would be a way to flush out Saddam's intentions. If he says no and still refuses to get out of Kuwait, we've exposed him. If he says yes, then we're ahead of the game."

"If we did that," Bush objected, "we'd put him in the position of saying that he's done this for the Palestinians. We'd be rewarding him. We'd be playing his game."

But Gorbachev persisted: "The situation in the Middle East will remain as uneasy as it is now until the problem is solved comprehensively."

Bush agreed that when the crisis was over, the United States and the Soviet Union together should sponsor an international conference on the region. But he insisted that there must be no public hint of any linkage between the conference and Soviet support for the American position in the Gulf.

This was an important moment in the history of both the Soviet-American relationship and U.S. diplomacy in the Middle East. In order to keep Gorbachev on board the anti-Iraq coalition, Bush was reversing America's forty-five-year-old policy of trying to keep the Soviets out of the Middle East. He was effectively agreeing in private to a linkage that he would continue to deny in public.*

Recognizing that he had gotten what he came for, Gorbachev beckoned to Bessmertnykh and whispered, "You and Shevardnadze work on this and wrap it up."

Gorbachev let Bush know that he was nearly as eager to get U.S. troops out of Saudi Arabia as he was to get Iraqi troops out of Kuwait. Operation Desert Shield had already achieved a number of strategic objectives: Saudi Arabia and the other Gulf states had not been invaded, and a world oil crisis had been averted. What was now needed was "new diplomatic efforts."

Bush agreed. He assured Gorbachev that U.S. troops would stay in the Gulf only until the UN resolutions had been carried out and the security needs of the area met: "And the sooner they are out of there, as far as I'm concerned, the better. . . . We have no intention of keeping

---

* Three months later, he said at a press conference, "The question is the aggression against Kuwait. There will be, and is, no linkage to the West Bank question. . . . The United States, of course, remains interested in a solution to that other question, but there is no linkage with what has happened in Kuwait or what *will* happen in Kuwait." Realizing how convoluted and unconvincing his statement must have sounded, Bush paused and jovially added, "Tough way to make a living!" The reporters laughed.

them a day longer than is required." Listening to this statement, Gorbachev managed to look both relieved and skeptical.

During the morning, Baker and Shevardnadze met in another room of the Presidential Palace. Shevardnadze said that Saddam Hussein was a "ruthless, brutal, evil man" who had, among other things, "lied" to Moscow about his intentions toward Kuwait. Baker replied, "We have to continue to build up international pressure on Saddam so that he sees no way out except to withdraw. We have to have a joint statement."

Shevardnadze nodded and said, "Yes. Otherwise it will look as if we're not as close together as we are. It's good that you have lowered public expectations these last few days. That way, whatever statement we write will be more effective."

"I've got a draft statement," Baker said, and he read Ross's draft aloud. There was no mention of an international conference.

Shevardnadze said, "That sounds good to me as far as it goes, but we'd also like to have something on the other issues, such as an international conference."

Baker balked. "An international conference is a buzzword," he said. "It's a symbol of linkage. Explicit linkage between a settlement of the crisis and an international conference would make Saddam seem like a hero. That's not the way to get a broader peace after the crisis. The way to do that is to show that Saddam's method of behavior doesn't succeed. . . . We're interested in practical steps to produce the outcome we want. We have to avoid playing into Saddam's hands or misleading him."

Shevardnadze said, "I can't disagree with that." Motioning to Tarasenko and Ross, he suggested, "Why don't we have Sergei and Dennis work on finalizing the language?"

As Shevardnadze spoke, Baker saw more sharply than ever the difference between Gorbachev and his foreign minister. Shevardnadze was far more apprehensive about the use of force inside the Soviet Union than outside, while Gorbachev was just the opposite. Gorbachev was urging a peaceful resolution of the crisis, implying that he would accept a compromise. Shevardnadze, by contrast, told Baker, "Anything that leaves Saddam Hussein intact with his horrific weapons would be disastrous."

At the end of the morning, Baker reconnoitered with Bush, who reported, "Gorbachev's big on linking a conference to his support on the Gulf." Baker said, "Here's the statement we did last night. Shevardnadze's agreed in principle. Dennis and his gang are supposed to go off and finalize it."

During a meeting with Richard Haass and Tarasenko on the joint statement, Ross said, "Let's focus on the last paragraph." As an old Middle East hand, Tarasenko was well acquainted with the Americans' sensitivity about an international conference: in October 1977, he had been involved in the writing of another such joint statement, which had been released by Cyrus Vance and Andrei Gromyko only to blow up in their faces.*

They agreed on language for a final paragraph that hinted at the need for a postcrisis peace conference to deal with the Arab-Israeli dispute. Tarasenko said, "Let me put it into Russian and sell it to our side."

Ross and Baker took the result to Bush, who said, "This is a great statement. I'd love it if we could get this. I just wonder if we will because Gorbachev came down so hard on linkage." Baker said, "Shevardnadze and Tarasenko have delivered before, so we'll see."

Tarasenko showed the draft to Shevardnadze, who approved it and showed it to Gorbachev. Primakov, Falin, and Gorbachev's foreign affairs aide Anatoli Chernyayev were also present. Shevardnadze took the statement out of their hands so that they could not fuss over it for too long. After making some minor changes, Gorbachev approved it on the spot.

Tarasenko returned the draft to Ross. "There's been a little damage done to it, but take a look at it," he said. Baker gave it to Bush, who noted that Gorbachev had made some marginal editorial changes but little more.

That afternoon, Bush and Gorbachev spent their first half hour together refining the joint statement. Gorbachev explained his changes and the insertion of some new language that would allow certain food supplies to continue going to Iraq: "We didn't want Saddam to be able to say that we were withholding food from Iraqi children to punish him." Bush agreed: "Absolutely."

---

* Vance and Gromyko publicly announced an agreement to reconvene, under U.S. and Soviet cochairmanship, a Middle East peace conference in Geneva. The initiative quickly turned into a debacle, amid an uproar from Israel and the American Jewish community. The Egyptians, who were the principal Arab players in the diplomatic drama at the time, backed away from the plan, leaving Vance frustrated and Gromyko furious.

Ross said to Tarasenko, "Let's finalize it. The two presidents have agreed on the language." Then Tarasenko produced a different version. The original statement had said that only total adherence to and implementation of the UN resolutions was acceptable, that nothing short of this would end Iraq's isolation. Now the first clause had been softened, the second omitted.

Ross instantly saw the fine hand of Primakov and his colleagues, who were intent on diluting the language. He told Tarasenko. "I didn't hear Gorbachev say that. I didn't hear those two changes." Ross asked Baker, "Can I have your copy?" Baker's version agreed with Ross's.

Ross advised Tarasenko, "Baker's copy is exactly the same as mine. If the two presidents have just worked out an understanding, we can't change what's been agreed to."

Bessmertnykh looked at the new draft and said, "You're right. Gorbachev didn't say this." The earlier, tougher language was restored.*

During his afternoon meeting with Bush, Gorbachev touched briefly on START, CFE, and Afghanistan but spent most of the time on the Soviet internal situation. He said that he intended to go foward with economic reform on the basis of the so-called Five-Hundred-Day Plan.

That very week, a group led by Stanislav Shatalin, an economist and member of Gorbachev's Presidential Council, had completed a new blueprint for economic reform, which called for the sale of huge numbers of state enterprises, the dissolution of state and collective farms, massive reductions in government spending (including a 10 percent cut in military spending and a 20 percent cut in the KGB), currency reform, and a new banking system. Shatalin recommended that all of this happen within five hundred days, though he realized that this aim was more of an ideal than a realistic timetable.

* The final version ended with the following language: "Our preference is to resolve the crisis peacefully, and we will be united against Iraq's aggression as long as the crisis exists. However, we are determined to see this aggression end, and if the current steps fail to end it, we are prepared to consider additional ones consistent with the UN Charter. We must demonstrate beyond any doubt that aggression cannot and will not pay. As soon as the objectives mandated by the UN Security Council resolutions mentioned above have been achieved . . . the Presidents direct their Foreign Ministers to work with countries in the region and outside it to develop regional security structures and measures to promote peace and stability. It is essential to work actively to resolve all remaining conflicts in the Middle East and Persian Gulf. Both sides will continue to consult each other and initiate measures to pursue these broader objectives at the proper time."

Explaining the plan to Bush, Gorbachev said, "The first four or five months will be critical. There will be serious reverberations in our society." He did not ask directly for U.S. credits or other financial aid as a quid pro quo for Soviet cooperation on the Gulf, but he said, "I'm going to need your help. Your attitude on this will be vitally important."

If Gorbachev had been hoping that his endorsement of the Shatalin Plan would open American coffers, he was disappointed. Bush merely offered to accelerate the normalization of the American-Soviet economic relationship as he had proposed at Malta and as the two presidents had agreed at their summit in Washington in June. Hinting at future economic aid to and investment in the Soviet Union, Bush added, "It would open up the door to other good things."*

At six o'clock that evening, the two leaders walked onto the stage at Finlandia Hall. Bush was asked if they had discussed holding an international peace conference to deal with the Palestinian problem. He cautiously replied that although it was "very important that that question be resolved," he felt strongly that the issue "should not be linked" to a solution of the Gulf crisis.

Asked if the talks had further improved their relationship, Gorbachev pushed the limits of what he and Bush had agreed they would say in public: "I don't know if I would be allowed to tell you a secret here. I haven't asked President Bush if he'll let me. But I must admit that I'm dying to take the risk and tell you."

The audience laughed. Bush failed to conceal his worry over what Gorbachev was going to say.

Gorbachev went on, "In our talks, the president said, 'You know, there was a long time when our view was that the Soviet Union had nothing to do in the Middle East, had no business being there.' This was something that we had to talk through during this meeting here in Helsinki. And what was said here is that it's very important for us to cooperate in the Middle East, just as it is on other issues of world politics."

Bush looked relieved: Gorbachev had given away no secrets. The Soviet leader was merely trying to increase the credit he would get at home for extracting a concession from Bush.

As they rode back to their hotel, Tarasenko exulted to Ross about

---

* That fall, Gorbachev refused to wage the political battle with economic conservatives in Moscow that would have been required to implement the Shatalin Plan.

the "miracle" they had accomplished: "We've really changed the course of U.S.-Soviet relations," he declared. "The future will never be the same, because we've established that we can truly be partners." Gorbachev told his staff that his talks with Bush had convinced him that the U.S. president intended to solve the crisis "by political means."

In public, Bush was restrained in his comments on the meeting. He did not wish to raise expectations about what the fragile Soviet-U.S. entente on the Gulf could achieve. As with the opening of the Berlin Wall, the fall of Eastern Europe, and German unification, his instinct was to let the event speak for itself. Nor did he wish to provide ammunition for Gorbachev's hard-line critics by gloating over how well the Helsinki meeting had gone from an American standpoint.

But during his Sunday-night air journey home to Washington, far from the prying cameras and tape recorders of the White House press pool, the president was in an expansive mood and confided to his aides that he felt "elated."

CHAPTER 13

"You Can't Back Off"

IN MOSCOW on Monday, September 10, 1990, Baker met with Shevardnadze to tie up loose ends from Helsinki and discuss other issues that had not found their way onto the presidential agenda there. Shevardnadze praised Baker for his recent visit to Damascus and his talks with Syrian President Hafez el-Assad, who had been a Soviet ally and U.S. enemy for decades: "This is very important," he said, "and I'm sure we can do something to help with Syria."

The secretary of state said, "We will need to have some kind of security structure in the Gulf once we get this crisis behind us." Reviewing trouble spots around the world, Baker focused on Havana: with Cuba serving as a rotating member of the UN Security Council that autumn, Castro's government would be able to make trouble for Washington over the Gulf.

Baker offered a sweetener intended to reciprocate Moscow's sensitivity to the U.S. position on the Gulf and at the same time, he hoped, make Castro slightly easier to deal with: "We're prepared to take steps on Cuba — confidence-building measures to demonstrate to the Cubans that the U.S. is no threat to their security. We are ready to notify Havana of all U.S. military exercises in or near Cuba in order to show that we're not trying to exploit the situation as the Soviet Union disengages." Shevardnadze was grateful.

Baker complained that with progress on CFE and START slowed almost to a standstill since the spring, "we're running the risk of having these negotiations become irrelevant." Shevardnadze said, "I agree. Let's make a big push when we meet in New York in two weeks."

On Tuesday, September 25, the Security Council debated Resolution 670, which would escalate the pressure on Iraq by halting commercial air traffic to and from both Iraq and Kuwait. It would also require UN member states to detain any Iraqi ships that defied the embargo and tried to enter their ports.

Before the vote, Shevardnadze spoke more harshly about Iraq than he had ever done before in public. The August 2 invasion, he said, had been an "act of terrorism . . . an affront to world order. . . . War may break out in the Gulf region any day, any moment." He even hinted that if diplomacy failed, the Soviet Union might support some kind of UN-led military action against Iraq. Only Cuba opposed the resolution.

In a private talk with Shevardnadze the next day, the secretary of state praised his speech. Both men agreed on the need for them to coordinate closely on the Gulf in order to increase the pressure on Saddam. While in New York, each met with a number of Arab foreign ministers in a joint effort to "wean" as many Arab states as possible away from Saddam.

Before Shevardnadze arrived in New York, Bush wrote to Gorbachev about the arms control deadlock. If START and CFE were not settled soon, he warned, there would be no agreement that year, which would damage the CSCE summit in November. Bush had previously told Gorbachev he would not attend the CSCE summit unless CFE was completed; now he urged him to instruct Shevardnadze to resolve all major outstanding issues on the two treaties.

In a meeting on Thursday, September 27, Baker and Shevardnadze cleared several technical hurdles on CFE.* START was not discussed.

---

* They narrowed the gap between their two positions on the "sufficiency rule," which held that no single nation should have more than a stipulated percentage of the total tanks, artillery, and other weapons allowed in Europe. (The United States had pushed for a maximum of 20 percent, the Soviets for 40.) They also resolved their differences over the total number of weapons to be allowed in various zones in Europe under a treaty in order to avoid concentrations of troops and weapons in any one area. Limits

Tarasenko confided to Ross, "It is getting to be very difficult to get decisions on this issue in Moscow. People are preoccupied with the Gulf and internal problems. Our military is reluctant to close on these treaties."

At a preparatory CSCE meeting in New York the following week, Shevardnadze told Bush that he was "very confident" that CFE would be ready to be signed in Paris in November. He hoped that START would be finished by the end of the year so that Bush could come to Moscow for a full-fledged summit with Gorbachev in January or February of 1991.

Despite Shevardnadze's outward buoyancy, Baker could tell that his counterpart's nerves were growing more and more frayed as a result of his long battles with the Moscow hard-liners over Germany, the Gulf, arms control, and the Baltics. During the public CSCE ceremonies, Baker offered what he considered to be a routine restatement of U.S. policy on the Baltics, warning against violence and calling for dialogue. This was hardly different from what he had been saying all along, but now it made Shevardnadze hopping mad.

Tarasenko took Ross aside and said, "My minister has taken this very personally. It has put him in a bad position at home. It will be used against him." Ross relayed the message to Baker, who was upset that Shevardnadze had reacted so emotionally to his boiler-plate. He apologized to Shevardnadze both in writing and in person, making it clear that he had not been trying to create any problems for him.

But Shevardnadze also had another reason to be jittery: Primakov had been lobbying Gorbachev for weeks to allow him to undertake a mission to Baghdad to see Saddam. The foreign minister had always rather liked Primakov and felt that he had promoted his career, but now he was furious at this meddling in Gulf policy.

At the Kremlin, Shevardnadze advised Gorbachev that a Primakov mission would send the "wrong signal" to Saddam, who would "interpret and exploit it in his own way."

But Gorbachev felt that Primakov might somehow divine a political

---

on aircraft and definition of what kinds were covered by an agreement were not settled; the Soviets still wanted to avoid restrictions on combat-ready trainers, some land-based naval aircraft, and other planes that the West wished to limit, while the United States continued to insist that carrier-based aircraft not be covered by the treaty.

solution to the crisis and thus get him off the hook with his own hard-liners. "Primakov wants to go, so let him go," said Gorbachev. Shevardnadze stormed back to his office at the Foreign Ministry and told his aides that he might have to quit his job: "We can't have two foreign policies!" he fumed.

On Wednesday, October 3, the two Germanys were officially united as the Federal Republic of Germany. In the wake of the Kohl-Gorbachev talks in the Crimea, the Two-plus-Four powers had in September agreed on a treaty to end the occupation rights of the four World War II victors.

Gorbachev summoned Bessmertnykh from Washington to Moscow to serve as his floor manager in steering ratification of the Germany pact through the Supreme Soviet. As Bessmertnykh later recalled, "It was very tough to get that treaty through. I suggested that we do it in a closed session. If it had been done in the open, the treaty would never have been ratified. Right-wingers would have gone to the microphones and blocked it."

In Baghdad on Friday, October 5, Saddam insisted to Primakov that Kuwait "historically belonged" to Iraq. He would not consider withdrawing from Kuwait until and unless his demands were met. He would let out those Soviet nationals with less than a year left on their Iraqi contracts (about one third of the total) but would not discuss the others. Soviet citizens were thus to be held hostage, along with Americans and others.

Primakov was baffled by Saddam's intransigence. He had predicted to Gorbachev that behind closed doors — and with the right interlocutor — Saddam would begin to deal. He concluded that Saddam's obsession with secrecy and security had so isolated him that he did not understand the full impact of the UN sanctions against his country.

On Saturday evening, Primakov flew back to Moscow and told Gorbachev that the Gulf crisis was nearing a "critical stage." Succumbing to one of the occupational hazards of the diplomat, he portrayed the results of his trip as rosier than they actually were: his mission, he said, had shown "small" signs of a "chance to turn the whole matter toward a political settlement."

Backed by KGB chief Kryuchkov and Prime Minister Pavlov, Gorbachev asked Primakov and Shevardnadze to draw up proposals that would advance the quest for a political solution. He said that these should be floated before Bush, Mitterrand, Assad, President Hosni Mubarak of Egypt, and King Fahd of Saudi Arabia. Finally, Primakov should raise them with Saddam in Baghdad.

Shevardnadze was irate that Gorbachev was assigning Primakov part of the portfolio that rightfully belonged to the foreign minister, but instead of lashing out in protest, he swallowed his pride. Galling as it was to have to endure Primakov's intrusions, Shevardnadze suspected that his rival might be even more dangerous if he were allowed to work his mischief without Shevardnadze at Gorbachev's side to keep an eye on him.

At the Kremlin on Monday, October 8, Primakov told Gorbachev that he had figured out a way to "save face" for Saddam without "rewarding" his aggression: they must convince the Iraqi dictator that if he pulled out of Kuwait, "a process would start, leading to a settlement of the Arab-Israeli conflict."

This, he said, would lead to the kind of "system of strategic security for the region" that Baker talked about. Saddam's old territorial and economic claims against Iraq, meanwhile, would also be adjudicated: "He would know ahead of time that talks with the Kuwaiti leadership would be organized within an Arab framework."

Primakov knew that the phrase "within an Arab framework" would be pleasing to Saddam's ears: it meant that the United States and the other Western coalition partners would be kept at arm's length while Saddam dealt primarily with Arab states, most of them weaker than Iraq and therefore vulnerable to his bullying.

Gorbachev told Primakov to pursue this plan, vague and lopsided though it was, with Western leaders and then with Saddam. But he imposed a stern condition: under no circumstances should Primakov allow the United States to think that the Soviets were backing away from the commitments Gorbachev had made to Bush at Helsinki.

At a meeting of the Supreme Soviet on Monday, October 15, members of the newly established Soyuz (Union) faction took the floor to lambaste Shevardnadze for the "surrender" of Eastern Europe and the decline of Soviet military strength. They complained that in New York Shevardnadze had spoken favorably of possible Soviet participation in a war against Saddam. If Soviet troops were sent to the Gulf, they warned, fifty million Soviet Muslims would rise up in fury against the Kremlin.

Shevardnadze fended off the attack by promising parliamentary consultation: "This is not 1979, a year of great tragedy, when the decision was made to send Soviet troops into Afghanistan. Any use of Soviet troops outside this country will require the consent of the Supreme Soviet."

On Tuesday, October 16, Dick Cheney arrived in Moscow as the guest of Defense Minister Yazov. The secretary of defense had received Yazov in Washington the year before and was now making a return trip. Relations between the two men were correct but far from close; there was nothing like the chemistry and sense of common mission that now united Baker and Shevardnadze.

In part, the mutual wariness between Cheney and Yazov was a function of their jobs. As secretary of defense, Cheney saw himself as responsible for maintaining American military preparedness at a level where the United States could quickly resume the task of deterring Soviet aggression if the hard-liners in the USSR were to come out on top after a power struggle. Cheney was a firm believer in his friend Scowcroft's favorite maxim — "Judge your enemy by his capabilities, not his intentions" — and he was convinced that Soviet military capabilities were still formidable.

As for Yazov, he believed it was his responsibility to keep Soviet military power from being sacrificed on the altar of *perestroika*. He made no bones about his unhappiness over the course of Kremlin policy. He felt that little good had come of Gorbachev's friendship with Bush, or Shevardnadze's with Baker, and he had no desire to develop a similar relationship with his own American counterpart.

Yazov kept complaining to Cheney about the decay of the Soviet military and the decline of the Soviet Union. Cheney knew he was supposed to react with sympathy, but he had difficulty doing so. He privately said, "Yazov is not warm and cuddly."

Yazov and his colleagues feted Cheney over dinner at a Defense Ministry dacha outside Moscow. When Cheney, in his toast, praised the awarding of the 1990 Nobel Peace Prize to Gorbachev, there was silence in the room. As Cheney later recalled, "It was as if I'd done something gross in the middle of the table. They were not enthusiastic about Gorbachev's prize — or about Gorbachev himself!"

The Soviets took Cheney to a MiG factory that was being converted to "peaceful purposes." One of the new products rolling off the assembly line was a Soviet version of the Cuisinart tabletop food processor. Cheney remembered, "It was about six feet high. It couldn't fit in any apartment in Moscow." He asked the factory manager, "Are there parts available for this?" The manager said, "We are having a terrible time getting them." Cheney wondered, "How about parts for a MiG fighter?" The reply: "No problem at all."

Like so many of the other words in the vocabulary of *perestroika*, *conversion* had yet to be given real meaning in Soviet economics. The system was still geared to churn out weapons of war; the military was the only consumer likely to be satisfied for a long time to come.

At the Kremlin, Cheney found Gorbachev "his usual aggressive self" but felt that he "seemed to be carrying a heavier burden than before." Gorbachev castigated Bush for his use of the U.S. Navy in the Gulf: "The president is a former navy man. Everyone in the U.S. government is obsessed with the navy."

When Cheney congratulated him on his Nobel Peace Prize, Gorbachev was churlish: "I suppose, coming from a secretary of defense, that should be taken as a disguised complaint!" Nevertheless, he ordered Soviet military officials to brief Cheney and his delegation on "everything the Iraqi military has."

Primakov flew to Europe to peddle his "peace plan." In Rome, Prime Minister Andreotti said that he would accept it if the Americans did.* In Paris, Mitterrand endorsed the notion that the prospect of a solution to the Palestinian problem would "help settle the Kuwait crisis," but he quickly added that he doubted Bush would agree.

Outraged that Gorbachev had allowed Primakov to undertake this mission, Shevardnadze decided to throw a monkey wrench into the machinery. Before Primakov went to Washington, Tarasenko sent Robert Zoellick a message for Ross: "Let Dennis know that Primakov is coming to Washington with a proposal that the minister and I don't like." Zoellick told Ross that his interpretation of the implied recommendation was "Shit all over it."

It was yet another watershed in the relationship between the two countries: the Soviet foreign minister and the U.S. State Department were conspiring to undermine the Kremlin's special envoy.

---

* Andreotti feared that the United States might attack Iraq before all possibilities for a political solution were exhausted. He noted that sand storms would lash the Arabian desert in March, making military action more difficult. In May, the annual pilgrimages to Mecca and Medina would start. If there should be a Gulf war, "tensions might increase in North Africa and the Mediterranean."

* * *

Arriving in Washington on Thursday, October 18, Primakov was taken immediately to the State Department, where he and Bessmertnykh met with Baker and Ross. As they talked, Primakov got the impression that Baker was stalling in order to ensure that any real business would be done during a White House meeting with Bush.

Obeying his instructions from Gorbachev, Primakov insisted that the Soviet Union would remain part of the UN coalition even if it came to war: "Understand that whatever happens, we'll be with you," he promised.

He then lectured Baker on his twenty-two-year acquaintance with Saddam Hussein. Given a choice between surrender and war, he said, the Iraqi leader would fight, no matter what the odds were against him. Using a spectacularly inappropriate metaphor, Primakov asserted, "Saddam has a Masada complex."

After the meeting, Ross followed Primakov to the Soviet embassy to talk with him more directly than was possible in a formal session in which both sides were speaking for the record. Primakov spelled out what he meant by "face-savers": assurances that after Saddam withdrew from Kuwait, there would be an international conference on the Palestinian question, and U.S. troops would leave the area. In addition, Saddam should be allowed to keep the two islands and the oil field under dispute with Kuwait; the details of such a package could be worked out with the Saudis.

Ross replied that this final suggestion was a "particularly odd feature — to have Iraq negotiating with Saudi Arabia over concessions by Kuwait. You're reaffirming Saddam's point that the Kuwaitis have no legitimacy of their own." Primakov shrugged, then allowed that once the talks started, perhaps the Kuwaitis could join in.

Ross said, "You know what Israel's position is on an international conference." A "regional conference" might be more feasible. As for Primakov's "face-savers," they would merely "be seen as rewards or payoffs. Saddam will be seen as having gained ground from the invasion, not lost. Now let me give you my analysis: All the things you're afraid of happening if we follow through with our policy will actually happen if we do what you're suggesting.

"Compromise will build up the imagery in the area that this guy has overcome all the odds, defied the superpowers. Only mystical powers could possibly explain that. That will pave the way for a much bigger war later. You'll make him a hero of unprecedented scale, especially

among Arab masses, if you let him get away with what he's doing. He'll
be the artiber of what happens in the future. And if you think *I'm* hard
on this, you ought to see how tough the *president* feels!"

After the meeting, Ross reported to Baker, "Unlike Shevy, who is
with us, Primakov has basically come here to see if there is any flexibility on our part that would give Saddam enough cover to get out of
Kuwait."

Primakov drove through a rainstorm to see Scowcroft at the White
House. He correctly perceived, as he later recalled, that Scowcroft was
"more interested in our perceptions of the situation in Iraq than in our
proposals for getting out of the crisis." In the middle of the meeting,
Bush suddenly appeared in Scowcroft's office. With his hand outthrust,
he explained that he had dashed over from the residence to say hello:
"I had to come by, knowing that you were here with General Scowcroft.
I'm looking forward to our meeting tomorrow morning."

On Friday morning, October 19, Primakov returned to the White House,
where the president, Baker, Scowcroft, Richard Haass of the NSC staff,
and others were gathered in the Cabinet Room. Bush had confided to
his aides that actually he had "zero enthusiasm" about this meeting, as
he did not want to "legitimize" what Primakov was up to. But he felt
he had to see him; after all, Primakov *was* an envoy from Gorbachev.

Bush told Primakov how "appreciative" he was that Gorbachev's personal representative had come to share information about his mission
to the Middle East. Primakov repeated his canned lecture on Saddam's
"Masada complex." Haass was disgusted by this reference, which
struck him as "half malaprop, half chutzpah."

Primakov warned the president, "Don't push Saddam into a corner. . . . We have to give him a face-saver without giving him a reward.
We've got to help him find a way to a political solution."

Bush replied, "I don't understand what you mean by giving Saddam
a way to find a political solution." He recited the catalog of Saddam's
crimes: rapes, pillages, babies removed from incubators.* It was "like
Hitler and the Nazis": "You give a face-saver to someone who's part
of the civilized world, but he's not part of the civilized world."

Adjusting his recommendation slightly to take account of Ross's ob-

---

* After the Gulf War, the oft-repeated allegation that invading Iraqi soldiers had removed babies from incubators in Kuwait City came under serious question.

jections the day before, Primakov proposed that Washington and Moscow "tell Saddam what we're prepared to do about the Arab-Israeli conflict." He announced, "Dennis Ross has an idea for a regional conference." Ross was appalled that Primakov would try to drag him into his effort to publicly link the Arab-Israeli dispute to the Gulf crisis.

Bush saw through Primakov's ruse. He declared, "I'm not going to give Saddam anything. . . . Go back and tell him you found an absolute stone wall here."

Still, the president did not wish to seem entirely dismissive of Primakov's ideas. He could not know for sure how much Gorbachev supported his envoy's efforts, and he was aware that he might have to deal with Primakov in the future as foreign minister. Thus, he told his Soviet visitor that he would not object if he returned to Baghdad to see Saddam, so long as he did so in order "to inform Saddam about the uncompromising position of the United States." He added, "If a positive signal should come from Saddam, it will be heard by us."

Straining to be polite, at the end of the two hours allotted for the meeting, Bush remarked that at least there seemed to be "something new" in the ideas that Primakov had presented. "Do you plan to stay on in Washington?" he asked. Primakov replied that he could stay if necessary. The president said, "I'll give you an answer in about two or three hours."

This was merely an attempt on Bush's part to show that he was taking Primakov and his mission seriously; he had no real intention of seeing the Soviet again. Forty-five minutes later, as Primakov lunched with John Sununu, Robert Gates made the brush-off official: "The president has asked me to inform you that you can decide for yourself what time you want to leave."

Before Primakov left Washington, the Saudi ambassador to the United States, Prince Bandar bin Sultan, asked to see him. Working closely with Bush and Baker, Bandar had been deputized to impress upon Primakov how one-sided a war between the U.S.-led coalition and Iraq would actually be. The implicit message was that the Soviet Union would be wise to stay on the winning side.

When Primakov began his incantation that the use of force in the Gulf would have "grave consequences," Bandar would have none of it. If it should come to war, he said, "everything will be over in a matter of hours. Do you know what happens to tanks in the desert? They are absolutely unprotected targets for the air force, in which we have an overwhelming superiority. They will burn like matches. Don't overestimate the fighting ability of the Iraqi army. . . . Don't exaggerate the number of [allied] casualties, either. This operation will be backed up by the most up-to-date electronics. It will be a surgical attack."

At Margaret Thatcher's request, Primakov stopped in London to brief her on his trip. At her official country house, Chequers, she subjected him to her own uncompromising hourlong monologue. Presuming that anything she said to Primakov would go directly to Saddam, she declared that any use of force would not only reverse the invasion of Kuwait but also "break the back" of Saddam and his military-industrial complex. Glaring at Primakov, she said, "No one should try to ward off this blow against Saddam's regime."

Primakov asked the prime minister when military action would start. She replied, "This I cannot tell you, since the military action should come as a surprise to Iraq."

When he returned to Moscow, Primakov told Gorbachev that the "barometer of the situation is clearly pointing to a military solution." Gorbachev asked him to fly on to the Middle East to appeal for the release of the roughly 5,000 Soviet nationals who were still in Iraq, including more than a hundred military advisers.

In New York, the UN Security Council was considering yet another resolution — number 674. It would demand that Iraq compensate Kuwait for the damages it had caused and release its hostages. The Soviet ambassador to the UN, Yuli Vorontsov, reported to Primakov by telephone that a vote could come as early as Friday, October 26.

The Iraqi foreign minister, Tariq Aziz, informed the Soviet ambassador in Baghdad that the "Iraqi leadership" took an "extremely negative" view of the resolution. If it passed, Primakov's invitation to Baghdad might be canceled.

Primakov cabled Aziz that he was "puzzled" that at this critical moment, just as the Soviet Union was trying to find a political solution, Iraq should be setting up obstacles. He had Moscow instruct Vorontsov to try to postpone the vote on Resolution 674 so that he could have time to see Saddam. Vorontsov succeeded in winning a delay.* Aziz then promised that if Primakov came to Baghdad, he would be received by the Iraqi president.

---

* The resolution was finally passed on Monday, October 29, with Cuba and Yemen opposed.

* * *

In Baghdad on Sunday morning, October 28, Primakov called on Saddam. Present was a glittering array of Iraqi leaders, all dressed in military uniforms. Saddam said, "I have especially invited my colleagues here. Let them listen to our talk. After all, among them are both hawks and doves."

Primakov handed Saddam a letter from Gorbachev reiterating the demand that he withdraw from Kuwait. In the presence of his colleagues, Saddam had nothing new to say, but after they were dismissed, Primakov was interested to note that the Iraqi leader stopped arguing that Kuwait "historically" belonged to Iraq and seemed to be more willing to speak about specific conditions for withdrawal.

When Primakov raised the subject of the Soviet hostages, Saddam summoned an aide and ordered him to report to him personally on any Soviet civilians who were being detained and wished to leave. As for Soviet military specialists, he said, all who had fulfilled their contracts could return home immediately. This may have sounded magnanimous, but in fact it merely served as a reminder that all the Soviets would have to remain in Iraq.

Saddam told Primakov that he wanted Mitterrand and Gorbachev, who at that moment was visiting France, to appeal to him "personally" for the release of their detainees. At the same time, he said, the French and Soviet leaders would have to affirm their commitment to a political settlement of the Gulf crisis, along with other Middle East problems. They would also have to renounce the use of force against Iraq.

Primakov replied that these demands were "unrealistic," but he promised to convey the message to Gorbachev and Mitterrand. He went on, "You have known me for a long time, and apparently you believe that I try to tell you the truth. A strike, a powerful strike against Iraq is unavoidable unless you announce your withdrawal from Kuwait and carry it out."

Saddam asked, "How can I announce the withdrawal of troops if I am not informed how the question of the removal of U.S. forces from Saudi Arabia will be resolved? Would the UN sanctions against Iraq be lifted, or would they remain in force? How would my country's desire for an outlet to the sea be ensured? Would there be some sort of linkage between an Iraqi withdrawal and solution of the Palestine problem?" Without knowing the answers to these questions, he said, he could not relax his position: "For me, that would be suicidal."

Early the next morning, Primakov cabled an account of the talks to

Gorbachev in Paris. As usual, he suggested that he had succeeded in evoking important new signs of Iraqi flexibility.

Whether or not he actually believed this, Gorbachev told reporters in Paris that "some signs are showing that Saddam may be heeding the will of the United Nations." The Soviet leader was characteristically trying to have it both ways, continuing to support the U.S.-led coalition, which was moving ineluctably toward war, even as he attempted to accommodate those in his own government who wanted to avoid battle at almost any cost. To the latter end, he let it be known that Iraq "might" be ready for an inter-Arab conference sponsored by the Saudis, aimed at reaching a political settlement of the crisis. UN sanctions might have to be strengthened, Gorbachev admitted, but the use of force would be "unacceptable."

As November began, Bush was still hoping that the economic sanctions and the threat of military action would cause Saddam to withdraw from Kuwait. But Scowcroft, Cheney, and Powell persuaded him to keep all options open by doubling U.S. forces in Saudi Arabia to ensure the success of a strike against Iraq.

Bush and Baker believed that Resolution 665 and Article 51 of the UN charter gave them the authority to wage war if necessary. But they were worried by Shevardnadze's repeated comparison of a Gulf war to Afghanistan and by Gorbachev's insistence in Paris that the use of force would be "unacceptable." They were also nervous about growing domestic opposition to the possibility of war, both in Congress and on the part of the public.

They therefore decided to try for a new UN resolution explicitly authorizing the use of force to fulfill the aims of the ten earlier resolutions. The United States held the rotating presidency of the Security Council in November, so Bush and Baker hoped to get such a resolution passed before the end of the month — especially since in December the presidency would pass to Yemen, a radical Arab state that was friendly toward Iraq.

On Saturday, November 3, Baker left Washington to ask the leaders of twenty different countries for money and political support for a possible war with Iraq.

The following Wednesday, November 8, in the briefing room of the White House, Bush announced that 200,000 new U.S. troops were being sent to the Gulf to ensure that the coalition had an "offensive military option."

*   *   *

That same day, in Moscow, Baker met with Shevardnadze at an elegant state guesthouse and laid out the rationale for a use-of-force resolution. Shevardnadze told him that now was not the time to take military action; rather, they must find "new ways" to show that Saddam himself had rendered a peaceful solution impossible. "Resort to force threatens to make Saddam into a hero," said Shevardnadze. Why not strengthen the sanctions instead?

Baker replied, "I don't think that will be enough."

Shevardnadze asked, "Have you really thought about what it will mean to use force? Have you asked all the right questions?" Baker sensed that Shevardnadze was once more thinking about the Soviet fiasco in Afghanistan: if the Soviet Union were ever again to commit troops beyond its borders, the foreign minister wished to be sure that it could achieve its objectives.

Shevardnadze went on, "If you go down this path — and I'm going to suggest to my government that we go down it with you — the critical factor here is that you must succeed. It must be decisive, and it must be unmistakable what the outcome is." How long would such a war take? What kind of armaments would be required?

The secretary of state called in a member of his delegation, General Howard Graves of the Joint Chiefs of Staff, to explain U.S. war planning with unprecedented candor. By the end of the briefing, Baker felt that Shevardnadze could be persuaded to support a use-of-force resolution. He was less certain about Gorbachev.

Shevardnadze called his president at his dacha at Novo-Ogarevo to arrange a meeting with Baker for that afternoon, and then he drove out to Gorbachev's compound to brief him on the morning session. When they were finished, Baker's motorcade snaked through the frosted pine and birch woods up the quarter-mile driveway to the great mustard-colored mansion.

Gorbachev greeted his guests under a large chandelier in the wood-paneled entry hall and then took them up a grand staircase to his ballroom-sized library. Sitting across from the Americans at a glass-topped table, he crossed the index and third finger of both hands and held them aloft, saying, "The first thing we must do is stick together. . . . If we let a thug like this get away with what he's done, then there'll be no hope for the new kind of international reality we'd like to see."

Baker was pleased by what he was hearing. He told Gorbachev, "We've seen no evidence that Saddam has begun to comply with the

Security Council resolutions." He discussed U.S. planning for military options in a freewheeling fashion that was intended to impress the Soviet leader as yet another demonstration of American openness.

Gorbachev said, "We will have difficulty with this — the idea that you're going to go in there — because, after all, the force that's going to be used is American, and you're asking the Soviet Union to approve the use of American force against a longtime ally of the Soviet Union." He added that he was "disappointed" that Primakov's second mission to Baghdad had produced no seriously encouraging signs.

Baker then made the case for a use-of-force resolution, basing his appeal on Gorbachev's own 1988 speech on the UN's future role in world affairs. Hadn't Gorbachev himself said that the world community must be governed by the "rule of law"? Saddam was testing the UN's "credibility" by defying the ten resolutions. He was flouting Gorbachev's vision of how an interdependent world should work. Baker concluded, "We can't have the UN go the way of the League of Nations."

Gorbachev looked him hard in the eye and said, "You understand now that if we pass a resolution on the use of force, and Saddam does not move, you will actually have to use force. . . . Are you really ready to do that right now?"

Baker answered that President Bush understood "perfectly" what he had to do, and was ready to do it.

Gorbachev replied by suggesting not one UN resolution but two. The first, to be voted on in late November, would authorize the use of force — after a waiting period of six weeks in which diplomacy would be given a last chance to work. Then a second resolution could be passed that would give the actual go-ahead for war.

Baker said that this approach could prove to be a serious mistake: "Two resolutions would mean we'd have to take this difficult use-of-force issue *twice* to the Security Council. . . . You'd never get a second resolution, and Saddam could toy around with it for a long time. . . . Two resolutions wouldn't put as much pressure on Saddam as a single strong one."

He offered a compromise: "We can build in a time period. We can have one resolution and say it doesn't actually become operative before a certain date."

Gorbachev refused to commit himself. As Ross later recalled, "When we left the dacha, we felt fairly confident that we had them on board. But we didn't have a firm commitment. The indications from Shevardnadze and Gorbachev's body language were that they were very strongly inclined to do this."

Shevardnadze and Baker returned to the guesthouse and talked late into the night. They could not agree on when force should be used, or with what limitations. But Shevardnadze liked the idea of an ultimatum, so long as there was a grace period. As in August, he insisted that the word *force* not appear in any new resolution.

At a late-night joint news conference in the gilded entry hall of the guesthouse, a reporter asked about the use of force. Shevardnadze conceded, "A situation may arise that will call for such an action."

Baker could barely conceal his delight. His aides discreetly jabbed one another in the ribs. Afterward, the secretary of state called Bush and reported that the United States "has a pretty good shot at getting them to go along with us."

The day after his talk with Baker, Gorbachev flew to Bonn to sign a nonaggression pact with Germany. He declared, "A new vision of the world has triumphed."

Three weeks later, the Germans elected Helmut Kohl as the first chancellor of their united nation. The Christian Democrats won 44 percent of the vote, the Social Democrats 33 percent, and Genscher's moderate Free Democrats 11 percent. Kohl pronounced himself "particularly happy that the result in the former East Germany is almost identical to that in the west."

At the White House on Wednesday, November 14, congressional leaders complained to Bush about the doubling of U.S. forces in the Gulf. To several of the congressmen, the United States seemed to be going it alone. After the meeting, the president, Baker, and Scowcroft agreed that a use-of-force resolution would be essential not only to keep the coalition together but to bring Congress along.

Bush cabled Gorbachev to explain his reasons for seeking a single resolution. He wrote that he would ask for Gorbachev's formal approval when they met at the CSCE summit in Paris five days hence.

The next day, in New York, Primakov told a reporter for the *New York Times* that the UN should delay a use-of-force resolution in order to allow a final negotiation effort. If that effort failed, a resolution should be passed and military action authorized almost immediately.

During a stopover in Brussels, Baker dismissed Primakov's comments, saying he doubted that the Soviet government really believed that another political initiative would do any good. Speaking anonymously to reporters, Baker's aides stuck the knife into Primakov, noting that he had not even been able to win the freedom of Soviet hostages in Iraq.

In mid-November, Bush, Baker, Gorbachev, and Shevardnadze were all in Paris, along with numerous other European leaders, for a CSCE meeting. On Sunday night, November 18, Baker showed Shevardnadze a draft resolution authorizing the use of force. "Can you live with this?" he asked.

The foreign minister read it and replied, "After our Afghanistan experience, that won't fly with the Soviet people." He suggested that another, less menacing-sounding phrase be substituted for "use of force."

Baker said that he did not want to run the risk of not saying exactly what was meant. He scribbled out five different euphemisms and then explained why none of them would do. Shevardnadze still favored language that would authorize force but also allow for other possible measures, such as diplomacy and new sanctions.

Baker said, "How about 'all necessary means'?" Shevardnadze quickly agreed. Then Baker had second thoughts. He worried that the phrase was "too indefinite." Shevardnadze said, "The United States knows what 'all necessary means' is. Don't embarrass us. Don't push us. Don't be extreme."

Baker explained that he wished to avoid ambiguity, as U.S. policy on the Gulf was still "volatile" at home. "We don't want a domestic debate on what the resolution means," he complained. But in the end he gave in to the formulation, reminding Shevardnadze that as a way of dramatizing the urgency of the situation, he would be representing the United States as Security Council president at the time of the vote. This would allow him to speak immediately after the balloting and to characterize the resolution as an unambiguous authorization to use force.

Shevardnadze said that he could not commit Gorbachev to the "all necessary means" language. "Your president will have to make the case to Gorbachev when they see each other tomorrow evening," he told Baker.

Baker frowned. He knew that if he could not tell the press that the Soviets had agreed to his language, reporters would conclude that the talks had hit a snag. Early on Monday morning, when asked about the results of the meeting, Baker gave a reply he would soon come to regret: "Stay tuned. You'll get an answer tonight."

Tarasenko assured Ross that Gorbachev would accept Baker's position, "but it must be done directly with the president."

That evening, Gorbachev dined with Bush at the U.S. ambassador's residence. Bush was planning to leave the next day for the Middle East, where he would share Thanksgiving dinner with troops in Saudi Arabia.

Gorbachev assured him, "We've been with you since Day One on the Gulf, and we'll continue to be with you." He said that he was ready to accept the idea of a single UN resolution but would prefer it to be "two-tiered": it could authorize force, but it should also explicitly state that there must be a "pause of goodwill" before such force was used.

Bush consented but insisted that the deadline be no later than New Year's Day. Gorbachev asked him not to make the Soviet approval public until after Aziz came to Moscow one last time. Gorbachev was anxious to avoid the appearance of following U.S. dictates.

Baker told Shevardnadze that Gorbachev's request put him in a difficult position: he had suggested to the press that there would be a final announcement that evening. Ross advised him to tell the press that it was important not to jump to conclusions because conclusions could prove to be wrong. Baker and Shevardnadze agreed to use this line.

After the Paris meetings, Shevardnadze wrote a confidential memo to Gorbachev underscoring the importance of Soviet support for an "all-necessary-means" resolution and a firm deadline in the near future. He wanted to keep it from Primakov, who he suspected might try to undo what he had accomplished. Fearing that Chernyayev might slip a copy to Primakov, Shevardnadze waited until he was on a plane with Gorbachev before pulling out the memo and showing it to his boss. After obtaining Gorbachev's approval, he sent appropriate instructions to Vorontsov at the UN.

Shevardnadze also took the precaution of visiting China to ensure that the Soviet Union would not be embarrassed by a Chinese veto of the new resolution in the Security Council. Baker, lobbying hard himself, sweetened the pot by inviting the Chinese foreign minister to Washington for the first such visit since the Tiananmen Square massacre of June 1989. The secretary of state even asked to meet with the Yemeni president, Ali Abdallah Salih, but he was rebuffed.

In Moscow on Friday, November 23, Gorbachev told reporters that there was "absolutely" no conflict between the Soviet Union and the United States on the Gulf. But he then warned once again against a military confrontation. Echoing Shevardnadze, he said, "This is not Vietnam. This is not Afghanistan. This is extremely serious."

At the UN on Saturday evening, November 24, U.S. Ambassador Thomas Pickering sent the other four permanent members of the Security Council — the Soviet Union, Great Britain, China, and France — a draft resolution that gave Iraq "one final opportunity" to abide by UN demands, and authorized member states to use "all necessary means" to implement the previous ten resolutions unless Iraq complied fully by the deadline, now fixed as January 15.

This would be only the second time in its history that the UN had agreed to invoke provisions of its charter to reverse aggression by force if other sanctions failed. The first time was in 1950, in Korea, an action made possible only because the Soviet Union was temporarily boycotting the Security Council and thus did not exercise its veto.

At the Kremlin on Monday, November 26, Gorbachev told the visiting Tariq Aziz, "If Iraq really wants a settlement in the entire region and is trying to avoid the worst, it must now openly declare, and demonstrate in its actions, that it is pulling out of Kuwait, freeing hostages, and in general not preventing anyone from leaving Iraq. Otherwise the UN resolution will be adopted — a tough resolution."

Gorbachev complained about the Soviet hostages still in Iraq, who now numbered about 3,300: "It is against the norms of ethics that people are being let out in groups of several dozen in some kind of trading." Aziz replied that "bureaucratic" problems had delayed the release.

The Soviet leader declared, "The fate of Iraq is in the hands of its leadership. Time is running out." Shevardnadze added that the use-of-force resolution would be the "last resolution" that the UN would pass on Iraq.

In New York on Tuesday, November 25, Baker, in his capacity as UN Security Council president, met with representatives of the other permanent members. Primakov tried to get him to postpone the vote on Resolution 678. Baker refused to consider a delay: in three days, the council presidency would pass to Yemen, which could block the measure until January.

On Thursday evening, before the vote, Shevardnadze said to Baker, "You know you can't back off once you start down the road. You will have to implement the resolution." Baker replied, "I'm afraid you're right."

With Baker in the chair, the council passed the resolution authorizing "all means necessary" on November 29.* As he had earlier told Shevardnadze he would do, Baker proclaimed, "Today's resolution is very clear. The words authorize the use of force, but the purpose . . . is to bring about a peaceful resolution of this problem."

At the White House the next morning, Bush announced that in order to "go the extra mile for peace," he would invite Tariq Aziz to meet with him and allied ambassadors in Washington at a mutually convenient time in mid-December. He would also suggest to Saddam that the Iraqi leader receive Baker sometime between mid-December and the UN deadline on January 15.

The Gulf crisis had retarded Bush's effort to reach out beyond Gorbachev to reform and nationalist leaders in the USSR. At a time when the Soviet president's consent to U.S. policy was critical, Bush did not wish to inflame Gorbachev by seeming to court his adversaries.

Separatist forces were now gaining strength throughout the Soviet Union, in republics both small and large. In July, after meeting with Boris Yeltsin in the Latvian coastal town of Jurmala, the three Baltic presidents vowed to keep pressing for absolute independence. Ukraine declared its sovereignty. The Armenian legislature rejected a decree by Gorbachev ordering that armed nationalist groups turn in their weapons or be disarmed by Soviet security forces.

In Moscow, newly infuriated by the secessionist movement, the Soviet military, the KGB, and other hard-liners were also angrier than ever about Gorbachev's cooperation with Bush on the Gulf. Furthermore, the goodwill of the West had brought Gorbachev virtually nothing in financial aid to mitigate the increasing crisis in the Soviet Union.

Worrying about his growing vulnerability, Gorbachev now made a choice that he would come to regret deeply the following year. With reckless self-confidence, in a crude and desperate attempt to buy some more time for his policies and for himself, he decided to move hard to the right. He calculated that he had extra latitude in that direction

* China abstained, and Yemen and Cuba voted against the resolution. After the vote, Baker sent a message to the Yemeni delegate saying, "That is the most expensive vote you ever cast." Yemen soon lost $70 million in U.S. foreign aid.

because the Americans, preoccupied as they were with the Gulf and eager for Soviet support of the coalition, were unlikely to protest a crackdown in the Baltics or an effort to turn back the clock in domestic politics.

At the end of November 1990, just as the UN authorized force in the Gulf, Defense Minister Yazov made an ominous appearance on Soviet television, announcing presidential measures to protect Soviet troops from a "massive outburst" of antagonism all over the Soviet Union: soldiers were authorized to use their weapons to defend themselves and their interests against harassment by local nationalists.

On Tuesday, December 2, Gorbachev fired his moderately progressive interior minister, Vadim Bakatin, and installed in his place Boris Pugo, a former KGB chief and party leader in Latvia. To serve as Pugo's deputy Gorbachev appointed General Boris Gromov, the last Soviet commander in Afghanistan. Gromov had been among Shevardnadze's loudest critics at the party congress in July and was now widely thought to harbor ambitions of "Bonapartism."

The following week, KGB chief Vladimir Kryuchkov went on Soviet television to warn that the Soviet Union was in danger of "disintegrating." Pledging that the KGB would fight "anti-Communist" elements at home and abroad with "all" its might, he solemnly declared, "To be or not to be — that is the choice for our great state." Gorbachev issued a presidential decree canceling reform measures passed by local governments that had "disrupted" the distribution of food and goods.

Alexander Yakovlev warned in public, "An offensive is under way by conservative and reactionary forces which are vengeful and merciless." Yuri Leavada, a commentator for *Moscow News,* said, "I think we are seeing a creeping militarized coup — not military, but militarized."

During their Paris meeting in November, Bush and Gorbachev had finally signed the CFE treaty. In some respects, the pact was the most impressive accomplishment in the history of arms control. To an extent unimaginable a few years earlier, it reduced the danger that a surprise attack would be launched against Western Europe.

Under the terms of the treaty, the number of tanks, artillery pieces, and armored combat vehicles that the Soviet Union could keep west of the Urals would be almost 70 percent less than the number deployed in the zone when Bush took office.

But the CFE treaty also showed how events could overtake the best efforts of statesmen. In early 1989, Brent Scowcroft had dared to postulate that if the West made a bold enough CFE proposal, the Kremlin might be induced to withdraw all of its ground forces from Eastern Europe. By the time the treaty was signed, in November 1990, Soviet units were already committed to a complete pullout from Hungary and Czechoslovakia in 1991 and from the eastern parts of Germany in 1994.

Many Western lawyers involved in CFE felt as though the contract they had been negotiating with the Warsaw Pact for years had suddenly gone into probate: the other party, quite simply, had died. A year earlier, in the fall of 1989, the Hungarians had made it clear that they had no intention of remaining in the Pact; by the time the CFE treaty was completed, of the original twenty-three states involved in the negotiations, one — the German Democratic Republic — had ceased to exist, and five others had changed their names.

Just as the final text of the treaty was being printed out at CFE headquarters at the Hofburg in Vienna, the Bulgarian ambassador, Lujben Petrov, anxiously phoned the chief American negotiator, James Woolsey, and said, "You must change the name of our country from the People's Republic of Bulgaria to the Republic of Bulgaria. Our parliament acted yesterday."

Woolsey's staff quickly stopped the printers, called up the document on an Apple computer, and, with a few keystrokes, made the necessary substitution.

In the wake of their "militarized coup," the Soviet generals took revenge on Shevardnadze by reopening certain issues supposedly resolved in the CFE treaty. Since it was pulling out of Eastern Europe, the Soviet military was more desperate than ever to keep what weapons it had inside the Soviet Union. Accordingly, Yazov moved to protect hardware earmarked by the CFE treaty for destruction.

Under pressure from the Defense Ministry, Soviet negotiators tried to exempt several thousand pieces of equipment from CFE, either by claiming that they were assigned to "coastal defense" or by designating them "naval infantry units," similar to those of the U.S. Marine Corps.

This was a clear violation of the CFE treaty's explicit stipulation that it covered all battle tanks, artillery, and armored combat vehicles. In early December, Woolsey and his CFE negotiating team traveled to Moscow in an effort to deal with a last-minute difficulty.

In the Moscow meeting, Woolsey found himself facing what seemed to be the entire Soviet high command — not only Yazov and his chief of the General Staff, Mikhail Moiseyev, but six other generals and a variety of colonels, all arrayed under a giant painting of Alexander Nevsky after the defeat of the Teutonic knights in 1242.

Yazov declared that he and his colleagues were determined to resist limits on naval infantry. Waving his finger at Woolsey, he said that any such curbs would be possible only as part of some *future* agreement that would also restrict U.S. aircraft carriers and submarines. Furious, Woolsey pushed Yazov's hand away from his face, almost striking it, and said, "Marshal, over my dead body!"

When this was translated, Yazov grinned at the other generals, pointed at Woolsey, and said, "Yes, Mr. Ambassador, perhaps so!" Woolsey accused the Soviets of trying to foist a "deliberately fraudulent interpretation" of the treaty on NATO. Yazov thumped his chest and proclaimed, "Over *my* dead body!"

At the Houstonian Hotel in Houston on Monday, December 10, Shevardnadze met with Baker for the twenty-third time since Baker's appointment as secretary of state.

Baker was startled by Shevardnadze's ashen face, the black wells around his eyes, and his general state of exhaustion. The foreign minister had been accompanied to Houston by a small battalion from the Soviet military-industrial complex. If Baker still had any doubts about whether there had been a serious move to the right in Moscow, they were soon dispelled.

Out of the blue, in repudiation of their previous understandings, Shevardnadze demanded a new Security Council resolution calling for an international conference on the Middle East. Baker told him that the timing was wrong: better to wait until after the Gulf crisis was over.

Shevardnadze's demand was so out of keeping with his previous approach that Baker realized his friend must be under heavy domestic pressure to get tough. In private, Shevardnadze himself said as much: didn't Baker understand the kind of beating he was taking in Moscow for his support of the U.S. position on the Gulf? That was why he was insisting on a new UN resolution. "I know you're concerned about linkage," he conceded. "But I think we shouldn't become prisoners of that term. I don't feel as strongly as you do about it. We need to think about the Middle East as a whole — not as a reward for Saddam Hussein, but as a way to compete with him. There ought to be a resolution that you're able to go with."

Baker replied, "We won't go with any resolution that mentions an international conference." Shevardnadze said, "Maybe it's best to postpone the whole thing." Baker responded, "That's what we've been trying to do. . . . I'd like to postpone it until after January 15."

Shevardnadze said, "It's fine to talk about that, but we're going to put a resolution on the table in three hours." He had already instructed Ambassador Vorontsov at the UN to put forward the proposed language. Baker warned, "If it has any reference to a conference in it, we'll have to veto it."·

Ross lectured Shevardnadze on what he saw as the dangers of linkage: it would embolden Saddam, infuriate the Israelis, and undercut the Bush administration. Surely this was not what Shevardnadze had in mind.

The foreign minister threw up his hands. "I understand your position!" he said. "I won't try to talk you out of it. But I do think you're wrong."

Baker said, "Dennis is going out to the region. We're working on the peace process. But we don't want a resolution that sounds as if it was designed in Baghdad." Shevardnadze replied, "Then there should be no resolution at all." Baker agreed: "That's just what I want."

Ross reminded them, "It's supposed to be considered in three hours." Shevardnadze said, "Let me direct Vorontsov to get a delay."

Having given his best impersonation of an old-fashioned, contentious Soviet diplomat, Shevardnadze then returned to his familiar conciliatory self. Noting that Israeli Prime Minister Yitzhak Shamir was in the United States, he said, "Should I see Shamir when I'm in Washington?" Baker told him that this would be helpful. He asked Ross to set up a meeting.

Shevardnadze also reported that during a forthcoming visit to Turkey, he expected to see Yasir Arafat, the chairman of the Palestine Liberation Organization, who was siding with Saddam in the Gulf crisis. "What should I tell him?" he wondered.

Baker said, "Tell him, 'You're in trouble, pal.' Tell him he's lost his financial base. The Gulf states want nothing to do with him. Look at Syria and Egypt. He's damaged the cause of the Palestinians severely. He's undercut the peace movement in Israel."

Ross said, "You might add that he's going to be on the losing side — and he ought to be. He should be thinking about his future, not just his present. People don't get rewarded for having been on the losing side."

Later, Shevardnadze asked one of Baker's top aides if the administration had any additional message for Arafat. The aide said, "Yes. Tell him, 'Screw you! Harsh letter follows.'"

During a break in the talks, Baker and Shevardnadze toured NASA's Johnson Space Center, stooping to climb through the hatch of a spacecraft mockup. Shevardnadze joked that someday they might negotiate in space: after all, they had met in almost every other venue.

That afternoon, there was another acrimonious session on CFE. Woolsey complained to Shevardnadze that the Soviets were moving military equipment east of the Ural Mountains instead of destroying it: "You've got to destroy the equipment beyond the Urals," he insisted. The two sides soon became enmeshed in arcane issues such as the types of military equipment to be eliminated.*

Baker was annoyed that Woolsey had brought the matter up, for it was bound to raise Shevardnadze's hackles at a time when Baker had more important business to do with him on the Gulf. Baker told an aide through clenched teeth, "Woolsey's screwed up. He's lost us about a day and a half's worth of work."

The secretary of state felt that the east-of-the-Urals question was a political rather than a legal issue. Even the Joint Chiefs of Staff were relatively unconcerned by it. Baker noted that one of the chiefs had advised him, "They're dumping the stuff there in order to let it rust."

As Baker had feared, Shevardnadze responded to Woolsey's complaint with another jut-jawed, no-compromise performance for the benefit of his military minders at the table. Afterward, Baker confided to his aides, "Shevardnadze and I have never had a meeting that left such a bad taste in my mouth."

Later, Tarasenko came to Ross's hotel room and said, "You have to understand that some of what my minister did, he had to do. Nevertheless, he feels badly about it."

Shortly afterward, as they flew together on an air force plane from Houston to Washington, Shevardnadze and the Americans had what

---

* The Soviet military moved more than 16,000 tanks east of the Urals so that they would not be subject to the treaty's requirement that all equipment beyond the permitted number be destroyed. The zone covered by the treaty extended from the Atlantic to the Ural Mountains. There was no prohibition on transfers out of the Atlantic-to-the-Urals region before the signing of the treaty in November 1990, nor was there any limit on the amount of equipment that could be kept east of the Urals. Nonetheless, Bush administration officials, particularly in the Pentagon, complained that by so obviously trying to save their tanks from destruction, the Soviets were engaging in a "sharp practice," or unscrupulous activity, contrary to the spirit if not the letter of the CFE treaty.

Ross called a "real schmooze session." Indirectly explaining his militance at the negotiating table, the foreign minister admitted that the fall of 1990 had been a "very difficult period" for him. The generals were finally staging their "counteroffensive," he said, paying him back for all the times he had gone over their heads to get Gorbachev's approval on arms control concessions. The reformers in Moscow were "vanishing," and Gorbachev himself, without even realizing it, was getting into deeper and deeper trouble. Bitterly, Shevardnadze said, "He always thinks he is the master of events."

On Wednesday, December 12, the foreign minister went to the White House, where Bush showed him that season's Christmas decorations. The president and Shevardnadze discussed their remaining differences on START but did not resolve them. Bush agreed to a three-day summit with Gorbachev in Moscow in mid-February, saying that he hoped the START treaty would be ready to sign by then.

Bush also approved U.S. credit guarantees for Soviet purchases of up to $1 billion in U.S. commodities, and proposed granting the Soviets minor economic and other aid, including medical supplies and technical assistance in food distribution. He waived Jackson-Vanik through July 1991 but noted that the new Soviet emigration law remained bogged down in the Supreme Soviet. He reiterated that he would not submit the Soviet-American trade agreement to Congress until the law was passed.

With this combination of supportive gestures and finger-wagging, Bush was trying to strike a balance between the requirements of his own domestic political position and Gorbachev's. Bush knew that if he seemed too eager to help his friend in the Kremlin and too indulgent of Gorbachev's tendency to vacillate and procrastinate, he would lose congressional and public support for his policy toward the USSR. Therefore, he had at least to appear to be holding the Soviet leader to a high standard of performance. "Tough love" — Marlin Fitzwater's catch phrase for the administration's attitude toward Gorbachev on the eve of the Washington summit — was still very much the order of the day.

In Moscow on Monday, December 17, Gorbachev opened a session of the Congress of People's Deputies with a speech that left little doubt about his militant new line. "We have underestimated the depth of our society's crisis," he began.

He asked for new executive powers to create a "strong government, tight discipline, and control over the implementation of decisions. Then we shall be able to ensure normal food supplies and rein in and stop interethnic strife. If we fail to achieve this, we will inevitably see greater discord, the rampage of dark forces, and the breakup of our state."

Two days later, on Wednesday, December 19, Boris Yeltsin told the same body, "Russia will not agree to this restoration of Kremlin *diktat*. The way out of this crisis requires honest dialogue, with equal rights, between the center and the republic. This does not mean the disintegration of the Union. On the contrary, this is the only way to save it."

That night, in his Moscow apartment, Shevardnadze tossed and turned in his bed, musing on the bruising year that was coming to an end. As he later recalled in a memoir, "The year 1990 had been equivalent to several decades. We lived through it without pausing for breath, preoccupied by numerous external worries and constant internal pressure."

The "first direct blows" against him, at the February Central Committee session, had "crescendoed into a campaign" by the July party congress, where he had been pilloried for losing Eastern Europe: "I was now the scapegoat. A creature and guardian of the system myself, who had risen to the top by using it, I was now a deviant, slated for ruthless treatment."

The demands of the Baltics, German unification, the Gulf crisis, and other issues had been "so intense" that at the time he had resolved "not to let the business of absorbing and parrying attacks distract me." He resented Gorbachev's failure to defend him from those attacks and to keep the hard-liners from undercutting him.

In recent months, Shevardnadze had had a "growing premonition that events would soon destroy our achievements, which had been made largely because my foreign partners trusted me personally. . . . At times it was hard for me to look them in the eye. I could not explain to them . . . the sudden complications and reversals, clearly stage-managed by someone in order to jeopardize agreements we had already reached."

Shevardnadze knew that Gorbachev had concluded that his usefulness as foreign minister was over, that he carried too much baggage to remain in his job.

The Soviet leader had already quietly suggested to him that he take up the new position of vice president of the Soviet Union. All too aware of Gorbachev's Machiavellian streak, Shevardnadze had instantly seen the trap. As vice president, he would be largely responsible for domestic policy. In the new, angry atmosphere in Moscow, that would make him the whipping boy in the crackdown that was sure soon to come.

Since Shevardnadze was a Georgian, his position would be especially difficult, for his own native republic was among the most restive. The other non-Russians would expect him to be sympathetic to their separatist causes, and the Russians themselves would mistrust him for exactly the same reason.

Before dawn, the foreign minister climbed out of bed and scrawled notes for a resignation speech. He confided his secret to his wife, his daughter, Tarasenko, and another aide, but not to Gorbachev. The Soviet leader had talked him out of resigning too many times before.* This time Shevardnadze was not going to give him a chance. He had made his decision.

On Thursday morning, December 20, Shevardnadze told the Congress of People's Deputies that he was about to make the "shortest and most difficult speech of my life." The day before, he said, some comrades had suggested a declaration "forbidding the country's leadership from sending troops to the Persian Gulf. . . . Those speeches have overfilled my cup of patience.

"What, after all, is happening with the Persian Gulf? . . . We have no moral right at all to tolerate aggression and the annexation of a small, defenseless country." No one in the Soviet government was "planning to send even one serviceman in a military uniform," but "if the interests of Soviet people are encroached upon, if just one person suffers," then "the Soviet side will stand up for its citizens."

He recalled that at the July party congress, eight hundred delegates had proclaimed their lack of confidence in him. "Am I personally undesirable?" he asked. "Comrades, a hounding is taking place. . . . I will put it bluntly: comrade democrats, in the widest meaning of the word, you have scattered. The reformers have gone to seed."

He noted Gorbachev's demand for new powers: "Dictatorship is coming. . . . No one knows what kind of dictatorship this will be and who will come — what kind of dictator — and what the regime will be like." Then he dropped his bombshell: "I want to make the following statement: I am resigning."

---

* In December 1989, Shevardnadze had threatened to resign when a military prosecutor tried to cover up the Kremlin's complicity in the Tbilisi killings of April. Only Gorbachev's powers of persuasion and apparent repudiation of the coverup at an emergency Politburo meeting prevented Shevardnadze from quitting.

There was a collective gasp from the hall. Shevardnadze went on, "Let this be — do not respond, do not curse me! Let this be my contribution, if you like, my protest against the onset of dictatorship. I express profound gratitude to Mikhail Sergeyevich Gorbachev. I am his friend. I am a fellow thinker of his. . . . But I think that this is my duty, as a man, as a citizen, as a Communist.

"I cannot reconcile myself to the events unfolding in our country and the trials awaiting our people. Nevertheless, I believe that dictatorship will not succeed, that the future belongs to democracy and freedom."

At five-thirty in the morning in Washington, Ross called Baker at his house on Foxhall Road and awoke him with the staggering news. Once he had absorbed it, the secretary of state remembered that at a recent meeting Shevardnadze had pulled him aside and told him in a lowered voice, "We have an absolute crisis. We could have a dictatorship very soon in our country." Baker recalled, "I never found anything he ever told me to be untrue."

Baker put in a call to Moscow but was informed that Shevardnadze, exhausted from the day's events, could not come to the telephone. Later the foreign minister told him, "I wanted to tell you before I resigned. I felt so badly. But I couldn't. I had come to this conclusion before, and each time I had been talked out of it." He had agreed to stay on as interim foreign minister through the February Bush-Gorbachev summit.

When Baker arrived at the State Department, he faced the press. Looking stricken, he said, "We would obviously be foolish not to take the warning in Minister Shevardnadze's resignation statement seriously."

Returning to his office, the secretary of state morosely speculated with his aides about whether Primakov might become the new foreign minister. Ross said, "Primakov has clearly been the stalking horse of the hard-liners against Shevardnadze on the Gulf. Primakov has always been a new thinker, so Gorbachev might think he can please the reformers, too. But he must know that a Primakov appointment would be a bad signal to send to us on the Gulf."

At the Soviet embassy on Sixteenth Street, Alexander Bessmertnykh wrote out by hand a message to Shevardnadze: "Dear Eduard Amrosievich, I suggest that you take back your resignation. It would be better for our foreign policy and for the general international situation. I feel this strongly. Keep your post. Sasha."

Lest anyone doubt Shevardnadze's predictions of an impending dictatorship, Kryuchkov took the podium on Saturday, December 22, to warn that Soviet citizens must "accept the possibility of bloodshed if we are to bring about order" in the republics. He charged that Western intelligence services were trying to "mastermind" the Soviet Union's collapse.

The Soviet Union was indeed coming apart at the seams, but not because of anything the CIA was doing. The republic of Moldavia, on the Romanian border, was in near rebellion. On Sunday, December 23, Gorbachev demanded that Moldavians abandon plans to establish their own army.

The Congress of People's Deputies gave Gorbachev most of his desired new powers, though it stopped short of creating a new all-Union body to enforce his decrees, as he had requested. To serve as Soviet vice president, Gorbachev chose a hard-drinking careerist, Gennadi Yanayev, who in his maiden speech assured the Congress, "I am a Communist to the depths of my soul."

At the White House, Bush and Scowcroft were shocked by the fortnight's events in Moscow. Scowcroft complained to Bush that Gorbachev was "still trying to find common ground between the reformers and the reactionaries, even though it doesn't exist." He reminded the president that the Soviets' Gulf policy "had Shevardnadze's fingerprints all over it"; with Shevardnadze gone, Gorbachev might back away from cooperation on the Gulf.

During the final week of December, just before his young wife gave birth to a son, Bessmertnykh came to the White House to bring Bush New Year's greetings from Gorbachev. The president told Bessmertnykh that he was worried about the continuing crisis in the Baltics, but, anxious to keep the Soviets on board in the face of a possible Gulf war, he refrained from criticizing Gorbachev's swerve toward a tough line at home.

On Thursday, December 27, before leaving by helicopter for New Year's weekend at Camp David, Bush declared to reporters, "Any time you move from a totalitarian, totally controlled state to an open state . . . you're bound to have problems. . . . Far be it from me to try to fine-tune the difficulties that they're having there."

As the president spoke, U.S. military officers at the Pentagon were planning an air strike on Baghdad. In Moscow, Soviet military and security officers were plotting a crackdown in the Baltics.

CHAPTER 14

"I Want to Preserve the Relationship"

S PENDING NEW YEAR'S DAY at Camp David, Bush telephoned
some of his most important foreign partners: François Mitterrand;
King Fahd of Saudi Arabia, the principal U.S. ally in the showdown with Iraq; and President Carlos Salinas de Gortari of Mexico,
with whose help he was trying to create a North American free trade
zone.

Bush asked Scowcroft, "What about Gorbachev?" Scowcroft replied
that he saw a political risk in such a call: the internal situation in the
Soviet Union was growing tenser by the day, especially in the Baltics.
What if Gorbachev was about to impose presidential rule, which
amounted to martial law? What if he was about to "knock heads and
spill blood"? A cheerful greeting from the president of the United States
on the eve of such a crackdown "wouldn't be too great."

Bush decided to make the call anyway. Throughout the fall and early
winter, Gorbachev had been his ally in the Gulf crisis, the most important challenge of his presidency. Scowcroft urged him to mention his
concern over the Baltics, but the president said he felt he had said
enough on the subject during his White House meeting with Bessmertnykh five days before.

When he was finally put through to the Kremlin, he spoke with Gorbachev for thirteen minutes. He limited himself mainly to wishing the Soviet leader well in the year to come. Gorbachev thanked him and several times referred to the severity of the troubles he was facing at home.

The next day, Wednesday, January 2, 1991, "Black Beret" riot-control troops belonging to the Soviet Interior Ministry seized the headquarters of the Communist party central committee in Lithuania, as well as the editorial offices and printing presses of a major publishing facility in Latvia. Their pretext was that these buildings were the property of the central Soviet authorities.

On Thursday, January 3, Ambassador Matlock went to see Vladimir Kryuchkov. He expressed the United States' "concern that the already tense situation in the Baltic states may be exacerbated by actions most unconducive to a peaceful outcome." The KGB chief brushed the warning aside.

Matlock also took Kryuchkov to task for his speech of a fortnight earlier, in which he had accused the CIA of covert operations intended to destabilize the Soviet Union. "Go back and check the facts," said the ambassador. "We're not trying to subvert your system."

Kryuchkov replied, "We don't tell our ambassadors everything we're doing, and I'm sure your people don't tell you everything."

Matlock said, "I know what *my* government is doing in the country where I'm accredited."

The following day, Matlock called on Gorbachev's foreign policy adviser, Anatoli Chernyayev, who was less smug and pugnacious than Kryuchkov. To Matlock, Chernyayev seemed deeply worried about the direction in which Soviet internal politics were moving.

On Monday, January 7, an ominous new report reached the State Department's operations center. The local Soviet military commander in the Baltics had informed leaders of the three republics that Moscow was dispatching elite paratroops to enforce conscription laws and round up draft dodgers and deserters, who numbered as many as 32,000.

Told of the news, Robert Gates and Condoleezza Rice rushed into Scowcroft's office to argue for a tough public statement from the White House. Scowcroft demurred. Like the president, he knew that more than ever, Soviet support for the UN coalition in the Gulf was crucial to the credibility of the U.S. threat to use force against Saddam Hussein.

In the Oval Office, Scowcroft confided to Bush and Baker that he could all too easily imagine the Baltic crisis "ripping the Soviets out of the coalition." But the president feared that a muted American response to the Kremlin's new militance toward the Baltics might be seen as acquiescense. Scowcroft said he would have his aides draft a public expression of "concern."

Bush asked Baker to move toward postponement of his summit with Gorbachev in Moscow, now planned for February. However, he said he did not want to appear to be "acting out of pique" or taking a "slap at Gorbachev"; Baker would need to find some way of presenting the postponement to the world as a "mutual decision" by Washington and Moscow.

In public, there was no hint of these contingency plans; Fitzwater told the press that the administration was "still planning" to go ahead with the February summit. But he added that the movement of Soviet military units into the Baltics was "provocative and counterproductive," and suggested that the Soviet government should "cease attempts at intimidation" and return to "negotiations conducted free of pressure and the use of force."

Despite the president's hope that the statement would not seem too inflammatory, the media treated it as a tough warning to the Kremlin. Watching a report to that effect on the "ABC Evening News" in his office, Scowcroft said, "That's exactly what I was afraid of. Now we're going to be in a full-scale pissing match with Moscow — just when we don't need it!"

After his meeting with Bush, Baker ordered cables to be sent to Moscow and Leningrad, instructing U.S. diplomats to "start asking questions" of Soviet officials about the meaning of the directive to use troops to round up draft resisters and deserters.*

Ambassador Matlock went to Smolensk Square to raise the matter with Shevardnadze, who looked troubled and said he knew nothing.

For the next several days, Scowcroft and Bush waited for the Soviets to retaliate for the Fitzwater statement by doing something to undermine the U.S. position at the UN on the Gulf crisis. But nothing happened, though TASS branded the statement an "unconcealed attempt

---

* The directive applied to Armenia, Georgia, Moldavia, and parts of Ukraine as well, but Washington was focusing on the Baltics as the only republics whose incorporation into the USSR the United States had never recognized.

to interfere in the internal affairs of the Soviet Union." This was a phrase out of the Cold War past. Officials at the White House and the State Department were struck by the speed with which the old Soviet propaganda machine had slipped into reverse, but they consoled themselves with the thought that at least Soviet policy in the Gulf remained unchanged.

As Soviet paratroops landed in Lithuania, Matlock called on Georgi Shakhnazarov, one of the few "new thinkers" who were still part of Gorbachev's inner circle. Shakhnazarov made a perfunctory attempt to defend the recent moves against the Baltics. Insisting that Gorbachev's economic reforms were still on track, he blamed the Balts themselves for creating the crisis.

Returning to the embassy, Matlock told his aides that Shakhnazarov seemed "hunkered down, extremely defensive, and not willing to be candid about what's really going on here. He's being loyal to his boss, but he's clearly worried."

In Moscow that same week, the retrograde new Soviet interior minister, Boris Pugo, received Edgar Bronfman, the chairman of Joseph E. Seagram & Sons, a producer of wine, liquor, and other beverages. In his capacity as president of the World Jewish Congress, Bronfman had praised the Soviets for the dramatically increased exodus of Soviet Jews, and urged the U.S. to suspend the Jackson-Vanik Amendment. Thus he was most welcome in Moscow.

Pugo told Bronfman that Baltic nationalists were threatening to "undermine the rights of the minorities." Like his fellow hard-liners, the interior minister was posing as a champion of the Russian minorities in the Baltics.

In early January, Baker flew to the Middle East and Europe in a last-ditch effort to head off a war against Iraq. As acting secretary of state in Baker's absence, Lawrence Eagleburger told Scowcroft it was time to summon Bessmertnykh to the State Department for a new warning on the Baltics. Scowcroft agreed but cautioned that "we've got to be careful that the Soviets don't go off the reservation" on the Gulf: "Keep it low-key. Don't make it into a big public thing."

When Bessmertnykh arrived at his office, Eagleburger informed him that in response to the dispatch of Soviet paratroops to the Baltics, he had already had dozens of calls from Capitol Hill demanding U.S. retaliation against Moscow. "Look, Sasha," he said, "you know perfectly well how serious a problem this is within the United States. You know that further progress in our relationship is going to depend on how this situation develops. I strongly urge you to tell Moscow to change its approach."

Bessmertnykh replied, "Larry, I've got to tell you: the situation is almost out of control." He added that he was "grateful" that the Bush administration was still proceeding with plans for the summit with Gorbachev the following month. Gorbachev had already yielded to pressure from Soviet conservatives on domestic policy; now he was trying to avoid a similar reversal in American-Soviet relations. If Washington were to impose linkage between the Baltics and the summit, it would make it even harder for Gorbachev to insulate his foreign policy from Soviet domestic turmoil.

Eagleburger cabled a report on the conversation to the traveling secretary of state. Knowing that Baker's aides would see the telegram, he omitted any reference to Bessmertnykh's comment about Gorbachev's losing control. A leak of such a sensitive remark not only would embarrass Eagleburger but might also damage Bessmertnykh's chances of succeeding Shevardnadze as foreign minister.

Bessmertnykh was the Americans' number one choice to be their next Soviet interlocutor, though no one expected him to be another Shevardnadze. As a career diplomat who had risen during the Gromyko era, Bessmertnykh could be relied upon to adapt to a return of the hard line, if it came to that. He lacked the independent political base and the close personal relationship with Gorbachev that had made Shevardnadze so much more than a cog in the Soviet apparatus, but he nonetheless seemed to be in the Shevardnadze mold. He was presumed to be a new thinker, and from his years in Washington, he was on friendly terms with key members of the Executive Branch and Congress. Baker recalled with approval that after his 1989 Wyoming meeting with Shevardnadze, Bessmertnykh had asked him to autograph a picture of the official party posing by Jackson Lake.

American analysts had by now divined that Bessmertnykh had two principal competitors for the post. One was Alexander Dzasokhov, a onetime ambassador to Syria who had become the member of the Politburo in charge of ideology. Clearly, the installation of the party's highest-ranking ideologist as foreign minister could foreshadow an effort to reinstate Communist precepts in Soviet foreign policy. The other candidate was Yevgeni Primakov, whose self-appointment as mediator in the Gulf crisis had won him no friends in the Bush administration.

During his trip, the State Department sent Baker a biography of Dzasokhov, in case he should need it suddenly. Bessmertnykh himself thought that Primakov would get the job, concluding, as he put it, that of all those around Gorbachev, "he's the pushiest guy in the crowd."

In Geneva on Wednesday, January 9, Baker held a long meeting with the Iraqi foreign minister, Tariq Aziz, which ended acrimoniously. War was now a certainty; the only question was when the coalition would launch its attacks.

Afterward, Baker assured Shevardnadze by telephone that the United States had made every effort to prevent hostilities. He added a warning about the Baltics: "I know this isn't an easy time for you personally, but you've got to know that the steps being taken in the Baltics will have the kinds of consequences we've talked about before. I hope you'll convey that to President Gorbachev."

Shevardnadze did not reply. Baker found his silence both "painful and eloquent." Wishing to end the conversation on a positive note, he told the Soviet how sorry he was that they would not be dealing with each other as fellow ministers anymore.

That same day, in Moscow, Shevardnadze met with Edgar Bronfman. Reflecting gloomily on the drift of events, he said he feared that what was happening in the Soviet Union might lead to the "greatest destabilization" in Europe. Looking out the window, he murmured to himself, "I can now understand how someone might immolate himself."

At the White House on Friday morning, January 11, Scowcroft told Bush that Gorbachev was trying to reach him by telephone to discuss the Gulf crisis. The UN deadline for Saddam Hussein to withdraw his forces from Kuwait was only four days away; Bush and Scowcroft suspected that Gorbachev was calling to ask for a delay in military action.

Scowcroft advised Bush to use the call to "lay down another marker" on the Baltics: he must reiterate his concern about the central Soviet authorities' "bullying" of the three republics. As soon as reporters learned of Gorbachev's telephone call, Scowcroft predicted, they would ask whether Bush had raised the issue of the Baltics. "The answer had better be 'yes,' or there will be hell to pay," he concluded.

Bush said, "Okay, I'll try to do it in a way that doesn't increase the danger of Gorbachev bailing out on us."

Once the call from the Kremlin came through, Gorbachev repeated his support for all the UN resolutions on the Gulf, including 678, which

threatened the use of force. He went through the motions of appealing
to Bush to postpone an attack. Mindful as ever of his conservative
critics, he wished to put himself on the record one more time as cham-
pioning a political solution.

In the course of the conversation, recalling Scowcroft's advice, Bush
raised the issue of the Baltics. "I want you to understand my concern,
my *deep* concern," he said, "about the need to ensure that there is a
peaceful resolution to the situation there." Recourse to violence would
halt and perhaps even reverse the progress of the last few years in the
relationship that they had both been working so hard to nurture.

Gorbachev replied that he, too, was concerned about how the situation was developing, and was still committed to finding a "rational
resolution." Portraying himself as an overworked crisis manager, almost
a victim of circumstances, he appealed to Bush's sympathy: "It's extremely difficult, and it's taking up much of my time and energy."

Bush repeated his hope that there would be a "dialogue" between
the Kremlin and the Baltics.

The same day, in Vilnius, the Soviet paratroops who had come to round
up draft dodgers moved suddenly to occupy Lithuania's main printing
plant. When protesters gathered in front of the building, the troops
began firing at random. Several people were shot.

After seizing two local police academies and the republic's Ministry
of Internal Affairs, the Soviet troops advanced on the television tower.
Lithuanian citizens surrounded both that building and the parliament
building, where President Landsbergis and many Lithuanian legislators
and draft resisters had been holed up for days. The citizens kept a vigil
into the night, many huddling around bonfires in the cold.

In Moscow on Saturday, January 12, Boris Yeltsin called the Russian
parliament into emergency session and got it to pass a strong condemnation of this latest turn of the screw in the Baltics.

Immediately afterward, Yeltsin explained to Ambassador Matlock,
"If the forces of the center can do this to the Balts, they can do it to
us."

Yeltsin took his parliament's protest to the Kremlin, where in a private meeting he and Gorbachev had an angry exchange. In order to
avert total disaster, the two men agreed to send a delegation to Vilnius
to mediate the conflict and ensure the resolution of the crisis "by political means."

*   *   *

By then, however, it was too late. Early on Sunday morning, January 13, Soviet units in Vilnius resumed their attack on the television tower, which had been broadcasting news every other hour about the mounting Soviet military pressure.

Near the tower, several hundred Lithuanians confronted two Soviet tanks and an armored personnel carrier. One tank swung its gun barrel over the heads of the demonstrators and smashed the windows of a parked bus. The other fired a blank shell, the explosion shattering nearby windows.

A young man climbed onto one of the tanks and straddled the gun barrel, which swung wildly as the tank rocked back and forth, trying to buck him off. Another man stood in front of the other tank and mockingly gestured for it to take aim at his head; the tank crew obliged. Many of the onlookers remembered Tiananmen Square. By the time the assault was over, several hundred Lithuanians were wounded, and fifteen were dead.

At the moment of the massacre, it was still Saturday evening in the United States. Word reached Washington by telephone and ham radio. George Kolt, director of the CIA's Office of Soviet Analysis, had gone out to dinner and neglected to take his beeper. The phone was ringing off the hook when he returned home.

After hearing the news, Curtis Kamman, the deputy assistant secretary of state for Europe, rushed to his office at ten-thirty to establish a working group that would help prepare an official U.S. response. Condoleezza Rice spent the night and early morning talking on the telephone with State and the CIA.

At one-thirty Sunday morning, Paul Goble, a State Department expert on Soviet nationalities, met with Endal Lippmaa, a minister of the Estonian government who, at that moment, was the senior Baltic official in the United States. Lippmaa said he was convinced that Moscow intended to reestablish its control over all three Baltic capitals: "Next week it will be Riga, the week after that, Tallinn."

At three o'clock in the morning, Rice received a call from Dennis Ross, who was with Baker in Turkey. Ross reported that the secretary of state hated to divert public attention from the impending showdown with Saddam Hussein but felt that the United States had no choice but to issue a public protest over the killings in Lithuania.

*   *   *

In Moscow, Sergei Stankevich, the reformist deputy mayor of the city, called the crackdown in Vilnius the "most serious blow against *perestroika* since it started." It was a "catastrophe for everything we've achieved in the last five years" and evidence that, just as Shevardnadze had warned, Gorbachev was imposing "systematic dictatorship."

Pro-reform, pro-democracy members of both the Russian and the Soviet parliaments marched through Red Square. At a rally, several thousand Muscovites denounced Gorbachev for allowing the murders in Vilnius — and Bush for having supported him so staunchly to date.

On Sunday afternoon, Matlock and the ambassadors of Britain, France, Germany, and Finland were summoned to the Foreign Ministry. Since traffic had been slowed by a falling snow, Matlock walked the short distance from Spaso House to Smolensk Square.

The envoys were ushered in to see Anatoli Kovalyov, the first deputy foreign minister, who had just met with Gorbachev. Kovalyov said he wanted the group to know that Gorbachev had not ordered the resort to force in Vilnius. The Soviet leader's policies had not changed; he was "still committed" to doing everything he could to avoid bloodshed.

Speaking for himself and his colleagues, Matlock replied that they were "shocked and dismayed": they could only hope that in light of what Kovalyov had said about Gorbachev's attitude, there would soon be a clear statement from Moscow on the illegality of what had happened in Vilnius, along with assurances that those responsible would be punished.

Roland Dumas in Paris and Hans-Dietrich Genscher in Bonn released identical statements demanding an end to the Soviet use of force. The British foreign secretary, Douglas Hurd, and the Belgian foreign minister, Mark Eyskens, warned the Kremlin that the European Community might well suspend a billion dollars in promised aid to the Soviet Union.

In Vilnius, before the long day turned to night, Landsbergis was already referring to it as Bloody Sunday. This designation was intended to recall an event in the history of the first Russian Revolution.

The original Bloody Sunday — January 9, 1905 — was one of the landmark dates of the twentieth century. A procession of workers marched on the Winter Palace in St. Petersburg to present Czar Nicholas II with a petition of grievances. Troops fired into the crowd, killing forty people. Other clashes around the city left hundreds more dead.

One consequence of the massacre was irreparable damage to the image of Nicholas as the "good czar." In present-day Moscow, this same title was often conferred — sometimes with sarcasm, sometimes with admiration — on Mikhail Gorbachev.

Boris Yeltsin flew to Tallinn, where he signed a "mutual support pact" with the Baltic states and appealed to "soldiers, sergeants, and officers, our fellow countrymen drafted into the army on the territory of the Russian Federation and now in the Baltic republics."

He warned that these troops might soon be "given the order to act against legally created state bodies, against the peaceful civilian population that is defending its democratic achievements." Citing a clause in the new Russian constitution, adopted only a month before, Yeltsin said that any such order would be "unlawful."

Back in Moscow, Gorbachev went apoplectic at Yeltsin's words, crying, "That son of a bitch! What's to be done about him?" One of Gorbachev's advisers shuddered, thinking his boss sounded like Henry II asking about Thomas à Becket, "Who will free me from this turbulent priest?"

Informed that there had been an anomymous threat to blow up his plane between Tallinn and Moscow, Yeltsin was driven to Leningrad and flew home from there. Beset by similar anxieties, a number of Yeltsin's colleagues in the Russian government increased the size of their bodyguards. Some Russian officials began carrying sidearms and sent their families to dachas in the country — as if that would put them out of harm's way if the KGB decided to round them up.

On Sunday morning, in the Situation Room at the White House, Robert Gates used a secure video link to speak with officials at State, Defense, and the CIA. Condoleezza Rice said, "Boy, what a coincidence! Just when we're all tied up with the Gulf, Gorbachev sends in the tanks." She recalled that in 1956, Nikita Khrushchev had cracked down on Hungary at a moment when he presumed the West was absorbed in the Suez crisis.

Gates replied that "whether it's deliberate or not," the Soviets "must understand we're not too distracted" by the Gulf crisis to react. David Gompert — who had become the principal European affairs expert on the NSC staff since Robert Blackwill's return to Harvard the previous fall — said, "This is a classic challenge to us as a superpower. We've got to prove to the world that we can walk and chew gum at the same time, that we can deal with two crises at once."

Bush returned to the South Grounds by helicopter from Camp David. Inside the White House, Fitzwater and Rice were waiting for him. Bush asked about the situation in Vilnius: "How bad is it?"

"Awful," said Rice. "They ran over a thirteen-year-old girl with a tank."

Hoping that Gorbachev was not directly responsible, Bush asked, "Do we know who ordered the attack?"

"No," she said, "but the buildup has been there for some time. There's no reason to believe the military was acting on its own."

Rice had drafted a statement for the president, which he studied and then went back outside to deliver for the cameras. It said that the resort to violence in Vilnius "threatens to set back or perhaps even reverse the process of reform" in the Soviet Union, "which is so important in the world and the development of the new international order." Improvising, Bush then added, "I talked to President Gorbachev not so many hours ago to encourage the peaceful change there, and not the use of force."

In the Oval Office, Bush put his hand on Scowcroft's shoulder and thanked him for urging him to mention the Baltics during his telephone conversation with Gorbachev the previous Friday. "It's a good thing we didn't let that subject slide," he said.

Scowcroft reported that the press was badgering him about whether the February summit with Gorbachev was still on. Meanwhile, the Soviets themselves were pushing for a firm date. He told Bush, "The longer we let this thing hang, the more of a charade it becomes."

The president did not want to cancel the summit in the immediate aftermath of Bloody Sunday. Such a move would appear to be in direct retaliation against Gorbachev for what had happened in Vilnius, an impression he wished to avoid on the eve of a Gulf war that was growing more likely by the hour.

Scowcroft and Gates seriously considered sending a presidential letter to Gorbachev rescinding the package of programs for economic assistance and cooperation that had been unveiled after Bush's December meeting with Shevardnadze. But Bush preferred to wait awhile and give Gorbachev a chance to undo the damage that had been done in Vilnius.

Gorbachev's efforts to defend himself in Moscow verged on buffoonery. In rambling statements to reporters and the Supreme Soviet, he denied any personal responsibility for the bloodshed while still endorsing the need for a crackdown. The real culprits, he said, were Landsbergis and the Lithuanian nationalists, who had staged a "nighttime constitutional coup." A peaceful resolution of the crisis, he said, would be difficult "when the republic is led by such people."

The Soviet president went on to test the credulity of even his staunchest supporters by insisting, "The report about the tragedy came as a surprise to all. I learned about it only later, when they woke me up." If, however, Gorbachev was telling the truth about not having approved the intervention in advance, this statement meant that he was no longer in control of the forces over which he was supposed to preside — just as Bessmertnykh had privately implied to Eagleburger.

In Washington, Condoleezza Rice was disgusted when she heard Gorbachev's extraordinary claim. She grimly joked with Gompert, "How about that? They didn't wake up Gorbachev — they woke *us* up instead!"

The CIA wrote a "Spot Commentary," or SPOTCOM, for the *President's Daily Brief,* a classified summary of the latest intelligence information. The brief concluded that Gorbachev must have approved the deployment of airborne troops to the region, even if he neither issued nor approved the order to shoot. He had pointed events in a direction that made some kind of violent confrontation almost inevitable. Thus, Gorbachev was "strategically if not tactically" responsible for the assault in Lithuania.*

In Moscow, Vadim Bakatin, who had been Boris Pugo's predecessor as interior minister, publicly demanded to know why Gorbachev would not completely dissociate himself from the Vilnius "putsch." Yelena Bonner, the widow of Andrei Sakharov, asked that her husband's name be stricken from any list of Nobel laureates that also included Gorbachev's.

Gorbachev was stung by the intensity and breadth of the world's reproach. Especially now that he had alienated or disillusioned virtually all of his various constituencies at home, he was desperate to preserve the ones he had built abroad. He was appalled to hear Bush, Kohl, and

---

* In its coverage of developments in the USSR, the *Daily Brief* had earlier referred regularly to the "conservative" forces that were seeking to turn back the clock. Bush, who considered himself a conservative, objected to the application of the label to Soviet hard-liners. The CIA started to use the term "traditionalist" instead, though that word, too, certainly applied to Bush. George Kolt preferred "Leninist," while Condoleezza Rice's candidate was "reactionaries." Fritz Ermarth recommended simply "bad guys."

Mitterrand declare that the events in Vilnius had jeopardized not only Western economic assistance but also Gorbachev's good standing in the club of world leaders.

In Washington on Monday, January 14, Marlin Fitzwater told the White House press corps that planning for the summit was now "up in the air."

The next day, in Moscow, Gorbachev met in his Kremlin office with a group that included several distinguished foreign visitors. Far from radiating his usual self-assurance, he struck those present as being profoundly worried about what was happening to his country and his reputation in the eyes of the outside world.

In a transparent effort to assure his guests that he was still being advised by one of his original partners in reform, he had Alexander Yakovlev seated at his right hand. But throughout the session, Yakovlev said little and looked glum.

Gorbachev promised the visitors that he was still committed to making the Soviet Union a "law-based society." He appealed for "understanding" as he tried to reconcile that goal with the "political realities" he faced. He compared himself to a voyager who was "out of sight of land" and feeling "seasick."*

In Washington the previous weekend, the rush to keep up with events abroad had deflected attention from the sudden departure of Ambassador Bessmertnykh. At four in the morning on Thursday, January 9, the Soviet embassy's duty officer had awakened the ambassador with an urgent summons from Gorbachev to return home and succeed Shevardnadze as foreign minister.

Gorbachev had come under pressure from the party's Central Committee and the military to appoint as his new minister a career diplomat rather than an independent figure like Shevardnadze. The growing

---

* The group was made up of representatives from an international foundation established in 1988 to promote East-West cooperation on human rights, economic development, environmental action, education, and culture. Andrei Sakharov had been among its founders. In addition to Yakovlev, the board included two prominent Soviet scientists, Roald Sagdeyev, the former director of the Soviet Space Research Institute, and Yevgeni Velikhov, the vice president of the Academy of Sciences, both occasional advisers to Gorbachev. The American members were Susan Eisenhower (who was married to Sagdeyev), former Senator Charles Mathias, former Secretary of Defense and World Bank President Robert McNamara, Armand Hammer, and two former university presidents, Theodore Hesburgh of Notre Dame and Jerome Wiesner of MIT.

Western anger over the Kremlin's stance on the Baltics had added weight to the argument for choosing someone who could reassure the outside world about Soviet foreign policy.

Asked to recommend a successor, Shevardnadze had offered Gorbachev three names, in order of preference: Yuli Kvitsinsky, a deputy foreign minister who had been ambassador to Bonn; Yuli Vorontsov, ambassador to the UN, who had been one of Dobrynin's deputies in Washington; and Bessmertnykh. Shevardnadze put Bessmertnykh third on his list out of concern that he might be too quick to trim his sails in shifting political winds.

But Gorbachev, still angry over the way Shevardnadze had resigned, was in no mood to take his advice. He picked Bessmertnykh because, as he told his aides, "the Americans trust this man, and that's important to us now."

On receiving Gorbachev's summons, Bessmertnykh raised the matter with his young wife, Marina, who tried to talk him out of accepting the post. She loved the diplomatic high life in Washington, and their son Arseni was only two weeks old. She knew there would be nothing but political trouble at home.

As a career *amerikanist,* Bessmertnykh was satisfied that he had already reached the pinnacle of his career. He was just beginning to feel comfortable as ambassador to Washington, and he feared that to become foreign minister at this uncertain moment would be to throw himself into a political "meatmincer."

In the end, however, he could not resist Gorbachev's offer. Nor was he sure he would like working for whoever Gorbachev's second choice might be. He said to Marina, "When the president asks you to do something, you've got to do it." She replied, "All right, it's up to you." He went to his desk and wrote out his acceptance in longhand, then had it sent by cable to Gorbachev.

On Sunday, January 13, Kvitsinsky telephoned Bessmertnykh in Washington and told him to be in Moscow in time for the morning staff meeting the next day. Bessmertnykh snapped, "That's impossible, even if you sent me a missile to ride home on! The best I can do is tomorrow afternoon."

That evening, he flew by commercial airliner to London, arriving at about six on Monday morning. Stopping at an airport newsstand, he saw splashed across the front pages of the London tabloids color photographs of tanks and mangled corpses in the streets of Vilnius. He had followed the reports of the crackdown the day before, but these first visual images of the carnage sickened him. He bought several copies, stuffed them into his briefcase, and boarded the connecting flight to Moscow.

In Washington, Bush and Baker knew nothing of the ambassador's promotion until Monday, January 14, when Japanese Foreign Minister Taro Nakayama, stopping at the State Department on his way to Moscow, told Baker that the Soviet embassy in Tokyo was reporting that Bessmertnykh was the new foreign minister. The secretary of state was both surprised and relieved.

Bessmertnykh arrived at Gorbachev's Kremlin office on Tuesday, January 15, at ten in the morning. Gorbachev shook his hand and said, "I'm presenting you to the Supreme Soviet [for confirmation] in thirty-five minutes. I hope you know what you're going to say. Also, you'd better give me some biographical data on you. The people in my office haven't given me enough to work with."

In near panic, Bessmertnykh scribbled out a summary of his career in less than a minute, then made a few notes for his speech to the parliament, in which he praised Shevardnadze. After he spoke, one legislator told him, "You made a mistake in saying all those nice things about Shevardnadze. He's not very popular here." Bessmertnykh replied, "I don't give a damn. It won't break my heart if I'm not confirmed." His nomination sailed through by a vote of 421 to 3.

Gorbachev was elated. Walking back to his office with Bessmertnykh after the vote, he said, "This is wonderful! It confirms the correctness of the basic course of our foreign policy. They support your dedication to new thinking! This is critical. It's absolutely vital!"

Back in Gorbachev's office, Bessmertnykh opened his briefcase and pulled out the newspapers he had bought in London. He said, "In agreeing to take this job, I'm committing myself to do the best I can. But this kind of thing may undermine our whole foreign policy."

Gorbachev's ebullience evaporated. Staring at a color photograph of the body of a Lithuanian who had been crushed by a tank, he said, "I'm very upset about the whole thing. It's terrible. I know that whatever we do in our domestic policy is going to have a huge effect on our foreign policy."

In his new office at the Foreign Ministry, Bessmertnykh received Matlock, who told him, "Look, Sasha, we both know Washington, and we also both know that if this business goes on in the Baltics, there's no way we can proceed with plans for a summit."

*   *   *

On Wednesday, January 16, Baker called Bessmertnykh from Washing-ton to congratulate him on his confirmation. Then, on Thursday morn-ing, at two o'clock Moscow time, the secretary of state called again. Bessmertnykh was asleep in his apartment near the Kremlin. He shook himself awake.

Baker said he was calling to notify the Soviet government that the UN coalition in the Persian Gulf would begin its attack on Iraq "very shortly."

His senses racing, Bessmertnykh asked, "What does 'very shortly' mean? Is it a matter of minutes or hours?" Baker replied that the co-alition would strike targets around Baghdad "within an hour."

Bessmertnykh said, "Can you do something to delay it? My president will need time. Please give us more time!"

Baker said, "I'm sorry, Sasha, but you know how things are with this kind of military action. The preparations are all very careful. The orders have been given, and I don't think there's any way to recall them."

Bessmertnykh called Gorbachev and told him, "The Americans have launched an attack against Iraq." The Soviet leader asked, "When is it going to happen?"

"Within the hour."

"Call Baker and see if you can get a delay of forty-eight or at least twenty-four hours," said Gorbachev. "Tell him it's my one personal request of Bush."

Bessmertnykh called Baker back and passed along the message. The secretary of state pledged to convey the message to Bush, but he said, "I've got to tell you, Sasha, I doubt there's time to do anything."

He put Bessmertnykh on hold in order to check on military devel-opments. When he came back on the line, it was to report that the skies over Baghdad were already ablaze.

Told that Operation Desert Storm had begun, Gorbachev tried once more to persuade Saddam Hussein to back off. Since telephone con-tact with Baghdad had been broken, he asked Bessmertnykh to cable the Soviet ambassador in Iraq to request an emergency meeting with Saddam. But the Iraqi leader had already disappeared into an under-ground bunker.

When intelligence officials at the Pentagon and the National Se-curity Agency intercepted and analyzed these Moscow-to-Baghdad communications, they suspected the Kremlin of exploiting Baker's advance notice to warn Saddam before the first bombs struck, perhaps even giving him time to seek safety and scramble his air force.

In his Kremlin office, before dawn on Thursday morning, Gorbachev gathered his national security team around a modern oval table of dark, smoothly polished wood. Bleary-eyed and unshaven, those present included Bessmertnykh, Vice President Yanayev, Defense Minister Yazov, KGB Chairman Kryuchkov, Valentin Falin, Primakov, Chernyayev, and Gorbachev's new spokesman, Vitali Ignatenko.

Yazov brandished maps showing the location of U.S. forces, then spread them out on the table. He was doing his best to minimize his embarrassment at having been caught by surprise. He said that "well in advance" of Baker's call to Bessmertnykh, Soviet military intelligence had deduced from its intercepts of conversations among pilots headed for the war zone that an allied air attack was imminent.

Gorbachev thrived on the atmosphere of international crisis. It gave him a respite from the conundrum he faced in the Baltics and allowed him to resume his favorite role as world statesman and peacemaker. As usual, he did most of the talking, saying, "It's a great pity that the problem couldn't be solved peacefully." He understood why the coalition had decided that Saddam had to be punished, he said, but the allies must avoid the "total destruction" of Iraq, which "would be worse for the world than the war itself."

Gorbachev and Yazov put Soviet armed forces along the southern Soviet border on alert. Bessmertnykh issued a public statement stressing that these military precautions were "solely" in response to the war in the Gulf and were "absolutely unrelated" to the ethnic and political turmoil in the Soviet Central Asian republics.

Gorbachev drafted a new message to Saddam saying that he had tried and failed to delay the start of the air war long enough to give him a final chance to withdraw from Kuwait. He fired off similar communiqués to the leaders of France, Britain, China, Germany, India, and a number of Arab states, as well as to Javier Perez de Cuellar, the secretary-general of the United Nations.

At the Soviet Defense Ministry, senior military officers watched CNN's daily coverage of the briefings from the Pentagon and the coalition's headquarters in Riyadh. A Soviet major interpreted as allied briefers on the screen reported one spectacular success after another.

*　　*　　*

From Moscow on Friday, January 18, Gorbachev telephoned Bush at the White House. The Soviet president conveyed his government's anxiety over the ferocity of the attack on Baghdad, but he was careful not to blame Bush for the escalation of the crisis.

Gorbachev said that the coalition had "made its point": Saddam Hussein had been given the thrashing he deserved. Now why not let up on him long enough for him to reconsider? Gorbachev promised that during such a pause in the bombing, he would use his own influence to persuade Saddam to withdraw.

Bush replied that a suspension of the air war would accomplish nothing beyond allowing Saddam to boast of having withstood the allies' attack.

On Saturday, January 19, with the Soviet Union seemingly quiet, for a change — at least compared to the Persian Gulf — Condoleezza Rice told her deputy Nicholas Burns, "I think I can get out of here early for once. Things seem to have settled down a bit."

But in Riga, where night had fallen, tracer bullets were lighting up the skies as fifty Black Beret troops shot their way into the headquarters of the Latvian Interior Ministry, allegedly to confiscate arms that were being illegally stored there. One person was killed inside the building, and four more died outside. Latvia's deputy prime minister, Ilmars Bisers, announced, "Civil war has begun!"

Claiming that a sniper was shooting at them, several Black Berets rushed into a hotel across the street and fired automatic weapons around the lobby. Upstairs were three U.S. diplomats, Robert Patterson, James Kenney, and Stuart Swanson, one of several teams from the U.S. consulate in Leningrad that were moving through the Baltics to monitor the crisis. Hearing the commotion, Swanson phoned colleagues in Leningrad with a message that was immediately flashed to Washington.

At the operations center at State, a duty officer said, "Here we go again. Things are getting hot!"

In public, Gorbachev once again denied personal responsibility and blamed the violence on the Balts themselves rather than on the troops who were doing the shooting. But in private, he took a very different though no less self-serving line, telling his aides that he was now "convinced" that the massacres in Vilnius and Riga were a political "provocation" against him personally — and "an attempt by reactionary forces to derail the process of reform."

*   *   *

In 1989, Scowcroft had quietly established a group to study the possibility of widespread violence erupting throughout the Soviet Union. He instructed Robert Gates to "put on your Kremlin-watcher's hat, dust off your crystal ball, and start asking some questions about what we do if various nightmare scenarios come true."

Gates had in turn formed two interagency committees — one of senior officials, under his own chairmanship, and the other of "working level" experts, run by Condoleezza Rice. Now that the worst seemed to be happening in the Baltics, the groups were meeting on an emergency basis. They quickly focused on one paramount issue: the disposition and security of Soviet nuclear weapons. What was the danger that rebel or dissident groups might seize weapons and use them for intimidation or worse?

The CIA reported on what it knew about the highly secret subject of Soviet "command and control" mechanisms and "permissive action links," which were designed to keep the authority and ability to activate nuclear weapons in a very few hands.

Thanks to intricate codes and identification devices, Soviet strategic weapons were thought to be under tight control; there was little danger that a breakaway republic could use strategic nuclear weapons on its territory to blackmail Moscow or, for that matter, Washington. Still, the group was concerned that unauthorized dissident groups might be able to gain control of tactical nuclear warheads, such as artillery shells, or chemical or biological weapons.

Briefed on these deliberations, Bush told his aides that the exercise had confirmed his strong conviction that secessionism must not be allowed to "get out of hand": it was essential that Gorbachev "remain in overall charge of the situation over there."

The Baltic massacres made it harder than ever for Bush to maintain his pro-Gorbachev policy. Senator Robert Byrd of West Virginia charged that the administration had "winked, nodded, and looked the other way" while Gorbachev worked his will in Vilnius and Riga. "Perhaps this was the price for ensuring Soviet cooperation in the Persian Gulf," said Byrd. "If it was, then it seems to me to have been a poor bargain."

Another Democrat, Bill Bradley of New Jersey, said, "It would be a sad irony if the price of Soviet support for freeing Kuwait was American acquiescence in Soviet aggression against another illegally annexed country."

The January 24 edition of the *National Intelligence Daily,* the CIA's classified summary and analysis of current events, included an article headlined "Crisis at the Turning Point." It said, "Gorbachev has started a conflict without a visible program and with scant prospect of long-term success. He will not easily escape the predicament for which he is largely responsible, and he may become its principal casualty."

At the Pentagon, Dick Cheney took several hours off from running the Gulf War to hear half a dozen Kremlinologists present an equally bleak assessment. During this session, George Kolt of the CIA declared, "Gorbachev is still better than the company he keeps. But the people he's hanging out with are now driving the process in a very disagreeable direction."

Cheney smiled faintly and observed, "A lot of what I'm hearing reminds me of something I once said that got me in a certain amount of hot water." He was referring to the incident in the spring of 1989 when his skeptical comments about Gorbachev on a television show had triggered a reprimand from the White House.

In the wake of the Baltic crackdown, Robert Gates was no longer quite so easily ridiculed as the "chief Gorbachev-basher" or as "Chicken Little."*

With some satisfaction, Gates still kept in his top desk drawer a copy of the pessimistic speech on Gorbachev that Baker had stopped him from delivering in 1989. After the first Bloody Sunday in Vilnius, Scowcroft had teased him, "You want to say 'I told you so' so badly you're about to burst!"

Gates did tell colleagues that while he was not particularly moved by the tragedy of the "good czar gone bad," he was distressed that because of the Gorbachev "debacle," many Soviet citizens would be forever disillusioned by democratization and the effort to create a market economy.

He noted that the Soviets' daily lives had in many ways been happier under the old Stalinist system. In the future, they would identify liberalization with chaos. "Now that Gorbachev has screwed it up," Gates maintained, "it'll be all the harder for some subsequent leader, more

* Gates remembered one article in particular, dated May 28, 1989. In it, David Ignatius of the *Washington Post* had recalled the adage that when an intelligence officer smells flowers, he looks around for a coffin. He went on, "Gates certainly has been looking for the coffin in the case of Soviet leader Mikhail Gorbachev. With his dour assessments, the NSC official has become to the world of Sovietology what Eeyore is to Pooh Corner — someone capable of finding a dark lining in even the brightest cloud."

determined and skillful than Gorbachev, to get his countrymen ever to support reform again."

At his White House office on Tuesday, January 22, Scowcroft received a small delegation of Baltic-Americans who were predictably furious about the relatively subdued official U.S. response to the killings in Vilnius and Riga.

Scowcroft tried to explain that the administration could do little to force the Kremlin to change its policies. Not only would anything the United States did be a "mere pinprick," he said, but it might also be "provocative and counterproductive."

Bush made a surprise "drop-by" appearance. Just as he had done before, during the Baltic tensions in the spring of 1990, he raised the specter of Hungary in 1956: imprudent Western support could "doom" the cause of Baltic independence. Scowcroft chimed in that by "lashing out," the United States might open a trap door under Gorbachev and ruin whatever chance there still was for reform in the Soviet Union. He then asked the visitors a leading question: would they really prefer a KGB-military dictatorship in the Kremlin?

Mari-Ann Rikken of the Estonian-American National Committee replied that it was the administration's own "hands-off" policy that was proving counterproductive. She complained that the administration was inadvertently sending a "signal to Moscow" that Soviet leaders might take to be tantamount to "appeasement."

His nerves taut after the months of pressures on him from every direction, Bush cut her off in midsentence: *"Don't — use — that — word!"*

Just as in the opening months of his administration, the president was now once again being accused of timidity in his conduct of U.S.-Soviet relations. In 1989, he had been criticized for his reluctance to engage with Gorbachev; now it was his reluctance to *dis*engage that was under fire.

In the Oval Office, John Sununu cautioned Bush, "This is turning into a major political problem for us." He listed conservative Republicans in Congress who were especially upset. "Carefully worded protests" about the Baltic crackdown were "not adequate," he said; the administration must "put teeth" into its complaints.

Bush raised the matter during a separate meeting with Scowcroft, who said, "John and his friends on the Hill want us to wave a bloody shirt. He's watching out for your political fortunes here. That's fine. But we've got to be careful not to make gestures without effect."

Bush replied, "Whatever we do, I don't want to do anything irrevocable. I want to preserve the relationship with Gorbachev as much as possible."

Gruesome as the Vilnius and Riga massacres were, they did not justify the historical comparison to Khrushchev and Hungary in 1956. Had Gorbachev followed Khrushchev's script, Landsbergis would have wound up forcibly retired from politics — in hiding, in jail, or dead. Instead, Gorbachev prevailed on the military to call off the tanks and leave Landsbergis's government alone.

Troops were still occupying the Vilnius television station, but the once-vaunted Soviet Army was reduced to patrolling a few hundred yards of fence around a single tower on the outskirts of a provincial capital, and with little effect: Lithuanians could still tune in to defiantly nationalistic broadcasts, since the radio station in Kaunas, their second-largest city, was still on the air.

Nor could Vilnius and Riga qualify as another Tiananmen. When their moment of truth came, in June 1989, Chinese leaders, impervious to world opinion, set the course of Chinese internal politics for years to come. By contrast, Gorbachev waffled — largely because he was so sensitive to what the outside world thought of him.

The unresolved crisis in the Baltics had become a metaphor for the conflict raging within the Soviet Union, and within Gorbachev himself. It was a standoff between the forces of the center and of secession, the forces of repression and of continuing reform.

By allowing Pugo and the military to use violence, Gorbachev had caused many of the democrats and the nationalists to give up on him. Yet by keeping the hard-liners from finishing what they had started in Vilnius, he alienated the Right as well. In January 1991, Gorbachev still commanded the middle ground between Right and Left, but his position was becoming increasingly lonely and precarious.

Despite his disinclination to undermine Gorbachev, Bush wrote the Soviet leader a private letter threatening to cut off all American economic assistance. Baker telephoned Bessmertnykh in Moscow and told him that under the circumstances, there was no point in pretending any longer that the summit could take place in February.

The administration kept secret the contents of Bush's letter to

Gorbachev and Baker's telephone call to Bessmertnykh. In public, the White House continued to avoid criticizing Gorbachev.

In Moscow, Matlock was given the task of handing Bush's stern letter to the Soviet leader. Following instructions, he said to Gorbachev, "It's hard to understand what's happening." He added that it would be difficult to continue the improvement of U.S.-Soviet relations "if you don't return to your line from the last summit." By this he meant Gorbachev's assurances that he was committed to a peaceful resolution of the nationalities problem.

Shaken and angry, Gorbachev told Matlock that there could only be "one law," the law of the Soviet state. The Balts must respect and obey it while pursuing their aspirations. Expressing "regret" over the bloodshed in Vilnius and Riga, he said he was "determined" to prevent the return of *proizvol* — the arbitrary rule and official lawlessness that had characterized the Stalin era. He asked Matlock to appeal to Bush and Baker for "patience" and "understanding."

CHAPTER 15

"You've Got to Understand"

ON SATURDAY, January 26, 1991, Bessmertnykh boarded a special Aeroflot plane at Vnukovo-2 Airport outside Moscow and flew to Washington for his first visit as foreign minister.

His recent conversations with Ambassador Matlock and the tough letter that Bush had just sent Gorbachev gave Bessmertnykh a sense of foreboding. He felt that a U.S. decision to withhold assistance to the Soviet Union would amount to the imposition of sanctions against Moscow.

Such a move, he believed, would weaken Gorbachev, whose prestige abroad was one of his few remaining political assets. An escalation of pressure from the West would also rile hard-liners, who would complain that the United States was trying to dictate to them how they should handle their internal affairs.

On landing at Andrews Air Force Base, Bessmertnykh would have liked to go to the apartment in the Soviet embassy where his wife and infant son remained for the time being. Instead, he asked to be driven to the State Department for a preliminary meeting with Baker. In his view, the situation was deteriorating so quickly that every hour counted.

*   *   *

Bessmertnykh's first order of business with the secretary of state was to put the finishing touches on the joint announcement postponing the summit. Baker had called him in advance and read him the proposed language, which avoided any mention of the Baltics: the two governments would present the postponement as a mutual decision, blaming the Gulf War and obstacles that had arisen in arms control.

On the Baltics, Bessmertnykh told Baker, "I sense you're on the verge of sanctions, Jim. If you go ahead with any plans like that, you'll be overreacting. You'll bring about exactly the effect that you don't want. Remember that the U.S. is always presented to our people as a country that supports Gorbachev. I know the U.S. can't sit tight and do nothing about Vilnius, but whatever you do should be well calibrated; it shouldn't be overdone."

The new foreign minister had brought with him Gorbachev's reply to Bush's letter. Baker noted that it lacked concrete assurances that the Kremlin would cease its violent repression of the Baltics. "You've got to understand, Sasha, how serious this situation is," Baker said. "We've got to take some sort of action."

He cited the wide margins by which resolutions supporting Baltic independence had passed the Congress, and explained, "You need to do something so that people won't think that the situation is doomed to go from bad to worse." The only way for the Kremlin to avoid suspension of U.S. economic aid, he told Bessmertnykh, was to add "substance to your claims of seeking a solution": "Our ability to hold the line against pressure depends on our being able to point to something specific, like a negotiating mechanism."

Exasperated, Bessmertnykh responded that the Kremlin should get credit for having introduced a secession law that guaranteed the right of the republics to leave the union if they chose to do so.

Baker retorted, "In its present form, your secession law is a device to *prevent* secession. People have to believe that whatever procedure you have makes secession possible." Wasn't there some way to modify the secession law so that it would have greater credibility, both within the Soviet Union and abroad?

Bessmertnykh did not rule out changes in the law: "Everything's possible — as long as it takes place in a constitutional framework." He appealed for patience until March 17, when a referendum was scheduled on the proposition that the Soviet Union should be preserved as a "renewed Union" with a strong center but greater autonomy for the republics.

He tried to convince Baker that the planned plebiscite was significant proof of Gorbachev's commitment to democracy: large numbers of Soviet citizens would, for the first time in their history, have a say in the nature of their state and the terms of debate over its future. He said, "If people vote, they will get used to the idea of working according to an orderly, legal process."

But March 17 was seven weeks away, and Baker knew there was no certainty that the vote would actually lead to changes in the secession law. Moreover, the central authorities might in the meantime tighten control over the Baltics.

Baker repeated to Bessmertnykh that it was important for the outside world to see "immediate and demonstrable" evidence that the crackdowns in Vilnius and Riga were not harbingers of a new Kremlin policy on the nationalities problem.

Bessmertnykh said, "I understand." He promised to ask his superiors in Moscow whether there was anything he could add to what was in Gorbachev's letter. After leaving the State Department, he cabled Gorbachev with Baker's objections and recommended that the Kremlin authorize him to give the Americans specific assurances that it was pulling back from the brink in the Baltics.

In reply to Bessmertnykh's cable, Gorbachev sent his foreign minister new instructions: he could tell the Americans that the Kremlin was taking "concrete steps to defuse the situation" in the Baltics. The paratroops dispatched to the region earlier in the month had already been withdrawn, and two-thirds of the Interior Ministry forces would be gone within days.

When he saw Baker again on Monday morning, January 28, Bessmertnykh reported that the Soviet leadership had accepted the "principle that all problems will be solved peacefully" and that the "use of armed force in political struggles is inadmissible." The violence unleashed against the citizens of Vilnius and Riga was "not presidential policy," he said. This was as close as Gorbachev was likely to come to repudiating the brutality of the security forces and the military in the two Baltic capitals.*

---

* On Gorbachev's behalf, Bessmertnykh also disavowed the "attempt of any committee or organization to claim power in a nonlegal manner" — a repudiation of the national salvation committees that were fronting for the hard-liners in the Baltics.

Impressed, Baker asked, "Can this be said publicly?" Bessmertnykh said that it could.

Baker rushed to the White House to brief Bush: "I think we've got something that we can work with here. I think the Soviets are ready to pull back, and they may even let us take credit for getting them to do it. That takes some of the pressure off us on having to hit them too hard for what they've done."

Bush was much relieved. His principal concern was that he not be forced by circumstances into distancing himself from Gorbachev — even if Gorbachev himself bore a large share of responsibility for what had happened.

That afternoon, Bessmertnykh came to the Oval Office, where he and the president sat in wing chairs near the crackling fire. As coffee was served, Bush said he was "delighted" that the new foreign minister was someone who knew the United States so well. He endorsed the formula Baker and Bessmertnykh had worked out for delaying the summit, while stressing that he still "very much" wanted to go to Moscow.

Working from notes, Bessmertnykh paraphrased Gorbachev's latest letter on the Baltics before handing it over to Bush. He said that his president was "determined" to keep both *perestroika* and the new era in Soviet foreign policy alive. Soviet internal reform was a "key factor" in making international cooperation possible, he asserted: "It has brought us to the point of trust."

The Soviet Union and the United States, he said, had already accomplished much and could do more in the future. Nothing must be allowed to obstruct this collaboration. The Soviet Union's ability to maintain the "cooperative approach" — demonstrated on the issues of Eastern Europe, German unification, and the Persian Gulf — "will depend on how the United States reacts" to the trouble in the Baltics.

On the surface, Bessmertnykh seemed to be delivering an appeal for patience and understanding. Yet when what he said was reduced to its essence, the import was that the Americans should stop making life difficult for the Kremlin on the Baltics, or else Gorbachev would find ways to impede the coalition in the war against Saddam Hussein.

Rather than give his listeners a chance to bristle at the veiled threat, Bessmertnykh moved smoothly and briskly along. He reiterated the Kremlin's basic, "principled" position: the Balts could have independence if they insisted, but only by following a "constitutional process." He added that he had been in touch with Gorbachev over the weekend, and that there were several things that the Soviet president wanted Bush to know beyond what was in the letter. Bessmertnykh then repeated what he had already told Baker about the removal of airborne divisions and Interior Ministry troops from the Baltics.

Bush informed Bessmertnykh that he had no doubt that Gorbachev was "sincere" in believing that he was handling the Baltic crisis in the most appropriate way. But the Soviet leadership must understand that there were "political facts for us as well."

He recalled that at Malta, in Washington, and in Helsinki, Gorbachev had personally assured him that he would deal with the Baltics peacefully. Now violence had been instigated by forces acting on behalf of Moscow. Naturally, there would be a "reaction" in the United States, especially from Congress. Surely Bessmertnykh had spent enough time in Washington to understand the "way things work here."

Once again, Bessmertnykh asked that the administration be patient until March 17. "Let's see what happens," he said. "At least the referendum will improve the overall atmosphere."

Bush replied, "That's certainly something all of us want."

Bessmertnykh noticed that Bush had several index cards with talking points typed out on them, but he was ignoring them and only shuffling them occasionally in his lap. Bessmertnykh concluded that had it not been for the new assurances he had conveyed from Moscow, the president would have read from the cards, and his message would have been considerably tougher.

The next morning, Tuesday, January 29, Bush and Baker met in the Oval Office to talk about the foreign policy passages in the State of the Union address that the president was to deliver that evening.

The address was devoted mainly to the war in the Persian Gulf. Bush planned to say that the international response to the Iraqi invasion of Kuwait proved that the "end of the Cold War has been a victory for all humanity."

Taking their cue from Gorbachev's latest private message, Bush and Baker decided to add a new passage to the opening of the speech. The president would tell Congress, "Our objective is to help the Baltic peoples achieve their aspirations, not to punish the Soviet Union. In our recent discussions with the Soviet leadership we have been given representations which, if fulfilled, would result in the withdrawal of some Soviet forces, a reopening of dialogue with the republics, and a move away from violence."

It was Bush himself who chose to describe as "representations" the assurances that Gorbachev had just relayed through Bessmertnykh. This word, he felt, implied U.S. skepticism, as did the next sentence in his new text: "We will watch carefully as the situation develops."

With Shevardnadze's resignation, Baker continued to wonder whether the Soviet Union would remain so firmly in the anti-Iraq camp. Anticipating Bessmertnykh's arrival, he had told aides, "We've got to find a way of making sure he's as much on board as Shevardnadze was. We can't let the Soviets wreck things now. We've got to lock Bessmertnykh into his predecessor's policy."

Just as the Americans had feared, Bessmertnykh came to Washington with instructions to seek assurances that the United States would end the Gulf War quickly and, if possible, in a way that would let Saddam Hussein off the hook.

During their first meeting, on Saturday, January 26, Bessmertnykh promised Baker that the Kremlin would not renege on its commitment to help dislodge Iraq from Kuwait. At the same time, he said, the Soviet leadership was concerned about the mounting civilian casualties in Iraq and their possible effect on Arab states and "our own Muslim republics." Gorbachev was under great pressure from southern areas of the Soviet Union: "Our president has been receiving letters and delegations," the foreign minister noted.

He tried to persuade the secretary of state to soften the Bush administration's apparent determination to eliminate Saddam: U.S. conduct of the war was "making Saddam Hussein into a sympathetic figure where he was not one before. We've got to convince people that the purpose of this war is not simply to destroy Iraq."

Bessmertnykh's last comment struck a chord in Baker. For some time, he had been asking his under secretary for political affairs, Robert Kimmitt, to draw out his counterparts, particularly Under Secretary of Defense Paul Wolfowitz, on how the Gulf War might end. Would the coalition have to send forces into Iraq itself? If so, how far would they go? How long would they have to stay? What would constitute victory?

Wolfowitz had seemed strangely reluctant to respond definitively to these questions. Kimmitt suspected that some at the Pentagon wished to reserve the option of going well beyond the eviction of the Iraqi army from Kuwait, perhaps even to the extent of ordering coalition ground forces to sweep all the way to Baghdad and drag Saddam out of his bunker.

Baker was worried by that possibility. Desirable though it would be to rid the region and the world of Saddam, the director's forcible removal from power was not an objective included in the UN resolutions. Nor was it certain that there was sufficient support for this goal on the American home front — particularly if it entailed a drawn-out war and high U.S. casualties. Baker did not want the United States to get into a position "where we go to Baghdad and can't get out."

The secretary of state therefore wished to use his conversations with Bessmertnykh to commit his own administration to a formula for ending the war that would be consistent both with its limited UN and domestic mandates and with the imperative of keeping the Soviets on board.

For his part, Bessmertnykh wanted, if possible, to make the UN mandate even *more* limited. The foreign minister warned that the Kremlin was thinking of introducing a new resolution in the UN Security Council — "something that will give hope that a political solution is still possible."

Baker recoiled. The last thing he wanted was a new round of wrangling over the contents of yet another UN resolution. The twelve resolutions of the previous autumn had the cumulative effect of demanding much more than Saddam's withdrawal from Kuwait. For example, Resolution 674, passed on October 29, demanded that Iraq pay for the devastation it had caused in Kuwait.

No one knew better than Baker how much diplomatic exertion had gone into the passage of those twelve resolutions. A thirteenth would give the post-Shevardnadze Foreign Ministry an opportunity to bid for support among Arab and Islamic nations opposed to the war, a comforting prospect for Saddam. Worse, a thirteenth resolution, showing the effect of the new priorities in Soviet diplomacy, might provide Saddam with a way to avoid clear-cut defeat and survive with his armies to fight another day.

But Baker did not raise these points with Bessmertnykh. He simply told him that the resolutions already in place were "just what's needed," and that another might "complicate things."

Bessmertnykh replied, "You've still got to change the image of what you're doing, and it's objective." He suggested as an alternative a statement released in the names of the Soviet and American governments. Relieved that Bessmertnykh was willing to drop the notion of a thirteenth resolution, and hopeful that a joint statement would help to guarantee Soviet support for Iraq's unconditional withdrawal from Kuwait, Baker consented.

*   *   *

During their second meeting, on Monday, January 28, Bessmertnykh produced drafts for two joint statements — one on the Gulf War and the other on the Arab-Israeli conflict.

The first had a number of features that were unacceptable to the Americans. It emphasized the need for a "political" solution to the crisis, which implied a compromise of the coalition's war aims. It implied that all Iraq had to do to end the war was declare its *intention* to withdraw from Kuwait.

The statement on the Arab-Israeli dispute also contained a number of semantic booby traps. It proposed that the United States join the USSR in endorsing the "national rights of the Palestinian people" — a well-worn code phrase for the establishment of a Palestinian state — and in calling for an international peace conference. Such a conference, Baker knew, would be seen as giving the Soviet Union a forum to champion its Arab clients against Israel.

Bessmertnykh and his colleagues were anxious to pressure Israel to be more accommodating in the peace process. They believed that Baker might be sufficiently fed up with the Likud government's policy of building Jewish settlements in the occupied territories that he would now approve some version of the statement.

As during the Bush-Gorbachev meeting in Helsinki the previous October, the secretary of state knew he must be careful not to endorse any formal linkage between the United States' insistence on Iraqi withdrawal from Kuwait and its hope that Israel might eventually concede territory to the Arabs. At the same time, he was eager to adjust U.S. policy in such a way as to create a new opportunity to jump-start Arab-Israeli diplomacy once the Gulf War ended.

He felt that the Soviet Union had contributed to a number of welcome trends in the Middle East. Soviet Jews were emigrating to Israel, and Soviet influence had helped to moderate the policies of Syria's Hafez Assad. Throughout the Gulf crisis, the Soviet Union and the United States had stood on the same side.

Baker realized that Bessmertnykh was under clear instructions to include the postwar Middle East in whatever statement came out of their talks. He told his aides that he was inclined to give the foreign minister a "combination of reward for past Soviet good behavior and incentive for future good behavior."

He asked Dennis Ross to work on drafting a joint statement with Pavel Palazhchenko and others in the Soviet delegation. Bessmertnykh noted sympathetically that Ross's old partner Tarasenko had left the ministry to work as a private citizen with Shevardnadze. "I'm sorry you don't have your friend to work with," Bessmertnykh said to Ross.

At the White House, reporters were asking Marlin Fitzwater whether Bessmertnykh had brought some kind of Gulf peace proposal with him to Washington. Fitzwater's foreign affairs deputy, Roman Popadiuk, called Condoleezza Rice to ensure that nothing was afoot.

Rice in turn called Ross and told him there was "some nervousness" around the White House that Bessmertnykh might be trying to use his visit to advance a "peace plan that will let Saddam off the hook."

Ross replied, "Don't worry. We're not at that stage yet. We may be able to put everything into a statement that shows that the Soviets are on the same wavelength as we are." Rice asked if there was yet any agreed-upon language for a communiqué. Ross said they were still working on it.

The final draft of the joint statement incorporated points that both sides wanted to make. To the relief of the Americans, it said that Bessmertnykh "agreed that Iraq's withdrawal from Kuwait must remain the goal of the international community."

Then came the two sentences that the Americans had felt they had to accept in return: "The Ministers continue to believe that a cessation of hostilities would be possible if Iraq would make an unequivocal commitment to withdraw from Kuwait. They also believe that such a commitment must be backed by immediate, concrete steps leading to full compliance with the Security Council resolutions."

Thus, for the first time since the war had begun, the U.S. government was suggesting that it might accept a ceasefire *before* all Iraqi troops were out of Kuwait.*

Then came a paragraph on the Arab-Israeli conflict: "Both Ministers agreed that without a meaningful peace process — one which promotes a just peace, security, and real reconciliation for Israel, Arab states, and Palestinians — it will not be possible to deal with the sources of conflict and instability in the region."

* Ross had inserted the verb *continue* in the first sentence to avoid the impression that there was any change in U.S. policy. He intended the passage to stipulate that Iraq would have to do more than merely promise to withdraw — it must take "immediate, concrete steps" to comply with all twelve UN resolutions. He noted that the United States was committing itself not to a ceasefire but to an enumeration of the conditions under which one "would be possible."

Ross was delighted at having discarded the usual Soviet language about Palestinian national rights and an international conference under UN auspices. He recalled that at Helsinki, in September, they had mentioned the Arab-Israeli conflict in the same statement as the Gulf crisis without being accused of linkage.

He regarded the passage as an addition to the diplomatic lexicon, one that would be useful to the furtherance of peace and, not incidentally, welcome to Israel. The phrase "real reconciliation" seemed to him to be an improvement on the usual references to peace, since peace in the Middle East generally meant merely the absence of war — that is, an armed truce. By putting the "Arab states" ahead of the Palestinians, he was trying to establish the principle that progress toward peace could be achieved only if one of Israel's neighbors — either Syria or Jordan — took the lead in the negotiations, just as Egypt had done in the Camp David process during the Carter administration.

As Ross and Baker fine-tuned the statement, it never occurred to them that its esoteric nuances might create a worldwide sensation.

On Tuesday afternoon, when Baker and Bessmertnykh met for the last time, Margaret Tutwiler assured the State Department press corps that they were scheduled to discuss only the dreariest details of arms control: the reporters could call it a day without any risk of missing a story. Not long afterward, she left for home herself.

During their meeting, Bessmertnykh told Baker that he wished to release the joint statement on the Gulf and the Middle East right away. Baker replied, "Sasha, there's no point in doing anything publicly the night of the State of the Union. Believe me, this won't get two lines in any American newspaper." He proposed that they wait several days.

But Bessmertnykh insisted. He warned that if they did not release the statement that evening, he would be obliged to submit it to Moscow for approval. "There may be some people in my bureaucracy who will like it less than I do," he said. "They'll want to revise it if they can."

Bessmertnykh tried to enlist Ross in his cause by suggesting that a delay might jeopardize Ross's language on the Arab-Israeli peace process. He told Ross, "I know why you put that in there. I've thought about it, and I agree with it. But I don't want to have to fight over this with my own bureaucracy. Let's finish it now and make it a fact."

Baker reluctantly agreed to have a copy of the joint statement posted in the State Department press office, where he presumed reporters would not even notice it until the next day.

But on his way out of the State Department, Bessmertnykh encountered a cluster of correspondents who had staked out the lobby in hopes of speaking to him. Never was a diplomat more pleased to be ambushed. Asked how the talks with Baker had gone, Bessmertnykh replied that they had gone very well indeed; in fact, they had even yielded a joint statement. Beaming, he pulled the document out of his pocket and read it aloud.

The reporters dashed to the telephones. To them, the statement offered not one sensational story but two: first, the United States had formally endorsed a ceasefire conditioned on a mere announcement by Iraq that it would pull out of Kuwait; and second, a passage about the Arab-Israeli peace process had been included. This smacked of just the kind of linkage between the two issues that Bush and Baker had been denying in public.

In the White House press room at seven that evening, Scowcroft and Fitzwater held a background briefing on the State of the Union message to be delivered by Bush two hours later. When Fitzwater called for a final question, a reporter raised his hand and said, "Mr. Baker and Mr. Bessmertnykh just put out a joint statement on the Gulf — "

Scowcroft interrupted: "I beg your pardon?"

"The Soviet Union and the United States just put out a joint statement on the Gulf saying that if Iraq pledges to withdraw from Kuwait, the war can stop. Does that mean that you aren't insisting anymore that Iraq should go completely from Kuwait, that they only have to pledge that they will do so?"

Scowcroft stonily said, "No, they have to leave Kuwait."

"Entirely?"

"Yes, of course."

Scowcroft stomped back to his office, where Popadiuk brought him a copy of the communiqué that Bessmertnykh had released. With pursed lips, Scowcroft read it. He found the stated conditions for the cessation of hostilities more stringent than his questioner had suggested, but the statement as a whole seemed to him closer to the Soviets' position on the war than to the Bush administration's. As for the paragraph on the Middle East, "it sure sounds like linkage to me, and it's going to sound that way to a lot of people," he predicted.

Scowcroft telephoned Baker and asked with deceptive casualness, as though he had not seen the text, "Jim, what's this about you guys releasing a communiqué over there?"

Baker said that he had been watching television, and that the news media were "overreacting": the statement had not been intended to signal any change in policy. Sensing that a major flap was imminent, Baker made an effort to treat the problem as a miscommunication between staffs. He noted that Ross had told Condoleezza Rice about the document in advance.

Hanging up, Scowcroft told his aides, "Get Condi and find out what the hell happened here!" He folded up his copy of the statement, put it in his pocket, and went to join Bush for the limousine ride up to the Capitol.

The president was just emerging from the White House makeup room when Scowcroft told him what had happened. Bush said, "Gee, it sounds like Jim got a little carried away over there." But by the end of the evening, when the fracas over the joint statement was threatening to eclipse coverage of his own State of the Union address, the president was furious.

Richard Haass, the NSC specialist on the Gulf and the Middle East, placed an urgent call to Rice. Indignant, she called Ross.

"How dare you say that I approved that statement!" she exclaimed.

Ross denied having said any such thing, and Baker later sheepishly admitted to Scowcroft that he had "overstated" the extent of the consultation between the White House and the State Department.

NATO envoys demanded appointments with Baker to register their puzzlement and displeasure over the communiqué. It sounded to some like a Soviet-American conspiracy. One diplomat asked, "How many ships and soldiers did the Soviets contribute to Desert Storm? Is *this* the post–Cold War order?"

Israeli leaders were also miffed, as they expected to be consulted in advance of any such vital statement. Still, they welcomed precisely those points of substance that Ross had worked so hard to include.

The *New York Times* columnist William Safire, who had more than once pilloried Baker as a giveaway artist, later called the communiqué the "surrender on the seventh floor," complaining that it "limited our war aims, gave the Soviets equal Mideast status at no cost and provided the Iraqi dictator his fig leaf of linkage."*

Baker's critics within the State Department cited the episode to demonstrate the folly of his secretiveness and excessive reliance on his inner

* Safire's column making this charge appeared on February 21, 1991.

circle. At the NSC and the Pentagon, where Baker's monopoly on the president's ear was so often resented, there was no little satisfaction that the secretary of state finally seemed to have overreached himself.

On Tuesday, February 12, the United States and its allies pounded Iraq with the heaviest bombardment since the start of the Gulf War. That same day, Yevgeni Primakov called on Saddam in Baghdad.

Primakov was determined to do all he could to deprive the United States of a total victory in the Gulf War, and thus to spare Saddam a total defeat. He urged the Iraqi government to "announce its readiness" to leave Kuwait and to specify a "period of time" during which the withdrawal would take place; in response, he said, the coalition would accept a ceasefire.

Saddam saw immediately that Moscow's terms for peace were far more flexible than Washington's. Still, he did not agree to the proposal outright. Removing the jacket of his military uniform and loosening his holster, he asked questions that to Primakov suggested concern about the practical consequences of acquiescence. When would the sanctions be lifted if he agreed to a withdrawal? How could he be sure that Iraqi soldiers would not be shot in the back as they left Kuwait?

Television cameras recorded the opening minutes of Primakov's meeting with Saddam, which included a warm embrace, and later his inspection tour of bomb damage around the city. The Iraqis broadcast these scenes around the world, implying that Primakov had come to Baghdad as a sympathetic friend of Saddam. In Moscow, several of Gorbachev's advisers were appalled to see Primakov playing into the hands of Iraqi propagandists.

As usual, Primakov found a silver lining even where there was none. He cabled Gorbachev that there were "rays of hope" and that Tariq Aziz was prepared to come to Moscow to pursue negotiations.

Gorbachev was now feeling more pressure than ever to distance himself from Shevardnadze's "soft" line on the Gulf. The Central Committee and the Politburo were agitating for a ceasefire, and party officials were openly expressing second thoughts about the wisdom of their government's support for the anti-Saddam resolutions in the UN, claiming that at a minimum, an abstention would have been better.*

---

* The Soviet journal *Questions of Military History* speculated that under a "different foreign policy" and a "different foreign minister," the Gulf War could have been

On the day Primakov saw Saddam in Baghdad, the reactionary news-paper *Sovietskaya Rossiya* complained that the government's decision in 1990 to back the UN coalition had "ended the USSR's existence as a superpower." The next day, senior political officers from the armed forces held a joint press conference with KGB border guards to de-nounce the "U.S.-led attempt to destroy Iraq."

With these pressures building on the Right, Bessmertnykh and his aides drafted a new letter for Gorbachev to send to Bush, aimed at putting the most favorable gloss on Primakov's conversation with Saddam. It noted that Saddam "did not dismiss the possibility of a withdrawal" and wished to "continue the dialogue" by sending Aziz to Moscow. The Soviet government would ensure that the "dialogue will not be used simply as a ploy to win time."

Then came the sticking point: "It would not be desirable to conduct any massive ground operations, if they are being planned, during the period of the Moscow talks."

During a telephone call on Wednesday afternoon, February 13, Bess-mertnykh alerted Baker to the main points in Gorbachev's letter. At seven o'clock that evening, Sergei Chetverikov, the deputy ambassador, came to the State Department to summarize the message in more detail before delivering it to the White House.

Baker realized that the Soviets were playing fast and loose with the joint statement he and Bessmertnykh had signed two weeks before. That statement had stipulated that a ceasefire would come after a withdrawal had begun; now the sequence was being reversed.

Baker told Chetverikov, "Announcing withdrawal isn't the same as withdrawing." The Soviet initiative, said the secretary, was "mighty fuzzy. It lets Iraq off the hook. That's exactly what we *don't* want to do."

In briefing the president on the letter, Baker stressed the many ways in which the Soviet plan either ignored or contradicted specific U.S. demands. Bush thought for a moment, then shook his head and said, "No way, José!"

Scowcroft was, as always, determined to avoid personal recrimina-tions and intramural finger-pointing. But Cheney was less restrained, remarking to associates that in his overeagerness to play peacemaker,

---

averted — presumably if the Soviet Union had played its usual role by blocking effective action in the UN.

Baker had given Gorbachev an opening to make mischief. Sununu complained to his own aides, "Baker bends over backward to please the Soviets, and now the Soviets are bending over backward to help Saddam. That's just great!"

On Friday, February 15, Baker phoned Bessmertnykh in Moscow to underscore the administration's unhappiness with Gorbachev's letter. He asserted once again that Saddam's withdrawal from Kuwait must precede any relaxation of military pressure on Iraq. He complained about Gorbachev's "departure from what we agreed to" in the January joint statement.

Bessmertnykh tried to put a better face on the situation. Surely their main goal was to end the crisis with as little bloodshed as possible, he said; seen in that light, the latest shift in Iraq's position should be "welcomed," not denounced.

The Kremlin formally lauded the Iraqi "initiative" as a reason for "satisfaction and hope." This upbeat assessment seemed as much a slap at Bush as a pat on the head for Saddam.

In Moscow, Primakov and other Soviet officials argued that the Americans were merely upset because they stood to be deprived of the devastating victory over Saddam they so desperately wanted. Primakov was eager to capitalize on the considerable fear among the American people and among the other coalition partners that a ground war — especially one that led to Baghdad — would be long and extremely bloody.

Many in the West believed that in complicating the coalition's prosecution of the war, the Soviet Union was demonstrating that it had abandoned "new thinking" and the other benign tenets of the Gorbachev-Shevardnadze foreign policy. William Safire wrote in the *New York Times*, "Cold War II has begun."

According to numerous reports, it was feared in Eastern Europe that resurgent Soviet hard-liners, particularly in the military, might try first to destabilize, and then to resume domination of, the Kremlin's former satellites.*

---

* Safire's column appeared in the *New York Times* on February 14. Next to it was a guest essay by Charles Gati, a professor of political science at Union College, reporting apprehension in Eastern Europe and quoting the foreign minister of the Russian Republic, Andrei Kozyrev: "If the forces of darkness prevail in the Soviet Union, Central Europe is next on their agenda."

                                    *   *   *

These fears were not allayed by the conflicting signals coming from
Moscow. On Monday, February 11, Gorbachev had written all the Warsaw Pact chiefs of state to propose that the alliance's military structure
be disbanded by April 1. The next day, however, the Soviet government
informed Poland that it would not be able to withdraw its forces from
that country as quickly as the Poles wanted. The Soviets claimed that
this was because they did not have housing or jobs for the returning
soldiers, but many Poles and other Eastern Europeans saw more sinister
forces at work.

On Saturday, February 16, Tariq Aziz began his talks in Moscow. The
following day, Bessmertnykh cabled the Soviet embassy in Washington
with an outline of Primakov's peace plan as now endorsed by Gorbachev.
    Chetverikov telephoned Baker to summarize the plan and then de-
livered it by hand to Ross. After reading the document, Ross called
Baker at the White House and reported that the Soviets had filled in a
few blanks: for example, under the plan, Saddam's withdrawal from
Kuwait was to take place over six weeks.
    But other central points were vague or had been ignored entirely.
There was, for instance, no provision for the return of prisoners of war.
Moreover, the Soviet initiative included an item that the United States
was determined to resist: open linkage to the Arab-Israeli dispute.
    Scowcroft told Bush, "Except for providing for a withdrawal, the
clearer this gets, the worse it gets. It's designed to make things as easy
as possible for Saddam."
    The president sent a message to Gorbachev expressing his misgivings
about the "imprecisions" in the Soviet plan and flatly rejecting any open
linkage to the Arab-Israeli dispute.
    By now the Soviet plan had been made public. Bush downplayed the
growing rift. He told the press that he "appreciated" Gorbachev's keeping him informed about what was happening in the Moscow talks, but
he added that the Soviet formula fell "well short" of what was needed
to end the war. Fitzwater assured reporters, "Our military campaign
remains on schedule."

On Tuesday, February 19, Baker telephoned Bessmertnykh in Moscow
and then followed up with a written message spelling out U.S. reservations about the Soviet peace plan. There must be an exchange of

prisoners of war, he said, and the Iraqis would have to provide maps showing the location of the minefields they had laid in Kuwait. In addition, the timetable for an Iraqi pullout must be limited to four days.

In the wake of the fracas over the joint statement in late January, Scowcroft had ordered the NSC staff to study Baker's talking points and written message in advance. Sununu remarked with satisfaction to his aides, "Baker's on a somewhat shorter leash these days."

The Soviets quietly conveyed Baker's demands to the Iraqi regime. But in public, they stepped up their propaganda campaign to make Iraq seem eager for peace, the United States determined to escalate the war, and the Soviet Union once again a commanding player in world politics.

In a television interview, Primakov parroted the accusation of the Soviet military that the United States was pursuing motives that went far beyond the mere liberation of Kuwait. "The slaughter must be stopped," he insisted. "I'm not saying that the war was not justified before, but its continuation cannot now be justified from any point of view. A people is perishing."

During the final fortnight of the war in the Persian Gulf, Bush and Gorbachev made unprecedented use of the telephone. To call Bush from Moscow, even Gorbachev had to go through an operator at the city's Central Post, Telephone, and Telegraph Office; since he often called in the middle of the night Moscow time, the operator generally was slow to come onto the line and sounded sleepy when she did. But she would snap awake when told who was on the other end.

It sometimes took as long as half an hour to put the call through to the White House. During that time, Gorbachev would pace back and forth in his office while an attendant fetched him sandwiches and a glass of milky tea in a pewter holder.

When Gorbachev called Bush on Thursday, February 21, he described a new refinement of the peace plan, to which Tariq Aziz, now back in Moscow, had already agreed. Bush warily said that he would have to consult with the other coalition partners on any such diplomatic development.

Playing to Primakov, who was sitting nearby, Gorbachev covered the mouthpiece of the receiver, winked, and said, "Now I'm really going to knock him for a loop!"

He proudly told Bush that in response to the American objections, as conveyed by Baker earlier that week, he would not insist on open linkage between the end of the Gulf War and the resumption of the Arab-Israeli peace process. Iraq's withdrawal from Kuwait would be "full and unconditional."

Bush still felt that the Soviets' offer gave Saddam too much time to get out of Kuwait, and that the plan effectively wiped clean the slate of Iraq's other obligations to the world. He reminded Gorbachev that withdrawal from Kuwait would bring Saddam into compliance with only one of the twelve UN resolutions. Under the Soviet plan, once Saddam's troops were out of Kuwait, all sanctions, reparations, and other demands embodied in the United Nations resolutions would be dropped.

Talking afterward to his aides, Bush summarized Gorbachev's position: "Saddam calls it quits in Kuwait, and all is forgiven."

Some versions of the Soviet plan suggested that Moscow would guarantee Saddam's personal safety. Learning of this provision of the plan, some American officials feared that a Soviet commitment to protect Saddam's life might even conceivably compel the Soviet Union to enter the war *against* the coalition.

Bush was not happy about this, either. In private, he told his aides that he hoped Saddam might suffer "some kind of a Ceausescu scenario," meaning the execution of the dictator by his own troops in a coup d'état.

After all the months of careful diplomatic maneuvering, Bush felt that Gorbachev was now trying to claim a commanding role in the crisis. He told his aides, "We've got to get this thing back under control. It's slipping away from us."

Sununu complained that Gorbachev was deliberately trying to "screw us." He ribbed Condoleezza Rice about all the trouble her Soviet "clients" were causing: "Can't you keep them under better control?" he asked.

Scowcroft believed that the Soviet hard-liners were bent on "trying to break the pattern of cooperation" that had developed under Shevardnadze, and on "trying to help us fail" in the Gulf. But he did not attribute these motives to Gorbachev himself. He considered the Soviet president to be somewhere in the middle, "straddling between Shevardnadze and Primakov."

Bush agreed that Gorbachev's peace efforts were not part of a "sinister plot": "He's trying to juggle a lot of things of his own, but he's not trying to do us in. . . . If he's not deliberately trying to give us a hard time, let's not give him one. No need to make him squirm."

In late February, the president and Baker were already thinking ahead to other issues that would require U.S.-Soviet cooperation in the near future, including the continuing transformation of Europe and the uncertain future of the Soviet Union itself. They also hoped for Soviet cooperation in exploiting any opportunities that might arise after the Gulf War to revive the Arab-Israeli peace process.

As Baker said during a White House meeting, "We're going to need these guys when the war's over to help us on the Middle East. Let's let them down easy on the Gulf, not rub their noses in the fact that we're telling them to butt out. If we're going to tell them to go away, let's make sure they don't go away mad."

Fitzwater was thus sent out to inform the White House press corps that the latest Soviet peace initiative was "helpful" and "useful." Afterward, he told his staff, "I guess we killed 'em with kindness out there. That's what the boss wanted."

On Friday, February 22, in a ninety-minute telephone call, Bush patiently explained to Gorbachev why the Soviet peace plan was inadequate. Its shortcomings, he said, were the fault of the Iraqis, who had refused to commit themselves to a truly unconditional withdrawal or to recognize the other UN resolutions.

At Colin Powell's suggestion, Bush publicly announced a twenty-four-hour deadline for Iraqi withdrawal from Kuwait. If it was not met, the coalition would be free to start the ground war at any time.

Although the president tried to assure Gorbachev that he was not being consigned to irrelevance at this climactic stage of the crisis, the Soviet leader was still upset by what he was hearing. In translation, Bush's words sounded harsh and reproving. Gorbachev asked an English-speaking aide who was listening in on the conversation whether Bush's "warmth" was getting lost in the translation. The aide said, "Yes, it's friendlier in the original." Gorbachev was somewhat relieved.

On Saturday, February 23, with the U.S. deadline imminent, there was a final spasm of Soviet-Iraqi bargaining. In Moscow, Tariq Aziz told reporters that Iraq would now "comply with Resolution 660 and therefore will withdraw immediately and unconditionally all its forces in Kuwait."

Even the Soviets saw through this Iraqi effort to avoid having to obey the other eleven UN resolutions. They floated still another plan, this time at the UN, based on "hints" from Tariq Aziz that Baghdad was prepared to meet at least some of the coalition's demands, but they were unable to confirm that this desperate improvisation even had Saddam's backing.

Bush called Gorbachev to thank him for his "efforts" and to explain why they were insufficient. Gorbachev tried to minimize the differences between the Soviet peace plans and the coalition's conditions, characterizing them as "details." Couldn't these be ironed out by negotiation? Certainly they did not justify an "escalation of combat operations to a new, even more destructive stage."

But Gorbachev, knowing that he had failed, was already looking to repair his strained relations with Bush. He praised his achievement in "implementing the will of the world community to overcome the serious obstacle to peace created by the Iraqi invasion," and assured him that the "ordeal" they were passing through would not obstruct his own determination to realize the "vision we share of a new world."

Bush thanked him. He said that if Gorbachev happened to be in touch with the Iraqis during the coming hours, he might remind them that they had scoffed at the January 15 UN deadline. With the coalition poised to begin a ground war, they should not make the same mistake again. In English, Gorbachev said, "Okay, good-bye."

Early on Sunday morning, February 24, Gorbachev was informed that the ground war had begun. This took him by surprise. Experts from the KGB, the Ministry of Defense, and his own staff had repeatedly asserted that while Bush would keep pounding Saddam from the air, he would not risk the high allied casualties that so many were predicting would occur in a ground battle.

The Soviet Foreign Ministry spokesman, Vitali Churkin, expressed official "regret" that the "instinct for a military solution had prevailed" and that a "real chance to solve the conflict peacefully has been missed."*

Quoted in *Pravda*, Defense Minister Yazov said that by seizing Iraqi territory, the coalition had now definitely exceeded its UN mandate. He charged that the United States was pursuing a larger, more sinister plan in the Middle East, one that might jeopardize the Soviet Union's own security interests. General Moiseyev of the Armed Forces General Staff told the military daily *Red Star* that the Gulf had become a "testing

---

* Churkin had replaced Gennadi Gerasimov, who had been reassigned as Soviet ambassador to Portugal.

ground" for advanced U.S. weaponry that would soon be provided to NATO and aimed directly at the Soviet Union.

The Iraqi army collapsed in less than seventy-two hours. Gorbachev could easily imagine his conservative opponents using this humiliation of a longtime client as further evidence that he had squandered Soviet power.

Gorbachev could also imagine the United States doing to Saddam Hussein what it had done to Manuel Noriega of Panama in December 1989. If a U.S.-led posse were to swoop into Baghdad, haul Saddam out of his bunker, and bundle him off to a jail cell — after the Soviet Union had done so much to try to save him — Soviet prestige would be sure to suffer another huge setback.*

On Tuesday, February 26, in a speech to factory workers in Minsk, Gorbachev struck a very different note from the conciliatory one he had sounded with Bush on the telephone a few days before. He warned that U.S.-Soviet relations were "very fragile": unless the co-alition leaders showed a "great sense of responsibility," he said, the overall improvement in the international climate could be seriously jeopardized.

Throughout the Gulf crisis, Bush's first priority had been the eviction of Saddam from Kuwait. The more certain he felt of achieving that objective, the more inclined he was to accommodate Gorbachev on what was to happen in the region afterward.

Despite Gorbachev's lurch to the right in December and his meddling in Gulf War diplomacy, Bush was still convinced that he was the best available leader of the Soviet Union. He did not wish to fan anti-Gorbachev sentiments in the Ministry of Defense or the increasingly restive republics.

In mid-March, when Baker toured the Middle East, he included a stop in Moscow to demonstrate to the world that the United States was grateful for Soviet support on the Gulf and eager to collaborate with the Kremlin in postwar diplomacy. He told his aides, "Let's see if we can help the Soviets get out from under the shadow of being tools of U.S. policy."

---

* Some on the Soviet side, particularly in the Foreign Ministry, did not share Gorbachev's concern. They argued that it would be best if the Americans did finish off Saddam — "destroy the beast in his lair," as several of them put it.

When the secretary of state arrived in the Soviet capital on Thursday evening, March 14, Bessmertnykh wasted no time in advising him that the best way for the United States to help would be to withdraw its forces from the Gulf region as quickly as possible. "There are those who criticized us for cooperating with you," he reminded him.

Baker was willing to do a favor for Gorbachev, but not for Saddam Hussein. Nor was he prepared to let the Soviets soften the retribution that the United States had in mind for the Iraqi leader now that the war was over. He showed Bessmertnykh a proposal that the Bush administration intended to submit at the UN.

The draft resolution demanded a heavy punishment for Saddam and stipulated that Iraq must destroy all biological and chemical weapons in its possession, as well as all ballistic missiles with a range of more than ninety miles. Furthermore, Iraq must agree not to develop or acquire any weapons of mass destruction in the future. Until Iraq accepted these constraints on its military, it would not be allowed to export its oil.

Bessmertnykh objected, saying that it was unfair to "single out" Iraq for a ban on weapons of mass destruction. Why should the world community discriminate against Iraq when other states in the area also had such weapons? "Our position is that arms control should apply to everyone in the region," he concluded.

He was referring, if indirectly, to Israel, the only Middle Eastern country with nuclear weapons. Bessmertnykh was trying to reintroduce linkage by treating Israel's deterrent of last resort as comparable to a terror arsenal that Iraq had already used not only against Iran but against its own Kurdish minority.

Baker replied that unless the coalition took advantage of the leverage it now had to impose stringent conditions, Iraq would eventually start rebuilding its war machine using its vast oil revenues. Singling out Baghdad was justified, he insisted: "The Iraqis are the ones who have brought the world to war. They're the ones who have used chemical weapons." To reinforce his argument, he noted that Hans-Dietrich Genscher had acknowledged that after World War II, the allies had been right in forbidding Germany to acquire weapons of mass destruction.

Bessmertnykh finally relented and agreed that these prohibitions against Iraq might be acceptable, so long as they constituted a "first step" in a process that would ultimately extend to the entire region. Linkage had once again receded into the background.*

* The provisions suggested by Baker were contained in UN Resolution 687, which was passed with Soviet support on April 3, 1991.

* * *

The next day, Gorbachev received Baker at the Kremlin. Like Bessmertnykh, he noted that the military, the Communist party, and Muslim minorities had all objected to Soviet cooperation with Washington in the Gulf: "Our policy, while principled, was not universally popular here. We've come through a test in our relations, and we passed the test because our approaches converged."

He added that he was glad the war had ended as quickly as it had, since he had "come under a lot of pressure." He hoped that the United States would remove its forces from the region soon. Bessmertnykh said that failing such a withdrawal of troops, "there will be those within the Soviet Union who will seize on this as proof that you are trying to use the Gulf as a launching pad for a buildup in the region."

Baker replied that the American government and public were eager for U.S. troops to return home as soon as possible, but that their demobilization would depend on the restoration of stability in Kuwait. This would in turn depend at least in part on what the United States and the Soviet Union could do together.

The secretary of state steered the conversation toward diplomatic cooperation on the Arab-Israeli dispute. After more than forty years of rivalry in the Middle East, he suggested, perhaps the United States and the Soviet Union could now work together to address the most persistent and dangerous of all the world's regional conflicts.

Baker said, "We want to see you work with us in the region on the diplomatic process. It would be a vivid demonstration that 'new thinking' is alive and well in Soviet foreign policy. It would show that 'new thinking' works, and would give you a role."

Gorbachev welcomed Baker's indication that Moscow would be a full partner with Washington in such a process. "We appreciate what you're doing," he said.

Bessmertnykh pledged that the Soviet Union would continue its recent efforts to move away from uncompromising championship of the Palestine Liberation Organization. He said that while the Soviet Union would still prefer an international conference on the Arab-Israeli conflict, it was willing to consider "other approaches" as well.

Dennis Ross felt that Bessmertnykh's comments justified what he and Baker had tried to accomplish in the now-infamous January 29 communiqué. Ross had hoped all along that the rhetorical shift in the Soviets' position — as reflected in their willingness to sign a joint statement that referred to the Arab-Israeli peace process without the usual invocation of Palestinian national rights and the demand for an international conference — might presage a major change in policy.

After the meeting, Baker, echoing Gorbachev, told reporters, "The relationship has gone through a test recently, and it has survived. That is good for the Soviet Union and good for the United States and good for the world."

CHAPTER 16

"He's All They've Got"

DURING THE PERSIAN GULF CRISIS, Bush had by necessity been bound to Gorbachev. Now that the war was over, his administration was divided over how best to deal with the increasingly complicated politics of the Soviet Union.

Condoleezza Rice and mid-level officials at the State Department had for months been pressing the president to "diversify our investments" by reaching out to Yeltsin and other reform and secessionist leaders. Rice advised Scowcroft that the diffusion of power beyond Moscow was speeding up: to deal with other Soviet leaders would be not only to recognize reality but also to advance the values of self-determination and democracy for which America stood.

Bush did not like the idea. Privately, he bridled at any action that might suggest to the world that he was turning his back on Gorbachev.

Scowcroft was less attached to Gorbachev than Bush was. But though he continued to worry about "overpersonalizing" relations with the Soviet Union, he shared Bush's reluctance to reach out too far or too often beyond the Soviet president. He felt that however fractious its republics, the Soviet Union was still a single country, and a country could have only one leader at a time.

As an old Balkan hand, Scowcroft was particularly sensitive to the danger that "romantic nationalism" could lead to turmoil or even civil war. More than ever, he and Bush agreed that under no circumstances should the United States do anything that might inadvertently provoke the violent breakup of the Soviet Union.

At an NSC meeting, Scowcroft said, "Our policy has to be based on our own national interest, and we have an interest in the stability of the Soviet Union. The instability of the USSR would be a threat to us. To peck away at the legitimacy of the regime in power would not be to promote stability."

Before resigning from her job in March to return to her Stanford professorship, Rice wrote Bush a memo in which she asserted that Gorbachev was by now probably the single most unpopular figure in the Soviet Union. But he was still the "linchpin" in a political system that was in growing danger of flying apart.

Only Gorbachev could serve as a "communications node between the extremes," she believed. Perhaps the officially instigated violence in Vilnius and Riga would shake the reformers out of their somnolence and open Gorbachev's own eyes to the folly of his alliance with the hard-liners. Rice concluded that the United States should continue to support him.

Bush read the memo and told several of his aides, "Condi's got it about right, I guess. It's not great for him or for us. But he's still all we've got. And all *they've* got, too."

Rice's replacement on the NSC staff was Ed Hewett. In one respect, it was a surprising choice: Hewett had been for ten years a senior fellow at the Brookings Institution, a think tank whose decidedly liberal reputation had often made it the target of conservative suspicions, criticism, and even, on one occasion during the Nixon administration, a criminal plot.*

It would have been virtually inconceivable for Bush to have anyone from Brookings serving at the White House at the beginning of his administration, when he was hypersensitive to criticism from the Republican Right. But by late 1990 and early 1991, with communism in

* During the 1973 congressional investigation into the Watergate scandal, John Dean, the former White House counsel, testified that two years earlier, Nixon's aides John Erlichman and Charles Colson had concocted a scheme to firebomb and burglarize Brookings in order to search the premises for politically sensitive documents. In the end, the plan was called off.

decline and the president's prestige in foreign affairs at its high point, ideology counted for less than it once had in the formulation of U.S. policy and the appointment of key officials in the administration.

Hewett was widely respected as an expert on the Soviet economy. He spoke Russian well, traveled frequently to the USSR, and knew many of the advocates of reform there. He was among the Kremlinologists whom Rice had selected to brief Bush at Kennebunkport three weeks after the inauguration, and in congressional testimony in October 1989, Baker had justified the administration's overall caution by citing Hewett's belief that the West had only a modest ability to influence Soviet reform.

Hewett had warned first Rice and then Scowcroft that it might be a mistake to pick him just for his economic expertise: "There may not be that much we can or should do in that area, given Gorbachev's inability to stick with a single plan or a single set of advisers."

Rice replied that she had never set much store in the prospects for American assistance to Gorbachev. On the contrary, she expected the Soviet economy to "fall apart completely" in the second half of 1991, and thought the president would need someone to explain what was happening.

Scowcroft agreed. "I don't think 1991 will be a period for great initiatives," he said, "but it'll be confusing, and I'd like a first-rate Sovietologist talking to the president about what's going on."

As Rice prepared to turn over her portfolio to Hewett, she ticked off the problems that she predicted would "complicate your life." High on the list was deciding what the administration's response should be to nationalism and secession. Very specifically, she identified the dilemma of "dealing with Yeltsin."

Scowcroft often muttered to colleagues that the very word *republic* sent shivers up his spine. But in recent months, the White House had been opening its doors to visitors from the republics and from the democracy movement in the Soviet Union.

Matlock had cabled Baker in January 1991 that Boris Yeltsin wished to join this parade. But this time Yeltsin was demanding assurance in advance that he would be "properly received" by President Bush. Matlock endorsed the idea but suggested that Bush avoid incurring Gorbachev's displeasure by inviting him personally; perhaps he could be invited instead by Congress or the National Governors' Conference.

Matlock had been making a strong effort to cultivate the Russian president. He dined with Yeltsin and his wife at Spaso House. Yeltsin in turn often asked Matlock join him at receptions and concerts. By telephone and cable, the ambassador kept stressing to Washington that the Gorbachev-Yeltsin relationship was "not a zero-sum game"; the administration could — and should — cultivate both leaders.

True, the two men detested each other, but they also needed each other. Matlock said that Yeltsin could be enlisted to win popular support for political and economic reform while Gorbachev shielded *perestroika* from the brunt of a conservative backlash. No one in Washington should presume that an invitation for Yeltsin to visit the White House would be "disloyal" to Gorbachev.

However, Matlock was informed by cable that the administration did not "believe the time is right" for a Yeltsin visit. The Soviet desk at the State Department had wanted to add that if Yeltsin came to Washington on his own, he could expect to be received "at the highest level" — meaning by Bush — but the White House had deleted this phrase from the cable, substituting the promise merely that Yeltsin "could count on a range of meetings with senior officials."

Matlock complained to his aides, "It's absolutely standard practice for the president to receive national opposition leaders. When Neil Kinnock visits Washington, he knows he'll get into the White House, just as Mario Cuomo or Teddy Kennedy can come to Moscow and be pretty sure of getting into the Kremlin. Why should we treat Yeltsin any differently?"*

While Yeltsin nursed a fresh grudge against the Bush administration, his foreign minister, Andrei Kozyrev, came to Washington in early February. Smooth, soft-spoken, fluent in English, Kozyrev was a veteran diplomat and Shevardnadze protégé who in 1990 had become part of the exodus from the Soviet central government to that of the Russian federation.

During a meeting with Baker, Kozyrev warned that the "success of repression and conservative elements" in Soviet internal politics would bring a "return to aggressive behavior internationally." He told Baker that it was in the American interest to shore up Yeltsin and the Russian Republic — not so much against Gorbachev personally (Kozyrev knew that was not a winning argument in Washington) but against the reactionaries who were gaining strength in Gorbachev's shadow.

* Kinnock was head of the British Labour opposition.

Kozyrev urged the Bush administration to promote the prospect of a new center-left, Gorbachev-Yeltsin coalition. This was music to Baker's ears. By now he and Ross felt that only by joining forces with Yeltsin could Gorbachev succeed against the reactionaries.

But two weeks later, in a Soviet television interview, Yeltsin lashed out at Gorbachev in a fashion that suggested he had little interest in making common cause with him. He accused Gorbachev of betraying the reforms he had begun and of adopting instead an "anti-people policy."

Yeltsin demanded that Gorbachev resign and turn over his power to the Federation Council, an interrepublic body on which Yeltsin himself, thanks to his prestige and the vast size of the Russian Republic, was the most influential figure. Striking back, Gorbachev accused Yeltsin of "declaring war" on the leadership of the Soviet Union.

During a meeting with his aides in the Oval Office, Bush observed, "This guy Yeltsin is really a wild man, isn't he?"

At the CIA, George Kolt, the head of the Office of Soviet Analysis, and Fritz Ermarth, chairman of the National Intelligence Council, offered a very different interpretation. They saw Yeltsin as being dedicated to a "Union built from below" — a looser, more democratic, and ultimately more durable confederation. Gorbachev, by contrast, was stubbornly, perhaps even irredeemably committed to preserving a "center-dominated Union" — a recipe for further strain between Moscow and the republics.

Ermarth argued that the Soviet Union was experiencing its own 1776, a revolutionary struggle for independence that would lead to a new constitution and federation. Scowcroft preferred a different historical analogy. He felt that the Soviet Union was comparable to the United States of 1861, on the verge of a civil war in which the issues were secession and stability. Where Ermarth saw Yeltsin as a Russian George Washington, Scowcroft saw Gorbachev as a Soviet Abraham Lincoln.

Scowcroft needled the CIA chief, William Webster: "Why doesn't George Kolt just make it simple and go work for Yeltsin?" Webster denied that the CIA was "pushing Yeltsin." The agency was just doing its job, he said: "Don't shoot the messenger."

Told that at the White House he and his colleagues had become known as "Yeltsin-lovers," Ermarth said, "I'm a Yeltsin *watcher*. Nothing more. It's an excessive attachment to personalities that got us into this fix to begin with. What we're talking about is competing visions for the future of the Soviet Union. And Yeltsin's makes more sense."

Scowcroft could not forget Yeltsin's boorish appearance a year and a half earlier at the White House. In March 1991, he warned Bush that however a new invitation might be couched, Yeltsin would boast to the world that he was coming to the Oval Office as Bush's personal guest.

The president agreed and added, "If it looks like we've asked Yeltsin here, it'll drive Gorbachev nuts."

Scowcroft laughed. "That's at least part of the reason why Yeltsin wants so much to do it," he said.

Bush replied, "Well, that's also why I *don't* want to do it."

Afterward, Scowcroft told his aides, "Yeltsin can come here, but we don't want any White House fingerprints on his visit. . . . We're not going to do anything that looks like we're casting our lot with Yeltsin against Gorbachev. Members of the Yeltsin Fan Club should remember that."

Gorbachev's strategy for keeping the Soviet Union together hinged on the referendum scheduled for Sunday, March 17. He would ask the Soviet people to approve the proposition that the Soviet Union should be preserved "as a renewed federation of equal sovereign republics in which human rights and freedoms of all nationalities will be fully guaranteed."

With a popular majority supporting that vague formulation, Gorbachev hoped to be able to claim a democratic mandate to redefine the Soviet Union in his own way and according to his own timetable. It was widely believed that his actual purpose was not to create a new federation at all, but to reaffirm the principal feature of the old one — the supreme power of the center over all fifteen republics.

Estonia, Latvia, Lithuania, Moldavia, Armenia, and Georgia announced their intention to boycott the referendum on the grounds that they did not need Moscow's permission to go their own way. These six republics comprised only about 10 percent of the total population of the Soviet Union, but they had a powerful ally in Yeltsin.

The Russian leader himself stopped short of saying publicly that he would vote against Gorbachev's resolution, but his allies on the left declared that a "no" vote would send a sobering signal to the Kremlin.

When Baker traveled to Moscow to meet with Gorbachev in mid-March, just before the referendum, he was determined to show that

U.S.-Soviet cooperation could enhance Gorbachev's world stature and bring crucial outside help to his domestic economy. The Soviet leader insisted that he was still "unfailingly committed to *perestroika*."

Baker was skeptical. He cited the KGB's new role in policing business ventures, the firing of Gorbachev advisers who advocated free markets, the rising influence of the Soviet military, and the assertion of Gorbachev's new hard-line prime minister, Valentin Pavlov, that foreign banks were conspiring to sabotage the Soviet economy. These developments, he said, were having a "chilling effect" on U.S.-Soviet relations, and raising questions about where Gorbachev was taking the country.

Gorbachev at first seemed impatient and annoyed at being contradicted. Then his manner abruptly changed. Growing very still, he stared at Baker and gave the hint of a smile. He said he recognized that the U.S. government might not be pleased with the pace at which he was moving or with every step he took along the way in the interests of "preserving a balance." He made no attempt to reply to the specific concerns Baker had raised, but he said there should be no doubt about his "ultimate direction." He would "not be diverted from the overall course" of Soviet policy; there would be "no turning back."

Baker pressed him about secessionism. He wished to know how Gorbachev would use the results of the March 17 referendum to "reach out in a positive way to the republics" — and particularly to the six that were boycotting it. "Couldn't you use your victory in the referendum as a vehicle to justify reaching out and cutting a deal with the republics on far more liberal terms?" he wondered.

Gorbachev dodged the question and instead filibustered about the latest draft of a new Union treaty. He expected "many republics" to support it, he said; this would be a "starting point" toward solving the nationalities problem, "and it will also help the economy."

Resuming his old role as a "former finance minister" (that is, secretary of the Treasury), Baker made the case that a healthy economy depended on a political arrangement among the republics that was both voluntary and stable. The old system had been too rigid; the new situation was too uncertain.

He explained that many potential Western investors were deterred from entering the Soviet market by fear of chaos and civil war: "If you want to bring in investment, and if you want people to risk capital, they need to know where the locus of economic decision-making is." Until that issue was clearly resolved, foreign governments and businesses would hold back. Baker said he recognized that the problem of economic reform was "laden with psychological, historical, and ideological baggage."

Gorbachev interrupted: "And it's also complicated by very strong vested interests." He was clearly referring to the Soviet military-industrial complex. With that behemoth looming over his shoulder, he was unwilling or unable to embrace more radical measures to reform the economy and the political system.

In keeping with his own inclination to establish links with figures other than Gorbachev, Baker, while in Moscow, tried to meet with politicians of as many stripes as possible. At Spaso House he hosted a dinner for Mayors Popov and Sobchak of Moscow and Leningrad; Stanislav Shatalin, author of the discarded Five-Hundred-Day economic plan; Zviad Gamsakhurdia, the passionately anti-Russian leader of Georgia; the prime ministers of Kirghizia and Armenia; and the president of Kazakhstan, Nursultan Nazarbayev.

Also present were two Russian intellectuals who represented the left wing of the Gorbachev faction: Alexander Yakovlev, who had once been Gorbachev's closest ally but now was drifting to the sidelines, and Fyodor Burlatsky, the pro-Gorbachev editor of the *Literary Gazette*. Their presence was intended to signify the American hope that there was still common ground among the Russian democratic movement, the republics, and the center. Over dinner and coffee, Shatalin expressed his deep pessimism about the future and his scorn for Gorbachev. Popov was more temperate, saying, "We can still do business with Gorbachev." That this qualified endorsement of the Soviet leader — a faint echo of Margaret Thatcher's comment in 1984 — came from one of Gorbachev's own countrymen was an indication of how far Soviet politics had evolved.

The only vigorous defender of Gorbachev that evening was Nazarbayev, who maintained that "in his heart" the Soviet president was still a reformer: as a flywheel between Right and Left, between centrifugal and centripetal forces, he must survive.

Baker agreed. At the end of the evening, he told his aides that he had found Nazarbayev the most practical and impressive of the guests.

Boris Yeltsin had sent word in advance that he wished to meet separately with Baker during his visit to Moscow. He wanted the Bush administration to recognize his status as the most important of the republic leaders and as the paramount champion of Soviet democracy now that Gorbachev had thrown in his lot with the Right. He invited Baker to visit him at the headquarters of the Russian Republic, the white marble skyscraper on the banks of the Moscow River that Muscovites called the White House.

Not wanting to offend Gorbachev, Baker notified Yeltsin that he would see him instead at the Spaso House dinner, suggesting that perhaps he might come early or stay on afterward for a private chat. As Ross said, "He can come for cocktails or coffee, as long as he stays for the main course."

Yeltsin refused. He boycotted the dinner and sent in his place Vladimir Lukin, a close ally and chairman of the Russian parliament's foreign relations committee. Lukin took Ross aside and complained that Baker's failure to call on the Russian president would contribute to the growing impression that the Bush administration favored Gorbachev over Yeltsin.

Ross told Lukin, "We didn't seek to get in the middle of this. The hope for democratic reform depends on a coalition of the reformers and the center." Lukin replied, "We need more signs of support from you if we're to be able to form such a coalition. We can't do it from a position of weakness."

On Saturday, March 16, Baker had lunch with his old friend Shevardnadze in the same apartment where they had first dined together, in May 1989. When Baker, Ross, Tutwiler, and the other Americans arrived, Shevardnadze cried out nostalgically, "Ah, the old team!"

About the immediate future Shevardnadze was pessimistic, saying that all the fears that had led to his resignation were now being justified: "There is still the danger of chaos and dictatorship," he insisted. Like Nazarbayev, he felt that Gorbachev remained essential, if only because there was no better alternative. "Still," he said, "we need a new generation of leadership." He had come to see Gorbachev as a transitional figure, and told Baker that in his judgment, a coup d'état against the Soviet president was "very possible."

The next day, Gorbachev barely won a majority of "yes" votes in his referendum. Given the loose wording of the resolution and the central government's massive efforts to ensure victory, he could not easily claim an overwhelming mandate for his policies.

*   *   *

That spring, the Soviets must have begun to wonder whether they should install a revolving door at the entrance to the VIP lounge at Sheremetyevo Airport. So many distinguished visitors came and went that it was surprising Gorbachev and other officials had any time at all to attend to their problems.

No sooner did Baker leave than Richard Nixon arrived. He was remembered in Moscow less for being the only American president to resign in disgrace than as the author of détente and a master of power politics. He could always count on being received at the highest level.

His first important session in Moscow, on March 21, was with Yevgeni Primakov, best known in the West as Gorbachev's emissary to Saddam Hussein during the Gulf War.

Primakov was a member of a newly created Kremlin "Security Council" charged with advising Gorbachev on everything from defense issues to economic reform.

Some had hoped that Gorbachev might weight the new council toward the reformist side in order to offset the preponderance of hardliners throughout the rest of the Soviet hierarchy, but in the end, the council's composition reflected the conservatives' growing strength.*

Primakov tried to convince Nixon that he and Gorbachev remained staunch reformers: "If I thought Gorbachev was abandoning reforms, I couldn't stay here for a day longer," he proclaimed.

He then launched into a complaint that the Bush administration's new policy of reaching out to the republics and the democrats was arousing fear, suspicion, and resentment in "some quarters" in Moscow. He said he sensed a "temptation" in Washington to "exploit our difficulties" and "play games with the republics." This new element in U.S. policy "puts us on the alert," Primakov declared, because it amounted to "interference in our internal affairs." He warned that the "destabilization of the Soviet Union would not be in the interests of the U.S."

When Nixon pressed him for specifics, Primakov referred to the high-level, high-visibility treatment that secessionist and oppositionist figures were now enjoying in Washington. He also denounced Baker's "decision to turn his visit here into a seminar with such a wide variety of those who are criticizing the central authorities."

* In addition to Primakov and Bessmertnykh, it included Defense Minister Yazov, KGB Chairman Kryuchkov, Interior Minister Pugo, Prime Minister Pavlov, and Vice President Yanayev. One of the few members who were clearly identifiable as liberals was Pugo's predecessor Vadim Bakatin.

Nixon also saw the KGB chairman, Vladimir Kryuchkov. During this period, Kryuchkov was in the habit of presenting visitors with souvenir envelopes bearing five-kopek stamps commemorating Rudolph Abel, Kim Philby, and others who had spied for the Kremlin against the West. He had the good sense to omit this ritual during his meeting with Nixon, who early in his career had led the charge against the accused Soviet spy Alger Hiss.*

Unlike Primakov, Kryuchkov made no pretense of being a reformer. "I've had as much democratization as I can stomach," he said, adding that there was still a "fundamental conflict" between the global interests of the United States and those of the Soviet Union. Referring to Soviet acquiescence in German unification, Kryuchkov lamented "our eagerness to take historical shortcuts" and cautioned that "democracy is no substitute for law and order."

He confided that he and Gorbachev had fallen into the habit of "arguing too often." He said he suspected that one day the Soviet president would fire him and end their arguments once and for all.

Nixon also met with Boris Yeltsin, and was impressed when the Russian president told him that he favored a series of swift, radical, and thorough steps to bring into being a free market economy. Yeltsin recognized that the end of subsidies and price controls would trigger inflation, and that the closing of inefficient factories would result in widespread unemployment. But he was confident that the citizenry would put up with these hardships.

He believed that the "key" to such reforms was a democratic election for the presidency of Russia, of the kind he intended to hold and win in June. "The people must feel that by choosing their leaders, they have participated in a process that leads to difficult but necessary measures," he said.

Vice President Gennadi Yanayev told Nixon, with more resignation than enthusiasm, that the next stage in the Soviet political drama would have to be a Gorbachev-Yeltsin alliance: "Gorbachev can take a step toward Yeltsin. Actually, he has no choice but to do so." He added that he had personally been in touch with Yeltsin's deputies "about how our two leaders can come together."

---

* Kryuchkov displayed amazing ignorance on certain subjects. Grumbling about *glasnost* and its impact on the KGB, he said that he envied his American counterpart, William Webster, "who's not supposed ever to meet with the press and is not allowed by law to talk to Congress."

At the Kremlin, Nixon called on Gorbachev in the same chamber in which he had once negotiated with Leonid Brezhnev. He was startled by the transformation in the Soviet leader since their first meeting, five years before. Then Gorbachev had radiated confidence; now he seemed discouraged, defensive, exhausted.

Gorbachev went into a long monologue about how the process of reform had moved too quickly in Eastern Europe, leaving people there with neither the protection of socialism nor the benefits of a market economy. Shifting the focus somewhat, Nixon asked whether Gorbachev's recent moves to accommodate the conservatives were permanent.

Gorbachev replied, "No, we're on a detour . . . but it's going to lead back to the main road." No doubt referring to the once-fashionable speculation in the United States about the old and new Nixon, the Soviet leader insisted that he was still the "old Gorbachev." He professed his willingness to cooperate with Yeltsin but asserted that the Russian president was "difficult to deal with."

Before Nixon left Moscow, a member of his traveling party, Dimitri Simes, received a call from Yuri Zimin, the senior KGB official responsible for liaison with the Nixon group. Simes was a Soviet-born U.S. citizen who was a Kremlinologist at the Carnegie Endowment for International Peace in Washington. Zimin arranged to see Simes in his hotel room.

When he arrived, Zimin said that he had a message for President Nixon from Kryuchkov. The message was that Gorbachev might soon be overthrown through the parliamentary process. Tired of the constant bickering between Gorbachev and Yeltsin, the Supreme Soviet, under the leadership of its speaker, Gorbachev's old friend Anatoli Lukyanov, intended to take power into its own hands.* Nixon should know that in this power play, Lukyanov would have the backing of the military and the KGB.

If this message indeed originated with Kryuchkov, the KGB chief may have been trying to use Nixon to telegraph Bush that a hard-line coup against Gorbachev was inevitable, and to advise him that the United States had better accommodate itself to that reality. On his return,

---

* Lukyanov had been Gorbachev's mentor in the party youth organization at the Moscow State University law school. In the 1970s, as a member of the Central Committee secretariat, he had supervised personnel matters in the military, the KGB, and the Interior Ministry, an assignment that assured him close contacts in those organizations when he rose to be Gorbachev's second-in-command in the legislature.

Nixon conveyed the message to Bush and Baker, but the president and the secretary of state did not give it much credence.

Meanwhile, a hard-line faction of the Russian parliament, alarmed by Yeltsin's rising influence, began working to muster enough votes among the deputies to oust him as parliamentary leader at a session scheduled for Thursday, March 28. Yeltsin's supporters countered by announcing that they would hold a rally in central Moscow on the same day.

Boris Pugo warned Gorbachev that unless stern measures were adopted, there would be a "coup d'état by mob violence": the rally was a direct challenge to Gorbachev's personal authority, and it must be resisted with a vivid reminder of how much power the Soviet president still had at his command.

With Gorbachev's consent, Prime Minister Valentin Pavlov issued a decree banning all public demonstrations in the capital for the next three weeks. Gorbachev augmented the ban by bringing troops and tanks into the capital.

Yakovlev tried to dissuade him from taking this confrontational course, arguing that a show of force would not succeed in intimidating the democratic opposition and would only confirm the widespread suspicion that in his desperation, Gorbachev had irrevocably thrown in his lot with the conservatives. Yakovlev noted that for months, Gorbachev had been warning about the dangers of confrontation and explosion; if he now used military force to suppress the demonstration, he would be fulfilling his own apocalyptic prophecy.

Even if disaster was avoided, Yakovlev said, a showdown between the military and peaceful demonstrators would backfire on Gorbachev by strengthening Yeltsin's popular base and ruining any chance that still existed for cooperation between the center and the opposition.

In Washington, during her regular briefing at the State Department, Margaret Tutwiler was bombarded with questions from reporters about what the administration was doing to defuse the situation in Moscow. She went to Baker and persuaded him to lodge a complaint with Bessmertnykh, "so that at least if the worst happens, we're on the record as having told them not to do anything."

By the time Baker got his call through, however, Bessmertnykh had left his office for the day, so Matlock delivered the message to the Foreign Ministry the next day. He told Bessmertnykh that since previous demonstrations in Moscow had been peaceful, it was "difficult to understand" why the central authorities had chosen to ban this one. It would be all the more difficult if there was bloodshed, he added.

When he heard about this message, Ed Hewett protested to Dennis Ross that the NSC had not been informed in advance. With Scowcroft's approval, Hewett advised Ross that it was not for State to make "a priori editorial comments about this kind of thing." Ross apologized for "short-circuiting the proper procedure."

The altercation underscored how proprietary the White House had become about any official American attempt to influence, or even comment on, Gorbachev's handling of his internal opposition. It was also a reminder that in the wake of the flap in late January over the Baker-Bessmertnykh communiqué, Baker now had somewhat less leeway to act on his own.

On March 28, while 100,000 Yeltsin supporters rallied near the Kremlin in defiance of Pavlov's ban, some 50,000 police and Interior Ministry troops waited in nearby side streets, ready to move in.

As it happened, the rally came off peacefully. Nonetheless, Yakovlev, Shevardnadze, and Mayor Sobchak of Leningrad all told a visiting U.S. senator, David Boren of Oklahoma, that the mobilization of the armed forces against the demonstrators was the single biggest mistake Gorbachev had ever made. Yakovlev said that the Soviet leader had jeopardized not only his relationship with Yeltsin but also his "place in history."

As with the Baltic crisis in January, Gorbachev had once again taken the advice of Pavlov, Pugo, Kryuchkov, and the other hard-liners, and once again he had seen their methods bring the country to the brink of chaos. Gorbachev's aides soon began buttonholing journalists and diplomats in Moscow to tell them, off the record, that their boss had had nothing to do with the debacle: it was all Pavlov's and Pugo's fault.

Having looked into the abyss and been horrified by what he saw, Gorbachev now moved toward a new alliance with Yeltsin and the democrats. On Tuesday, April 23, he met at his dacha in Novo-Ogaryevo with the presidents of nine republics: Russia, Ukraine, Belorussia, Kirghizia, Tadzhikistan, Turkmenistan, Kazakhstan, Uzbekistan, and Azerbaijan.

Officially, this was just another meeting of the Federation Council, the supposedly advisory body that Gorbachev had created to keep the

Soviet Union together. But the session had more the quality of a surrender ceremony.

Gorbachev consented to an accord dubbed the Dacha Agreement, which increased the autonomy of those nine republics that were still willing to remain in the Union and gave them more authority over decision making for the USSR as a whole. The agreement also laid the ground for a revision of the new Union treaty to make it easier for the six other republics — the three Baltics, Armenia, Moldavia, and Georgia — to secede.

The Novo-Ogaryevo meeting led to a new piece of political shorthand, "Nine-plus-One." As the term suggested, Gorbachev, representing the central government, was outnumbered and increasingly isolated. The undeniable leader of the "Nine" was Boris Yeltsin.

At the White House, Bush was being advised to move much closer to Yeltsin. Ed Hewett felt that the United States had been too "reactive" to the rapidly changing situation in the Soviet Union; it was time, he said, to adopt a more "forward-leaning" policy toward the republics, including Russia.

Visiting the Oval Office in April, Matlock stepped up his campaign for a Yeltsin invitation to Washington. He told Bush that while the Kremlin was unquestionably committed to a foreign policy that was in the American interest, the republics — not all, but some, particularly Russia — were pursuing internal policies that the United States should also encourage.

Matlock noted that democratization had proceeded further and faster in the republics than in the Soviet Union as a whole. Reflecting the people's will, the republic governments were "putting pressure on the military-industrial complex." If the United States continued to embrace the central government and shun the republics, it would in effect be giving aid and comfort to the forces of reaction.

Now more than ever, Matlock continued, Gorbachev and Yeltsin needed each other. Despite all the bad blood between them, they were natural allies: "Neither can survive without the other. Their fates are linked." Once again he asked for authority to tell Yeltsin that Bush would receive him. The president did not oppose such a meeting, but neither did he make a commitment.

On Monday, April 22, Richard Nixon lunched with Bush at the White House. The former president knew that his successor was reluctant to let go of Gorbachev. In private, he said, "Being the gentleman that he is, George Bush is not going to throw over his old friends." Thus he was careful to couch his message in terms that would not alienate Bush.

Like Matlock, Nixon argued for Yeltsin not as an alternative to but as an important ally for the Soviet leader: Gorbachev still had his hands on the levers of traditional power, but Yeltsin now had an indisputable claim to the support of the people. Peculiar and even "obnoxious" though Yeltsin might seem to many Americans, he had the "right chemistry with the Russian people." After all, Nixon joked, drinking and womanizing had never been liabilities for Russian politicians.

He added that whatever legitimate reservations Bush might have about Yeltsin's character or his program, "people take him seriously. They're willing to follow him. The more seriously we take him, the more seriously Gorbachev will have to take him."

After Nixon left, Bush said, "I think he's got a point about Yeltsin."

Three days later, the CIA's Office of Soviet Analysis sent the president a review of the latest developments in the Soviet Union, under the heading "The Soviet Cauldron." Scowcroft, Gates, and Hewett had asked for this highly classified study, which turned out to be the most explicit and detailed scenario to date of how a hard-line coup might unfold against Gorbachev.

The paper observed that Gorbachev's "traditionalist colleagues" — Yazov, Pugo, Kryuchkov, and the others — seemed to be "distancing themselves from him." It was becoming all too easy to imagine their forming a "committee of national salvation," overthrowing Gorbachev in a "putsch," and arresting and perhaps murdering prominent democrats such as Yeltsin and Popov, in a "premeditated, organized attempt to restore a full-fledged dictatorship."

However, the "long-term prospects of such an enterprise are poor," the study concluded, "and even the short-term success is far from assured." The key factors would be how much support there was for the putsch among the rank and file of the Soviet military and how much resistance the democratic forces put up.

The CIA was not supposed to make recommendations on policy, but the paper clearly implied that Bush should do everything he could to shore up Yeltsin and help him deter those figures who might already be planning a right-wing coup.

Scowcroft was unpersuaded. He still felt that the CIA was a hotbed of Yeltsin partisans whose view of the Soviet problem as "traditionalists versus democrats" was "simplistic."

*   *   *

On Friday, April 26, Robert Dole and George Mitchell, the Republican and Democratic leaders of the Senate, sent Yeltsin an invitation to visit Washington in late June.

The Soviet desk at State drafted a new cable to Matlock instructing him to tell Yeltsin that President Bush "looked forward" to seeing him in the Oval Office if he came. Once again Scowcroft spiked the cable, saying that it sounded too much as though the White House itself were issuing an invitation.

Hewett put up a fight. When Scowcroft once again mentioned Yeltsin's boorishness during his 1989 visit to the White House, Hewett replied, "The guy you're talking about now represents a significant portion of the aspirations of the Russian people. We need a change in attitude toward a changed man."

On Thursday, May 9, during a meeting with Scowcroft and Gates, Hewett argued that U.S. policy was based on a "false dichotomy" between the Union and the republics. Things were changing very fast, and the United States must not lag too far behind. It was possible for it to expand contacts with a wide variety of leaders in the Soviet Union without becoming a pawn in the game that was going on between the republics and the center.

With undisguised reluctance, Scowcroft approved more "outreach" to the republics — but with a caveat: "Don't undermine the center or jeopardize our relations with Gorbachev. If you can assure me on that, I'll be a happy man."

Baker and Scowcroft authorized Matlock by cable to tell Yeltsin that he would be welcome in the Oval Office. Even in these instructions there was a reminder of how apprehensive Bush still felt about the matter: before Matlock talked to Yeltsin, he was to inform Gorbachev's foreign minister of what he was about to do.

When Matlock complied, Bessmertnykh said that it would not be "necessarily upsetting" if Bush received Yeltsin. What mattered was that President Bush use the occasion to reiterate American support for the central government and to urge Yeltsin to cooperate with Gorbachev.

CHAPTER 17

"I Really Hit Him over the Head"

I
N THE SPRING of 1991, Gorbachev was pressing Bush to reschedule the meeting in Moscow that had been postponed because of the Baltic crisis. Bush decided to use Gorbachev's eagerness as leverage to win concessions on two arms control treaties — the CFE agreement, signed in 1990, and the unfinished START treaty, which was supposed to be the centerpiece of their next summit.

Although the Iron Curtain and the Warsaw Pact had passed into history, Bush and Gorbachev were still arguing over how many warheads should go onto an ICBM and how to interpret the fine print in CFE. The Soviet armed forces had not given up on the idea that the USSR was a global superpower; for its part, the Pentagon was girding itself for the possible collapse of Soviet reform and perhaps even the revival of Soviet expansionism.

With a reelection campaign looming in 1992, Bush did not want to give hawks of either party an excuse to accuse him of having done Gorbachev any favors in arms control. Moreover, U.S. negotiators in both CFE and START were confident of getting their own way on most of the lingering disputes. As Reginald Bartholomew, the under secretary of state with responsibility for arms control, put it, "We've been spoiled by Shevardnadze."

Many Soviet hard-liners agreed. They saw CFE and START as elements in Shevardnadze's — and Gorbachev's — overall surrender to the West. Now they saw their chance to strike back. On several points, they tried to wriggle out of agreements reached by Shevardnadze; where that seemed impossible, they tried to get the United States to pay them back for earlier concessions.

The remaining hurdle in CFE was the Soviet military's continuing effort to exempt 3,000 pieces of equipment on the grounds that they were assigned to newly created "coastal defense" units or to four "naval infantry regiments." This was one of the issues that had cast a cloud over Baker's negotiations with Shevardnadze in Houston in December 1990.

At Malta, in December 1989, Gorbachev had tried in vain to persuade Bush to include naval nuclear weapons, especially sea-launched cruise missiles, in START. Now the Soviet military was pushing hard on this point. Defense Minister Yazov had told Nixon in March that he and many of his colleagues regarded the CFE treaty as "one-sided and unfair." He frankly admitted that the Soviets were retaliating for the United States' refusal to include many of its own naval weapons, particularly sea-launched cruise missiles, in START.

General Moiseyev, the chief of the General Staff, had similarly advised the former president, "Your side has steadfastly refused to deal with naval armaments in arms control. We have been disappointed, and we have had to take appropriate measures."

More than once, representatives of the Soviet Foreign Ministry privately admitted to their American counterparts at the negotiating table in Geneva that they had become mouthpieces for the Defense Ministry back in Moscow. But the hard-liners were negotiating on behalf of an alliance that was being disbanded. The country's mounting internal problems motivated the Soviet political leadership to resolve as many disagreements as possible with the outside world.

As the wrangling continued, the Soviets offered to freeze at existing levels the number of naval-infantry armored combat vehicles (ACVs) that would be excluded from the CFE limits. The Americans took this as a tacit admission by the Soviets that they had been trying to violate the treaty, coupled with a promise that they would not do so again. The United States refused to agree to the proposal, insisting that ceilings already established under the treaty had to be respected.

When Bessmertnykh saw Baker in Moscow in mid-March, he suggested that they take another crack at the problem. Baker said, "I don't know what there is to talk about. Twenty-two countries have signed this treaty, and only one country has changed the rules. There's a basic principle involved here, and we're not going to back off on it."

Bessmertnykh pleaded with him: "I've been working on this issue very hard." He hinted that he was having a great deal of trouble with the military. "Please, let's have our experts meet." That night, James Woolsey, the U.S. negotiator on CFE, squared off against General Moiseyev in another fruitless round of talks.

The next day, Bessmertnykh told Baker that Moiseyev wanted to see Woolsey again. Baker said, "What's the point in having another replay of your side telling us how it's not going to change its position?" Bessmertnykh replied, "Let's see what happens." Baker hoped this meant that Gorbachev had intervened to break the deadlock.

Moiseyev jovially began the session by remarking that Woolsey seemed "well served" by his interpreter, Jean Arensburger, adding, "This isn't surprising since there are many things women can do as well as or better than men."

Woolsey decided that the general needed instruction not only on treaty law but on the sensitivities of women. He told Moiseyev that another female member of his delegation owned a coffee mug inscribed, "Men are only good for one thing — and how important *is* parallel parking, anyway?"

Arensburger had the satisfaction of translating this put-down into Russian, along with an explanation of the exotic Western concept of parallel parking. Moiseyev looked puzzled at first and then broke into good-natured laughter. The women of the U.S. delegation later presented him with the coffee mug.

Moiseyev had brought with him several small concessions. He hoped for an old-fashioned trade-off: in exchange for being able to exclude their naval infantry from CFE, the Soviets would agree to withdraw from the European zone a limited amount of other equipment that they had been intending to keep in storage depots. But Woolsey insisted on compliance with the terms of the treaty as signed.

Baker then met with Gorbachev and bore down on the Soviet position, declaring that there was "nothing in the negotiating record to justify" the exclusion of the disputed equipment.

Gorbachev said, "Let's not argue anymore. I've got a proposal." He upped the ante, doubling the numbers on the coastal defense equipment that would be covered by the treaty and thus bringing the two sides even closer together. But he would not budge on the naval infantry equipment. Baker said he wanted his own experts to study the new numbers.

The next day, Baker said to Bessmertnykh, "This is a step in the right direction, but it still doesn't solve the problem. The issue here is not whether you can have forces that you call coastal defense or naval infantry. The issue is that our presidents have signed a treaty that mandates certain numbers.

"The integrity of the treaty depends on maintaining the integrity of those numbers. It doesn't matter to us how you reach the limits. If you have to maintain naval infantry units, then do so. But you've got to take forces from some other category."

Woolsey told the Soviets, "You can resubordinate your tanks to the Boy Scouts if you want, but they still count."

Back in Washington, Baker reported to Bush on his meeting with Gorbachev: "I really hit him over the head," he said. After describing his frustrations in dealing with Moiseyev, he concluded, "We've got to keep Gorbachev himself involved." He advised Bush to negotiate directly with his Soviet counterpart through a new round of presidential correspondence.

Bush said, "Okay, I'll write him and tell him, 'Look, we've come this far. We're almost there. Don't blow it.' "

Bush ordered the creation of a panel of top-ranking U.S. arms control experts who were to convene regularly in the White House Situation Room. The meetings were chaired by Arnold Kanter of the NSC. No one was supposed to refer in writing to the panel's existence; its members began calling themselves the Un-Group.*

The Un-Group drafted a letter for Bush to send to Gorbachev. It made it clear that the United States was counting on the Soviet leader to overrule his generals on CFE. Reiterating what Baker had already told Gorbachev, Bush's letter said that if Moscow wished to keep a certain amount of equipment in what it chose to call coastal defense or naval infantry units, it would have to remove the same amount from

* Principal members, in addition to Kanter, included Under Secretary of State Bartholomew; James Timbie, a veteran arms control specialist at the State Department; and Stephen Hadley, an assistant secretary of defense.

other units. Both sides must abide by terms of the treaty as signed in November.

Replying to Bush, Gorbachev slightly bettered the proposal he had made to Baker in Moscow on the coastal defense divisions. As a gesture of "goodwill," he pledged not to increase the amount of equipment attached to naval infantry brigades. Bush responded by urging Gorbachev to solve the naval infantry question the same way he had the coastal defense problem — by accepting the Western position.

For years, U.S. negotiators had used the bargaining tactic of warning Soviet leaders that American conservatives might thwart any arms control treaty that they considered to be too "soft." Now that the Soviet Union was becoming a more democratized society, Gorbachev used the same device in reverse: he cautioned that the Soviet military might oppose — and the Supreme Soviet refuse to ratify — a CFE treaty that contained any concessions beyond those he had already made.

On Thursday, April 25, during yet another peace-brokering tour of the Middle East, Baker flew to Kislovodsk, in southern Russia, for a one-day meeting with Bessmertnykh. The foreign minister had suggested the mountain resort town because it was closer for Baker to fly to than Moscow, and also because it was one of Bessmertnykh's favorite spots — the equivalent, he felt, of Baker's scenic hideaway in Wyoming.

Much of the meeting was spent on the Arab-Israeli conflict. Bessmertnykh found it gratifying that he and his American counterpart were tinkering with the language of documents that would eventually lead to the joint U.S.-Soviet sponsorship of a regional peace conference: "Jim, we're working here like regular staff members, really getting something accomplished," he said.

Baker replied, "Sasha, you really are part of the solution now. You're not part of the problem anymore. That's a big payoff on the way you and your colleagues have changed the foreign policy of your country."

Nonetheless, Bessmertnykh at first tried to defend the interests of the USSR's traditional clients, the Palestinians, insisting that the PLO and UN must both have important roles in the talks. When Baker and Ross told him that neither idea would fly, he quickly backed off and said, "Let us work on the PLO and tell them the facts of life."

On CFE, Bessmertnykh's hands were still tied by the Soviet military. Shortly before Kislovodsk, he had proposed to Gorbachev that Moiseyev be given responsibility for the next round of talks with the Americans; that way, the general and his uniformed comrades would have to take the blame if the negotiations broke down and the treaty slipped away.

Gorbachev had liked the scheme. He, too, was exasperated by the whole subject of naval infantry: better this time not just to include the military at the table but to put Moiseyev in the hot seat across from the Americans. Let him experience American adamancy firsthand and then explain to his president why he could not force the Soviet position down the Americans' throats. Maybe that way Moiseyev might come around.

However, when Bessmertnykh suggested to Baker that the two governments let their "senior experts" — which obviously meant Moiseyev on the Soviet side — have another go at breaking the impasse in Geneva, Baker balked. Now that the two presidents were "working the problem," why should it be relegated to a lower level?

"I've done as much as I can," said Bessmertnykh. Even though the matter was "in the presidential channel," it would be "useful to have Moiseyev address the problem with your people. Let's bring him into this now."

Ross told Baker after the meeting, "It might work. Bessmertnykh doesn't have Shevy's political clout or weight, so he has to maneuver more bureaucratically. This arrangement requires Moiseyev to take the blame but also to have a stake in the agreement."

The Kremlin made a formal proposal to send Moiseyev to Geneva in an attempt to break the impasse on naval infantry. Scowcroft, Gates, and Kanter had a better idea: bring Moiseyev to Washington and let him meet with Bush. Gates said, "That way, we can give him a firsthand look at how dug-in the president himself is on this issue." Bush wrote Gorbachev to invite Moiseyev to Washington.

Months of give-and-take — with the Soviets doing most of the giving — had by now reduced the amount of equipment in dispute to 753 naval infantry armored combat vehicles in two areas, Murmansk and the Crimea.

On Monday, May 20, Moiseyev brought to Washington another partial concession: all naval infantry equipment, including the 753 ACVs, would count against the overall CFE ceilings. A corresponding number of vehicles would be withdrawn from Europe, but they would be taken from storage depots, not active units. This would effectively increase the amount of equipment the Soviets could have in active units and decrease the amount they were expected to keep in storage.

The next day, Bush saw Moiseyev in the Oval Office. He told him there was a great deal riding on the resolution of the outstanding issues. If the Soviets persisted in trying to back out of an agreement they had already made, it would raise "basic questions" about the direction of policy in the Soviet Union. It would even raise questions about who was really in charge in Moscow. "I don't want to see questions raised," said Bush.

Moiseyev responded with a lengthy pledge of fealty to *perestroika* and Gorbachev. He assured Bush that he understood the concern on the American side and was "completely supportive of what our president is trying to do." Bush said afterward that he had found the general's performance "fairly convincing."

That same day, Moiseyev went to the Pentagon and called on his American counterpart, General Colin Powell, with whom he had met four times over the past eighteen months. Adopting the confidential tone of one soldier speaking to another, Moiseyev complained about how difficult it was to deal with civilians.

If they had to give up the disputed armored combat vehicles, he said, the naval infantry units would "lose their integrity." They would be unable to move troops around easily and with relative safety in a "potentially hostile environment."

For months, Moiseyev and other Soviet military officers had been dropping hints about the various emergencies that might create such an environment. For the units around Murmansk and Leningrad, the bogeyman was trouble in the Baltics; for those in the south, disorder in Armenia, Azerbaijan, or Georgia. Now Moiseyev told Powell quite explicitly that the Soviet Union needed the ACVs to "keep the population under control."

Powell replied, "Misha, this issue isn't worth the time we're spending on it, and you know it." He was not about to let Moiseyev play the Pentagon off against the State Department. He asked the general not to bring his complaints about civilians to him: "Go back across the river and talk to Reg Bartholomew."

The Americans tried out another idea for solving the naval infantry issue. The CFE treaty contained a provision allowing ACV "lookalikes" — vehicles that were based on the same chassis as armored combat vehicles but were modified in ways that either reduced or eliminated their troop-carrying or combat capability. The Soviet Union could retain the 753 troublesome naval infantry ACVs if it agreed to modify that many other vehicles by converting them from troop carriers to "look-alike" ammunition carriers, which were permitted by the treaty.

Moiseyev dismissed the idea, saying that the dignity of Soviet infantrymen required that they not be transported in *"telyogi"* — horse-drawn wagons.

After Moiseyev's departure, Bush sent Gorbachev yet another letter, this one saying that while he appreciated the spirit in which the general had come to Washington, in his view the Soviet delegation was still holding out for an unacceptable reinterpretation of the treaty. Bush noted that Bessmertnykh and Baker were to meet in Lisbon at the beginning of June to sign a peace accord ending the civil war in Angola; he urged Gorbachev to let that meeting become a deadline for closing the gap on CFE.

On Monday, May 27, by telephone, the president told Gorbachev that the difference between the two sides was now "very narrow." If the Soviets would just "move a little bit," plans could proceed for the Moscow summit.

Gorbachev replied that he had received Bush's letter and had "given instructions" for Bessmertnykh to take some "new ideas" on CFE to Lisbon. After the call, Scowcroft grinned at Bush and said, "I think the other guy just blinked."

On Saturday, June 1, at the U.S. embassy in Lisbon, Bessmertnykh handed Baker a letter from Moiseyev reviewing the latest Soviet position. Even though he spoke fluent English, Bessmertnykh read the letter aloud in Russian, letting an interpreter translate it. He wished to be sure that the Soviet concession was couched in the military's own language, so that no one could charge that something had been lost in translation.

Calling on his experience as a contract lawyer, Baker was equally meticulous. He went over the Soviets' English translation of the letter phrase by phrase to make sure there were no tricks or traps. There were none. The Soviets had accepted the "look-alike" solution to the ACVs.*

---

* Also at issue were 1,700 armored personnel carriers (APCs), which were supposed to provide security for Soviet strategic missile launching sites. The Soviets maintained that CFE should not pertain to these vehicles at all, since they were not attached to conventional forces. Western officials at first took the position that an APC assigned to protect a strategic site one day could be used for the invasion of Western Europe the next, but in the end they agreed that these vehicles — provided that they numbered no more than 1,701 — could fall under the existing treaty exemption for internal security equipment.

Moiseyev later told Powell that he had decided he could live with the compromise just as he was leaving Washington in May: "I solved the problem in my head as we were taking off." Powell said, "Gee, Misha, that's great, but it would have been even better if you'd solved it while you were still on the ground."

Baker dispatched Woolsey to Moscow to draw up agreements on all other outstanding matters.* After five days of bargaining, everything was ready to be signed, including documents enshrining the Soviet commitment to limit, and count against treaty ceilings, coastal defense and naval infantry equipment. These also incorporated a pledge that in the future all equipment would count toward the limit, regardless of the type of unit to which it was assigned. In honor of Woolsey, this was informally dubbed the "Boy Scout paragraph."

On Friday, June 14, the agreements — essentially refinements of a treaty signed seven months before — were formally ratified at an "extraordinary conference" of CFE ambassadors in Vienna, held in the same hall where the negotiations had begun, in March 1989.

With CFE finally resolved, Bush turned his attention to the impasse over START. The most troublesome issue was a consequence of the success the negotiators had had in achieving the goal of "de-MIRVing" — that is, reducing the number of warheads on top of intercontinental rockets.†

One way to reduce warhead totals was to develop a new generation of ICBMs expressly designed to carry fewer MIRVs than their predecessors. This option could be easily verified, in that each side could monitor the testing and deployment of the other's new missiles and ensure that it had only the number of MIRVs allowed.

But building new missiles from scratch was extremely expensive. A

Western negotiators reasoned that it was in everyone's interest to assure the security of Soviet strategic forces, especially now that the Soviet Union was in turmoil.

* For example, both sides agreed that on a one-time-only basis, the Soviets could move some vehicles beyond the Urals, so long as they destroyed the same number of pieces already there.

† START imposed a ceiling of 4,900 on each side's ballistic missile warheads. To meet that requirement, the USSR was expected to reduce its ICBM warheads from 6,595 to 3,028, and its SLBM (or submarine-launched ballistic missile) warheads from 2,810 to 1,872. Once the treaty was ratified, the Soviets would have to dismantle ballistic missiles at a rate of one every sixty-six hours for seven years. The United States was agreeing to substantial reductions as well (in ICBM warheads, from 2,450 to 1,444, and in SLBM warheads, from 5,056 to 3,456), but with the revolution in the East, American military strategists calculated that they would need far fewer nuclear weapons than before.

far cheaper and faster way to de-MIRV was to "download," or remove warheads from existing missiles. The Reagan administration had first proposed a downloading provision in 1987, to enable the United States to meet START ceilings by converting the Minuteman III from a triple-warhead to a single-warhead ICBM.

However, when the Soviets engaged in their own version of down-loading, they generated anxiety and suspicion among the Americans. U.S. intelligence knew that two existing Soviet missiles, one land-based and the other submarine-launched, were capable of carrying more war-heads than the number with which they were usually deployed.*

At the December 1987 Reagan-Gorbachev summit in Washington, the United States agreed to give the Soviets the benefit of the doubt in both cases — much to the disapproval of Brent Scowcroft, then a pri-vate citizen, who noted that the Soviets could easily and quickly add warheads to these missiles and thereby greatly increase the threat they posed to the United States.

This danger was known as "breakout" — the ability of one side to break out of the restraints imposed by the treaty. In the spring of 1991, breakout was what a prudent American strategist such as Scowcroft worried about when he contemplated the possibility that Gorbachev's reforms might backfire, leading to the reemergence of a militaristic, predatory Soviet Union.

As Bush's national security adviser, Scowcroft would have preferred to ban downloading altogether, but under pressure from the Pentagon, he accepted the idea of permitting each side to download only one type of missile. The United States would be allowed to download the Min-uteman III from three warheads to one; the Soviets would be allowed to download a submarine missile, the SS-N-18, from seven to three.

But the Kremlin held out for a provision that would allow it to download two other missile types in addition to the SS-N-18. The Americans deduced, partly on the basis of highly sensitive intelligence information, that this was because the Soviets were secretly developing two new missiles — again, one land-based, the other submarine-

---

* At issue were the SS-18, the largest of the Soviet ICBMs, which American intelligence believed to be capable of carrying twelve or even fourteen warheads rather than the ten with which it was operationally deployed, and the SS-N-23, which had originally been designed to carry ten rather than the four warheads with which it was deployed. (NATO designated Soviet ballistic missiles "SS," meaning surface-to-surface, followed by a num-ber indicating when the missile was first observed. If the missile was submarine-launched, the letter N, for *naval*, was added to the designation.)

launched — which, for complex technical reasons, would be banned under START unless there was a lenient downloading provision.*

As for the SS-N-18, the Soviets did not want it to count against the downloading limit at all. In December 1987, they had classified it as a seven-warhead missile, but by September 1990 they were insisting that it existed in two versions — one with seven warheads, the other with three — and claiming that they had converted all the seven-warhead models to three-warhead ones. Since the conversion had taken place before the conclusion of START, the Soviets argued that the SS-N-18 should be considered a three-warhead, not a seven-warhead, missile.

There was also a disagreement over how many warheads could be removed from the arsenals by means of downloading: the Soviets wanted more than twice as many as the Americans were willing to accept.† Many U.S. analysts felt that in order to diminish the danger of breakout from downloading, it was more important to restrict the warhead total than the number of missile types involved; it was their belief that if the START treaty was ever to be completed, the United States would probably have to let the Soviets download all three types. But in meeting after meeting, Scowcroft kept saying that no START treaty at all was better than one in which the Soviets got their way on downloading.

Neither Secretary of Defense Cheney nor General Powell was so adamant on this issue. Cheney knew that the Pentagon would come under more and more domestic political pressure to trim its budget and revise its weapons programs, now that the Soviet threat was receding. He was attracted to downloading for the same reason his Soviet counterparts were: it was a relatively cheap way of reducing strategic forces.

There was also another factor in Cheney's mind. An independent commission, mandated by Congress and chaired by Stanford physicist Sidney Drell, was concerned about the safety of the propellant system used in the Trident II SLBM. It had recommended a less volatile pro-

---

* The issue of downloading overlapped with the question of how to define a new type of missile. To qualify as a permissible new type, an improved version of an older missile had to differ from its predecessor in specified ways. By the standards on which the United States was insisting, the two missiles the Soviets were developing — successors to the SS-24 (the rough equivalent of the American MX) and the SS-N-20 — did not qualify as new types. Thus, the Soviets were hoping to fit them into their allotment of downloaded upgrades of existing types.

† The Soviets initially proposed an effective total of around 2,200 downloaded warheads, including those that would come off the SS-N-18. The United States favored a limit of about 1,000.

pellant, which would not permit the rocket to carry so many warheads. To meet this recommendation, Cheney wanted to retain the option of downloading the Trident II from eight to six warheads.

As for Powell, he did not fully share the fear of many of his colleagues' that the new Soviet Union would give way to a reincarnation of the old, malevolent one. About downloading and breakout, he told Cheney in the spring of 1991, "I'm not as exercised about it as Brent. That's not for technical or military reasons, but for political reasons.

"The situation is changing so fast and so profoundly that someday we'll wonder why we ever argued over this. With everything that's going on over there, I have a hard time convincing myself I should stay awake at night worrying about the Sovs' future breakout capability."

In Geneva, Richard Burt, the chief U.S. START negotiator, was frustrated. He would send suggestions to the administration on how to resolve the sticking points. He would reach tentative deals with his Soviet counterpart, Yuri Nazarkin, only to have them slapped down by Washington, often on personal instructions from Scowcroft.

In January 1991, on a visit to Washington, Burt tried to persuade Baker that there was a real danger of their losing the START treaty altogether. But the secretary of state was distracted by the war in the Persian Gulf, and besides, he was not about to tangle with the White House on an issue that was so close to Scowcroft's heart.

After returning to Geneva, Burt decided to make one last attempt at a compromise with the Soviets on downloading: the Americans would let the Soviets have their way on the number of missile types that could be downloaded if the Soviets would accept a tight limit on the number of warheads that could be removed by that method.

Burt tried to sell the idea in Washington. Baker, eager to split the remaining differences and get on with a summit, gave Burt's proposal his tentative blessing, but once again Scowcroft turned it down flat. "It isn't worth having this treaty if there's going to be a danger of breakout," he insisted. Shortly afterward, Burt resigned from the government.

By the end of the spring, Baker was worried that the long-delayed Bush-Gorbachev summit in Moscow would be held hostage to the "absurd and trivial" issue of downloading. "For years we've been trying to get the Soviets to cut back on warheads," he complained. Now they're finally willing to go along, and we're saying, 'Hey, wait! Here are some rules to make it harder for you to do!' "

CHAPTER 18

"Business Is Business"

B Y THE SPRING of 1991, the Soviet economy was in deeper crisis than ever. The country's gross national product and its standard of living had fallen steadily since Gorbachev first came to power; in the eyes of many long-suffering Soviet citizens, *perestroika* was to blame.* Gorbachev and his colleagues had begun dismantling the old system but had failed to introduce, or even clearly visualize, a new one.

The Soviet leader called this state of affairs "transitional." But even as he vowed repeatedly to decentralize control of the economy, an interlocking network of ministries was fighting to block reform. Official rhetoric about privatization meant little in the absence of laws to define and protect private property. To complicate matters further, Gorbachev still saw himself as a good Communist, to whom the very idea of private property was anathema.

Just as he was constantly engaged in tactical maneuvers between

---

* In 1989, the Soviet GNP was thought by Western experts to be growing by an anemic 1.4 percent annually; by 1990, it was thought to be declining by 2.5 percent. A further decline of 4.4 percent was expected in 1991, with a drop of 14 to 20 percent predicted for 1992.

conservatives and liberals on issues involving the future of the Union and its political structure, in economics, too, Gorbachev instinctively sought a hybrid system. When he and his advisers uttered the new magic word *market*, they almost always qualified it with a modifier such as *managed* or *regulated*, which implied some kind of compromise between the philosophies of Karl Marx and Adam Smith.

Since 1987, Gorbachev had run through a stream of economic advisers who had urged him to make basic changes in the system — Abel Aganbegyan, Leonid Abalkin, Nikolai Petrakov, and Stanislav Shatalin. While their programs varied, they all believed that the government must decontrol prices to reflect the actual costs of production and availability of goods; otherwise, they maintained, all talk of moving to a market economy was meaningless and deceptive. The Kremlin would be unable to introduce free markets unless and until it was willing to slash subsidies for inefficient enterprises and stop printing vast quantities of rubles to finance the huge budget deficit.

At the end of 1990, Gorbachev had tilted to the right not only in politics but in economics as well. By then, Shatalin and the other reformers were either on the sidelines or, in some cases, closely allied with Boris Yeltsin in planning to overhaul the laws of the Russian Republic.

By the spring, Gorbachev was relying on Communist conservatives, who warned that the inflation resulting from decontrol of prices, and the unemployment attendant on the closing of inefficient factories, would cause social unrest and political upheaval in the Soviet Union.

Chief among these advisers was the stout, crew-cut prime minister, Valentin Pavlov, who embraced precisely the sort of "command-administrative methods" that Gorbachev repudiated in rhetoric but often relied on in practice. Pavlov not only resisted fundamental reform but believed that many of its advocates were either knowing agents or unknowing dupes of a conspiracy masterminded by Western capitalists.*

It was at Pavlov's urging that Gorbachev in January 1991 had signed a decree granting the KGB authority to enter and search enterprises suspected of the hoarding of goods, price gouging, currency speculation, and other forms of black-marketeering and "economic sabotage."

---

* In a February 12, 1991, interview in the trade union journal *Trud*, Pavlov charged that a cabal of Western banks had been buying up black-market rubles and dumping them back into the Soviet economy in order to cause hyperinflation and start price riots. The ultimate goal, he concluded, was the overthrow of Gorbachev and the takeover of the government by radical reformers.

"Black market" was a pejorative term for what in fact was the free market that reformers saw as the country's salvation. Since Soviet law was so vague and contradictory about what was permitted and what was not, the police measures instituted by Pavlov had an inhibiting effect on entrepreneurship.

Still, Pavlov's crackdown was far from unpopular. For all their disillusionment with communism, many Soviet citizens had yet to erase from their political consciousness the image of the fat, villainous Western banker, clutching his moneybags and trampling on the backs of the workers.

Small private enterprises — or "cooperatives" — were charging whatever they could get for their goods or services. Since their prices were much higher than those in state stores, they were seen as profiting at the expense of the "people."

In his campaign for the presidency of Russia, even Yeltsin had to be careful not to go too far in his public support for the market reformers.* Most Soviet citizens knew that reform, at least in the short term, could mean misery for millions of people.

Bush remained opposed to the idea of giving extensive financial aid to the Soviet Union. In the absence of a credible plan for Soviet reform, he believed that U.S. aid would merely help communism stave off bankruptcy.

During his visit to Washington in late May, Yeltsin's foreign minister, Andrei Kozyrev, agreed. In a private meeting at the State Department, he said, "Any money you give to the center will not only be wasted, but worse than that, it will keep afloat a system that should be allowed to sink." He added that the $33 billion in German assistance to the Soviet Union since 1989 had simply bought the existing system an "extra year of life."

Even if someone had been able to design a program of financial aid that would have ensured the end of communism in the Soviet Union, there would have been serious obstacles on the American side. In the United States, foreign aid was traditionally one of the most unpopular uses of public funds; in 1991, with the country burdened by the largest deficit in its history, there was more domestic political resistance than ever.

---

* One of Yeltsin's conservative opponents for the Russian presidency, former Prime Minister Nikolai Ryzhkov, used the slogan "A vote for Yeltsin is a vote for capitalism."

Even those U.S. senators and congressmen who were willing in principle to help the cause of Soviet reform warned Soviet visitors to Washington that they would not support any substantial aid so long as the Kremlin was engaged in activities hostile to American interests and American values. The three examples most often cited were the repression of the Baltics, the allocation of a vast portion of the Soviet GNP to military spending, and the roughly $13 billion a year that the Kremlin channeled to leftist regimes in Afghanistan, Angola, and, above all, Cuba.

Scowcroft had another reason to be skeptical about sending massive aid to the USSR. He was determined that the United States and its Western partners should nurture the new, fragile democracies in Eastern Europe, and he did not want to see funds diverted from that cause to what seemed like the far less promising prospect of Soviet reform or, worse, to an ongoing subsidization of the Soviet command system.

Bush himself shared all those concerns, and he was also worried about the tumultuous political environment inside the Soviet Union. When the subject of Soviet aid came up at a White House meeting, he shook his head and said, "I think we'd better wait for events to clarify themselves."

Yet the issue of aid would not go away, largely because Soviet officials kept raising it. They needed to feed their own people. In late March, Gorbachev wrote Bush a letter appealing for $1.5 billion in loans with which to purchase American grain on the international market.*

He presumed that the United States would be quick to agree. After all, the loans would cost the American taxpayer nothing unless the Soviet Union defaulted, and would benefit American farmers, who would be at the head of the line to sell their produce to the Soviet Union.

Viktor Komplektov, a journeyman Foreign Ministry *amerikanist* who had replaced Bessmertnykh as the Soviet ambassador to Washington, told American officials that without an emergency purchase of grain from abroad, there could be famine in the Soviet Union as early as the summer of 1991. Further communications from Gorbachev to Bush were increasingly strident, virtually accusing the president of backing away from his avowed support for *perestroika*.

---

* The letter was brief and so vague that U.S. officials at first thought Gorbachev was asking for $500 million in addition to the billion-dollar credit the U.S. had granted in December 1990. Only after seeking clarification from the Soviet government did they realize that he wanted $1.5 billion in *new* loans.

At a White House meeting in late April 1991 with Baker, Scowcroft, and Secretary of the Treasury Nicholas Brady, Bush complained about Gorbachev's hectoring: "The guy doesn't seem to get it. He seems to think that we *owe* him economic help because we support him politically. We've got to give him a lesson in basic economics. Business is business. Loans have to be made for sound financial and commercial reasons."

On Monday, April 29, Bush explained to a group of farm-state broadcasters that the laws governing the lending of public money to foreign governments required certain standards of creditworthiness, and that anyone looking at the Soviet Union's growing balance-of-payments deficit would have to doubt its ability to service its debts in the future.

Bush said that "regrettably," the Soviet Union had not begun the market reforms "that I think Gorbachev aspires to" and "that I know . . . Mr. Yeltsin aspires to."

The Soviet embassy in Washington sent a report on Bush's remarks to Moscow. Gorbachev read it and fumed. Untutored as he was in Western economics, *creditworthiness* sounded to him like a synonym for *trustworthiness*, in which quality Bush seemed to be saying that the Soviet Union was deficient.

Nor did Gorbachev like Bush's implication that Yeltsin was more committed to market reforms than he was. He asked his advisers whether Bush was dropping his policy of support for the Kremlin in the expectation that the situation in the Soviet Union was about to get worse. Had the president lost confidence in him personally? he wondered.

In early May, Gorbachev protested directly to Matlock: didn't Bush realize the impact that his negative words had inside the Soviet Union? They were contributing to the impression of an incompetent leadership presiding over a country that was falling apart. Bush was undermining Gorbachev's credibility among his own people. Matlock sent a cable to the State Department warning that Gorbachev had been stung by Bush's comments.

In a visit to the Oval Office on Monday, May 6, Shevardnadze, now a private citizen, advised Bush that the coming three or four months would be crucial. Gorbachev was finally making common cause with Yeltsin and the democrats; now that he was moving in the proper direction, he deserved a show of support from the West.

Shevardnadze added that the American reluctance to grant grain credits seemed to have brought about a "dangerous pause in the relationship, and if it's allowed to continue, there could be backsliding" in the Soviet Union. He feared that Gorbachev might either lose his grip on power or panic and tack again toward the conservatives.

That same day, Shevardnadze lunched with Baker at the State Department. He recalled that in the early days after its accession to power, in 1985, "our team" — meaning Gorbachev, Yakovlev, and Shevardnadze — had been faced with a choice between "two models for *perestroika*." They could drastically overhaul the economy by introducing radical price reforms and market mechanisms virtually overnight, or they could phase in the same reforms and mechanisms over twenty years: "We had a choice between shock therapy and gradual medicinal treatment."

Believing that the first option would put Soviet society under too much strain, they had settled on the second instead. Shevardnadze told Baker that with the wisdom of hindsight, he now realized that this decision had been a fundamental mistake: "We should have moved more rapidly." A swifter, bolder version of *perestroika*, he said, might have spared the central government the humiliating prospect of the breakup of the Union, which now seemed almost inevitable.

Shevardnadze also suggested that had the Kremlin proceeded in 1988 or 1989 with the version of the new Union treaty that it was now trying to promote, even the Balts and his fellow Georgians might have embraced it. Having given Shevardnadze exactly this advice in 1989, Baker had to restrain himself from saying, "I told you so."

In Moscow, Gorbachev declared to the visiting press lord Rupert Murdoch that the Bush administration was risking the possibility that the "world will again plunge into a Cold War or semi-Cold War."

On Wednesday morning, May 8, the NSC staff sent a copy of Gorbachev's comments to the president, who said, "Gee, I guess we've got a misunderstanding developing here." He decided that he had better say something to reassure Gorbachev that there had been no change either in American policy or in his feelings toward him.

That day, Bush was to meet with three Baltic leaders — President Landsbergis of Lithuania, Prime Minister Edgar Savisaar of Estonia, and Prime Minister Ivars Godmanis of Latvia. When a reporter asked what he would say to the visitors, Bush replied that he would "tell them that we have a strong and, I think, good relationship with President

Gorbachev. . . . When you look at the accomplishments of Mikhail Gorbachev, they are enormous.

"Yes, the Soviet Union is fighting difficult economic times. But I am not about to forget history. And what Gorbachev did in terms of Eastern Europe, what he's done in terms of *perestroika* and *glasnost,* has my respect. So we will deal with the facts as they come to us. But I don't want to see a breach in a relationship that is very strong, that's served us extraordinarily well in recent times."

In the Cabinet Room, Bush pressed the Baltic leaders to negotiate with the Kremlin, lest the central government impose crippling economic sanctions on them. Godmanis, who served as the principal spokesman for the group, asserted confidently that Yeltsin would not let that happen. "Russia will be our protector," he said: Yeltsin and Kozyrev had privately promised not to permit "economic blackmail to be imposed on the Baltic states."

For a moment, Bush was speechless. The leaders of the breakaway republics now seemed to feel that only Yeltsin stood between them and a vengeful, repressive Gorbachev.

On Saturday, May 11, Gorbachev spoke to Bush on the telephone. This was the first time the two men had talked since the end of the Gulf War. Gorbachev stressed his hope that Bush would approve the additional grain credits he had asked for; continued American reluctance would make him wonder whether the U.S. government still fully backed his reforms.

Bush assured him that there was "nothing political" in the delay; it was strictly an economic matter. He said he would dispatch a delegation to Moscow, headed by Richard Crowder, the under secretary of agriculture, and including Ed Hewett, of the NSC staff, and Eugene McAllister, the assistant secretary of state for economic and business affairs.

The mission's stated purpose was to assess the crisis in Soviet agriculture and to assay long-term Soviet farming needs, but it was also intended to demonstrate to Gorbachev that Bush was taking seriously his request for emergency help. At the same time, it enabled the administration to stall on deciding how to respond to Gorbachev's demands for grain credits.

The delegation went first to Ukraine, which annually produced a surplus of grain that it exported to the other republics. The increasingly nationalistic government in Kiev did not want the United States to make it any easier for the Kremlin to buy from American farmers instead. Ukrainian leaders also knew that if the central government borrowed $1.5 billion from the United States, it would expect all the republics, including Ukraine, to share in the obligation of repaying the debt.

In Stavropol, the city in southern Russia where Gorbachev had worked as a party boss, the delegation met with the owner of thirty-six chicken farms, who explained that the biggest problem afflicting Soviet agriculture was a shortage not so much of bread for the populace but of feed grain for livestock and poultry.

"The big problem with this country isn't hungry people," Crowder observed sardonically to several other members of the traveling party. "It's hungry cows and chickens."

On Saturday, May 25, Matlock took the delegation to the Kremlin for a two-and-a-half-hour meeting with Gorbachev, who was still angry about the delay on the grain credits. Crowder asked Gorbachev to instruct his government to be more forthcoming with the data necessary to determine Soviet creditworthiness.

Gorbachev snapped that the matter was simple: the Soviet Union had always paid its debts for agricultural purchases in the past. He had made a "personal request" to Bush for assistance; why was any more information necessary?

He went on to complain that he was getting mixed signals from Washington. Bush and Baker still seemed supportive, but it looked as though "conservatives" in the administration were against him and what he was trying to do. One example was the "well-known anti-Soviet" Robert Gates, whom Bush had just nominated as director of the Central Intelligence Agency.

Matlock could not let this comment pass without a response. He said, "Mr. Gates is less anti-Soviet than Chairman Kryuchkov is anti-American." Hewett added, "Bob Gates is a lot better than you think." Gorbachev shot back, "There's no point in talking about this. I've got my opinion of Gates, just as you've got yours of Kryuchkov."

On their return to Washington at the end of May, Crowder, Hewett, and McAllister advised Bush to proceed with the grain credits. They pronounced themselves satisfied with Soviet assurances that any grain purchased with the American loan would be fairly distributed among the republics and the Baltic states.

Except for emergency transfusions of cash, such as the additional grain credits, Gorbachev and his current set of economic advisers had no coherent idea of exactly what form a Western aid program should take. For its part, the Bush administration wanted to encourage reform but did not know how best to go about it.

Into this vacuum rushed a small group of academics who, in most cases, had only slight experience on the fringes of policy-making in the Soviet and American governments. After months of networking and brainstorming, they came up with a plan they dubbed the "Grand Bargain."

According to this scheme, the West would pledge to provide, in prescribed stages, various forms of economic help, beginning with food, medical aid, and technical assistance and eventually progressing to large-scale financing for the rebuilding of the country's infrastructure. The estimated cost of the program would be $15 to $20 billion a year from 1991 to 1993, a burden to be shared by the United States, Europe, and Japan.

In exchange for this aid, the Soviet government would commit itself to taking specific steps toward reform, including privatization, the phasing-out of government price controls, the reduction of subsidies to industry, and the push toward full convertibility of the ruble.

The principal Soviet author of the Grand Bargain was Grigori Yavlinsky, a former deputy prime minister of the Russian Republic and the coauthor, with Shatalin, of the Five-Hundred-Day Plan. Since the fall of 1990, Yavlinsky had been in frequent contact with Graham Allison, the Harvard political scientist. With the help of Robert Blackwill, now a Harvard lecturer, Allison had been trying to interest the Bush administration in his own ideas for how to channel Western aid to the Soviet Union.

Allison and Blackwill concentrated their efforts to promote the Grand Bargain on Blackwill's old colleague Robert Zoellick, who at the start of 1991 had been appointed the under secretary of state for economic affairs.

Zoellick had strong doubts. He found it difficult to imagine that the Soviet government, particularly in the hands of men such as Pavlov, would be willing to undertake the kind of sweeping, rapid measures that the plan called for. He also thought it was unrealistic to expect the industrialized democracies to come up with anything like $20 billion a year.

Nonetheless, he listened to the pitch for the Grand Bargain. Allison and Blackwill represented a constituency — the academic foreign policy elite — that Zoellick wanted to keep on the administration's side, and furthermore, he was intrigued by the bright young reformer Yavlinsky and the role he might play in the future of the Soviet Union.

Allison and Blackwill proposed that the Group of Seven leaders invite Gorbachev to attend their next summit, scheduled for London in July. This would demonstrate to the world that the West recognized that it had a stake in the success of *perestroika*.

The idea of the G-7's giving Gorbachev a seat at the table found little support in Washington. Zoellick feared that Gorbachev's presence might distract attention from other urgent business, such as the coordination of G-7 trade and monetary policy to stimulate a recovery from the recession in the West. It would also build up impractical hopes about how much the outside world could do to help the Soviets out of their economic crisis.

In April, Yavlinsky received an invitation to attend a two-day economic conference in Washington later that month. Before accepting, he checked with Primakov, whose multiple portfolios now included responsibility for international economic policy within Gorbachev's new Security Council.

Yavlinsky said privately on several occasions that he considered Primakov a "snake," but he also knew that he was one of Gorbachev's most trusted advisers. Primakov, in turn, thought Yavlinsky bright but brash and naive, a peddler of blue-sky nostrums. Still, he was aware that Yavlinsky was well regarded within Yeltsin's circle and among Western economists. He calculated that Yavlinsky's involvement in the Washington conference might help advance the Kremlin's latest effort to satisfy domestic and international demands for economic reform.

Pavlov had that month unveiled what he called the "anticrisis plan," a program that paid lip service to various goals favored by both radical reformers and Western governments: a balanced budget, accelerated privatization, convertibility of the ruble, and the creation of a federal banking system. However, it was short on specifics and had as an immediate effect the strengthening of the central government's authority to ban strikes and to "stabilize" prices in order to avert hyperinflation. Only later, and then only gradually, would the central authorities let prices float freely, and permit the widespread privatization of property.

As the republics began pressing their claims to sovereignty, Pavlov amended the plan to shift some of the responsibility from Moscow to the other capitals in the Soviet Union. But the essential concept remained the same: power to control the economy lay mainly with the center.

Over whisky in Primakov's apartment, Yavlinsky and Primakov collaborated on an open letter to the G-7 governments in which they made the case for Western aid. The letter called for "joint efforts" by Soviet and Western experts to draft a plan for "effective interaction between the reformist leadership of the USSR and the Group of Seven." As the Kremlin hastened the transition to a market economy, the West would "prepare its parallel plan of action" for economic assistance.

Primakov and Yavlinsky mentioned no figures but cited a precedent for what they had in mind: the massive help that the United States had given Japan and West Germany immediately after World War II. This left no doubt that they were thinking of an "interaction" that would require tens of billions of dollars a year.

They asserted that if the Soviet Union had to abandon communism and build a free-market economy on its own, "the excessive social tensions expected to accompany transformation on such a scale inside a military superpower would present an unjustified risk for both the country and the entire world."

This was a veiled threat: if the West refused to help, chaos and privation in the Soviet Union could result in a tidal wave of refugees sweeping into Western Europe, and perhaps even lead to civil war among the republics, some of which were armed with nuclear weapons.

For decades, the United States and the West had worried about the threat posed by the military strength of the Soviet Union. Now, overnight, they were being told by the Soviets themselves — or at least by two of Gorbachev's advisers — that it was the political and economic *weakness* of the USSR that endangered Western security.

During his mid-May telephone call to Bush, Gorbachev proposed sending a delegation to Washington to explain what his government was doing to "hasten, broaden, and deepen" reform of the Soviet economy. Primakov would lead the group, accompanied by Yavlinsky and Soviet Deputy Prime Minister Vladimir Shcherbakov.

After the call, Scowcroft told Bush, "Primakov is a lot of things, but he's not a stellar 'new thinker.' " Neither was Shcherbakov. In addition to being Pavlov's right-hand man, he was head of the Ministry of Economics and Prognosis. This was the successor to the State Ministry of Planning, or Gosplan, which had long exerted control over virtually all aspects of the Soviet economy.

Scowcroft, Gates, Hewett, and Zoellick all presumed that Primakov and Shcherbakov were bringing Yavlinsky with them as window dressing to make the administration more receptive to Pavlov's "anti-crisis" plan. Hewett telephoned Graham Allison in Cambridge to ask him what he thought of his partner's being included in an official Kremlin delegation.

Allison called Yavlinsky in Moscow. It was the first Yavlinsky had heard of the idea.

At the Kremlin on Saturday, May 18, Allison and Yavlinsky presented an outline of their Grand Bargain to Chernyayev. Gorbachev's aide told them, "I'm not an economist. But I know when something works, and the system we've got simply doesn't work. What you're talking about offers us a way of making a break with the past."

Allison took Yavlinsky to Washington to meet unofficially with Zoellick and Dennis Ross on Tuesday, May 21. Yavlinsky explained that even though he was personally closer to the reformers around Yeltsin, he still believed in Gorbachev: "Mikhail Sergeyevich gave us our freedom," he said. "Some dissidents, like Sakharov, earned their freedom on their own, but the rest of us Gorbachev saved. I want to do what I can to help him."

Yavlinsky added that the West, too, should help Gorbachev. He noted that while the Soviet leader had introduced concepts such as "new thinking" and "mutual security," it had taken the United States to give content and direction to those slogans by making concrete proposals for arms control treaties and the settlement of regional conflicts. Now the West should do the same thing in economics. It should help Gorbachev "fill in the blanks" in his program.

Zoellick replied that transforming the Soviet Union's economy would be much more difficult than altering its foreign policy. He noted that Jeffrey Sachs, a Harvard economist whom Allison had recruited to work on the Grand Bargain, had publicly suggested figures as high as $300 billion. Such an astronomical price tag would discredit not only Allison and Yavlinsky's plan but the prospect of any Western assistance at all. "You've got to avoid looking like you're holding out a tin cup," Zoellick told his visitors. Instead, Yavlinsky should strike the pose of a "patriot trying to save his country."

Yavlinsky replied that he had no desire to see the West write big checks to the Soviet Union, at least not right away: "Do not give us any money up front. You'd only be putting my children in debt. You have to use the *promise* of money *in the future* to make us do what we must do *now*."

*   *   *

Zoellick, Ross, and Hewett agreed on a strategy for the upcoming visit of the Kremlin delegation. Primakov might be the chairman, and Shcherbakov might be the representative of Pavlov's government, but the Americans should lose no opportunity to make it clear that Yavlinsky was the only member of the troika whose ideas the administration considered promising.

On Monday, May 27, Bush called Gorbachev to tell him he was looking forward to an "interesting week of talks" with the Primakov group. At Hewett's urging, Bush made a conspicuous point of mentioning Yavlinsky as someone he was especially eager to meet and hear from.

To reinforce that message, Zoellick sent a cable to Matlock in Moscow instructing him to tell Primakov in no uncertain terms that Yavlinsky's "active participation" was crucial to the mission's success.

Primakov had already made several attempts to exclude Yavlinsky in advance from some of the more important meetings in Washington. When Yavlinsky threatened to complain directly to Gorbachev, Primakov relented, though he and Shcherbakov continued to insist that since they alone represented the Soviet government, they should do most, if not all, of the talking.

Soon after arriving in Washington, Primakov took Hewett aside and said in a confidential tone, "You know, Ed, Yavlinsky works for me"; therefore Hewett should not be surprised if the young man was kept in the background.

Having anticipated this ploy, Hewett objected. He said he had been listening when Gorbachev emphasized to Bush on the telephone that Primakov and Yavlinsky were coming to Washington *together,* as equals. Primakov retorted that he had been listening on the Kremlin side, and Gorbachev had said no such thing.

The Americans expected Primakov to put in a formal request for Western aid, perhaps attached to an announcement of reform measures along the lines of those suggested in the Grand Bargain. Had the Soviets brought a proposal, the administration would have responded with nothing more than a promise to study the plan carefully.

But Primakov made no such request; in fact, he seemed more interested in refuting the impression that the Soviet Union was looking for handouts. He assumed a pose as the envoy of one superpower who wished to discuss with officials of the other superpower an issue that was equally vital to both sides.

In a private meeting with an interagency group of administration economic experts headed by Michael Boskin, chairman of Bush's Council of Economic Advisers, Primakov said, "We're not beggars. We're not on our knees. . . . We're here to exchange views. . . . We're all in this together. . . . You're always talking about interdependence. Well, here is a chance to prove that it exists."

Primakov's strategy was to convince the Bush administration of Gorbachev's seriousness about economic reform, with an eye to improving the chances of a favorable Western response to later specific Soviet requests for aid. The first of these requests would presumably come when Gorbachev made his case to the G-7 in London.

As it turned out, Primakov's mission had just the opposite effect. It revealed how contradictory and inadequate the central government's approach to the economy was — and how little cooperation there was between official managers, represented by Primakov and Shcherbakov, and more impatient reformers such as Yavlinsky.

The Americans bluntly told Primakov that they did not think much of Pavlov's "anticrisis plan." It suffered from the same fundamental flaw that had always afflicted the Soviet economy: centralized planning and control, with market mechanisms to be installed by government decree. Zoellick said, "You can't use command-administrative methods to introduce a market system. That just won't work." Then he called on Yavlinsky to give his views.

Yavlinsky made no secret of his own distaste for the plan: "Our purpose is not to support or adjust a failed system. It is to create a new one." He urged a "prompt and decisive break with regulated prices" and "aggressive privatization" of state property. Shcherbakov objected, saying, "Moving in a superradical way is unrealistic."

Primakov told the Americans, "What my two colleagues are saying differs only on questions of tactics, but the concept is the same." However, Yavlinsky's further interjections drew from Primakov angry looks and reminders that "Mr. Yavlinsky is under instructions from our president."

Finally, Primakov took Zoellick aside and said that Yavlinsky's views were not "representative of our government." He added that Pavlov's plan "isn't as bad as you think."

When Baker received the Soviet delegation, on Wednesday, May 29, he spelled out a number of modest, tentative steps that the administration was prepared to take to show that it sincerely wanted to encourage reform. "We have the potential to do more as we become convinced that you're serious about moving toward a market economy," he suggested.

Like the "basket of initiatives" that Bush had unwrapped with much fanfare for Gorbachev at Malta, the new American package contained mostly old ideas. Bush had been promising since the Washington summit a year before to waive the Jackson-Vanik Amendment and send a new trade agreement to Congress — but now here that proposal was again, a classic example of selling the same horse twice. The United States had already signaled its support for special associate status for the Soviets in the International Monetary Fund, but now Baker renewed that offer as well.

Baker said that a significant American private investment in the Soviet energy industry would have to await clarification on the relationship between the center and the republics. Congress was still unwilling to ratify the new trade agreement until the Soviet parliament cleared away remaining ambiguities in the emigration law.

Repeating an old refrain, Baker reminded Primakov that he was a former finance minister. His "real worry" about Pavlov's plan, he said, was that "it won't work, and you won't achieve good results." He echoed what Shevardnadze had said several days earlier about the Union treaty, asserting that if something like the Pavlov plan had been introduced two years before, "you might have had more than nine republics with you today." By now, such half measures had been overtaken by events.

Primakov responded with generalities: the "Nine-plus-One" agreement between Gorbachev and the leaders of the republics had created "favorable conditions" for "radical reform." Once there was a new Union treaty — Primakov predicted that it would be signed within weeks — the republics' rights and a significant degree of sovereignty would be assured, and "centrifugal forces will be replaced by centripetal ones."

He believed that once the republics recognized the benefits of maintaining a "single economic space," they would back away from their earlier demands and remain part of a Soviet commonwealth, bound to Moscow by a healthy and convertible ruble.

Hearing this, the Americans became more skeptical than ever. They knew that rather than being a single economic space, the Soviet Union was in fact a single economic disaster zone, deteriorating with every passing week. This was one of the principal reasons that so many of its subjects were trying to escape, either individually or collectively, as entire republics moved to secede. It was precisely the all-but-worthless ruble, as much as fear of the KGB and resentment of Kremlin domination, that was driving everyone away from the center.

Hewett saw not only a flaw in Primakov's logic but also a trap: the notion of a single economic space embraced not just the nine republics that were negotiating with Gorbachev on the new Union treaty but also the six that were intent on total secession — the Baltics, Georgia, Armenia, and Moldavia. He asked Primakov whether those six would be "free to leave."

Primakov said, "Yes, but there will have to be negotiations." He made it clear that these talks would be time-consuming. Also, he added ominously, the Kremlin would have its own claims to make against any republic that opted for secession.

Just as Hewett and the other Americans had suspected, Primakov's concept of a single economic space seemed to be part of a larger political strategy to prevent the breakup of the Union.

Baker spoke about the "political context" and the "political environment" in which the Bush administration would consider the question of aid. He was referring to U.S. domestic politics: unless the Soviet Union eased up on the Baltics and abandoned its support for Castro and its lavish defense spending, he said, it would be "unrealistic" to expect the American people and their representatives in Congress to endorse any steps to bolster the Soviet economy.

On Friday morning, May 31, Bush received Primakov, Shcherbakov, and Yavlinsky in the Oval Office. Predictably, Primakov and Shcherbakov had tried to cut Yavlinsky out of the meeting, but the White House had insisted on his inclusion.

The president began by repeating his desire to see the West "engage" with the Soviet economy, and his hope that the United States could find a way to be "supportive of real reform."

Prompted in advance by Hewett, Bush made a point of addressing Yavlinsky and asking for his views. Yavlinsky reviewed the case for immediate, sweeping price reform and privatization.

Glowering, Primakov said that Yavlinsky's recommendations were "too radical." He later told Bush that Yavlinsky was a "smart young man" with "interesting views," but "not always practical." He stressed that he alone spoke for Gorbachev.

At the end of the morning, Bush held a photo opportunity in the

Rose Garden with championship swimmers from the University of Texas. When reporters asked about the Soviet economic mission, Bush tried to be both nebulous and gracious: "I liked what I heard," he said. He added that he had the impression that the Soviets were "undertaking what for them is — what the world will see is — radical economic reforms."

Primakov was delighted. Despite the qualification, this was just the sort of presidential endorsement he had been looking for. Allison and Yavlinsky, meanwhile, were aghast. They felt that Bush's public comments had undermined their weeklong closed-door effort to nudge the Soviets away from Pavlov's plan and toward something like the Grand Bargain.

Actually, the week had merely reduced the administration's already limited interest in the Grand Bargain. The ill-disguised tensions between Yavlinsky and the other Soviet visitors heightened suspicions among Zoellick, Ross, Hewett, and Boskin that Yavlinsky had little standing where it counted back in Moscow. The Grand Bargain, whatever its conceptual merits, lacked the necessary political backing on the Soviet side to make it interesting to Washington.

In any event, Bush was not eager to commit the United States to giving large-scale financial assistance to the Soviet Union, and the Primakov mission, he felt, provided him with a splendid new reason not to do so. He told Scowcroft, "These guys really don't have their ducks in a row, do they?"

At the beginning of June, flying to Budapest, the first stop on a tour of Eastern Europe, Dan Quayle granted an interview to four reporters who were accompanying him on *Air Force Two*.

Quayle dismissed as a "nonstarter" any plan that entailed direct cash assistance to the Soviet Union. He said that the Bush administration would not subsidize an "inefficient, bankrupt economic system": "Until the Soviet Union makes some of the systematic reforms that are necessary, you can put as much money as you want in there, but it's not going to help." He singled out the Yavlinsky-Allison plan for particular scorn: "Harvard has got more ideas out there than there are problems."

Published in the *Washington Post* on Wednesday, June 5, the Quayle interview reflected what high administration officials were saying in private. But it also shattered Bush and Baker's public efforts to keep up the appearance of a U.S. government that generally supported Gorbachev, had an open mind about how the West might encourage reform, and was willing to consider aid to the Soviet Union — so long as the American position was expressed in the future tense and the conditional mood.

On the same day that Quayle's remarks appeared in the *Post,* Gorbachev appealed almost desperately for Western help in his Nobel Peace Prize lecture in Oslo: "If *perestroika* fails," he said, "the prospect of entering a new peaceful period of history will vanish, at least for the foreseeable future." He added that the Soviet Union had the "right to count on large-scale assistance to assure its success."

At the White House, Bush told Baker, Scowcroft, Gates, and Treasury Secretary Nicholas Brady that the Primakov mission had confirmed his impression that the idea of providing large-scale financial assistance to the Soviet Union was a "loser," until and unless the Kremlin committed itself unambiguously to sweeping reform.

However, he said, "I still don't want to appear to be slamming the door in Gorbachev's face," since that would only embolden Soviet hard-liners, damage the fragile entente between Gorbachev and Yeltsin, and cause European leaders to complain that Washington was being intransigent.

The president said he could easily imagine Gorbachev's showing up at that summer's G-7 meeting in London with a "half-baked reform plan like the one Primakov brought here." Convinced that such an approach would "just guarantee a rejection," he opposed Gorbachev's being invited to London — for Gorbachev's own good, he insisted.

But Gorbachev himself had meanwhile been lobbying Kohl and Mitterrand, and in turn they prodded Bush and the new British prime minister, John Major, to let the Soviet leader come to London as a sign of Western support for him and his program. The G-7 leaders worked out protocol for the meeting to minimize the impression that Gorbachev was attending the summit as anything other than a guest.

On Wednesday, June 12, Boris Yeltsin was elected president of Russia by 57 percent of the eighty million votes cast. For the first time in its history, Russia had a democratically elected leader.*

* Gorbachev's choice, former Prime Minister Ryzhkov, won only 17 percent. Vladimir Zhirinovsky, an extreme nationalist with pronounced neofascistic views, won 7 percent. The champion of the hard-line Communists, General Albert Makashov, and Gorbachev's old interior minister, Vadim Bakatin, together won less than 4 percent.

Yeltsin announced that he would visit the United States in late June. The Soviet Foreign Ministry issued a statement saying that there was "no reason" to interpret Yeltsin's U.S. trip as a challenge to the Gorbachev government; rather, it should serve to strengthen U.S.-Soviet ties.

When Yeltsin's foreign minister, Andrei Kozyrev, traveled to Washington to prepare for the trip, Ed Hewett privately warned him that while in the United States Yeltsin must do "nothing to hurt Gorbachev." If he created the impression that the Bush administration was undermining the Soviet president, "it won't be a great visit."

CHAPTER 19

"We're Counting on You"

ON MONDAY, June 17, 1991, Prime Minister Pavlov addressed the Supreme Soviet. He strongly suggested that the Grand Bargain was part of a conspiracy to sell out the motherland to foreign interests: "I know a few gentlemen from Harvard University. They do not know our way of life. We can hardly expect them to explain everything to us."

Pavlov said that under the Harvard plan, the Soviet Union would have to "stand in line with Israel and Nicaragua." He declared, "Whoever wants to do that is welcome to, but not me!"*

In his own address to the parliament, Vladimir Kryuchkov of the KGB portrayed the Grand Bargain as part of a vast Western plot to destabilize the Soviet Union. "Among the conditions," he noted, "is the implementation of fundamental reforms in the country, not as they are envisioned by us but as they are dreamed up across the ocean."

---

* Pavlov's comments sounded eerily like George Bush's criticism of Michael Dukakis in his acceptance speech at the 1988 Republican National Convention: "He sees America as another pleasant country on the UN roll call, somewhere between Albania and Zimbabwe." During the campaign, Bush also accused Dukakis of getting his ideas on government from a "Harvard Yard boutique."

Pavlov indicated to the deputies that after six years of exertion, Gorbachev was in failing health. He called on them to transfer much of Gorbachev's presidential authority, especially in the economic sphere, to him: "The president's working day is fourteen hours long. If we load him up with everything, he simply won't be able to deal with it all — even if there were forty-eight hours in his day!"

The hard-line Soyuz (Union) leader, Colonel Viktor Alksnis, agreed that Pavlov's proposed measures were needed for the "preservation of our present state."

Kryuchkov, Pugo, and Defense Minister Yazov all accused Gorbachev of deliberately neglecting his constitutional duty to defend the country against the capitalist West. Kryuchkov charged that Western intelligence services had for years been buying influence among Soviet liberal intellectuals and political reformers, paying huge sums of hard currency for articles, interviews, books, and lecture tours. Shevardnadze and Yeltsin, he said, had taken particular advantage of this practice.

The KGB chief further claimed that "sleeper agents" planted by the CIA in the 1970s now held important positions in the Kremlin, where they stood poised to fulfill the plans of their Western masters, "aimed at the breakup of Soviet society and the disruption of the socialist economy." The Western powers were preparing to "demilitarize and even occupy" the Soviet Union.

Kryuchkov said he had shown KGB evidence of this conspiracy to Gorbachev, but the Soviet leader had refused to consider it. Just as Stalin had ignored warnings of an imminent Nazi attack in June 1941, Gorbachev was turning a blind eye to the Western threat fifty years later, and in so doing endangering the Soviet Union.

Emerging from a closed-door session, several liberal deputies described what was happening as a "constitutional coup d'état."

During the Supreme Soviet session, Shevardnadze saw several American visitors at his new foreign policy think tank, quartered in what had until recently been the embassy of Chad.* He blamed the United States for fanning the flames of the "constitutional coup": many U.S. officials — particularly in Congress, he claimed, but Baker, too — had been "provocatively" trying to link Western aid to further Soviet foreign, domestic, and defense concessions.

---

* The Americans were part of a delegation from the Aspen Institute for Humanistic Studies, led by Dick Clark, a former Democratic senator from Iowa.

"Just as I had feared," Shevardnadze said, "such pressure tactics have played into the hands of those who have the power to get rid of democracy, which is still young and fragile in this country. If you say, 'Let the Baltics go and we'll give you fifty billion dollars,' the reactionary forces and the military will say, 'That's it! Let's finish with this whole political experiment!' "

Shevardnadze said he could well imagine Pavlov's persuading the Supreme Soviet to grant him "emergency powers." Then Kryuchkov, Pugo, and Yazov would use their troops to dissolve the parliament. "If you persist in trying to impose conditions," the former foreign minister told the Americans, "the reactionaries will sweep us aside. You'll find yourselves dealing with some beastly dictator, and you'll end up spending a lot more on defense than what Gorbachev is asking you for now."

Jack Matlock felt that Pavlov's "constitutional coup" proved how vulnerable Gorbachev had actually become: the only politician in the country who had a wide base of popular support was Boris Yeltsin.

Yeltsin was now in Washington. Matlock told his aides, "The timing can't be an accident. It's like that great tradition in the Third World: the plotters make their move when the number one guy is off on a trip somewhere. Only in this case, it's Yeltsin who they want to make sure is out of town."[*]

Matlock went to the Kremlin and asked Anatoli Chernyayev, "What do you think about the drift of things? Don't the opponents of reform seem to be pressing their case awfully vigorously? Might they be preparing to take unconstitutional measures?"

Chernyayev was unconcerned about a possible coup. He dismissed as "ludicrous" the idea that a faceless apparatchik like Pavlov would challenge a master politician like Gorbachev. Matlock persisted, saying he was disturbed by rumors that Kryuchkov and Yazov and their battalions were behind the intrigue.

"Don't worry," Chernyayev assured him. "The situation is fully under control."

On Thursday morning, June 20, the reform mayor of Moscow, Gavril Popov, sent word to Matlock that he must see him privately right away.

Highly agitated, Popov rushed over to Spaso House. After he and

* In fact, this method of coup d'état was not limited to the Third World: in 1957, Nikita Khrushchev had nearly been overthrown by hard-liners while on a visit to Helsinki.

Matlock sat down, Popov pointed to the ceiling and made a scribbling gesture. This was a signal familiar to all experienced westerners in Moscow: the mayor wished to say something important on a sensitive subject and was concerned that their conversation was being bugged by the KGB.

Matlock pulled a small spiral-bound notebook from his pocket. While the two men carried on an innocuous-sounding conversation, Popov wrote out his message: Matlock must immediately warn Yeltsin that there was to be an attempt the next day to oust Gorbachev and transfer governing powers to Pavlov.

This was all Popov wrote. He trusted Matlock to fill in the blanks: since Yeltsin was the leader of the democratic forces that could be expected to oppose such a coup, it was imperative that he abort his visit to Washington and rush back to Moscow to help thwart the hard-liners. Popov wanted Yeltsin to know that the warning had come from him; otherwise, he might not take it seriously.

Matlock scrawled out a question: who besides Pavlov was involved?

Popov's answer: Kryuchkov, Yazov, and Lukyanov. Matlock was not at all surprised by the first two names and only slightly taken aback by the third. Lukyanov was Gorbachev's old friend and law school classmate, but it had been rumored for months that he was playing a double game against the Soviet leader.

Popov crumpled up the sheets of paper and pocketed them. Standing up, he shook Matlock's hand vigorously and, before leaving, said in a near whisper, "We're counting on you!"

Matlock scribbled out an account of what had happened and summoned his deputy, James Collins, who took the piece of paper back to the embassy. Using a system called STU-3, the most secure telephone circuit available, Collins relayed Popov's warning to Lawrence Eagleburger, who was in charge of the State Department while Baker was in Berlin at a meeting of foreign ministers.

Eagleburger told Collins to put his report in writing and send it by NODIS — "no distribution" — cable to Washington. Then he hurried off to the White House to break the news to Bush and Scowcroft.

In the meantime, the operations center at State flashed a copy of Collins's cable to Baker in Berlin. At that moment, Baker and Bessmertnykh were concluding a joint press conference in the garden of the U.S. ambassador's residence.

As Bessmertnykh was leaving, Dennis Ross read the cable, then pulled Baker aside and showed it to him. Baker and Ross agreed that Popov's warning must be taken seriously: the mayor was close to reformist elements in the military, the party, and the KGB, and his prediction dovetailed with what had happened in the Supreme Soviet earlier in the week.

The U.S. government was in a tricky position. It was obliged to honor Popov's request and pass the warning on to Yeltsin, but it had better also alert Gorbachev directly. Otherwise, the United States would be in the position of passing messages behind Gorbachev's back between two of his critics about a matter of supreme concern to him. It would seem as if in a moment of crisis, Bush had simply thrown in his lot with the Yeltsin camp and then sat idly by as Gorbachev collapsed.

This raised the question of how they should notify Gorbachev. A telephone call from Bush would be dangerous since the KGB presumably eavesdropped on all conversations between the Kremlin and the White House. Baker decided instead to send a message to Gorbachev through Bessmertnykh. He was acting on the assumption that the foreign minister would be outraged by the notion of a right-wing coup and would pass the word discreetly to the Soviet president.

Baker returned to his quarters at the Inter-Continental Hotel to call Bush on a secure telephone link. Already briefed by Eagleburger about the planned coup, Bush shared Baker's concern that Gorbachev not be bypassed. He had asked Eagleburger to have Matlock inform Gorbachev about Popov's warning in person.

After speaking with the president, Baker telephoned Bessmertnykh. "I have something important to tell you," he said. "I want to do this in person. Can you come by in a few minutes?"

At first, Bessmertnykh resisted, presuming that Baker merely wished to discuss some detail he had forgotten about during their earlier conversation. He said, "Jim, I've got an appointment with the foreign minister of Cyprus in a few minutes. Can't this wait?"

Baker replied, "Sasha, I really think this is necessary. It's something quite new and important."

"Could I send someone else over to your place?"

"No, Sasha, it has to be you. And it should be very discreet."

To avoid attracting attention, Bessmertnykh left his bodyguards behind and took a regular Soviet embassy car rather than his ministerial limousine. An elevator was being held for him at the Inter-Continental, ready to whisk him up to Baker's suite, where the two men met alone for five minutes.

Baker told Bessmertnykh that the U.S. government had "picked up" information from a source it considered "reliable" that conservatives were about to attempt a coup against Gorbachev. All the U.S. officials handling the matter had agreed not to name Popov as their source in any conversations with those close to Gorbachev or with Gorbachev himself.

Baker went on, "We're in no position to vouch for the information, but it's so important that we thought you should know it. I leave it to you to decide what to do with it." Matlock had already requested an appointment to inform Gorbachev in Moscow, he said, "but we want to make sure there are two channels."

Bessmertnykh thanked Baker and bustled off, promising, "I'll communicate this right away." Knowing that the KGB could tap any call he made to Gorbachev, Bessmertnykh resolved to pass on the message in a more oblique way. From the Soviet embassy in Berlin, he telephoned Chernyayev at the Kremlin and said, "Matlock will request an appointment with Mikhail Sergeyevich. Please get him in right away."

"Matlock has just arrived," said Chernyayev. "What's this all about?"

"Listen to what he says. You know I'm in Berlin, where I just had a talk with Baker. That's all I can say."

It was Thursday evening in Moscow when Chernyayev ushered Matlock into Gorbachev's office. The Soviet president was about to be driven to his dacha.

Matlock told Gorbachev that he was under instructions from Washington to convey a "report that President Bush feels merits your attention": it was "more than rumor, although we cannot confirm it." Matlock conveyed the essence of Popov's information, without making any reference to Popov as the source and without actually naming the four men he had identified as the plotters.

Gorbachev thanked Matlock for the message but made it clear that he thought American concerns about his political survival were excessive. He conceded that some of his colleagues, especially Pavlov, had been engaged in "certain maneuverings" in the Supreme Soviet. Pavlov, while a "good economist," was "inexperienced" in politics; Gorbachev seemed amused at the notion that anyone in the Soviet government could overthrow him. But he asked Matlock to thank Bush for the "friendly gesture" and to assure him that he "need not worry."

Matlock cabled Washington, noting that nothing in Gorbachev's voice had suggested any anxiety.

By now it was Thursday afternoon in Washington. At three o'clock, Yeltsin's car pulled up to the White House. Two years before, Condoleezza Rice had met him at a side entrance and slipped him in through the basement; this time it was Bush who welcomed the Russian president, in a Rose Garden ceremony.

Despite all that had happened during the previous six months as a consequence of Gorbachev's lurch to the right, and despite the powerful new evidence of Yeltsin's emergence as a champion of democratic ideals and free markets, Bush still stuck by Gorbachev. It made little difference that he could no longer cite the excuse of the war in the Persian Gulf and the need to keep the Soviet Union on board the coalition.

Stepping up to the lectern to welcome the Russian leader, Bush mentioned Gorbachev's name more often and more favorably than Yeltsin's own. He said that no one should forget that it was Gorbachev's "courageous policies of *glasnost* and *perestroika*" that had made possible the end of the Cold War. "I want to be very clear about this," Bush concluded. "The United States will continue to maintain the closest possible official relationship with the Soviet government of President Gorbachev."

When Bush took Yeltsin into the Oval Office, he told him about Popov's warning. Yeltsin was not greatly alarmed, but he suggested that they should put in a call to Gorbachev and alert him to the danger.

This suggestion pleased Bush since it freed him of the awkward duty of acting as an intermediary. He ordered a call to be put through to the Kremlin, but by then it was too late in Moscow to reach Gorbachev.

After saying good-bye to Bush, Yeltsin acidly told an aide, "He certainly seemed eager to get on the phone with his friend." He went on to comment that Bush still seemed to be "under the illusion" that everything depended on his personal relationship with Gorbachev. He compared Bush to one of the many gullible religious believers in Russia who had fallen under the influence of a famous and popular television faith healer named Anatoli Kashpirovsky.

As he emerged from the West Wing, Yeltsin spoke with reporters. Conceding that "we still have forces back home that want to go back to the era of stagnation," he vowed that Russia would "not allow any reversal of the course of history." As for Gorbachev's efforts to hold the USSR together, Yeltsin said, "There is no way for one man to preserve the Soviet Union."

In off-the-record remarks at a reception at the Soviet embassy, Yeltsin proclaimed the "end of the Marxist experiment in Russia."

The next day, Friday, June 28, Gorbachev was in good form. Having been absent from the meetings of the Supreme Soviet earlier in the week, he now swept into the hall and delivered a rhetorical broadside against his critics. The parliament struck down Pavlov's "constitutional coup" by a vote of 262 to 24.

Speaking to reporters afterward, Gorbachev made sure that he was flanked by Yazov, Kryuchkov, and Pugo, who were grim and silent. With a large grin, the Soviet leader pronounced his verdict on the week: "The 'coup' is over."

That day, Bush finally reached Gorbachev on the telephone to report on his meeting with Yeltsin. He began the conversation by saying that he hoped all was well after the "trouble" Gorbachev had apparently been having with some of his colleagues. So eager was Bush to convey the openness and trust that were the hallmarks of his relations with Gorbachev that he accidentally let slip that the source of the warning had been Popov.

Gorbachev was anxious to dispose of the matter so that Bush would not let the episode affect his opinion about Gorbachev's prospects. He thanked Bush for his interest and gloated that he had given his foes a "good thrashing." Quickly he turned to a more acute concern: how had Bush's meeting with Yeltsin gone?

In fact, on this visit Yeltsin had impressed Bush with his gravity and his determination to bring democracy to Russia. But on the telephone with Gorbachev, Bush was careful not to sound too enthusiastic.

The next day, Saturday, June 22, Bessmertnykh returned to Moscow from Berlin and caught up with Gorbachev during a ceremony at the Tomb of the Unknown Soldier, next to the Kremlin Wall. He asked for a few minutes alone "to report on my trip to Berlin."

The two men walked back to Gorbachev's office together, but they confined their conversation to pleasantries since Pavlov was walking nearby. Once his office door was closed, however, Gorbachev told Bessmertnykh that he appreciated Bush's handling of the rumor; the U.S. president had been "considerate and sensitive."

Nevertheless, Gorbachev said he hoped Bush would be "very careful" not to let Yeltsin exploit his new access to the Oval Office as he maneuvered against the Kremlin.

Gorbachev noted that Bush had mentioned that Mayor Popov was the source of the warning. Popov's secret approach to Yeltsin through the Americans seemed to bother Gorbachev as much as the possibility that Prime Minister Pavlov had actually been plotting against him.

Several weeks later, when Gorbachev encountered Popov at a reception, he took him aside and demanded, "What did you call Bush for?"

Popov replied, "I *didn't* call him! You must be misinformed."

This was literally true, since Popov had conveyed the warning to Matlock, not to Bush directly. But he was furious at the Americans for identifying him as the source of the message. Popov concluded that in giving priority to his friendship with Gorbachev, Bush had endangered genuine Soviet reformers who were trying to avert political catastrophe.

Believing that he had whipped Pavlov and the conservatives into line, Gorbachev now returned his attention to the G-7 summit to be held in London in mid-July. He was more desperate than ever to elicit a vote of confidence from the leaders of the Western democracies.

Knowing that Yavlinsky was far more respected in the West than anyone in Pavlov's cabinet, Gorbachev decided to give the young economist a prominent place in his official delegation to the G-7 summit coming up in London. During a briefing for the Moscow press corps, Gorbachev's spokesman, Vitali Ignatenko, announced that the "Primakov-Yavlinsky Plan" would be the basis of Gorbachev's presentation to Bush, Kohl, and the other G-7 leaders.

On Saturday, June 22, Primakov and Yavlinsky met with Gorbachev and Chernyayev to review the latest iteration of the plan, which called for a Western promise to assist the USSR in exchange for a Soviet pledge to accelerate reforms. The following Tuesday, Gorbachev summoned them back to the Kremlin for yet another meeting, this one also attended by Graham Allison.

The Soviet president lavished praise on their "masterpiece" of "intellectual brainstorming." It was the "best report I've seen" and would be "invaluable" to him in preparing his presentation for London. He told Yavlinsky that he was ready to accept "90 percent" of the plan.

Flying on a Boeing 727 borrowed from Ann Getty, a generous donor to Harvard's Kennedy School of Government, Allison and Yavlinsky toured Europe to promote their plan in advance of the G-7 summit. European and Japanese officials listened politely but were as skeptical as ever about Gorbachev's commitment to making profound changes in his economy. In fact, Yavlinsky himself remained skeptical; he knew that Gorbachev was exploiting him to advance the idea of economic aid for the Soviet Union.

When Gorbachev sent him a draft of a letter that Primakov and Chernyayev had written for him to send to the G-7 leaders, Yavlinsky found it a bitter disappointment — full of generalities, a rationalization for more half measures, more in keeping with Pavlov's "anticrisis plan" than with the Grand Bargain. He sent word to Gorbachev that he would not go to London only to be used again the way Primakov had used him in Washington in May.

Both Bush and Gorbachev were still eager to complete a START treaty so they could hold a summit in Moscow that summer. In early June, Baker suggested to Bush that the remaining issues on START might best be resolved through the device that had worked so well for CFE — a correspondence at the highest level, between the two presidents.

This would lift the negotiations over the heads of the Soviet military — and perhaps, Baker quietly hoped, over the head of Scowcroft, who was still holding out against any American flexibility on the issue of "downloading" warheads from existing missiles. The most that Scowcroft was ready to concede on this point was the possibility that the United States might accept a more lenient provision in the future.

On Thursday, June 6, Bush included a suggestion to this effect in a letter to Gorbachev, which Baker delivered to Bessmertnykh in Geneva. The foreign minister told Baker that he did not believe they were moving fast enough on START to have a treaty — and therefore a Moscow summit — by the end of June. They had better begin thinking about late July instead.

Replying to Bush's letter, Gorbachev held out for the right to download three types of missiles per side, rather than the one per side that Scowcroft was insisting on. But in keeping with a proposal that Richard Burt had made in Geneva earlier in the year, he tried to make the Soviet position more palatable by offering to reduce by half the number of warheads that could be removed by downloading.

Most U.S. analysts continued to feel that a low warhead total was a more useful and more relevant "currency" for downloading than the number of missile types, so they thought this an important concession. But Scowcroft held his ground.

At the White House, even some of Scowcroft's own aides joked about his intransigence. Arnold Kanter said, "Desert Storm must have gone to your head, Brent. You're in the habit of achieving total victory on every issue in every negotiation." Other members of the NSC staff fantasized about kidnapping Scowcroft and holding him incommunicado for a few days — just long enough to secure Bush's approval for the necessary compromise.

When Bessmertnykh saw Baker in Berlin on Thursday, June 20, he said, "My president is trying to be responsive to your president. We're looking for a similar approach on your side, but we're not seeing much."

In Geneva on Wednesday, June 26, the Un-Group met with a Soviet team led by Bessmertnykh's deputy for arms control issues, Alexei Obukhov. Bush had assured Gorbachev that Reginald Bartholomew, who chaired the Un-Group when it served as a bargaining team, would have wide latitude to deal on the spot. Gorbachev had said the same was true of Obukhov.

But in fact, the Americans were struck yet again by how little freedom the Soviet diplomats had to negotiate. Obukhov was accompanied by Lieutenant-General Fyodor Ladygin, chief of the Treaty and Legal Directorate of the Soviet General Staff, who clearly had the final say on any concessions that were to be made. There was small progress on some issues, but none at all on downloading.

On Friday, July 5, Bush wrote Gorbachev to urge one last effort by Baker and Bessmertnykh in Washington to surmount the final hurdles in START. While drafting the letter, Baker and Ross had discussed the best way to get Moiseyev to come. They reasoned that no deal would be possible unless he was in on it and unable to complain about it later.

Bush's final letter made it clear to Gorbachev that Bessmertnykh should attend the talks only if he was truly empowered to bring the negotiations to a conclusion. Following the script he had used in CFE, the U.S. president suggested that Bessmertnykh bring with him the top "experts" on the Soviet side — an unmistakable hint that Moiseyev be included in the delegation. Two days later, Gorbachev agreed.

When Bessmertnykh arrived in Washington with Moiseyev, he at first tried to withhold Soviet consent on all other outstanding issues until the United States caved in on downloading. Instead, Baker persuaded him to allow the negotiators to close on as many questions as possible: "You don't need to worry about us pocketing concessions," he promised. "We recognize that nothing's agreed until everything's agreed."

*   *   *

By now the Un-Group was in the position of mediating between two generals — Scowcroft and Moiseyev. Scowcroft considered downloading a matter of overriding strategic importance: the "good" Soviets who were now willing to sign a START treaty must not be allowed to bequeath to some future "bad" Soviets the chance to reload missiles with warheads that had been downloaded under the terms of START.

For his part, Moiseyev saw lenient downloading rules as an economic and practical necessity. The Americans had already figured out that he must be especially concerned about two missile systems that were still in top-secret development in the Soviet Union but whose existence had been deduced by U.S. intelligence.

The Un-Group devised a scheme that would loosen the restriction on new types of missiles and thereby allow the two secret programs to continue; the U.S. negotiators hoped that in return, Moiseyev might agree to Scowcroft's tough position on downloading.

On Friday, July 12, when Baker floated the idea, Bessmertnykh pronounced it "interesting" and Moiseyev said he would like to "study it more closely." The Un-Group put the proposal on paper and sent it to the Soviet embassy.

The Soviet experts did not like it; Obukhov went so far as to call it a "trick" to "get us to accept the essence of their position." The Soviets were all the more annoyed because they now realized that U.S. espionage had penetrated their veil of military secrecy and obtained key information on their new missile systems. Obukhov said to several of his colleagues, "You know what this proposal means? It means the Americans know something they shouldn't know."

On Saturday morning, in a conference room near Baker's office, Bessmertnykh and Moiseyev reminded Baker that it had been agreed long before that neither side would "seek unilateral advantage" over the other. Echoing Obukhov's pronouncement, they labeled the latest American proposal a "cheap trick."

Baker rejected the Soviet accusation. He and his colleagues had made a good-faith effort to break the impasse, he said; all the Soviets had to do was say that the proposal did not meet their needs.

He then took Bessmertnykh into his office for a private talk. The foreign minister told him that the American compromise was mere "craftiness": "You presented what you wanted us to believe was a softening of your position, but there were thorns in the softness." Then his tone shifted. He almost pleaded for American concessions: "You must understand, Jim, there are certain limits in my freedom to maneuver."

Baker telephoned Bush and Scowcroft, who were spending the weekend in Kennebunkport. A conference call was arranged so that Cheney and Powell could join in. Baker said he had tried to get the Soviets to accept Scowcroft's position on downloading, but added that there was no longer any point in "trying to squeeze every last drop of blood out of this stone."

He proposed that the Soviets be allowed to download three types of missiles, provided that the number of warheads involved was significantly limited. Baker maintained that this solution ought to be acceptable: all the technical experts agreed that the number of warheads, not the number of types of missiles, constituted the "measure of merit where downloading is concerned."

Cheney and Powell consented. Knowing he was beaten, Scowcroft withdrew his objections. Bush said, "Well, it sounds like we've finally wrapped this thing up."*

In fact, one problem remained. If the devil was in the details of nuclear arms control, this was nowhere more true than in the final detail of START.

CIA and Pentagon experts believed that the Soviet SS-25 single-warhead mobile ICBM was capable of carrying extra warheads. The Soviets denied this. To settle the question, the Americans wished to monitor a test of a new version of the SS-25 over a longer range than was used for other ICBMs.[†] Baker and Bessmertnykh relegated this arcane matter to their specialists, who promptly dug in their heels.

Bush and Gorbachev were scheduled to have a private lunch together in London on Wednesday, July 17. Shortly before leaving Moscow, Gorbachev told Bessmertnykh and his military advisers that he did not want to have to do any actual negotiating on START during his meeting with

---

* In the final treaty, the Soviets were permitted to download the SS-N-18 plus two additional unspecified types of missiles, so long as the total number of warheads affected was no more than 1,250, of which no more than 500 could be mounted on the two additional types.

† At issue here was another U.S. worry about breakout. The SS-25 was a three-stage intercontinental version of the SS-20 intermediate-range missile. Since the SS-20 had three warheads, U.S. experts were concerned that it would be relatively easy for the Soviets to "upload" the SS-25 by taking advantage of what they believed to be its excess throw-weight potential. To establish whether the SS-25 did indeed have extra throw-weight capacity, the United States wanted the SS-25 successor tested at 11,000 kilometers. The Soviets retorted that the 10,000 kilometers used for other ICBMs was adequate.

Bush, lest it appear that he was selling out Soviet military interests for whatever financial aid the West might care to offer. Accordingly, he wanted the problem of the SS-25 test solved before he saw Bush. But up until the time he left, the Soviet military-industrial complex was still refusing to meet the Americans' demand.

On the morning of the day Gorbachev was to meet with Bush, Moiseyev and Yazov were still trying to persuade senior experts to accept the American position. At the Soviet embassy in London, Bessmertnykh paced the floor and looked at his watch. With the Bush-Gorbachev luncheon only an hour away, he finally called Moscow and asked Moiseyev and Yazov, "What the hell are you guys doing there? We must have an answer!"

Thirty minutes later, Moiseyev and Yazov notified him that their colleagues had at last capitulated. Bessmertnykh informed Gorbachev, "We've just managed to squeeze what we need out of our people." Gorbachev replied, "Good. Go explain it to the Americans."

Bush, Baker, and Scowcroft were waiting for the Soviets at Winfield House, the splendid U.S. residence donated after World War II by the Woolworth heiress Barbara Hutton. Bessmertnykh rushed there and announced, "This is the end of a ten-year-long journey, Mr. President."

Bush turned to Baker: "Are we really there, Jim?" Baker answered, "Yes, I think so." But Scowcroft said, "Let's check with Washington." The text of the treaty language to which the Soviets had agreed was sent to the White House. After a telephone poll of the Un-Group, Arnold Kanter cabled an approval to London exactly two minutes before Gorbachev's ZIL limousine pulled up the gravel driveway in front of Winfield House.

Emerging from his car, Gorbachev glanced down at his blue suit. Seeing that the jacket was wrinkled, he gave it a tug. He squared his shoulders, took a deep breath, and strode forward to shake Bush's hand.

The international press had written that Gorbachev was coming to London "hat in hand" and with a "begging bowl," looking for large-scale Western assistance; the "Communist pauper" meant to throw himself on the charity of the "princes of capitalism." Gorbachev detested these images, no doubt in part because they contained such a large measure of truth.

Over the preceding months, Bush had tried to caution the Soviet president not to expect large-scale financial assistance, whether in the form of a hard-currency fund to help stabilize the ruble, a rescheduling of the Soviet Union's foreign debt, or loans for the purchase of consumer goods. In a letter he wrote to Gorbachev in early July, Bush had tried to make it clear that help would be limited to technical assistance in the distribution of food, defense conversion, and energy conservation.

In Washington, Ed Hewett had underscored this message to Andrei Kokoshin, deputy director of the USA-Canada Institute, who was helping to prepare Gorbachev for the G-7 meeting. "Whatever you do, Andrei," he advised, "don't ask for money up front as a down-payment on reform. Think of reform as a precondition for greater Western participation in your economy later on."

On the eve of his departure for London, Gorbachev had told several of his aides that he wondered why he was making the trip at all; he had no intention of being "humiliated" or "lectured to like a schoolboy."

When Gorbachev lunched with Bush at Winfield House, he immediately went on the offensive. The most important issue, he said, was "what kind of Soviet Union you want to see in the future." He and his advisers had long since agreed that it was in the long-term interest of the Soviet Union for the United States to be healthy and prosperous — "but it's not clear that you want the same for us," he said pointedly.

Bush replied, "I'm sorry that's unclear." He said there should be no doubt that the United States wanted to see a "democratic, market-oriented Soviet Union."

In his meetings with the other G-7 leaders, Gorbachev heard much the same thing: he had the West's good wishes, but these would not translate into actual money to shore up the ruble and permit the Soviet Union to stock its shelves with consumer goods. He left London feeling patronized and rebuffed.

Soon after the G-7 summit, Scowcroft told Bush, "Gorbachev came to collect what he obviously felt was his due, but he never really made his case. It's almost as though he doesn't recognize the severity of the problems, which might explain why he doesn't acknowledge the need for really drastic solutions."

The president sadly agreed: "The guy kind of bombed, didn't he? It's funny. He's always been his own best salesman, but not this time. I wonder if he isn't kind of out of touch."

By dispensing with the last obstacle in START, Bush and Gorbachev had cleared the way for a Moscow summit at which the treaty could be signed. Bush was eager to get the meeting out of the way before he took his annual August vacation in Kennebunkport. Thus, the summit was quickly scheduled for the last two days in July.

The real test of Bush's statesmanship in this instance would lie in his response to the changes sweeping the fifteen republics of the USSR. The Moscow summit would be his first visit to the Soviet Union as president, and for months, U.S. officials had been arguing that he should visit the capital of an outlying republic as well.

Bush himself was ambivalent about the idea. As he privately said, he was still convinced that the "complete, sudden bust-up" of the Soviet Union would be in no one's interest. He could understand and even endorse further diffusion of responsibility and authority from Moscow to the republics, but he hoped that "some kind of Union" would survive. The best format for this, he thought, would be the loose federal structure that Gorbachev seemed committed to achieving under his new Union treaty.

At the same time, largely because of his reluctance to embrace Baltic independence earlier in the year, Bush was under domestic political attack for siding with Gorbachev and the center against the forces of self-determination. With the start of a presidential election year only five months away, his advisers wanted him to blunt that charge by making a "gesture" toward the republics.

As the capital of the largest non-Russian republic, Kiev was the most obvious candidate for a stopover after Moscow. In May 1972, after his own first presidential visit to Moscow, Richard Nixon had gone there for a day. But Ukraine was then an obedient province of the Soviet empire; now, nineteen years later, it was well on its way to secession.

During a discussion of the Kiev stop, Bush told Baker, Scowcroft, and Sununu, "Whatever we do, I don't want to make trouble for Gorbachev, so let's handle it with that in mind."

When State Department planners advised the Soviets of Bush's wish to visit Kiev, they soft-pedaled it, comparing the trip to the brief stops Gorbachev had made in Minneapolis and San Francisco in 1990. The Foreign Ministry informed Matlock that there would be no problem with such a visit.

Then in Washington, on Friday, July 19, Sergei Chetverikov of the Soviet embassy called Ed Hewett with an "urgent message" from Moscow: since Bush was interested in spending a day outside of Moscow, perhaps he would agree to come to Stavropol and spend some time in the lovely mountain resort, as Kohl had done the previous summer —

or perhaps the two presidents and their wives could relax, Camp David–style, in the informal surroundings of Gorbachev's dacha.

Chetverikov said he knew that "at the working level," the Americans had been thinking about going to Ukraine. But this was "not such a good idea," he confided; tensions were high at the moment, and a visit by Bush to Kiev would be "hardly practical." Later, Chetverikov brought a teletype printout of this message to the White House.

The exact origins of this last-minute appeal for Bush to drop Kiev from his itinerary were unclear. The message was not addressed directly to Bush, nor was it signed by Gorbachev. Still, Chetverikov told Hewett that he should consider it a "presidential message."*

Hewett relayed it to Scowcroft, who at that moment was flying with Bush to Turkey. He and the president worked out a reply stating that they did not wish to exacerbate the growing strains between the Kremlin and Ukraine. If the Soviet government insisted, Bush would agree to scrub the Kiev visit.

But the American reply added that since the Ukrainians had already been told that Bush was coming, the Soviet government would have to accept the blame for the cancellation. In wording the response this way, Scowcroft and Hewett hoped to force the Soviets to back down and withdraw their objections to a Kiev trip.

Told what was going on, Matlock deliberately telephoned the State Department over a circuit on which he knew the KGB would be listening. He said, "Do these guys in the Soviet government know what they're doing to themselves? They'll just make things worse with the Ukrainians, and they'll be clobbered by public opinion everywhere, including in the U.S.!"

At Baker's behest, Matlock delivered a similar warning to Bessmertnykh at the Foreign Ministry. "Sasha, this is all very puzzling," he complained. "You've got a public relations disaster brewing here. The cancellation of the Kiev stop will become *the* story out of the summit."

Bessmertnykh professed total surprise: "Jack, I promise you I don't know what this is about. Let me see what I can do."

---

* Months afterward, Foreign Ministry officials insisted that they had sent the "presidential message" at the behest of the Kremlin, implying that either Gorbachev or Chernyayev had wished to sound out the Americans on their willingness to drop Kiev from the schedule. Kremlin officials in turn blamed ministry overzealousness or mischief making. High officials of the U.S. embassy in Moscow credited the latter view, while members of Bush's NSC staff suspected their least favorite Gorbachev adviser, Yevgeni Primakov.

After Matlock left, the foreign minister called Gorbachev for guidance. The Soviet president was unwilling to risk the embarrassment of asking Bush personally not to go to Ukraine. Annoyed, he instructed Bessmertnykh, "Just forget about it. Tell the Americans not to worry and to go ahead with their plans. If the president wants to go to Kiev, I'm sure he'll be welcome there."

There was a touch of bitterness in his voice. It seemed all too likely that Bush would receive a warm welcome in Kiev — warmer, certainly, than the one he would get in Moscow — since the Ukrainians were sure to interpret his presence as a vote of support for their separatist cause.

CHAPTER 20

"We're Not Going to Let Him Use Us"

A T SHEREMETYEVO AIRPORT outside Moscow, on Monday evening, July 29, 1991, Vice President Gennadi Yanayev and a small honor guard stood on the tarmac to greet George and Barbara Bush as they emerged from *Air Force One*.

The next morning, Bush called on Gorbachev in Saint Catherine's Hall in the Kremlin, where the two men had first met six years earlier, after the funeral of Konstantin Chernenko. Still smoldering over the failure of his trip to London, Gorbachev complained about the reluctance of the West to lift Cold War restrictions on the transfer of sophisticated technology to the USSR.

He remarked that recently the U.S. government had obstructed the laying of fiber optic lines across the Soviet Union. "You've got all these nice words about how you want us to succeed," he said bitterly, "but when it comes to specifics, you put up roadblocks."

Gorbachev further complained that Bush and the other G-7 leaders had offered only "special associate status" in the IMF. What did that mean? It sounded to him like second-class citizenship. As a "major power," the Soviet Union was entitled to full membership.*

---

* On July 23, the World Bank and the IMF had announced that the Soviet government

Bush tried to turn the tables on his host by noting how difficult Soviet authorities were making it for American firms to do business in the USSR. Jurisdictional disputes between Moscow and the republics, and red tape at all levels, were "dampening enthusiasm for investment and joint ventures."

Gorbachev could not conceal his continuing loss of power. To a small private Kremlin luncheon with Bush, he had invited Boris Yeltsin, President Nazarbayev of Kazakhstan, and several officials of the central government: Pavlov, Bessmertnykh, Moiseyev, Chernyayev, and Valeri Boldin, head of his personal staff. Gorbachev hoped that this event would satisfy his visitor's desire to meet with Yeltsin, even as it reduced his rival's status to that of merely the leader of one of the fifteen republics.

But at the last minute, Yeltsin refused to attend, announcing that he would not be part of a "faceless mass audience." Since Russia was pursuing its own foreign policy with the United States, any business he had with Bush would be taken up during his own separate session with the American president.

Yeltsin took some of the sting out of this obvious rebuff of Gorbachev by declaring that he would sign the new Union treaty, a step that seemed to increase the chances that the Soviet Union might survive, albeit in a different, looser form.

After the luncheon, Bush went to the new office that Yeltsin had been given in the Supreme Soviet building on the Kremlin grounds. There Yeltsin kept him waiting for seven minutes. Scowcroft muttered, "Bad form. How long are we supposed to wait for His Highness?"

Bush's one-on-one meeting was scheduled to last only fifteen minutes, but Yeltsin stretched it to forty. He told Bush that as soon as the new Union treaty was signed, the Russian Republic and the United States should expand their economic "cooperation" in a variety of fields. By this he meant that the United States should increase its direct assistance to Russia.

---

had written them to apply formally for full membership in the two bodies. The letter was dated July 15, the day before Gorbachev arrived in London. The United States and other Western governments had already warned Moscow not to expect full membership because of the two-steps-forward-one-step-back pace of Soviet economic reform; not surprisingly, the two organizations tartly characterized the Soviet application as "premature."

Baker, Sununu, Matlock, Hewett, Ross, and Nicholas Burns of the NSC staff were then ushered into the room, along with Yeltsin's aides. Yeltsin repeated many of the same points he had just made privately to Bush. This led the Americans to wonder whether the real purpose of the one-on-one session had been simply to inflate Yeltsin's image and to needle Gorbachev.

Although the two sides had agreed in advance that there would be no press conference afterward, when Yeltsin and Bush emerged from the room, the beaming Russian president told a group of waiting reporters and camera crews that he had high hopes for "normalizing" American-Russian ties. He added that Bush had "agreed" with him on economic cooperation.

Bush felt sandbagged. He did not wish to confirm the impression that behind Gorbachev's back, he and Yeltsin had opened a new era in direct U.S.-Russian relations, but neither did he wish to contradict him. Thus, he ignored Yeltsin's comment about the future and said instead that the Russian president had made "a big hit" during his trip to Washington the month before.

A reporter called out, "President Yeltsin, why didn't you attend the meeting with President Gorbachev?" Before Yeltsin could respond, Bush turned to him and said, "We've got to go. I'm late." As he climbed into his limousine, Bush complained to Scowcroft that he had been "ambushed" by the Russian leader: "Yeltsin's really grandstanding, isn't he?"

That evening, Gorbachev gave an official dinner for the Bushes in Saint Vladimir's Hall in the Great Kremlin Palace. Yeltsin waited until the last minute to make his grand entrance, then tried to escort Barbara Bush in to dinner. With a steely smile, the First Lady preserved a semblance of protocol by keeping Raisa Gorbachev between herself and Yeltsin as they went to their tables.

At the end of the evening, Bush grumbled to his aides that Yeltsin had been a "real pain," exploiting him in order to "upstage Gorbachev." Scowcroft said, "That guy's got to be told we're not going to let him use us in his petty games!"

Hewett took Matlock aside and asked him to speak to Yeltsin's foreign minister, Andrei Kozyrev: "Tell him that there are certain agreed-upon norms of gentlemanly behavior. Let's not get into the habit of surprising each other."

*   *   *

On Wednesday morning, July 31, Bush, Baker, Scowcroft, and Gates were driven to Gorbachev's dacha at Novo-Ogaryevo, where for nearly five hours they held intensive discussions with the Soviet president, Bessmertnykh, and Chernyayev. The Soviets were all tieless and in sweaters.

The agenda was well in hand. On the Middle East, Baker and Bessmertnykh were collaborating more harmoniously than ever, having recently hammered out an agreement to cosponsor an Arab-Israeli peace conference in October.* Negotiators in Geneva, meanwhile, had put the final touches on the START treaty.

Bush was prepared for Gorbachev to bring up old Soviet anxieties about the U.S. antimissile defense program. But today the Soviet leader seemed reluctant to waste time or U.S. goodwill on this or other traditional points of contention, such as Cuba or the size of the Soviet defense budget.

Instead, in a performance reminiscent of those put on by Shevardnadze in his meetings with Baker, Gorbachev unburdened himself to Bush about what was happening inside the Soviet Union. He referred ominously to the civil war that for weeks had been consuming Yugoslavia.† Since Bush was so interested in visiting Kiev, Gorbachev wanted him to consider the possibility that Ukrainian secessionism might lead to a Yugoslav-type civil war — only spread across eleven time zones and a territory dotted with nuclear weapons.

Then came an unexpected reminder of how close to the surface were the forces of violence in the Soviet Union. Stationed at the traveling White House headquarters at the new German-owned, white and chrome Penta Hotel, Nicholas Burns of the NSC learned from Baltic representatives in Moscow that an unidentified group of armed men had raided a Lithuanian customs post, forced six guards to lie on the floor, and then shot each of them in the head.

The immediate assumption was that the outrage was the work of the Black Berets, who had taken part in the January massacres in the Baltics.

---

* Bessmertnykh had not wished to specify "October" in the agreement, merely "the fall." Baker had Ross explain that committing to October would "give us momentum and put all the parties in a position where they would have to respond." Bessmertnykh raised the matter with Gorbachev, who consented.
† Slovenia and Croatia had declared their independence, and in response, Serbia had invaded Croatia with the Serbian-dominated Federal Army, partly on the pretext of protecting its Serb minority.

Burns telephoned Hewett at Novo-Ogaryevo, where he was sitting with Sununu and Ross in a dacha near Gorbachev's.

Sununu insisted that he be the one to rush in with a note for the president about the murders. When Gorbachev asked what the interruption was all about, Bush read him the message.

Furious at this blot on his summit — and humiliated that Bush should be the one to inform him of violence on what he still considered to be Soviet soil — Gorbachev said, "This is the first *I've* heard about it!" He sent Chernyayev to find out what had happened.

Later Gorbachev told Bush that an investigation of the incident was under way. He promised that his government would do everything it could to "avoid such excesses" in the future.

Some in the American party wondered whether some of the hardliners who had failed in the June "constitutional coup" might have engineered this latest incident to embarrass Gorbachev during his meetings with Bush. Several of Gorbachev's own advisers shared this suspicion.

That afternoon, Bush and Gorbachev returned to the Kremlin for the signing of the START treaty in the marble and gilt Saint Vladimir's Hall. The two leaders signed the forty-seven-page treaty and seven-hundred-page protocols using pens made of metal taken from missiles banned under the INF treaty.

Bush proclaimed that they were reversing a "half century of steadily growing strategic arsenals." Gorbachev responded, "Thank God, as we say in Russian, that we stopped this."

As the ceremony was ending, Gorbachev's adviser-interpreter Pavel Palazhchenko whispered to a colleague, "If only the conflicts and tensions we've got in our own country could be tidied up as neatly as the ones we've had with the outside world."

On Thursday morning, August 1, when Bush and his entourage boarded *Air Force One* to fly to Kiev, they were joined by Vice President Yanayev, a Kremlin protocol official, a KGB colonel, and Victor Komplektov, the Soviet ambassador to the United States. Once the Soviets had resigned themselves to this one-day trip, they had asked Bush to take along a small number of escorts from the central government, presumably to underscore the point that Ukraine was still part of Moscow's domain.

During the two-hour flight, the Soviet passengers were assigned one of the new plane's spacious conference rooms and served a sumptuous lunch, which Yanayev washed down with several scotches. A chain-smoker, he grumbled about not being allowed to light up during the flight. Ever the good host, Bush looked in on his guests to make sure they were comfortable and well cared for.

Since Yanayev was the senior member of the group, Bush tried to engage him in conversation. It soon became apparent, however, that Yanayev had nothing of substance to impart and no inclination to talk business, so Bush took him on a tour of the high-tech airborne presidential command center, showing off his bedroom with its mechanical window shades and even the presidential toilet. Yanayev confined his comments to "Very nice" and "Very interesting."

Leaving the Soviets to themselves again, Bush told his aides that Yanayev seemed a "friendly sort of guy" but definitely "not a heavy hitter." He added that Yanayev was living up to the assessment that U.S. intelligence had offered of him before this trip: an old-fashioned apparatchik unlikely to play a vital or independent role in the political life of his country.

Like most Americans, Bush was accustomed to referring to the republic he was about to visit as "the Ukraine." Ukrainians themselves, however, had for some time been campaigning to drop the definite article, on the grounds that it connoted colonial status, like "the Lebanon" or "the Gambia." Impatient with the nationalist firebrands of the Soviet Union, Scowcroft had on one occasion carped, "What about *the* Netherlands? For that matter, what about *the* United States?"

But Matlock knew how strongly the Ukrainians felt. During the flight to Kiev, he warned Hewett that if Bush referred to "the Ukraine," the White House would be "bombarded with letters from lots of irate Ukrainian-Americans." Hewett told the president, "I know it feels funny to say it that way, but it means a lot to these people." Loath to offend either his hosts in Kiev or the roughly 750,000 Ukrainian-Americans in the United States, many of whom usually voted Republican, Bush promised to comply.

After landing outside Kiev, the president and his party traveled by motorcade into the city. The streets were lined with thousands of cheering well-wishers; women held up bouquets of flowers, babies, and loaves of bread and bags of salt, a traditional sign of greeting. Bush looked as if he were campaigning in Pittsburgh, Cleveland, Detroit, or

Chicago, which to some extent he was, since all of those cities had large Ukrainian-American populations. Waving back, he exclaimed, "Hey, this is great!"

Just as Gorbachev had feared, this welcome was in sharp contrast to the one the U.S. president had just received in Moscow, where much of the populace regarded him as just one more foreign dignitary coming to pay homage to the most unpopular man in the Soviet Union.

The Kiev crowds pressed Bush to support them against Gorbachev, waving the blue and yellow flags of an independent Ukrainian state and holding placards in Ukrainian and English saying, "MOSCOW HAS 15 COLONIES" . . . "THE EMPIRE OF EVIL IS LIVING" . . . "53 MILLION UKRAINIANS DEMAND INDEPENDENCE" . . . "IF BEING PART OF AN EMPIRE IS SO GREAT, WHY DID AMERICA GET OUT OF ONE?"

When the motorcade reached the center of Kiev, Bush got out and met with Leonid Kravchuk, the barrel-chested chairman of the Ukrainian parliament. A longtime Communist and minion of Moscow, he had lately, with exquisite timing, turned on a dime and made himself a champion of the nationalist cause.

The meeting lasted less than an hour, with no joint press conference afterward; U.S. officials did not want a repeat of the president's experience with Yeltsin in Moscow. Kravchuk spent much of the session explaining to Bush that even in the rich farming country of Ukraine, waste, corruption, and a faulty transportation system kept as much as 30 percent of the harvested grain from reaching the market.

In spite of American efforts to keep the Kiev visit from offending Gorbachev, Ukrainians took advantage of Yanayev's presence to thumb their noses at the Kremlin. Hewett observed that the Soviet vice president was treated more like the "chairman of the All-Union Leprosy Association." At a luncheon for the U.S. and Ukrainian delegations, the working languages were English and Ukrainian. Since Yanayev knew neither, he looked alternately puzzled, bored, and annoyed. At least he was allowed to smoke.

Bush's address to the Ukrainian parliament had been in the works for several weeks. The president had advised his aides that he wished to use the speech to promote negotiations between Moscow and the republics, without encouraging secessionist movements that Gorbachev would not tolerate and the United States could not support.

After perusing a draft, Bush inserted several passages of his own, each intended, he told Scowcroft, to make the speech "more sensitive to Gorbachev's problems." He was worried that "Gorbachev's accomplishments are being lost in all this talk about independence."

The result was a glowing endorsement of Gorbachev's vision for the future of the Soviet Union. In his speech, Bush referred to his listeners as "Soviet citizens" and defended the leader he had just left behind in Moscow: "President Gorbachev has achieved astonishing things, and his policies of *glasnost, perestroika,* and democratization point toward the goals of freedom, democracy, and economic liberty."

Bush never explicitly denounced the cause of Ukrainian secessionism per se, but he repeatedly hinted that he was not enthusiastic about the idea. Implying that Ukraine and other republics would be wise to remain in a Soviet federation, he said, "As a federation ourselves, we want good relations, improved relations, with the republics."

Bush went on to say, "Freedom is not the same as independence. Americans will not support those who seek independence in order to replace a far-off tyranny with a local despotism. They will not aid those who promote a suicidal nationalism based on ethnic hatred."

Ukrainians who were shocked by this last phrase did not realize that the U.S. president was merely reaffirming a private formulation that Baker had first expressed to Shevardnadze in July 1989. Bush was repeating this declaration now as a particular warning to the newly elected president of Georgia, Zviad Gamsakhurdia, who was behaving dictatorially and cracking down on numerous minorities. But Bush also knew that there were similar ethnic passions in Ukraine, and his warning thus applied to his listeners in Kiev as well.

Disgusted, Ivan Drach, a leader of the Ukraine independence movement, complained to reporters, "Bush came here as a messenger for Gorbachev. On the issue of Ukrainian independence, he sounded less radical than our own Communist politicians. After all, they have to run for office here in Ukraine, and he doesn't!"

In a column published on August 29, William Safire of the *New York Times* dusted off the old accusation that Bush was being too timid and characteristically siding with the forces of the status quo against those of democratic change. As Exhibit A, Safire cited what he called the president's "dismaying 'Chicken Kiev speech.' " The sobriquet was almost immediately adopted by others, and it stung Bush severely.

Gorbachev's new Union treaty was to be signed by Yeltsin and Nazarbayev in Moscow on Thursday, August 20. The Soviet president hoped that leaders of other republics would add their signatures later.

Made public five days before the date of signing, the treaty mandated the transfer of so much authority to the republics as to mark the end of the historical, centralized Soviet Union. Also included were several concessions by the Kremlin to the republics on taxation, natural resources, and control of the state security apparatus. These all came as unpleasant surprises to hard-liners in Moscow.

For almost three years, Bush and his administration had probed the limits of Gorbachev's ideological tolerance and political power. Analysts at State, Defense, and CIA had long wondered where exactly lay the line that Gorbachev could not cross.

Could he really, for instance, introduce democratic choice in Soviet elections, infuriating and terrifying apparatchiks from one end of the Union to the other? Dare he break the Communist party's monopoly on political power? Could the system tolerate a free press? Could the Soviet people stand to hear the truth about their own past? Could they adjust to some version of private property and free-market economics?

Then, too, could Gorbachev end the decade-long occupation of Afghanistan? Could he pull the plug on Soviet support for the Sandinistas in Nicaragua and pressure them into elections they would very likely lose? Could he permit "fraternal" regimes to topple in Eastern Europe and thus surrender the buffer zone that Stalin had created after World War II? Could he force the retirement without honor of the Warsaw Pact?

In the past, many U.S. experts had presumed that if a red line existed, it ran between East and West Germany: surely, they reasoned, Gorbachev could not let the two Germanys unite or allow a united Germany to be a full member in NATO. But those experts had been proved wrong.

Now that the Union treaty was about to be signed, Western diplomats and policymakers wondered whether Gorbachev could survive one more such momentous change.

There had been talk of a coup d'état for months. Shevardnadze had predicted one when he resigned in December. In June, Mayor Popov had warned Matlock that the hard-liners were poised to move against Gorbachev.

But with every false alarm, every threatened coup that failed to materialize, Gorbachev seemed more confident of his invincibility, and therefore less inclined to take the rumors and warnings seriously.

On Sunday, August 18, he was nearing the end of a vacation with his wife, daughter, son-in-law, and granddaughter at his lavish hillside retreat at Foros, on the Black Sea. That afternoon, he worked on the speech he was to deliver at the signing of the Union treaty, in Moscow, two days hence.

Suddenly, his chief bodyguard appeared with the news that a delegation had arrived from Moscow and was asking to see him. Immediately suspicious, Gorbachev picked up a telephone to call for help. The phone was dead, as were all the others he tried.

By now, the visitors had pushed their way into his office. They included Gorbachev's own trusted chief of staff, Valeri Boldin, and Oleg Baklanov, a secretary of the Central Committee and a leading tribune of the military-industrial complex.

Telling Gorbachev that they represented the "State Committee for the State of Emergency," the men demanded that he sign a decree turning over presidential power to Yanayev. When he refused, they put him under house arrest.

CHAPTER 21

"I'm Afraid He May Have Had It"

BUSH HAD FLOWN from Kiev directly to Maine, where he planned to spend the month "recreating," as he put it. When he read intelligence bulletins the weekend of August 18–19, he saw several signals that something might be going badly wrong in the Soviet Union.

The *President's Daily Brief* for Saturday, August 17, led with a report that Soviet hard-liners seemed to be mounting some last-minute opposition to the new Union treaty. It went on to note that on Friday, Alexander Yakovlev had warned that an "influential Stalinist group" was planning a "party and state coup." The *Daily Brief* concluded, "There is an increasing danger that the traditionalists will want to provoke a situation that will justify the use of force to restore order." These plotters "would hope to co-opt Gorbachev as part of the effort, but this time he may turn against them and side with the democrats."

Later, another intelligence report, this one based on highly classified sources, including satellite espionage, raised a troubling question: why hadn't Gorbachev left the Crimea to fly back to Moscow on Sunday for the Union treaty signing ceremony?

*   *   *

At Kennebunkport on Sunday evening, local lobstermen and Secret Service agents put up barriers against Hurricane Bob, which was throttling the mid-Atlantic coast. Inside the gray-shingled house, as Bush prepared to retire, he heard rain pounding the roof. He was planning to get up at dawn to play eighteen holes of golf at the Cape Arundel Country Club with Scowcroft and Roger Clemens, star pitcher of the Boston Red Sox.

The president had scarcely closed his eyes when the white telephone on his wooden night table rang. It was 11:45.

Scowcroft was calling from his room at the Nonantum Hotel in town. At eleven-thirty, he had been in bed watching CNN and had seen a report, based on a TASS announcement, that "ill health" had compelled the replacement of Gorbachev by Vice President Yanayev. Scowcroft had decided not to bother the president until there was confirmation and amplification.

Now he told Bush that CNN had reported a second TASS announcement that Yanayev and the rest of the junta, including Pavlov, Kryuchkov, Yazov, Pugo, and Baklanov, had imposed a six-month "state of emergency" in the Soviet Union.*

Bush exclaimed, "*My God!*"

Presuming that the report was true, Scowcroft advised the president that the United States must not, of course, endorse the new leadership in Moscow. But Bush must also realize that history suggested that when a coup was backed by so many powerful figures, it was likely to succeed. The West might have to do business with these people, so "we don't want to burn our bridges with them."

Bush wondered how the coup should be characterized in any public statement by the administration. Scowcroft replied that words such as *illegal, illegitimate,* and *unconstitutional* would be too provocative; he and the president finally settled on the more neutral-sounding *extra-constitutional.*

By telephone, Scowcroft told his spokesman, Roman Popadiuk, to use that word with the reporters who were nearly breaking down his door with demands for an official U.S. response to the shocking news from Moscow.

---

* The other two members of the "Emergency Committee" were Vasili Starodubtsev, chairman of the conservative Farmers' Union, and Alexander Tizyakov, a party loyalist who served as president of the Association of State Enterprises.

Popadiuk warned Scowcroft that by morning, the president would have to say something himself: "You can't have him go golfing, reacting to the most momentous event in our lifetimes on the golf course." Scowcroft said, "It might be raining in the morning anyway."

Baker was in bed with his wife at their Wyoming cabin when the State Department's operations center called with the news. Susan Baker recalled that Kuwait had been invaded at the start of the previous year's August holiday; now she said, "There goes another vacation."

"Don't worry, honey," said her husband. "I'll be back here in no time. It won't be like last year." Baker found it hard to believe that this crisis would last. In recent visits to Moscow, he had been struck by how deep and broad the changes of the last few years were; his intuition told him that the conservatives had long since lost control of the situation, and that their bid to seize power had come too late.

Remembering that Shevardnadze had predicted a hard-line coup, Baker was tempted to call him and say, "You told us so." But he thought better of the idea: as long as the new regime was in power, he would be doing Shevardnadze no favor to call him on an open telephone line.

Unable to sleep, Baker pressed the operations center for the latest developments. He called Dennis Ross, on vacation in New Hampshire, and Robert Zoellick, who was traveling in Scotland.

Ross reminded his boss that the Soviet military was no monolith; they must not presume its full complicity in the coup or even its willingness to back the junta. Like Soviet society as a whole, he said, the military was now deeply divided along ethnic and other lines, which might keep it neutral in a conflict affecting the central government. If that turned out to be the case, the coup would probably fail.

Zoellick noted that the administration must be careful not to say anything publicly that might grant the plotters legitimacy. "We won't lose anything by taking a tough line at the beginning," he maintained. "If they consolidate their power, they'll need outside help and acceptance later, so they'll swallow anything we say early on."

General Colin Powell was asleep in his home at Fort McNair in Washington when a duty officer from the Pentagon's national military command center called him and said, "It's a coup!"

During the Persian Gulf War, Powell had grown used to such late-night alarms. Putting down the telephone, he allowed some time to pass to ensure that he was wide awake and thinking carefully. His most immediate concern was the danger of a surprise attack: no U.S. official could know who now had the "little suitcase" containing codes that could allow Yanayev or Yazov to launch ICBMs against North America.

Powell asked for the latest "real-time" intelligence on the disposition of all Soviet missiles, bombers, and submarines: "Is there any change in the alert status of any forces?" The Pentagon assured him that there was none.*

At the CIA, George Kolt established a task force to monitor and analyze the cables that were now pouring in on the Soviet coup. For months, the agency had been hearing that Gorbachev was suffering from emotional and psychological tension, so the first TASS statement on the coup, at eleven-thirty, had made Kolt wonder whether the Soviet leader might actually be sick. But the second statement left no doubt in his mind that Gorbachev's setback was not medical but political.

At 12:45 Monday morning, Kolt told David Gompert of the NSC staff, "We're calling this a coup." Whether it would succeed would depend on the ability of Yeltsin and the other democrats to resist, as well as on the Soviet military's response and the reaction of the West.

Later, the CIA was criticized for having failed to "predict" the takeover. In recent months, agency experts had indeed suggested a "low probability" of a hard-line coup, but that was because they did not believe that such a coup could succeed. Just as they had concluded a year earlier that it would be stupid for Saddam Hussein to invade Kuwait, so they had presumed that the hard-liners would not slit their own throats by attempting to oust Gorbachev.

Kolt called Scowcroft in Kennebunkport and stressed the importance of the Western reaction to the coup. The CIA generally tried to avoid the appearance of meddling in policy, but Kolt was obliquely appealing for a strong American condemnation of the plotters and a statement of support for Yeltsin.

When Fritz Ermarth arrived at Langley, at around one o'clock Monday morning, he began tapping away at the keyboard of his computer

---

* Once the coup was well under way, top-secret American intelligence sources revealed that some Soviet Strategic Rocket Forces regiments were engaged in unusual activities involving the deployment of mobile ICBMs. Under a worst-case interpretation, this was at first cause for alarm, but Pentagon experts soon concluded that the unit commanders were in fact taking steps intended to avoid the appearance of threatening behavior, and to make absolutely certain that the missiles remained under control.

terminal, which was linked to the agency's data bank. He reviewed what U.S. spy satellites and communications intercepts had uncovered in recent days about movements by the Soviet army and the KGB.

Ermarth was startled by what was *not* in the reports. There was no evidence of the telltale stirrings that might have been expected before a coup. The plotters had made no serious preparations; there had been no massive redeployment of troops and tanks, no interruption of communications, no jamming of Western radio broadcasts, no roundup of popular reform leaders.

At two in the morning, Ermarth exclaimed to his colleagues, "Hey guys, there are no dogs barking!" Kolt replied, "Yeah, we've noticed that, too." Ermarth said, "You'd think these guys could bring off something like this rather smartly. After all, they've been practicing since January." They reminded one another of Popov's June warning and expressed their regret at not having taken it more seriously at the time.

Ermarth drafted a "Spot Commentary," or SPOTCOM, for the president. It noted that the coup had a ragged, ill-prepared, impromptu quality. Ermarth gave odds on the outcome: he saw a 10 percent chance that the Kremlin would revert to an Andropov-style regime, a 45 percent chance that the coup would lead to an open-ended stalemate between the plotters and the reformers, and a 45 percent chance of an "early fizzle."

At the White House, Gompert and Hewett sipped coffee and paced around the windowless Situation Room. Gompert, a former destroyer officer, suggested that he and Hewett set up rotating "port and starboard watches" for the duration of the crisis.

Hewett did not think it would go on for long: "This is a group that can't possibly last for more than a month or two. They'll get done in by the economy. They can't buy off the workers with promises of wage increases and welfare. The economic collapse will accelerate."

By dawn in Moscow, military units, including hundreds of tanks, had taken up positions on key streets, at major intersections, and on bridges. The coup leaders issued decrees prohibiting large gatherings, setting curfews, banning opposition political activity, and imposing restrictions on the press.

At five o'clock on Monday morning in Kennebunkport, Scowcroft called the president and said, "You're going to have to say something

to the press, and it would be better not to do it on the golf course."
The president agreed. It was raining anyway. Popadiuk arranged an
early-morning presidential news conference.

At six-thirty, Scowcroft climbed into his rented Oldsmobile, drove
to the president's house, and stowed his rain gear in the hall closet next
to jackets, overcoats, and souvenir hats from every previous Bush campaign. Wearing a navy-blue blazer and a tie adorned with gold presidential seals, the president greeted him in the living room. He was
already working the telephone.

Bush talked to James Collins, the ranking U.S. diplomat in Moscow
since Matlock's recent retirement from the Foreign Service. Matlock's
designated replacement, Robert Strauss, the powerhouse Washington-
Dallas lawyer and former Democratic party chairman, had yet to be
sworn in.

Collins informed Bush that he had just been to the "White House" —
the Russian parliament — where Boris Yeltsin and several of his top
aides had been holed up through the night. In the early hours of Monday morning, Yeltsin had denounced the coup, branding its leaders as
traitors. The building, which was almost directly across the street from
the new U.S. embassy complex, was surrounded by military vehicles,
but Collins reported that he had been able to get past the blockade and
into the parliament to meet with Yeltsin and Kozyrev. He added that
all the Americans in the Soviet capital were believed to be safe.

"Thanks very much," said Bush. "I'm glad you're there."

Calling from Wyoming, Baker told Bush that the United States
should have an ambassador on the scene in Moscow, and Bush agreed
that Strauss should be sworn in as quickly as possible and rushed there.
Baker called the new envoy at his vacation home in Del Mar, California.

The previous winter, when Matlock had announced that he was retir-
ing, Bush and Baker had considered for the appointment a number of
other diplomats who spoke Russian and knew the Soviet Union well.
The State Department's leading candidate, Edward Djerejian, then the
U.S. ambassador to Syria, had to be ruled out because he was of Armenian extraction: at Kislovodsk, with some embarrassment, Bessmertnykh had questioned Baker about whether Djerejian could really
be objective about the Kremlin's growing rift with Armenia, or about
the bloodshed between Armenia and Azerbaijan.

Bush and Scowcroft wanted to send someone whom Gorbachev was likely to see as the president's personal representative. Condoleezza Rice was considered, as was Dennis Ross, who had no interest in the job. When Bush and Baker settled on Strauss, a fellow Texan, Gorbachev had the desired reaction: he viewed the appointment as a vote of confidence in himself.

Strauss knew that he had been appointed largely to guarantee a direct channel between Bush and Baker and Gorbachev; now, with the Soviet leader out of power, he began to wonder whether he was the "right guy for the job." But on his flight from California to Washington, he warmed to the task: "I guess I *could* tell those motherfucking sons of bitches off!"

All day Monday, Yeltsin continued to defy the coup and to rally support. Braving the danger of army snipers, he came out of the parliament building and addressed a crowd of tens of thousands of Muscovites who had gathered amidst the tanks and armored personnel carriers. Yeltsin repeated his charge that Yanayev and others had seized power illegally; he also called for a general strike against the state of emergency. Eduard Shevardnadze and other prominent democrats came to the building to show their solidarity.

Pavlov, citing illness, abruptly resigned as prime minister and as a member of the Emergency Committee. Foreign reporters in Moscow began to joke about an outbreak of "coup flu."

Back in Washington, Bush was working the telephone. He spoke first with his key European allies — John Major, François Mitterrand, and Helmut Kohl — and later with Lech Walesa of Poland, Vaclav Havel of Czechoslovakia, Turgut Ozal of Turkey, Ruud Lubbers of the Netherlands, Jozsef Antall of Hungary, Brian Mulroney of Canada, Giulio Andreotti of Italy, Toshiki Kaifu of Japan, and Felipe Gonzalez Marquez of Spain.

Walesa, Havel, and Antall were concerned that the hard-liners in Moscow might find a way of instigating similar upheavals in their respective countries. Bush urged them to avoid taking any preemptive action that might appear provocative, while promising to make it clear in his own statements that whatever happened in the Soviet Union, the United States considered the advent of democracy in Eastern Europe irreversible.

Major predicted that the new regime in Moscow would be out in a matter of months, if not sooner, and Mitterrand ventured that "this may be the first time a coup fails" in the Soviet bloc.* Bush recalled his own encounter with Yanayev on the trip to Kiev three weeks earlier, and noted that Vice President Quayle had met his Soviet counterpart at the funerals of King Olav V of Norway in January and Prime Minister Rajiv Gandhi of India in May. Quayle had pronounced Yanayev "not a ball of fire," but "reasonable."

Bush told Major and Mitterrand that from what he and Quayle had seen of Yanayev, "he's not such a bad guy, but pretty much of a lightweight." Mitterrand agreed, adding that Yanayev was "probably nothing more than a puppet" of the other seven members of the Emergency Committee.

Prime Minister Gonzalez of Spain pressed Bush to try to reach Gorbachev directly, if only to be able to publicize the effort in order to show that the United States had not given up on the deposed leader.

Of all the leaders Bush spoke to, Kohl was the most upset. The chancellor knew how much the Soviet hard-liners had hated Germany's unification within NATO, and he wondered whether they might use the Soviet troops that were still in eastern Germany to make trouble. He urged Bush to insist that the new Soviet leaders abide by their international obligations and respect human rights. Kohl also asked the American president to stress Gorbachev's important place in the history of the world.

At the beginning of the day, Bush was prepared for the worst. He was anxious to offend no one, especially the man who was now at least the titular leader of the Soviet Union, Gennadi Yanayev. Scowcroft reinforced the president's natural inclination to trim his sails until the situation was clearer.

In the Bushes' living room at Kennebunkport, Scowcroft reported that the indications coming out of Moscow were mixed. The U.S. embassy had not sighted armored personnel carriers on the streets until a few hours before — a good sign, since the usual script for a military takeover called for tanks to roll as soon as the first announcement was made.

Scowcroft passed along the CIA's view that the plotters had not got their ducks into a row, although he added, "That's all just speculation

---

* In public, Mitterrand was far more cautious. He called on the putsch leaders to respect "life and liberty" but refrained from outright condemnation of the coup until late Tuesday, August 20.

at this point, no doubt with some wishful thinking mixed in." Yanayev and his coconspirators could well prove to be the next government of the Soviet Union, he reminded Bush: "You've got to be careful. We may have to deal with these guys."

On the phone to Bush from Wyoming, Baker had recalled sitting next to Yanayev during the Moscow summit, and suggested that he was "not a very convincing ringleader."

Knowing that he was sure to be asked about Yanayev by the press, Bush said, "Maybe the thing to do is go easy on him at first."

Just before eight in the morning, a somber Bush appeared before reporters and camera crews in a cottage normally used by the Secret Service. Following Kohl's advice, he said that he expected the Soviet Union to "live up fully to its international obligations" and called Gorbachev a "historic figure, one who's led the Soviet Union toward reform economically and toward a constructive and cooperative role in the international arena."

But Bush stopped well short of an outright denunciation of the men who were now in charge of the Kremlin. Using Scowcroft's formulation, he described the seizure of power as "extraconstitutional." He noted hopefully that the Emergency Committee had promised that reform would continue, but he admitted, "I don't know whether to take heart or not. I think at this point what we do is simply watch the situation unfold, and we state and restate our principles, and we'll see where matters go. It's all still unfolding."

A reporter asked what the president thought of Yanayev. Bush replied, "Well, my gut instinct is that he has a certain commitment to reform. . . . But I think it's not he that is calling the shots. . . . I've said over and over again that we did not want to see a coup backed by the KGB and the military."

Then he added, "I think it's important to know that coups can fail. They can take over at first, and then they run up against the will of the people."

And what of Yeltsin's demand for a general strike? "Well, we'll just have to see what happens on that. . . . I hope that people heed his call." Would he fly back to Washington? Bush turned snappish: "I'm not interested in show business. Not interested in make-work." He pointed out that there was an excellent communications setup at Kennebunkport.

Had he tried to talk to anyone in the Soviet leadership on the hot line? The president bristled even more at this query: "We're not going to overexcite the American people or the world. And so, we will conduct our diplomacy in a prudent fashion, not driven by excess, not driven by extreme."

Bush added that people associated the hot line "with some kind of military problem between the Soviet Union and the United States. And do you think I want to suggest that to the American people or to the people in Europe? *Absolutely not!*" He broke off the session rather abruptly, saying, "All right, you got it. Don't say we never give you any news here."

No sooner did Bush and Scowcroft return to the president's living room than they began picking up signs that the press conference had laid an egg. Commentators were comparing it to Bush's restrained response to the Tiananmen Square massacre: was the president simply going to tolerate the Soviet coup as well?

Scowcroft told Bush, "We may have a problem developing here." Recalling the criticism the president had received for remaining on vacation in Kennebunkport during the first month of the Persian Gulf crisis, Scowcroft persuaded him to fly back to Washington for a highly visible day of presidential leadership.

Air Force One took off at midmorning. From Washington, Robert Gates called Scowcroft aboard the plane to read him a letter from Yeltsin to Bush, sent through James Collins. Yeltsin wanted Bush to "demand the restoration of the legally elected organs of power," and a "reaffirmation" that Gorbachev was the leader of the Soviet Union.

Gates told Scowcroft, "I think the message is clear. He wants us to go a bit further in condemning the coup and supporting the anticoup forces."

At that moment, citizens were pouring into the streets of Moscow to defend Yeltsin's headquarters against the army units surrounding the parliament. The Emergency Committee had just held its own press conference, which had reinforced the view that it was a gang that couldn't shoot straight. When Yanayev read out a statement, his hands were shaking, and journalists in the audience suspected that he and several other members of the committee were drunk — a suspicion that was later confirmed.

This ridiculous performance strengthened Scowcroft's inclination to condemn the plotters more harshly than Bush had done in Kennebunkport. He advised the president that "someone from the administration" must exercise immediate spin control by talking to the pool of White House reporters at the rear of *Air Force One*.

Bush said, "I don't think *I* should have to go back there." Popadiuk volunteered Scowcroft, who agreed, with a caveat: "I'll be as negative about this thing as I can, while recognizing that we might have to live with these guys." The president approved the tactic.

Over the roar of jet engines, Scowcroft declared to the press that the coup was "quite negative": "It's our feeling that the Soviet people want the reforms to continue. And from all we can judge, this group intends to halt or at least slow them down. . . . What we support is a return to the reform programs that were under way when this coup took over."

As *Air Force One* flew to Washington, other air force planes were on their way to pick up Dick Cheney, on vacation in Canada, as well as Baker and Strauss, who was to be sworn in as ambassador to Moscow in the White House Rose Garden on Tuesday morning.

In his Pentagon office, Colin Powell kept one eye on CNN and another on the intelligence reports that were still flowing in. Both sources told him that the tanks and armored personnel carriers on the streets of Moscow were showing no signs either of combat readiness or of political purpose. He exclaimed, "These guys have been sent into Moscow without a mission!"

Powell called Cheney, who was then airborne, and said, "The bottom line is that this is an incomplete coup. Something has happened, but it hasn't gone according to the book." At the CIA, Ermarth concluded, "This thing is being perpetrated by a bunch of losers. It's going to flop."

In the first hours after the coup, the Soviet Foreign Ministry had cabled to its missions abroad the text of the Emergency Committee's declaration. Victor Komplektov, the Soviet ambassador in Washington, was instructed to deliver a letter from Yanayev to Bush conveying the committee's desire for good relations with the United States, its commitment to continue the process of reform, and its assurances that Gorbachev was safe.

Komplektov called on Eagleburger at the State Department at noon and Gates at the NSC shortly thereafter. He carried out his mission with a gusto that led both his embassy colleagues and U.S. officials to conclude that he had welcomed the coup.

Komplektov told Eagleburger and Gates that he "appreciated" the "understanding" with which President Bush had handled the situation so far. It was a compliment the Americans were not happy to hear, since it suggested that Komplektov — and the putschists in Moscow — had indeed taken Bush's mild Monday-morning statement as an expression of willingness to accept the coup.

Eagleburger gave the envoy a written message on behalf of the administration insisting that the coup committee adhere to Soviet international obligations and continue political and economic reform. But even if they met these standards, he said, the coup leaders should not expect the United States to recognize them as the legal government of the Soviet Union any time soon.

At five o'clock on Monday afternoon, in the Roosevelt Room of the White House, Bush chaired a meeting of deputies of the major departments. He ordered that all American-Soviet exchange programs be suspended, but in such a way that they could be easily resumed. If the coup failed, he wanted to be able to restore normal relations quickly.

The CIA's deputy director, Richard Kerr, listed the dogs that were still not barking in Moscow: communication links with the West remained in operation; Yeltsin was holed up defiantly in his White House; on the streets, soldiers were climbing down from their tanks and trying to calm angry Muscovites.

Kerr said, "In short, Mr. President, this does not look like a traditional coup. It's not very professional. They're trying to take control of the major power centers one at a time, and you can't pull off a coup in phases."

Stung by public criticism that he had seemed too tolerant of the coup, the president was eager to toughen his stance. Looking over a draft statement that had been prepared for him to read, he recalled the anxiety on the part of Walesa, Havel, and Antall that the Soviet hard-liners might try to regain control of their countries. He said, "I don't see anything in here about Eastern Europe."

In the White House briefing room, Bush now spoke words he had shied away from only that morning, such as *unconstitutional* and *illegitimate*. He endorsed Yeltsin's call for Gorbachev's restoration and outlined his own demands: the coup leaders must continue the Soviet Union's movement toward democracy; respect its constitutionally elected leaders and not violate human rights; observe all treaties; and refrain from using force against the republics or other "democratically elected governments" — a reference to Eastern Europe.

He had "no interest in a new Cold War," he said, but would "avoid in every possible way" actions that might give the coup committee any "legitimacy or support."

The Russian foreign minister, Andrei Kozyrev, whom Yeltsin had dispatched to Western Europe, telephoned Allen Weinstein of the privately funded Center for Democracy in Washington, who had lately been cultivating relations with Yeltsin's circle. Kozyrev dictated a statement calling the initial Western reaction to the coup "ambiguous and even disappointing," and emphasizing that this was "no time for appeasement." Bush's carefully hedged morning statement, Kozyrev suggested, had played into the hands of the coup plotters, who "believed for a time that their efforts had deceived the West." However, Kozyrev added, "more recent statements . . . have corrected that misconception."

In his Monday-morning letter to Bush, Yeltsin had asked the president to establish "operational contacts" with him during this crisis. This was a clear appeal for Bush to telephone him at the Russian White House. But Bush and his NSC advisers were reluctant to oblige. They felt they should attempt to reach Gorbachev first; otherwise, it might appear that the administration had written off the Soviet leader's chances of returning to power.

The White House operator put through a call to the Kremlin, hoping to be patched through to Gorbachev in the Crimea: "President Bush is calling President Gorbachev." A voice at the other end said, "Just a moment, please." After a pause, the Moscow operator came back on the line and said blandly, "I'm sorry, but he's unavailable now." The White House tried again several times over the course of the day, in vain.

On Monday evening, Hewett told Scowcroft, "Brent, we've given it our best shot on trying to reach Gorbachev. Now it's time to put in a call to Yeltsin. He's clearly key to the outcome of this thing, and we should register our support directly with him."

Before dawn on Tuesday in Moscow, troops outside the Russian parliament clashed with hundreds of citizens, some of whom hurled Molotov cocktails at the armored vehicles. Three of the protestors were killed and several more injured before the military units pulled back.

In Washington, Bush started the day early. In his hideaway study adjoining the Oval Office, Bush typed out a note to himself: "Keep in touch with Boris Yeltsin." Soon he had the Russian president on the telephone. Exuberantly he called out, "Boris, my friend!"

Yeltsin bellowed, "I am *extremely* glad to hear from you!" He reported that Soviet troops were surrounding the Russian White House: "We expect an attack, but your call will help us." The crowd of supporters on the street near the building, he said, had grown to 100,000.

Bush said, "We're anxious to do anything we can to be helpful. Do you have any suggestions?"

Yeltsin replied, "The main thing is moral support. We need to hear statements that will call the attention of the world to our plight."

Bush said, "All right, we'll do that. We'll do whatever we can. We're praying for you."

Referring to Bush's statement of Monday evening, Yeltsin said, "I heard about what you said yesterday. It's important for our people to have this kind of support."

Bush asked Yeltsin where he thought various other Soviet political figures stood on the coup. Of particular interest were Bessmertnykh and Moiseyev, whose role was especially important since Yazov, his immediate superior, had thrown in his lot with the plotters.

Yeltsin reported that Bessmertnykh had so far been "neutral"; he seemed to be waiting to see who came out on top. Moiseyev, meanwhile, was carrying out the policies of the Defense Ministry. In other words, he was at least passively supporting the putsch.

After hearing Yeltsin's voice, Bush began to believe that there might yet be a hero in this drama, one who would actually vanquish the villains — and it was not Gorbachev, but Yeltsin. As glowing reviews of his tougher Monday-evening statement poured in, the president told Scowcroft that he felt hopeful enough to return to Kennebunkport: "I think we can go back up there with a clear conscience," he said.

Aboard *Air Force One* on the flight north, the president's intensely partisan son George was exultant. The younger Bush saw the Soviet crisis as a reminder that the world was still a treacherous place, and that his father's experience in foreign policy was still important. Encountering a reporter in the back of the plane, he asked, "Do you think the American people are going to turn to a Democrat *now?*"

On Tuesday evening, the Americans concluded that if the Soviet military was planning an attack on Yeltsin's headquarters, it would come before dawn. Turning over his watch to Gompert, Hewett went home and told his wife, "If we can just get through the night without an attack, this thing could be over real soon."

In the Situation Room, Gompert used both CNN and U.S. intelligence reports to monitor the movement of troops, tanks, and war planes. It looked as though a major show of force was imminent against the Baltics and against Yeltsin. In an ominously familiar action, Soviet troops seized radio and television stations in Lithuania and Estonia.

Gompert typed out a tough statement for release in case the worst happened. It would announce the immediate severing of all economic ties with the Soviet Union and call on Soviet soldiers not to obey their commanders.

But by Wednesday dawn in Moscow, there still had been no attack. From Kennebunkport, Scowcroft worked with Gates and Hewett in Washington to prepare for a second conversation between Bush and Yeltsin at nine o'clock that morning.

All three men agreed that by surviving the night, the Russian president had grown immensely in stature. Gates said, "He's now a key figure as never before."

However, when Bush spoke to Yeltsin, the Russian president did not seem certain that the crisis was over. The Russian White House, he said, was still surrounded by KGB special forces. Prompted by Scowcroft, Bush asked once again about Moiseyev and the military. Yeltsin sounded optimistic that they were going to back down.

In fact, the coup was dissolving into farce. That morning, Kryuchkov and Yazov had rushed to Vnukovo Airport, outside Moscow, where they were joined by Gorbachev's traitorous old friend Anatoli Lukyanov. They commandeered an Aeroflot jetliner and took off for the Crimea — whether to negotiate with Gorbachev or to beg for his mercy was unclear.

Just after they took off, a delegation led by Yeltsin's vice president, Alexander Rutskoi, followed in a second plane. At Foros, Gorbachev refused to receive the first visitors. When the second group arrived from Moscow, it put the KGB and Defense chiefs under arrest.

Back in Moscow, Yeltsin loyalists, accompanied by armed men, rounded up the other plotters. They found Yanayev in a drunken stupor in his Kremlin office.

One of those assigned to the posse charged with arresting Boris Pugo was Grigori Yavlinsky, who had rushed back to Moscow from a

vacation in Ukraine to help defend the Russian White House. To avoid
capture, Pugo shot his wife, then himself.

After Robert Strauss was sworn in as ambassador, on Tuesday morning,
he left for Moscow aboard a small air force jet. At two o'clock Wednesday afternoon, local time, Strauss arrived at Sheremetyevo Airport. On
the way downtown, his armored Cadillac was stopped for nearly half
an hour to let pass a column of Soviet army vehicles pulling out of the
city. At that moment, Strauss realized that the coup was over.

By now, the new U.S. embassy complex was almost inaccessible behind the barricades erected to protect the nearby Russian White House.
To get to it, Strauss's car had to snake down sidewalks and alleys.

When the new ambassador arrived at his office, he had to make his
first policy decision. Yeltsin's government was flying several foreign envoys down to see Gorbachev at Foros, and Strauss had been invited to
go along. After his long journey, the last thing he wanted to do was
board another airplane — especially an Aeroflot one, and in the midst
of a crisis. Instead, he sent James Collins, who got to the airport only
to be told that Gorbachev was about to return to Moscow.

In Kennebunkport on Thursday morning, Bush ordered his aides to try
to call Gorbachev again. This time, to Scowcroft's astonishment, the
Soviet operator said, "We'll switch you down to the Crimea." As
the call was patched through, Bush was roaring around the harbor in
the *Fidelity.*

Summoned to shore, he raced to his bedroom and picked up the
telephone. Barbara stood nearby in a jogging suit. When Gorbachev
greeted him, Bush said, "Thank God! I'm so relieved to hear your
voice! . . . I hope Raisa came through this all right. . . . Barbara and I
are thinking about both of you."

Gorbachev boasted of his courage on Sunday: "They asked me to
resign, but I refused!" He said he had been frustrated over his isolation:
"My bodyguards remained faithful, but there was nothing they could
do. There was no way out of here. Even the way out by sea was blocked
by ships."

Gorbachev said he was just finding out what had happened in Moscow; his communications with the outside world had been restored only
an hour before. He told Bush that he had already talked to Yeltsin,
Kravchuk, and Nazarbayev, who had all played "useful" roles in the
previous several days.

He thanked Bush for taking a "position of principle" against the coup but characteristically reserved the greatest credit for himself. The coup's success, he said, had been prevented by everything he had done over the past several years: because of the new relationship he had engineered between the center and the republics, "things like this can't succeed."

He was exhilarated by his return to command and eager to get back to Moscow: "There's a lot to be done. . . . I have some tough decisions to make," he said. He had just given orders to General Moiseyev to "put everything back in order."

This last comment startled Bush and the other Americans listening in on the call. Hadn't Yeltsin indicated that Moiseyev had played at best an ambiguous role in the coup? After Bush hung up the telephone, Scowcroft said of Gorbachev, "He may have some surprises in store for him when he gets home."

On his return to Moscow, Gorbachev quickly turned his triumph into a debacle. He did not bother to stop by the Russian White House to thank Yeltsin for his deliverance. Appearing before the press, he sounded like Rip Van Winkle: instead of making himself the spokesman for the monumental change that had just occurred in the political life of the Soviet Union, he merely pretended that the past ninety-six hours had never happened. Now that he was back at his post, he seemed to be implying, life could go back to normal.

Apparently not recognizing that the Soviet Communist party had effectively destroyed itself, Gorbachev vowed to "work for the renewal of the party." Not until three days after his return was he persuaded to try to save his political career by resigning as General Secretary, disbanding the Central Committee, and handing all party property over to the Soviet parliament, which promptly voted, 283 to 29, to ban all party activities.

While crowds in the streets waved czarist Russian flags and chanted Yeltsin's name, Gorbachev closeted himself in the Kremlin and made televised speeches. He failed to comprehend that the citizenry was celebrating not his victory but the putschists' defeat. Never again would he be able to pose as the sole figure on the Soviet political scene who could deal with the dark forces on the right.

The "Yeltsin-lovers" at the CIA were scathing in their assessment of Gorbachev's behavior after his return to Moscow. One of their commentaries held that the Soviet leader displayed a "naive and egocentric quality" and seemed "unable to absorb news contrary to his ambitions."

In a private meeting with experts from around the government, Fritz Ermarth delivered what sounded like a postmortem not just on the coup but on the entire Gorbachev era. He predicted that the developments of the week would speed up the decommunization of the Soviet Union, the "deconstruction" of the party and the KGB, and the building of Russian statehood.

As for Gorbachev himself, his notion of a Soviet presidency was no longer viable. If he was lucky, said Ermarth, "Yeltsin may let him be a head of state in the manner of Queen Elizabeth."

With none of the same jocularity, Bush and Scowcroft were reaching the same conclusion. Watching television together in Kennebunkport on Friday, August 23, they saw Gorbachev and Yeltsin standing side by side before the Russian parliament, ostensibly to demonstrate that they were finally cooperating with each other.

Gorbachev admitted that he had not yet read the list of Russian proposals he held in his hand. Yeltsin poked his finger in Gorbachev's face and demanded gruffly, "Well, read them!"

Scowcroft sadly shook his head at the scene, musing, "It's all over." He said that Gorbachev was "not an independent actor anymore. Yeltsin's telling him what to do. I don't think Gorbachev understands what's happened."

Bush agreed: "I'm afraid he may have had it."

On Saturday, August 24, Marshal Akhromeyev hanged himself in his Kremlin office. He left a note saying, "Everything I have worked for is being destroyed."* Later, when Baker told Shevardnadze that he had been sorry to hear about the suicide, Shevardnadze made it clear he did not share the sentiment. He reminded the secretary of state that Akhromeyev had been one of the chief stumbling blocks on arms control: "He was the one who made it so difficult."

---

* For some time afterward, Akhromeyev's death was the subject of rumor and suspicion, in part because it was more common for Soviet general officers to commit suicide by shooting themselves. Right-wing oppositionists circulated the theory that he had either been murdered or told that unless he committed suicide, his family would suffer. This latter rumor was based on a cryptic line addressed to his family in his suicide note: "I always placed the interests of the state above yours, but now I am doing the opposite."

Gorbachev's first choice to succeed Yazov as defense minister was General Moiseyev, but Yeltsin's view that Moiseyev had allied himself with the coup soon prevailed. Almost as soon as he was appointed to the post, Moiseyev was fired and replaced by the commander of the air force, General Yevgeni Shaposhnikov.*

Bessmertnykh did not last much longer. On the Sunday of the coup, the members of the junta had summoned him back to Moscow from vacation and asked him to join their committee. The foreign minister refused but failed to speak out forcefully in public against the coup. Instead, he stayed away from his office, pleading illness and letting his deputy, Yuli Kvitsinsky, sign the cable instructing Soviet ambassadors around the world to convey the committee's pronouncement to their host governments. Yeltsin and his advisers wrote Bessmertnykh off as a political coward who was keeping his options open under the guise of protecting the institutional interests of the ministry.

When Gorbachev returned from the Crimea, Bessmertnykh was waiting at the airport to greet him. The next day, the Soviet leader called him to the Kremlin and told him to stay on at his post. But on Friday, Gorbachev telephoned and said, "I've gotten the impression that you were somewhat passive during those three days."

Bessmertnykh protested: "That's completely wrong, Mikhail Sergeyevich! I don't know what you've been told, but I was the only one of your close colleagues who passed the real test. No one else was around. They were all on vacation. But I was here, and I did my best to protect our policy."

Gorbachev said, "I've got information to the contrary." Bessmertnykh replied, "Well, Comrade President, if you believe what you've been told, then obviously I'll have to resign."

Bessmertnykh announced his resignation to his staff and then sat down in his office for a previously scheduled interview with ABC's Ted Koppel. With a camera crew recording the moment for broadcast, Bessmertnykh telephoned Baker in Wyoming, where it was four-thirty in the morning. He said, "Jim, it's a very important piece of information for me, but I think it will be also for you. I have just resigned."

Astonished that he had just lost another Soviet diplomatic partner,

* When Colin Powell met with a group of visiting Soviet officers at Harvard on September 9, he took the senior member of the group aside and asked him to convey greetings from him and his wife to Moiseyev and his wife in Moscow.

Baker said, "I'm sorry to hear that, Sasha. I'm sorry to hear that this has happened. I thought we'd begun to work well together."

Exploiting the opportunity to start clearing his name, Bessmertnykh went on to assure Baker that he had behaved "honorably" during the coup and would always be the "man of *perestroika* and 'new-thinking' policy."

Baker had no idea that millions of TV viewers would soon be listening to the conversation.

For months afterward, Bessmertnykh insisted to all who would listen that during the coup he had suffered not from some "diplomatic illness" but rather from a very real attack of kidney stones: he had done his best to shield the Foreign Ministry from the plotters and the KGB. Bessmertnykh blamed his dismissal on Primakov, whom he accused of intriguing once more to win the post of foreign minister for himself.*

U.S. officials were inclined to give Bessmertnykh the benefit of the doubt and suspect the worst of Primakov. Whatever the truth was, Gorbachev gave the job of foreign minister to Boris Pankin, a relatively obscure apparatchik who had served as Soviet ambassador to Prague and whose principal credential was that he had publicly opposed the coup while it was taking place.

In Kennebunkport, Bush and Scowcroft realized that Gorbachev was severely — perhaps mortally — wounded, but they did not like the way Yeltsin seemed to be moving in for the kill. When Prime Minister John Major came to visit in late August, Bush told him that he thought Yeltsin was "pushing awfully hard, rubbing Gorbachev's nose in the dirt."

Scowcroft agreed with that assessment. He reminded colleagues that even before the coup, "Yeltsin came pretty close to destroying Gorbachev. Now the jury is out on whether Gorbachev will be able to recover. The guy is now fighting for his political life."

In the flush of their victory over the coup plotters, some of Yeltsin's

---

* If the first cable, signed by Kvitsinsky, was the principal piece of evidence in the case against Bessmertnykh, a second cable dated August 19, over Bessmertnykh's signature, gave at least some weight to his side of the story. It called on ambassadors to "work in these complicated times to carry out their professional duties to protect the foreign policy interests of the USSR . . . in accordance with policy as defined by constitutional bodies: the Supreme Soviet, the presidency, and the Cabinet of Ministers." Bessmertnykh later noted that the coup committee was pointedly omitted from the list. The next day, in response to rumors that KGB station chiefs were generating support for the coup in various capitals, Bessmertnykh sent another cable warning ambassadors to take orders from no one but the Foreign Ministry.

political allies had suggested that Russia might claim parts of the territories of neighboring republics in order to protect ethnic Russians who lived there. Scowcroft seized on this as evidence of Yeltsin's "lust for land," even though the Russian president himself had quickly disavowed such ambitions.

Like Bush, Scowcroft recognized that because of the coup, much of Gorbachev's power had now shifted to Yeltsin. In public, he praised Yeltsin's political skills and democratic beliefs, but in private meetings with the British visitors, he referred to the Russian president as an egoist, a demagogue, an opportunist, and a grandstander who had never resisted a chance to use his meetings or phone calls with Bush to upstage Gorbachev.

CHAPTER 22

"What We Have Accomplished Will Last Forever"

THE AUGUST COUP had both frightened and emboldened secessionists throughout the Soviet Union. Leaders of the movements for democracy and independence had glimpsed what awaited them if the hard-liners returned to power: in the Baltics, investigators found lists of hundreds of local leaders whom the Soviet authorities had tagged for execution.

Now that the weakness of Gorbachev and the central government had been exposed, there was a stampede for the exits. The governments in Tallinn, Riga, and Vilnius renewed their campaign for international recognition, and several European nations quickly agreed to establish full diplomatic relations with the Baltic states.

On Saturday, August 24, 1991, the Ukrainian parliament approved its own declaration of independence. Other republics followed: Belarus, Moldova, Azerbaijan, Uzbekistan, Kyrgyzstan, and Tadzhikistan.* Yelt-

---

* As they approached independence, Byelorussia, Moldavia, and Kirghizia changed their names, much as Ukrainians were insisting on dropping the article in front of the English rendering of their country's name. The new designations were all intended to make these lands sound less like provinces of the Russian empire and more like independent countries of proud heritage.

sin's Russia signed its own political and economic treaties with Ukraine and Kazakhstan.

Desperately trying to keep ahead of events, the Soviet Congress of People's Deputies moved toward the creation of a confederation of sovereign states. Under this arrangement, Gorbachev would serve as chairman of an executive committee responsible for foreign policy, security, and law enforcement. Five republics, as well as the Baltics, boycotted the parliament's opening session.

In Washington, Bush and Scowcroft still hoped that the Soviet Union would survive in some coherent form — preferably a federation of republics with strong economic and military ties to the center. The alternative, they feared, was "atomization" and collapse into interethnic conflict.

Scowcroft noted that the centrifugal forces now surging throughout the Soviet Union could conceivably tear apart the Russian Republic as well, since it harbored numerous enclaves of non-Russians. The large populations of ethnic Russians scattered throughout the non-Russian republics posed a further complication. With his background in Yugoslavia, Scowcroft saw new parallels between the situation there and the one in the USSR.

Bush and Scowcroft regarded the Baltics as something of a special case. The Soviet Union had annexed them more recently than the other republics, and the United States had never formally recognized their incorporation. Bush hoped that once Moscow acceded to Baltic independence, the unraveling of the Union would slow down, at least for a while.

In late August, Bush wrote Gorbachev a letter urging him to recognize the Baltic states as soon as possible. He said that once the Soviet Union did that, the United States would follow suit. In letting Gorbachev dictate the timing of American recognition, Bush was trying to shore up the Soviet leader's increasingly shaky position.

On Monday, August 26, Bush told reporters, "I am not going to move precipitously. . . . I don't want to be a part of making a mistake that might contribute to some kind of anarchy inside the Soviet Union."

Gorbachev promised Bush he would recognize Baltic independence by Friday, August 30, but then he asked for more time. On Saturday, August 31, Bush called President Landsbergis in Vilnius and pledged that U.S. recognition was imminent. But two days later, Gorbachev still had not moved.

Unable to wait any longer, Bush formally recognized the Baltics on Monday, September 2. He said publicly, "When history is written, nobody will remember that we took forty-eight hours more than Iceland or whoever else it is."

Four days later, on Friday, September 6, the new Soviet provisional executive body, called the State Council, recognized the Baltics. Curtis Kamman of the U.S. State Department was in Landsbergis's office in Vilnius when an aide rushed in and gave Landsbergis the TASS dispatch from Moscow.

"Mr. President," said Kamman, "it looks like you have some good news there."

"Yes," said Landsbergis, beaming, "it certainly is!"

Despite everything that had happened, Bush remained queasy about the fading of Gorbachev and Yeltsin's ascendancy. He and Scowcroft believed that Yeltsin, having thrown in his lot with the forces agitating for the Soviet Union's dissolution, would be unable to succeed Gorbachev as the leader of the central government; as leader of Russia, with its tradition of overpowering its smaller neighbors, he was distrusted by the leaders of the other republics.

Talking with reporters in Kennebunkport on condition that they not identify him as their source in their stories, Scowcroft was asked when the Bush administration would finally abandon Gorbachev for Yeltsin. He replied, "When it looks like Gorbachev is irrelevant." Bush and Scowcroft were among the few who still felt that this moment had not yet arrived.

In the *Washington Post* on Sunday, September 1, Ann Devroy reported from Kennebunkport that "senior advisers to President Bush" were "expressing profound anxiety here about the prospect of losing as a diplomatic partner a Soviet Union led by Mikhail Gorbachev and the emergence, instead, of unproven charismatic leaders such as Russian President Boris Yeltsin."

Her article quoted a "senior administration official" as saying that Yeltsin had an "instinct for the demagogic" and a "passion to do 'what plays' among the populace." The anonymous attribution fooled no one. Appearing on CNN's "Newsmaker Saturday," Scowcroft went public with his concern, saying it was "not clear exactly to what end" Yeltsin would use his power.

From Moscow, Ambassador Strauss called Eagleburger and Tutwiler at the State Department and complained, "This Yeltsin-bashing is really stupid! It doesn't help Gorbachev or anyone else. The *last* thing Gorbachev needs is for Yeltsin to add this to his list of pretexts for disliking him."

Beyond his personal feelings for Gorbachev, Bush also had another reason for wanting to see the process of disintegration slowed: he still believed that a strong central government was necessary to assure reliable control over the Soviet Union's nuclear arsenal. He feared that if the center gave way, Soviet nuclear weapons could wind up in the hands not only of breakaway republics but also of renegade military units.

In late August, the president decided to propose a postscript to the START treaty that he and Gorbachev had signed only a month before in Moscow. He reasoned that the August coup had dealt the Soviet military-industrial complex a serious setback because two of its leading figures, Yazov and Baklanov, had been so prominent in the putsch. Yeltsin, for his part, was intent on a drastic reduction in military spending, and Ukraine wished to become a nuclear-free zone.* Bush felt that the United States could thus afford a further scaling-back of its own weaponry.

Dick Cheney was uneasy about undertaking further strategic arms reductions. He argued that the breaking apart of the Soviet Union would only add to the huge pressures from Congress and the American people to make radical cuts in the Pentagon budget. During a meeting with Bush and Scowcroft in Kennebunkport, he worried that a START-plus treaty would be "premature" and "imprudent." The NSC staff began calling Cheney the "defensive secretary."

Bush was adamant. Cheney returned to the Pentagon with instructions for Powell and the Joint Chiefs to prepare a list of new disarmament measures that they could tolerate. They responded by proposing the removal of short-range nuclear weapons from surface ships and submarines — a tactical and largely symbolic concession to the old Soviet insistence on naval arms control.

The president wanted more. In mid-September, the Pentagon agreed to a proposal for cuts in land-based weapons on both sides. Two categories of Soviet nuclear weaponry would be covered: short-range mis-

* The Ukrainians had pursued this aim even before the coup. On several occasions earlier in the year, members of their independence movement, Rukh, had come to Washington to ask the Pentagon for information on the location of Soviet nuclear sites in Ukraine, so that they could petition the Kremlin for their removal.

siles, many of which were based around the Soviet periphery, and land-based strategic missiles with multiple warheads, located in Ukraine, Belarus, Kazakhstan, and Russia.*

Bush revealed his proposal to the world in a televised address on Friday evening, September 27. Part of his aim was to strengthen Gorbachev's hand in dealing with the Soviet military; he knew that the Soviet generals would be more likely to make concessions to the United States if they were part of a two-way agreement. He was also offering Gorbachev a fig leaf behind which to conceal the withdrawal of nuclear weapons from the non-Russian republics.

Gorbachev hailed Bush's offer as a "major step" and replied with a new proposal of his own that he hoped would return him to the center of the world stage. But few listened. The Soviet Union was breaking up, and there was nothing that either Bush or Gorbachev could do about it.†

At the end of October, Bush and Gorbachev met in Madrid for the Middle East peace conference that the United States and the Soviet Union had agreed to cosponsor. It was a diplomatic breakthrough of major proportions in two respects: first, it represented the first time that all the principal parties in the conflict came together for sustained negotiations; and second, it furnished dramatic proof that the United States and the Soviet Union, after decades of rivalry and hostility in virtually every area of the world — notably including the Middle East — were now working together.

The peace conference was emblematic of the new U.S.-Soviet "partnership," giving real meaning to the word that Gorbachev had, to the surprise and discomfiture of many Americans, introduced into the vocabulary of their relations in 1989.

Had the Moscow hard-liners not moved against him in August, Gor-

---

* In its treatment of MIRVed ICBMs, the proposal was essentially a repackaging of the one Bush would have made to Gorbachev at Malta but for Cheney's opposition. By September 1991, elimination of the MX was an easy concession for Bush to offer to the Soviets, because the U.S. Congress was even more hostile toward funding for the program than it had been in 1989.

† The START treaty remained in limbo for many months. When Boris Yeltsin came to Washington for his own summit meeting with Bush in June 1992, he agreed to additional and even more dramatic reductions in the former Soviet arsenal. In the fall of that year, Lawrence Eagleburger, then acting secretary of state, sent the START treaty to the Senate with a letter saying, "The history of the Cold War will not be over until START is ratified and has entered into force." The Senate approved it by a vote of 93 to 6 on October 1, 1992.

bachev would have cited the Madrid meeting as a triumph of his rapprochement with the West, one of the many dividends that would have
been impossible while the Soviet Union was fighting the Cold War with
the United States in the Middle East.

Instead, Gorbachev came to Madrid a shadow of his former self.

By October, the Soviet treasury was so depleted that the United States
had to pay many of the Soviet delegation's expenses in Madrid. Even
the makeup of the delegation itself showed how weak Gorbachev had
become. It included Vladimir Lukin, the Yeltsin ally who chaired the
Russian parliament's foreign relations committee, and Lakim Kayumov,
the foreign minister of Tadzhikistan.

Gorbachev lamely told the Americans that Kayumov, who spoke
Persian and Arabic, "knows the part of the world that we're discussing
here." In fact, Kayumov's inclusion was a gesture on Gorbachev's part
toward one of his vanishing constituencies: the Central Asian republics.*

During private talks with Bush in Madrid, Gorbachev was barely
interested in discussing the Middle East at all. Instead, he prattled on
obsessively about the "complexity" of the crisis he now faced at
home. He declared that it would be "stupid" and "disastrous" for the
leaders of the republics to continue on their secessionist course, and
insisted that the situation in the Soviet Union was "moving in the
right direction" — though not even he seemed really to believe that
anymore.

Bush later confided to Scowcroft, "It was as though Gorbachev was
looking to me for support and, at the same time, practicing on me
arguments that he needs to use back home."

After their meeting, Bush and Gorbachev made one last appearance
together before reporters. Trying to cheer up his old friend, Bush said,
"You're still the master!" But in that context, the comment seemed more
patronizing than flattering.

Back in Washington, Scowcroft told colleagues that Gorbachev now
represented nothing more than the "ghost of the center." Nevertheless,
he added, U.S. policy now should take its cue from the Hippocratic
oath: "We should do nothing that causes Gorbachev any harm." Baker

---

* That fall, the United States asked the Soviet Union to cosponsor a UN resolution
repealing the "Zionism is racism" resolution passed with Soviet support in 1975. Gorbachev demurred. His deputy foreign minister, Vladimir Petrovsky, privately told the
Americans that he would have liked to help, but Muslims in the Central Asian republics
would not stand for it.

suggested to his aides that the only question that remained was whether the breakup of the Soviet Union would be violent or peaceful — "a crash or a soft landing."

Gorbachev stubbornly pursued the signing of the Union treaty that had triggered the August coup. Virtually everyone else knew that the document was a dead letter; the leaders of the republics felt that it left far too much power in the hands of the center.

Since August, Yeltsin had taken one unilateral step after another, all of which would have violated Gorbachev's treaty had it been in force. In November, he pushed through the Russian parliament a measure seizing control of the republic's economy and natural resources.

Twice that month, Gorbachev met with Yeltsin and leaders of other republics in an attempt to persuade them to sign his Union treaty. When they refused, Gorbachev lashed out at them for "pursuing their own agendas." He was right: their agenda was independence.

On December 1, Ukrainians were to vote on seceding from the Soviet Union. No one doubted what the outcome would be.

Had Bush followed the instincts that had first guided him in the case of Baltic independence immediately after the August coup, he would have waited to adjust U.S. policy until after the Ukrainian referendum, or perhaps even until after the Soviet government had accepted the referendum's results. But Gorbachev was not the only world leader whose political position had deteriorated since August.

Bush was growing anxious about the start of the next presidential election year, now only a little more than a month away. In early November, the people of Pennsylvania had sent him a disturbing message: in a special election to fill the Senate seat of Republican John Heinz, who had been killed in an airplane crash, the liberal underdog, Harris Wofford, defeated Bush's handpicked candidate, former Attorney General Dick Thornburgh.

Polls showed that many Pennsylvania voters of East European descent had backed Wofford to protest Bush's laggard recognition of Baltic independence. Bush did not want to make the same mistake with Ukraine. He was still smarting over William Safire's lampooning of his address in Kiev as the "Chicken Kiev speech." One newly announced presidential candidate, Governor Bill Clinton of Arkansas, criticized Bush for being slow to endorse the Soviet republics' demands for independence.

At the White House on Tuesday, November 27, Bush met with senior foreign policy advisers. He decided to recognize Ukrainian independence "expeditiously" after the referendum, without waiting for Moscow's blessing as a "precondition." The next day, the president announced his intention to a delegation of Ukrainian-American visitors, who promptly leaked it to the press.

When Gorbachev heard that Bush had in effect recognized Ukrainian independence four days before the Ukrainians themselves even voted on the issue, he felt devastated. He knew this would be a near-fatal blow to what was left of the Soviet Union, as well as to his own prestige.

Gorbachev asked Chernyayev, "How could Bush do this?" Other aides pronounced the U.S. president guilty of "betrayal."

During a call to Bush, Gorbachev controlled his temper. He said he was "disappointed" that the United States had acted so "prematurely," adding that many in Moscow had taken Bush's statement as an effort to "stimulate separatism in Ukraine."

Gorbachev lambasted Yeltsin for reneging on his April endorsement of the Union treaty. He told Bush, "Mr. President, I worked for several years with President Reagan and now for three or four years with you. We've known each other a long time. Can you say that after agreeing on something Gorbachev ever reneged?"

Bush said, "No, never." He was too polite to point out that in the tumble of events since the August coup, April was a lifetime ago.

Baker conceded to his aides that Gorbachev's complaint about the U.S. position on Ukrainian independence had some merit; it was a bad precedent for the United States so baldly to "jump the gun." Dennis Ross told him, "This is what happens when the political side of the White House starts to take over."

Scowcroft agreed, admitting, "I think we've signaled a more forward-leaning policy than we had in mind." He warned the president that by shifting sides so blatantly, "we may prejudice relations between Kiev and Moscow."

On Sunday, December 1, Ukrainians voted overwhelmingly for independence and made Leonid Kravchuk their first popularly elected president.

Yeltsin was determined to keep Ukraine and Russia together as part of some larger political entity. He feared that if he did not move quickly,

Ukraine would break all ties with Moscow and claim those Soviet armed forces and nuclear weapons that were on its territory.

On Saturday, December 7, Yeltsin quietly met with Kravchuk in Minsk, the capital of Belarus, along with the president of that republic, Stanislav Shushkevich. The three leaders resolved to declare that the Soviet Union no longer existed. In its place would be a "Commonwealth of Independent States" whose capital would be Minsk.

After Yeltsin telephoned Bush to give him the news, Shushkevich — the host of the meeting but the third-ranking member of the threesome — called Gorbachev. He reported that he and the other two leaders had endorsed a document, which he wanted to read to him. Gorbachev interrupted: what was he talking about? Shushkevich said, "Well, you know, it has already been gaining support. . . . We've had a conversation with Bush."

Gorbachev exploded: "You've been speaking with the president of the United States of America, and the president of your own *country* knows nothing about it? *Shame* on you!"

On Monday evening, December 9, during a cocktail reception at Spaso House, Pavel Palazhchenko and other top aides to Gorbachev denounced the Minsk agreement as the "second coup."

American officials heard rumors that when Yeltsin flew back to Moscow the night after signing the commonwealth agreement, he was so drunk that he had to be carried off his plane, and his bodyguards used brute force to prevent photographers from taking pictures.

Whatever the veracity of these reports, the Russian president was in full command of his faculties when he met with Gorbachev. "You've been off meeting in the woods, shutting down the Soviet Union," complained the Soviet leader. "Some people in this country have even interpreted it as a kind of political coup, carried out behind the back of the supreme soviets of the republics. The president of the United States learned about all of it before the president of the USSR!"

In November, Gorbachev had managed to wangle Shevardnadze into returning as Soviet foreign minister, replacing the hapless Boris Pankin. Now Shevardnadze called Tarasenko and other aides into his office and said that the Soviet state was finished. Returning to his old job, he said, had been a "grave personal mistake."

The former East German boss Erich Honecker likewise saw which way the wind was blowing. After German unification, fearing that he would be tried for manslaughter in the deaths of East Germans who had tried to cross the Berlin Wall, the old man had persuaded Gorbachev to fly him to the Soviet capital. Now that Gorbachev and the Soviet Union were about to collapse, Honecker sought asylum in the Chilean embassy in Moscow.*

On Friday, December 13, the present authors met with Gorbachev for eighty minutes. Gorbachev's aides had summoned them to Moscow for a final interview with the Soviet leader for this book. In the wake of the Minsk agreement, Gorbachev tried one last time to mobilize his sole remaining constituency — his Western audience.

Shortly after noon, Gorbachev's new spokesman, Andrei Grachyov, told the authors that they could come to the Kremlin at three o'clock, provided that the conversation could be expanded to include an interview on current events that would appear in the next week's issue of *Time*.

Along with *Time*'s Moscow bureau chief, John Kohan, and Felix Rosenthal, a Soviet citizen who had long worked for the magazine, the authors were driven to the Kremlin gate. Rosenthal informed the guard that they had come to see "Mikhail Sergeyevich."

The third floor of the yellow Council of Ministers building was deathly quiet and smelled of fresh paint. The previous day, two foreign cameramen had reportedly bribed their way into a meeting between Gorbachev and the Soviet press. Now one of Gorbachev's aides insisted to the authors, "I want it put on the record that the president is not giving this interview for hard currency."

Pavel Palazhchenko ushered the group into the cavernous office that had been occupied in turn by Stalin, Khrushchev, and Brezhnev. Gorbachev showed them to the purple-teak oval table where he had sat with the unshaven Yazov and Kryuchkov on the first night of the Gulf War, looking at maps of the U.S. bombing campaign. Tea and cookies were served.

Gorbachev's demeanor during the previous day's session with Soviet reporters had been so melancholy that some of those present had called

---

* The Chileans offered Honecker this hospitality out of gratitude for his similar favors to Chilean leftists exiled during the dictatorship of General Augusto Pinochet. But in July 1992, they forced him to leave. Since no other embassy would take the old man, who was now suffering from cancer, he was shipped back to Berlin for criminal trial. Before leaving Moscow, Honecker raised his right fist in a final, defiant Communist salute.

it "Gorbachev's last press conference." Thus, the authors had arrived expecting a swan song.

Instead, Gorbachev was determined to show that he was far from ready to surrender. Asked if he would be president of the Soviet Union three days hence, when an excerpt from the interview would appear in *Time,* Gorbachev laughed, then said, "On Monday? I'm sure I will!"

He denounced Yeltsin's Minsk agreement as "unconvincing, ill-founded, badly formulated," adding, "If we start tearing this country apart, it will just be more difficult for us to come to terms with one another."

Gorbachev argued for the restoration of his Union treaty. He pulled a document from a pink folder labeled URGENT: "Look here! It's a report on the Supreme Soviet of Ukraine discussing the Minsk agreement. They ratified it without discussion, then added several amendments." He was suggesting that Kravchuk was resorting to old, heavy-handed methods to ram the agreement through the Ukrainian parliament.

He said, "Three republics have no right to say that the Soviet Union is dead. This reminds me of Mayakovsky. One of his characters didn't like America. He wanted to close it down. I have received many telegrams asking what is happening behind the backs of the president and the people. In 1937, troikas made decisions about the lives of one, two, three individuals. Now they are deciding the future of the entire country."*

Gorbachev was asked about statements made by the Bush administration that seemed to support the Minsk agreement. Noting that Bush and Baker had professed to "consider the process taking place in this country as our internal affair," he complained that the secretary of state had been "much too hasty in saying that the Soviet Union no longer exists."†

---

* Gorbachev was probably thinking of Mayakovsky's long 1926 work "My Discovery of America," but in fact, none of the poet's characters much liked the United States. Born in 1893, Vladimir Mayakovsky passionately embraced the Bolsheviks and spewed forth anticapitalist and anti-American propaganda in his writings. In 1930, disillusioned with Stalinism, he killed himself and was hailed by Stalin as the "best and most talented poet of our Soviet epoch." The troikas referred to by Gorbachev materialized at the height of Stalin's purges.
† The previous Sunday, appearing on CBS's "Face the Nation," Baker had said, "I think the Soviet Union as we've known it no longer exists." The phrase "as we've known it" had apparently been lost in the translation that reached Gorbachev.

"Things are in flux here. While *we're* still trying to figure things out, the United States seems to know everything already! I don't think that's loyalty — particularly toward those of us who have favored partnership and full-fledged cooperation."

Gorbachev said he supported the "preservation of the Soviet Union as a country. I'm against cutting this country into different pieces like a pie and washing it down with tea or whisky or coffee." Picking up a white scratch pad, he angrily drew a circle with crisscross lines through it. "Who has the right to cut this country into pieces?"

He said he was "firmly convinced we are making a mistake" in allowing the dissolution of the Union: "If the process gets out of hand, then I'll have buried everything to which I've devoted the best years of my life."

Gorbachev was clearly disgusted with Yeltsin. On Sunday night, after signing the Minsk agreement, the Russian president "didn't even call me. I found out that he had talked to George Bush and not to me. There was no need to draw Bush into this. It's a question of Yeltsin's moral standards. I cannot approve or justify this style of behavior."

He went on, "You have to deal with other leaders on the basis of trust. Sometimes it's not a signed treaty but just a political agreement in principle, which is superior to any treaty. Without it there can be no trust with anyone."

Referring to Yeltsin, Kravchuk, and leaders of the other republics who had been making trips abroad, Gorbachev said, "There is a danger that some politicians are just entering the world of real politics. People forget that it was I who encouraged them to travel. I'm not shy about saying that. Maybe some people thought I had just asked them to take a letter to President Bush. I don't think my partners actually understood that I wanted them to get to know them. They figured, 'Well, if Gorbachev is sending these people over here, that must mean that Gorbachev is finished and we should side with the new leaders.' "

At the end of the interview, Gorbachev's anger gave way to a mixture of resignation and self-congratulation: "As far as my work is concerned, the main purpose of my life has already been fulfilled. I feel at peace with myself. I've lived through such experiences that I feel absolutely free. At the same time, I feel that the experience I've accumulated should be fully used for the freedom of my country and international relations. And I feel strong enough to go on."

Just before saying good-bye, Gorbachev wryly noted that someone earlier that week had asked him if he was happy. "Happy?" he scoffed. "That's a question to be asked of a woman!"*

As Gorbachev was meeting with the authors at the Kremlin, Yeltsin telephoned Bush with a cheerful report on the progress toward a new commonwealth.

Bush listened politely but had little to say in response. After hanging up, he instructed his staff to get Gorbachev on the phone. Ever since the August coup, he had made it a rule that whenever he heard from one of the two rival leaders, he would call the other; that way, he could not be accused of taking sides or allowing either one to play him off against the other.

By the time Bush's call reached Gorbachev at his dacha, it was eleven-thirty at night Moscow time. The Soviet leader sounded groggy and grumpy: "Good day, George — or actually good evening, because, you know, it *is* evening here," he said.

Bush said he had heard from Yeltsin and now wanted to hear from Gorbachev himself how things were going. Gorbachev launched into a twenty-minute monologue. Still downplaying the Minsk agreement, he called it "just a sketch, an improvisation. Many questions remain unanswered."

The new commonwealth, he said, would need a "system of laws regulating public order, defense, frontiers, and international obligations." His own participation, which he was more than willing to pledge, would be essential to "impart a legal and legitimate character to the process of the transformation of the state."

He said that the three leaders' statement at Minsk that the Soviet Union had ceased to exist was "facile" and "bullying." But he then acknowledged that his Union treaty was indeed all but dead, and that further discussion of the future had been rendered "virtually impossible. The agreements between me and the leaders of the republics have been discarded."

Gorbachev once again insisted that he had been "moving in the right direction" before Minsk. Granted, there was "some difficulty" with Ukraine, but he would have been able to work that out, too, if only he

---

* Excerpts from the interview dealing with the Minsk agreement ran in *Time*'s December 23 issue. On the cover was a photograph of Gorbachev shaking his fist, with the headline, "Gorbachev Says He'll Fight On, But He's Already: A Man without a Country."

had had a chance. But with the announcement that a commonwealth was being formed behind his back, he had been ambushed by his political inferiors: "All of this looks like the work of amateurs. They have rejected my role!" He was willing to concede, however, that "even if I do not share their approach, I understand the situation."

Having vented his spleen, Gorbachev reassured Bush that the Soviet military and its nuclear forces were still under control. He and Yeltsin were cooperating on that subject, if on nothing else.

As if to suggest that he intended to remain in power, he used the phone conversation to put in a new bid for Western economic assistance. January and February promised to be brutal months for the Soviet people, he said, and he was afraid there would be no food on the shelves in the stores.

Bush told him that Baker was on his way to Moscow and would study the situation more closely.

This mention of Baker's name set Gorbachev off again. He demanded to know why the secretary of state was already writing the obituary of the Soviet Union. Bush let the matter slide.

At the White House, after his conversation with Gorbachev, Bush said to Scowcroft, "This really is the end, isn't it?" Scowcroft replied, "Yeah, Gorbachev is kind of a pathetic figure at this point."

The next day, Saturday, December 14, Pavel Palazhchenko and his wife invited the authors of this book to their apartment on the outskirts of Moscow. Before luncheon, Palazhchenko grimly reminisced about the August coup. Had it succeeded, he said, he would have taken a job as a night porter.

He recalled that to take his mind off the unfolding tragedy in August, he had watched two videocassettes, which he now inserted into his tape machine to show the authors. One was a ballet, the other a collection of National Football League highlights, broadcast by CBS in 1985.

After luncheon, Palazhchenko asked his wife to leave the room so he could convey a "very confidential message" to the authors. He would not say on whose behalf he was performing this task, though he was not, he maintained, "speaking for Gorbachev." The interpreter was following a careful script that was intended to help protect Gorbachev while preserving the Soviet leader's deniability.

Palazhchenko asked the authors to write the message down and to deliver it only to "President Bush, Secretary Baker, or Dennis Ross."

They should not reveal that it had come from him, only that it was from "someone" on Gorbachev's staff.* The message was this:

"The president [Gorbachev] is keeping all of his options open. It is possible that he might accept some role in the commonwealth. But he will not accept it if it is done in a humiliating way. The leaders of the United States and the West should find a way to impress on Yeltsin and the others the benefits of keeping the president involved and the importance of doing so in a way that is not offensive to his dignity.

"At the same time, it is quite possible that he will have to resign. There is a 30 to 50 percent chance that he will be a private figure within a few weeks. Some people are fabricating a [criminal] case against him. It is important that Yeltsin not have anything to do with that and that he not permit anything to happen that would harm the president. Once again, the leaders of the United States should impress that point on him. The above is a personal view, never discussed with the president."

On Sunday afternoon, December 15, in the early-winter darkness and swirling snow, Baker and his party landed in Moscow. The previous evening, the five Central Asian republics had agreed to join the commonwealth. This was the final nail in the coffin of the Soviet Union.

The authors called on Dennis Ross later that day in his room at the Penta Hotel. Without divulging its provenance, they read aloud from Palazhchenko's message. Ross took notes, then glumly nodded, saying, "I'm not surprised. I think I know who it came from."

After the authors left, Ross went to Baker's room and passed on the text of the message. Baker asked who he thought had sent it. Ross replied that his first guess was Palazhchenko; his second was Gorbachev's old ally Alexander Yakovlev.

Baker said, "Well, we've got to follow up on this. . . . We've got to raise it with both Yeltsin and Gorbachev. Still, we can't get in the middle of it."

On Monday morning, December 16, Baker and his aides met with Boris Yeltsin. Seated next to the Russian president was General Shaposhnikov, the new chief of the Soviet armed forces. This told Baker all he needed to know: the army had thrown in its lot with Yeltsin, Russia, and the commonwealth.

Yeltsin and Shaposhnikov went out of their way to assure the secre-

---

* Palazhchenko has since granted permission for the authors to reveal this episode.

tary of state that Soviet nuclear weapons would remain under central control in the new commonwealth.

At a certain point in the conversation, Baker started to say that the United States would look with disfavor on any effort by Yeltsin's government to gather damaging information on Gorbachev or to put him on trial. He began, "Many people will be watching what's going to happen to Gorbachev."

Yeltsin stopped him, saying, "Gorbachev has done a lot for this country. He needs to be treated with respect and deserves to be treated with respect. It's about time we became a country where leaders can be retired with honor!"

Reassured, Baker felt that Yeltsin was trying to make it clear that as a newly fledged world leader, he was aware of the responsibilities he was assuming.

That afternoon, Baker met with Gorbachev. Ross was both startled and moved to discover that Shevardnadze and Yakovlev had also come to this farewell session: despite all of their struggles with Gorbachev over the years, they were closing ranks with him at the end.

Gorbachev correctly noted that the former Soviet republics that were now calling themselves states were not truly independent of one another at all — nor would they be for a long time to come, he added. After centuries under the czars and seven decades under a rigidly centralized Soviet system, their economies, communications, distribution networks, and natural-resource systems were linked in a web that could not be dissolved overnight.

The Soviet president still clung to the notion that he might serve as an honest broker between Russia and Ukraine, between the Slavic states and those of the Caucasus and Central Asia, and between the republics and the Soviet army. By now, however, that possibility was alive in no one's mind but his own.

Gorbachev told Baker, "There may have been miscalculations and even serious mistakes on my part, but that's not the point. I see a role for myself using the political means available to me to prevent even greater disintegration in the process of creating the commonwealth.

"Time is running out, and we have to act quickly. I want the leaders of the republics to succeed, though I don't believe they can. Still, I want them to, because if they don't, all that we have accomplished will be in jeopardy. And so will the future itself."

Baker acknowledged that a great many questions had been left unanswered. For example, since there were to be at least ten different sovereign states, each with its own foreign policy, "it's difficult to see how the Commonwealth of Independent States can have a common defense policy."

Gorbachev brightened. "You're right, Jim!" he exclaimed. "I anticipated this. My prophecies are beginning to come true very quickly. I've already had to intervene. I've spoken with Kravchuk and Yeltsin several times. Kravchuk has declared himself the commander in chief [of Soviet armed forces in Ukraine]. I can't help being worried.

"Russia may decide to put its foot down and say it's sick and tired of this whole mess. What then? If the republics do not come to terms, disintegration could escalate, and the result could be dictatorship. The people are in such desperate straits that they might even support dictatorship."

Realizing that he had unintentionally reignited Gorbachev's fury at Yeltsin, Baker tried to cool him down: "I have to tell you that what we've heard about the command and control of nuclear forces has been very reassuring."

Gorbachev said, "Yes, on that subject the world should be reassured."

Baker reminded the Soviet leader that the United States could not and would not "interfere in your internal affairs." At the same time, he lavished praise on Gorbachev: "There is no question that you've earned your place in history. There's a revolution going on here, but you set everything in motion."*

The following morning, Tuesday, December 17, Gorbachev announced that at the end of the year 1991, the Soviet Union and its governmental structures would cease to exist.

On Monday, December 23, the last leader of the Soviet Union prepared to tape a resignation speech. He had his hair cut for the occasion. Then Yeltsin arrived unexpectedly at the Kremlin for an eight-hour knockdown, drag-out negotiation with Gorbachev over procedures for handing over power and the terms of Gorbachev's pension and retirement.

Afterward, Chernyayev and Palazhchenko angrily told Gorbachev that Yeltsin had just staged "yet another coup." Gorbachev upbraided them: "You can't say that. This is happening according to the consti-

---

* Baker's aides had briefed their boss that in his Thursday "last press conference" with Soviet reporters, Gorbachev had taken pride and consolation in the claim, "I started this process."

tution." He decided to deliver his resignation speech live to the world on Christmas Day.

On Tuesday, December 24, Gorbachev gathered together his senior staff and urged them to follow his example: "Restrain your emotions as much as possible."

The next day, Gorbachev took a brisk stroll around the Kremlin grounds, surprising several groups of Russian tourists who called out their good wishes. Before entering his office, he received Ted Koppel of ABC, who was in the Soviet capital to do a program on Gorbachev's final days in power.

Koppel asked him how he felt about George Bush. Gorbachev chose not to dwell on his recent grievances against Washington; instead, he recalled the vice president who had ridden with him in a limousine in Washington almost exactly four years earlier, and how well they had seemed to hit it off.

Gorbachev went on, "Today is a culmination of sorts. I'm feeling absolutely calm, absolutely free. . . . Only my role is being changed. I am not leaving either political or public life. This is happening probably for the first time here. Even in this I have turned out to be a pioneer. That is, the process we're following is democratic.

"My resignation from the office of the presidency doesn't mean political death. . . . Everything is normal because I've made my decisions. And you know, the psychological stress is hardest before you make the decision."

At the White House, Ed Hewett and Nicholas Burns were working on a short statement for release at the moment of Gorbachev's resignation. They lauded the Soviet leader's "intellect, vision, and courage."

Gorbachev, the statement declared, had been "responsible for one of the most important developments of this century — the revolutionary transformation of a totalitarian dictatorship and the liberation of his people from its smothering embrace." His policies had established a "solid basis from which the United States and the West can work in equally constructive ways with his successors."

At Camp David, Bush looked over the draft, then arranged a conference call with Baker, Scowcroft, Fitzwater, his new chief of staff, Samuel Skinner, and his pollster, Robert Teeter. Scowcroft argued that Gorbachev's resignation was "too important to kiss off with a statement from Marlin's office"; the president should speak to the nation himself, on television.

Bush agreed. But what should he say? Referring to the Hewett-Burns draft, Teeter said, "This statement *is* the speech. Get those two guys who wrote the statement to turn it into a speech." Scowcroft called Hewett at home and said, "Merry Christmas! We need a speech by nine o'clock tomorrow morning."

Hewett and Burns returned to the White House and worked in the Situation Room until three o'clock Christmas morning. Six hours later, from Camp David, Bush held another conference call with Baker and Scowcroft to tinker with the text.

That afternoon, in Moscow, it was already dark outside the French windows in Gorbachev's office when the Soviet leader picked up a white telephone and called Bush at Camp David.

December had always been a milestone in their relationship. In December 1987, they had had their first extended conversation in the Soviet embassy limousine. In December 1988, at Governors Island, Gorbachev had appealed to the president-elect for support. In December 1989, they had held their first summit, at Malta. In December 1990, they had bargained by phone and letter over the scope, timing, and objectives of the Gulf War.

When Gorbachev's call came through, it was ten in the morning at Camp David. Gorbachev had waited in order to give the Bush family a chance to open their Christmas presents. He had just sent Bush a private farewell letter.

He had written, "Today, as I complete the discharge of my duties as President of the USSR, I would like to share some thoughts and sentiments with you. I will say frankly that I have mixed feelings today. I have serious misgivings and anxieties about the fate of the country whose unity I tried to preserve, and about the future of the new international relations which we have worked so hard together to build. Much will now depend on the viability of the commonwealth.

"I want very much to believe that the democratic gains of recent years will be preserved and that the peoples of my country will go forward together on the basis of the commonwealth. Many times in the past, in the face of difficult challenges, you and I acted with decisiveness and responsibility to keep developments on the right track. In the future, dramatic turns are still possible. I count on you always to make balanced and wise decisions.

"I will help those who have now assumed the burden of responsibility for the cause of reforms and democratic changes. But support and assistance should first of all be provided to Russia. This is because the economic situation there is the worst, and because everything will depend on that republic.

"I am confident that partnership between the United States and Russia, and other new states, has a future. You and I have laid down solid groundwork for the development of relations on the basis of trust and cooperation, out of awareness of our great responsibility to the entire world. I hope that our personal friendship, developed in the years of important work we did together, will continue. Raisa and I cherish the warmest memories of our meetings with Barbara and have sincere feelings of sympathy and respect for her. Please convey to her our very best wishes. We will be delighted to see you both again."

Now, on the phone, he said, "My dear George, greetings! Let me begin with something pleasant. Merry Christmas to you and Barbara and your family!" In addressing Bush, the Soviet leader several times used *ty*, a pronoun reserved for friends, family, and close colleagues.

Gorbachev said that he was about to make his final address to the nation as president. He explained, "I'm still convinced that the existence of sovereign republics within the framework of the Union would have made it more possible to solve rapidly the main problems facing us. But events have now switched to a track that is different from what I was hoping for and holding out for. I'll do all I can to make the Commonwealth of Independent States an effective entity. The principal issue here is setting up mechanisms for interaction."

In addition to recognizing the republics as newly independent states, Gorbachev said, the United States must also maintain state-to-state relations with the commonwealth as a whole: "We must promote cooperation rather than disintegration and destruction. This is our common responsibility. I emphasize this point." He asked for special economic assistance to Russia, which would "bear the brunt of reforms."

Turning to the subject that he knew was at the front of Bush's mind, Gorbachev reported that he had arranged for an orderly transfer of the dark-brown *chemodanchik* — the "little suitcase" containing the authorization codes for the use of Soviet nuclear weapons — to the "president of the Russian Republic." Gorbachev could not bring himself to utter Yeltsin's name.

He went on, "I attach great importance to the fact that this aspect is under effective control. I've signed a decree on this issue that will come into effect immediately after my final statement. You may therefore feel at ease as you celebrate Christmas, and sleep quietly tonight.

"For my own part, I am not running away to hide in the *taiga* [the heavily forested wilderness of Siberia]. I will remain active in politics and in public affairs. I want to help the processes that are under way in this country and to promote 'new thinking' in world politics."

Noting that U.S. reporters had asked him about their relationship, Gorbachev told Bush, "I want you to know that I value very highly our cooperation, partnership, and friendship. Our roles may change. In fact, they will definitely change. But the relationship that we have developed and what we have done together will remain forever."

Bush replied, "I'd like to assure you that we will stay involved in your affairs. We will do our best to help, particularly the Russian Republic, given the problems that it's now facing and that could get critical in the winter. I'm very glad to hear that you are not 'hiding in the *taiga*' and will continue to be active in politics and public affairs. I am sure that this will benefit the new commonwealth."

The president said that he had written a letter of his own to Gorbachev: "In this letter, I express my conviction that what you have done will go down into history and that future historians will give you full credit for your accomplishments.

"I am pleased to note what you have said regarding the nuclear weapons. This matter is of crucial international importance. I welcome the way you and the leaders of the republics have handled it. I also note your words that the transfer of this authority to Yeltsin is proceeding constitutionally. I want to assure you that we will continue to cooperate very closely on this important matter."

He recalled the summer's day he had spent with Gorbachev at Camp David: "The horseshoe pit where you threw that ringer is still in good shape! I hope our paths will cross soon again. You will be welcome to come and we will be glad to welcome you, once things settle down, perhaps here in Camp David. My friendship toward you remains and will remain that way always as events continue. There should be no doubt on that score."

Bush said that "of course" he would "deal respectfully, openly, positively, and I hope progressively with the leader of the Russian Republic and the other republics. We shall move toward recognition, with full respect for each republic's sovereignty. We will work with them on the whole range of issues as we have worked with you.

"But this will in no way affect my determination to stay in touch with you and listen to the suggestions you will have to make in your new capacity, and to keep alive our friendship with you and Raisa. Barbara and I value that friendship greatly. And so, on this special day of the year, at this historic crossroads, I salute you and thank you for all that you have done for the world. And thank you for your friendship."

Moved by the conversation, Bush was somewhat taken aback when he later learned that Gorbachev had allowed Koppel and his ABC crew to videotape the Kremlin side of the call. The president shook his head and chuckled: even at the end, the master showman in Moscow could not resist playing to his international audience.

Two hours after speaking with Bush, Gorbachev addressed the citizens of fifteen former Soviet republics and the world. Looking into the television camera, he said, "Dear fellow countrymen, due to the situation that has evolved as a result of the formation of the Commonwealth of Independent States, I hereby discontinue my activities in the post of president of the Union of Soviet Socialist Republics. I am making this decision out of considerations based on principle. I have firmly stood for independence and self-determination — for the sovereignty of the republics — but at the same time for the preservation of the [Soviet] state and the unity of the country. Events have now taken a different course. The policy that has prevailed is one of dismembering this country and breaking up the state — and I cannot agree with it."

Gorbachev then defended himself from the charge that he had unleashed the forces of chaos. Recalling the inertia he had inherited from his predecessors, he said, "All the halfhearted reforms — and there were a lot of them — fell through, one after another. This country was going nowhere, and we couldn't possibly live the way we had been living. We had to change everything."

After a lengthy defense of his policies, he ended his address with a peroration that included notes of bitterness toward his rivals and even a hint of self-criticism as well as graciousness, eloquence, and optimism: "I am leaving my post with apprehension, but also with hope, with faith in you, your wisdom and force of spirit. We are the heirs of a great civilization, and its rebirth into a new, modern, and dignified life now depends on one and all.

"I wish to thank with all my heart all those who have stood with me all these years for the just and good cause.

"Some mistakes could surely have been avoided. Many things could have been done better. But I am convinced that sooner or later our common efforts will bear fruit, and our peoples will live together in a prosperous and democratic society."

Moments later, the flag of the Union of Soviet Socialist Republics atop the Kremlin was lowered for the last time.

As night fell, Bush returned from Camp David to the White House for a nine o'clock television address from the Oval Office. In it he praised Gorbachev and announced diplomatic recognition of Russia, Ukraine, and other republics. He called on God to "bless the people of the new nations in the Commonwealth of Independent States."

Of the Cold War, Bush said that "for over forty years, the United States led the West in the struggle against communism and the threat it posed to our most precious values." Choosing his words carefully, he now said, "That confrontation is over."

However, a month later, in January 1992, when Bush delivered his State of the Union address to both houses of Congress, he was no longer so mindful of Gorbachev's sensitivities. Eager to take the credit for international accomplishments in an election year, he declared triumphantly that the United States had "won the Cold War." He received a standing ovation.

Watching from retirement, Gorbachev was heartsick. He told Tom Brokaw of NBC that he had to "criticize my friend George Bush": "I do not regard the end of the Cold War as a victory for one side. If what he says is because of the election campaign, I can easily forgive that. But if he really thinks that way . . . I cannot agree. . . . The end of the Cold War is our common victory. We should give credit to all politicians who participated in that victory."

EPILOGUE

I N MAY 1992, Gorbachev flew to California for a two-week tour of the United States, accompanied by his wife, Raisa, his daughter, Irina, and Pavel Palazhchenko, who, along with a few other aides, had followed him from the Kremlin into private life. Thanks to the American publisher Malcolm Forbes, Jr., Gorbachev and his party made the trip aboard the gleaming black *Forbes* magazine jet, *Capitalist Tool*.

The itinerary included stops at the Chicago Mercantile Exchange and the New York Stock Exchange, intended to celebrate Gorbachev's role in ending his country's long, unhappy experiment with communism. The professed purpose of the tour was to raise money for the Foundation for Socioeconomic and Political Research, the "humanitarian" institute Gorbachev had established in Moscow to underwrite various good works, such as student exchanges, scholarly symposia, and improvements in Russian health care. He referred to it as the "Gorbachev Foundation."

Back in Moscow, many of Gorbachev's critics grumbled that he was in fact trying to line his own pockets and to undermine the state visit Boris Yeltsin was to make to America a month later, the first ever by the president of an independent — and post-Communist — Russia.

Bush had ordered his aides to give Gorbachev royal treatment, including a grand evening at the White House that was to be a state dinner in everything but name. The president was motivated by a genuine feeling of friendship for the deposed leader, but he also had another motive for emphasizing the visit: his reelection campaign was well under way, and he welcomed the chance to remind Americans how he had helped to relieve them of the gravest external threat that the United States had ever faced.

When Yeltsin discovered that seventeen State Department officials were to escort Gorbachev around America, he was furious. His ambassador to the United States, Vladimir Lukin, informed the Bush administration that Yeltsin would take it as a personal insult if Gorbachev were treated like a head of state when he got to Washington. The president responded by scaling back the White House dinner for Gorbachev to a small, private meal.

Gorbachev's party arrived at the White House on Friday, May 15. It was a warm spring evening, not unlike the one on which he had arrived for his first full-fledged summit with Bush almost exactly two years before. But this time there was no twenty-one-gun salute, no marine band playing the Soviet national anthem.

Gorbachev, his wife and daughter, and Palazhchenko were whisked in through the back entrance of the mansion and brought up by elevator to the First Family's quarters on the second floor. The president had also invited his son Neil, as well as James and Susan Baker and Brent Scowcroft. To avoid angering Yeltsin, Bush had decreed that no photographs of the dinner be released to the press.

As he had done so often over the past two years, the president recalled Gorbachev's now-famous ringer during their horseshoe toss at Camp David. And as usual, Gorbachev took over the conversation. He reminisced with pride and nostalgia, but no bitterness, about his life and career. He credited himself with ending the "era of stagnation" and bringing "real politics" and "real democracy" to Russia, but he also criticized his own "lack of decisiveness" on economic reform.

He told Bush and the other guests that his only wish now was to make the Gorbachev Foundation a center of the highest quality for scientific and humanitarian work. He said nothing to suggest any thoughts of a political comeback. After the dinner, Bush gave Baker a valedictory assessment of his former partner: "A class act, that guy. A lot to admire there — a lot to miss."

*   *   *

A few days earlier, Gorbachev had visited Stanford University, just as he had after the 1990 summit. During a reception at George Shultz's house, Palazhchenko pointed to several Stanford professors and whispered to his boss that they were distinguished experts on the Soviet Union. Beaming, Gorbachev marched over to them and demanded, "Well, did any of you ever imagine that all this was going to happen?"

"All this" referred to the end of Soviet communism, the Soviet Union, and the Cold War. For a long moment, no one knew quite what to say. Breaking the silence, a Soviet-born professor of Russian literature, Gregory Freidin, tossed the question back to Gorbachev in Russian: "What about *you*, Mikhail Sergeyevich? Did *you* ever imagine it?"

For an instant, Gorbachev was nonplussed. Then he threw back his head and laughed.

The moment captured the irony and the complexity of Gorbachev's role in the last three years of the Cold War, and of his position in history. He was responsible for much of what had happened — including, not incidentally, the rise of Boris Yeltsin — yet he had neither foreseen nor intended the outcome.

In his 1943 study *The Hero in History,* the social philosopher Sidney Hook draws a distinction between the "eventful leader," under whose rule important developments occur, and the "event-making leader," who unleashes forces and then acts as their master and shaper.

During his first four years in power, Gorbachev was an event-making leader. He came to office in 1985 determined to substitute "real politics" for terror as the organizing principle of Soviet life. Until the end of 1988, he retained a degree of control over the forces of change he had so boldly set in motion.

Over the next three years, Gorbachev's role was more ambiguous: he was more than an eventful leader but less than an event-making one. In the fall of 1989 he exhorted the rulers of Poland, East Germany, and other satellite countries to follow his lead, loosen the chains of totalitarianism, and emulate Soviet *perestroika* and democratization. Just as important, he signaled that he would not use Soviet tanks to rescue them from their own people's impatience and wrath. In that crucial respect, he was the Commissar Liberator.

But Gorbachev had never anticipated that within months, the whole of Eastern Europe would fly out of the Soviet orbit, or that the Warsaw Pact would crumble. He went from being a bold initiator of revolution to being a baffled witness of its consequences.

Through 1990 and 1991 — as Gorbachev acknowledged to Bush

over their final dinner at the White House — his leadership became even less heroic. He vacillated in both politics and economics, turning against Soviet reformers, democrats, and nationalists. He tried alternately to preempt and to mollify the forces of regression, forming alliances of convenience with them. Most notoriously, he let the hard-liners massacre civilians in Vilnius and Riga in January 1991.

Fortunately, and to his lasting credit, Gorbachev ultimately pulled back from the abyss, unwilling in the end to be part of a reimposition of terror. Rather than keeping the Faustian pact he had made with the Right, he shifted back toward the Left during the spring and summer of 1991. Thus he strengthened the forces that first provoked and then prevailed against the hard-line coup of August 1991 — the same forces that in the end swept him from power.

In August 1992, three months after Gorbachev's American tour, George Bush began his acceptance speech at the Republican convention in Houston with a lengthy hymn to himself as the hero of the end of the Cold War: "Germany is united, and a slab of the Berlin Wall sits right outside this Astrodome. . . . The Soviet Union can only be found in history books. The captive nations of Eastern Europe and the Baltics are captive no more. . . . This convention is the first at which an American president can say, 'The Cold War is over, and freedom finished first!' "

As the delegates cried, "USA! USA!" Bush defended himself against charges that he had spent too much time on foreign policy: "I saw the chance to rid our children's dreams of the nuclear nightmare, and I did. Over the past four years, more people have breathed the fresh air of freedom than in all of human history. . . . These were the two defining opportunities not of a year, not of a decade, but of an entire span of human history. I seized those opportunities for our kids and our grandkids. And I make no apologies for that!"

This, of course, was partisan overstatement. In a calmer moment, not even Bush himself would have denied that but for Gorbachev, Yeltsin, and the forces of Soviet reform and democratization, the United States in August 1992 would still have been poised against a militant Soviet Union. Lampooning Bush for claiming to have ended the Cold War, Bill Clinton compared him to a rooster taking credit for the dawn.

Nevertheless, Bush indeed made an indispensable contribution to the Cold War's end. From January 1989 through December 1991, he coaxed the Soviet Union toward worldwide surrender. He did so largely by exercising restraint and refraining from pushing the Soviet government too hard, thus never giving Moscow a pretext to reverse course.

Yet despite his claims of diplomatic mastery, Bush was not uniformly commanding. He paid a lasting price for the "pause" in U.S.-Soviet relations in early 1989: when he belatedly began to engage with Gorbachev that May, he appeared to be doing so under pressure from public opinion, Congress, and his NATO allies. The delay strengthened the lingering, damaging impression that this was a president who tended to follow rather than lead.

At Malta, Bush was artful in reassuring Gorbachev that if he reformed his society, let the satellites go their own way, and withdrew Soviet forces around the world, the United States would not see it as weakness on the part of the USSR or use it to gain an advantage. Bush also demonstrated good sense in refusing the demands by both Gorbachev and many in the United States for massive Western economic aid to the Soviet Union. More than many other American leaders, he understood that Gorbachev and his advisers had only the dimmest conception of free markets and that underwriting their ill-conceived programs would be a waste of money. Bush showed an impressive awareness that Western aid might prolong the survival of the old system and result in a backlash in the West against help in the future, when it might actually do some good.

In refusing Gorbachev's pleas, he nonetheless managed, by stressing the personal rapport that he and the Soviet leader had developed, to soften the blow to Gorbachev's ego and limit the damage to his domestic prestige.

The confidential relationship that began at Malta allowed Bush and Gorbachev to say things to each other that they could not say in public. The extraordinary trust that developed between them allowed them to work together to wind down the era of superpower confrontation.

Through crisis after crisis, Bush bolstered Gorbachev's self-confidence and convinced him that the West would not exploit his many troubles. For his part, Gorbachev helped Bush understand Soviet domestic problems. Bush's forbearance was especially significant during the Bloody Sundays in Vilnius and Riga, when the relative mildness of the official American response may have made it easier for Gorbachev to prevent the crackdown from spreading and gradually to shift course back toward the reformers.

Still, the Cold War might not have come to so quick and so peaceful a conclusion had Bush and Gorbachev chosen different foreign ministers. On concrete issues ranging from arms control to the resolution of regional conflicts, James Baker and Eduard Shevardnadze proved even more determined than their superiors to take risks to end the Cold War.

As with other important diplomats throughout history, Baker's motives had little to do with ideology. Rather, it was his sensitivity to American domestic politics that told him that Bush's initial passivity was causing the administration harm. Later, he reveled in the chance to use his natural instincts for deal-making. And although he never gave even so much as a hint to this effect in public, he almost certainly wished to compile a record as a world statesman that would serve him well should he ever decide to run for president.

Perhaps no one was more surprised than Gorbachev himself that during the last three years of the Cold War, Shevardnadze turned out to be so much more than a handservant to his diplomacy. Moved largely by sympathy for the nationalists in his native Georgia and by horror over the bloodshed in Tbilisi, Gorbachev's foreign minister pushed his boss further than he would have gone on his own toward acceptance of the eventual breakup of the Soviet Union.

On arms control, Eastern Europe, German unification, and the Persian Gulf crisis, Shevardnadze was braver than Gorbachev in standing up to the hard-liners in the Communist party, the KGB, and the military. In the end, Shevardnadze was the opposite of Pyrrhus: having lost many battles along the way, he finally won the war.

In their handling of German unification, Bush and Baker were primarily concerned with shoring up their fellow conservative Helmut Kohl and thus staying on the good side of a vital ally. They failed to give full consideration to the potentially disruptive consequences of quick unification — consequences that would become apparent during the two years after 1990.

However, having made the decision to back Kohl, Bush and Baker deserved credit for demanding from the start that a unified Germany remain in NATO, thus assuaging European fears about a less predictable and more powerful German state. Perhaps the single most important accomplishment in Bush's overall handling of the Soviet Union was the way he guided and cajoled Gorbachev into overcoming both his own reluctance to agree to German membership in NATO and the formidable domestic opposition within the USSR to such an arrangement.

The unprecedented collaboration between Moscow and Washington on the Persian Gulf crisis in late 1990 and early 1991 sprang in part from fortunate timing. Had Saddam Hussein invaded Kuwait a fortnight earlier, when Gorbachev and Shevardnadze were still embroiled in the German issue, the Soviet leaders might not have felt able to consider joining the coalition against Iraq. It had been hard enough for them to countenance the defection of East Germany from the Warsaw Pact to NATO; now the United States was asking them to turn against a Soviet ally of long standing in the Persian Gulf.

Soviet-American cooperation in the United Nations Security Council made possible the international community's prompt, effective response to Saddam's aggression. Had the Soviet Union exercised its veto, as in days of old, the United States might have faced a difficult choice between acting alone or not acting at all.

While the relationship at the highest levels of the American and Soviet governments brought numerous benefits to both sides and to the rest of the world, it also had grave defects. These were starkly evident by 1991. By attaching such importance to their personal ties, Bush and Gorbachev had both become less sensitive than they should have been to what was happening at the grass roots of Soviet and American politics.

Because Gorbachev knew he had Bush's support, he made less effort than he might have otherwise to come to terms with his rival Boris Yeltsin. He was so out of touch that he grossly underestimated the depth of the Soviet people's hatred of the Communist party and their impatience for more daring leadership. This caused him to make what he later judged to be the fatal mistake of lurching to the right during the winter of 1990–91.

Bush was so determined not to add to the pressures on Gorbachev that he paid insufficient attention to the rise of competing centers of power within the Soviet Union, including more vigorous proponents of democratization and economic reform. For two years he kept saying, in effect, that Gorbachev was the best of all possible Soviet leaders — the one whose beliefs were most compatible with American ideals.

But by the spring of 1991, that was demonstrably no longer true. It was Yeltsin, not Gorbachev, who was willing to repudiate the Communist party, endorse the right of all the republics to go their own way, and support the radical measures necessary to introduce genuine democracy and free market economics.

Charles de Gaulle once said that John Kennedy was the mask of America but Lyndon Johnson was its real face. If Gorbachev was the mask of Russia and Yeltsin its real face, Bush preferred the mask. Gorbachev appealed to his preference for dealing with the man who was at the center and at the top, for the politics of gradualism and evolution over those of revolution. As a result, Bush clung to Gorbachev long after he should have apprehended that Yeltsin's vision for the future of the Soviet Union was far more in the American interest.

Gorbachev had the capacity to see the absurdity of the old system, and the courage to begin tearing it down. But when the time finally came to replace it, he wavered. Yeltsin was more resolute and more willing to follow through on the logic of the reforms Gorbachev had begun. And because he was so much more popular than Gorbachev, he was more likely to maintain a base of public support for his program.

It took the coup of August 1991 to convince Bush that Gorbachev was yesterday's man and that it was time to reorient American policy toward Yeltsin and the republics. Only then did Bush try, as gracefully as possible, to ditch his old partner and make up for lost time with the radical challenger.

During the 1992 presidential campaign, Bill Clinton and other Democrats criticized Bush for standing by Gorbachev for too long, and for letting friendship blind him to the erosion of Gorbachev's power and the rise of other political forces in Moscow and the ever more restive republics.* But in staying with Gorbachev as long as he did, Bush increased the chances that Gorbachev himself would remain in power long enough to achieve his greatest accomplishment: the peaceful transfer of power to a leader committed to the death of the Communist party and the dismantlement of the Soviet Union.

Almost a year after Gorbachev's resignation, many of those who had played a part in the end of the Cold War had landed in unexpected places. The people of an independent but embattled Georgia had brought back Eduard Shevardnadze as their president. From an office in Tbilisi adorned with Christian icons, he lectured his countrymen on democracy and civil liberties and tried to mediate an end to their multiple blood feuds.

Shevardnadze's successor as Soviet foreign minister, Alexander Bessmertnykh, had installed himself in an office on the ground floor of his

* In the spring of 1992, Bush told the conservative journalist Richard Brookhiser, "I know there's some current kind of conventional wisdom that we stayed with Gorbachev too long. I would say that the transition has been peaceful — not without some bumps in the road, but the transition has been peaceful. And the coup failed. I think we handled it about right." Excerpts from this interview appeared in the August 1992 *Atlantic*.

predecessor's old Moscow think tank. In the manner of the Ancient Mariner, Bessmertnykh implored all who would listen to believe his claim that he really had not been involved in the August coup.

Still in office at the Kremlin were several of Gorbachev's former aides who had privately denounced Boris Yeltsin as a traitorous "drunk" in December 1991, after the declaration of the Minsk agreement and the creation of the Commonwealth of Independent States.

Yevgeni Primakov took over as head of the Russian Intelligence Service, the successor to the KGB. Valentin Falin, who in 1990 had charged Shevardnadze with accepting bribes to permit German unification, turned up in, of all places, the united Germany, where he pursued a variety of business ventures and was said to be pondering whether to become a German citizen.

At the end of 1992, Mikhail Gorbachev suffered a new humiliation at the hands of his old political foe Boris Yeltsin, and George Bush lost the presidency to a challenger who gave him credit for a largely successful foreign policy but accused him of neglect and failure in dealing with the American economy.

During the fall, Russia's highest judicial body, the constitutional court, conducted hearings into the history of Communist rule. As general secretary of the party for its last six years, Gorbachev was naturally summoned to testify. He refused, saying he would not participate in a "political" trial "even if I am brought to the court in handcuffs."

In retaliation, the Russian authorities moved to evict Gorbachev's foundation from its building and yanked his passport, preventing him from traveling to South Korea. Only when the German government, which owed Gorbachev so much, protested his treatment was he permitted to attend the funeral of former chancellor Willy Brandt in Berlin.

In the midst of this acrimonious confrontation with the man who had replaced him in the Kremlin, Gorbachev issued a statement comparing himself to the Jews who had for years been refused visas to leave the USSR: "The first Soviet president has been turned into the first political 'refusenik' of Russia."

Meanwhile, Bush was fighting an uphill battle for reelection. Like Winston Churchill after World War II, he counted on the continuing support of voters who had followed him during a great international struggle. But like the British people in 1945, Americans in 1992 were not inclined to return their leader to office simply out of gratitude for his accomplishments abroad. Quite the contrary: the end of the Cold

War left them free to turn their attention to the home front, where Bush, by his own implicit admission, had fallen short. The president pledged to tackle the American recession and the federal budget deficit in a second term with the same sure-handedness with which he had managed the collapse of Soviet communism and the crisis in the Persian Gulf in his first four years in office. Underscoring his shift to domestic policy, Bush persuaded James Baker to resign as secretary of state and become the White House chief of staff.

Baker's first task was to secure Bush's reelection. In early October the campaign was still in trouble. Several right-wing congressmen urged the president to exploit the "revelation" that Clinton had visited Moscow while a graduate student at Oxford in early 1970. In light of Clinton's opposition to the war in Vietnam, Bush hoped to encourage suspicions that there was something unpatriotic, even traitorous, about his trip to the Soviet capital. Appearing on CNN's "Larry King Live" on Wednesday, October 7, Bush challenged Clinton to "level with the American people" on why he had gone to Moscow "one year after Russia crushed Czechoslovakia."

The insinuation backfired. The president who had played such a key role in ending the Cold War was widely accused of a desperate resort to 1950s-vintage red-baiting. The tactic enhanced the impression that Bush was badly out of touch and contributed to his resounding defeat on Tuesday, November 3.

Long before, when he had expected to serve two full terms in the White House, Bush had resolved that his presidential library and museum should be built at Texas A&M University, the site of his first speech as president on American-Soviet relations, in which he had declared his intention to move "beyond containment." Among the items considered for exhibition in the museum were a graffiti-covered segment of the Berlin Wall, a brass naval clock from the USS *Belknap* at Malta, a fountain pen used to sign the instruments of German unification, guns once fired on Iraqi soldiers, and the Camp David telephone on which Bush had heard Gorbachev declare that the Union of Soviet Socialist Republics was extinct.

At the beginning of 1993, Bush and Gorbachev found themselves once more united: repudiated by their own peoples, the two men who had presided over the end of the Cold War hoped for final vindication by history.

SELECTED BIBLIOGRAPHY

While this book is, as noted in the preface, based primarily on interviews with participants in the events described and on access to the classified diplomatic record, the following published and broadcast materials were of especial use:

American Enterprise Institute. "The Gulf Crisis" (television, three hours, 1991).

Annenberg Washington Program. "Television and the Gulf War" (transcript of symposium, Washington, D.C., September 26, 1991).

Ash, Timothy Garton. *The Magic Lantern: The Revolution of '89 Witnessed in Warsaw, Budapest, Berlin and Prague.* New York: Random House, 1990.

Aslund, Anders. *Gorbachev's Struggle for Economic Reform.* Ithaca: Cornell University Press, 1991.

Bialer, Seweryn, ed. *Politics, Society and Nationality Inside Gorbachev's Russia.* Boulder, Colo.: Westview Press, 1989.

Bialer, Seweryn, and Michael Mandelbaum. *The Global Rivals.* New York: Vintage, 1989.

British Broadcasting Corporation. "The Second Russian Revolution" (television, six hours, 1990–1991).

Bush, George, with Victor Gold. *Looking Forward.* New York: Doubleday, 1987.

Committee on Foreign Affairs, U.S. Senate. *Soviet Diplomacy and Negotiating Behavior, 1988–1990: Gorbachev-Reagan-Bush Meetings at the Summit.* Washington: Library of Congress, Office of Research Coordination, 1991.

Dallin, Alexander, and Gail W. Lapidus, eds. *The Soviet System in Crisis.* Boulder, Colo.: Westview Press, 1991.

Doder, Dusko, and Louise Brandon. *Gorbachev: Heretic in the Kremlin.* New York: Viking, 1990.

Gaddis, John Lewis. *The United States and the End of the Cold War.* New York: Oxford University Press, 1992.

Gati, Charles. *The Bloc That Failed: Soviet–East European Relations in Transition.* Bloomington: Indiana University Press, 1990.

Goldman, Marshall I. *What Went Wrong with Perestroika.* New York: Norton, 1991.

Gorbachev, Mikhail. *The August Coup: The Truth and the Lessons.* New York: HarperCollins, 1991.

Green, Fitzhugh. *George Bush: An Intimate Portrait.* New York: Hippocrene Books, 1989.

Gwertzman, Bernard, and Michael T. Kaufman, eds. *The Collapse of Communism.* New York: Random House, 1990.

Horelick, Arnold L., ed. *U.S.-Soviet Relations: The Next Phase.* Ithaca: Cornell University Press, 1986.

Hyland, William G. *Mortal Rivals: Understanding the Hidden Pattern of Soviet-American Relations.* New York: Simon and Schuster, 1988.

——— . *The Cold War Is Over.* New York: Random House, 1990.

Kaiser, Robert G. *Why Gorbachev Happened: His Triumphs and His Failure.* New York: Simon and Schuster, 1991.

Medvedev, Zhores A. *Gorbachev.* New York: Norton, 1986.

Oberdorfer, Don. *The Turn: From the Cold War to a New Era.* New York: Poseidon Press, 1991.

Public Papers of the Presidents: George Bush. 3 vols., 1989–1991. Washington: U.S. Government Printing Office.

Shevardnadze, Eduard A. *The Future Belongs to Freedom.* New York: Free Press, 1991.

U.S. News & World Report. *Triumph Without Victory: The Unreported History of the Persian Gulf War.* New York: Times Books, 1992.

INDEX

Abalkin, Leonid, 108, 375
ABC (American Broadcasting Company), 17, 117*n*, 439, 459, 463
"ABC Evening News" (TV program), 300
Abel, Rudolph, 355
ABM (antiballistic missile) treaty, 117, 118, 119. *See also* arms control
Aboimov, Ivan, 171
Academy of Sciences (Soviet Union), 310*n*
Acheson, Dean, 26
Acland, Sir Anthony, 46
ACVs (armored combat vehicles), 363, 367, 368, 369. *See also* arms control
Adami, Eddie Fenech, 128, 150
Adenauer, Konrad, 188
Afghanistan, 105, 122, 170, 179, 288; Gorbachev and, 23, 30, 123*n*, 158, 225, 265, 419; occupation ended, 30, 56; Baker-Shevardnadze talks on, 61, 62, 180, 243, 251; Soviet aid to, 105, 377; Shevardnadze quoted on, 123, 273, 284; Gulf crisis/War compared to, 273, 280, 281, 284, 286
Africa, 225
African National Congress (ANC), 198
Aganbegyan, Abel, 375
Agriculture, U.S. Department of, 205

aircraft (based in Europe) as issue, 38, 78, 79. *See also* arms control
Air Force, U.S., 12, 116*n*, 144, 150, 212; in Gulf War, 297, 314, 315, 333, 340
Air Force One (presidential plane), 70, 88, 89, 94, 234, 260, 411, 415, 430, 431, 434
Air Force Two (vice-presidential plane), 6, 390
Akhromeyev, Marshal Sergei, 80, 162, 221, 237, 261; at Baker-Gorbachev meetings, 66, 182, 183, 212; in U.S., 83, 145, 203, 225, 227; as courier, 94, 97; death of, 438
ALCMs (air-launched cruise missiles), 116*n*, 155*n*, 183*n*, 212–213. *See also* arms control
Alksnis, Colonel Viktor, 394
Allison, Graham, 56, 382–383, 385, 390, 401
American Association for the Advancement of Science, 48
American Express, 228
American Foreign Policy Council, 254*n*
Andover Bulletin, 17
Andreotti, Giulio, 235, 274, 427
Andropov, Yuri, 7, 35, 82, 124, 425; Bush meets, 5–6

Angola, 30, 56, 369, 377
Antall, Jozsef, 427, 432
anti-Semitism. *See* Jews
APCs (armored personnel carriers), 369*n*.
    See also arms control
Aquino, Corazon, 136, 150, 158
Arab-Israeli dispute, 62–63, 212, 225–226,
    261, 339; and peace conference, 31, 280,
    343, 446–448; Gulf crisis linked to, *see*
    Gulf crisis/War; Soviet-U.S. partnership in
    settling, 343, 446; Baker-Bessmertnykh
    conferences on, 366, 414. *See also* Middle
    East
Arabs, 175, 264*n*, 314; Arabist views on Gulf
    crisis/War, 247, 251, 253, 269, 272, 280,
    326, 327, (inter-Arab conference sug-
    gested) 280. *See also* Islam; Middle East
Arafat, Yasir, 291, 292
Arbatov, Georgi, 147–148, 160
Arensburger, Jean, 364
Argentina, 254
Arias, Oscar, 156
Armenia, 300*n*, 352, 368, 426; earthquake
    in, 12, 57*n*, 159; nationalism in, 175,
    216, 287; boycotts referendum, 350; in-
    dependence of, 359, 389
arms control, 25; Gorbachev and, 7, 10, 39
    (*see also* Gorbachev, Mikhail Sergeye-
    vich); Geneva conferences, 7, 363, 367,
    373, 402, 414; Bush and, 8, 10, 37, 50,
    120–121, 178, 181, 207, 209, (Open
    Skies proposal) 71, 72, 189, 220, (speech
    on) 446 (*see also* CFE [conventional
    forces in Europe]; START treaty); SDI
    (strategic defense initiative), 10, 113–114,
    117, 119; Soviet disregard of, 12 (*see also*
    Soviet Union); "zero option," 35–36, 38
    (*see also* Reagan, Ronald); Baker and, 40
    (*see also* Baker, James A., III); SALT trea-
    ties, 61, 113, 117; "third zero," 76;
    Thatcher and, 76–77, 78, 79; Cheney
    and, 116, 117*n*, 120, 146, 372–373, 405,
    445, 446*n*, (NATO) 74–75, 77; chemical
    weapons, 119–121, 155, 181, 189, 222*n*,
    316, 342; German, 188, 236, (post–
    World War II) 342; in Iraq after Gulf
    War, 342; Moscow summit linked to, 362,
    369, 373, 402, 407; U.S. "Un-Group,"
    365, 403, 404, 406. *See also* CFE (con-
    ventional forces in Europe); CSCE (Con-
    ference on European Cooperation and
    Security); NATO (North Atlantic Treaty
    Organization); nuclear policies; START
    treaty
Aronson, Bernard, 57, 105, 193*n*
Asimov, Isaac, 218
Aspen Institute for Humanistic Studies,
    394*n*

Aspin, Les, 145, 147
Assad, Hafez el-, 268, 272, 328
Associated Press, 67
Association of State Enterprises (USSR),
    422*n*
Atlantic Charter, 129*n*
Atlantic Council, 235. *See also* NATO
    (North Atlantic Treaty Organization)
Atlantic Monthly magazine, 472*n*
Austria, 81, 132
Azerbaijan, 175–176, 358, 368, 426, 442
Aziz, Tariq, 278, 285, 286, 287, 333, 334;
    Baker meets, 303; in Moscow, 336, 337,
    339

Bakatin, Vadim, 176, 288, 309, 354*n*, 391*n*
Baker, James A., III: enters State Depart-
    ment, 11–12, 19, 20, 26–27, 32, (re-
    signs) 474; and Kissinger plan, 13, 19,
    20, 21, 45–46; and NSC, NSR-3, 26, 45,
    48; Shevardnadze and, 28–29, 52, 60,
    67, 93, 97, 98, 171, 237, 273, 438,
    ("conspiracy" between) 274, (Shevard-
    nadze resigns) 296, 303, (prediction of
    coup) 353, 395, 419, 423, (Shevardnadze
    blames) 394–395, (end of Cold War) 470
    (*see also* MEETINGS WITH SHEVARDNADZE,
    below); Thatcher and, 29, 31; view of
    Gorbachev, 31, 39, 46, 93, 104–105,
    121, 125, 163, 317, (survival questioned)
    27, 33, 42, 55, 98–100, 122, 123–124,
    147, 177, 182, 241–242, ("outpropo-
    saled") 67, 68, 74, 144, (and *perestroika*)
    122, 179, 180, (warned, notified of coup)
    357, 423, (and Ukraine) 449 (*see also*
    meets Gorbachev, *below*); and NATO,
    36, 39, 75, 76, 166, 188, 232–239 *pas-
    sim*; and arms control, 40, (CFE) 53, 67–
    68, 77–79 *passim*, 189–190, 222, 269,
    363–370 *passim*, 402, (chemical weap-
    ons) 120–121, (START) 146, 373 (*see
    also* START treaty), (Soviet concessions
    withdrawn) 203, 209, 212–213; vs. Che-
    ney, 55, 116, 147; meets Gorbachev,
    (1989) 55, 58, 59–68, 78, 155, (1990)
    182–186 *passim*, 193, 211–219 *passim*,
    225, 281–283, (1991) 343–344, 350–
    353, 457–458, (1992) 466; and Central
    America, 56–57, 66, 72, 105; and Mid-
    dle East, 62–63, 259–260, 264, 328,
    (visits) 268, 422, 341, (need for Soviet cooper-
    ation) 339; as "finance minister," 64,
    351; visits France, 93–98, 99; and Bal-
    tics, 102, 197, 208, 209–212, 218, (rhet-
    oric on) 174–175, 325, (Soviet policy
    questioned) 202, 204, 205, 217, 300,
    305, (restates U.S. policy) 270, 322–323,
    (summit postponed) 319, (meets Bes-

smertnykh) 321–324; and Yeltsin, 104–
105, 348, 361, (meets in Moscow) 352–
353, 456–457; and foreign policy vs.
campaigning, 107, 470; foreign policy
speeches, 121–122, 123, 124–125; and
Malta, 126–127, 130, 144–145, 146,
153–163 passim; and German unity, 157,
169, 183–190, 191, 192n, 198, 230,
232–233, 236, 239; and Romania and
Bulgaria, 170–171, 180; and Soviet
Union, (use of military against nationalism) 176, (reform) 347, 359, 387–389,
(aid to) 378, 381, 387–391 passim (see
also visits Russia; and Moscow political
crises, below); and Gulf crisis/War, 243–
251 passim, 256, 257, 268, 275, 276,
285, 292, 305, 373, (use of force) 252–
255, 280–284, 287, (linked with Middle
East conference) 259–260, 263–264,
290–291, 328–333, 342, (meeting with
Saddam suggested) 287, (meets Aziz) 301,
303, (attack begins) 313, (ceasefire considered) 326–327, 334, (joint statement
on) 330–337 passim, 343, (Soviet peace
plan) 334–335, 336–337, 339, (postwar)
342; visits Mongolia, 245, 246; as UN
Security Council president, 280, 284,
286–287; and Bessmertnykh, 302, 312,
319–320, 334, 342, 357, (meetings with,
on Baltics, Gulf War, arms control) 321–
332 passim, 364–369 passim, 396–398,
402–406 passim, 414, (Bessmertnykh resigns) 439–440; visits Turkey, 305; visits
Russia, 342–344, 350–353, 354, 364–
365, 366, (and Moscow summit) 408,
409, 413, 414, 429, (after Minsk agreement) 455, 456–458; meets Kozyrev,
348–349; and Moscow political crises,
357–358, ("constitutional coup") 396–
398, (coup) 423, 426, 429, 431, (breakup
of Soviet Union) 447, 452, 457–458,
459–460, 474; at Lisbon meeting, 369;
at foreign ministers' meeting (Berlin),
396–398, 403; and Strauss as ambassador, 426–427; resigns as secretary
of state, becomes White House chief
of staff, 474. See also State, U.S. Department of
  MEETINGS WITH SHEVARDNADZE, 155,
163, 176, 221, 236, 414, 418; Vienna
(1989), 34, 39–41, 42; Moscow, (1989)
55, 61–65, 67, 353, (Feb. and May
1990) 177, 179–182, 193n, 210–211,
212–213, 218, (Aug.–Nov. 1990) 248,
268–269, 281–283, (March 1991) 353,
354; Paris, (1989) 94–97, 99, 101, 110,
(1990) 241–242, 284, 285; Wyoming
(1989), 99, 109–112, 116, 119–124 pas-

sim, 127–128, 181, 243, 302; Malta
(1989), 157; Ottawa (1990), 189–190;
Namibia (1990), 197–198; Washington,
(1990) 202, 203, 218–223 passim, 228,
(1991) 379, 388; Bonn (1990), 207–209,
210, 218; Copenhagen (1990), 230; East
Berlin (1990), 232–233; Irkutsk (1990),
242–243, 244–245; New York (1990),
269–270; Houston (1990), 290–293, 363
Baker, Susan, 59, 63, 248, 423, 466
Baklanov, Oleg, 420, 422, 445
Baltic republics, 294; Soviet view, 101, 110,
322, 395, (hard-liners/Black Berets) 228,
299, 315, 358, 368, 414, 442, (and perestroika) 306, (Yeltsin and "mutual support pact") 307, (recognizes) 444 (see
also Gorbachev and, below); U.S. view,
102, 198–203, 211–212, 318, 469, (CIA)
142, 309, 316, 317, (Congress) 198, 206,
209, 216–223 passim, 318, 322, (Baker
restates policy) 270, 322–323, (public
protest) 305, (U.S. aid) 306, 308, 310,
319, 321, 322, 377, 435, (monitors crisis)
315, (recognizes) 443–444; Bush and,
102, 164, 165, 174–176, 194–205 passim, 287, 297–304 passim, 468, (meets
leaders) 206–207, 379–380, (acquiescence in policy feared) 300, (after crackdown) 308, 309, 316, 318–320, 325,
(meets Bessmertnykh) 324–325, (domestic criticism) 408, 448, (recognizes) 443–
444; Gorbachev and, 102, 165, 208, 216,
222, 234, 314, (and perestroika) 111,
163, 164, 174, 324, (ultimatums, threats)
173–175, 194–206, 210, 211–212, (U.S.
as mediator) 202–203, (and U.S. trade
agreement) 204, 205, 217, 223, (crackdown) 228, 287–288, 297–312 passim,
317–323 passim, 346, 358, 468, 469–
470, (denies responsibility) 308–310,
315, 320, 323, (as metaphor) 319, (plebiscite planned) 322–323, (troops withdrawn) 323, 324–325, (Baltic leaders'
view) 380, (during Bush's visit to Moscow) 415, (after coup) 443; Malta meeting and, 163–164, 165; declare
independence, 173, 193–195, 210, 287,
359, 389, 442; Yeltsin and, 173, 287,
304, 307, 380; as issue in Gulf crisis,
298, 303–304, 305, 316, 324; linked to
summit, 300, 302, 308, 310, 312, 319,
321; and choice of foreign minister, 311;
public opinion of crisis, 316, 318, 322,
346, 408, 448; total secession sought, 322,
389; Dacha Agreement and, 359; and Gorbachev vs. Yeltsin, 380; after coup, 435,
442. See also Estonia; Latvia; Lithuania
Bandar bin Sultan, Saudi prince, 277

Barbarossa (Clark), 236
Bartholomew, Reginald, 144, 362, 365*n,* 368, 403
Batista, Fulgencio, 241
Beckwith, David, 168
Belarus (Byelorussia), 193, 358, 446; and change of name, 442*n;* Minsk as capital of new commonwealth, 450
Belgium, 190, 306
Belknap, USS, 150, 154, 160–161, 475
Belogonov, Alexander, 256
Bering Strait, international park along, 223*n*
Berlin Wall. *See* Germany
Berra, Yogi, 205
Bessmertnykh, Alexander, 127, 165, 217; on U.S. policy, 29, 227, 426; as ambassador to U.S., 80, 213–214, 377; and Germany, 132–133, 271; and Gulf crisis/ War, 262, 275, 301–302, 313, 314, 326– 336 *passim,* (linked to peace conference) 265, 342–343, (joint statement) 330–337 *passim,* 343, (advises withdrawal) 342; and Shevardnadze's resignation, 296, (as successor to) 302–303, 310–313, 321; and Baltics, 297, 298, 312, 321–325, (Gorbachev's weakness) 302, 309, (summit postponed) 319–320, (meets Bush) 324–325; meetings with Baker, *see* Baker, James A., III; on Soviet "Security Council," 354*n;* and Moscow political crises, 357–358, 396–398, 401, (coup) 434, 439–440, 473; and Yeltsin, 361; and Bush's trip to Soviet Union, 409– 410, 412, 414; resigns as foreign minister, 439–440
Bessmertnykh, Arseni (son), 297, 311, 321
Bessmertnykh, Marina, 297, 311, 321
Big Four. *See* World War II
Billington, James, 32
Birkenau concentration camp, 86–87*n*
Bisers, Ilmars, 315
Bismarck, Otto von, 188
Black Berets (Soviet Union), 299, 315, 414
Blackwell, Robert, 5, 6, 7, 25*n;* as National Intelligence Officer (CIA), 141–142, 143
Blackwill, Robert, 31, 34, 46, 51, 53, 93, 147, 227, 307; and arms control, 25–26, 36, 38–39; and NSR-3, NSD-23, 43, 69; and Bush's speeches, 70, 71, 86, 87, 88; and Yeltsin-Bush meeting, 103; and aid to Moscow, 106, 382–383; and Malta, 126–127, 143, 149, 150, 151, 220; and German unification, 136, 139, 188, 192, 234–235
Bloody Sunday (1905), 306
Boldin, Valeri, 412, 420
Bolsheviks. *See* communism/Communist party

Bonner, Yelena, 309
Boren, David, 358
Boskin, Michael, 387, 390
Boston Red Sox, 422
Bradley, Bill, 316
Brady, Nicholas, 26*n,* 53, 54, 205, 378, 391
Brazauskas, Algirdas, 173
Brezhnev, Leonid, 5, 6, 23, 110, 123*n,* 170, 356, 451; Gorbachev compared to, 7, 12, 36, 149; and CSCE, 148
Brezhnev Doctrine, 134, 158, 170, 171
Brinkley, David, 17, 117*n*
Britain, 46, 68*n,* 172; Gorbachev speaks in London, 49; and German unification, 82, 137, 169, 187, 207; and Gulf crisis, 286, 314; and Baltics, 306. *See also* Major, John; Thatcher, Margaret
Broder, David, 73
Brokaw, Tom, 112, 160, 464
Bronfman, Edgar, 301, 303
Brookhiser, Richard, 472*n*
Brookings Institution, 22, 122*n,* 346
Brzezinski, Zbigniew, 140–141
Bulgaria, 136*n,* 169*n,* 180, 289
Burlatsky, Fyodor, 352
Burns, Nicholas, 315, 413, 414–415, 459– 460
Burt, Richard, 116, 119*n,* 144, 146*n,* 373, 402
Bush, Barbara, 5, 73, 90, 176, 191, 225, 228, 436, 461, 463; quoted on press, 260; visits Soviet Union, 411, 413
Bush, George: in 1988 campaign, 3–4, 9– 10, 13*n,* 70, 114, 140, 393*n,* (advisers) 8, 20, 41; as vice president, (meets Soviet leaders) 3–4, 5–11, 65, 108, 165, 411, 459, 460, (and Reagan's aides and policies) 4, 8, 9, 10, 35, 114, (visits Eastern Europe) 53*n,* 81*n,* 86, 87, (and chemical warfare) 119, 120*n;* as ambassador to UN, 4, 151; as director of CIA, 4, 12, 43, 126, 155; resigns from Trilateral Commission and Council on Foreign Relations, 5; attitude of, toward history, 87, 187–188; visits China (1977), 129*n;* as conservative, 309*n. See also* AS PRESI-DENT-ELECT/PRESIDENT; RELATIONS OF, WITH SOVIET UNION; RELATIONSHIP WITH GOR-BACHEV; SPEECHES, *below*

AS PRESIDENT-ELECT/PRESIDENT, 117*n,* 176, 346; quoted on hopes for accomplishment, 17 (*see also* SPEECHES, *below*); first news conference, 19; first foreign visit, 21; dismisses Reagan appointees, 26, 32; criticism of, 31, 50–51, 61, 71– 74 *passim,* 107, 200, 306, 418, 430, 469, (approval vs.) 107, 165, 347, 408, 448, (by Gorbachev) 274, 464; and Central America, 56–59 *passim*, 105, 151, 156, 164, 168; Baker's closeness to, 63, 166; first initiative, 71 (*see also* arms control); first major foreign policy success, 80; visits Germany and England, 81; visits Poland and Hungary, 85–92; visits France, 92–93, 284, (G-7 meetings) 93, 401; and Baltics, *see* Baltic republics; reelection campaign of, *see* election campaigns, U.S. (*1992*); and chemical warfare, 120–121, 155; conflict within administration, 124–125; meetings with heads of government, 128, 190–192, 234–237, 284, (personal relationships) 166, 258, 399, 469, 471–472; and conflict of interests, 129*n;* and German unification, 137, 138–139, 156–157, 168–169, 184, 230, 267, (communicates with, meets Kohl) 187–192, 193, 213, 221, 235; and coup attempt in Philippines, 150, 167; Quayle's divergence from, 168; and Gulf crisis, 245, 271, 274, 275, 331, 345, 471, (first priority in) 341, (*see also* Gulf crisis/War); visits Middle East, 285; telephones foreign partners, 298; and free trade zone, 298; Council of Economic Advisers of, 387; first visit to Soviet Union, 408–418; and Soviet coup, 422–423, 426–438, 440–441; recognizes republics, 443–444, 448–449. *See also* RELATIONS OF, WITH SOVIET UNION; RELATIONSHIP WITH GORBACHEV; SPEECHES, *below*

RELATIONS OF, WITH SOVIET UNION, 10, 11–18, 32, 40, 41, 126; meets Shevardnadze, 9, 108–109, 117, 118, 225, 293, 308; Kennebunkport seminar, 21, 22–24, 140, 347; NSR-3, NSD-23, 24–26, 43, 45, 49, 50, 69–70; Baker's view of, 27, 41–42; and the *pauza*, 28–29, 80, 165, 469; and NATO, 36, 37, 74–81 *passim*, 164–165, 188, 192, 469, (Germany in) 231, 240, 470–471, (London summit) 234–237, 240; criticized, 50–51, 61, 71, 72, 74, 107, 418; and Eastern Europe, 53*n*, 54, 81–93 *passim*, 107, 131–143 *passim*, 157, 205, 267; and Baltics, *see* Baltic republics; and Berlin Wall, 135, 136, 138, 143; policy after Malta meeting, 167–168, 170; and trade agreement, 205–211 *passim*, 217–227 *passim*, 233, 293, 388; and aid, 237, 241, 266, 293, 376–391 *passim*, 469; and Middle East policy, 262, 264, 266; Gulf War and postwar, 287, 339–341, 345, 354 (*see also* Gulf crisis/War); and Bessmertnykh, 312, 406; and Yeltsin, 347–349, 350, 352, 471–472, (meets) 103–104, 108,

399–401, 412–413, 446*n*, (and Moscow political crises) 359–360, 397, 430–434, (invited to Washington) 361, (telephone calls) 433–434, 435, 453, 454; meets Moiseyev, 368, 412; first visit to Soviet Union as president, 408–418; and Strauss as new ambassador, 426–427; coup and, 432–434, 443; recognizes Ukraine, 448–449; and breakup of Soviet Union, 448–453 *passim*, 454–455, (discussed) 109, 297; Minsk agreement and, 450. *See also* RELATIONSHIP WITH GORBACHEV, *below;* arms control; Cold War

RELATIONSHIP WITH GORBACHEV: meetings (before Bush presidency), 3–4, 7, 8, 10–11, 65, 165, 173, 460; Bush's view of, 7–10 *passim*, 24, 92–96 *passim*, 150, 165–168, 260, 418, (arms control) 67, 86, (vs. Yeltsin) 87, 104, (after Baltic crisis) 308, 309, 316–324 *passim*, 479–480, 554, (after coup) 445–447, 467, 471–472, 474 (*see also* perestroika); letters from Bush, 13, 16, 137, 407, 462, (on Cuba) 57, 58, 59, 60, (on arms control) 79, 80, 127, 269, 365–369 *passim*, 402, 403, (on summit) 94, 97, 319–320, 321, (on Baltics) 201–202, 206, 319–320, 321, 443, (on Gulf crisis) 283, 460; telephone calls, 18, 193, 227, 240, 298–299, 308, 449, (on arms control) 177–178, 183, 369, (on Gulf crisis) 303–304, 315, 337, 339, 340, 460, (on aid) 384, 386, (on coup, breakup of Soviet Union) 400, 433, 454–455, 460–463; and Middle East peace conference, 31, 258–266 *passim;* Thatcher and, 49–50, 78, 81, 107–108, 166, 201; "secret pact" charged, 52; letters from Gorbachev, 59, 66, 137, 377, (on arms control) 75, 118, 366, (on Baltics) 322–323, 324, (on Gulf) 334, 335, (on resignation) 460–461; Bush criticized, 71, 74, 274, 306, 464, 469, 472; Gorbachev's view of, 71, 125, 162, 212, 459, (on *pauza*) 28–29, 49–50, 165, (criticizes Bush) 274, 464, ("betrayal") 449; Kremlin view of, 82, 273, 399; "partnership," 82–83, 122, 446, 453, 461; and Baltics, *see* Baltic republics; Yeltsin and, 103, 399; "ambivalence," 107, 408; at Malta, *see* Malta, Bush-Gorbachev meeting at (1989); in defeat of communism, 135, 162; and arms control, 162–163, 178, 181, 365 (*see also* arms control); Gorbachev's survival questioned, 168, 176–178, 228, 241, 242 (*see also* Gorbachev, Mikhail Sergeyevich); informal meeting suggested (1990), 213; Washington/Camp David meetings (1990), 214, 215–228,

Bush, George (*continued*)
237, 239, 258, 266, 325, 388, 461, 466,
(plans for) 127, 128, 155, 181, 188,
198–205 *passim,* 209, 213, 215; "tough
love," 216, 293; Gorbachev's need for
support, 218, 298–299, 392, 469; and
U.S. aid, 237, 241, 266, 377–392, 406–
407; Moscow summit urged, 243, 270,
293, 296, (linked to Baltic crisis) 300,
302, 308, 310, 312, 319, 321, (postponed) 322, 324, 362, (linked to arms
control) 362, 369, 373, 402, 407, (re-
scheduled) 408, (Bush attends) 411–415,
429; Helsinki meeting (1990), 258–259,
260–267, 268, 272, 325, 328, 330; Paris
meeting (1990), 284–285, 288; in Gulf
crisis/War, 287, 303, 313, 339–344, 345,
399 (*see also* Gulf crisis/War); postwar,
345–346; Moscow political crises, 356–
357, ("constitutional coup") 396–401
passim, (coup) 422–423, 426–438, 440–
441; London meeting (1991), 405–407;
and trip to Soviet Union (1991), 408–
418; Madrid meeting (1991), 446–448;
and breakup of Soviet Union, 448–449,
452–455; Washington meeting (1992),
466–467
    SPEECHES: public rhetoric, 4, 9–10, 80,
175, 198–200 *passim,* 260, 464; inaugural address (1988), 17; Hamtramck
(1989), 54; U.S. Chamber of Commerce
(1989), 55; Texas A&M (1989), 69–71,
93; speechwriters and, 70, 71, 78, 86;
New London (1989), 78; Mainz (1989),
81; Warsaw (1989), 89; UN (1989),
120–121, 181; welcoming Gorbachev to
Washington (1990), 216; State of the
Union (1991), 325, 330, 331, 332;
Ukrainian parliament, Kiev (1991), 417–
418; TV, on arms control (1991), 446;
TV, on Gorbachev's resignation (1991),
459–460, 464; State of the Union (1992),
464
Bush, George (son), 434
Bush, George (grandson), 11, 18
Bush, Jeb (John Ellis, son), 11, 18
Bush, Neil (son), 466
Bush, William ("Bucky," brother), 128–129
"Bush Doctrine," 54, 70, 158
Byelorussia. *See* Belarus
Byrd, Robert, 316

Cambodia, 56, 94, 105, 122, 151, 225,
243
Camp David: Bush-Kohl meeting at (1990),
190–192; Bush-Gorbachev meeting at
(1990), 224–227, 228, 237, 461, 466
Camp David agreement, 330

Cannon, Lou, 50–51*n*
Capitalist Tool (*Forbes* jet), 465
Carnegie Endowment for International
Peace, 356
Carpendale, Andrew, 246
Carter, Jimmy, 20, 27, 47, 100, 140, 241;
Bush denounces policy of, 4–5; and arms
control, 11, 113
Carvey, Dana, 135
Casey, William, 48
Castro, Fidel, 241, 268; Gorbachev visits,
57–58, 62; Soviet aid to, 59, 105, 156,
180, 225, 389. *See also* Cuba
Caucasus, the, 175–176, 287
Cavazos, Lauro, 26*n*
CBS (Columbia Broadcasting System), 452*n,*
455
Ceausescu, Nicolae, 86, 169–170, 171, 181
Center for Democracy (Washington), 433
Center for Strategic and International Stud-
ies (Washington), 55
Central America, 56–62 *passim,* 65–66,
105, 122, 151; Iran-*contra* scandal, 12,
48, 56–57; Bureau of Inter-American Affairs release, 72; discussed at Malta, 156,
158, 164, 167, 168; U.S. invasion of Panama, 170–171, 222. *See also entries for
individual countries*
Central Asian republics, 314, 447, 457; join
commonwealth, 456. *See also* Baltic republics; Belarus (Byelorussia); Moldova
(Moldavia)
Central Intelligence Agency. *See* CIA
CFE (conventional forces in Europe): 1989
talks, 35, 53, 67–68, 78, 79; Bush and,
37–38, 75–76, 77–80, 362, 368, 403;
Gorbachev and, 39, 67–68, 78, 85, 144,
183, 265; treaty, 155, 164, 189, 190,
212, 222, 235, 269–270, 362–370, 402;
Germany and, 236; "sufficiency rule,"
269*n;* treaty signed, 288–289, 292*n*. *See
also* arms control
Chad, embassy of, 394
Chamberlain, Neville, 206
Chamber of Commerce, U.S., Bush speaks
to (1989), 55
Chamorro, Violeta, 193
chemical weapons, use of, 119–120, 245.
See also arms control
Cheney, Richard, 126, 204, 431; view of
Gorbachev, 48–49, 54–55, 65, 147, 274,
317; and arms control, 116, 117*n,* 120,
146, 372–373, 405, 445, 446*n,* (NATO)
74–75, 77; and Gulf crisis/War, 248,
280, 317, 334; visits Moscow, meets
Gorbachev, 273–274
Chernenko, Konstantin, 6–7, 29, 411
Chernobyl disaster, 159

Chernyayev, Anatoli, 16, 264, 285, 299, 314, 385, 412, 449, 458; and coup, 395, 398; and "Primakov-Yavlinsky Plan," 401, 402; and Bush's trip to Soviet Union, 414, 415

Chetverikov, Sergei, 256n, 334, 336, 408–409

Chile, 451

China, 166; Tiananmen Square massacre, 83–84, 85, 96, 99, 136, 138n, 140, 200, 285, (Baltic massacres compared to) 305, 319, (Bush's response) 430; Bush visits (1977), 129n; and Gulf crisis/War, 285, 286, 287, 314

Christian Democrats (Germany), 198, 209, 283

Chrysler Corporation, 228

Churchill, Winston, 46, 114, 129n, 253, 474

Churkin, Vitali, 340

CIA (Central Intelligence Agency), 5, 6, 25n, 58, 90, 112, 163, 242; Bush as director, 4, 12, 43, 126, 155; predicts Gorbachev's rise, ponders power, 7, 419, 437–438; view of Yeltsin, 47–48, 142, 143, 349, 360, 424, 437; and arms control, 71, 406; briefs Bush before Malta, 139, 141–142, 143; Office of Soviet Analysis (SOVA), 142–143, 305, 349, 360; and Baltics, 142, 307, 309, 316, 317; Soviet accusations against, 242, 297, 299, 394; and Kuwait, 243, 244, 424; SPOTCOM of, 309, 425; and Moscow political crises, 360, (coup) 424, 425, 428, 431, 432, 437; Gates as director, 381

Cicconi, James, 70

CIGA (Italian hotel chain), 129

Clark, Alan, 236

Clark, Dick, 394n

Clark, Joe, 79

Clemens, Roger, 422

Cliburn, Van, 85, 218

Clinton, Bill, 448, 469, 472, 474

CNN (Cable News Network), 54, 168, 178, 422, 431, 435, 444, 474; Soviet use of, as news source, 246, 314

Coast Guard Academy (New London), Bush speech at (1989), 78

Cold War, 26, 32, 63, 187, 245, 301; Bush quoted on, 9, 19, 89, 205, 325, 433, 464, 468; end of, 13, 51, 89, 165, 166, 207, 235, 446n, (and "nostalgia" for) 107, 170, (moment of ending) 238–239, (danger of) 243, 249, (gains from) 247, 447, (credit for) 464, 468–469, 470, 472, 474; Scowcroft quoted on, 17, 51, 75; 1962 crisis, 56; and "Open Skies," 71, 72 (see also Open Skies proposal); as stable period, 106, 192; Quayle on, 122–123,

124; Gorbachev and, 149, 172, 219, 229, 411, 446, 464, 467; diplomacy following, 206; and "Cold War II," 335, 379, 433

Collins, James, 396, 426, 430, 436

Colson, Charles, 346n

Columbia University, 14

communism/Communist party, 5, 297, 452n, 470; anticommunism, 8, 23, 25n, 30, 62, 102, 140, (in Eastern Europe) 86, 186, (KGB vs.) 288; military buildup feared, 17; in Hungary, 23, 81n, 90, 91, 169n; Gorbachev and, 24, 162, 374, 375, 471, (criticized by) 14, 173, 233–234, (Gates's view of) 124, (speaks at anniversary) 132–133, (as general secretary, re-elected, resigns) 149, 234, 437, (in Baltics) 173, 210, (and political power) 419; Central Committee, 28, 72, 170, 182, 239, 356n, 420; (Gorbachev meets, addresses) 173, 177, 178, 179, (criticizes Shevardnadze) 294, (and Gulf War) 333, (disbands) 437; ousts Khrushchev, 32; in 1989 and 1990 elections, 47, 193; CIA view, 48; in Latin America, 56; in China, 83; in Poland, 84, 87, 88, 102, ("reform") 53; in Cambodia, 151; in Lithuania, 173, 199, 299; in the Caucasus, 175; public demonstrations against, hatred of, 178, 182, 471; Twenty-eighth Party Congress, 233; Yeltsin quits, declares unconstitutional, 234, 473; and Gulf War, 333, 343; decline/fall of, 346, 384, 417, 437, 438, 465, 467, 473, (NSR-3 hope for) 44, (in East Germany) 132, 135, 136, 139n, 168; foreign aid and, 376; court inquiry into, 473–474

Congress, U.S., 59, 89, 240, 302, 347, 469; and defense of Europe, 76, 119n, 146; and Baltic crisis, 198, 206, 209, 216–223 passim, 318, 322; and Gulf crisis, 280, 283; Bush speaks before, (1991) 325, (1992) 464; and aid to Soviet Union, 389 (see also Jackson-Vanik Amendment); and arms cuts, 445, 446n. See also Senate, U.S.

Congress of People's Deputies. See Soviet Union

containment policy, 24, 25n, 50, 106; and "beyond containment," 69, 70, 72, 81. See also Soviet Union

Control Data Corporation, 228

Coors, Joseph, 140

Costa Rica, 156. See also Central America

Council of Europe, Gorbachev speaks to (1989), 85

Council on Foreign Relations, 4, 5

Croatia, 414n

Crowder, Richard, 380–381

Crowe, Admiral William, 83, 120, 122; and CFE, 74, 75, 76, 77; and Lithuania talks, 195, 200, 203

CSCE (Conference on Security and Cooperation in Europe), 189, 191, 233, 270; Gorbachev urges, 148, 149; State Department view of, 184, 185, 219*n;* convenes, 230; Bush attends, 269, 283, 284

Cuba, 241, 256; and Cold War, 56, 192; Soviet aid to, 56, 66, 70, 105, 180, 211, 218, 225, 377, 389, 414; Gorbachev visits, 57–58, 59, 62; aids Sandinistas, 60, 72, 156; U.S. gesture toward, 268; and Gulf crisis, 269, 278*n,* 287

Cuomo, Mario, 348

Cyprus, 128, 225

Czechoslovakia, 21, 91, 169*n,* 191; 1968 invasion of, 14, 112, 134, 149, 158, 169–170; Soviet troops to leave, 289

Dacha Agreement. *See* "Nine-plus-One"

Davis, John, 53

Dean, John, 346*n*

Defense Department, U.S., 146, 307, 419

de Gaulle, Charles, 79, 108, 472

de Klerk, F. W., 197–198

de Maiziere, Lothar, 207

Demarest, David, 70

De Michelis, Gianni, 190

Democratic party, 56, 112*n,* 140, 434, 472; Bush denounces policy of, 4–5; complains of U.S.-Soviet relations, 6

Deng Xiaoping, 83, 99, 129*n*

Department of Education, U.S., 26*n*

détente. *See* Soviet Union (U.S. relations with)

Devroy, Ann, 81, 444

disarmament. *See* arms control

Djerejian, Edward, 426

Dobrynin, Anatoli, 15–16, 71, 153, 213, 229, 311

Dole, Robert, 3, 361

Drach, Ivan, 418

Drell, Sidney, 372

Dubinin, Yuri, 49, 73, 127, 131, 177, 198; quoted on Bush, 176, 214; Bessmertnykh replaces, 213–214

Dukakis, Michael, 10, 20, 55, 56, 393*n*

Dulles, John Foster, 25*n*

Dumas, Roland, 137, 189, 232, 256, 306

Dzasokhov, Alexander, 302–303

Eagleburger, Lawrence, 27, 46, 73, 77–78, 109, 138*n;* and post–Cold War world, 106–107, 123, 170, 446*n;* visits China, 138*n;* and Gulf crisis/War, 249, 253; and Baltics, 301–302, 309; and Popov warn-

ing, 396, 397; and Soviet coup, 431–432, 444

Eastern Europe, 76*n,* 105; Gorbachev and, *see* Gorbachev, Mikhail Sergeyevich; Kissinger plan for, 13–17, 19–20, 21, 45–46; 1989 revolution in, 14, 82, 156, 166, 170; Soviet Union in, 38, 74, 75, 428, 470, (troop cuts) 10, 39, 85, 289, ("loss" of) 15, 191, 203, 233, 272, 294, (support of/aid to) 188, 194, 209, 219*n,* 230, 238, ("cooperative approach") 324, (renewed fears of) 335–336, 432; Bush and, 53*n,* 54, 81–93 *passim,* 107, 131–143 *passim,* 157, 205, 267; U.S. forces in, 74; Berlin Wall falls, *see* Germany; and NATO, 235. *See also* Baltic republics; Warsaw Pact; *entries for individual countries*

East Germany, 46, 86, 451; Gorbachev and, 82, 132–137 *passim,* 467, ("loss" of) 15, 138, 182, 186, 203; German unification and, 136–139, 168–169, 184–188 *passim,* 207, 209, 231–232, 234; elections and, 169, 184, 190*n,* 198, 283; Soviet troops in, 219*n,* 428, (cut) 39*n;* West German aid to, 238; German Democratic Republic created, ended, 239, 289. *See also* Eastern Europe; Germany

East Prussia, 191

Egypt, 291, 330

Eisenhower, Dwight, 24–25*n,* 49, 71, 87, 187, 200, 241

Eisenhower, Susan, 176, 179, 310*n*

election campaigns, U.S.: *1968,* 122*n; 1972,* 20, 27; *1976,* 5; *1980,* 113; *1984,* 6, 27; *1988,* 3, 13*n,* 56, 70, 107, 114, 140, (rhetoric of) 4, 9–10, 393*n,* (Bush's advisers) 8, 20, 41; *1992,* 107, 116, 362, (Baltics and) 408, 448, (end of Cold War and) 464, 468–469, 472, 474; *1996,* 107, 122

elections: Soviet Union, *see* Soviet Union; Nicaragua, 57, 59, 62, 106, 193, 419; Israeli proposal for, 62–63; Poland, 84, 86; Hungary, 90, 91; East Germany, 169, 184, 190*n,* 198, 283; Lithuania, Gorbachev quoted on, 174; West Germany, 191; Ukraine, 193, 448; all-Germany, 209, 232, 283

El Salvador, 56–57, 58, 72, 151, 156

Erlichman, John, 346*n*

Ermarth, Fritz, 103, 142, 143, 309*n,* 349, 424–425, 431, 438

Esalen Institute (California), 102

Estonia, 101–102, 174, 196, 305, 307, 379; declares independence, 210, 287, 442; boycotts referendum, 350; Soviet actions in, after coup, 435. *See also* Baltic republics

Estonian-American National Committee, 318
Ethiopia, 5
European Community, 205, 306
Evans, Rowland, 54, 55, 198
Export-Import Bank, 154
Eyskens, Mark, 306

"Face the Nation" (TV program), 452*n*
Fahd, king of Saudi Arabia, 272, 298
Fairbanks, Douglas, Jr., 218
Falin, Valentin, 28, 29, 186, 220, 264, 314; and Germany, 190, 239, 240, 473
Falkland Islands, 254
Farmers' Union (USSR), 422*n*
Federal Republic of Germany: West Germany as, 15, 137 (*see also* West Germany); united Germany as, 271 (*see also* Germany)
Fidelity (speedboat), 255, 258, 436
Finland, 6, 306; Gorbachev visits, 125, 134
Fitzwater, Marlin, 50–55 *passim*, 92, 126, 131, 134, 308, 331, 459; as Reagan's spokesman, 10; "drugstore cowboy" comment, 72–73, 85; at Malta, 153, 160, 161; on Baltics, 175, 194, 196, 201, 300; and "tough love," 216, 293; on planned summit, 310; and Gulf crisis/War, 329, 336, 339
Five-Hundred-Day Plan. *See* Soviet Union (economic problems)
Fonda, Jane, 218
Forbes, Malcolm, Jr., and *Forbes* magazine, 465
Ford, Gerald, 5, 6, 47, 103, 113; Bush and CIA under, 4, 43; and Kissinger, 12, 13, 27; and détente, 49, 166
Foreign Affairs (periodical), 56
Foreign Policy Association, 121
Foundation for Socioeconomic and Political Research. *See* Gorbachev Foundation
Four Powers (Big Four). *See* World War II
France, 206, 306; and CFE, 68*n*, 78; and NATO, 76–77, 185, 240*n*; and German unification, 82, 137, 169, 187, 207; Paris meetings, 92–93, 94–98, 99, 279–280, 284–285, 288; and Gulf crisis/War, 279, 286, 314
Free Democrats (Germany), 283
Freidin, Gregory, 467
Friedman, Thomas, 45

Galbraith, John Kenneth, 218
Gamsakhurdia, Zviad, 52, 352, 418
Gandhi, Rajiv, 428
Gates, Robert, 103, 277, 381; on "pause" in policy, 25, 28*n;* view of Gorbachev,

47–48, 66, 99, 147, 220, 317–318, (Baker's reaction) 48, 55, 122, 124–125, 317; and CFE proposals, 77, 78, 367; and aid to Moscow, 106, 384, 391; and Bush-Gorbachev meetings, 126–127, 130, 143, 144, 155, 216, 414; and Baltics, 299, 307, 308, 316, 317; and Moscow crises, 360, 361, (coup) 430, 431, 435
Gati, Charles, 335*n*
GATT (General Agreement on Tariffs and Trade), 151, 154
Gazeta Wyborcza (Poland), 85
Geneva conferences. *See* arms control
Genscher, Hans-Dietrich, 79, 306, 342; and German unification, 185–191 *passim*, 209, 230, 232, 283, (meets Bush) 138–139
Georgetown University, 106
Georgia, 6, 110, 300*n*, 352; as Shevardnadze's homeland, 28, 52, 61, 63, 197, 295, 470; violence in, 51–53, 95, 96, 295*n*, 368, 418, 470; boycotts referendum, 350; independence of, 359, 389; Shevardnadze as president of, 473
Gephardt, Richard, 135
Gerasimov, Gennadi, 106, 132–137 *passim*, 165, 237, 340*n*
Gere, Richard, 191
German Democratic Republic. *See* East Germany
Germany: nationalism in, 15, 186; unification of, (Western view of) 82, 136–139, 168–169, 218, 267, (Gorbachev/Soviet Union) 137, 156–157, 183–192 *passim*, 198, 209, 218–221 *passim*, 270, 294, 324, 355, 419, 470, 473, ("Two-plus-Four" proposal) 184–185, 187, 189–190, 207, 232, 271, ("too fast") 198, 470, (all-Germany elections and) 209, 232, 283, (official) 271; Berlin Wall, and fall of, 131–138 *passim*, 143, 166, 184, 219, 267, 450, 468; as member of NATO, 183–193 *passim*, 207, 219–220, 221, 227, 230, 428, 470–471, (Gorbachev accepts) 231–240 *passim*, 419; in World War II, 183, 186, 236, 238; arms control in, 188, 236, (post–World War II) 342; in post–Cold War diplomacy, 206; Gorbachev signs nonaggression pact with, 283; and Baltics, 306; and Gulf War, 314; aids Soviet Union, 376. *See also* East Germany; West Germany
Getty, Ann, 401
Gillespie, Dizzy, 218
Gingrich, Newt, 200
glasnost, 14, 71, 131, 142, 155, 203; Bush on, 11, 155, 162, 380, 399, 418; Khru-

glasnost (continued)
shchev and, 32; expected result of, 33;
military, 64; "Jewish conspiracy" under,
181; impact of, on KGB, 355*n*
Goble, Paul, 305
Godmanis, Ivars, 379–380
Goldman, Marshall, 22, 23
Gompert, David, 307, 309, 424, 425, 434–435
Gonzalez Marquez, Felipe, 427, 428
Gorbachev, Irina (daughter), 465, 466
Gorbachev, Mikhail Sergeyevich: and Reagan, *see* Reagan, Ronald; meetings, relationship with Bush, letters and telephone calls, *see* Bush, George: RELATIONSHIP WITH GORBACHEV; seen as coming leader, 6, 7, 29–30, 467; and nuclear policy/ arms control, 7, 10, 39, 78, 144, 146*n*, 178, (Reagan and) 8, 35–36, 37, 112–119 *passim*, (Bush's reaction to) 8, 50, 80, 114–120 *passim*, 162–163, (CFE) 39, 67–68, 78, 85, 144, 183, 265, 288–289, 363–370 *passim*, (as "gesture") 66–68, (disbelieved/authority doubted) 73, 204, (START treaty) 116, 119, 155, 162, 189, 265, 405, 407, (counterproposal) 183, 189, (U.S. forces in Europe) 193, 220, (Tacit Rainbow) 212–213, (Soviet reaction to) 293, (and downloading) 371, 402–403, 406; and human rights, 7, 23, 167, 385; public relations of, 8–9, 68, 72, 122, 221; speeches by, *see* SPEECHES, *below;* U.S. officials' views of, 12–13, 26, 44, 349–350, 419, (Gates/CIA) 25, 47–48, 55, 66, 99, 122, 124–125, 141–143, 147, 220, 317–318, (Matlock) 32–34, 85–86, 395–399, (Cheney) 48–49, 54–55, 65, 147, 274, 317, (Quayle) 73, 122, 168, ("Gorbocentric" policy) 103, (Eagleburger) 106, (Rice) 222, 346, (after coup) 438, 444 (*see also* survival questioned, *below;* Baker, James A., III; Scowcroft, Brent); Kissinger and, 13–16, 19, 105, 166; criticism of, (by party and ethnic groups) 14, 173, 182, 216, 233–234, 240, 306, 353, (by Yeltsin) 108, 177, 178–179, 234, 294, 349, (by aides) 219, 293, 358, (reaction to) 222, 309–310, (by nationalists) 287–288; and Germany, (East Germany) 15, 82, 132–138 *passim*, 182, 186, 203, 467, (German unification) 136, 137, 138, 156–157, 168–169, 209, 221, 234, 247, 271, 419, (signs nonaggression pact) 283 (*see also* and Eastern Europe; and NATO, *below*); identified with, quoted on *perestroika*, 22, 92, 94, 213, 348, 351, 391 (*see also perestroika*);

and Eastern Europe, 22–23, 84, 86, 91, 134, 158–159, 167, 467–468, (troop cuts) 10, 39, 85, ("loss" of) 203, 233 (*see also* and Germany, *above;* Baltic republics; Warsaw Pact); and Afghanistan, 23, 30, 123*n*, 158, 225, 265, 419; survival questioned, 25, 47, 141–143, 168, 176–178, 181, 195, 228, (coup threatened) 22, 353, 356–358, 360, 419, (Baker questions) 27, 33, 42, 55, 98–100, 122, 123–124, 147, 177, 182, 241–242, ("constitutional coup") 394–401, 415, (quoted on) 451–452 (*see also* coup against, *below*); and NATO, 26, 74–75, 168, (German unification and) 183–191 *passim*, 207, 219–220, 231–240 *passim*, 419; and the *pauza*, 28–29, 41, 60, 165; Thatcher and, 29–31, 49–50, 78, 81, 166, 201, 236, 352, (Moscow meeting) 107–108, 109, 137; Shevardnadze and, *see* Shevardnadze, Eduard; and Yeltsin, *see* Yeltsin, Boris; and Georgia, 51–52, 96, 295*n*; meets Baker, (1989) 55, 58, 59–68, 78, 155, (1990) 182–186 *passim*, 193, 211–219 *passim*, 225, 281–283, (1991) 343–344, 350–353, 457–458, (1992) 466; "testing,". 56, 60, 121, 134; and Central America, 60, 65–66, 72, 167, 168, 225, 419, (visits Cuba) 57–58, 59, 62; economic problems, 64, 95, 159–160, 351–352, (as threat to survival) 33, 181, (Western aid sought) 92–93, 236–242 *passim*, 266, 377–387 *passim*, 391, 401–402, 406, 407, 455, (and trade agreement) 210, 216–217, 222, (reforms attempted) 214, 265–266, 352, 374–375, 378–382, 384, 385, 412*n*, (withdrawal of Western aid considered) 306, 308, 310, 319, 322, ("Primakov-Yavlinsky Plan") 401–402; world view of, 72, 73–74, 85, 309–310, 319, (as "historic figure") 24, 428, 429; and "peace offensive," 74; visits China, 83; and Group of Seven (G-7), 92, 383–384, 387, (London meeting) 391, 401–402, 407, 411; and nationalism, 108, 109, 110, 175, 181, 287–288, 309, 468 (*see also* Baltic republics); visits Finland, 125, 134; visits Italy, 148, 149, 150; and the Caucasus, 175–176, 287; and "renewal," 179; meets Kohl, 187, 188, 238, 239, 240, 271; as executive president of Soviet Union, 194–195, 199, (opposition to) 203, 208, 212, 214, 219–221, 349, (and choice of vice president) 257, 294, 297, (and referendum, 1991) 350, 351, 353, (learns of Minsk agreement) 450, (resigns) 458–459, 463, 472, 474; meets E. Kennedy, 199–200; and trade agreement with U.S., 205, 206, 211, 217, 218, 221, 222, 227; peace prizes awarded to, 222, 273, 274, 309, 391; visits midwestern and western U.S., 228–230, 408; meets Rho Tae Woo, 229; re-elected general secretary of party, 234, (resigns) 437 (*see also* communism/Communist party); in Gulf crisis, *see* Gulf crisis/War; Middle East peace conference suggested, 262, 263–264 (*see also* Middle East); meets Cheney in Moscow, 274; visits France, 279, 280, 284; Bessmertnykh and, 302, 309, 310–314, 321–325; Nixon meets, 356; Moscow political crises, 357–359, (coup planned) 356, ("constitutional coup") 394–401, 415; Dacha Agreement ("Nine-plus-One"), 359, 388; and Union treaty, 359, 379, 408, 418–419, 420, 448, 449, 451; coup against (August 1991) 419–420, 421–436, 468, 473, (returns) 436–441, 443–448; and Strauss as ambassador, 427; final days in office (December 1991), 449–464; authors meet with, 451–454; quoted on breakup of Soviet Union, 452–453; resigns, 458–459, 463, 472, 474, (Bush's speech on) 459–460, 464; visits U.S., 465–468; refuses to testify, denied passport, 473–474

SPEECHES: UN (1988), 10, 37, 39, 57n, 60, 137, 147, 282; London (1989), 49; Council of Europe (Strasbourg, 1989), 85; Warsaw Pact (1989), 86; Communist anniversary (East Berlin, 1989), 132–133; Rome (1989), 148–149; New Year's (Moscow, 1990), 172; Central Committee (Moscow, 1990), 178; Congress of People's Deputies (1990), 194, 293–294; TV, on Gulf crisis (1990), 252; Supreme Soviet (1991), 308, 400; Minsk, on Soviet-U.S. relations (1991), 341; Peace Prize lecture (Oslo, 1991), 391; TV, on resignation (1991), 463–464

Gorbachev, Raisa, 23, 215, 218, 225–230 *passim,* 413, 436, 461–466 *passim*

Gorbachev family in World War II, 183

Gorbachev Foundation, 465, 466, 473

Gorky (Soviet cruise ship), 153, 160, 161, 164

Grachyov, Andrei, 72, 186, 451

"Grand Bargain." *See* Soviet Union (Western aid to)

Graves, General Howard, 281

Greenspan, Alan, 121, 140

Gregg, Donald, 6

Gromov, General Boris, 288

Gromyko, Andrei, 63, 186, 264, 302

Grosz, Karoly, 90

Group of Seven (G-7), 92, 383–384, 387; London meeting, 391, 401–402, 407, 411

Grunwald, Henry, 40

Guardian (London newspaper), 79

Gulf crisis/War: Iraqi invasion of Kuwait predicted, verified, U.S. response, 243, 244–267, 424; UN in, 245–246, 262, 269, 271, 278, 314, 327, 329n, 330, (Soviet support of) 249–256 *passim,* 265, 275, 283–286 *passim,* 299–303 *passim,* 333, 334, 340, 342n, 471, (Saddam's view of) 278, 279, 280, 282, (deadline) 303, 339, (attack begins) 313, (Bush proposal) 342; use of force, 247, 252–256 *passim,* 269, 277–284 *passim,* 286, 287, (Operation Desert Storm begins) 116n, 313–314, 317, 340, (U.S. troops) 249–251, 257, 261, 262–263, 275, 279–285 *passim,* (Soviet troops) 251, 281, 295, (naval action) 252, 253, 256, 257, 269, 274, (air strikes) 297, 314, 315, 333, 340, (credibility of threat) 299, (Iraqi army collapses) 341; Soviet Union/Gorbachev and, 250–251, 257, 263–265, 296, 335, 345, 451, 460, (as Iraqi ally) 243, 247, 255, 341, 471, (as U.S. ally) 245, 249–262 *passim,* 266, 277–285 *passim,* 298, 328, 341, 342n, 471, (hostages) 249, 251, 271, 278, 279, 284, 286, (missions and messages to Saddam) 270–282 *passim,* 302, 313–314, 315, 333, 334, 336, 354, (Soviet reaction to, delay asked) 282, 285–287, 303–304, 313–315, 326, 340–342, (Shevardnadze resigns) 295, 296, 297, 326, 470, (peace plans) 329, 333–335, 336–340, (joint statement) 330–337 *passim,* 343, (ground war begins) 340–341; linked to Arab-Israeli dispute/international conference, 256–266 *passim,* 272, 275–280 *passim,* 290–291, 328–333, 336, 338, 342–344; Iraq blockaded, 256, 269 (*see also* use of force, *above*); Helsinki meeting, 258–259, 260–267, 268, 272, 328, 330; Bessmertnykh and, *see* Bessmertnykh, Alexander; withdrawal of Iraqi troops discussed, 275–280 *passim,* 286, 303, 316, 329, 331, 338, 339; public opinion on, 280, 283, 284; deadline in, 282–283, 285, 287, 291, 303, (fixed) 286, 339–340; U.S. overtures to Saddam discussed, 287 (*see also* Saddam Hussein); Baltics as issue in, 298, 303–304, 305, 316, 324; Baker meets Aziz, 301, 303; Operation Desert Storm begins, *see* use of force, *above;* summit postponed, 322; Bush's speech on, 325–326; ceasefire considered, 326–327, 334; peace plans, joint state-

Gulf crisis/War (*continued*)
   ment, *see* Soviet Union/Gorbachev and,
   above
Gysi, Gregor, 168

Haass, Richard, 249, 264, 276, 332
Hadley, Stephen, 365*n*
Hammadi, Saadoun, 252–253
Hammer, Armand, 179, 218, 310*n*
Hamtramck, Michigan, Bush speech at (and
   Hamtramck Concept), 54
Harriman, Pamela, 218
Hartman, Arthur, 6, 7
Hartman, Donna, 6
Harvard University, 22, 307, 390, 393;
   Russian Research Center, 22; Kennedy
   School of Government, 56, 401
Hauslohner, Peter, 246
Havel, Vaclav, 14, 427, 432
Heinz, John, 448
Helms, Jesse, 107*n*, 199
Helsinki: CSCE conference in (1975), 148;
   Bush-Gorbachev meeting in (1990), 258–
   259, 260–267, 268, 272, 325, 328, 330
Henry II, king of England, 307
Heritage Foundation, 140
Herodotus, 31
Hero in History, The (Hook), 467
Hesburgh, Theodore, 310*n*
Hewett, Ed, 22, 23, 122*n*, 346–347, 392;
   and Moscow political crises, 358, 360,
   361, 389, (coup) 425, 433, 434, 435,
   (Gorbachev's resignation) 459–460; and
   U.S. aid, 380–386 *passim*, 390, 407; and
   Bush's trip to Soviet Union, 408–409,
   413, 415, 416, 417
Hills, Carla, 205
Hiss, Alger, 355
Hitler, Adolf, 101, 140, 206, 255, 276
Hodnett, Grey, 142–143
Hoffman, David, 20, 71, 130
Honasan, Colonel Gregorio "Gringo," 158
Honecker, Erich, 39*n*, 86, 132–133, 168,
   450–451
Hook, Sidney, 467
Hoover, Herbert, 6
Horelick, Arnold, 139
Howe, Geoffrey, 31
human rights issue, 70; Gorbachev and, 7,
   23, 167, 385
Hungarian Freedom-fighters Day, 8
Hungary, 46, 170; parties/elections in, 22–
   23, 90, 91, 169*n*; reform government of,
   81, 82, 86, 91, 132; Bush visits (1989),
   85, 89–92; 1956 invasion of, 123, 135,
   (Baltic crisis compared to) 195, 200, 205,
   307, 318, 319, (Soviet troops to leave)
   289; quits Warsaw Pact, 289

Hurd, Douglas, 185, 189, 232, 306
Hutton, Barbara, 406
Hu Yaobang, 83

Iacocca, Lee, 228
ICBMs (intercontinental ballistic missiles),
   115, 119*n*, 146*n*, 362, 370–371, 405–
   406; limited, 113, 144, 145, 446*n;* Soviet
   deployment in coup, 424. *See also* arms
   control
Ignatenko, Vitali, 314, 401
Ignatius, David, 317*n*
India, 314
INF (intermediate-range nuclear forces),
   18*n*, 35, 36; treaty, 415. *See also* nuclear
   policies
Institute for the Study of the U.S.A. and
   Canada (Moscow), 111, 147
Institute of World Economy and Interna-
   tional Relations (Soviet Union), 175
Internal Affairs (film), 191
International Monetary Fund (IMF), 388, 411
Iran, 98, 119, 175, 245, 261
Iran-*contra* scandal, 12, 48, 56–57. *See also*
   Nicaragua
Iraq: Soviet alliance with, 63, 243, 247,
   255, 341, 471; invades Kuwait, 116*n*,
   243, 244–245, 424, 471; vs. Kurds, 119–
   120, 245; hostages in, 249, 251, 271,
   278, 279, 284, 286; blockaded, 256, 269;
   vs. Iran, 261; U.S. attack on, feared,
   threatened, 274*n*, 277, 278, 280, 286;
   PLO as ally of, 291; Saudi Arabia as ally
   against, 298 (*see also* Saudi Arabia); Gorbachev warns against destruction of, 314;
   army collapses, 341. *See also* Gulf crisis/
   War; Saddam Hussein
Ireland, 30
Islam, 175, 251, 272, 326, 327, 343. *See
   also* Arabs
Israel, 230, 258, 259, 264*n*, 291, 393; Soviet pressure on, 328; nuclear weapons
   of, 342. *See also* Arab-Israeli dispute;
   Jews; Middle East
Italy, 128, 129, 190; Gorbachev visits,
   speaks in, 148, 149, 150
Ivashko, Vladimir, 234
Izvestia, 32

Jackson, Jesse, 218
Jackson-Vanik Amendment, 23, 151, 154,
   156, 293, 301, 388
Jakes, Milo, 169*n*
Japan, 141, 312, 382, 384, 401
Jaruzelski, General Wojciech, 53, 84–91
   passim, 102, 169*n*
Jews: Soviet, emigration of, 23, 212, 217,
   225–230 *passim*, 301, 328, 473 (*see also*

Jackson-Vanik Amendment); anti-Semitism in Soviet Union, 181–182, 207–208, 226. See also Israel
John Paul II (pope), 149
Johnson, Lyndon B., 5, 87, 112, 472
Joint Chiefs of Staff, 83, 195, 246; and arms control, 74–75, 120, 292, 445
Jordan, 330
Justice Department, U.S., 26n

Kadar, Janos, 81n
Kaifu, Toshiki, 237, 427
Kamman, Curtis, 122, 305, 444
Kanter, Arnold, 152, 365, 367, 403, 406
Kashpirovsky, Anatoli, 399
Kassenbaum, Nancy, 198
Kayumov, Lakim, 447
Kazakhstan, 96, 358, 412, 443, 446
Kellogg-Briand Pact (1928), 223
Kendall, Donald, 32, 228
Kennan, George, 50
Kennebunkport seminar on U.S.-Soviet relations (1989), 21, 22–24, 140, 347
Kennedy, Edward, 199–200, 201, 348
Kennedy, John F., 5, 24, 87, 187, 472; and Soviet relations, 11, 40
Kenney, James, 315
Kerr, Richard, 432
KGB, 5, 155, 175, 234, 242; vs. Gorbachev, 22, (supports Yeltsin) 47; bugging by, 34, 49, 409; Shevardnadze and, 41, 61, 245, 247, 470; and Baltics, 197, 199, 299, 318; and Gulf crisis/War, 245, 247, 287, 314, 334, 340; spending cut, 265; warns of internal crisis, 288, 393, 394; Russian fears of, 307, 389; new role of (policing business), 351, 375; glasnost and, 355n; and coups, 356, 396–398 passim, 425, 429, 435, 438, 440; succeeded by Russian Intelligence Service, 473
Khmer Rouge, 95n
Khomeini, Ayatollah Ruhollah, 241
Khrushchev, Nikita, 16, 111n, 149, 307, 319, 395n, 451; Kennedy and, 11, 40, 56; ousted, 32; Eisenhower and, 71
Kiev, Ukraine, Bush speech in (1991), 417–418. See also Ukraine
Kim Il Sung, 249
Kimmitt, Robert, 27, 244, 246, 256n, 326
Kinnock, Neil, 172, 348
Kirghizia. See Kyrgyzstan
Kirkpatrick, Jeane, 140
Kissinger, Henry, 12, 27, 113, 218–219; and Kissinger plan, 13–17, 19–20, 21, 45–46; and Solzhenitsyn, 103; criticizes Gorbachev, 105, 166; and German unification, 138

Kissinger Associates, 12, 27
Kochemasov, Vyacheslav, 132
Kohan, John, 451
Kohl, Hannelore, 190
Kohl, Helmut, 128, 198, 206, 309, 401, 408; and Lance missiles, 35–36, 76–77, 79; and German unification, 138, 139, 184, 207, 209, 232, 235, 236, 240, 271, 283; meets Gorbachev, 187, 188, 238, 239, 240, 271; Bush communicates with, meets, 187–192, 193, 213, 221, 235, (and Soviet coup) 427, 428, 429; and aid to Soviet Union, 236, 237, 238, 391
Koivisto, Mauno, 125, 260, 261
Kokoshin, Andrei, 147–148, 407
Kolt, George, 142–143, 305, 309n, 317, 349, 424–425
Komplektov, Viktor, 377, 415, 431–432
Koppel, Ted, 439, 459, 463
Korea, 225, 286; North Korea, 122, 229; South Korea, 229, 473
Kornienko, Georgi, 186
Kovalyov, Anatoli, 306
Kozyrev, Andrei, 335n, 380, 392, 413, 426, 433; Baker meets, 348–349
Kravchuk, Leonid, 417, 436, 450, 452, 453
Krenz, Egon, 133–139 passim, 168, 169n
Kryuchkov, Vladimir, 41, 242, 288, 297, 299, 381; and Gulf crisis/War, 247, 257, 271, 314, 451; on "Security Council," 354n; meets, sends message to Nixon, 355, 356; in political crises, 356, 358, 360, ("constitutional coup") 394, 395, 396, 400, (coup) 422, 435
Kurdish minority in Iraq, 119–120, 245
Kuwait: Iraq invades, 116n, 243, 244–245, 424, 471; withdrawal of Iraqi troops discussed, 275–280 passim, 286, 303, 316, 329, 331, 338, 339. See also Gulf crisis/War
Kvitsinsky, Yuli, 239, 311, 439, 440n
Kyrgyzstan (Kirghizia), 352, 358, 442

Labor party (Israel), 225
Labour party (Britain), 172, 348n
Ladygin, Lieutenant-General Fyodor, 403
Lance missiles, 35–36, 39, 67, 76, 77, 79, 139; plans canceled, 207. See also arms control
Landsbergis, Vytautas, 174, 194–208 passim, 211, 242, 444; in crackdown, 304, 306, 319, (Gorbachev blames) 309; Bush meets, calls, 379–380, 443
"Larry King Live," 474
Latin America, 56–57, 59. See also Central America
Latvia, 101–102, 196, 288, 379; declares independence, 210, 287, 442; crackdown

Latvia (continued)
in, 299, 315, 319, 320, 323, 346, 468, 469; boycotts referendum, 350. *See also* Baltic republics
League of Nations, 282
Leavada, Yuri, 288
Lebanon, 98, 105
Lenin, V. I., 149, 173, 186, 214, 309n. *See also* Marxism-Leninism
Levy, David, 259–260
Libya, 49, 63, 130
Li Chiang, 129n
Liedtke, J. Hugh, 129n
Ligachev , Yegor, 186, 195, 234, 473
Li Peng, 83
Lippmaa, Endal, 305
Literary Gazette (Soviet Union), 352
Lithuania, 101, 175, 176, 208, 218, 379; declares independence, 173, 193–195, 287, 442; Gorbachev and, 194–205 *passim*, 211–212, (visits) 173–174, (crackdown) 299, 301–312 *passim*, 317–323 *passim*, 346, 468, 469; as factor in trade agreement, 206, 209, 211, 217, 222, 223, 233; boycotts referendum, 350; murders in, 414–415; Soviet actions in, after coup, 435; Bush recognizes, 443–444. *See also* Baltic republics
Lithuanian Freedom Day, 8
Looking Forward (Bush), 13n, 34
Lubbers, Ruud, 427
Lugar, Richard, 159–160n
Lukin, Vladimir, 353, 447, 466
Lukyanov, Anatoli, 356, 396, 435

McAllister, Eugene, 380, 381
McGovern, George, 20
"McLaughlin Group, The" (TV program), 31
Macmillan, Harold, 30
McNamara, Robert, 310n
Madrid, peace conference at, 445–447 (*see also* Middle East)
Mainz, West Germany, Bush speech at (1989), 81
Major, John, 391, 427, 428, 440
Makashov, General Albert, 391n
Malik, Yakov, 4
Malta, Bush-Gorbachev meeting at (1989), 131, 153–168, 258, 363, 446n, 460; plans for, 34, 93–94, 97, 126–131, 139–152; promises made at, 174, 193, 195, 201, 217, 266, 325, 388, 469
Marx, Karl, 375
Marxism-Leninism, 57, 82; as threat, 25; *perestroika* as form of, 122; disavowed, 169; "end" of, 400
Maslennikov, Arkadi, 204, 206, 242n

Mathias, Charles, 310n
Matlock, Jack, 31–32, 80, 94, 179, 230, 256; view of Gorbachev, 32–34, 85–86, (in "constitutional coup") 395–399, 401, 419; recommendations disregarded, 34; Shevardnadze meets, 40, 60, 127, 170–171, 300, 301; and the Baltics, 202, 299, 304, 306, 312, 320, 321; and Yeltsin, 347–348, 359, 360, 361; and U.S. aid, 378, 381, 386; and Bush's trip to Soviet Union, 408–410, 413, 416; retires, 426
Maxim Gorky (Soviet cruise ship). *See* Gorky
Maxwell, Robert, 228
Mayakovsky, Vladimir, 452
Mazowiecki, Tadeusz, 102, 169n
Meckel, Markus, 232
"Meet the Press" (TV program), 51, 170
Mexico, 298
Meyer, Stephen, 22, 140
Michel, Robert, 168
Middle East, 98, 105, 128; international conference on, 31, 258–266 *passim*, 343, 446–448; U.S. and, 62–63, 259–260, 262, (Soviet charges) 340; Soviet Union and, 175, 212, 247, 259, 262, 264, 279; Baker visits, 268, 341; Bush visits, 285. *See also* Arab-Israeli dispute; Arabs; Gulf crisis/War; *entries for individual countries*
Minsk agreement, 449–456 *passim*, 473
MIRVs (multiple independently targetable reentry vehicles), 144–146, 370–371, 446n. *See also* arms control
MIT (Massachusetts Institute of Technology), 22
Mitchell, George, 73, 107, 135, 221, 361
Mitterrand, François, 78, 206; Bush meets, telephones, 76–77, 128, 298, 427–428; and NATO, 79, 235; Gorbachev letter to, 92; and aid to Soviet Union, 237, 310, 391; and Gulf crisis/War, 272, 274, 279
Mladenov, Petur, 136n, 169n
Modrow, Hans, 134, 139n, 169n
Moiseyev, General Mikhail, 54, 80, 290, 340; and arms control, 363–370 *passim*, 403, 404, 406; Bush meets, 368, 412; in coup, 434, 435, 437, 439
Moldova (Moldavia), 174, 297, 300n, 350; secession of, 359, 389; change of name, 442n
Molotov, Vyacheslav, 210
Mongolia, Baker visits, 245, 246
Moscow News, 288
Moscow State University, 356n
Moscow summit meeting. *See* Bush, George: RELATIONSHIP WITH GORBACHEV
Mubarak, Hosni, 272

Mulford, David, 53n
Mulroney, Brian, 215, 216, 237, 427
Murdoch, Rupert, 379
Murphy, Admiral Daniel, 5, 114
Muslims. *See* Islam

Nagorno-Karabakh (Azerbaijan), 175
Najibullah, Mohammad, 62, 180
Nakayama, Taro, 312
Namibia, 56, 197, 236
NASA Johnson Space Center, 292
National Governors' Conference, 347
National Intelligence Council, 103, 142, 349
National Intelligence Daily, 317
National Intelligence Estimate (NIE), 141, 143
National Press Club, 9
National Review, 45
National Security Agency, 313
National Security Council. *See* NSC
NATO (North Atlantic Treaty Organization), 35–36, 128, 138, 166, 256, 332, 371n; Gorbachev and, *see* Gorbachev, Mikhail Sergeyevich; Bush and, 36, 37, 74–81 *passim,* 164–165, 188, 192, 231, 469, 470, (London summit) 234–237, 240; limits proposed, 39; "needless crisis" in, 50; as political (rather than military) force, 163, 186; Germany as member of, *see* Germany; and Open Skies proposal, 189; CSCE seen as "replacement" for, 191; new mission of, 192; as Soviet "problem," 198, 341; Atlantic Council of, 235; and CFE treaty, 290. *See also* arms control
Navy, U.S., 116n, 119n, 130, 145, 162–163, 219; Sixth Fleet, 150, 154, 161; in Gulf War, 252, 253, 256, 257, (government "obsession" with) 274
Nazarbayev, Nursultan, 96, 352, 353, 412, 418, 436
Nazarkin, Yuri, 373
Nazis, 183, 186, 232, 276, 394
NBC (National Broadcasting Company), 112, 135, 160, 170, 259, 464
Nemeth, Miklos, 90, 92
Netherlands, 190
neutron bomb, deployment of, 5. *See also* nuclear policies
Nevsky, Alexander, 290
New London, Connecticut, Bush speech at (1989), 78
"Newsmaker Saturday" (TV program), 444
Newsweek magazine, 176
New York Mets, 4
New York Times, 45, 46, 71, 73, 198, 254, 283, 332, 335, 418

Nicaragua, 30, 65, 70, 225, 393; Iran-*contra* scandal, 12, 48, 56–57; Sandinistas in, 56–62 *passim,* 72, 105, 151, 156, 193n, 419; elections in, 57, 59, 62, 105, 193, 419
Nicholas II, czar of Russia, 306–307
"Nine-plus-One," 359, 388
Nixon, Richard, 4, 13, 27, 87, 113, 140, 187; and détente, 12, 166, 354; Watergate, 346; visits, reports on Moscow, (1972) 408, (1991) 354–357, 359–360, 363
Nobel Peace Prize (1990), 273, 274, 309, 391
Non-Aligned Movement, 129
Noriega, General Manuel, 170, 249, 341
North Korea, 122, 229. *See also* Korea
Novak, Robert, 54, 55, 67n, 198
NSC (National Security Council), 50, 130, 150, 184, 205, 379, 380, 409n, 413; Scowcroft with, 12, 20, 26, 27, 337, 346; conflict with State Department, 20, 26, 45, 47–48, 143, 358, (over January 1991 joint statement) 332, 333, 337; Blackwill with, 25, 53, 143, (replaced by Gompert) 307; Rice with, 53, 332, 346; and arms control, 152, 365, 445; and coup, 424, 431, 433
NSD-23 (National Security Directive), 69–70
NSR-3 (National Security Review), 24–26, 43–45, 49, 69
nuclear policies, 5, 38–39; Gorbachev and, 7, 8, 36, 50, 66–68, 222–223n, 405; U.S., 35, 76, 79, 112–117, (Navy) 130; "football" and "little suitcase," 224–225, 424, 461; reciprocal, 236, ("risk reduction") 233n; Baltic crisis and, 316; Gulf crisis and, 342; after breakup of Soviet Union, 445–446, 450, 457, 458. *See also* arms control
Nunn, Sam, 145, 147
Nyers, Rezso, 90, 91, 92, 169n

Oberdorfer, Don, 72, 81
Obukhov, Alexei, 403, 404
Olav V, king of Norway, 428
Olympic Games, 156, 179
Omelichev, General Branislav, 212, 222
Open Skies proposal, 71, 72, 189, 220. *See also* arms control
Operation Desert Shield, 249, 262
Operation Desert Storm, 116n, 313–314, 317, 340. *See also* Gulf crisis/War
Operation Just Cause, 170
Organization of Economic Cooperation and Development, 154
Ottawa: Bush visits, 21; arms control

Ottawa (*continued*)
  meeting in, 189–190; Gorbachev visits,
  215
Ozal, Turgut, 427

Palach, Jan, 14
Palazhchenko, Pavel, 95, 154, 159, 226,
  328, 415, 450, 451, 458; authors meet,
  455–456; visits U.S., 465, 466, 467
Palestine, 62, 261, 266, 275, 279, 328, 330,
  366. *See also* Arab-Israeli dispute; Arabs
Palestine Liberation Organization (PLO),
  291, 343, 366
Palmer, Mark, 46, 91
Pamyat (nationalistic organization), 182,
  208
Panama, U.S. invasion of, 170, 171, 222,
  249
Pankin, Boris, 440, 450
Paris meetings. *See* France
"Party of Democratic Socialism" proposed,
  234
Patterson, Robert, 315
pauza (pause), the, 28–29, 41, 60, 80, 165,
  469
Pavlov, Valentin, 247, 271, 351, 354n, 412;
  in political crises, 357, 358, ("constitutional coup") 393–401 *passim,* (coup)
  422, (resigns) 427; and economic reform,
  375–376, 382–390 *passim,* 402
Pavlov, Yuri, 105, 193n
Payson, Joan Whitney, 4
peace prizes awarded to Gorbachev, 222n,
  273, 274, 309, 391
Pennzoil Corporation, 129n
Pepsico, 32, 228
peredyshka (breathing space), 17n
Peres, Shimon, 225
perestroika, 29, 440; Bush and, 11, 60, 94,
  100, 139–140, 147, 380, (supports) 55,
  70, 107, 131, 154–155, 169, 216, 399,
  418, (demonstration of support urged)
  157, 165, 237, 377, (Baltic crisis and)
  206, 217, (worries about) 260; success
  questioned, 11, 65, 210, 221, (by Castro)
  58, 156; Gorbachev identified with, 22,
  94, 213, 348, (quoted on) 92, 111, 157,
  164, 172–178 *passim,* 351, 391; NSR-3
  view, 24, 44; "first," Khrushchev and,
  32; and economic woes, 33, 374; as
  viewed by U.S. officials, 40, 65, 122, 142,
  179, 180, (and Western aid) 237, 383;
  arms cut as part of, 66; and Eastern Europe, 91, 133, 467; Soviet view of, 96,
  110, 139–140, 273, 306, 379, (Yeltsin)
  104, (Moiseyev) 368; Baltic crisis and,
  111, 163–164, 174, 306, 324; and conversion, 274

Peresyokin, Major General Alexander, 203
Perez de Cuellar, Javier, 314
Persian Gulf, 229. *See also* Gulf crisis/War
Petrakov, Nikolai, 375
Petrov, Lujben, 289
Petrovsky, Vladimir, 447n
Pfaltzgraff, Robert, 22
Philby, Kim, 355
Philippines, the, 136, 221; U.S. intervention
  in, 150, 158, 167, 170
Pickering, Thomas, 246, 253, 256, 286
Pinochet, General Augusto, 451n
PLO. *See* Palestine Liberation Organization
Poland, 136, 140, 157, 180, 190n, 336;
  1989 revolution begins in, 53, 54, 82,
  132, 467; elections in, 84, 86; Bush visits,
  85–89; coalition government, 102, 169n;
  border of, with Germany, 191, 192
Politburo, 33, 64, 108, 123n, 186, 233,
  295n, 302; East German, 134, 139n; and
  Gulf War, 333
Polozkov, Ivan, 214
Popadiuk, Roman, 50, 125, 130, 161, 329,
  331; and news of coup, 422–423, 426, 431
Popov, Gavril, 241, 242, 352, 360; warns
  of coup, 395–401 *passim,* 419, 425
Popular Front (Azerbaijan), 175, 176
Portugalov, Nikolai, 186, 239
Powell, Charles, 30
Powell, General Colin, 246, 248, 253, 280,
  339, 439n; and arms control, 368, 370,
  372, 373, 405, 445; and Soviet coup,
  423–424, 431
Pozsgay, Imre, 90, 91
Pravda, 32, 165, 175, 340
President Reagan: The Role of a Lifetime
  (Cannon), 51n
President's Daily Brief, 309, 421
Presock, Patty, 177
Pretoria, 198
Price, Meredith, 17
Primakov, Yevgeni, 409n, 440, 473; as
  spokesman, 175–176, 257, 259; as Shev-
  ardnadze's rival, 211, 257, 272, 274,
  285, 296, 302–303; at high-level meetings, 212, 237, 264; criticizes Gorbachev,
  219; and Gulf crisis/War, 257, 259, 261,
  265, 285, 286, 314, 335, 338, (missions
  to Baghdad) 270–282 *passim,* 302, 333,
  334, 336, 354, (Bush meets) 276–277,
  (Thatcher meets) 278, (and use of force)
  283–284, 337; Nixon meets, 354; and
  reform, 354, 355, 383–384, 386–387,
  388–390, 391, ("Primakov-Yavlinsky
  Plan") 401–402
Prunskiene, Kazimera, 206–207, 208, 211,
  241, 242
Pugo, Boris, 288, 301, 309, 319, 354n; and

political crises, 357, 358, 360, ("constitutional coup") 394, 395, 400, (coup, suicide) 422, 435–436

Qaddafi, Muammar al-, 130, 149
Quayle, J. Danforth, 52–53, 126, 248, 390–391, 428; on Gorbachev, 73, 122, 168; meets Yeltsin, 103, 104; and SDI, 117*n*, 119; on Cold War, 122–123, 124; and divergence from Bush, 168
Questions of Military History (Soviet journal), 333–334*n*

Rakowski, Mieczyslaw, 102, 169*n*
RAND Corporation, 139
Reagan, Nancy, 228
Reagan, Ronald, 24, 43, 63, 109, 126; Gorbachev meetings with, 3, 10, 18*n*, 34, 85, 141, 228, 371, 449, (Reykjavik) 8, 113–114, 130, 147; Bush as vice president under, *see* Bush, George; and Iran-*contra*, 12, 56; relations of, with Soviet Union, 18, 20, 25, 28–33 *passim*, 47, (Bush administration and) 14, 16, 29, 32, 49, 50 (*see also* and arms control, *below*); and NSC, NSR-3, 26, 27, 45; and CIA, 48, 90; criticizes Bush's foreign policy, 50; Castro's view of, 58; Polish view of, 86; and arms control, 112–119 *passim*, 120*nn*, 146, 371, (Bush's view) 8, 35, 114, ("zero option") 35–36, 38; and SDI, 113, 114, 117
Red Brigade, 128
Redford, Robert, 218
Red Star (Soviet military daily), 340
Republican party, 5, 20, 25*n*, 36, 41, 200, 318; Bush and, 4, 114, 346, 416; 1996 plans, 122; National Convention, (1988) 393*n*, (1992) 468, 474. *See also* election campaigns, U.S.
Reykjavik talks, 8, 113–114, 130, 147
Rice, Condoleezza, 51–53 *passim*, 69, 91, 105, 345, 427, 474; briefs Kennebunkport seminar, 21, 22–23, 347; and Bush-Yeltsin meeting, 103–104, 399; and Bush-Gorbachev meetings, 127, 130, 143, 150, 151, 227; and Baltic crisis, 205, 299, 305–309 *passim*, 315, 316; view of Gorbachev, 222, 346; and Gulf crisis, 257, 329, 332, 338
Ridgway, Rozanne, 19–20, 26, 45
Riga. *See* Latvia
Rikken, Mari-Ann, 318
Robinson, James, 228
Roh Tae Woo, 229
Romania, 86, 169, 170–171, 180, 297
Romanov, Grigori, 6, 30

Roosevelt, Franklin D., 28*n*, 43, 46, 87, 129*n*
Rosenthal, Felix, 451
Ross, Dennis, 53, 65, 105, 109, 266, 349, 427; Baker chooses, 20–21, 26, (and Baker's policy) 60, 61, 97, 107, 124, 179, 233, 248; and arms control, 39, 213, 292, 293, 367, 403; and Middle East, 63, 98, 263, 264, 275, 291; and Bush's speeches, 86, 87, 88; and Malta, 143, 144, 147; and Germany, 184, 187, 233, 237; and Baltic crisis, 202, 203–204, 208, 270, 305; and Gulf crisis/War, 245–248 *passim*, 261–265 *passim*, 270–277 *passim*, 282, 285, 328–330, (January 1991 joint statement) 332, 343, (peace plan) 336; and Shevardnadze, 296, 353; and Moscow political crises/coups, 358, 397, 423, 449, 455, 456; and U.S. aid, 385, 386, 390; and Bush's trip to Soviet Union, 413, 414*n*, 415; in 1992 campaign, 474
Rowan, Henry, 139
Rukh (Ukrainian independence movement), 445*n*
Russian Intelligence Service, 473
Russian Republic, 348–349, 358, 412; Yeltsin as president of, 193, 375 (*see also* Yeltsin, Boris); and referendum, 350, 351, 353; U.S. policy toward, 359, 412; nationalism vs., 443; nuclear weapons in, 446, 461
Rutskoi, Alexander, 435
Ryzhkov, Nikolai, 214, 376*n*, 391*n*, 473

Sachs, Jeffrey, 385
Saddam Hussein, 119, 305, 324; invades Kuwait, 243, 244–264 *passim*, 424, 471; pressure on, 269, 281, 282–283, 290, 299 (deadline) 303, 340; Primakov missions to, 270–282 *passim*, 302, 333, 334, 354; Gorbachev messages to, 279, 313–314, 315; overtures to, 287, 334; allies of, 291; elimination/punishment of, 326–327, 341, 342; Soviet peace plan and, 329, 333, 334–335, 336–338. *See also* Gulf crisis/War; Iraq
Safire, William, 198, 332, 335, 418, 448
Sagdeyev, Roald, 117, 176, 179, 310*n*
Sakharov, Andrei, 309, 310*n*, 385
Salih, Ali Abdallah, 285
Salinas de Gortari, Carlos, 298
SALT treaties. *See* arms control
Sandinista regime. *See* Nicaragua
"Saturday Night Live" (TV program), 135
Saudi Arabia: and Gulf crisis, 249, 250, 251, 261, 262, 275, 277, 298, (U.S.

Saudi Arabia (*continued*)
troops in) 279, 280, 285, (inter-Arab conference) 280
Savisaar, Edgar, 379–380
Schlesinger, James, 140
Schweitzer, Peter, 254*n*
Scowcroft, Brent, 34, 124, 125, 138*n*, 177, 225; as Ford adviser, 6, 12, 27; view of Gorbachev/Soviet Union, 13, 17–24 *passim*, 37, 67, 93–94, 99, 123, 200, (nationalist crises) 51, 102, 174, 198–204 *passim*, 298–308 *passim*, 317, 318, 408, 416, 443, (breakup of Soviet Union) 102, 109, 298, 346, (Yeltsin) 103–104, 105, 349–350, 360, 361, 444, (U.S. aid) 106, 377, 378, 384, 390, 391, (study group) 316, (diffusion of power) 345–346, 347, (political crises) 360, 361, 396, (after coup) 422–441 *passim*, 443, 447, 449, 455, 459–460; and NSC, NSR-3, NSD-23, 20, 24–25, 26, 45, 47, 69; and troops in Europe, 37–39, 74, 75, 77, 288–289; and Eastern Europe, 46, 54, 74, 75, 88, 92, 136, 139; and "Bush Doctrine," 54, 70; and Cheney, 55, 74–75, 77, 146, 273; and Malta, 126–131 *passim*, 139–153 *passim*, 161; and German unification/NATO, 190, 192, 234, 236; and Gulf crisis/War, 245–255 *passim*, 261, 276, 297, 300, 303, 334, (use of force) 280, 283, 299, (January 1991 joint statement) 331–332, 337, (peace plan) 336, 338; and arms control, 367, 369, 371, 373, (START, SDI) 115–116, 117*n*, 127, 402–406 *passim*, 445, (chemical warfare) 120; and Bush's trip to Soviet Union, 409, 412, 413, 414, 417
SDI (strategic defense initiative). *See* arms control
Seagram, Joseph E. & Sons, 301
Secret Service, U.S., 130, 429
Seitz, Raymond, 190, 217
Senate, U.S., 61, 189, 199, 206; Foreign Relations Committee, 50; Finance Committee, 121. *See also* Congress, U.S.
Serbia, 414*n*
Shakhnazarov, Georgi, 16, 82, 301
Shamir, Yitzhak, 225, 226*n*, 230, 291
Shaposhnikov, General Yevgeni, 439, 456
Shatalin, Stanislav, 375; and Shatalin (Five-Hundred-Day) Plan, 265–266, 352, 382
Shcherbakov, Vladimir, 384, 386, 387, 389
Shcherbitsky, Vladimir, 108
Shevardnadze, Eduard, 66, 71, 140, 300, 329, 348; Bush meets, 9, 108–109, 117, 118, 225, 293, 308; and Baker, *see* Baker, James A., III; and Middle East conference, 31, 259, 263–264, 290–291;

and Gorbachev, 40–41, 294–295, (defends) 177, 178, 210, 234, 242, 243, 301, 378–379, (criticizes) 293, 295–296, 306, (predicts coup against) 353, 395, 419, 423; comments of, to press, 49, 54, 160; and Georgian crisis, 52, 470; and CFE/arms control, 78, 80, 117–121 *passim*, 148, 155, 197, 209, 270, 292–293, 363, 438; and Iran, 98; quoted on Afghanistan, 123, 273, 284; and Malta, 127, 131, 153; and Germany, 133–137 *passim*, 157, 184–190 *passim*, 207, 220, 234, 239–240, 470–473 *passim*; and Eastern Europe, 180–181, 470, ("loss" of) 272, 294; and Baltics, 197–198, 202, 204, 207–210 *passim*, 294; and trade agreement, 209, 210–211, 218, 223; and Gorbachev-Roh meeting, 229; and Gulf crisis/War, 244–248 *passim*, 249–257, 259–265 *passim*, 269, 270–272, 274, 333, 338, 470, (compared to Afghanistan) 273, 280, 281, 284, 286, (and use of force) 282–283, 284, 286, 295, (visits China) 285; criticized, 257, 272, 288, 294, 394; resigns, 295–296, 297, 419, (returns to office) 450; successor to, 310–313, 326, (Primakov seen as) 211, 257, 296, 302–303; and political crises, 358, 379, 388, ("constitutional coup") 394–395, (coup) 427, 438; and breakup of Soviet Union, 470; as president of Georgia, 473
Shevardnadze, Nanuli, 63, 248, 295
Shmelyov, Nikolai, 111
Shultz, George, 26, 29, 31, 47–48, 63; visits Moscow, 6, 7; criticized, 9, 27–28, 41; Gorbachev visits, 229, 467
Shushkevich, Stanislav, 450
Siberia, 95, 118
Sicily, 128
Sidey, Hugh, 167
Simes, Dimitri, 356
Simons, Thomas, 19–20, 53
Sinatra, Frank, 218; and "Sinatra Doctrine," 134, 136*n*
Skinner, Samuel, 459
Slava (Soviet cruiser), 152, 153
SLBMs (submarine-launched ballistic missiles), 146*n*, 370*n*, 372. *See also* arms control
SLCMs (sea-launched cruise missiles), 116*n*, 119*n*, 155*n*, 162, 183*n*. *See also* arms control
Slovenia, 414*n*
Smith, Adam, 375
SNF (shorter-range nuclear forces), 36, 39, 76, 79, 80. *See also* nuclear policies
Sobchak, Anatoli, 241, 242, 352, 358

Social Democrats (Germany), 283
Socialist party (Hungary), 169n
Solidarity movement, 53, 82–88 passim, 89n, 90, 102
Solzhenitsyn, Alexander, 103
Somalia, 5
South Africa, 197–198
South Korea, 229, 473. See also Korea
SOVA (Office of Soviet Analysis). See CIA (Central Intelligence Agency)
"Soviet Cauldron, The" (CIA report), 360
Sovietskaya Kultura, 32
Sovietskaya Rossiya, 334
Soviet Space Research Institute, 310n
Soviet Union: U.S. relations with, (détente) 4, 12, 48, 49, 85, 166, 354, (and "Cold War II") 335 (see also economic problems; U.S. view of, below; Bush, George: RELATIONS OF, WITH SOVIET UNION; Cold War; Reagan, Ronald); changes in leadership, 5–7; internal crisis warned of, 6, 102 (see also COLLAPSE OF, below); in Eastern Europe, see Eastern Europe; Czechoslovakia; Hungary; Poland; Rice lectures in, 21; and Afghanistan, see Afghanistan; emigration from, 23, 212, 217, 223–230 passim, 293, 301, 328, 388, (Gorbachev denied passport) 473–474; as MFN (most favored nation), see Western aid to, below; and Nicaragua, 30, 56, 57, 65, 70, 72, 105, 156, 193; economic problems, 33, 64, 95, 159, 412n (and U.S. trade agreement) 205–211 passim, 217–227 passim, 233, 293, 388, (Five-Hundred-Day Plan) 265–266, 352, 382, (crisis deepens) 374–392, (GNP) 374, 377, (Gosplan) 384, ("anticrisis"/Pavlov plan) 387, 388, 390, 402, (coup and) 425, 448 (see also perestroika); U.S. view of, 34, 47, 52, 72–73, 122, 123–124, (Kissinger) 15, (containment/"beyond containment") 24, 25n, 50, 69, 70, 73, 81, 106, (use of military vs. nationalism) 176, (study group formed) 316, (need for cooperation) 339, (reforms) 345, 347, 387–389; elections in, 46–47, 64, 122, 124, 214, 215, 295, 319, 391, (Ukraine) 193, 448, (plebiscite planned) 323; Congress of People's Deputies, 46, 49, 64, 122, 175, 297, 443, (Yeltsin as member, addresses) 102, 294, (Gorbachev addresses) 194, 293–294, (Shevardnadze addresses) 295–296; rise of Yeltsin in, 47, 214, 215 (see also Yeltsin, Boris); "testing," 55–56, 60, 61, 121, 134; and Cuba, see Cuba; and the Baltics, 101, 110, 299–302, 435, 444, (Black Berets in) 299, 315, 414 (see also Baltic republics); -Japanese conspiracy feared, 141; and arms control, 147–148, 183, 189, 190, 270, 438, 470, (disregard of) 12, 105, 289–290, (as "gesture" by Gorbachev) 66–68, 73, 181, ("linkage" and) 112, 117–119, 406, (disputes START) 117, 123, 144–146, 197, 209, 362–363, 370–373, (concessions withdrawn) 203, 209, 212–213, 292–293, ("nuclear risk reduction") 233n, (1991 negotiations) 362–373, 402–406, (in coup) 424n, 445–446, 456, (Yeltsin and) 445, 446n, 449–450, 456, 458; Western aid to, 155, 238, 266, (MFN status) 23, 71, 217, 222, 223, 230, (G-7 and) 92–93, 401–402, (questioned) 106, 241, 469, (tied to reforms) 141, 158, 236, 237, 293, 401, 406, (economic crisis and) 242, 287, 376–392, 407, 455, (Baltic crisis and) 306, 308, 310, 319, 321, 322, (Gorbachev appeals to U.S.) 377–382, 384, 386, 391, 407, 455, ("Grand Bargain") 382, 385, 386, 390, 393, 402, (Yeltsin's view) 412; and U.S. presence in Europe, 163, 220; Quayle on totalitarianism of, 168; and German unification, see Germany; and the Caucasus, 175–176, 287; anti-Semitism in, 181–182, 207–208, 226; German invasion of (World War II), 183, 186, 236, 238; and Gulf crisis, see Gulf crisis/War; Five-Hundred-Day Plan, see economic problems, above; Soyuz (Union) faction of, 272, 394; Supreme Soviet, 272–273, 293, 312, 366, (Gorbachev addresses) 308, 400, (plans coup) 356, (Pavlov and) 393, 395, 398; on UN Security Council, 286 (see also United Nations); as U.S. partner in Arab-Israeli dispute, 343, 446; diffusion of power in, 345, 347–349, (Gorbachev-Yeltsin coalition/alliance) 349, 353, 355, 358–361 passim, 378, 391; Federation Council, 349, 358; referendum (March 1991), 350, 351, 353; "Security Council" of, 354, 383; Moscow political crises (1991), see COLLAPSE OF, below; GNP, Gosplan of, see economic problems, above; "end of Marxist experiment" in, 400; "Emergency Committee" of, 422n, 427, 428, 429, 430, 431; State Council formed, 444; Commonwealth of Independent States formed, 450–464, 473; Union ceases to exist, 458, 464, 467, 470. See also Brezhnev, Leonid; communism/Communist party; Gorbachev, Mikhail Sergeyevich; KGB; Politburo; Stalin, Joseph; Yeltsin, Boris
    COLLAPSE OF: Soviet warnings, 6, 234, 242, 273, 288, 393, 394; nationalist up-

Soviet Union (*continued*)
risings, 51–53, 96, 295n, 368 (*see also* Baltic republics); U.S. fears, 102, 142, 298, 443, 445–446, 448; U.S. provocation avoided, 109, 346; republics declare independence, 173, 193–195, 210, 287, 359, 389, 442–443; Shevardnadze's fears, 242, 243, 295–297, 303, 306, 353, 379, 388, 395; Yeltsin and, 294, 444; coup planned, 356; political crisis, 357–359; Union treaty (proposed), 359, 379, 388–389, 408, 412, 418–419, 420, 448; "constitutional coup," 394–401, 415; coup, 421–441, 447–448; Minsk agreement, new commonwealth, 449–464, 473; Gorbachev quoted on, 452–453
SPOTCOM ("Spot Commentary"), 309, 425
Stalin, Joseph, 61, 101, 140, 210, 451, 452n; Gorbachev compared to, 22, 149, 173, 199, 317, 394; foreign policy of, 32, 238, 419; at Yalta, 46, 129n
Stanford University, 229, 372, 467
Stankevich, Sergei, 306
Starodubtsev, Vasili, 422n
START treaty: Baker-Shevardnadze/Bessmertnykh talks, 112, 116–117, 119, 128, 155, 181, 183, 203–204, 209, 212–213, 222, 243, 269–270, 402–406 *passim;* Bush and, 114–117, 127, 146, 155, 362; Gorbachev and, 116, 119, 155, 162, 189, 265, 405, 407; Soviet Union disputes, 117, 123, 144–146, 197, 209, 362–363, 370–373; Malta and, 128, 144–147 *passim,* 155, 162–164, 193, 363; Tacit Rainbow, 212–213; compromise on, 223n; downloading, 371–373, 402–405; signed, 407, 414, 415, 445; postscript to, 445–446. *See also* arms control
Star Wars. *See* arms control (SDI)
State, U.S. Department of, 9, 63n, 303, 378; Kennedy-Johnson, 5; Kissinger and, 13n; view of Soviet Union, 34, 47, 52, 72–73, 122, 123–124, (diffusion of power) 345, (financial aid) 376; and nuclear power/arms control, 39, 222, 223, 365n, 368; and Poland, 53; Bureau of Inter-American Affairs, 72; view of Yeltsin, 104–105, 345, 348, 444; and Malta meeting, 144; and CSCE, 184, 185, 219n; and Baltics, 194, 305, 307, 444; and Gulf crisis/War, 244, 251, 256n, 275, 299, 301, 321, 334, (linked with peace conference) 330–332; and Moscow political crises, 357–358, (coup) 431; and Bush's trip to Soviet Union (1991), 408–409; and limits of Gorbachev's power, 419. *See also* Baker, James A., III; NSR-3 (National Security Review)

State of the Union speeches: (1991), 325, 330, 331, 332; (1992), 464
Steinhoff, Lena, 130
Stettinius, Edward, 28
Stevenson Amendment, 154
Strategic Defense Initiative (SDI). *See* arms control
Straub, Bruno, 90
Strauss, Robert, 426, 427, 431, 436, 444
Sudetenland, 191
Suez crisis, 307
Sullivan, Michael, 112
Sununu, John, 52, 72, 78–83 *passim,* 89, 126, 141, 226, 277; in 1988 campaign, 8; and "Bush Doctrine," 54; and Malta, 149, 153; and Gulf crisis/War, 276, 335, 337, 338; and Baltics, 318; and Bush's trip to Soviet Union, 408, 413, 415
Susann, Jacqueline, 5
Swanson, Stuart, 315
Sweden, 159
Syria, 62, 63, 105, 291, 302, 330, 426; Baker visits Damascus, 268. *See also* Middle East
Szuros, Matyas, 123

Tacit Rainbow cruise missile, 212–213. *See also* arms control
Tadzhikistan, 358, 442, 447
Tallinn. *See* Estonia
Tarasenko, Sergei, 65, 98, 153, 202, 295, 329, 450; on U.S. policy, 52, 71, 97, 120, 264, 266–267; on Soviet military demands, 203–204, 208, 213, 233, 237, 292; and Gulf crisis/War, 244–245, 247–248, 263, 265, 270, 274, 285
TASS (Soviet news agency), 300, 422, 424, 444
Tbilisi. *See* Georgia
"Team B," 4, 5
Teeley, Pete, 43
Teeter, Robert, 9, 460
Telschik, Horst, 192, 209
Temple, Shirley, 93
Texas A&M University: Bush speech at, 69–71, 93; Bush library at, 474
Thatcher, Margaret, 128; and Gorbachev, 29–31, 49–50, 78, 81, 166, 201, 236, 352, (Moscow meeting) 107–108, 109, 137; and arms/troop cutback, NATO, 76–77, 78, 79, 235–236; and aid to Soviet Union, 237; and Gulf crisis/War, 253–254, 278
"third zero," 76. *See also* arms control
"This Week with David Brinkley" (TV program), 17, 117n
Thomas, Helen, 192, 260
Thomas à Becket, 307

Thornburgh, Richard, 26n, 448
Tiananmen Square. See China
Timbie, James, 365n
Time magazine, 40, 167, 452, 454n
Tizyakov, Alexander, 422n
Tower, John, 48, 117n
Treasury Department, U.S., 26n, 17, 53, 205
Trilateral Commission, Bush resigns from, 5
Truman, Harry, 25n, 28n, 87, 187
Trud (Soviet trade union journal), 375n
Tufts University, 22
Turkey, 305, 409
Turkmenistan, 358
Turner, Ted, 218
Tutwiler, Margaret, 26, 98, 107, 109, 161, 244, 330, 353, 474; in Moscow political crises, 357, 444
TV Marti (Cuban exile station), 58
"Two-plus-Four" proposal. See Germany (unification of)

Ukraine, 95, 108, 183, 300n, 380–381; elections in, 193, 448; independence of, 287, 358, 442–443, 452, 454, 457, (Bush recognizes) 448–449; Bush visits, speaks in (1991), 408–410, 414, 415–418; nuclear weapons in, 445, 446, 449
Ulam, Adam, 22
"Un-Group," U.S. See arms control
Union College, 335n
United Nations, 94n, 311, 447n; Bush as ambassador to, 4, 151; Gorbachev speech at (1988), 10, 37, 39, 57n, 60, 137, 147, 282; Bush addresses (1989), 120–121, 181; Shevardnadze addresses, 121; South Korea admitted to, 229n; in Gulf crisis, see Gulf crisis/War; Cuba as member, 268; Security Council presidency, (U.S.) 280, 284, 286–287, (Yemen) 280, 286; and Middle East conference, 290, 291 (see also Middle East)
United States: and Soviet Union, see Soviet Union; public opinion in, 10–11, 31, 74, 107, 165, 408, 469, (on Eastern Europe) 15, (on Gulf War) 280, 283, 284, (on coup) 430; nuclear policy, 35 (see also nuclear policies); forces of, in Europe, 36–39, 74, 75, 77, 189, 191, 235, 257, (Gorbachev on) 163, 220; and Central America, see invades Panama, below; Central America; Cuba; Middle East policy, 62–63, 259–260, 262, (Soviet charges) 340, (partnership with Soviet Union) 343, 446; and Iran, 98; view of Baltics, see Baltic republics; "Gorbocentric" policy, 103; in Philippines, 150, 158, 167, 170; invades Panama, 170–

171, 222; and German unification, 185, 187, 207; and arms control, 189 (see also arms control); in Persian Gulf, see Gulf crisis/War; and Russian Republic, 359, 412. See also Bush, George: AS PRESIDENT-ELECT/PRESIDENT; election campaigns, U.S.; Reagan, Ronald
USA-Canada Institute, 407
U.S. News & World Report, 20
University of Denver, 21
University of Texas, 390
UPI (United Press International), 192, 260
Urbanek, Karel, 169
Uzbekistan, 358, 442

VAAP (Soviet copyright agency), 34n
Vance, Cyrus, 264
Varennikov, Valentin, 199
Velikhov, Yevgeni, 117, 310n
Versailles Treaty, 186
Vershbow, Alexander, 45
Vietnam: and Cambodia, 56, 94n, 105; Gulf War compared to war in, 286
Vilnius. See Lithuania
Vlasov, Alexander, 214
Voice of America, 51, 52
von Stade, Frederica, 221
Vorontsov, Yuli, 278, 285, 291, 311
Vorotnikov, Vitali, 193

Walesa, Lech, 53, 84, 87–88, 89, 167, 427, 432
Walker, George Herbert, 21
Walters, Vernon, 169
Warsaw, Poland, Bush speech at (1989), 89
Warsaw agreements, 53
Warsaw Pact, 105, 109, 137, 169n, 185; Gorbachev and, 13, 37, 86, 108, 136, 140–141, 148–149, 168, 234, 419, (Germany as member) 219, 231, 471, (proposes disbanding) 336; NATO vs., 35–36, 75, 236; and troop cuts, 37, 39, 70, 75; as political (vs. military) force, 163; and Romania, 169, 170; and Open Skies proposal, 189; collapse of, 232, 234, 289, 362, 419, 468
Washington/Camp David meetings (1990). See Bush, George: RELATIONSHIP WITH GORBACHEV
Washington Post, 20, 50n, 71–73 passim, 81, 130, 131, 258–259, 317n, 390–391, 444
Washington Times, 168, 254–255
Watergate scandal, 346n
Watson, Samuel, 114
Watson, Thomas, Jr., 100
Webster, William, 48, 126, 142–143, 349, 355n

Weinstein, Allen, 433

Wellesley College, 22

West Germany (Federal Republic of Germany), 15, 46, 137, 384; Lance missiles in, *see* Lance missiles; Bush speech in (Mainz, 1989), 81; and German unification, 157, 183, 187, 232, 271; elections in, 191; aids East Germany, 238. *See also* Germany

Wiesner, Jerome, 310*n*

Wilson, Woodrow, 91

Woerner, Manfred, 235

Wofford, Harris, 448

Wolfowitz, Paul, 326

Woolsey, James, 289–290, 292, 364–365, 370

World Bank, 89, 310*n*, 411–412*n*

World Jewish Congress, 301

World War I, 15

World War II, 12, 137, 140, 157, 169, 206, 219; Nazis/Germany in, 183, 186, 236, 238, 394; Big Four of, 184, 185, 232, 271

Wyeth, Andrew, 218

Yakovlev, Alexander, 140, 175, 288, 310, 352, 379; meets Kissinger, 14, 15; on Baltic states, 101, 111, 173; at Malta, 153, 161; defends Gorbachev, 178, 186; and political crises/coup, 357, 358, 421, 456

Yalta agreement, 46, 129*n*, 184

Yanayev, Gennadi, 297, 314, 354*n*, 355; Bush meets, 411, 415–416, 417, 428; seizes presidential power, 420, 422, 424, 427–430 *passim;* letter to Bush, 431; arrested, 435

Yavlinsky, Grigori, 382–390 *passim,* 401–402, 435

Yazov, Dimitri, 41, 176, 195, 257, 273, 288, 354*n;* and arms control, 289–290, 406; and Gulf crisis/War, 314, 340, 451; and political crises, 360, ("constitutional coup") 394, 395, 396, 400, (coup) 422, 424, 434, 435, 439, 445; meets Nixon, 363

Yeltsin, Boris: in elections, 47, 193, 214, 215, 376, 391; CIA view of, 47–48, 142, 143, 349, 360, 424, 437; as challenge to Gorbachev, 47, 108, 177, 193, 214, 294, 392, 471, (Gorbachev's view of) 106, 215, 226, 307, 350, 356, 461; Bush's view of, 87, 103, 104, 167, 413, (ascendancy) 241, 242, 444–445, 471–472; visits to Washington, (1989) 102–103, 106, 108, 350, 361, 399, (seeks visit, in-
vited, 1991) 347–348, 350, 361, (1991) 392, 395, 396, 399–401, 413, (1992) 446*n,* 465–466; Bush meets, 103–104, 108, 399–401, 412–413, 446*n;* State Department view of, 104–105, 345, 348, 444, (Baker and) 352–353; criticizes Gorbachev, 108, 177, 178, 179, 234, 294, (demands resignation) 349; and Baltics, 173, 287, 380, (protests action) 304, ("mutual support pact") 307; as president of Republic, 193, 215, 226, 307, 353–357 *passim,* 375, 391–392, 444, (quits, abolishes party) 234, 473, (after dissolution of Union) 456, 458, 465–466, 467, 471–472, 474; coalition/alliance with Gorbachev discussed, 349, 353, 355, 358–361 *passim,* 378, 391, (and Union treaty) 412, 418, 448, 449, 451; and referendum, 350; Baker meets (in Moscow), 352–353, 455–457; Nixon meets, 355; and political crises, 356–360, ("constitutional coup") 395–397, 399–400 (*see also* and coup, *below*); in "Nine-plus-One," 359; and economic reforms, 375, 376, 378; criticized, 394, 441, 473; view of Bush, 399; and coup, 424, 435, 437, (defies) 426, 427, 432, (letter to Bush) 430, 433, (Bush telephones) 433–434, 435, (and Gorbachev's return) 436–441 *passim;* demands general strike, 429; recognizes independent republics, 442–443; as Gorbachev's successor, 444–445, 456–457, 458, 461, 465–466, 467, 471–472, 474; and arms control, 445, 446*n,* 449–450, 456, 458; forms commonwealth (Minsk agreement), 450, 452, 453, 454, 456, 473, (telephones Bush) 453, 454

Yemen, 246*n,* 252, 253, 256, 278*n;* and UN presidency, 280, 286; and Gulf crisis, 285, 287

Yerevan. *See* Armenia (earthquake in)

Yeutter, Clayton, 127, 205

Yugoslavia, 27, 106, 443; civil war in, 414

Zapata Petroleum, 129*n*

"zero option." *See* arms control

Zhao Ziyang, 83

Zhirinovsky, Vladimir, 391*n*

Zhivkov, Todor, 136*n,* 169*n*

Zimin, Yuri, 356

Zionism, 447*n. See also* Arab-Israeli dispute

Zoellick, Robert, 39, 56, 98, 184, 423, 474; and Baker, 26–27, 107, 109; visits Moscow, 121, 140; and Malta, 127, 143, 151, 153; and Gulf crisis/War, 245, 246, 274; and U.S. aid, 382–387 *passim,* 390

THREE EVENTFUL YEARS: A CHRONOLOGY

1989

Jan. 20: George Bush is inaugurated.
Jan. 23: Bush calls Mikhail Gorbachev to promise no "foot-dragging" in the improvement of U.S.-Soviet relations.
Feb. 12: Bush sees experts in Kennebunkport: "Suppose, God forbid, that [Gorbachev's] heart stops tomorrow. Is there *perestroika* after Gorbachev?"
Feb. 13: Bush orders a "pause" in diplomacy with Moscow.
Mar. 7: In Vienna for their first private meeting, James Baker tells Eduard Shevardnadze, "We really hope that you succeed."
Mar. 26: Boris Yeltsin is elected to the Soviet parliament.
April 6: In a private meeting with Margaret Thatcher in London, Gorbachev denounces Bush's "pause" as "intolerable."
April 9: Soviet troops break up a Georgian nationalist demonstration in Tbilisi; at least twenty are killed.
May 11: During their first private meeting in Moscow, Baker complains about Gorbachev's efforts at one-upsmanship.
May 12: At Texas A&M, Bush gives his first presidential speech on the Soviet Union, pledging to move "beyond containment."
June 4: Demonstrations after Gorbachev's trip to Beijing, the first Sino-Soviet summit in thirty years, lead to the massacre in Tiananmen Square.
July 9–13: Bush is feted by crowds in Poland and Hungary.
July 18: Flying from Paris to Washington, Bush scrawls a secret invitation to Gorbachev to meet with him "without thousands of assistants hovering over our shoulders."
Aug. 22: In Vilnius, the Lithuanian parliament declares the 1940 Soviet annexation of the Baltics illegal. In Warsaw, after a call from Gorbachev, Polish Communists announce the formation of a coalition government with Solidarity.
Sept. 12: Bush refuses to receive Yeltsin in the Oval Office and instead stages a "drop-by" during Yeltsin's meeting with Brent Scowcroft.
Sept. 21: During his first meeting with Bush as president, Shevardnadze implores him to ignore Yeltsin's doomsaying about Gorbachev: "Don't believe everything you hear." Afterward the foreign minister leaves for meetings at Baker's Wyoming cabin on START, chemical weapons, regional conflicts, and Soviet separatism. Baker advises, "Cut the Baltics loose!"
Oct. 6: Gorbachev sees East German leader Erich Honecker in East Berlin and urges him to adopt a

program of reform. Later he tells aides that Honecker "can't stay in control" and must go.
Oct. 16: 100,000 East German protesters march through Leipzig.
Oct. 18: Honecker is deposed in favor of former security chief Egon Krenz.
Oct. 25: Gorbachev, in Helsinki, proclaims what his Foreign Ministry spokesman calls the Sinatra Doctrine, promising that the USSR will allow satellite states to "do it their way."
Nov. 1: Gorbachev, in Moscow, calls for Krenz to speed up reform and open borders to "avoid an explosion."
Nov. 9: The East German government opens the Berlin Wall. Bush says, "I'm not going to dance on the wall."
Nov. 13: Henry Kissinger privately warns Bush, "If the Germans see us as obstructing their aspirations, we'll pay a price later on."
Nov. 28: West German Chancellor Helmut Kohl unveils a plan for German unification.
Dec. 2–3: At the Malta "seasick summit," Bush and Gorbachev make a secret compact on the Baltics: Gorbachev pledges to avoid violence, while Bush promises not to "create big problems" for him.
Dec. 5: A new Czechoslovak cabinet is formed; the majority is non-Communist.
Dec. 6: Krenz resigns as East German leader.
Dec. 20: Lithuanian Communists declare independence from the Moscow party leadership.
Dec. 25: Nicolae Ceausescu is executed after the Romanian revolution begins.
Dec. 29: Vaclav Havel is elected president of the Czechoslovak parliament.

1990

Jan. 11: Gorbachev visits Vilnius in an effort to halt the pro-independence movement.
Jan. 15: Gorbachev dispatches troops to Azerbaijan after anti-Armenian riots. Bush privately tells Soviet Ambassador Yuri Dubinin that he supports the move "completely."
Feb. 9: In a private meeting with Gorbachev in Moscow, Baker proposes a "Two-plus-Four" mechanism to solve the problem of German unification.
Feb. 13: American, Soviet, British, and French representatives agree on "Two-plus-Four" during a meeting in Ottawa.
Feb. 25: Demonstrations throughout the USSR signal a growing impatience with Gorbachev on both the Right and the Left.
March 11: The Lithuanian parliament declares independence; Gorbachev denounces the move as "illegitimate and invalid." In private, Scowcroft says that the U.S. wishes the Balts well, but there is a "lot more at stake" in U.S.-Soviet relations.